OXFORD READINGS IN CLASSICAL STUDIES

The series provides students and scholars with a representative selection of the best and most influential articles on a particular author, work, or subject. No single school or style of approach is privileged: the aim is to cover a broad overview of scholarship, to cover a wide variety of topics, and to illustrate a diversity of critical methods. The collections are particularly valuable for their inclusion of many important essays which are normally difficult to obtain and for the first-ever translations of some of the pieces. Many articles are thoroughly revised and updated by their authors or are provided with addenda taking account of recent work. Each volume includes an authoritative and wide-ranging introduction by the editor surveying the scholarly tradition and considering alternative approaches. This pulls the individual articles together, setting all the pieces included in their historical and cultural contexts and exploring significant connections between them from the perspective of contemporary scholarship. All foreign languages (including Greek and Latin) are translated to make the texts easily accessible to those without detailed linguistic knowledge.

D1602663

OXFORD READINGS IN CLASSICAL STUDIES

Aeschylus
Edited by Michael Lloyd

Ovid
Edited by Peter E. Knox

The Attic Orators
Edited by Edwin Carawan

Lucretius
Edited by Monica R. Gale

Catullus
Edited by Julia Haig Gaisser

Seneca
Edited by John G. Fitch

Vergil's *Eclogues*
Edited by Katharina Volk

Vergil's Georgics
Edited by Katharina Volk

Homer's *Odyssey*
Edited by Lillian E. Doherty

Livy
Edited by Jane D. Chaplin and Christina S. Kraus

Persius and Juvenal
Edited by Maria Plaza

Horace: *Odes* **and** *Epodes*
Edited by Michèle Lowrie

Horace: *Satires* **and** *Epistles*
Edited by Kirk Freudenburg

Thucydides
Edited by Jeffrey S. Rusten

Lucan
Edited by Charles Tesoriero, with Frances Muecke and Tamara Neal

Xenophon
Edited by Vivienne J. Gray

All available in paperback

Oxford Readings in Classical Studies

Greek and Roman Historiography

Edited by
JOHN MARINCOLA

OXFORD
UNIVERSITY PRESS

OXFORD
UNIVERSITY PRESS

Great Clarendon Street, Oxford OX2 6DP

Oxford University Press is a department of the University of Oxford.
It furthers the University's objective of excellence in research, scholarship,
and education by publishing worldwide in

Oxford New York

Auckland Cape Town Dar es Salaam Hong Kong Karachi
Kuala Lumpur Madrid Melbourne Mexico City Nairobi
New Delhi Shanghai Taipei Toronto

With offices in

Argentina Austria Brazil Chile Czech Republic France Greece
Guatemala Hungary Italy Japan Poland Portugal Singapore
South Korea Switzerland Thailand Turkey Ukraine Vietnam

Oxford is a registered trade mark of Oxford University Press
in the UK and in certain other countries

Published in the United States
by Oxford University Press Inc., New York

British Library Cataloguing in Publication Data

Data available

Library of Congress Cataloging in Publication Data
Library of Congress Control Number: 2010940326

Typeset by SPI Publisher Services, Pondicherry, India
Printed in Great Britain
on acid-free paper by
MPG Books Group, Bodmin and King's Lynn

ISBN 978–0–19–923349–6 (Hbk.)
978–0–19–923350–2 (Pbk.)

1 3 5 7 9 10 8 6 4 2

Preface

There have been substantial changes to the study of the historical writings of the Greeks and Romans over the past forty years. New approaches to the ancient texts and new questions posed of them have illuminated previously neglected aspects of ancient historians' work, and in not a few cases have led to fundamental re-evaluations of the aims and approaches both of individual historians and of ancient historiography as a whole. Because Greek and Roman historical texts have been studied both by practising (modern) ancient historians and by literary scholars, one can sometimes see radically divergent views on how the ancient historians worked and what they saw as their task. The present collection can give only a small sample of work done in Greek and Roman historiography in the last generation, and faced with so large and multi-faceted a topic, I have chosen to focus on three particular areas that I consider important (more is said about each in the Introduction): the complex nature of constructing the past; the question of the extent to which ancient historiography concerned itself with historical truth (as we might understand that term); and the relationship between history and other genres, especially poetry. Because other volumes in this series have covered or will cover individual historians, my criterion for inclusion here has been that an essay concern itself with general matters involved in the writing of history in the ancient world. Even Loraux's article, despite its title, treats the larger issue of the use of and approach to ancient texts; and if the name of Thucydides recurs with some frequency throughout this collection, that is simply a reflection of his enormous influence on the genre in antiquity.[1]

Aside from compilation of a single bibliography and the homogenization of spelling and references, my editorial intrusions are as

---

[1] I am not unaware that some will be surprised that I have not included any essay by Arnaldo Momigliano. My action intends no disrespect towards this great scholar; the reader will find him often cited in the bibliography, and Momigliano himself ensured easy access to his work by the many collections he published of his own essays (see Introduction, n. 4).

follows: I have translated all words and phrases in foreign languages, either ancient or modern, except when the meaning of the word(s) is obvious from the surrounding text, or when such translations would serve no purpose; I have replaced references to foreign-language books and articles with an English version if such exists; and I have referred to the most recent edition of secondary works (again, when such exist). I have indicated my additions throughout by the use of curly brackets, thus: {}.

My first thanks for this volume must go, of course, to the authors of the essays themselves. Those still living (the majority) were offered the opportunity to write a short addendum, and in most cases they availed themselves of this. Thanks are due also to the translators, Mark Beck, Cécile Dudoyt, and Gail Trimble, who provided excellent versions of the originals. For advice and assistance of various kinds I thank Harriet Flower, K. Scarlett Kingsley, Christina Kraus, Elizabeth Meyer, Christian Mileta, Roberto Nicolai, Michael Peachin, Christopher Pelling, and my research assistants, Guy Boudreaux and Caitlin Ulmer, who helped in turning the older articles into electronic form. I owe a special debt of gratitude, as always, to Laurel Fulkerson, who helped in the editing of translations, patiently discussed many matters (intellectual and practical) with me, and consistently offered sage counsel.

At the Press I thank Hilary O'Shea who first approved (so long ago now!) the topic for a volume in this series, and Jenny Wagstaffe, Dorothy McCarthy, and Tessa Eaton who have been unceasingly courteous and helpful in the myriad details that go into the making of a book. For errors of any sort that remain, I alone am responsible.

Tallahassee, March 2010   J.M.

Table of Contents

III. History and Poetry

Abbreviations

Ancient authors and their works are cited according to the usual conventions found in H. G. Liddell and R. Scott, *A Greek–English Lexicon*⁹ (Oxford 1940), P. G. W. Glare, ed., *Oxford Latin Dictionary* (Oxford 1982), and C. T. Lewis and C. Short, *A Latin Dictionary* (Oxford 1879). Lucian's *How to Write History* is abbreviated *h.c.* throughout. Journals are cited according to *L'Année Philologique* with the usual modifications in English. The abbreviations below are used for frequently cited works or series.

ANRW	H. Temporini et al., edd., *Aufstieg und Niedergang der römischen Welt* (Berlin–New York, 1972–)
CAF	T. Kock, *Comicorum Atticorum Fragmenta*, 3 vols (Leipzig, 1880–8)
CAH	*Cambridge Ancient History*
CIL	*Corpus Inscriptionum Latinarum* (Berlin, 1863–)
FHG	C. Müller, *Fragmenta Historicorum Graecorum*, 5 vols (Paris, 1841–70)
FGrHist	F. Jacoby et al., *Die Fragmente der griechischen Historiker* (Berlin, 1923–58; Leiden, 1994–)
GCS	*Die Griechischen Christlichen Schriftsteller der ersten drei Jahrhunderte* (Leipzig, 1897–)
GGM	C. Müller, *Geographi Graeci Minores*, 3 vols (Paris, 1855–82)
Gomme, *HCT*	A. W. Gomme, A. Andrewes, and K. J. Dover, *A Historical Commentary on Thucydides*, 5 vols (Oxford, 1956–81)
IG	*Inscriptiones Graecae* (Berlin, 1873–)
ILLRP	A. Degrassi, *Inscriptiones Latinae Liberae Rei Publicae*, 2 vols (Florence I², 1965; II, 1963)
ILS	H. Dessau, *Inscriptiones Latinae Selectae*, 3 vols in 5 (Berlin, ²1892–1916)
Kaibel, *CGF*	G. Kaibel, *Comicorum Graecorum Fragmenta* (Berlin, 1899)

Kassel–Austin, *PCG*	R. Kassel and C. Austin, edd., *Poetae Comici Graeci* (Berlin–New York, 1983–)
LCL	Loeb Classical Library
ML	R. Meiggs and D. M. Lewis, *A Selection of Greek Historical Inscriptions to the End of the Fifth Century B.C.* (Oxford, 1969; repr. with addenda, 1988). Inscriptions are cited by document number
OCD	*Oxford Classical Dictionary* (Oxford, ²1970, ³1996)
OCT	Oxford Classical Texts
PG	J.-P. Migne, *Patrologiae Cursus, series Graeca* (Paris, 1857–66)
*PIR*²	E. Groag et al., *Prosopographia Imperii Romani Saeculi I, II, III* (Berlin, ²1933–)
POxy	*Oxyrhynchus Papyri* (London, 1898–)
R/O	P. J. Rhodes and R. Osborne, *Greek Historical Inscriptions: 404–323 BC* (Oxford, 2003). Inscriptions are cited by document number
RE	A. von Pauly, G. Wissowa, and W. Kroll, edd., *Real-Encyclopädie der classischen Altertumswissenschaft*, 84 vols (Stuttgart, 1893–1980)
SEG	*Supplementum Epigraphicum Graecum* (Aalphen et alibi, 1923)
*SIG*³	W. Dittenberger, *Sylloge Inscriptionum Graecarum*, 4 vols (Leipzig, ³1915–24)
TLL	*Thesaurus Linguae Latinae* (Munich, 1900–)
Tod, *GHI*	M. N. Tod, *A Selection of Greek Historical Inscriptions*, 2 vols (Oxford, 1946–8). Inscriptions are cited by document number
Walbank, *HCP*	F. W. Walbank, *A Historical Commentary on Polybius*, 3 vols (Oxford, 1957–79)

Introduction

I

Classical historiography is fortunate to have had so many great scholars engaged in its study: Friedrich Creuzer in the nineteenth century; Eduard Schwartz and Hermann Peter in the late nineteenth and early twentieth century; Felix Jacoby and Arnaldo Momigliano in the twentieth century. The last two in particular have cast a long shadow over subsequent scholarship, although for different reasons. Jacoby, without doubt the greatest scholar ever of Greek historiography, is best known for a series of brilliant books, articles, and full-length studies of some of the major Greek historians, and, even more so, for his astonishing collection of the fragments of the lost Greek historians, which may fairly be said to be the twentieth century's most impressive monument of classical scholarship by an individual scholar.[1] Yet this collection was unlike any other compilation of its kind, in that Jacoby arranged the lost historians not alphabetically or chronologically, but rather according to generic rubrics that mirrored his own understanding and interpretation of the development and growth of Greek historiography.[2] His model, which also influenced theories of the development of Roman historiography, for long

[1] On Jacoby's life and work see Chambers (1990) and the essays collected in Ampolo (2006). His major studies of the Greek historians are collected in Jacoby (1956b). A new on-line edition of Jacoby's collection, under the general editorship of Ian Worthington and by various hands, is now appearing; it contains the Greek texts, English translations, and updated commentaries. Though it will certainly make these fragmentary historians more accessible, scholars will nonetheless need to continue to consult Jacoby's edition.

[2] Jacoby (1909) outlines the rationale for the collection; the schema is followed with a few (important) modifications in Fornara (1983) 4–46.

held the field, although doubts about it have recently been raised.[3] Momigliano, for his part, moved with unmatched brilliance and insight over the whole of ancient—and medieval and modern!—historiography, and his impressive collections of papers show that there was hardly any aspect of the history and historiography of the ancient world that he left untouched. Among his many interests, one of the strongest was in tracing lines of development both within classical historiography and between classical and modern historiography.[4]

While in no way wishing to diminish or simplify the complex thought of both of these great scholars, I think it is fair to say that each believed that history-writing in antiquity was an activity not dissimilar in kind or purpose from its modern counterpart.[5] They believed that ancient historians conducted on-going research, made good-faith efforts to eliminate their personal prejudice, tried to find out what actually happened, and produced works of history that gave a fairly accurate and reliable account of events. In asserting this, however, it was necessary to separate out the 'serious' historian from the 'frivolous' or misguided one, who 'corrupted' or 'adulterated' history: the latter used history for flattery or vituperation, included tall tales, legendary accounts, and fantastic stories, cared little for truth, and wrote primarily to entertain rather than instruct readers. Yet the assumption of a consistent and easily recognizable dichotomy between 'serious' and 'non-serious' history not only privileged the testimony of certain historians over that of others, but also failed to consider the various (and sometimes contradictory) ways in which the ancients employed history.

This traditional approach to ancient historiography, still widely held by many scholars, has been assailed from a variety of quarters,

---

[3] See Fowler (1996) 62–9; Humphreys (1997); Marincola (1999); Porciani (2001); Luraghi (2001a) 4–8.

[4] There are numerous collections of Momigliano's essays in a variety of languages, but everything eventually appeared in his *Contributi alla Storia degli Studi Classici e del Mondo Antico* (9 vols. in 11 parts; Rome), 'the greatest landmark of classical and antique learning witnessed since the Second World War' (Bentley (1997) 476). For Momigliano's influence and importance in the field of historiography see (i.a.) Weinberg (1988); Dionisotti (1989); Steinberg (1991); Miller (2007).

[5] Most easily seen in the title of Momigliano's posthumously published Sather lectures, *The Classical Foundations of Modern Historiography* (Momigliano 1990).

which is not surprising, given the intense debate over the last forty years concerning the nature and purpose of all historiography, not just ancient. A few of these new approaches have not necessarily been hostile to the traditional picture, in that they tried to deepen or complicate established views by considering aspects previously ignored or unknown. Others, however, were very much on the attack, questioning even the epistemic value of history itself.[6] Post-modern approaches in particular have questioned the value of narratives or meta-narratives, as well as the relationship between literary texts and an external world that they supposedly represent; and it is now commonplace to point out that narrative history, with its use of plot and characterization, with its attempts to connect the dots of evidence by means of a 'story' with beginning, middle, and end, inevitably entails techniques of fictionalization which compromise the truth-value of history.[7]

Space precludes discussion of these important issues, but it may not be out of place to mention three of the most significant challenges to the traditional picture of ancient historiography, which are further discussed in the following sections and in a number of the essays in this volume. First, it has been noted that the relationship between past and present in classical antiquity was different from that of the modern world. As Nietzsche observed long ago, the ancients lacked the distance necessary for a truly historical perspective, and more recently scholars have examined in particular cases how the works of the ancients consistently betray a kind of

---

[6] The major historiographical issues from antiquity onward are surveyed in the essays in Bentley (1997); for a brief overview of important trends since the Enlightenment see Bentley (1997) 395–506, reprinted separately as Bentley (1999); Clark (2004) provides an exceptionally clear and cogent survey and analysis of contemporary literary theories that bear on the writing and practice of history. For discussion with ancient historiography particularly in mind, see Cameron (1989); Batstone (2009); and Wheeldon (1989) who has many good observations on the contrast between moderns' concerns with the writing of history and those of the ancients.

[7] See, perhaps most famously, White (1971); cf. White (1989). Ronald Syme, considered by many to be the greatest twentieth-century historian of ancient Rome, remarked more than once on the necessity of fictional techniques in the writing of history (see below, for example, p. 317), but he seems neither to have exercised himself much over the question nor to have given any indications of how such fictionalization might operate in his own work.

'unhistorical thinking',[8] in which the past looks remarkably like the present. Second, it has been emphasized that the discovery of the past was, for ancients as well as moderns, not a simple and straightforward task; on the contrary, interest and inquiry were directed by memory (both individual and societal), unconscious presuppositions (again, individual and societal), technologies of recording (oral vs. written), social pressures, and the values of the historian's own society. Finally, it has been argued that the role and importance of rhetoric in the ancient educational system makes for a fundamental gulf between ancients and moderns.

II

The articles in the first section of this book are all concerned with how the past is constructed, both by the ancients themselves for their own history and by modern scholars for the history of the ancient world. Perhaps the most fundamental shift over the last thirty years has been the recognition, with all of its attendant consequences, of a significant break between ancient civilization and our own. Today this is an obvious truism, but it was not always so. The attempt to de-familiarize classical antiquity has changed deeply the way we approach ancient texts, including historiographical texts. It seems fair to say that even the best scholarship of the twentieth century found it difficult to disengage from the belief that history was in some way for the ancients what it was for us (not to mention the fact that history itself seemed a straightforward and transparent activity), such that even sympathetic portraits of ancient historians had a touch of condescension about them, as if moderns were so much clearer about what history was or should be, or how it should function in society. But the grave identity crisis which the discipline of history has undergone in our time has led many to rethink old paradigms and to be aware of the fragile and tentative nature of any construction of the past. Self-evident truths have turned out, upon closer inspection, to be neither self-evident nor necessarily true.

Loraux's striking and polemical formulation—'Thucydides is not our colleague'—caught this tone just right, and in the article that

---

[8] The phrase is that of Wiseman (1979) 41–53.

opens this collection she subjects some well-established 'methods' of dealing with classical texts to critical scrutiny, pointing out that there is no such thing as a 'neutral' demonstration. She emphasizes that texts are ineluctably bound to their contexts, and cannot be removed or isolated from that context, nor can they be analysed in a way that takes no thought for how the text as a whole works; on the contrary, every analysis must consider the generic and other conventions that have influenced the text's formulation and production.

This contextual approach can be seen in a number of the articles that follow. The modern historian, for example, is exhorted to distance himself from his subject, to not assume that his or her values were those of the subject under study. In antiquity, by contrast, as is shown in the chapters by Gehrke, Thomas, von Ungern-Sternberg, and Timpe, the ancients (including their historians) felt a close and indissoluble bond between themselves and their forebears, between their present and their past. In the ancient city-state the past was omnipresent, in monuments and temple dedications, in religious rites and festivals; the élite, both Greek and Roman, preserved their own family histories and traced their descent back to the heroes of epic poetry. On a larger scale, cities and territories looked to the stories of their past to assert or justify their claims in the present. Newly-created states could not exist in a timeless, pastless present, and so throughout antiquity there was a strong urge, indeed one might say a necessity, given the socio-political realities of the ancient world, to invent historical connections or modify and adapt existing ones—to construct, in Gehrke's formulation, 'intentional history'.

The newer approaches to historiography mentioned above can also be seen in this first section of articles. One of the most important areas of study for classical scholars in the last generation has been that of oral tradition. First pioneered in the study of African tribal societies, the work of oral historians has come to influence many historiographies. Whereas earlier scholars might dismiss the historical value of oral tradition,[9] recent scholars have concerned themselves much more with the dynamics of oral tradition, with the

---

[9] For an illuminating contrast between the approaches of Gehrke, Thomas, von Ungern-Sternberg, and Timpe in this volume and an earlier essay covering some of the same issues, see Finley (1975), an important article but one bedevilled by a modern superiority complex.

ways in which an oral society is in fundamental ways different from literate ones. Understanding oral tradition and its interaction with a developing literacy and a culture of writing helps to explain a number of characteristic features of classical historiography, including the nature of what is preserved and even the shape of our surviving histories, as Thomas makes clear in her chapter on the genealogists.[10]

Intersecting this interest in important ways is the role that memory plays in the shaping of a society's relationship to its past. Scholars have shown—and here we return to context—that memory is not a mechanical and inert process but one that is dynamic and innovative, and which is constantly guided by the interests in the present of the particular family or tribe or city or nation that 'remembers' the past. Memory is not identical with history, yet it nonetheless plays a fundamental role in the sorts of things that are thought worthy of being recorded and elaborated.

The different ways of knowing and experiencing the past in antiquity were also not limited by specifically 'historical' texts. Interest in the past can be seen in any number of genres in both Greece and Rome, and in texts we would hardly call historical. Poetic, religious, and legal texts, as shown by Cornell and Timpe, had important roles to play in the formation of the historical tradition, and clear lines of demarcation separating historical from non-historical texts are difficult to establish in practice.

Finally, there was the person of the historian himself, and the approaches he brought to constructing his narrative of the past. Formed by tradition, by education, by the spirit of his time, by his own interests, and by the desire to equal or surpass his predecessors, the historian is seen by the ancients as fundamental to the entire historiographical enterprise. As Schepens shows in his chapter, the ancient historian's attitude towards his sources and his practice of 'source-criticism' were very different from those of a modern historian: whereas modern source-criticism focuses on what is to be gained objectively from the sources, ancient concerns revolved

---

[10] The importance of considering oral tradition when treating classical historiography is well brought out in the essays collected in Luraghi (2001b).

around the subjective means by which one acquired and assembled one's material. This emphasis meant that the main interest was in how historical knowledge came to be acquired and in how the historian himself was disposed towards the subject-matter of his history, which in turn led to an overriding concern with the historian's intellectual and/or moral qualities, with his character and way of life. Any construction of the past in antiquity was, therefore, always mediated through the person of the historian.

III

Part II of this collection concerns ancient notions of historical truth and falsehood. Such concepts as historical truth are not simple, of course, and come freighted with cultural baggage. In the case of ancient historians, scholars have focused particularly on the rhetorical education given to young men in antiquity and on the place of history in that education. It is important to remember that the writing of history in classical antiquity was not performed by a professional class, by scholars who had been led through a prescribed curriculum and then examined or tested by other professionals.[11] All the historians of antiquity were products of an education that had become systematized in the fourth century BC and continued to late antiquity.[12] The 'curriculum' of the putative historian was no different from that of the putative poet, orator, or indeed even philosopher. This is not to say that history did not necessarily have a particular approach to the past, one that could be distinguished from that of poetry or oratory, nor that the historian was not expected to bring a certain viewpoint or ethic or orientation to his work; but it is to say that ancient historiography was much more open to, cognizant of, and influenced by the other genres practised by

[11] Malitz (1990); Meissner (1992) 191–3, 208–14.
[12] For ancient education see Morgan (1998), and the essays collected in Too (2001); it is not the case, of course, that ancient education remained exactly the same over the centuries; nonetheless, there is a remarkable consistency.

men of letters.[13] We today might be surprised to read that a great
English historian was profoundly influenced by, and modelled himself on, Shakespeare, or that a great German historian saw himself as
vying with Goethe. In antiquity, by contrast, the historians were often
portrayed—and often portray themselves, albeit in subtle ways—as
rivals of the great poets, especially Homer.[14]

Since the narrative histories produced by ancient historians are
clearly influenced by the rules and practices of rhetoric and rhetorical
training, the debate has largely concentrated on the extent and nature
of this influence. One school, which we might call 'minimalist', is well
exemplified by Brunt's article on Cicero and historiography, in which
he argues that the ancients clearly distinguished historiography both
from oratory and poetry, two fields with which it was often compared, and that ancient historiographical standards, while not exactly
those of the modern day, are nevertheless congruent with many of the
aims and aspirations of history as it is written today. The ancients—
not just their historians—were aware of the difference between the
true, the false, and the plausible, even if they did not in every case
observe such distinctions. They knew that history was the realm of
the 'true', while oratory that of the 'plausible', and they could point to
instances where history had been corrupted by family pride or other
pressures attendant on the historian. The use of rhetoric is not
incompatible with a desire for veracity, however, and if one looks at
a historian such as Thucydides, one can see both an impressive
rhetorical style and a commitment to historical truth. The issue of
overriding importance is whether one used rhetoric for 'good' or
'bad' ends.

By contrast, the other school, here represented by Woodman's
analysis of the some of the same passages treated by Brunt, sees the
influence of rhetoric as all-pervasive and, in many instances, deter-
minative of the approach that ancient historians took towards the
past. Woodman argues that historians in antiquity saw truth as the

---

[13] In not a few cases, the ancient historian had also written non-historical works:
Polybius wrote biography (Pol. 10.21.5–8) and a work on tactics (9.20.4); Asinius
Pollio wrote tragedy (Hor. *Odes* 2.1); Tacitus wrote a biography (*Agricola*) a dialogue
(*Dialogus de Oratoribus*), an ethnographical treatise (*Germania*), and, perhaps rather
surprisingly, a book on jokes (Fulg. *Expos. Serm. Antiq.* 54).
[14] See note 16.

opposite not of falsehood but of partiality, and this, to begin with, conditioned the way that they approached history. The narration of a historical work was no different in essence from that of the *narratio* of a speech, where, in a similar way, events were set out in chronological order with antecedent circumstances and consequences. In a speech the orator's aim before the jury was plausibility, not truth, and the historian, who had been trained in rhetoric, did not take a different approach when writing history, but rather here too tried to construct a plausible account of events. This 'construction' includes the task of 'fleshing-out' a story for which there was only a bare amount of information, and such rhetorical activity would inevitably lead to the invention of unhistorical (from our point of view) details. Not for nothing, Woodman maintains, did the ancients see poetry, oratory, and historiography as three different species of the same genus.

Luce also notes that for the ancients truth was defined negatively, as the absence of favouritism or bias (again, the emphasis on the person of the historian is visible), and he observes as well that a sensitivity to just this aspect of the historian's character and work is pervasive in antiquity, such that we are not dealing with an isolated phenomenon or the pet peeve of a particular individual. On the contrary, history, with its task of immortalizing great deeds, was precisely the place where it was felt that an unscrupulous historian might attempt to make events greater or more impressive than they were, or where he might seek to justify or cover up the more questionable actions of his subjects. The image that often recurs in ancient discussions is that the historian must be an impartial judge or an ideal juryman, and it may not be coincidental that this again returns us to the realm of the courts, although here the historian is not the pleader but the one hearing the pleas of the contending parties and judging.[15]

But if the truth is not a simple matter, then neither is falsehood. For as Wiseman points out, the ancients meant a number of different things when they considered that someone was lying, any one of which could be portrayed as the opposite of truth. There were, of course, *mythoi*, myths, which might shade into fiction, or travellers' tales which consisted of exaggerated descriptions and situations; but there was

---

[15] For the historian as judge, see also Butti di Lima (1996).

also lying for dramatic effect and for the pure pleasure of story-telling; and one could also 'lie' by giving either too much detail or too little.

Finally, there is the question of the audience and their expectations. Gabba argues that in the period after Thucydides the committed political history championed by that historian lost its *raison d'être*, and people became much more interested in the fantastic, the unusual, and the paradoxical, interests that were sparked by the discovery of new 'exotic' lands in the wake of the conquests of Alexander and Rome. There was a particular fascination with islands as the locations of utopias, or as venues for paradoxical events and fantastic inhabitants. Much of this utopian literature had no real historical content, but it was taken up by later writers and given prominence in works of history (such as that of Diodorus). Similarly, the writings of the local historians, with their interest in individual city-states or lands, could indeed preserve records that had been kept in local archives, or elucidate the interpretation of inscriptions or monuments, but they were just as likely to include also records of miracles or portents, 'events' that had been important to the self-definition of the city-state (returning us to Gehrke, above), but which were not, of course, factual. Throughout antiquity many accepted without question any available information, and in this way 'false' history was disseminated along with 'true'.

IV

The final section deals with the relationship between historiography and poetry, a relationship that contained elements of both emulation and hostility. The influence of poetry on history was enormous. It was perhaps inevitable that the great prestige of the *Iliad* and *Odyssey* in the ancient world, and the pre-eminence of Homer, should ensure that historiography, like nearly every other genre in Greece (and Rome), had an important relationship to epic. The two earliest historians, Herodotus and Thucydides, who became the models for later historians, themselves modelled their works in important ways on Homer, and the formal devices of epic that they adopted—the largely third-person narrative, the use of circumstantial detail, delineation of causes and consequences of actions, and speeches delivered in direct discourse by the characters themselves—became the characteristics of all later historiography.[16] So great was the influence of poetry in general and epic in particular that, as Canfora demonstrates, historians imitated the epic cycle by establishing a 'chain' of their own, in which it became common for one historian to pick up his narrative where a predecessor left off. Even here they were following the example of the master, Thucydides, who by his narrative of the fifty years between the end of the Persian wars and the beginning of the Peloponnesian, 'joined up' his history to that of Herodotus.

This symbiosis was possible in part because, as Walbank points out, Greek epic poetry was about the great heroes of the past, and the characters and events depicted therein were thought by the ancients to have been historical persons; one might acknowledge that poets embellished or exaggerated, but no one in antiquity ever doubted that Achilles existed or that the Trojan War had taken place. Tragedy too influenced the writing of history, developing, as it did, at the same time as the genre of history: like historiography, tragedy was a 'descendant' of epic, and put 'historical' people on stage, so it is not surprising that some historians wrote history that reminded readers either of tragedy or of epic.

In addition, poetry and history had similar concerns and aims. The most obvious one was instruction: history was meant not only to inform readers about the past but also to serve as some sort of guide for the future, whether that be in intellectual understanding, the appropriation of exemplary models, or the regulation of one's own behaviour in the public arena. Yet it was not only in terms of instruction that history and poetry came together. Both also employed vivid representation and sought to engage their readers on a deep emotional level. Although many scholars consider these techniques to be characteristic of only a limited number of histories (which in turn are consigned to realms outside of 'mainstream' historiography), Walbank makes clear that both of these interests are fundamental to nearly all types of literary endeavour in antiquity, historiography included, and he argues that it is not justifiable to speak of a 'tragic' school of history (in which

---

[16] On Homer and historiography, Strasburger (1972) is fundamental; for the *Odyssey* in particular, see Marincola (2007a).

emotionalism and vividness were demanded) as some sort of separate type of history different from the rest.

At the same time, however, it was not the case that historiography merely assimilated itself to poetry; on the contrary, many historians strove vigorously to demonstrate the superiority of their approach to the past to that of Homer and the poets. Ancient historiography is full of comments excoriating the poets or ridiculing their credibility and exaggerations, and professing a superior method of understanding the past, even the distant ('epic') past. Hecataeus, Herodotus, and Thucydides all express contempt for the poetic tradition and laud their own 'superior' versions of events. Yet at the same time, as Funke points out, their reliance on, and continual re-engagement with, poetry created a kind of schizophrenic relationship[17] with poetry, whereby their methodological statements praise history over poetry, while in individual passages they use poetry as an important source for their work, sometime with little regard for the critical stance that they earlier espoused. Much of this can be seen in the historians' use of Homer, whose importance necessitated the development of a methodology that could extract historical truth from the epic poems; and, as Funke shows, this is the same relationship visible in the Christian historians of late antiquity, who bring a similarly divided loyalty to their own sacred scriptures. This was, of course, only one of the ways that Christian historians built on and developed the interests and methodologies of their classical predecessors.

V

Two final points to keep in mind. First, of the vast output of ancient writings on the past we possess but the smallest fraction.[18] It is true that we have the works (or in some cases substantial portions) of those

[17] The phrase is mine, not his.
[18] For a sense of what has been lost, at least on the Greek side, see Strasburger (1977); the losses on the Latin side, while numerically inferior, are nevertheless sobering, as a glance at Peter's *HRR* or the treatment of lost historians in Bardon (1952–6) *passim* shows.

historians considered by the ancients themselves to be the best: on the Greek side, Herodotus, Thucydides, and Xenophon; on the Latin side, Sallust, Livy, and Tacitus.[19] Most ancient histories, however, have perished, and what survives is not necessarily representative: local history, for example, the account of an individual city-state or ethnic region, was a prominent, important, and much-practised genre for centuries, but not a single local history survives in full or even in large measure.[20] By contrast, narratives of battles and wars are over-represented, forming the vast majority of surviving histories from the ancient world. This means that our analyses of ancient historiography are based on a tiny sample, and the discovery of a new historiographical papyrus, especially for the poorly represented genres, could easily change our entire understanding.

Second, although there was no historiographical 'curriculum' in antiquity, there were theoretical writings on history. The earliest one that survives, Dionysius of Halicarnassus' essay *On Thucydides*, written in the late first century BC, is largely a critique of the language, structure, style, and arrangement of Thucydides' history, although it also contains a few remarks on the historian's reliability, research, and relationship to truth.[21] We also have from Dionysius a letter to a certain Pompeius which contains capsule evaluations of Herodotus, Thucydides, Xenophon, Philistus, and Theopompus.[22] Plutarch's *On the Malice of Herodotus*, written in the early second century AD, is a wholesale assault on Herodotus, accusing him of distortion, bias, and a kind of sinister approach in general to the deeds he narrates. Plutarch seeks to 'correct' and 'improve' Herodotus' account by using evidence he finds in other sources and by adopting a highly

[19] On the canon of Greek historians, see D. Hal. *Imit.* 3 (II.207–10 U–R); Cic. *de Orat.* 2.55–58; Quint. 10.1.73–5; for Latin historians, Quint. 10.1.101–4; see further Radermacher (1919) 1876; Momigliano (1972) 279 n. 1; Nicolai (1992) 249–339.

[20] On local history see Jacoby (1909) 49–59; id. (1949) *passim*; Porciani (2001); Clarke (2008).

[21] For an English translation with commentary see Pritchett (1975); translation also in Usher (1974–85) I.463–633; French translation with notes in Aujac (1991) 41–125, 145–62. Cf. Dionysius' *Second Letter to Ammaeus* (translation in Usher (1974–85) II.405–33; cf. Aujac (1991) 125–44, 163–5), which contains additional remarks on the style and language of Thucydides.

[22] Translation in Usher (1974–85) II.353–99; French translation with notes in Aujac (1992) 69–99, 161–6; full commentary in Fornaro (1997).

polemical manner.[23] Finally, in the mid-second century AD, Lucian's essay, *How to Write History*, the sole surviving general treatment of the writing of history, contains both a satirical attack on some of Lucian's inept contemporaries and a series of admonitions for the prospective historian on how he should approach his task in composing a worthwhile history in the manner of Thucydides.[24] It would be fair to say that the reaction of modern scholars to all three works has been lukewarm at best. It is particularly noteworthy that in all of them only passing reference is made to that aspect of history-writing generally considered by moderns to be paramount, namely inquiry and research. Perhaps because of this generally disappointing showing, covetous eyes have often been cast towards lost works on historiography,[25] but it is uncertain whether these lost discussions would have either been any more insightful than the ones we possess, or espoused viewpoints not represented somewhere in our surviving evidence.[26] In any case, scholars are generally agreed that the best repository of information on the ancients' approach to the writing of history is the very large number of remarks made by the historians themselves in the course of their histories, such as Polybius' attack on

[23] Translation with notes in Pearson (1965); French translation with notes in Lachenaud (1981); the English translation and commentary of Bowen (1993) is of use mainly for historians and has little sympathy with or interest in what the work tells us about ancient historiography: see Marincola (1994a) and (1994b).

[24] Text and translation with notes in MacLeod (1991) 198–247, 283–302; other commentaries include Avenarius (1956) and Homeyer (1965); the *Habilitationsschrift* of Porod (2009) is now the most comprehensive commentary on Lucian's work.

[25] Works entitled *On History* or the like are known for Theophrastus (Diog. Laer. 5.47), Praxiphanes (Marcell. *Vit. Thuc.* 29), Metrodorus of Scepsis (*FGrHist* 184 F 2), Caecilius of Caleacte (*FGrHist* 183 F 2), Theodorus of Gadara (*FGrHist* 850 T 1), the third-century AD sophist, Tiberius (Suda, s.v. 'Tiberios' [T 550 Adler]), and, on the Latin side, Varro's *Sisenna uel de Historia* (Gell. 16.9.5). In the Lamprias catalogue of Plutarch's works we also find tracts entitled, 'How We Discern the True History' (No. 124), and a four-volume 'On Neglected History' (No. 54), but nothing is known of either and the latter does not sound like a theoretical work on the writing of history.

[26] See Avenarius (1956) 171–2 for doubts that these lost works concerned themselves with historiographical methodology. A recently published papyrus fragment, *POxy* 4808, contains capsule evaluations of historians and mentions Onesicritus, Chares, Cleitarchus, Hieronymus of Cardia, and Polybius. The judgements expressed there focus mainly on the reliability of the individual historians (rather than their styles), but the categories of evaluation are easily paralleled in the surviving tradition.

the Sicilian historian Timaeus of Tauromenium, where Polybius details what he sees as the proper method of writing history.[27] Although all the historians' remarks have never been systematically assembled and analysed,[28] there have been numerous studies which have collected either the remarks made by a particular author on the topic of history or the comments made by different authors on a particular topic, and, as will be seen, many of the essays in this volume are based on just such collections.

[27] Polybius' remarks in Book 12 of his history, like many by the historians in the course of their work, come in intense polemic with predecessors and contemporaries, and must thus be treated with great caution: see Walbank (1962) on Polybius' polemic; Marincola (1997) 218–36 on polemic in general; and Brunt (1980b) and Lenfant (1999) on the dangers of trusting fragments in reconstructing lost works.

[28] Jacoby had intended to collect these in a separate volume at the beginning of his *Fragmente*, but he did not consider such testimonia to be particularly valuable: cf. Jacoby (1909) 84.= (1956) 20–21: 'the little that there is from antiquity on the theory and method of historiography'.

Part I

Constructing the Past: Myth, Memory, and History

1

Thucydides is not a Colleague*

Nicole Loraux
English translation by Cécile Dudoyt

What *is* an 'ancient text'? Is it a document or a monument?[1] As a document, it is a means of access to a long-gone and yet ever-present reality recorded in the carved lines of a certain decree that time has not erased,[2] or in the pages of a certain historical work wherein is stored, undamaged, for the benefit of posterity (which is us), the truth about the Peloponnesian War.

As a monument, the ancient text is forever raised in the garden of the Humanities, surviving the joint corrosion of time and successive

---

* This is the text of a paper given at the symposium *Lucien Goldmann et la sociologie de la littérature aujourd'hui* (Paris, 15–18 March 1979) organized by the University of Paris VIII–Vincennes and the *Ecole des Hautes Etudes en Sciences Sociales*. I have kept these remarks in their original form for the occasion, and it does not escape me that as they change addressees, they might come to look incomplete: first presented to sociologists of contemporary literature, they were meant to suggest to readers of texts (for whom, as discussion showed, history was the main issue) that, conversely, for historians of antiquity the text is an urgent and repressed issue. I would add that it was obviously not my intention to deliver a final verdict on the ancient text in general, and that I have tried for efficiency's sake to keep to texts that are classical both by their period and by their history. The text of my report will be published in the *Actes* of the symposium. {Never published, to my knowledge.}

[1] Here the two terms are meant in their most common sense; they should not be endowed initially with the meaning given to them in Foucault (1969) 13–15.

[2] Admittedly, the Greeks were incomparably harder to please, twenty-five centuries ago, than we are now, concerning the quality of an inscription which was for them no more than a century old. A lucky chance gave us the stone on which a dedication quoted by Thucydides (6.54.7) is carved. How should we interpret the ancient historian's verdict that the inscription 'can still be seen in indistinct letters', when *we* have no difficulty deciphering the lettering? (See ML 11, with ample bibliography.)

readings. Our relation to it bears the stamp of admiration: we extol its beauty. Thus, a certain scholar who decried Athenian funeral orations for belonging to a genre full of *topoi* (in other words, 'boring') did not hesitate to shield from this general condemnation the *epitaphios* delivered by Pericles in Thucydides' Book 2, on the grounds that it is a 'beautiful' text, a great text. The unchanging topicality of ancient texts is also upheld: they are put on an equal footing with the great works of art in which the all too human nature of human beings is disclosed. In the rarefied atmosphere of classical culture, Sophocles communicates with Shakespeare.

An ancient text—is it raw historical data *or* pure literature?

Sociologists of literature, accustomed as they are to working on important works of art without so much as a shiver, will doubtless think that such an alternative is too abrupt not to be slightly forced in its formulation. It is true that every single text is bound to operate always both as a document and as a work of art. Ancient texts do not escape this twofold determination, and in defining his *History of the Peloponnesian War* as 'a treasure for all time' (*ktêma es aei*),[3] Thucydides was opening his text from the outset to the ambiguities of the Greek category of 'value', halfway between utilitarian considerations and reverential awe.[4]

It remains the case that in treating an ancient text, this alternative forces itself on one with uncommon strength.

Because they are forced to work with gaps—there are no archives, no proceedings of the *ekklesia*, and because oral speeches predominate (which depend on someone's good memory to leave any trace at all)—sociologists of ancient Greece are not at liberty to choose their material. Especially when they work on the classical period, they are bound to fall back on a wealth of exceptionally dense texts in which they must seek both the meaning and the whole universe of references necessary for the text itself to make any sense; in sum, to treat the text as a document in order to extract from it a context likely to throw some light on that very same text considered as a product of speech and thought. It is a paradoxical and awkward situation, usually bypassed by readers of ancient texts, who conveniently neglect either one or the other of these two approaches: history and

---

[3] Thuc. 1.22.4.   [4] See Gernet (1968) 93–137.

literature, either the context without the text or the text without the context.

Readers of ancient texts may indeed find it very difficult to free themselves from the dilemma of choosing between utilitarian perspectives and a feeling of reverential awe. For the alternative from which they try to escape is inscribed by the Greeks in all the texts intended for posterity: 'a treasure for all time' is something to be used endlessly and without more ado,[5] but also something to be admired. Tragedies purge the immutable passions of human beings, but they also dramatize crucial historical issues specific to the Athenian *polis*. For instance, the *Eumenides* recounts the triumph of the father's law, well beyond history; but the play can also be seen in the context of Athens of 458 BC as a warning against reducing the political power of the Areopagus: one has a choice.

One has a choice... òr at least this is what in France is professed in the field of Greek studies, portioned as it is between 'historians' and 'literary scholars' with remarkably little bickering over boundaries. Yet it would be imprudent for anyone to venture bravely, as sociologists of antiquity do, into the no-man's land where those boundaries get blurred.[6] Must such an apportionment be seen as a consequence—the consequence of the entity 'Greece' as applied to the academy—or is it rather a purely accidental encounter between a subject and an institution? I shall not set out to answer this question today, however worthy of systematic enquiry it might be. Let me only observe that this typically French bipartition has a history which reduces the part played by chance in this skirmish between subject and institution. The way French historians of antiquity are recruited is also worth scrutinizing. As paradoxical as it may seem, historians are genuinely losing ground to an important minority of 'literary scholars'; converted to history and to

---

[5] Cf. de Romilly (1956).

[6] This horror of interfering with disciplines is considered here as an essentially French phenomenon, in so far as the strict separation between History and Literature is usually ignored in Great Britain, Germany, or the United States, at least as far as institutions are concerned. An illustrious body, the *Comité Consultatif des Universités*, wields supreme power over the careers of academics and makes sure that researchers working on Antiquity do not mix together Literature, History, and Philosophy, each of which discipline corresponds to a different *département*.

the sacrosanct separation of History and Literature, these new historians, who have nothing to do with New History, hope to redeem their past as literary specialists through no end of 'seriousness', a seriousness obsessed with the study of institutions, presupposing the use of 'serious' material: mostly epigraphy or, whenever texts considered 'literary' are involved, the most prosaic and mundane among them.

Paradoxically, with the exception of archaeology (the assumed realm of *realia* but a largely silent continent), the historian of ancient Greece is condemned to work mainly on textual materials. Yet however nourished by texts, the field of 'Greek history' owes its very existence to a repression of the question of the status of the text.

To be sure, historians and literary specialists will object that there are texts and there are texts. The distinction (whether it is imperative or simply empirical is hard to say, although either way it has the force of law) between pure texts and 'zero degree' texts, between texts and documents makes a triumphant reappearance.[7] Historians deal with documents—epigraphic documents, of course, as if the fact of inscriptions on stone had once and for all resolved the documentary status of lines thus engraved, so that no one would ever dare to imagine that they could constitute a text. At any rate, the course of study for teacher certification in classical literature does not make room for the reading of inscriptions.[8] On the other hand, literary scholars have texts, as rarely as possible considered as documents and referred to in a context other than the strictly chronological. Undoubtedly, the academic splitting up of 'Greece' as a subject is slightly more complicated. Scholars reserve the right to choose from the whole corpus of texts (always in a manner simultaneously imperative and empirical), determining which are prestigious—these are virtually useless to the historians' quest for *realia*, and constitute the prerogative of literary scholars, or are otherwise given over to

---

[7] Here again I give these words their most basic meaning, which alone allows the opposition to work implicitly.

[8] Bollack (1975) 5–6 n. 19 mentions that candidates to the *agrégation* in Literature or in Grammar are never taught how to read a critical apparatus. Shall I add that the lack of training in the reading of decrees, by reproducing the most classical definition of what a text is, seems to me even more outrageous?

philosophers, the third partner in crime)[9]—and which texts are good for historians because they are thought to be more or less already written from the viewpoint of political or social historians. This is how the poetry of Hesiod, the Homeric hymns, and tragedy are assigned to literary scholars, which does not exclude the possibility of a further distinction within Hesiod's works or in the corpus of Attic tragedies, and which assigns to historians the *Works and Days* as being presumably rich in information on the everyday life of small Boeotian farmers,[10] or Euripides' plays, deemed too 'psychological' to be great but considered as convenient mirrors of Athenian history in the late fifth century, while simultaneously literary scholars claim as their own the *Theogony* and Sophocles' tragedies, as being too ill suited to chronological speculations. To the philosophers go most of Plato's dialogues and Aristotle's works without a fight. But here too, another distinction assigns 'properly philosophical' works (O sleep-inducing opium!), such as the *Parmenides* or the *Metaphysics*, to philosophers, while historians are content to occupy themselves with the *Laches*, the *Laws* (the analysis of which philosophers are more than ready to grant them) or, even better, the *Athenian Constitution*, which escapes the ban on the rest of Aristotle's works to the point that both sides completely ignore the fact that it was written by a philosopher.[11] In the end, the textual territory of the historian is made up of every text with a realistic or prosaic feel, or whose supposedly serious informational qualities allow them to be treated as documents, even at the cost of an ever implicit methodological *epochê* {suspension of judgement}. Obviously, historical writings

[9] Philosophers stand at a distance from the traditional pair formed by historians and literary scholars, if only because they are always ready to translate texts into the language of philosophy, characterized by a certain timelessness. It should also be said that whereas literary scholars are allowed to teach History in universities, this permeability does not seem to apply to philosophers.

[10] Hesiod's works can be divided further: the split can run through *Works and Days*, in which the myths at the beginning are easily appropriated by the literary crowd, who without regret give up to historians everything related to inheritance and the precepts of rustic life.

[11] The *Laches*, the *Laws*: the historian does not dare to appropriate these texts except in the best of cases. On the *Constitution of Athens*, Day and Chambers (1962) is an outstanding exception, which at last views the *Athenaiôn Politeia* as a philosophical work; we will not venture to say that historians of Greece have adopted the solid core of these analyses easily.

come first, since it is taken for granted that the historian of the fifth or fourth century BC is the colleague of present-day academics. It has to be said nonetheless that the Father of History, with his suspicious lightness, does not enjoy the same reputation[12] as Xenophon, the lucky journalist, or above all, as Thucydides, model of accuracy. After historical, writings come higgledy-piggledy: comedies (deemed closer to 'reality' than the tragic genre and thought to contain ready-made information on the people of Athens,[13] Athenian women and slaves); the speeches of Attic orators (even though there could well be an argument between literary scholars and historians about Isocrates and Demosthenes, there is a general consensus that the countless juridical particulars of Isaeus' speeches confine them to 'history'); the *Politeiai* (Constitutions) or what is left of them, a scanty corpus in which, next to Aristotle's *Constitution*, the *Constitution of the Athenians* written by an unknown oligarch receives the lion's share of attention.[14]

One could draw the complete cartography of how texts are allocated to various branches of Greek studies. I have limited myself to a few indications, although it does not escape me that they tend to simplify an ever-fluctuating redivision, as far as details are concerned: thus I have deliberately left aside difficult cases, such as the Homeric poems, which have fostered endless rivalries between literary scholars and historians, and among historians themselves, between advocates of irreconcilable definitions of the discipline called History;[15] or the debate on the *Politics*, which both historians and philosophers think they have a right to explore separately, mostly ignoring each other. In a majority of cases, however, the implicit redivision aims at avoiding meeting points or intersections at all cost. In this context, a scholar such as Wilamowitz, who was as interested

---

[12] On the other hand, historians who claim affiliations with anthropology give Herodotus all due attention: see Hartog (1980).

[13] I am thinking of the famous book of Ehrenberg (1962).

[14] This text is given many different names depending on scholars' predilections: 'pseudo-Xenophon', because the pamphlet has been transmitted to us among the works of Xenophon; 'the old oligarch', a nickname dear to English scholars (for instance, Gomme (1962)), or, most recently, '*L'émigré*' (Hemmerdinger (1975)).

[15] Two points of view: Bollack (1975) and Vidal-Naquet (1963); on Homer between poetry, history and archaeology, see section VI of Finley's bibliography (adapted by P. Vidal-Naquet): Finley (1978) 230–3.

in the legend of Phaedra and Hippolytus as in the demotics of Athenian *metoikoi*, as fascinated by Plato as by Sappho and Simonides or the Constitution of Athens, would be at a loss to find his place.

*

Such a distribution may have no other function than obscuring the obvious: an ancient text is probably even more liable than any other literary work to be transformed into a document, because nothing is more alien to the 'spiritual universe of the *polis*'[16] (which constitutes for us the very essence of the 'classical' city) than the notion of a literary work as expressing an individuality:[17] tragedy, history, oratory, comedy even, are civic genres or, in other words, oral institutions rooted in the city. Yet since writing is constantly claimed as a conquest in fifth-century Athens, there is no such thing as a writing that is purely documentary; nothing is written which is not presented as marked by discourse.[18] In this regard, even the most 'documentary' of documents—I mean a decree, the most prized possession of political history—is also a text. In a similar way, readers would have to be very naive indeed to take literally the claims on which historical writing, the writing most taken with accuracy, prides itself, and to credit it from the beginning with the characteristics it claims as its own: a refusal to be seduced by the charms of poetry and rhetoric, an effort to distance itself from Herodotean accounts which seem concerned only with pleasure,[19] and a definition of history as a transparent rendering of 'actual facts'.[20] Such are the principles behind which the work of Thucydides is hidden (since, as might have been guessed, we will focus on Thucydides' work). Thucydides' history strongly defines its own practices, and strikes us as a document. In other words, to the eyes of modern readers, it offers all the guarantees

---

[16] I borrow the expression from the title of chapter 4 of Vernant (1962).

[17] See the remarks I made about funeral orations as a genre in Loraux (1986) §V.3. Let me say again that these remarks concern texts of the classical period, principally those of the fifth century, because some features of Hellenistic literature appeared as early as the fourth century.

[18] For instance, a decree is always presented as the transcription of a speech in the people's assembly: 'so and so said', etc.

[19] See Thuc. 1.21–2 and the remarks of Vernant (1974) 195–250, esp. 200–3.

[20] Thuc. 1.21.2 ('to consult reality itself', *ap' autôn tôn ergôn skopousi*) and 2.41.2 and 41.4 ('the truth of deeds', *ergôn aletheia*).

of seriousness required of historical writings. Yet for readers to accept whatever the text says about itself is to show an untimely readiness to occupy the position Thucydides wants them to take, precisely so that they will not want to question the 'historicity' of his writing.

I want to make it crystal clear from the start that no text can avoid being approached as a document. Yet in order to evaluate how the understanding of a text changes when it is considered primarily and absolutely as a document (whether a tragedy by Sophocles or one of Demosthenes' speeches, a dialogue by Plato no less than an exposition by Thucydides[21]) I will analyse three examples, all taken from the corpus of writings traditionally considered documents. My aim is to show the limits of such a reading and to suggest some of the issues one should bear in mind in order to avoid the pitfalls of semantic positivism. I have chosen two texts, one to which the name of text is usually denied, and one which is readily labelled a document: a decree and a few pages by Thucydides. Along with these two sample *exempla*, I will discuss a few lines by Aristophanes, which scholarly tradition usually has no qualms extracting from the plot of the play in order to make of it a dossier, one of those ready-made dossiers that delight political and social historians of Greece.

I shall begin with an allegedly pure 'document' or at least considered such; more exactly, two documents considered 'pure': a decree and a piece of judicial eloquence. Two testimonia of a single decision of the people's assembly: a historian's dream ... but let us not anticipate.

My first example is *Against Theozotides*, one of Lysias' speeches, or rather what is left of it. There are only two lacunose fragments, but their meaning could not be clearer. At the moment when democracy was restored in 403, and in the context of a complete redefinition of Athenian citizenship on the narrow basis of Pericles' law of 450, an

---

[21] I mean to recall Marrou's definition of a document in Marrou (1954) ch. 3, 'L'histoire se fait avec des documents', 67–96, and in particular 77): 'I call a document every source of information out of which an historian's mind has successfully drawn something useful for the knowledge of the human past, seen from the angle of a given question ... There is no saying where a document begins and ends.' In fact, it is impossible to read a text, however shrouded in the deepest reverence, with the single intention of limiting oneself to its 'immanent meaning'; the readings of some Greek tragedies by Vernant and Vidal-Naquet (1972) make this clear.

orator and a political figure named Theozotides proposed a decree
seeking to exclude illegitimate (*nothoi*) and adopted children from
benefiting from the law on war orphans.[22] Apparently, the measure
fits perfectly with other legislation designed to restrict citizenship[23]
in the present and in the future. Lysias' speech can thus be read as a
defence of the *nothoi* {F 129 Carey}:

for at the Dionysia, when the herald announces the orphans and the names
of their fathers, stating also that the fathers of these youths died in the war
fighting on behalf of their country and proving themselves brave men, and
that the city was supporting them until adulthood, will he then make a
separate announcement concerning adopted and illegitimate sons, saying
that the city would not support these young men on account of Theozotides? [...] Won't this be arrogance and a great slander for the city? And
when Cleomenes [...], judges, captured your Acropolis...

The fragment ends there, just as the orator is about to recall with
pathos the golden age of Cleisthenes, where the citizen body was
defined by enlarging it.

This was all we knew when, in 1971, an American archaeologist
published an inscription which, despite its fragmentary state, was
beyond doubt the decree in question.[24] It became apparent then
that the formulation of the decree was perceptibly different from
what could be gathered from the fragments of Lysias' speech. Certainly from the mention of a *dokimasia* (an inquiry into legitimacy)
which orphans had to undergo (line 15), one can infer that the
benefit granted by the decree was to be limited only to the legitimate
children of Athenian citizens. But harmony between the decree and
the speech ends here. For the decree is not a new law carved by the
Athenians in stone, but a decision purely circumstantial: the future
is not in question, only the present time and its immediate issues.
Far from revisiting the status of war orphans, the decree refers to it

[22] The law provides that the city will raise (more precisely, that it will see to their
trophê, their food, or in other words their development) the children of Athenian
citizen fallen on the battlefield. See Thuc. 2.46.1; Plat. *Menex.* 249a5–6; Aesch. *Ctes.*
154.
[23] This is how Gernet (1926) II.234–6 understands the decree in the preface to
Against Theozotides.
[24] Stroud (1971){= *SEG* XXVIII 46}.

as to a norm within which a very awkward particular case has to be situated,[25] that of the sons of Athenians who fell fighting against the oligarchy. Let us not mistake the situation: it is not the sons so much as their fathers who pose problems for the city. Because civic ideology and the contemporary atmosphere all tended to make *homonoia* (concord) their password, and the evils of the past (the evils of civil war, *stasis*) as opposed to the only lawful form of war (war waged against an external enemy, *polemos*), were to be forgotten for good,[26] it is awkward to include democratic rebels who fell during the *stasis* among the glorious cohort of citizens fallen in combat, and in the formulation of the decree the official terminology according to which the deaths of warriors is recounted in the vocabulary of value is replaced by the abrupt language of facts. The first lines of the decree reveal the mood pervading the whole text, a dedication to 'all the Athenians who died a violent death (*apethanon biaiôi thanatôi*) during the oligarchy, trying to rescue democracy'— a beautiful death and a united city are not mentioned; instead, the text tells about political strife, one regime against another and about violence. Because they were outside the city—their opposition to the heinous but 'legal' *polis* of the Thirty had excluded them—the democrats are rewarded for their benefaction (*euergesia*) through their children.[27]

Could the discrepancy be more glaring between what the decree says, when one considers the language it employs, and Lysias' speech?[28] Reading only the speech, one would infer that a restriction was placed

[25] Stroud (1971) 287 and 294 clearly saw that such expressions as *kathaper tôn en tôi polemôi* ('in the same way as those dead in battle') and *kathaper tous orphanous* ('in the same way as orphans') mean that the sons (*paides*) in question are not the same as the war orphans (lines 16–17, 19, 6, and 9).

[26] Such was the potent rallying cry of the last years of the fifth century, in which one can choose to see an uplifting example of social consensus or an astonishing case of repression of an awkward incident by the collective memory: see Loraux (1976) 1285–6.

[27] *Euergesia*: line 7; one should remember that until the end of the fifth century *euergesia* effectively refers to the good done to the city by a *stranger*. *Andragathia* {manly bravery}, consistent with official phraseology of the praise of war dead, appears in the following line only.

[28] Stroud (1971) 285 observes that this decree is written in rather more 'colourful' language than that found in most Attic decrees of this period: this fact should be interpreted rather than simply mentioned.

on Athenian citizenship; reading the decree without the speech, one could forget the sons in favour of their fathers and underestimate how the decision of the people affected the general policy adopted concerning *nothoi*.

I will not dwell on the actual reasons for this discrepancy; the investigation would lead us too far into historical reconstruction. I would rather consider it as a symptom likely to shake historians out of the reassuring belief that 'reality' can be grasped through texts, whereas it is in actual fact full of contradictions. There are no such things as unmediated *realia* or privileged documents through which one can get direct access to *the* actual truth. Ancient historians rarely have at their disposal discordant documents that force them to take into account the complexities of any given event, and so they sometimes run the risk of taking coincidence for necessity, and of treating the only document at their disposal as if it were in actual fact a unique document, where an historical phenomenon could be grasped in its totality. The dialogue of the deaf that arises from the decree of Theozotides and the speech of Lysias wakes the historian's failing vigilance: a single document is hardly a document at all. There should always be another document less to provide some confirmation than to question the outline which the first document seems to call for.[29] Moreover, one might add that all documents need to be deciphered and constituted as documents in the closest way possible not to what is actually said but to what is inscribed between the lines: like Lysias' speech, Theozotides' decree *is* a text; readers have only to accept this to read it as such.

The problems raised by texts immediately recognized as texts, i.e. as 'classical' texts, are bound to be of a different nature—or so it would seem, because both sides are in complete agreement that a classical text is a text that one should read. The correct distance that readers should keep towards such a text remains to be determined. At which distance will the text make sense for a reader of the twentieth century without losing its rootedness in the ancient Greek city? A microscopic reading, one matching each word to a vast context of significations, undoes the text; by focussing on Greek culture as a whole,

---

[29] In this regard, Marrou's remarks ((1954) 128–33) are extremely suggestive.

the text runs the risk of losing its autonomy. Conversely, reading a Greek text from too far away, be it a comic, tragic, or historical text, cuts it from its generic moorings which should serve as a means of relating the text to the city's shared representations.

Neither too close nor too far from the city: such is the space careful readers have to build if they do not want to reduce the text either to its documentary function or to its monumental aspect. This imperative is particularly crucial for such texts as Aristophanes' comedies, functioning as sources of information on Greek society and everyday life, but also read as timeless classics of Greek literature which are texts judged sufficiently rich to provide their own criteria of evaluation. There is a passage in Aristophanes' *Lysistrata*, a few lines that illustrate the situation in exemplary fashion.

Women have seized the acropolis. They are besieged by men who first want to get back the treasure of the city but soon yield to a lust far more pressing than their greed. In the meantime, at the gates of the citadel, two choruses confront each other, a chorus of old men bemoaning the boldness of the women, and a chorus of Athenian women singing the glory of the women of Athens (*Lys.* 638–47):

> For we, all you citizens, begin
> with useful words for the city;
> reasonably, since the city nurtured me in splendid luxury.
> As soon as I was seven, I was an Arrêphoros,
> and then, when ten, a Grinder for the Foundress,
> and shedding my saffron robe, I was a Bear at the Brauronia,
> and once, being a beautiful girl, I was a Basket-bearer,
> wearing a necklace of dried figs.[30]

The chorus is well known among historians of Athenian religious institutions, who, seeing it as a precious document on women's initiations in Athens, extract it from the play without misgivings, as if the comic poet had simply wanted to assemble a dossier on the education of Athenian girls for the benefit of future scholars. They discard also, without a qualm, the prelude in which the women say they offer 'valuable advice' for the city (but since it is valuable to the

---

[30] Here I take up the broad outlines of an argument made in detail in Loraux (1980), where all bibliographical references about this text as a document about initiations are given.

understanding of initiations, what more could we ask?). Scholars discuss the 'information' given by Aristophanes and compare it to knowledge gleaned elsewhere. Interestingly, the operation receives the blessings of literary scholars of *Lysistrata* who voluntarily abandon to the historian what they see as a chunk of reality in the midst of fiction. Reality belongs to historians, the rest is literature . . . But as a result of this division into spheres of influence, the fact that the text at hand is actually an extract from a comedy is utterly forgotten. In other words, to excise from the *Lysistrata* a 'chorus describing women's institutions' is a necessary but partial way of reading. It is important to shed light on what the chorus says through a reference to the institutions it evokes but this goes only halfway. The essential question is yet unanswered: why such a reminder in a comedy—a comedy, what's more, about women on strike?

In order to answer the question, readers are not free to choose between reality and fiction. They have to distinguish what is real and what comes from the plot. Comparing what the women say to reality, we soon realize the glaring departure between what is known concerning the number of *Arrêphoroi* (only two young Athenians girls) and the *Lysistrata*, where 'the chorus argues *as if* the Athenian women actually *were* the city'.[31] Then readers would certainly want to go back to the beginning of the chorus when the women say they are going to tackle 'valuable' issues for the city. A further step and one will have to wonder why the women have withdrawn to the acropolis, removing themselves from male desire and playing at travelling back in time to be young servants of Athena again. All this they do, they explicitly claim, in order to bring men to unconditional surrender, and this indeed eventually happens. But the women also remind the men at this point that although they are excluded from political life, they nonetheless have a close bond with the city and its goddess.

Only now can one begin to answer the following question: why mention initiation rites in a comedy? Obviously, for an Athenian audience the chorus was not a 'document'. But while the Athenians did not need to be informed about institutions they knew perfectly well, they probably went to the theatre in order to laugh at them, to

---

[31] Vidal-Naquet (1974) 154.

laugh without danger at the city and its practices, to laugh at a fiction which still preserves reality. The intrusion of women in the political life of the city is fantasy, and an audience could laugh without anxiety at the distortions which these women inevitably brought to institutions which, since they did not aim at accommodating the erotic strategies of Athenian matrons, did not welcome all the young girls of Athens to the Acropolis.

The question of genre has thus found an answer *in extremis*. But readers who do not ask it from the start will in all likelihood not go all the way to answer it. I would say on this matter what Aristotle said of the city: even if it comes at the end of a development inscribed in chronological time, it is nonetheless present first as a necessity: such is the paradox of the question of genre that, although last to be tackled, must be asked from the beginning, and no one can avoid it without running the risk of taking seriously a development which, even if it does not make us laugh, was certainly meant to release the joy of the Athenians, because it subverts a venerable institution. One risks missing the comic in a comedy. Of course, this means one has to admit that laughter has a history and that, if timeless comedy undeniably exists (Aristophanes' obscenities and ribaldry are probably of this kind), there are also comic devices unique to the Greek city. The chorus on female initiations then becomes a second-degree document, a document on what laughing meant at Athens... What reading, even 'literary', could afford to omit understanding of the Athenian meaning of the word 'comedy'? Read in this way, the text taken as a text becomes a document: it awaits only a reader to constitute it as such.

Yet there is, or so it seems, a kind of text which spares historians the effort. The work is, so to speak, already done, since the 'inquiry has given itself as its aim a rational explanation, independent of metaphysical or mythological interpretations'. Thucydides' history, in which one can reputedly read the 'birth of modern historical thought',[32] is thought to provide a completely reliable guide to present-day historians of Greece. It is true that Thucydides' account

---

[32] Quotations from Will (1972) 513–14. Even this most sensible of historians, whose critical mind is at work when he deals with contemporary historical productions, seems to renounce all distance and to enter Thucydides' text unselfconsciously.

is indeed the canvas of all analyses of the events of the Peloponnesian War,[33] and of every historical study of the period that separates this conflict from the two Persian wars, a period universally named following Thucydides—the *Pentekontaetia* {Fifty Years}—and universally narrated according to his account, sometimes with a remark saying that this 'fundamental source' is 'sadly brief and incomplete'.[34]

Since Thucydides is supposed to have conceived of history just as we do, the only valid approach to his work is thought to be that of proximity, and since, amongst peers, proximity does not exclude criticism, a friendly critical dialogue, or even a harsh one is sometimes conducted with the Athenian historian twenty-five centuries later, to reproach him for his 'omissions' and the incomplete nature of his work.[35] In order to avoid some certitudes of positivism, however, it would be advisable to realize that there are no omissions in Thucydides if one takes into account his project to associate history and reason; from this point of view (that of the historian of the fifth century), the account of the *Pentekontaetia*, just like his study of the Peloponnesian War, is complete.[36] Omissions, silences, gaps exist only *for us*, who do not conceive history in the same terms as he does.

We are the ones who believe that the excursus in Book 1 on the early ages of Greece recognizes no flashbacks or regressions,[37] because the 'Archaeology' aims at describing an unbroken line of progress which leads toward Athens and its maritime empire. We, again, are the ones who, based on our own demands of history, enter without difficulties into a mode of exposition praised for having preferred the rational to the 'embellishments' of Athenian official

[33] If one were to push this logic to its limits, there would be no other mode of exposition than the re-exposition of Thucydides.

[34] Will (1972) 125 (in the fn.); see also 516: 'one regrets sometimes in Thucydides a tendency to expurgate'.

[35] See for example Gomme's criticisms (*HCT* I.361–413) of Thucydides' account of the *Pentekontaetia*.

[36] *History and Reason in Thucydides* is the title of a study by J. de Romilly (1959). On the *Pentekontaetia* as a 'complete' text, I side with R. Winton's analysis of this text (in an unpublished study: *The Athenian Empire, the Archê of the Athenians and the* Pentekontaetia) as an illustration of the Athenian character as described in the Corinthian speech in 1.68ff.

[37] Cf. de Romilly (1966) 161.

discourse,[38] or who put aside the religious (or even the irrational) in history and proceed, on the contrary, to enumerate facts and events passed over in silence by Thucydides or hidden behind a rationalizing explanation. It is perfectly true that, when the historian evoked the capture of Skyros by the Athenians, he said nothing of the return of the remains of Theseus, whose bones Cimon wished to install in the agora in Athens to commemorate Theseus as founder of the city. He said nothing of it because Athenian internal politics were not his immediate concern, especially not when carried out with such heroic and legendary ado. In the same way, whereas Thucydides described with an anthropologist's precision the Athenian public funeral for men fallen in battle, he painstakingly ignored all religious dimensions because he wanted to insist on their thoroughly civic and thus laic dimension. Hence we do not owe what information we have on funerary competition (*agôn epitaphios*) to him, even though it was a key part of the ceremony. Conversely, by reading him we know everything about the *agôn epitaphios* instituted by the inhabitants of Amphipolis to celebrate the Spartan Brasidas, or about the purification of Delos by the Athenians, who revived the musical competition of the ancient Ionians. But the presence or the absence of such 'pieces of information' has to be understood in the light of the logic of the narration of the war, which in reality are not information but signs: for Thucydides, they were the events of external politics that could shed light on Athenian behaviour or on the sentiments of the rest of Greece concerning the Athenians.[39] The same logic, consisting of a rational explanation of human behaviour, covers with reasonable explanations a number of practices that modern historians would

[38] In a similar way, Strasburger (1958) opposes the account of the *Pentekontaetia* in Thucydides to those in official *epitaphioi* (funeral orations).

[39] Skyros: 1.98.2 (cf. Plut. *Thes.* 36.1–2); public funerals: 2.34 (see Loraux (1986) §I.1); Brasidas: 5.11 (with Gomme, *HCT* III.654–6); purification of Delos: 3.104.5 (with Gomme, *HCT* II.414–15). At a public reading of this study in P. Vidal-Naquet's seminar (February 1980), Mr Carl Schorske observed to me that religion sometimes resumed its central place within the city of Athens in Thucydides: absent from the description of public funerals, it plays an important part in the account of the departure of the expedition to Sicily (6.32). In fact, the difference of treatment between the two episodes is easy to account for: whereas the public funeral ceremony has to be purely political, the departure of the fleet, in a frantic city soon to be plunged into consternation by the profanation of the mysteries, is both a tragic event and a manifestation of political irrationality in which prayers fit perfectly well.

explain in light of rites of initiation, and which, having been sifted, enter the historian's narrative because they are deemed 'useful' for the actions. For instance, Thucydides mentions the besieged Plataeans who attempted a sally, marching in the dead of night with only one shoe 'for security against sliding in the mud'. But social historians do not believe him, and, remembering the ephebe Jason with his single sandal, surmise that this nocturnal outing must be part of an initiation.[40]

It could be that to historians raised on his work Thucydides speaks as a colleague to colleagues. Or does he speak rather as a master to disciples? The question deserves to be asked...but a day will (or should) inevitably come when, renouncing the formulaic repetition of the master's discourse, those who have adopted Greek categories without discussion in the name of historical rationality will refuse to accept a ready-made document, and they will want to return Thucydides' *History* to its status as a text, taking in this way enough distance to constitute it as a document. Then and only then will historical work not be ready-made but ready to be invented.

Restoring Thucydides' history to its status as a text in order to treat it as a document on historical writing in the fifth century: to express such a remark is not to indulge in paradox but to take a step towards understanding what an ancient text is. At a time when writing gradually replaced the spoken word both as means of communication and as a guarantor of truth, what is the status of a *graphê*, a writing which proclaims itself as such, against the illusions of speech?[41] Not without contradictions, to be sure: in order to understand the present of *erga* {deeds}, *logos* {speech} remains the essential device of History. Speech, or rather speeches, but speeches reconstructed by writing and speeches that the historian presents as truer than reality.[42] And yet, in this confrontation between what is said and what is written, speech takes its revenge more than once: only speech provides historians with registers such as grandeur, directly inherited from epic poetry,[43] or from the narratives of *erga*

---

[40] Thuc. 3.22.1–2, with the remarks of Vidal-Naquet (1978).

[41] See Weil (1975) and esp. Longo (1978).

[42] Cf. Thuc. 1.22.1.

[43] As Canfora (1977) clearly saw, grandeur in Thucydides is 'a fundamental category of historical knowledge'.

already codified in official eloquence;[44] when history becomes a chronicle of the vicissitude of *logos* in a world dominated by war, this 'master of violence', it is speech that well and truly becomes the secret hero of historical writing. It happens, nonetheless, that speech can gain autonomy. It escapes from the written work and reduces written history to a protocol of facts: the most famous instance, because doubly exemplary, is the funeral oration pronounced by Pericles in Book 2. It is usually considered both as the model of the *epitaphios* genre and as an *analogon* {analogue} of the entire work.[45] Such a phenomenon of autonomy bears witness to a still predominantly oral culture in which the threads of writing do not contain the *logos* well, because the *logos* has been, as it were, imported.[46] This is an important matter but one that would lead us too far towards the Platonic practice of discourse (pastiche? apology? document?), yet (and this is essential) this speech, which presents itself as a hymn to the city, proclaims the superiority of the spoken word transformed into memory over writing that has been reduced to a stele, a mute stone.[47]

The funeral oration: 'document' of Athenian democracy, or, to be comprehensive, one which is taken as such in the developments of twentieth-century historians; yet at the same time and in a manner indistinguishable, it is also a spoken monument to the glory of Athens, studied only with the respect due to *prosopopoieae* {impersonations} of the past. In this text—which tempts one with such success to forget that it is one—the project of constructing 'a possession for all time' takes form: the monumental project is a trap for posterity, into which the reader cannot but fall. 'We will be the

---

[44] See for example the exploits of young and old men under the direction of Myronides (Thuc. 1.105.4), which comes straight from a similar catalogue of exploits in the *epitaphioi* (developed at length in Lysias' *Epitaphios*).

[45] See Loraux (1986) §IV.2.

[46] Here I should mention the problem of Greek authors quoted by other Greek authors. Quotation, as is necessary in an essentially oral culture, was done from memory and did not imply absolute faithfulness to the letter of the text. To my mind, this practice should be considered in relation to the Aristophanic and later Platonic device of imitating a speech to the point of having the imitation taken for an authentic sample of the genre; scholars detach the *epitaphios* in the *Menexenos* from its context, and count the discourse on love in the *Phaedrus* among Lysias' works...

[47] Thuc. 2.43.2–3, with Longo (1978) 536.

wonder not only of men of today but of aftertimes', says Pericles, says Thucydides, says the work of Thucydides—the exemplary mouthpiece of the desire for immortality at work in Greek texts of the classical era.[48]

It is this above all that makes difficult the reading of Thucydides, namely the design of the historian to write a text in such a way as to make readers forget that they are reading a text, which presents itself as a privileged document, as a window opening onto Greek 'reality'. Yet at the same time it closes access to this reality as to the reality of the text, in placing before the reader who is already overcome a monument of speech.[49] Because the confusion of monument and document is here at its peak, Thucydides' text is transformed into a tomb, the tomb of Athens, the tomb of the city. As such, it has its sights on readers to come, because it gives them a place, a role, just as steles in Greek cemeteries incited passers-by to become the repository of a dead man's memory. It says to the reader, 'remember and go to some useful task':[50] some useful task, such as writing the history of events that 'will in the future take similar or analogous forms because of human nature',[51] in other words, to write under the influence of Thucydides' historical categories.

In order to escape the prestige of authority, in order to remove the impediment, there is always a strategy for reading. In this instance, there is no other way than considering the text itself as a document. This procedure yields a twofold benefit: one not only understands how history was written in the fifth century BC, but also hopes to address to this prestigious text questions other than those it suggests and which have been seized upon by modern historiography, according to which Athens is installed as the centre of Greek studies, Pericles' funeral oration as the most exact description of democracy, and Thucydides as 'the most reliable historian'.[52]

---

[48] Thuc. 2.41.4.

[49] On history as monument, see Immerwahr (1960).

[50] Here I parody the last verse from the epitaph of a young aristocrat fallen in combat (Tettichos: *IG* I². 976).

[51] Thuc. 1.22.4.

[52] On the history of this status, which begins in Thermidorien times and is finalized with V. Duruy, see Loraux and Vidal-Naquet (1979). The quotation is from P. Ch. Lévesque (ibid. 208).

One can above all hope, since this remains the aim of historians, to come back to the facts: to the Peloponnesian War, of course, but also to Athenian democracy, better armed to understand a system in which civic genres are rooted in the heart of the tension between deed and word.

There is no ancient text that could not serve as a document. But historians who would want to avoid the fact that their documents *are* texts lose the most precious document of all: the text as a coherent system of signs and pointers towards reading, for only with this can historians deal with information without asking useless questions of it.

Necessity is law: freed (if not deliberately) from the fantasy that pure documents could exist, the historian of classical Greece has to learn how to read text–monuments that play at being documents, treasures once and for all collected by the Greeks for their own use— is a Greek ever tired of repeating his identity?—and for the edification of readers to come. Such is the awkward situation one must put up with. It offers certain advantages, however, and the historian of Greece in the byways of research can enjoy the pleasure of the text.

The dominance of texts certainly bends historical enquiry into a perspective in which everyday life does not easily fit. The historian can be left with a feeling of nostalgia for everything that texts have not preserved and has not found a place in historical memory, in the fictitious reality specific to comedy, or in the distortions and ambiguities of the tragic. No text, and an ancient text even less than any other, is a complete document. Nonetheless, the idea of a well ordained suite of written works, in which texts can have a part next to documents of another nature is a delusion best left behind from the start. There is no such thing as a 'unified discourse, in which everything—narratives, epigraphic documents, finds from archaeological excavations—would miraculously fit together'.[53] The confrontation between two parallel documents, a piece of oratorical eloquence and an epigraphic text, reminded us of that.

But there is no transparent speech either, in which documents would take their place without meddling with the threads of the plot

---

[53] I borrow this formulation from Vidal-Naquet (1980) 175.

or the weaving of the narration, and without being altered by their textual setting. This is not to say that Aristophanes' comedies or Thucydides' historiography contains no material for historians, i.e. no documents of the first degree such as those inscriptions inserted into the account of the Peloponnesian War, or such as that evocation of female initiations which serves as the *parabasis* in *Lysistrata*. Yet I would want to say that we only truly have access to these documents, in the end, after delimiting the place that the historian means to occupy as a reader of texts.

2

Myth, History, Politics—Ancient and Modern

Hans-Joachim Gehrke
English translation by Mark Beck

I

The central and elementary points of discussion in politics and history are always the questions concerning the causes of armed military conflicts: wars and civil wars.[1] They achieve special force when they bring into play the aspect of guilt and combine with it very concrete moral and juridical consequences. The resolution of the

---

[1] This essay (which does not presume to be more than the concept indicates) is primarily the fruit of countless conversations and intensive reflection provoked and fostered by the Freiburger Altertumswissenschaftliche Graduiertenkolleg 'Vergangenheitsbezug antiker Gegenwarten', in particular a seminar in Summer Semester 1992 on the topic, 'Myth as Argument in the Foreign Policy of Greek States'. For the topic dealt with here, the close interdisciplinary cooperation of classical philology, classical archaeology, and ancient history has been especially indispensible. I therefore owe a great debt of gratitude to all of my colleagues and especially to my students. A first brief version of this essay appeared in the periodical *Damals* which was then still under the professional direction of my student Kai Trampedach. The sub-sections of this article could be entitled: (I) Myth as Argument; (II) Myth as History; (III) History as Myth. Scheer (1993) appeared after the completion of this manuscript, and since empirical elaboration has been largely dispensed with in this essay, I call particular attention to this thoughtful and detailed work. In general, the 'mythical-historical' theme has been intensively investigated in recent years, especially with a view to Hellenistic and Imperial Asia Minor, and in association with the local minting of coins there, the so-called Greek Imperials. Weiss (1984) demonstrated some time ago what meaningful and adaptable graphic results could be obtained.

question of war guilt {*Kriegsschuldfrage*} in the peace treaty of Versailles burdened the Weimar Republic with a heavy indemnity, as is well known, and even in recent times the dispute about the causes and the outbreak of the First World War, this 'mother catastrophe' of our century, has remained topical.

Yet this type of dispute is basically as old as the approach to history itself. That is to say, we find elements of a discussion about war guilt already in the *pater historiae*. Herodotus raises the question at the beginning of his great work—'for what reason' Greeks and barbarians waged war against one another—and relates thereupon the Persian viewpoint: it was alleged that Phoenician sailors had once abducted Io, the daughter of the King of Greek Argos, and Greeks had taken revenge with the abduction of the Phoenician princess, Europa, from Tyre. Thereafter, however, the Greeks allegedly took the first step by leading Medea away from Colchis. They did not return her despite the demand that they do so and this indirectly caused Paris of Troy for his part to seduce the Spartan woman Helen. Instead of letting these stories about women pass, as would have been reasonable (not one had been abducted against her will anyhow!), the Greeks then began a large-scale expedition, the Trojan War. That was reputedly the beginning of enmity between the Greeks and the barbarians.[2]

It is easy to recognize the usual underlying sagas that naturally were known to the public. Io in this instance, however, is not the priestess of Hera who has been transformed into a cow, just as Europa has very little to do with a Zeus in the form of a bull. And Medea is anything but a demonical and highly active sorceress. The myths are stylized here in a special way, virtually cut to shape. They are transported into the world of the normal, the known, and readily imaginable. Phoenician traders like those with whom Io got involved sailed into a Greek port and then sailed out. The demands for the redemption of a legal entitlement ($\delta\acute{\iota}\kappa\eta\nu\ \delta\iota\delta\acute{o}\nu\alpha\iota$) were just as commonplace as the discriminatory allusions to the behaviour of women. In this way the myths were deprived of their mystique, and in exchange they were 'charged' with reality, and thereby rendered plausible. These variants of a rationalization of myths practised

---

[2] Hdt. 1.1–5.

already prior to Herodotus present an immediately obvious relationship between past and present. Back then things were no different than they are today.

This example very clearly demonstrates how myth in antiquity could also be instrumentalized politically. Myth is employed in certain situations involving conflict, and, above all, it is used in order to elucidate certain questions of law, or to substantiate certain legal claims: Who began the conflict? Who bears primary responsibility? To whom does the object that is the source of conflict belong? The abduction of women is rarely the event in question (although at the beginning of the Peloponnesian War such stories were also coined about Pericles and Aspasia in the mockery of Old Comedy);[3] more often moveable property was the cause, such as livestock, but also particularly land.[4]

Those were quite elementary and decisive questions in which the concern was to discover who had the best legal title. The upshot of this was to ask the question about the first wrong committed or even about the first owner. One thus endeavoured to surpass the respective age that the opponent advanced for his claims with an even older one, by continuously pushing the age back into the past. Contemporary history and the immediate context were not, or only partially, required here. It was necessary to descend deep into the shaft of the past, the *praeteritum*. Virtually by necessity people turned to myth.

Herodotus' discussion reveals, however, yet another no less characteristic aspect. It says something about the groups that find themselves in conflict, that face each other as parties in conflict, or as such

---

[3] Aristoph. *Ach.* 515–39 (cf. Plut. *Per.* 30.4). It is not unthinkable, by the way, that Herodotus' proem was the force behind this caricature of the outbreak of war.

[4] All of this was, however, not only a question of historiography and literature but also a common factor in everyday politics. In a legal battle concerning the ownership of territory between the Cretan *poleis* of Itanos and Hierapytna in the third decade of the second century BC, the *polis* Magnesia on the Maeander—because of kinship relations that were established purely mythically: cf. n. 43—assumed the role of arbitrator at the wish of the Roman senate. From the text of the inscription one can discern the criteria according to which land claims were generally decided. In first place stands traditional ownership ($\pi\alpha\rho\grave{\alpha}\ \pi\rho\sigma\gamma\acute{\sigma}\nu\omega\nu$); purchase ($\mathring{\alpha}\rho\gamma\upsilon\rho\acute{\iota}\sigma\upsilon\ \delta\acute{\sigma}\sigma\iota\varsigma$) follows; then conquest ($\delta\acute{\sigma}\rho\alpha\tau\iota\ \kappa\rho\alpha\tau\acute{\eta}\sigma\alpha\nu\tau\epsilon\varsigma$) and transmission by a more powerful ruler or leader ($\pi\alpha\rho\acute{\alpha}\ \tau\iota\nu\sigma\varsigma\ \tau\mathring{\omega}\nu\ \kappa\rho\epsilon\iota\sigma\sigma\acute{\sigma}\nu[\omega\nu]$) (Kern (1900) 105, 105–6). It was, therefore, a matter of proving that one had inherited something 'from ancestors'.

also first enter into and understand themselves to be in conflict. The presentation of the argumentation in Herodotus rings true only if it is based on the division between Greeks and barbarians. Only then is it possible to attribute the misdeeds of the Phoenicians and the Trojans to the Persians and make all Greeks responsible for the ones committed by the abductors of Medea and Europa. Indeed the (Herodotean) Persians assert that they were not the instigators at all, but it was rather the Phoenicians who had begun with the abductions. They allow themselves to be charged with the deed of the Phoenicians because they understand themselves to be representatives of all barbarians, in this case a huge conflict group.

This is a clear indication of the specific historical constellation in which the interpretation of these myths belongs, i.e. the historical constellation of the Persian Wars and the understanding of them as a Greek–barbarian conflict. This leads us to a further important, and likewise elementary function of myth in politics: it was essential and obviously necessary for the constitution and integration of political and social units. It contributed to the creation of identity. In our example, we already find ourselves on a universal, that is global, level: that of the polarity between Greek and barbarian (non-Greek), which encompasses the entire world. It is a question of identities that were politically rather diffuse, but indeed, in the Greek world and doubtless beyond, definitely perceived. But the use of myth was in no way restricted to this realm. We find it also, and especially on the level of the most important basic unities, in the *polis* as well as in its internal organization, the so-called *phylai* {tribes}, and in the inter-*poleis* alliances, i.e. the so-called federal states (κοινά, συμπολιτεῖαι), the 'international' cultic leagues (*Amphiktyones*) and the bi- and multilateral alliances (συμμαχίαι). What counted here, along with age and its prestigious venerability, was above all kinship. To put it more precisely, the older and the more venerable the kinship ties, the greater the increase in solidarity and loyalty that could be counted on or appealed to. And because this concerned identity and self-conception, in general it was necessary to go as far back as possible into the past, to the roots and the origins of these ties.

The family tree of Hellen and his descendants and other relatives, for example, permits clear statements about the Hellenic identity of groups, lineages, and *poleis* or about their relation to the Greeks since the time of Hesiod (seventh century) at the latest: whoever could trace his lineage to Hellen's sons Dorus and Aeolus, and his grandson Ion (from his son Xuthos) was, simply, a Hellene. The only requirement was to be Dorian, Aeolian, or Ionian in order to 'automatically' possess Hellenic identity. And Macedon, the 'progenitor' of the Macedonians, was a nephew of Hellen[5]—a very apt characterization of the proximity and yet difference of Greeks and Macedonians in the archaic period. Already at this point in time intellectual ordering, organization, rationalization, and construction were underway. But this arose from observations about reality (Macedon's residence, for example, is indicated precisely) and influenced this reality reciprocally because it provided a firm and, as such, very widely accepted definition: one could easily find oneself here.

This was even more easily possible, as the fictive kinship relations continued in the *polis*, in its organizational structures, and in the daily lives of its inhabitants: the *phylai* that existed in the *poleis*, as the name signals, were defined as descent groups. We are talking about gentilician *phylai*. They are already for their part connected with the 'tribes' that understood themselves to be descendents of Hellen: the Dorians were divided into Dymanes, Pamphyloi, and Hylleis, the Ionian *phylai* were associated with Ion's sons Geleon, Aigikores, Argadeus, and Hoples. Thus the internal form and the external classification of the polis were melded together in an elemental way.

If various *poleis* concluded an alliance, then this did not occur without the mythical background. It was obviously not sufficient to point to a common political interest. Indeed prior to the 'rational orientation to a system of discrete individual ends,'[5a] reference had to be made to affective bonds established by kinship and above all to the obligation to provide help and solidarity that results from this relationship. In the early fifth century the *poleis* Thebes and Aegina had allied themselves against an ambitious Athens that was becoming increasingly dangerous to them. At the same time we encounter a mythical version, in which both were allied by kinship ties. Asopus, the god of a river emptying into the sea at the Peloponnesian city of

[5] Hes. *Cat.* F 7 M–W.
[5a] {Translator's note: I am using here A. M. Henderson's and Talcott Parson's paraphrase translation of Max Weber's term *Zweckrationalismus* (*Max Weber: The Theory of Social and Economic Organization*, Oxford 1947).}

Sicyon and, in an older version, the father of the nymph Aegina, is simply identified with the river of the same name, the Asopus in Boeotia. Aegina is thus the sister of the nymph Thebe[6] and the alliance between Aegina and Thebes is therefore an act of support based on ties of kinship. In the Peloponnesian War the main adversaries, the Athenians and the Spartans, attempted, in part very successfully, to 'politicize' the above mentioned Ionic and Doric identities as the internal underpinnings of their respective systems of alliances.[7]

These examples offer insight into an important factor involved in making reference to myth: its religious component. Since the fifth century, for example, Apollo Patroös was regarded as the father of Ion, and his cult thus extended beyond the polis. There were likewise cults that were specific for Ionic and Doric Greeks, e.g. the Apaturia and Carnea. The Apaturia was the festival—understood in a very elementary way—of the sub-units of the *phylai*, of the *phratries* ('brotherhoods'). In every case the cult had a powerful impact and determined the feeling of identity in the respective communities and *poleis* in conjunction with the myth associated with it, regardless of whether it was a cult matter that preceded the formation of the respective groups and units, and was then in part reinterpreted, or whether it was first conceived in its entirety later, and was then retrojected into the past. The myth was not venerable solely because of its age but because of its indispensable and constantly vibrant relationship to the religious sphere.

---

[6] Pind. *Isth.* 8.16ff., cf. Hdt. 5.80. The neutrality of the Argives during the Persian wars (480 BC), which in and of itself is readily understandable as being based on political interests (Hdt. 7.148–9), was, however, also associated with their supposed mythical kinship with the Persians (Perses, their 'progenitor', as the son of Perseus, son of Danae and Andromeda: thus the Persians were the descendents [ἀπόγονοι] of the Argives). This mythical kinship at a later date was also decisive for an Argive-Persian friendship (Hdt. 7.150ff.). In this context even the Greek conception was placed in the mouth of the Persian king Xerxes, who said that it would not be fitting for the Persians to take the field against their ancestors, nor for the Argives to fight against them (οὔτε ὦν ἡμέας οἰκὸς ἐπὶ τοὺς ἡμετέρους προγόνους ἐστρατεύεσθαι, οὔτε ὑμέας ἄλλοισι τιμωρέοντας ἡμῖν ἀντιξόους γίνεσθαι, ἀλλὰ παρ' ὑμῖν αὐτοῖσι ἡσυχίην ἔχοντας κατῆσθαι, Hdt. 7.150).

[7] Cf. Smarczyk (1990) 501ff.

This was especially true of (still) unfinished political organizations that were in the process of formation or even expansion. The state of the Aetolians in western Greece furnishes a clear example. It was a relatively recent 'product' of historical development; the Aetolians were still widely regarded in the fifth century as semi-barbarians and rather uncivilized savages.[8] In the early Hellenistic period their Confederacy attained great importance in terms of its political power through its consistent anti-Macedonian politics and its service in the defence of central Greece against the Galatians. Around the middle of the third century it was ranked as a major Greek power. For the Aetolians, the sanctuary of Apollo at Thermos was simultaneously their centre and the crystallization point for their neighbours who were organized in the form of 'confederate states' or 'cantons'. For this new state an old story was especially vital. The Aetolians therefore took up the very old and rather commonplace myths from Calydon, one of their member states. A major event of the saga located there was generally well known in Greece, the hunt for the Calydonian boar. This boar was hunted by a large party of heroes under the leadership of Meleager of Calydon, and it was Meleager who finally killed it with a throw of his spear.[9]

This Meleager became an identification-figure for the later Aetolian Confederacy. The boar's tooth or lower jaw and the spear formed the symbols of the Confederacy, virtually a state coat of arms that was obviously understood as such without difficulty throughout the entire world. One can even assume that the lower jaw and spear were 'preserved' as relics in the above mentioned central sanctuary[10]—just as weapons from the Trojan War were given to Alexander the Great during his visit to Ilion, and the graves of Achilles and Patroclus were shown to him.[11] The reality of myth as an element of life for political units was therefore even concretely visible and tangible.

---

[8] Cf. Antonetti (1990).

[9] The oldest version of the myth, already rather detailed, is found in Hom. *Il.* 9.529ff.

[10] I base this example on the penetrating observation of Jördens and Becht-Jördens (1994).

[11] Arr. *Anab.* 1.11.7, 1.12.1; Diod. 17.18.1; Plut. *Alex.* 15.8; Just. 11.5.12; Ael. *VH* 12.7.

When viewed in its entirety every Greek was thus 'located' in a network of various classificatory relations. He could feel at home where he was, surrounded and supported by various relatives, and he could always feel, indeed comprehend and 'enact', this closeness in cult and ritual. This mode of classification thus had a very fundamental and real character, and a high degree of efficacy. Typically, ethnology has identified genealogies and kinship lines that are anchored in a comparably mythological way, even with quite similar structures, as characteristic of the feeling of belonging experienced by many tribes or peoples. This, therefore, very obviously reflects a fundamental anthropological constant, indeed not a ubiquitous one, but a widespread form of self-verification and self-definition.

Myth at any rate, this 'theme with variations' (Hans Blumenberg), was simultaneously familiar to the Greeks and distant, mundane and venerable, topical and remote. Well-known versions were valid, but they could be modified through new versions or supplemented. New kinship ties could be established at any time. Zeus and Heracles and Apollo, etc. could have innumerable sons.[12] The political relevance of myth is therefore unquestioned.

At any rate we may not render the meaning of myth absolute. Its value in the realm of political argumentation is on the one hand very high, but it is not absolutely decisive or the primary form of argumentation in every respect. Herodotus himself furnishes clear examples of this: after the presentation of the argumentation concerning the cause of the Persian Wars, he pushes aside the entire discussion and begins with the individual whom he personally 'knows' to have first committed injustice against the Greeks.[13] He means, of course, Croesus. In addition to the mythical realm another realm comes into play here, that of ἱστορίη {*historiē*} which is accessible through research. We can and will name it 'history'. Consequently, it takes its place beside myth in Heradotus or confers upon myth a different status.

Myth also encounters limitations in concrete political argumentation, as likewise becomes clear in Herodotus' narrative.[14] Prior to the decisive land battle against the Persians at Plataea (479 BC), an

---

[12] Cf. on this in general Gehrke (1986) 87.
[13] Hdt. 1.5.3.   [14] Hdt. 9.26ff.

argument arose over who should receive the most honourable position in the battle line after the Spartans. The Tegeans from Arcadia, the oldest allies of the Spartans, argued in favour of their claim by reference to 'old and new'. They emphasized the former, however, namely the great deed of one of their mythical kings, Echemus, who had defeated in single combat Hyllus, the son of Heracles, one of the traditional 'fathers' of the Doric–Spartan people. The Athenians, who laid claim to the second place of honour, countered with their 'old' achievements, *inter alia* the protection of the Heraclids and the fight against the Amazons, all well known myths in classical tragedy. Nevertheless they laid greater emphasis on a 'new' deed, the successful military engagement that they had waged all alone against the Persians in the battle of Marathon. And, in the way Herodotus presents the matter, this justification clearly appears to be decisive. The argumentative value of myth in politics was dependent on the respective situation and the specific circumstances.

II

Even if myth (and its value for self-conception and as argument) did not dominate in an unrestricted way and without competition, its significance can nevertheless hardly be underestimated. It offered in the world of politics, as we saw, two great advantages above all in the realm of the self-conception of groups and the safe-guarding of claims against others, i.e. in the areas of identity and conflict. With legendary traditions one could not only insist on one's rights and justify one's reputation as well as one's claims, but also establish alliances and demand political and military aid by reference to the very ordinary obligations of kinship solidarity and with appeal to the feelings of closeness that are connected to it. Additionally such bonds cloaked in the garment of myth could also be represented and propagated especially well externally. For since the time of Homer at the latest, the mythical realm was also a realm of communication in which the Greeks could understand one another, so to speak. When Herodotus (2.53) says that Hesiod and Homer had created for the Greeks their gods, this is valid *mutatis mutandis* also for myth. Poets, bards, writers, and artists participated substantially in its formation and conveyance. They 'administrated' myth, as it were, and nearly canonical authority was conferred upon the works of those who were pre-eminent among them. They contributed substantially to the development and organization of 'cultural memory' and their works were in this respect 'foundational texts' (Jan Assmann), comparable in their function to, for example, the religious texts of Egyptian and Jewish cultural circles.

Myth, as a trusted realm of the past, was for the Greeks their history, and was not distinguished in principle (and at most only partially) from what is regarded as history today.[15] This was true everywhere. It was very common and gave everyone, individuals as well as groups, a place in a well-ordered network of coordinates. Typically it was even possible to incorporate the Romans into the Greek legendary context. As is well known, they were regarded as the descendants of the Trojans (by way of Aeneas). The Acarnanian Confederation in western Greece was supposed to have attempted to extract profit from this in the third century. Since in the *Iliad* the Acarnanians are not named, they could not have fought against Troy. That was exactly what they referred to when they called for Roman aid against their Greek neighbours, the Aetolian Confederacy. Allegedly even a Roman embassy visiting the Aetolians had intervened in support of the Acarnanians because 'they alone had given no aid to the Greeks against the Trojans, their ancestors.'[16]

When later the Romans, who for their part had a completely different relationship to the past, were present politically and militarily in the Greek world, they moved closer to the Greeks in the mythical realm. One encounters a version of Roman history where Arcadians, i.e. Greeks, had already settled on Roman soil. As a result the Romans had Hellenic ancestors and were therefore related to the Greeks. In his historical work the *Origines* (*Origins*), the Roman Cato the Elder himself, not exactly suspected of philhellenism, regarded Sabo, the progenitor of the Sabines (and Sabine women!), as a Spartan. He thus placed the Romans partially in a Greek line of

---

[15] Cf. on this the superb summary in Graf (1993) 121ff.
[16] Just. 28.1.6.

descent.[17] As the title of his work and also the fragments show, he generally adopted the procedure of deriving (mythical) roots from the Greeks and transferring them to the history of the Italic tribes and cities.[18]

The basis for this specific approach to myth was to be found in the 'belief' in myth and the idea that it contained a piece of history: one's own history. For on the one hand the mythical realm was absolutely constituted as such: intellectuals and artists dealt with myth, they constructed it, worked on it, and understood it often as another world, as an opposing world, as an exemplary world, and they conveyed this. On the other hand, the Greeks recognized themselves in myth not only as in a mirror, but also as directly connected to it, in the sense of an historical continuum. Myth was, however, also temporally structured, and the succession of generations was an integral element precisely because of the ties of kinship. In the family trees of royal houses and the nobility, in the conception of communities of descent, there was a close connection with the mythical world, and the respective intervals and locations can also be measured temporally. The citizens of Greek cities saw in this their history, a panhellenic history, but also a history of their individual units. This does not necessarily have anything at all to do with 'real' history or that which we professional historians today consider to be history, and attempt to determine and reconstruct. Often absolutely nothing was known about this history.

History, as conceived by ancient contemporaries, was therefore derived essentially from myth. Added to this was what was rudimentarily known about 'real' history (e.g. about the Persian Wars, the Peloponnesian War, etc.) and what had not infrequently been clothed in the garment of myth and 'mythicized'. As history that was believed, the stories and sagas were, however, of considerable and not seldom decisive significance for real life and political behaviour. I would like to suggest for it the name 'intentional history' and employ it in what follows. The concept of intention, as it is understood here, is borrowed from ethno-sociology, above all the concept

[17] Cato, *HRR* F 51 (= Serv. ad *Aen.* 8.638), on which cf. Gehrke (1994) 601.
[18] On Cato in this respect, see especially Kienast (1954) 107ff.; Badian (1966) 8–9; Timpe (1970/71) 5ff.

of Wilhelm Mühlmann, who emphasized the aspect of self-classifi-
cation and consciousness, of subjectivity and even intentionality
(and the self-stylization connected with it) as essential factors in
the determination of tribes or comparable large ethnic groups.[19]
The medievalist Reinhard Wenskus demonstrated the applicability
of this concept for the history of the Germanic tribes especially
during the Migration period {*Völkerwanderung*}.[20] Accordingly it is
reasonable to characterize history in its assumptions as intentional
and then, following Wenskus ((1961) 9), to understand intentional
history as that which in a group is '*known*' about the past, 'how the
past is *evaluated*, and what it *means*'—independent of what historical
research in the modern sense thinks about this. In so far as this
history created identity for the respective groups and communities,
and established its existence as it were, it is possible also to characterize it as 'hot memory' {*heisse Erinnerung*}, following Jan Assmann
who moreover identifies myth with 'foundational stories' and very
clearly points out the character of such a myth that creates meaning
and values: 'Myth is a story that one tells to orient oneself vis-à-vis
oneself and the world, a truth of a higher order that is not merely
right but also makes normative demands and possesses formative
power.'[21]

In any case, in examining the ancient tradition, we have to allow
the boundaries between myth and history to fall as much as possible.
On the one hand even highly critical historians such as Thucydides
never doubted the historical reality of the Trojan War and other
important mythical constellations. At best (but by no means consistently) one called into question or reinterpreted the miraculous and
fantastic element of myth and rationalized it in the light of one's own
conceptions in the fashion already practised in the early Ionic intellectual revolution (as Hecataeus first did). Herodotus' discussion of
who was to blame for the war attests to this. Io is, as already
indicated, not the cow persecuted by Hera, Europa is not abducted

[19] Mühlmann (1938), esp. 108ff., 124ff.
[20] Wenskus (1961), esp. 1ff. {The *Völkerwanderung* was the period of the great
migrations of the Germanic peoples from about 300–900 AD, including, but not
limited to, the barbarian invasions attendant upon the fall of Rome.}
[21] Assmann (1992) 66ff.; citation from p. 76.

by the besotted bull Zeus, Medea is not the sorceress in the vicinity
of the Golden Fleece.[22] Again and again we encounter, especially
in authors who are close to philosophy, e.g. Strabo and Lucian,
the feeling of uneasiness associated with μυθῶδες {*muthōdes*}, with
the all-too-fabulous element in the old stories.[23] Never, however, are
myth and history strictly separated; never is the historical realm
distinctly delimited from the mythical realm.

Conversely, historical events, especially great deeds of war, are also,
often very quickly, 'mythicized', that is conceived of and represented
as mythical events: the victories of Marathon, Salamis, and Plataea
over the Persians were particularly well-suited for this. Miraculous
signs played a part, gods took part in the battle, humans accomplished superhuman feats. It was therefore not offensive when Miltiades, the hero of Marathon, was pictorially represented with gods
and heroes. In the Painted Stoa (*Stoa Poikilē*) in the Athenian Agora
(so-called because of its famous paintings), one could see four
thematic complexes: the battle of Oinoe, an event probably from
the middle of the fifth century; the battle of the Athenians under
Theseus against the Amazons; a gathering of the Greek kings after the
capture of Troy on the occasion of the rape of Cassandra by Ajax; and
the battle of Marathon. This last represented a concrete situation in
the battle: the combatants, i.e. the Athenians, Plataeans, and the
various units of the Persian army were recognizable. But:

here is also a portrait of the hero Marathon, after whom the plain is named,
and Theseus represented as one rising from the earth, and Athena and
Heracles... Among the warriors in the painting, the most conspicuous is
Callimachus, who was elected Athenian polemarch, and Miltiades, one of
the generals, and the hero Echetlus.[24]

The complete amalgamation of mythical and historical occurrences,
the 'historicization' of myth and the 'mythicization' of history, is
manifest and conspicuous here.

In addition, how self-evident and commonplace this blending was
is shown by the fact that Aeschylus brought a drama about the

---

[22] Cf. also Graf (1993) 121–2.
[23] See, e.g. Str. 1.2.35, 10.3.7, 10.3.23, Luc. *h.c.* 60, with Homeyer (1965) 279–80;
on μυθῶδες in Thucydides, see Graf (1993) 123.
[24] Paus. 1.15.3.

victory over the Persians to the stage that was reserved for myth. At the same time this presented the opportunity to work through great historical events and the fundamental experiences connected with them, to give them meaning, and to explain what was mysterious and wondrous. One's own success, which could hardly be grasped, was ultimately ascribed to the excesses and *hubris* of the Persian king towards the gods, i.e. to divine punishment, without the minimization of one's own contribution. The connection of Greekness with freedom was thereby deeply etched in Greek and Athenian self-conception. Precisely in the context of such important occurrences, such as the Persian Wars, myths and legends could rapidly develop and entwine around the leading personalities. All manner of cunning ruses and tricks were already ascribed to Themistocles,[25] the strategic father of the victory, shortly after the battle of Salamis. His indisputable political insight and the Greek passion for the deliberate trick, for $\mu\eta\chi\alpha\nu\dot{\eta}\mu\alpha\tau\alpha$ {contrivances} and $\tau\dot{\epsilon}\chi\nu\eta$ {skill, craft}, were combined in a portrait in which a second Odysseus practically emerges before our eyes.

Such things happened repeatedly, precisely in connection with important occurrences that affected and concerned people and their livelihood and that were surprising and unexpected. Thus the deeds of Alexander the Great and his Successors especially were later celebrated as the achievements of mythical heroes. With them another dimension of the amalgamation of myth and history is simultaneously reinvented before our eyes: the historical actors stylize themselves according to myth. Even the boundaries between the mythical and the concrete, historical event became blurred here among the actors.[26] They acted as if they themselves were mythical heroes, they virtually entered into competition with them. Heracles

---

[25] On the tradition about him cf. the brief sketch in Frost (1980) 3ff.

[26] On Alexander in this respect cf. especially Heuss (1977) 29ff., particularly 35; additional information in Gehrke (1990) 139–40. Cf. further the virtually Homeric single combat of Ptolemy against the Indian tribe of the Aspasians (Arr. *Anab.* 4.24.3ff.) or Lysippus' representation of the fight with the lion, a work that Alexander's comrade-in-arms Craterus dedicated to Delphic Apollo (*Fouilles de Delphes* III.4.137; Plin. *HN* 34.64; Plut. *Alex.* 40.5) and that naturally suggested an association with Heracles' first labour.

and Achilles, even Dionysus, were the point of reference for Alexander's plans. This relationship was always present and was always presented in the form of displays of a thoroughly ritual character. After landing in Asia Minor, Alexander proceeded immediately to the small and insignificant Ilion that lived primarily on the fame of its 'Trojan' past. There he sacrificed to Athena Ilias and dedicated to her his arms. In compensation he received weapons that, as mentioned above, were allegedly from the time of the Trojan War. Notably he conducted expiatory sacrifices for the slaughter of King Priam by Neoptolemus, whom he regarded as his ancestor. Here already the mere reference to the myth has become an element of personal identification. The affirmation of the relationship becomes even clearer when Alexander crowned the (supposed) grave of Achilles with a wreath, just as his closest friend Hephaestion crowned that of Patroclus.[27]

These types of heroizations also occurred in everyday life, beyond the realm of 'great politics' and the events associated with it. It is characteristic of this that deeds of the quality of Heracles' achievements were attributed to great athletes, above all, naturally, to those who had multiple victories at Olympia: Pausanias tells of the boxer Euthymus from Locri in south Italy, who had been a three-time Olympic victor in boxing in the first half of the fifth century and whose statue he still saw. He reports that Euthymus not only achieved great things as an athlete, he also fought with a hero after his return to Italy. In Temesa every year the most beautiful maiden was given, i.e. sacrificed, to a *daimôn* honoured in cult. 'Euthymus came to Temesa, and there the custom for the *daimôn* had just been conducted. He learnt of her plight and desired to enter the temple and see the virgin. As soon as he saw her, he was seized first with pity, then with love. The maiden swore she would marry him if he could save her, and Euthymos awaited in arms the appearance of the *daimôn*.'[28] Typically Euthymos was then also regarded as the son of the river god Caecinus (the river on the border between Locri and Rhegium).[29]

---

[27] Cf. the reff. in n. 11 as well as the summary in Gehrke (1990) 12–13.
[28] Paus. 6.6.7ff.   [29] Paus. 6.6.4.

The connection between great athletic accomplishment and her-
oization was so widespread that in the wake of the rationalizing
interpretation of myth, Heracles was seen as a former sports cham-
pion. The list of the Olympic victors included him,[30] and he was even
celebrated as the founder of the Olympic Games, as portrayed especially in Pindar's *Olympian* 10. Theogenes of Thasos, in his day a
famous competitor of Euthymos', was thus also regarded as the son of
Heracles. Virtually magical powers were ascribed to a statue that
depicted him, and he himself was in part honoured as a god of
healing.[31] One sees here how the proximity of divine and human
spheres, viewed as a specific characteristic of Greek culture, is connected with this concreteness of myth. At any rate there was no
principal division under this aspect, no boundary between myth
and event, between saga and history.

Even where myth or the myths, i.e. whatever people said, were
subjected to the criticism of the thinking mind and investigatory
search for truth (as for the first time in the Ionic ἱστορίη of Hecataeus
and Herodotus), mythical occurrences were not regarded as ahistorical or ignored as such, but rather only in so far as they were resistant
to rational comprehension or eluded the inquiries of research.[32] If
shortly thereafter, Thucydides wanted to open the eyes of the Athenians to the establishment of their democracy and sought therein to
replace the contribution of the tyrant slayers Harmodius and Arito-
geiton with the unpleasant truth (especially in the Peloponnesian
War) of Spartan intervention against the Athenian tyrants,[33] then he
will have had hardly any success. Too much of a spell had been cast
over this great event through the fascination of myth.

In general this was also true of Greek culture: one always had a
story, even when one, according to our criteria, did not know one's
past at all. To put it differently, one knew one's past very well. It was
that which everywhere impinged upon one's eyes and ears in the
world of portraits and statues, in the milieu of poems and songs.
That is the reason, by the way, that we modern historians grasp much
more clearly this intentional history than genuine history. We can see
this most clearly in the periegete Pausanias: like every good tour

[30] Jüthner and Brein (1965) 129.   [31] Paus. 6.11.2ff.
[32] Graf (1993) 121ff. and cf. above.   [33] Thuc. 1.20.2; 6.54ff.

guide today, he begins his description of new regions and locations in each case with a historical outline. This consists primarily of mythological genealogies and legendary prehistory; it becomes historical, in our sense, usually only with the treatment of events from the time of the Persian Wars. This is a later reflection of the fact that Greek history in important areas first became comprehensible through Herodotus, i.e. with the collection and fixation of older traditions in the scope of the depiction of the Persian Wars. The previous period of time could still be grasped only in myth or in events mythically overvalued: thus, according to our conceptions, events that were completely deformed (e.g. the Lelantine War and the Messenian Wars).[34]

Modern historical criticism, which acknowledges its obligation to the aforementioned 'founding heroes' Hecataeus, Herodotus, and Thucydides, is correctly cautious with respect to this entire complex. It can in actual fact hardly be sceptical enough, if the aim is to reconstruct the historical event in the most refined way possible. It will place much more trust in archaeological discoveries or historical–linguistic observations than in the ancient tradition. One must

[34] This of course does not mean—in so far as misunderstandings may be prevented—that the point was reached more or less with Herodotus when orality simply changed into literacy, as is readily assumed today. Herodotus' principles of research were decisive. They placed personal investigation and inquiry in the foreground and not so much—as obviously was the case in Hecataeus and certainly Thucydides (especially in the so-called 'Archaeology')—the critical penetration of the old myths that had already been transmitted in literature. The correspondence of the picture of earlier depicted history with the typical oral-tradition pattern (time of origin—'floating gap'—recent past) by Jan Vansina (1985) is thus not attributable to common structural characteristics, but more likely to chance or dependent on an individual decision, namely Herodotus'. This does not deny that a great deal of orally transmitted information was preserved by Herodotus and was then transmitted further from a 'written' point of origin. The reconstruction, however, that proceeds orality—Herodotus—literacy is too beautiful schematically to be true. Generally one should guard against rendering the medial aspect (orality versus literacy) more or less absolutely. Schott (1968) 166ff. cites a number of common structural characteristics between our observations and those of ethnology (the bearing of the past on the present and its events; its significance for the legitimization of legal claims and for identity, especially in intercultural contact; the fluid boundaries between myth and history). The existence of elaborated conceptions of time with corresponding points of reference and modes of calculation is obviously decisive. In this regard Herodotus attained special quality (see Strasburger 1956). For this, however, the archaic period had 'done the preparatory work'.

take care, however, not to completely ignore the ancient tradition for this reason; quite the contrary. Precisely if we consider its status, how that status arose from previous traditions, we will confer special value on them, in particular in the realm of what we today call the history of mentalities. If one asks, in short, which explicit and implicit, conscious and unconscious, rational and affective conceptions and attitudes influence the thought and feelings of people and motivate their actions, then one must also and especially inquire about their respective self-conception. For example, what image of themselves danced before the eyes of the Athenians as individuals, but above all as Athenians? What commitments did this imply? What behaviour did it demand? Such questions point one back in the direction of the tradition, towards intentional history. This was indeed much more closely connected with their self-conception than history in our sense, because it had developed in close connection with concrete life situations and with the processing of elementary experiences.

It is thus not only worthwhile but also necessary for the understanding of ancient history and culture, to inquire into this intentional history—and also into myth. In the case of Athens this is especially possible because we are in possession of rich material, above all dramas and funeral orations (*epitaphioi*) that enable us to reconstruct the conceptions of an Athenian from his history, and thereby an essential element of his self-image, with the orientations and obligations that result from those conceptions. One finds there the basic ideal to be the fight against the powers of disorder, savagery, and barbarism for one's own freedom and for Hellenic freedom as well as for the protection of the weak. Many facets, however, become apparent when inquiries are made regarding the diverse elements and their historical origin. Nicole Loraux made a first attempt in this direction in her stimulating book about the *epitaphioi*.[35] Here, but also for other *poleis*, there still remains much work to do, work

[35] Loraux (1986); cf. also the collection of material in Schröder (1914); Jost (1935); and further the references in Gehrke (1976) 49 n. 67. Graf (1993) 136–40 sketches the Theseus myth as a study of the intentional history of Athens. In a general way the topic dealt with here has been subjected to a stimulating treatment by Cartledge (1993). The observations of Bowie (1986) are also important in this context: he infers large-scale elegies with 'substantial narratives of their city's history'

which must rely on the fruitful cooperation of philology, archaeology, and history. The reason for this lies in the medial side of our
topic, as becomes immediately clear when one sees in what way and
in which forms this intentional history is transmitted to us.

Intentional history as myth had, as has already been suggested
numerous times, yet another, aesthetic side: myth was much more
attractive than real history! That was not surprising, as myth indeed
sprang ultimately from artistic and poetic inspiration. Singers and
poets, and then painters and sculptors, had an impact on myth.
In this sense the first historian was Homer, the *Iliad* definitely
an historical book—of intentional history. Almost immediately,
therefore, historiography transmitted epic motifs and continued to
develop and examine them critically. We can observe this still in its
founding heroes, Herodotus and Thucydides, and it is also seen in
the epic tradition. As was the case between myth and history, the
borders between their most important media—epic and historiography—were also fluid. History was thus placed within an intellectual discourse. It developed its own independent methodology, but
also remained an integral part of aesthetic and literary communication: the association between history as science and history as art
form was not as strictly separated as we are accustomed to think.

It is also possible to observe how historiography is repeatedly
subject to predetermined literary conventions. Under the influence
of the great Athenian *rhetor* and stylist Isocrates it was 'rhetoricized'
in the fourth century BC, as is well known. Later, in the early
Hellenistic period, one spoke of the new direction of 'tragic historiography'. Both in its objectives, as well as its use of language, this was
fiction as we would understand it, not the rigid search for ἀκριβές
and ἀλήθεια, for exactitude and truth; rather, it sought affect and
effect.

It remained *à la longue* the dominant direction, as Lucian shows in
his polemical attempt to establish the dedication to truth and usefulness, rather than exaggeration and bias, as the primary element
of ἱστορίαν συγγράφειν, the writing of historical works. The figure of

that were presented at public festivals, with which 'the city as a whole defined its
corporate identity and paraded its internal history' (34: I thank Reinhold Bichler,
Innsbruck for this reference).

Alexander the Great and the period of the Diadochs' battles, which was so full of reversals, established or at least decisively reinforced the predilection for the miraculous and sensational presented in an appropriate style. Significantly, the roots of popular Alexander history such as the Alexander Romance were probably to be sought in Cleitarchus.[36]

It is easy to see that this literary and artistic character of historiography considerably promotes the mythicization of history or rather the identity of myth and history in intentional history. The world of stories and pictures renders available a nearly unlimited supply of motifs and *topoi* that could be varied and transferred—one is reminded of the fairy-tale element of slaying the monster in the story of the Olympic victor Euthymus. This then was not initially an 'invention' of Hellenism, but entirely characteristic of the association with the past, a return to roots, so to speak.[37] For long before historiography, history indeed, as just mentioned, had been conceived of and presented in the medium of literary–artistic communication.

This had significant consequences also for the subject matter and structure of intentional history. Whatever arose from artistic inspiration, i.e. for example what was staged by a tragedian of the fifth century in literary engagement with older variants, could thereafter—independently of the author's objectives—be taken as historical fact and made an essential part of intentional history. This was promoted in particular by the fact that one always saw something prophetic embodied especially in the poets; a special wisdom, and a special knowledge. Other artists, writers, and philosophers could also profit from this esteem, and it is therefore not surprising when Plato clothes many of his messages in the garment of myth or even presents them in the form of a 'myth-history' structured in a chronologically exact way—with such great effect that the search for sunken Atlantis was and is repeatedly undertaken.[38] In reality this concerns pseudo-history. And on principle this was also not different for the variants

---

[36] The foundations for this topic have been laid by Schwartz (1903) and Jacoby (1922). On tragic historiography, see esp. von Fritz (1956) and Walbank (1960) {= Ch. 14, below}; in general cf. now the overview in Meister (1990) 80ff.

[37] Cf. Patzek (1992) 158–9 for an equivalent relationship in Homer.

[38] On this cf. Vidal-Naquet (1993) 61ff.

and versions that were promulgated by other authors and artists. If, however, the conglomerate that had been fashioned was taken up and believed, it was history, and was then also known as such or was at least accessible in so far as it was no longer alterable. One had to engage with such versions, if one wanted to say or reconstruct something else. Especially weighty were variants derived from authoritative writers such as Homer or Hesiod, whose works, as discussed above, had the character of foundational texts. But it was in no way limited to these texts. Various parts of early Macedonian history were based on tragedies that Euripides had composed at the court of King Archelaus.[39] History could, therefore, be 'creatively' supplemented (euphemistically speaking). It oscillated between what was fixed and therefore unchangeable (the older versions just mentioned) and reinterpretations or pure inventions (to put it less euphemistically).

It is hardly difficult to imagine what these preconditions and possibilities meant for the relationship between myth and politics—especially in view of a public whose historical knowledge was rather limited (even with respect to intentional history). Since this intentional history represented a central argument for legal claims, legitimization in conflicts and wars, appeals for aid and alliances, and for the ranking of cities, it seemed reasonable to organize and expand it, and thereby strengthen one's own positions. For these reasons we can still frequently observe today the concrete historical situations in which a myth arose. If suddenly, in a Greek list at Delphi visible also to the Greek public, a hero Triphylos is related to the progenitors of the Arcadians, then this is a reaction to the political aspirations of the Arcadian Confederacy directed at Triphylia, the neighbouring country to the west, in the 360s BC.[40] Great care was applied by all participants to conceptualize and interpret, and thereby also to normatively shape in an 'intentional–historical' way, Rome's involvement in the world of Greek politics in the latter part of the third and

---

[39] Cf. now especially Borza (1990) 172–3.

[40] The information about Arcadian genealogy in Paus. 8.1ff. should be compared with the Arcadian dedication, *Fouilles de Delphes* III.1.3; on the historical interpretation, see now Kopp (1992) 157ff.

the early second century using mythical references (Rome—Perga-mum—Troy; Rome—Achaea—Arcadia).[41]

That, likewise, had consequences for the concrete association with history and for the role of historians. A dispute over fertile agricul-tural land between the *poleis* of Samos and Priene that went on for decades and is known to us through inscriptions from the temple of Athena in Priene from the second century BC provides in its outlines a graphic example for this state of affairs.[42] In the scope of an 'international' legal dispute, in which the island republic of Rhodes served as arbitrator, the ambassadors of the parties in conflict deliv-ered their arguments. *Inter alia* the earliest ownership of the disputed territory also played a role. For this reason one delved deeply into the intentional history of the region, or rather of the Ionic cities, to an event completely anchored in myth, the destruction of an older city and the distribution of its territory. In all this historians, or more precisely their works i.e. (ἱστορίαι), virtually became witnesses (μάρτυρες) in a trial. The Samians called to witness a Milesian historian by the name of Maiandrios, while the Prienians refuted their arguments by citing seven other historians, including four Samians, in whose works another version of the distribution was to be found that was unfavourable to the Samians. It thus became a matter of a 'false statement' by the other 'witness': the *Histories* of Maiandrios were ψευδεπίγραφοι, forged or distorted!

This blow to the credibility of witnesses (to put it in legal terms) is, from an historical and modern point of view, an example of com-parative source criticism: the parallel tradition is utilized as a control and possible signs of bias (political affiliation) are then also consid-ered so as to decide between two variants. Historical works here have absolutely the same value that documents concerning bestowals and endowments had in comparable legal disputes in the Middle Ages

---

[41] On this Mavrogiannis will make substantial contributions {= Mavrogiannis 2003}; cf. for now Mavrogiannis (1989/90).

[42] *Inschriften von Priene* 37; further references in Chaniotis (1988) 129–30. An-other important example is the previously mentioned border dispute between Itanos and Hierapytna (Chaniotis (1988) 4). In deciding this the [ποιη]τῶν καὶ ἱστοριογράφων ἀποδείξεις {'writings of poets and historians'} (Kern (1900) 105.65) played an important role.

and the modern era; and forgery and the reproach of forgery were correspondingly common.

Even if the subject was not war and conflict at all, but rather 'only' the rank and reputation of the *polis*, great care was taken. When, towards the end of the third century BC, the citizens of Magnesia on the Maeander established a great religious festival in honour of their goddess, Artemis 'with the white brow' (*Leucophryênê*), and sought simultaneously to acquire for their *polis* the dignity, prestige, and security of a 'holy city', they commissioned historians to compose their own foundation history which especially emphasized their origin and kinship relations to other Greeks. The official text was chiselled into stone and put on display in a great hall in the central square of the city together with the letters and decisions of the rulers, *poleis*, and alliances that recognized the important role of the festival games. To these inscriptional documents belongs also an 'Alliance of Cretans' which authenticated an important detail of the foundation history, but had been fabricated specifically for this purpose and was given a date around nine hundred years older than it was.[43] For us modern historians it is, to put it bluntly, forged, or at any rate fictitious; it seems almost futile to seek an authentic core in this version. Yet for the Magnesians and their contemporaries it was 'history'. It was also structurally oriented towards their roots, the earliest past, in which identity, original kinship connections, and ancient relationships were created. And it amply fulfilled its argumentative aim, and was thus highly effective.

Everything was possible in and with intentional history: the internal discourse of historians, the debate about known traditions and their employment for political objectives, even their creative supplementation, not only by ingenious suppositions, but also through manifest falsifications. Myth, which was also always a realm for

---

[43] The texts are published in Kern (1900), nos. 16–87. For the matters discussed here, the dedication decision no. 16 (on which cf. now Ebert 1982) and the foundation history no. 17 (see also Kern 1894) are very important; on the historical interpretation, see Prinz (1979) 111ff.); the fictitious *psêphisma* {decree} of the Cretan *koinon* is no. 20. An inscription from Xanthos is likewise a very illustrative document for a corresponding engagement with 'history' in a political context: see Bousquet (1988).

artificial and intellectual creativity, provided the ideal framework for this.

III

If we conceive of myth as intentional history, as history that is an essential element of self-verification, the fixing of one's place, and the creation of identity and its preservation, then very striking parallels from the modern era, even the present, arise concerning the question of its political function. Jan Assmann, in his extensive and in-depth reflections on collective memory cited above, has discussed in detail the 'case' of Israel.[44] In particular the people of Israel provide an especially impressive example for the circumstances discussed here, even though in some respects it is different and connected with other assumptions, above all of a religious nature. Here we seize upon, in a specific form, a continuity in the preservation of tradition that encompasses thousands of years and rests upon memory that is anchored in a consciously cultivated belief in the bond with Yahweh. The memory of God's care for his people, in religiously founded festivals and rites, in the circle of the family, and in the synagogue, is transmitted from father to son, from the older to the younger. It predisposes Jews, with a quite singular poignancy, to speak of 'we', of 'our' departure from Egypt to the Promised Land, of 'our' Babylonian Captivity, 'our' fight against the Hellenistic monarchs and Roman emperors, of 'our' Diaspora and persecution up to the Holocaust and the foundation of a new state.

Mythical elements also are found everywhere in the tradition. But archaeological investigations too are not only scientific endeavours but also searches for evidence in terms of self-verification. They are directed at the traces that have been left behind and they also serve, specifically for this purpose, to confirm and to concretize or supplement the tradition preserved in holy writings and in religious customs. Simultaneously they provide the opportunity to substantiate historically fixed claims to land and to legitimize them in contemporary politics.

---

[44] Assmann (1992) 196ff.

What is markedly pronounced here, in view of the specific Jewish understanding of history, is found, however, nearly everywhere with very similar structures. In the field of conflict in the Middle East, the Israelis are by no means the only ones who instrumentalize history and archaeology politically. The same is also true *mutatis mutandis* of their current opponents. And the question as to which population groups are understood as ancestors or relatives who settled (e.g. in the second and early first millennium), in Palestine, Israel, and the Levant,[45] is discussed not only with scholarly vigour, but also with political passion. The reference to the past has a creative and foundational function; following what was said above, it concerns a 'hot memory'.

In other regions the same circumstances have acquired a particularly oppressive topicality, as a look at the Balkan catastrophe shows. Here too, especially here, especially in the present constellation of conflict, memory is 'hot': the Croatian guerrilla can declare before running cameras, '*We* Croatians have defended Europe against the Turks for centuries.' And his and his comrades' readiness to commit acts of violence is fostered and legitimized not least of all by this assumption and the feelings that accompany it. The sombre myth of annihilation at the Battle of Kosovo, a central event of Serbian history, and especially of the intentional history of the Serbs, obstructs a sober and appropriate treatment of the difficult problems of Kosovo to the point of rendering it impossible. And, as in the Macedonian question,[46] the structure of the arguments is downright ancient up to the smallest detail: it concerns borders, i.e. land and rights. Important, indeed decisive, is the age of the claims. The opponents therefore place themselves in close relationship to their ancestors, the Macedonians. They thereby associate themselves with the oldest conceivable historical group that is distinguished by a high level of prestige. History is the argument, but with the elementary categories of kinship and genealogy. It thereby reveals itself as intentional history.

Here, then, the much discussed question in historical circles as to whether the Macedonians were Greeks becomes a political one.

---

[45] Cf. the overview in Malamar (1992) 35ff.
[46] On this, cf. Rondholz (1993).

Interestingly this was the case already in the study of ancient history in Germany in the nineteenth century when leading historians, not least Johann Gustav Droysen, saw in the 'unification' of Greece by the Macedonians a clear parallel to the unification of Germany by Prussia.[47] And so, just as the Prussians were indisputably Germans, the Macedonians must also have been Greeks; since it certainly concerned the same national issue. At that time it was only a question of analogies, nevertheless it was discussed with some vehemence. Today in the southern Balkans it concerns the Macedonians' own cause, and emotionality there encounters almost no limits.

It is especially characteristic that here too—as we have already established for antiquity—signs and symbols of the past play an essential role. Archaeological findings thus can attest to age and identity, they are claimed by both sides, and attain the status of coats of arms and symbols of state: an emblem—a star known to us from ancient Macedonian shields, coins, and the golden cinerary urns from the graves in Vergina—has thus become a important object of contention. It is interpreted as an ancient Macedonian dynastic or regal symbol.[48] Above all it is portrayed again and again, and becomes through various media (including stamps and coins) a common image with a specific meaning. It has also become a visible expression of intentional history and develops its own political dynamic; it becomes an object of contention between Greece and her northern neighbour which calls itself the 'Republic of Macedonia', while in Greece it is commonly called Skopje after its capital.[49]

---

[47] See especially Droysen (1920) 11ff.; id. (1877) I.1.29–30, 44ff.; on the interpretation, cf. especially Landfester (1988) 138; further references (and a critique of the 'overuse' of the analogy in the interpretation of Droysen's concept) in Wagner (1991) 54ff.

[48] Cf., e.g., Andronikos (1981) 224 ('probably the royal emblem'). In the meantime the star is interpreted as the Macedonian sun and connected with the fairy-tale history (cf. Hammond and Griffith 1979: 7) of the early Argeads in Hdt. 8.137ff.; cf., e.g., Borza (1990) 81: 'One wonders if this story were the inspiration for the Macedonians' adoption of the radiate sun (or star) as a national [*sic*!] symbol.' The problematic nature of such interpretations has now been demonstrated by the richly illustrated analysis of Mitropolou (1993).

[49] Cf. Rondholz (1993) 877. On the immense significance of symbols in general (hymns, flags, coats of arms) which can represent the entirety, so to speak, see Hobsbawm (1983) 10ff.

Soberly considered, it is obviously absurd, given post-antique history and especially more recent developments, when the former Yugoslavian Republic of Macedonia ties itself to ancient Macedonia. But the opposite side does not primarily argue in this way. A history of great antiquity, lost in dark, mythical, prehistoric times, is required. It obviously must be the case that Macedon for thousands of years or from the very beginning, was and is Greek. On the other hand, in the so apparently scurrilous recourse on the part of the Republic of Skopje, one recognizes the urgent, even elementary need for a historical identity, for intentional history. Such an intention is generally quite detectable, particularly where a nation is *in statu nascendi*, so to speak, and/or where because of political conflicts it sees itself endangered in its identity, integrity, and development.

Thus, as already mentioned, the examples sketched here are representative, particularly in our time, where the world order that seemed to be so rigidly cemented is in flux again. Before the plenary assembly of the United Nations on 23 September 1991, the then President of the United States, George Bush, explained: 'People who for years had been denied their pasts have begun searching for their own identities . . . This revival of history ushers in a new era.'[50] Everywhere national identity is becoming a topic that is important and widely experienced as existential.[51] And particularly for this reason people strive to descend deep into the 'well of the past', to beginnings and oldest ancestors. Thus one has recourse almost unavoidably to myths, and so today one also sees the unity of myth and intentional history. Historical linguistics and archaeology, our other means of access to earliest times, are integrated into this conception of the past, and become, for their part, a component of intentional history.

Admittedly we—i.e. we historians of central and western Europe—have no reason to feel correspondingly superior in view of this. Indeed,

---

[50] President George Bush, cited from the epigraph in Cartledge (1993).

[51] Hobsbawm (1990) now offers an important overview of this complex of themes, within the historical context of nation-building and nationalism. Hobsbawm previously ((1983) 14–15, 266ff.) had already made clear that the history of developing nations in particular is also a field for 'invented traditions', and cites there (267) Massimo d'Azeglio's famous dictum of the post-Garibaldi time: 'We have made Italy; now we must make Italians.'

the modern science of history, which consciously and rightly refers to the above-mentioned 'Enlightenment' tendencies and methods within ancient history, has strongly delimited its scope vis-à-vis the instrumentalization of the past, the creative development and formation of intentional history, and the construction of myth and legend for political purposes. Fabrications, distortions, and fictions are easy to detect. In his famous Sorbonne lecture of 11 March 1882 concerning the question 'What is a Nation?' (still today one of the most lucid discussions of this topic), Ernest Renan perceived progress in the study of history as a 'danger' to nationality.[52] But he also noticed very clearly that a nation also needs a 'common store of a rich legacy of memories': critical history causes problems; intentional history is required. In view of this tension we must in no way be too optimistic. We have not exorcised the demons.

In the blossoming of the critical science of history {*Geschichtswissenschaft*} lay and lies the blossoming of historical construction and mythicization. We have in part experienced how history was instrumentalized for totalitarian purposes, be it in Communism, Fascism, or National Socialism: an instrumentalization that consisted precisely of history running to myth, the myth of continuous class struggle, of 'wandering Jews', of the dominance of the 'Nordic races', and whatever other such myths of the twentieth century may also exist. These are extreme cases. They do not stand up to scholarly examination. But does scholarship always have the opportunity to be tested? Were scholars ready to do this? Wasn't it also scholars who together created these constructs and lovingly arranged them—like their anonymous 'ancestors' who fashioned for the *polis* of Magnesia on the Maeander its history?

There is yet a second reason not to be too optimistic with regard to the science of history and its possibilities. Even a professional involvement with history itself can easily lead to intentional history. The boundaries can also become blurred here; occasionally they can become almost as fluid as those between myth and history in

---

[52] Renan (1882) 7–8: 'Forgetfulness and I would say even historical error are an essential factor in the formation of a nation, and it is thus that the progress of historical studies is often a danger for nationality.' Historical research, he thought, would bring to light the momentous events that had stood at the beginning of the establishment of the state and the nation.

antiquity. Whoever as a historian is sufficiently honest and self-critical is familiar with how one can give or has given, even occasionally must give—even *intra muros*—different interpretations to historical circumstances and processes. This can be seen even in the reconstruction of details, in naked factuality, e.g. the concrete and elementary question about the sequence of events, about chronology, the 'backbone of history'. For it is a matter of priorities that then do not remain purely temporal. One remembers what role the question of the *prius* of Bolshevik or National Socialistic terror played in the so-called *Historikerstreit*.{52a}

That our understanding of history between science and intentionality, between *historiē* and myth, can change so remarkably even within the profession too, is connected with the conditions under which it came into being; to a certain extent it is inherent in it from the beginning.[53] What we today call the scientific approach to history has its roots in the Romantic period of the late eighteenth and early nineteenth centuries, a time in which there was concern about self-verification and the establishment of position in the units, the nations, that were newly forming and defining themselves: self-verification arose here precisely in the view of history as one's own, a history that could not be confused with someone else's. The *Monumenta Germaniae Historica* initiated by Baron von Stein in 1819, 'the most important collection of medieval textual sources of German history' (Brockhaus) stood from the beginning and still stands today under the motto *Sanctus amor patriae dat animum* {'The sacred love of country gives courage'}. Honest and exact investigation of the past was to be the basis: a postulate still valid today. It is also, however, affected again and again by the requirements of intentional history.

[52a] {The 'dispute amongst historians' (*Historikerstreit*) was the controversy in Germany in the late 1980s over the interpretation of the Holocaust; the particular matter referred to here is the German historian and philosopher Ernst Nolte's claim that Nazi atrocities were a reaction to the earlier (*prius*) genocide of the Bolsheviks.}

[53] Heuss (1959) 56, 64–5 points to the first half of the nineteenth century, when 'history as a science could refer systematically to history as memory [this corresponds rather exactly to what is here called 'intentional history'], when it pursued simultaneously as its relevant concern the aim of correcting and replacing an existing "memory"' (64).

To self-discovery belonged also at that time the separation of 'others'. In the Napoleonic Wars the struggle between the Romans and the Germans was not only a metaphor for the conflict between the French and the Germans, but also a part of their respective national history—in the case of Germany, virtually its glorious beginning. Scholars not infrequently had to (and have to) be self-forgetting in order to allow the necessary room for expert precision, sobriety, and honesty. Indeed, they would like to keep themselves free, in their ranks and in their most innate duty, even partially from well-founded emotionality; intentional history rendered and renders itself effective in another manner, in such different media as school-books, monuments, soap-box speeches, television programmes, etc., and for its part it limits considerably the impact of scientific history. It is 'hot memory', it satisfies elementary needs, it appeals to feelings and is therefore more attractive than dry research every time. Only an attractive presentation of history, e.g. in good historiography, may function here as a corrective. But even if there is (or would be) something like this, it would not be sufficient because it does not depend on affect and appearance, not on—as Thucydides puts it—an ἀγώνισμα ἐς τὸ παραχρῆμα ἀκούειν, an entry in a competition for the moment, but rather on a lasting possession, a κτῆμα ἐς ἀεί.[54]

The conscious flight to myth and esoterica, today in vogue and even in scholarly circles socially acceptable, will also not be of any use, since it only casts out the devil with Beelzebub.[55] Critical and methodological discipline is required, independent of a pleasing presentation and emotional comfort; laborious investigations are necessary and complicated thought processes are demanded, which might be supposed eventually to overcome memory and intentionality in particular. Whether, then, by means of an historical awareness, a new sublimated, collective memory emerges, one which no

[54] Thuc. 1.22.4.
[55] An instructive example of this approach is Gugenberger and Schweidlenka (1993). The authors are historians and the printing was subsidized by Austrian funds for the promotion of scientific research. They diagnose—certainly correctly—an amazing re-mythologization in the present. Their therapy, however, is not based on rationality—they reject the 'pure rationalists...from Sir Karl Popper and Hans Jonas to Günther Glotz and Jürgen Habermas' (25)—but rather on positive, cosy myths. In the presence of irrational fears they do not expect doubts in our mind; rather, they wish to calm us with the false security of an 'archaic legacy'.

longer 'needs to succumb to social instincts as seen through the lens of historicism' and that gains its 'overall intellectual relevance' from its relationship with history, may be left undecided. Given the power and the magic exerted by intentional history, one may nowadays be satisfied with the power and the stringency of the criticism. At any rate intentional history will not disappear without the *sapere aude* {'daring to reason'}.

In short, when we see today how in many places, particularly in more recent or newly formed nations and in still unresolved political situations, e.g. in the Balkans, in the Near East, in North Africa, or in the 'successor states' of the Soviet Union, early history and archae-ology are employed, virtually mythologized, as a contribution to the foundation of legal positions and the creation of identity—in unity and separation—we need only remember the nineteenth century. There too the spade exposed one's own history and opened the way to 'our' ancestors. He who today smiles about the Macedonian sun should have a look at the monument to Arminius.

Twenty years ago, when in Detmold—in Arminius' shadow, so to speak—the ancient historian Dieter Timpe presented the results of his *Arminius-Studies*, which, using a stringent interpretation, made the 'liberator of Germany' into a 'rebellious auxiliary officer',[56] he felt impelled, on the occasion of the publication of his lecture, to separate himself from the 'pseudo-religious intellectual fantasies of the folklore sectarians and the teuto-maniacal edification literature surrounding the monument to Arminius' and to reject the 'indigna-tion of those patriots' who 'with a sure sense discern "the soiling of one's own nest" when the discussion of this material is not accom-panied by the familiar background music of a *Luren*.'[57]

This may mark the place of the ancient historian vis-à-vis inten-tional history: in enlightenment and criticism. Since Thucydides at

---

[56] Timpe (1970).

[57] Timpe (1973) 5; he continues (5–6): 'Historical research will respect and foster true historical consciousness where it is expressed in the honouring of local and national heroes; it will shed light upon itself and thus seek to make itself the catalyst of historical education. The illusory and politically malevolent ideology of national paganism, by contrast, cannot either be fostered or have light shed upon it; least of all can it be made the catalyst of historical education.' {The *Luren* is a German and Scandinavian musical instrument of the Bronze Age.}

the latest—as remarkable as this may sound after two and a half millennia in a largely history-less time—the historian's task is to destroy, not create myths and legends. Therein lies the most important legacy of the ancient world for the historian who feels responsible towards his era and his environment, and who therefore wishes to introduce the possibilities of his field into public discussion. Looking back to these beginners and 'ancestors' is a central element of *his* self-verification, his intentional history.

ADDENDUM

It was already apparent at the time that this article was being written that the issues addressed in it were receiving increased attention in then current scholarly debates. Comparable concepts, such as *lieux de mémoire* {'sites of memory'} were spreading further and in the meantime there was a large area of research that dealt with *Geschichtspolitik* {the advancement of partisan interpretations of history} and the role of collective memory. That cannot be described in detail here. For ancient history one might mention only the books of Jonathan Hall ((1997) and (2002)) and the recently published work of Nino Luraghi on the Messenians (2008), which in my view deserve special mention. Since I myself in the years since this article was written have consistently engaged with the issues here, I may refer to a few of my articles which can serve also to indicate the development and current state of discussion: see Gehrke (2001), (2003), (2005), (2007), and (2008).

3

Genealogy and the Genealogists

Rosalind Thomas

Greek legendary genealogy may exert little attraction. We would not regard it as a form of entertainment, and if we look at it as historians, it seems to offer little in comparison with other materials. So it is neglected. But it is crucial to recognize how popular at least legendary genealogy was in Greece and how it was thought to provide proof or explanation for the present. These beliefs have a fundamental bearing on oral tradition, since memory and, therefore, oral tradition are formed and re-formed by prevailing attitudes: it is the beliefs about legendary genealogy (for instance) which mould family tradition. It is also against this background that one must see the activity of the genealogists. The role of the prose genealogists—and therefore of written methods—in coordinating and perhaps rewriting the oral family traditions into consistent and lengthy genealogies requires more precise attention.

Legendary genealogy was certainly popular. Polybius (9.1.4) distinguishes the various kinds of history and attaches a certain kind of reader to each one. Somewhat to our surprise, genealogy is linked with the man who just likes listening ($\tau \grave{o} \nu \ldots \phi \iota \lambda \acute{\eta} \kappa o o \nu$), as opposed to the curious and those with antiquarian interests ($\tau \grave{o} \nu \ldots \pi o \lambda v \pi \rho \acute{a} \gamma \mu-$ $o \nu a \; \kappa a \grave{\iota} \; \pi \epsilon \rho \iota \tau \tau \acute{o} \nu$) and the statesman ($\tau \grave{o} \nu \; \pi o \lambda \iota \tau \iota \kappa \acute{o} \nu$). Genealogy is just entertainment. Plato tells us (*Hipp. Mai.* 285d) that Hippias of Elis found the Spartans delighted most in the genealogies of men and heroes, the ancient founding of cities, 'and, to put it briefly, all forms of antiquarian knowledge (*archaiologia*)'.

Hippias contrasts these subjects with others, such as music and maths, which the Spartans did not want to hear. It is implied that enthusiasm for genealogy was rather old-fashioned—or rather that the Spartans did not share the advanced tastes that the sophists expected from their audiences in the late fifth century. Legendary genealogy was the subject of much poetry, of which Hesiod's *Theogony* and the *Catalogue of Women* are the best surviving examples.[1] The heroes of Homer cite their genealogies before engaging in conflict.[2] Clearly, genealogies were not the dull lists we tend to imagine. Interspersed with some elaboration for one or two of the figures, as in Glaukos' genealogy, they form the bare bones of a story or narrative. This is seldom appreciated.[3] Against this background the prose genealogists cannot be regarded simply as antiquarians.

The few criticisms of genealogy that occur serve rather to highlight its evidently widespread popularity. Polybius' remark implied a certain contempt for genealogy as truthful history. Another Hellenistic writer, Asclepiades of Myrleia, a grammarian (*c.* 100 BC), seems to have gone further (Sext. Emp. *Gramm.* 1.252). He regarded genealogy as even more false than comedy and mime which were only 'seeming true'. But since he was speaking in the rhetorical terminology of Hellenistic grammarians, the value of this scepticism is unclear.[4] He does at least imply that there was a lot of 'false history' around. Indeed, genealogy continued to thrive. More revealing is the criticism made by Plato in the *Theaetetus* (174e–175b), sometimes quoted without much comment as a solitary stand against the habit of boasting of one's genealogy. He makes fun of those who boast of their ancestors ($\tau\grave{\alpha}\dots\gamma\acute{\epsilon}\nu\eta\ \acute{\upsilon}\mu\nuο\acute{\upsilon}\nu\tau\omega\nu$), citing seven rich *pappoi*; and

---

[1] See West (1985) ch. 1.

[2] Most impressive are those of Glaukos, *Il.* 6.145–211, which extends to six generations, and that of Aeneas, *Il.* 20.200–41 (eight generations). Others are a great deal shorter: Achilles, *Il.* 21.188f. (two generations to a god), Idomeneus, *Il.* 13.448–53; Krethon and Orsilochos, *Il.* 5.541–9 (two generations from the river Alpheios); Telemachus, *Od.* 16.117–20; Theoclymenos, 15.225–56, and Diomedes, *Il.* 14.113–27 (four generations).

[3] West (1985) explains enjoyment in genealogy by simple 'delight' in factual knowledge for its own sake, which may also have an element of truth. But again, genealogy is more than facts.

[4] See Gabba (1981) {= below, Ch. 12}. On Asclepiades, see Slater (1972); however, Fornara (1983) 10f. points out the rhetorical background to Asclepiades' statement and interprets 'genealogical story' rather differently.

he mocks the man who 'proudly cites descent through twenty-five ancestors back to Heracles' (175a). This is the most articulate and straightforward criticism of the custom—which may have been common by Plato's day.[5] The grounds on which Plato argues his point are therefore very significant. If one looks more closely at what he says, one sees that he does not argue on the grounds of historical truth: he does not say that these lengthy genealogies cannot possibly be true. He only points out that amongst all those myriads of ancestors some will be kings, some beggars. Though a man may cite his descent from Heracles through twenty-five generations, it is in fact entirely a matter of chance what kind of man he will be. This criticism leaves intact the assumption that these genealogies are true. The claimed descent is accepted. It is only the inference drawn from the descent that Plato questions.

If genealogies, then, were mostly regarded as 'true' in antiquity, in what sense were they true?

Genealogy is often an explanation or expression of a relationship that is non-historical. For instance, in Plato's *Theaetetus* (155d) we find the following remark: 'He who said Iris [messenger of heaven] was the daughter of *Thaumas* [wonder] made a good genealogy (οὐ κακῶς γενεαλογεῖν)'. That is, one of the ways of expressing a relationship or similarity between two things or two concepts is to put it in genealogical terms. Plato was in fact referring to Hesiod's *Theogony* where this device is used repeatedly.[6] The genealogical relationship seems to be merely conceptual or metaphoric, yet it is expressing something that is also 'true'. In another example from Plato (*Symp.* 178a–b) genealogy is used in a different way: Eros, it is said, must be the oldest of the gods because we do not know his father.[7]

---

[5] The passage may suggest that by the time of this late dialogue, it was more common for people to have worked out their line of ancestors back to a hero. Perhaps the development of historiography, chronological awareness and increased application of written methods encouraged families to ensure the links were there. But this may be taking too literally Plato's exaggerated picture leading up to his more serious criticism of the custom's premise.

[6] Examples in *Theog.* 211ff. and 383ff.; Fränkel (1975) 96ff.; West (1985).

[7] In general, see Haedicke (1936), introduction; Philippson (1944); van Groningen (1953). Such symbolic relationships are hardly absent from the modern world: cf. the 'marriage' recently celebrated in New York between the Statue of Liberty and Christopher Columbus to symbolize the links between New York and Spain (*The Times*, 13 October 1986).

This readiness to express ideas and related concepts in genealogical terms is paralleled by the Greek use of genealogy to explain links between human groups. Friendship between cities may be explained or justified on the grounds that their respective eponymous ancestors were related. Present circumstances are often supposed to correspond to the legendary past.[8] This could effect a circular process and one which recurs with other kinds of oral tradition. For if legendary ancestry corresponds to the present, that correspondence would apparently confirm that the legendary past had relevance for the present.[9]

Tribes and cities had eponymous ancestors who were often extracted from the name of the tribe or city. The importance of the eponymous ancestor was so great that original ancestors were made as back formations from the names of tribes.[10] For instance, Doros and Ion were the eponymous heroes of the Dorians and Ionians and they were connected genealogically to Hellen, the eponym of the Hellenes. The old Ionian tribes clearly did not derive from heroes' names (e.g. Hopletes, Geleontes), but by the time of Herodotus (5.66) they had acquired eponymous heroes whose names (Hoples, Geleon) were again back formations from the tribal name. They were said to be the sons of Ion. Legendary genealogy thus clearly expressed

[8] Cf. Bickerman (1952); Nilsson (1951) collects numerous examples in which cult or legend are changed for 'political propaganda' in order to express in legend what is felt should be the case in the present. {See also above, Ch. 2.}

[9] Cf. Vansina's examples ((1985) 157 and 187) of oral traditions connected to monuments or other visible remains: stories grow up to explain the monuments or geographical formations, then the stories are said to be confirmed by those material objects—the monuments are in fact cited as proof. Gabba (1981) and Wiseman (1986) have interesting discussions of the often similar role of monuments in the 'traditions' of early Rome.

[10] Nilsson (1951) esp. 65ff. on eponymous ancestors and later examples. The heroes of the new Cleisthenic tribes at Athens do not seem to be regarded as ancestors. But the language of Demosthenes' *Epitaphios* (28ff.) comes very close to treating them as ancestors, as he finds in each eponymous hero a particular source of inspiration for his tribe. Cf. especially the use of *syngenê* (28) and *archêgos* of Oineus, Kekrops, and Hippothios (30, 31), though Erechtheus is called only eponym (27). *Archêgos* surely carries a strong implication of first origins or original ancestry. Cf. Thomas (1989) 213–21 on the *demos*' acquisition of legendary ancestry. Numerous anthropological examples of legendary ancestors who correspond to divisions of tribes or regions and which change when the divisions are reduced in Goody and Watt (1968); West (1985) collects others.

the contemporary divisions of society. This may not have been regarded as a literal statement of blood relationship, yet that is how it is expressed and it is hard to see how the idea of a merely metaphorical ancestor could be maintained for long—there surely can have been no distinction made. By their nature eponymous ancestors had to correspond to the number of present-day tribes (or whatever group they represented). Thus, they could also change as the situation changed.

In an interesting and stimulating study, van Groningen has drawn some of these phenomena together to stress how Greek ways of thought were based upon the past and how often present reality is explained by the past.[11] In some sense this must obviously be true. But as he himself shows, the 'past' is influential in a rather restricted way. Often it is the 'beginning' which is regarded as significant, rather than the past in a wider sense, implying the whole of past history and perhaps some sense of historical change. In the case of genealogy it is less misleading to talk instead about the influence of the model of the family and of inheritance from the original family ancestor. It is not the past as such that seems to be the basis of these expressions I have been discussing—that seems to import implications of historical awareness that are perhaps out of place. The emphasis lies rather upon the idea of inheritance and the importance of family relationships—particularly those of the legendary period. This seems to be the basis of the genealogical linking of concepts that we see in Plato and Hesiod. Such links were naturally explained in terms of family links or genealogy.[12]

This same assumption seems to lie behind certain statements of ancient writers about historical figures, statements we regard as non-historical. For instance, it is often pointed out what reckless assumptions ancient biographers make about the kinship links of those whose lives they describe. Ancient writers who wrote in a similar genre often appear in the ancient biographies as related in some way. Not all these links can be historical.[13] But the assumption behind this

---

[11]   Van Groningen (1953), esp. ch. 5.
[12]   See further Haedicke (1936). It is questionable whether the elaborate genealogies in the *Theogony* imply that Hesiod's contemporaries had similar genealogies.
[13]   See Fairweather (1974), who argues the case to its limits.

cavalier treatment (which we see merely as invention) is an interesting one, however contemptuous one may be of the biographers' lack of historical sense. For here again similarity in outlook and in writing is made to connect with, or reflect, kinship. (It may also reflect the fact that profession was often inherited from father to son.)[14] One biographer, Hermippus, even thought Thucydides was descended from Peisistratos. Why? Because of Thucydides' treatment of the period of the tyranny and the tyrannicides, which to Hermippus could only suggest family relationship and descent (Marcell. *Vit. Thuc.* 18).

Genealogy supplied proof of status and prestige. It seems hardly necessary to stress that the importance attached to ancestry by Greek aristocrats means that it was likely to be changed and falsified. But this was compounded by the fact that it was legendary ancestry which was regarded as the significant ancestry, not recent genealogy of historical times. Legendary ancestry was beyond the range of reasonable memory, so it could not be disproved.[15] But more important are the beliefs I have just been discussing that legendary ancestry should correspond to present-day circumstances.

The significance of legendary ancestry I have stressed repeatedly, and most of the discussion above confirms it. So here I shall only add that legendary ancestry was important because it was the beginning of the family which was thought to characterize it later. A fragment of Aristotle, surprisingly, expresses precisely that idea (*On Nobility* [*Peri eugeneias*], F 94 Rose³): 'But not even those descended from good (*agathoi*) ancestors are noble (*eugeneis*), only those who have among those ancestors originators who are good (*agathoi*).' (οὐ μὴν ἀλλ᾽ οὐδ᾽ οἱ ἐκ προγόνων ἀγαθῶν εὐγενεῖς πάντως, ἀλλ᾽ ὅσοις τυγχάνουσιν ἀρχηγοὶ τῶν προγόνων ὄντες <ἀγαθοί>.) The ancestors in between were comparatively insignificant.[16] Prestige through birth is an

[14] E.g. in families of seers like the Iamids or Melampodids (*Od.* 15.225–55); Haedicke (1936) 32f. When Socrates says he is descended from Daidalos (Plat. *Alcib.* 1.121a) this must be explained by the fact that his father was a stone mason—the expression of paternal profession in legendary terms.
[15] What constitutes 'proof', however, in an oral context, is an interesting question. See Thomas (1989) 34–8 for the slow acceptance of writing as proof, and see also below, p. 179: membership of a *phratry* or *genos* would be important.
[16] Bethe (1935) ch. 8; Haedicke (1936) 13f.; van Groningen (1953), stressing the beginning or *archê* in Greek thought.

essentially aristocratic value.[17] But for the Greek aristocrat it is not so much the long line of ancestors, each named in succession—the 'pedigree'—that is prestigious, as the original ancestor.

The corollary to the idea that legendary ancestry reflected the present circumstances of the family in some way was that the ancestry could change in what we would take to be a wholly ahistorical manner. One of the clearest and most interesting examples is that of the Iamids. When the Iamid seer Teisamenos was given an exceptional grant of Spartan citizenship (Hdt. 9.33), a Spartan element was incorporated into the legend surrounding the Iamid eponymous ancestor, the seer Iamos. This took the form of the woman Pitane, who is inserted into the legendary genealogical tree in Pindar's ode for an Iamid descendant, *Olympian* 6.[18] Thus, legendary genealogies do not always remain stable but may change with the later fortunes of the family.[19] While the incorporation of further elements has no basis in actual historical genealogy, it has clear enough basis in the feeling that the beginning of the family sets its character. Confusion could obviously result.

Legendary genealogy by itself could be of intense interest to the audiences of both genealogical poets and prose writers. In fact, it has contemporary relevance without any explicit reference to present-day descendants and thus without continuation of the genealogy

---

[17] Loenen (1926) has an interesting discussion of other aspects of 'nobility'. Much later, Dionysius of Halicarnassus (first century AD) remarks on the ignoble, 'he cannot even trace his family back to the third ancestor' (D. Hal. *A.R.* 4.47.4): perhaps a commonplace about having no heroic ancestor or no ancestors beyond the grandfather; or implying a later concern in the Roman period with tracing back ancestors step by step.

[18] On this, see Thomas (1989) 107. Another example is the Philaids' addition of the Lapith Koronos to their genealogy (Thomas (1989) 167 n. 28). For a similar alteration to a king-list (Argead), see Greenwalt (1985). Cf. the genealogy of Hippokrates which goes back to the healing god Asklepios, though Asklepios was only worshipped in Cos from 400 BC.

[19] Cf. the extreme example of fluid genealogy, which exactly reflects present-day organization, among the Tiv of Nigeria: Bohannan (1952). Van Baaren (1972), however, gives an example of a genealogy which was officially unchanged, but when a change of ruler necessitated alteration to the 'traditional' genealogy, the priests slowly and almost imperceptibly changed it until it 'fitted' the new ruler. Other studies of genealogy: Vansina (1985) 160f. and 182ff.; Person (1972); Lewis (1962); de Mahieu (1979).

down into the historical period. The legends could not help being significant to later audiences, and alterations which we might take to be only of antiquarian interest may have had important political implications.[20] If aristocratic pride concentrated on legendary fore-bears, explicit continuation down into the historical period was simply not necessary. Therefore, oral traditions were unlikely to record continuing genealogies to make that link, for that kind of memory was not necessary to reinforce the main functions of the legendary ancestors. So, in the case of Athens' claim to Salamis, the argument rested upon the notional event in the legendary period combined with the vague continuity assumed between the original hero Philaios and his descendants later resident in Attica. Plato and Solon were said to be descended from Codrus, though there was some doubt about the identity of a crucial link, Solon's father.[21] The original ancestor could be known and believed in, even if intervening links were not.

At this point we might see our modern insistence on the interven-ing links as one made possible or necessary by a highly literate society and a highly developed sense of written proof. *We* wish to know how a family could prove its heroic ancestry to satisfy others. But such proof as was necessary probably lay in the fact that everyone 'knew' of the heroic ancestor; alternatively, the legendary hero might be enshrined in cult or confirmed by a descendant's membership of *genos* {tribe} or *phratry* {brotherhood} and the way the hero corre-sponded to present-day circumstances. If an aristocrat belonged to a descent group centred on a *phratry* or a *genos*, his ancestry would be confirmed by his very membership of that group and therefore his descent from whatever hero was involved. We see descent and ge-nealogy as representative of the historical 'truth', but Greek genealogy expresses more than that: it was not necessary to cite the intervening links back to the Trojan War for legendary ancestry to have its full force. We must simply accept that family tradition could accommo-date a void between the great legendary forebears and the recent,

---

[20] West (1985) ch. 1 also stresses contemporary relevance.

[21] Plut. *Sol.* 12; Diog. Laert. 3.1: Plato's mother was descended from Solon, Solon from Neleus, and Poseidon, Solon's father from Codrus. Plutarch gives the alternative identity of Solon's father.

more prosaic past, while we demand historical verification of each genealogical link. The modern aristocrat might revel in the immensely complicated web of a written family tree; the Greek aristocrat would tend to think of his heroic ancestor and thus of his ultimate descent from a god. The difference is partly connected with the use of writing, as well as beliefs about the first ancestor. For it is possible to trace the elaborate ramifications of genealogy, and indeed to demand proof of each link, in a highly literate society with complex written records.

Here we must return to the question of full genealogy. It is sometimes recognized that the Greeks saw great significance in the legendary origins of a family at the expense of their recent past. But the background of oral transmission, less often appreciated, considerably alters the way we see these traditions and the whole subject of ancient genealogy.

Legendary ancestors may have become enshrined in poetry, and so their memory was not entirely left to the vagaries of the most fluid type of oral transmission, that without a verse text. But even this poetry was meant to be heard and was not until the late sixth century made the subject of detailed enquiry and comparison. So inconsistencies and illogicalities could continue to exist in the great mass of poetry that dealt with legendary genealogy. Oral poetry and oral tradition can accommodate inconsistencies far more easily than a written text which is meant to be read. Legendary origins could change, as we have seen. But they could be altered the more readily because the traditions were transmitted in an essentially oral manner.[22]

This concentration on legendary origins has many parallels in other oral traditions and societies. As we saw, we should expect to find telescoping in such family tradition. Greece did not have the incentives or actual mechanisms for remembering without writing immensely complex genealogies down to the present that anthropologists sometimes find. In any case, the legendary ancestor was most important in Greece. Where we can check, memory of ancestors

---

[22] When literacy was introduced among the Somali, an unfortunate result was that it became harder for them to alter genealogies to suit the present: Lewis (1968).

more than four generations back is very shaky, if it exists at all.[23] Even Plato's family tree had lost two generations of the sixth and early fifth centuries, and the sixth-century figures at the end of the Philaid genealogy were extremely doubtful. Neither length nor accuracy can be expected. We should assume that most families with legendary ancestors probably had genealogical information only about the legendary period surrounding the ancestor and about the recent past—and in exceptional cases perhaps some muddled knowledge of ancestors between the recent and legendary periods: but not necessarily a full genealogy from the present day to the legendary period.

How, then, do we regard the activities of the prose genealogists? It will be clear by now that I believe their work must be seen as the application of literate methods of study to poetic and essentially oral material that could be contradictory by its very nature. The full genealogies that we occasionally find are, I think, to be connected closely to the activity of these genealogists: they are largely the product of recognizable methods of sorting out conflicting geneal- ogies to fit them into a coherent and chronologically plausible framework of generations. The apparent elaboration of genealogy (especially by the prose genealogists) in the late sixth and early fifth centuries has, of course, been noted before. But the only attempt to explain the phenomenon in terms of family tradition sees it as the product of a narrowing circle of aristocratic families who, therefore, needed more urgently to prove their legendary ancestry. Erudition was called in to provide the continuous stemmata—erudition in the form of the genealogists.[24] It is certainly right to emphasize that genealogists' work was of great importance to their contemporaries, as we have seen. But their activities, particularly their provision of full genealogy down to the present day, must also be seen as an application of written methods to a mass of oral traditions which were neither factually nor chronologically stable.

---

[23] Contrast Wade-Gery's optimism ((1952) 92): 'A distinguished family would know its own pedigree, as we see from Pindar often, from Herodotus 6.125, 131 (Alcmaeonidai)' and (he adds) in the cases of Heropythos, Hecataeus, and Hippok- rates. This confuses pedigree, and thus *full* genealogy, with legendary ancestry. Pearson (1942) 9–10 is more cautious but still over-optimistic.

[24] Bethe (1935) 57f. and 69, followed by Haedicke.

I shall first briefly outline what little we know about the activity of the prose genealogists.[25] The five main ones are Hecataeus (*FGrHist* 1), Acusilaus of Argos (*FGrHist* 2), Pherecydes of Athens (*FGrHist* 3), Hellanicus (*FGrHist* 4; 323a), and Damastes of Sigeum (*FGrHist* 5). Of these, Hecataeus was the earliest we know of (late sixth century) and he apparently set the pattern that the later ones followed, proclaiming his distinction in his preface (F 1). Their interests are primarily in the legendary and mythical past, as the fragments and testimonia show. They concentrated upon tracing the genealogies of certain heroic families, for instance the Aiacids, the Heraclids or the Deucalionids. Their overwhelming concern seems to be in tracing legendary genealogy, not in reaching down to the present day.[26] Indeed, it is its subject-matter which makes it likely that genealogy was one of the earliest kinds of prose literature in Greece.[27]

While we have only fragments of their works, which might there-fore not be representative, ancient testimony confirms that they were primarily dealing with the legendary genealogies of poetry. Clement of Alexandria (*FGrHist* 2 T 5) objected that Eumelus of Corinth and Acusilaus simply turned Hesiod's poetry into prose and published it as if the contents were their own. Josephus (*Ap.* 1.16) notes the divergences: 'It would be superfluous for me to instruct those who know better than I do how often Hellanicus disagrees with Acusilaus about the genealogies and how often Acusilaus corrects Hesiod.' The subject-matter was that of the genealogical and epic poets. But the task involved putting into order a great mass of often confused and contradictory material. As I have already said, different areas or groups produced differing 'versions' of the legends or legends about

[25] They have attracted little discussion, and what there is, is sometimes partial and confusing. Most important are the fragments themselves and Jacoby's commentary; also Jacoby (1909) and (1947) on Pherecydes; Fornara (1983) 4–12 (mostly con-cerned with the separation of the legendary past from the 'historical period').

[26] Fornara (1983) 4–5 is confusing: 'For it is a reasonable inference that Hecataeus drew a boundary between "heroic times" and "historical times"—the point at which the genealogical approach could be replaced by the exercise of historical memory.' But as the full genealogies show, legendary genealogy could be joined to 'historical' genealogy. Murray's scepticism (1987) as to how much Herodotus (or others) explicitly distinguished *logos* from *mythos* is also relevant here.

[27] Jacoby (1947); Fornara (1983).

the same characters with different implications. These reflected the various claims made through the legends, as well as actual changes made in these genealogies to reflect later circumstances. The genealogists collected together this information and produced in a systematic manner a version that was at least consistent with itself (see below, p. 85), a stupendous task.[28]

This information was naturally of great interest to contemporaries: though legendary, such genealogy could not help being relevant. One must therefore regard the prose genealogists not simply as antiquarians or as forerunners of the chronographers, mainly interested in chronology (see below, p. 86). Their subject had an intrinsic interest for those groups who believed themselves descended from any of the heroes included. One must therefore also expect them to produce versions of genealogies which favour the claims of their own city and other groups: this is why they disagree with each other (e.g. Acusilaus, *FGrHist* 2 FF 5–6), continuing in the same tradition of using legendary genealogy for contemporary claims (for an example of this in the legendary Philaid genealogy, see Thomas (1989) 161–73).

One wonders, then, how the full genealogies or *any* references to later history actually fitted into their work. And did they often continue legendary genealogies to the present day? We can only answer this last question by repeating the overwhelming emphasis in the fragments on the legendary period—which had contemporary relevance by themselves. But we simply cannot know the position of the very few genealogies that did continue. Jacoby put Hellanicus' mention of Andocides' ancestry in his *Atthis* (history of Athens), not his genealogical works (*FGrHist* 4 F 170 = 323a F 24), and thought it improbable that he gave all the intervening links: it thus came in retrospectively, introduced via an historical person, Andocides' grandfather. The Philaid genealogy of Pherecydes (*FGrHist* 3 F 2) was probably introduced into a mythical history of Greece via Ajax or Philaios.[29] Legendary interest is still predominant. Indeed, one

[28] West (1985) gives genealogical tables at the back; cf. n. 32 below.
[29] As Jacoby (1947) 32 n. 48: Pherecydes is primarily interested in the prehistory of the clan. F 146 is the only other contemporary allusion in extant Pherecydes apart from the Philaid genealogy. On Andocides' 'genealogy', Jacoby, commentary on Hellanicus, *FGrHist* 323a F 24—he is not connected with the Kerykes (against Toepffer 1889).

suspects in reading these fragments that what people really wanted to hear was not a continuation down to the prosaic present generation but continuation *back* from the hero to a god. In several proud citations of genealogy (e.g. Hecataeus') that is the emphasis—Alcibiades (Plat. *Alcib.* 1.121a) says he is descended from Eurysakes and therefore from Zeus.

The genealogists' methods demand the use of writing. It is barely appreciated, if at all, that their methods are essentially literate ones and that the genealogists' work must represent new uses of writing and literacy.

Hecataeus in his famous preface to his *Genealogies* (*FGrHist* 1 F 1a) declared that 'the tales of the Greeks are many and absurd'. The usual interpretation is that Hecataeus intended to rationalize the absurdities of legend,[30] but Fornara has recently pointed out that he also criticizes the plurality of tales: genealogies were numerous and contradictory and this Hecataeus intended to rectify.[31] Whether this is the correct interpretation of Hecataeus or not, the vast number of competing and conflicting legendary genealogies confirm that such plurality was a major problem for any genealogist. It would be interesting if Hecataeus had himself commented upon it. But one must add to this picture that the original genealogies were products either of pure oral tradition or of poetry which was orally delivered;[32] such diversity, plurality, and contradiction could exist, in part, precisely because the genealogies were orally delivered or transmitted. The correction of their inconsistencies and chronological implausibilities by the genealogists needed written study. Inconsistent relationships can be voiced and believed in different poems (or areas), especially if they each correspond to some contemporary situation or belief. Oral tradition can accommodate contradictions comparatively

---

[30] E.g. von Fritz (1967) I.71.

[31] Fornara (1983) 6: 'The preface may be explained as a criticism of the inconsequence of the genealogical tradition in the strict sense of the word.'

[32] Even if there was a written text, it was not approached and studied in that form (and cf. Thomas (1989) 48, for uses of a written text which might involve *oral* transmission from the text). This applies to the immensely complicated *Catalogue of Women*, whose author synthesized disparate traditions: West (1985) 166 thinks the tradition in which local genealogies of the eighth century evolved into the sixth-century *Catalogue* was not likely to have been an exclusively oral one. This is surely true—though he gives no argument for it—for the reasons I am discussing.

readily and each version can be regarded separately as 'true'. The plurality Hecataeus complains of is that of oral tradition, as are the inconsistencies he implies. Such inconsistencies can only become glaring and worrying when traditions are brought together and compared—which is easier in writing—and when one definitive version is attempted (again, a 'definitive' version is very much easier to obtain by means of writing). Acusilaus himself seems to have been aware of this new significance of writing. He seems to have claimed that he composed his *Genealogies* from bronze tablets which his father dug up in the garden.[33] It is an interesting attempt to claim written and documentary sources for an early work of coordination. Against the background we have been describing, it seems to indicate some awareness of new uses of writing in treating the old legendary material of poetry (cf. Thomas (1989) 34–8 for other extensions of writing in the fourth century).

The mass of genealogical relationships for the legendary period produced glaring problems of synchronization. Figures who were supposed to be contemporaries during the Trojan War might turn out to be in different generations. Various authors tried to explain Theseus' supposed rape of Helen of Troy, which implied particularly absurd chronology.[34] Genealogists had to solve these problems. One solution used by Hellanicus[35] was to suppose that there had been two people of the same name and (presumably) that the more famous one had ousted the other from memory. This method (not unknown in modern scholarship) also levelled out the generations and, by adding extra ones, produced a coherent and plausible schema for the legendary period. The very idea of synchronizing generations like this requires written methods and probably a written mode of study. For writing made it easier—perhaps even possible—for the different relationships expressed in different poems to be brought together. The generations could be worked out, counted and synchronized; the chronology had to be plausible. In a completely oral context it is doubtful if the need for synchronization would even be felt, still less

---

[33] *FGrHist* 2 T 1 (Suidas).
[34] It could be calculated that Theseus was 50, Helen still a child: Hellanicus, *FGrHist* 4 F 168a = Plut. *Thes.* 31.
[35] Pearson (1942) 9ff.

fulfilled. Synchronization revealed confusion. The coordination of the disparate material requires written and graphic forms.[36] Though a crude method, such synchronization also formed incipient chronology. The genealogists' chronological interests may be overstressed, particularly since modern historians are interested in the beginnings of Greek chronology, related to early historiography. The genealogists' predominant interests were in 'correcting' the legendary genealogies so relevant to their contemporaries. This tends to be ignored.[37] However, their writings did obviously have chronological implications which they surely realized. Calculations of chronology would use the same written methods of synchronization. In fact, chronological complications may have been revealed by the attempts to make the legends cohere. There are other problems with the chronological emphasis which one should mention here, if only briefly. Genealogical telescoping would make accurate dating from genealogy impossible. Could the genealogists have tried to use genealogy to work out chronology back to the Trojan War, as is sometimes thought? This seems unlikely, too. By the time of Herodotus (2.145.4) the Trojan War was dated to the thirteenth century, yet it is notorious that neither the full genealogies nor the Spartan king-lists could be made to extend much beyond the tenth century BC, whether they were calculated with a thirty- or forty-year generation. The Philaids, for example, had twelve ancestors back to the Trojan War. Thus, dating of the Trojan War could hardly have been derived by calculations from the genealogies, though they did purport to go back to a generation contemporary with the Trojan War or earlier.[38] On the

[36] We do not know precisely how the genealogists coordinated the material. Pherecydes' genealogy is couched in continuous prose though it is essentially a list. Heropythos' genealogy is written out as a bare list, as is Klearchos' (Thomas (1989) 159 n. 9). See further on the list, p. 91 below.

[37] E.g. Pearson (1942) 9–10, 'The only way of establishing a chronological basis for mythology was to construct parallel family trees for the various families beginning with the divine ancestor of each one', implying that chronology was the dominant interest.

[38] Thus Snodgrass (1971) 10ff. He suggests 'some kind of barrier to this type of recollection in the region of the tenth century BC'. I would say it was not so much a barrier to recollection as a process of forgetting, telescoping, and reconstructing that, when calculated, happened to result in a span of four or five hundred years. We can hardly use these telescoped genealogies purporting to go back to the Trojan War to

contrary, it would seem that the dating of the Trojan War would be a reason to stretch and lengthen the genealogies, perhaps even to exaggerate the length of a single generation. Its dating must have been based on some other kind of calculation.[39] Whatever that basis, however, we begin to discern how the genealogists' work could raise suggestions and problems concerning chronology which others could take up, even if the genealogists themselves were not primarily interested in those aspects.

The other element I would stress in the genealogists' method is that it is not merely a matter of synthesis; it is creative in the most literal sense. The genealogists do not simply take the lineages from the poets and put them together. The method I have outlined above actually infers new generations, in effect inventing new figures.[40] That is, the organization of consistent genealogy may involve manipulation and addition, even if the basic material is preserved in poetry. The process of setting out a stemma in written form may entail apparently logical but invented additions.

We recognize that this occurs in the genealogists' treatment of the legendary period, but less readily that it must apply just as well to their treatment of the historical period. If one accepts their (necessary) manipulation of legendary genealogy, it is in principle likely that they should use similar methods for any genealogies that continued into the historical period. But one may go further. To produce a full genealogy down to the historical period they had to use

date the Ionian migration (as Wade-Gery does, followed by Snodgrass). More literally, Burn ((1935) 131 and 146) used them to date the fall of Troy to *c.*1010 BC, which highlights the difficulties!

[39] Snodgrass ((1971) 12–13) suggests another source, perhaps oriental (but nothing specific): 'The forty-year generation would then be a by-product, not a cause of the dating of the Heroic Age'. Herodotus' preoccupation with the Greek time-scale compared to the Egyptian in Book 2 (e.g. 2.142–6) suggests how worrying fifth-century thinkers found their chronology. Herodotus suggests (2.146.2) that the 'births' of the Greek gods were in fact calculated only from the time when the Greeks first heard about them from Egypt. On generation calculations in historiography, see Mitchel (1956) (with next n.); Prakken (1943); Strasburger (1956).

[40] Cf. Mitchel (1956) 49, 'the genealogists were only recorders of what they uncovered in traditional materials' (my point is that oral tradition probably would not provide it in the right form). Later he explains the deteriorating chronological schema of Herodotus for the centuries before the Persian Wars, as a matter merely of perspective and interest. Contrast Jeffery (1976) 34–6.

family tradition. This was even more fluid than the poetic sources they used for the legendary period, and it is unlikely that much of it can have been preserved in poetic form. It is clear that there must have been large gaps in knowledge of any one family line and figures in the tradition who were known of but not clearly connected to the family stemma in family memories. Still worse, they had to be connected somehow to an Homeric hero over a wide span of time, which in most cases was far longer than our conventional 'Dark Ages'—since, as we have seen, genealogical memory actually falters in many cases as early as the sixth-century ancestors of a family.[41] The genealogist's task in ordering such oral family traditions was even more 'creative' than his treatment of the purely legendary genealogies from the poets. In the Philaid genealogy of Pherecydes we see one such artificial construction which has ordered the family memories into an impressive linear genealogy from Philaios to Miltiades.

This brings us back to the question of the precise effect a written genealogy may have had upon oral family traditions. Recent anthropological studies have provided interesting confirmation of the role of writing in the formation of many genealogies and other kinds of list, and it will be illuminating to consider these first, before we reach final conclusions about the Greek genealogies.

Henige (1974) has made an extensive study of certain kinds of oral tradition that imply the measurement of time, particularly king-lists and genealogies. This study examines many of the ways in which oral tradition distorts chronology—it achieves, for instance, telescoping and artificial lengthening by treating contemporary rulers as successive ones or by imputing very long reigns. A drawback of this approach is that many of the most impressive examples of these lists occur in societies which are (or were) not entirely illiterate when the lists were first written down.[42] It is often very difficult to determine how far they are actually products of *purely* oral tradition, yet for a long time it has been assumed that they are simply written

---

[41] Herodotus puts the Trojan War over 800 years before his time (*c.*1250?); so even by fifth-century time-reckoning there was a wide gap.

[42] An extreme example is the twelfth-century (AD) chronicle of Kashmir (see Henige (1974) 49), which has very long reigns, or any of the other Indian examples.

versions repeating faithfully long-lived 'oral traditions' transmitted (orally) for generations or centuries. So Henige's study often leaves it unclear whether these king-lists or genealogies might have been elaborated with literate methods or at least after the society ceased to be entirely illiterate. But for certain types of example he does point out the effects of literacy. For instance, he stresses that 'the extensive manipulation of genealogies for synchronistic symmetry... could not have been carried out in an oral society. Indeed, its need would not have been perceived... [M]uch of the genealogical oral traditions available from Africa are the products of an era of at least restricted literacy.'[43] (This quotation encapsulates the confusion produced by calling genealogies elaborated through writing 'oral traditions'.) Genealogical data were also often produced in response to the British colonial administration,[44] again at a period when literate methods were beginning to be used more widely.

Since then, there has been more careful study of the role of writing (or lack of writing) in genealogical tradition. Of course, there are impressive examples of careful transmission and recitation of genealogies, particularly in Polynesia.[45] But these are not found in all societies. Genealogical information is often merely general knowledge and not recited in isolation for its own sake. There is a crucial difference between 'genealogical information' which has been collected together from various snippets of information and 'a genealogy' recited or regarded as such. If one speaks of distortion or change in a genealogy, one is in a sense speaking from a modern literate standpoint, assuming that there is an 'original text', as it were, from which there are deviations. But if genealogy in a certain society is always tied to a practical issue, as it often is, and not recorded separately, then it is misleading to speak as if there were a whole genealogy which could be thought of in isolation from the practical

---

[43] Henige (1974) 26. He also mentions (23) the Greek historians of the sixth and fifth centuries and their use of the 'grid effect' (i.e. synchronization of generations).

[44] Henige (1974) 12. But he also explains artificial lengthening (39ff.) as either unconscious or because of 'the universal propensity to revere antiquity for its own sake'.

[45] Vansina (1973) 32, stressing the importance of social mechanisms in preservation; Vansina (1985) 95f. and 182ff. is more cautious. An instance is known from Polynesia of recitation involving over 700 names and thirty-four generations (Smith (1921), 16ff.).

application of the relationships.[46] It is therefore important to remember that when field anthropologists produce complex genealogies, they are often constructing artificially a genealogy which, pieced together from isolated information, may not correspond to the way in which their informants see their family and ancestral relationships.[47] Here I would particularly stress the effect of a written and graphic form on these oral traditions (rather than emphasizing simply the difference in outlook of researcher and informant).[48] Behind all these observations lies the problem that the process of forming a written genealogy from oral tradition may involve the ordering of information not necessarily remembered in that precise form and the recording in a 'definitive version' ('definitive' because it is in writing) of information that was not stable. The actual form of the written genealogy may alter the form of the oral traditions. (One

[46] Finnegan (1970) 198, a point akin to that made about telescoping above. This applies to the classic case of shifting genealogy (or 'structural amnesia') according to present-day reality, that of the Tiv (above, n. 19). Finnegan's point is that changes are not dependent on lapses of memory or distortions, precisely because the genealogical knowledge is always tied to a practical issue. In many societies genealogies are never recited as a whole all at once: those parts which are relevant may be discussed and reconstructed by consensus, Vansina (1985) 95f. and 182ff. Cf. also Vansina's experience with Kuba traditions ((1985) 95). He says he misjudged the coherence of the royal 'annals', for the Kuba do not give a full performance of their whole dynastic history at any one time—much of it consists of anecdotes of kings told in various circumstances.

[47] Miller (1980) 18f. But rather uneasily, he takes genealogy to be merely a cliché, a way of expressing a certain element in a genealogical metaphor: the oral narrators could understand the true meaning behind the metaphor (i.e. they could translate it), and only modern historians misunderstand. But I find it very hard to believe that the narrators could keep separate in their own minds the historical reality and a metaphor very close to a possible reality. Cf. Vansina (1985) 44f. and 137ff. on interpreting clichés: some can be meant literally.

[48] Cf. Barnes (1967), esp. 118–21: he distinguishes genealogies—the actual family trees—from pedigrees, the accounts of their genealogy which an individual or family would give. But with unconscious irony he points out *both* (i) the genealogy of the ethnographer may misrepresent the relations as conceived by the informants (e.g. as patrilineal when they are not) *and* (ii) how there are various ways of setting out genealogical charts (which give rather different emphases through their graphic form). Though he does not say so, this seems to be an excellent illustration of the fact that genealogical charts are essentially written and graphic formulations of relationships which were not necessarily conceived like that, and in particular that they may impute merely through their form a western and literate idea of a 'family tree'.

need only think of the conventions of modern genealogical tables which stress descent in the male line.) In addition, the collection of varying pieces of information perhaps not seen as connected by the informants actually highlights omissions and shows inconsistencies which had happily existed in oral form—and these must then be eliminated.

Goody has done stimulating work on early uses of literacy and the list which draws together some of these ideas, relating his observations to the overall development and effect of literacy.[49] He has pointed out that lists, whether genealogical lists or king-lists, are essentially a written phenomenon; simple lists, which are non-syntactic, do not occur much in a completely oral society and they are not a 'natural analytical category' by themselves.[50] Genealogy is the most likely type of list in such a society, but since it would thus exist in an oral form alone, it could not be finite, with a definite form in the way that a written list is. It would not have the independent existence that a written list could have. Oral lists would not be very long.[51]

Such suggestions have prompted re-examination of certain king-lists which were once taken to be pure products or oral tradition. For instance, Henige himself returned to the Ganda and Nyoro king-lists to suggest that they were in fact 'oral' only in the sense that they were collected in spoken form.[52] Originally they may even have been a product in some way of early Arabic literacy.[53] It is striking that the Ganda king-list grows in length dramatically from the first written

[49] Goody (1977), esp. 108; followed by Miller (1980) and Vansina (1985) 179–81. Here Goody moves away from the strict 'autonomous' model of literacy presented in Goody (1968): Thomas (1989) 15–34. Goody (1986) 67 explores further the potential of writing or rather, as he sees it, 'the nature of writing' which 'means that each activity is transformed in significant ways by its introduction'.

[50] Oral lists are kept when they have social meaning, but they are never very long, except when there has been some feedback from writing, Vansina (1985) 179ff. Cf. also Goody (1986) 54 and (1987) 114ff.

[51] For length, cf. the genealogical list of Heropythos: one name out of fifteen was left out by the first scholar who recorded it, and that was even with the help of writing.

[52] Miller (1980), on 'The Disease of Writing', 240ff.

[53] Literacy and the resulting 'harm' to indigenous oral traditions are mostly associated simply with the European colonial presence, and contact much earlier with the Arabs' literate culture in large parts of Africa is often grossly underestimated. Cf. Finnegan (1977), who stresses how very few (if any) 'oral societies' now studied have actually had no contact with literacy at all; also Henige (1982) 80–7; Goody (1987) ch. 5.

record made of it by a European in 1865. The first list was short, but it developed as time passed, acquiring a great many new names, until by 1901 it was much augmented. That its contents agreed with another king-list had seemed to guarantee its authenticity. But in retrospect this consistency was a suspicious sign that both lists were products of similar environments where writing was becoming increasingly common. As Henige says, 'literacy was actually having its greatest impact at precisely the moment that remembrances of the past were undergoing their final mutations'. These augmented king-lists were perhaps not based on oral tradition at all; certainly their increasing length was made possible by the presence of writing.[54] The flowering of the list was contemporary with European presence and growing literacy, not a final relic of oral tradition shortly to be stunted by the coming of literacy.[55]

Much research remains to be done on this whole subject, especially on the precise rather than the overall, effect of writing in this sphere (see Thomas 1989: 15–34, for provisos).[56] However, it is clear that writing itself may help order information which in its oral context may not be remembered in that form; that the list as we think of it is almost always a literate phenomenon, one particularly associated with early literacy; that such lists may grow dramatically in length from their oral origins under the conditions of early literacy; and that while writing encourages the accretion of names on a list, it also shows up gaps and inconsistencies.

If we return to the Greek genealogies, these studies confirm what we suspected of their formation. The very process of constructing a written genealogy from family tradition must often have involved the ordering of disparate information, some in genealogical form, some remembered without context. Production of a stable genealogy

---

[54] It is not always clear how the names were added and where they came from. Henige is vague on this (though the overall pattern is clear) except for the use made of royal and semi-royal tombs to augment the list.

[55] Another example of this combination in Oliver (1955) 111–17, who shows that the oral traditions reached a peak only in the twentieth century, particularly with the publication of Ganda oral traditions; cf. remarks in Goody (1987) chs. 3, 4.

[56] Cf. recent work on early medieval king-lists and genealogies. Dumville (1977) examines the roles of ideology and learning in the construction of genealogical schemes and king-lists. Bede, *HE* 3.1 comments that those who count the length of kings' reigns have agreed to delete the reigns of Edwin's apostate successors.

obviously prompted the inclusion of figures whose position in the family tree was unclear or unknown. We saw an example of this in the Philaid genealogy. Moreover, the other, more complex elements in producing a genealogy—such as chronological or generational calculation, appropriate lengthening of the line and inclusion of duplicated figures of the same name—are the product of applied written methods, that is, written study beyond the simple recording in writing itself. Greek family traditions did not remember such genealogies unaided. Especially problematic was the gap—which we must assume was usual—between the legendary Homeric ancestors and the recent, historical members of the family. The necessity to bridge the gap in a plausible number of generations called most urgently for the help of genealogists. Here Heropythos' genealogy seems to be exceptional, but we must judge it against the cumulative evidence and inferences from other family traditions or genealogies. It did not extend to an Homeric ancestor, nor is it explicitly associated with the genealogists (though we have no way of knowing otherwise). So, at least the chronological inconsistencies produced by an Homeric hero were not present. The original ancestor, Kyprios, must have had special importance to the family. But since we have no external evidence whatsoever of Heropythos' family, we should suppose that in his case, too, the same processes of memory, telescoping and forgetting would have occurred, if his family tradition was transmitted in a similar way to all the others we have examined.[57] Even his genealogy only 'extends' as far back as the tenth century. The full genealogies (or instances of numbered generations) back to a god or hero were in part a product of the applied literate methods of the professional genealogists.

A further distortion is introduced by the linear form of a genealogy, since in its extreme simplification it allows only a list of fathers and sons.[58] Genealogical information in linear form would be

[57] Wade-Gery took Eldios as a Semitic name, and other names in the list may not be Greek: in which case one may wonder if the genealogy belongs to a different tradition which encourages the preservation of genealogies (in writing?) from an early period; cf. Momigliano's remarks ((1966) 19f.) on the Jewish imperative to remember their past. Even so, what I have said about the significance of genealogy for status and family character and the formation of a written list would still hold.

[58] Such linearity implies that the lateral links of the family and ancestors were not considered socially important: if they were, perhaps we should expect appropriate family memories.

misleading even in oral tradition; when a linear genealogy is constructed in writing the problem is exacerbated. The elongation of the line I mentioned above is partly encouraged by the linear form—so that collateral members might be included.

But there is a further element of distortion in the linear genealogy. Not only may a linear genealogy be formed by including members not of the direct line: a list that represents some kind of succession to office may also be interpreted or assumed to be one of father–son succession. Henige produces numerous examples where king-lists purport to show a continuous line of fathers and sons over a long period of time, whereas other evidence shows that brothers sometimes succeeded. So the process is similar to the one by which brothers become included in a linear genealogy. This has the effect of lengthening the chronological time span, since successive generations are thus indicated by the line. Yet, where lines of succession can be checked (e.g. in the British royal family) it is extremely rare to find continuous father–son succession for many generations. The holders of office invariably have to include others.[59] Thus, in Greece, for example, the Spartan king-lists purported to represent fathers and sons in succession, at least for the period about which little was known (Hdt. 7.204). Each was presented both as a king-list and a linear genealogy of the appropriate house.[60]

I suspect a similar background to the list of priests of Poseidon Erechtheus from the *genos* of the Eteoboutadai.[61] Pseudo-Plutarch tells us (*Vit. X Orat.* 843e–f) that the *genos* was descended from Boutes and Erechtheus, son of Ge and Hephaestus, and 'most recently from Lycomedes and Lycurgus' (fifth- to fourth-century figures):

[59] Henige (1974), esp. 42ff. and ch. 2.
[60] Also Hdt. 8.131. Huxley (1962) 117–19 and (more sophisticated) Cartledge (1979) App. 3 attempt in various ways to sort out the genealogy/king-lists. The line of each is satisfyingly linear only for the early kings about whom least is known. They then branch out in the latest generations, forming an interesting parallel to the Philaid genealogy. The early Eurypontid line includes suspicious names, Eunomos and Prytanis. Herodotus does not say the list of 8.131 was a king-list for the recent generations, but Pausanias (3.7.2) called the Agiad list a king-list of fathers and sons. He does the same of his Eurypontid list which is rather different from that of Herodotus. The King Soos is again suspicious and there seems to have been some attempt to even up the generations of the two houses. Henige (1974) App. C has an interesting discussion of the problem.
[61] On the family of Lycurgus, see Davies (1971) no. 9251.

And this genealogy (*katagogê*) of the family of the priests of Poseidon exists on a complete tablet (*pinax*) which lies in the Erechtheum ... and there are wooden statues of Lycurgus, the orator, and his sons ... His son Habron dedicated the tablet, who received the priesthood from the *genos* (λαχὼν ἐκ τοῦ γένους) and handed it over to his brother Lycophron.

By his use of *katagogê* ('bringing down', i.e. 'pedigree', 'genealogy'), the author shows that the *pinax* represented *both* a list of the priests and a genealogy of the family from Boutes and Erechtheus down through Lycomedes to Lycurgus, the orator: the implication is that the whole list was interpreted as a linear genealogy of father–son succession.[62]

The way in which *genos* priesthoods were handed down is unclear,[63] but it is certain that the list of priests, taken to be a genealogy, was very misleading. Pseudo-Plutarch gives us evidence in the same paragraph of precisely the kind of non-linear succession which was obscured in the list of priests and turned into a linear genealogy— and obviously, if it happened once, it had done so before. For he says (see extract, above) that Habron who set up the tablet ceded the priesthood which he had received to his brother Lycophron. So the succession is not the simple linear one implied by the rest of the list; and the assumption that the list represents the linear descent from

---

[62] Lists of priests might be particularly prone to this kind of distortion if the priesthood was held by a *genos*. *SIG*³ 1020, the first century BC list of priests of Poseidon at Halicarnassus, purports to list the priests going back to the foundation by the legendary Telamon. It says (lines 1–2) that it was copied from an ancient stele. Cf. the later decree from Eleusis honouring the daduch Themistocles (20/19 BC; Clinton 1974: 50ff.): it gives his predecessors, his father and eight other ancestors. What is interesting is that it then says: 'And before all these, Hermotimus and Hierocleides were daduchs before the registering (*anagraphê*) of the Kerykes on the tablet.' So the contemporary record presents an extremely complex family tree, in which successors do not form a linear line; but for daduchs before the written record (i.e. end of third century) all is very vague. See Jacoby (1949) 280 n. 39 and 358 n. 26. In general, on lists in shrines, see Jeffery (1961) 59ff.; ead. (1976) 34–7; and Jacoby (1949) 58.

[63] At least occasionally apportioned by lot rather than inheritance: Dem. 57.47. But it is unknown how common this was. The phrase used above seems in the context to imply the lot here, too. It is still uncertain whether Habron or Lycophron was the eldest son of Lycurgus (see Davies (1971) 351f.): either way the priesthood was passed by one brother to another, and probably the only candidates were Lycurgus' sons (Humphreys (1985)).

Boutes is clearly incorrect.[64] A similar observation and explanation may be made of the famous line of Egyptian priests whose statues Herodotus said he was shown in Thebes (2.143). The statues represented three hundred and forty-five priests who, it was insisted, had succeeded each other in continuous father–son succession from the earliest period. Thus, both the creation of linear genealogy and the assumption of linear genealogy from lists of succession form gross distortions which stem in part from their creation in written form in the first place.[65]

These, then, are some of the ways in which written genealogy may have affected the original oral traditions. In the first place, the mere collection in writing may increase the amount of information that is thought relevant. This may result in an impressive accretion to the genealogy of names of people who were not clearly remembered themselves or whose genealogical position was not clearly recalled. The form of the genealogy also has an effect. A linear genealogy in its simple form may exaggerate the tendencies of lengthening and addition of extraneous figures—as we saw in the Philaid genealogy. It may also be confused with lists of offices, so that a list of priests may be taken to represent both a list of 'office-holders' and a linear genealogy: this we saw in the case of the priests of Poseidon Erechtheus. Beyond this, the use of writing may encourage—indeed make possible—the comparison of different genealogies, the counting of generations and the construction of a plausible sequence of generations. These methods we know the genealogists used at least for the legendary period. But one may extend it to the case of the full genealogies down to the historical period. For a Greek aristocratic

[64] Cf. again the complex line of daduchs at Eleusis (n. 62). We do not know the provenance or reliability of the list itself. It may have derived from an earlier list of priests or from a list partly reconstructed artificially (Plutarch implies the first, like the statues). Since the list was regarded as the family genealogy, it represents family tradition (and manipulation?). But more complicated, it is also an official list of priests of the sanctuary, perhaps kept by the sanctuary.

[65] This obviously bears on other early Greek lists, e.g. the list of priestesses at Argos, the Olympic victor list or the Athenian archon list. Were they remembered for a long time before being written down (as Jeffery (1976) 35–6, citing the role of *mnêmones*)? When were they written down, and were the early reaches partly reconstructed from memory and speculation? This needs much further examination. I outline some preliminary points in Thomas (1989) 287–8.

family it was extremely rare to have a full genealogy back to legendary times. And genealogical information certainly began to be very inaccurate four or five generations back from the present day. Where such genealogy occurs, we may suspect that information in it has been gathered together from the family's oral traditions, ordered and improved to produce a coherent and plausible stemma. The genealogies we find are thus the product both of written record itself and of the organization that comes—or may come—from literate study of that material.

*

I have tried to build up a picture of Greek genealogy of the sixth and fifth centuries, the one form of family tradition that seems to have extended over an extraordinarily long period of time. Such genealogy has interesting implications for the possible effect of the written word on the oral traditions and for the activities of the early proto-historians of Greece in constructing a written framework for the past. The direct evidence is sparse, but for that reason it is important to look the more closely at what there is. My argument has necessarily been a cumulative one, supported by detailed examination of particularly illuminating examples.

Genealogical information was both popular and important for the Greeks, but it was genealogy primarily of the legendary period. Genealogy was seen as an explanation of observed relations which was far removed from historical 'fact'; and legendary genealogy was believed to explain or to correspond in some way to the later descendants, whether tribe, city or family. Thus it was liable to change as circumstances changed. Similarly, one should expect in the conditions of oral transmission that the great concentration upon the legendary period would produce a vast gap of forgotten history or generations between the legendary period and the recent past, with telescoping of the two extremes. This is what we find, and it seems most striking in the case of family tradition, since we are well used, from our standpoint, to lengthy and complex genealogies that reach back over centuries. But full genealogy, a list of ancestors purporting to be complete from the legendary hero, seems to have been exceedingly rare in Greek family tradition. Indeed, much evidence suggests that there was knowledge of the legendary and recent ancestors, but a dim period of ignorance between which was not bridged and did not need to be: the heroic ancestor was enough, and there was no need to know or prove the intervening links.

But there were some full genealogies, and they prompt interesting and far-reaching suggestions about the role of writing and written coordination in elaborating and crystallizing the oral traditions. The genealogists themselves concentrated mostly upon legendary genealogy—the same preoccupation with the heroic period. This was of intense relevance to their contemporaries and could reflect contemporary 'propaganda' and argument. Again, there was no necessity to continue the genealogies down to the present day explicitly. However, it is no coincidence that the few examples of full genealogies occur in the work of the genealogists (except, apparently, for Heropythos' genealogy). I have therefore suggested that such genealogies are essentially constructions of the genealogists and their written and graphic methods. They collected and organized oral family tradition which was often disparate, remembered in non-genealogical form, illogical, or contradictory. They used the essentially written methods of generation counting and synchronization to produce lengthy and impressive genealogies. Plato's construction of his family's recent genealogy shows a similar process on a smaller scale. The application of written methods to family tradition showed up its gaps and illogicalities. I have examined in detail some of the possible effects of both writing and written study on this kind of material in Greek family tradition. The Philaid genealogy both illustrates this process and suggests some reasons for it. Pherecydes crystallized in writing a genealogy that encapsulated both legendary propaganda and later historical figures who enhanced the family's glory. Both parts were peculiarly appropriate to the early fifth century, and the written genealogy preserved in definitive form the family's view of its past at one particular time. It also contains evidence of literate manipulation of generations, partly for chronological reasons, a process that often occurs when oral tradition is transferred into written genealogy.

The full Greek genealogy is therefore essentially a written and artificial construction of the genealogists: it crystallizes the claims made through genealogy in that period and orders and elaborates the material with methods that are literate and graphic ones. The genealogists' activities represent an extension and new application of writing and writing study to the oral traditions—albeit in one limited sphere. Though not themselves interested primarily in chronology, the genealogists highlight the extreme problems of reckoning any chronology from such oral traditions and indeed producing any chronological framework for Greek history. They offer a foretaste of the problems of early historiography derived from oral tradition.

ADDENDUM

Agathon of Zakynthos' inscription claiming 30 generations of *proxenoi* from Kassandra, (mentioned in Thomas (1989) 159 n. 9) is now discussed by Fraser (2003), who argues that it is partly a riddle or joke, noting the extraordinary fact (missed in the written text alone) of the male reproductive organ in the middle of the inscription.

Important new bibliography includes Fowler (1996); id. (1998); Calame (1987); Möller (1996); ead. (2001) has much on genealogy and çhronography. Hunter (2005) is an important collection of articles. For the continuing importance of legendary genealogy in *polis* identity and interstate relations into the Hellenistic period and beyond, see Curty (1995), with a catalogue of inscriptions; Jones (1999).

4

Some Aspects of Source Theory in Greek Historiography

Guido Schepens

The elaboration of a source theory as we know it from the *Quellen-kunde* in our traditional handbooks of historical method is a comparatively recent phenomenon in the history of historiography, and one without precedent in ancient and medieval historical writing. The organized reflection on the methodological foundations of historical knowledge, to which the systematic description and classification of the various kinds of historical evidence belong, cannot be separated from that stage in the development of historical thought—mainly the nineteenth century—in which it has tried to assert itself as an independent and self-conscious discipline.[1]

Because of the modern connotations of the concept of 'source theory', due caution must be exercised in linking the term to the summary and often implicit indications found in the ancient historians on the definition and classification of historical evidence. It is by no means my intention to suggest the existence of a lost, but reconstructable, treatise on the various forms of historical information, one that could be regarded as a prototype of the modern *Quellen-kunde*. It is beyond doubt—even though the works 'On History' by Theophrastus and Praxiphanes may have dealt with historical methodology[2]—that the best that ancient historiographical theory

[1] Cf. Johnson (1926) esp. 101–40.
[2] Cf. Walbank (1972) 36 n. 20.

has to offer has been invested empirically in the historical works themselves.[3] This does not, however, make the study of this theory any less interesting, imaginary, or anachronistic; for how could the ancient historians discuss the requirements of historical πολυπραγμοσύνη {effort} without being able to refer to a kind of common notion, and therefore to a certain theory, of historical information? *Reservatis reservandis*, the term 'source theory' is accordingly used as an expedient in the present study, which is an attempt to reduce a few peculiarities of the ancient approach to the problem of historical evidence to a common denominator.

In comparison with modern *Quellenkunde*, ancient source theory undoubtedly displays peculiar traits, which demand our special attention.[4] There is more to it than just a conspicuous shift in the relative importance attached by ancient and modern historians to certain forms of information (it is common knowledge that written documents, among them the archives that are the starting point of modern historical research, ranked only third in ancient historiography, after oral tradition and eyewitness reports).[5] There is also a fundamental difference in the approach to the matter of historical sources. Even a superficial look at the main categories in which the definition and classification is undertaken—ὄψις {autopsy} and ἀκοή {oral report} on the one hand, and 'records' and 'remains' on the other—will make this clear. Ὄψις and ἀκοή appear as the essential terms of a paradigm *sui generis*, which has nothing in common with the modern arrangement of source materials.

Needless to say, the problem here posed is deeply rooted in the evolution of historical method and in the history of historiography from antiquity to the present.[6] To deal with all its aspects is plainly beyond the scope of this paper. I have confined myself to a survey of the main characteristics of the ancient approach to 'sources' with the aid of examples taken from Greek historiography; these traits in turn provide the basis for the subsequent discussion of a few typical instances of arrangement or classification of the evidence.

---

[3] Cf. Strasburger (1966) 11–12.
[4] See e.g. Peremans (1950) 17–18; id. (1955).
[5] Cf. Lacroix (1951) 224–7. The use of 'documents' in ancient Greek and Roman historiography is extensively covered in Biraschi et al. (2003); see also Rhodes (2007).
[6] See Ernst (1957).

Before proceeding, however, it should be noted that the contemporary scholar, who has been taught, as it were, to identify the modern division of the evidence with the basic principles of historical methodology, is quite understandably somewhat taken aback by the lack of comparable concepts and classifications in the methodological tradition of ancient historiography. It seems almost as if the crude essentials for the rigorous writing of history were unknown to the Greek and Roman historians. Serious criticism to that effect has sometimes been levelled, mainly by an earlier generation of scholars, at the still underdeveloped method of the ancient historians. Wilamowitz's and Howald's critiques of Polybius are cases in point: according to them the historian from Megalopolis had not the slightest notion of 'sources' or 'source criticism'.[7] However, the fact that ancient source theory cannot be given a self-evident explanation within the confines of modern historical method is in itself by no means sufficient grounds for rejective or demeaning criticism. Due to a feeling of superiority founded on an unspoken belief in the continual progress and perfection of historical science and its techniques, we are sometimes all too easily inclined to regard the present state of historical scholarship as the quintessence of all that preceded it, which thereby becomes worthless. However, as will be apparent from the ensuing study, the recognition of a basic distinction between two types of historical research—in H. Strasburger's terminology, the distinction between the *Primärforschung* {primary inquiry} of the ancient historian and the *Sekundärarbeit* {secondary work} of his modern colleague[8]— should rather be the point of departure for an equitable evaluation of ancient source theory on its own terms.

Let us start, then, with a discussion of the specific approach to the information problem by ancient and modern historians. Although it is difficult, in the absence of a generally received definition, to sum up the essence of the modern notion of 'historical source' in a few lines, the observations of G. J. Henz can serve as a valid point of departure for a more precise description of the phenomenon 'source' as such.[9] According to this scholar, general source theory aims to

---

[7] Wilamowitz (1908) 14; Howald (1944) 108–9.
[8] Strasburger (1966) 12.
[9] Henz (1974).

contemplate 'the general possibilities of historical knowledge with an eye towards objectivity, i.e. taking into consideration the possibilities offered by the sources for an objective interpretation of the material they relate'.[10] In this description of source theory, the restrictive clause 'with an eye towards objectivity' seems particularly important to the definition of 'historical evidence': source theory does not describe all the means employed in the process of acquiring historical knowledge, but only those that exist as a material object, i.e. in time and space. This definition leads to the conscious exclusion of all things immaterial, which cannot be defined in spatial or temporal terms. Consequently, the historical source can exist only by virtue of its material connections.[11]

This definition of historical evidence as the objective, material medium between the historian and past reality echoes those found in the classical handbooks of historical method. Thus A. Feder, for example, postulates as the fundamental principle of source theory that its aim is to study the various *objective* historical sources; the description of the *subjective* means, i.e. the various capabilities and activities of the person involved, such as perception, judgement, and faith, is beyond the compass of historical methodology.[12] To sum up, modern source theory, in excluding the *Erkenntniskräfte* {powers of knowledge}, strives toward a definition and systematic description of the *Erkenntnisstoff* {material of knowledge}.[13]

Ancient source theory, on the other hand, as it can be reconstructed from the most representative pronouncements of the Greek historians, appears to aim at precisely the opposite of the modern definition. It takes no account of the objective aspect and explicitly discusses the subjective means in their diverse forms. From the birth of Greek historiography with Herodotus this methodological tradition assumes its characteristic features. As sources for his description of the land, people and history of Egypt, the *pater historiae* mentions ὄψις {autopsy}, γνώμη {judgement}, ἱστορίη {inquiry}, and [ἀκοή]

---

[10] Henz (1974) 2–3; cf. 17.
[11] Henz (1974) 6.
[12] Feder (1924) 83. Cf. Spieler (1970) 49–50; further examples of modern definitions of 'Quellenkunde', 52 n. 74.
[13] Cf. Keyser (1931) 46 n.1.

{oral report}.[14] It is remarkable that in the phrase μέχρι μὲν τούτου ὄψις τε ἐμὴ καὶ γνώμη καὶ ἱστορίη ταῦτα λέγουσά ἐστι, the terms 'my own sight, judgement, and inquiry' constitute the subject of the periphrastic and emphatic λέγουσά ἐστι {are saying}, a particularity of the Greek expression usually lost in modern translations.[15] Essentially, then, ὄψις, γνώμη, and ἱστορίη are to be understood as *active* faculties deployed by the historian in his inquiry.

Let us for a moment leave γνώμη aside—we will return to this term below—and have a look at the objective material that Herodotus assembles by way of ὄψις, ἱστορίη, and ἀκοή. It is immediately clear that the amount of information thus collected was both large and varied. It is not our task here to give a complete survey of Herodotus' sources.[16] Suffice it to say that his ὄψις brought him into contact with archaeological and epigraphical evidence, with manners and customs, with ethnological characteristics, and with the geographical features, climate, fauna, and flora of foreign lands. Through ἱστορίη, which should be taken in the narrower sense of the questioning of informants,[17] Herodotus was able to obtain the testimony of, for example, eyewitnesses and *epichorioi* {native inhabitants}. The term ἀκοή/ἀκούω, finally, introduces the written[18] as well as (mainly) the oral reports that Herodotus prefers to present on the authority of others, without

[14] Hdt. 2.99. Herodotus defines the notion ἀκοή by stating that he will recount the history of Egypt κατὰ τὰ ἤκουον {in accordance with what I heard}.

[15] E.g. Godley (1920) 385: 'Thus far all I have said is the outcome of my own sight and judgement and inquiry,...'; Legrand (1944) 130: 'Jusqu'ici ce que je disais est tiré de ce que j'ai vu, des réflexions que j'ai faites, des informations que j'ai prises...'; cf. Stein (1893–1908) I.108: 'ὄψις, one's own vision and the knowledge acquired from it; γνώμη, one's own judgement and the insight based on reflection'; ἱστορίη knowledge obtained by asking around and enquiry'. These and other interpretations of Hdt. 2.99 emphasize, from a modern point of view, the *result* or the *object* of Herodotus' inquiry, whereas literally he declares: 'Thus far it is my own sight and judgement and inquiry that say this'. Cf. Schepens (2007) 44–5.

[16] See Verdin (1971) 1–53. Hedrick (1993) and (1995) have made pertinent observations on the wide range of historical sources that, according to the characteristic approach of the ancient historians, are 'pressed' into one or the other of the basic categories of the seen (ὄψις) and the heard (ἀκοή).

[17] See Verdin (1971) 4–5 on the difference with the more general sense of '*historiē*' as used in the proemial phrase ἱστορίης ἀπόδεξις; cf. Schepens (2007) 40–2.

[18] That the reading of written sources also belongs to ἀκοή is clear from Pol. 12.27.2–3. See also Peter (1911) 88 and n. 1. For the scholarly debate on the question whether ancient Greeks and Romans read aloud or silently see Johnson (2000).

necessarily believing them. The critique that 'Herodotus himself rarely draws clear distinctions between the specific categories of historical evidence'[19] appears somewhat irrelevant because it is formulated from a modern viewpoint. A more equitable appreciation of Herodotus' intention is expressed in J. C. Bähr's remark that in 2.99 the historian is trying to draw an *accurate distinction* between the sources from which he derives his knowledge and that throughout his work he remains true to his habit of acknowledging sources.[20]

Another highly instructive text for the particular Greek approach to the information problem is the passage from Thucydides in which the subjective way to historical knowledge as well as the objective means thereto are mentioned together. The phrase in question is part of the speech given by the Athenian envoys who happened to be in Sparta just before the outbreak of the Peloponnesian War (1.73–78). 'Now', say the Athenians, 'what need is there to speak about matters quite remote, whose only witnesses are the stories men hear rather than the eyes of those who will hear them told? But concerning the Persian War and all the other events of which you have personal knowledge, we needs must speak, even though it will be rather irksome to mention them, since they are always being paraded.'[21] Here it is said that, as regards the very distant past (τὰ πάνυ παλαιά), the hearing of stories (ἀκοαὶ λόγων) provides much more testimony than the eyesight of the listeners (ὄψις τῶν ἀκουσομένων).[22] To such an unusual formulation one can from a modern viewpoint rightly remark, with J. Steup, that the μάρτυρες {witnesses} of the past are not the ἀκοαί {hearings}, but (the content of) the λόγοι {stories}.[23] The expression ἀκοαὶ λόγων {hearings of stories}, however, makes the typically Greek view on historical sources immediately clear; the relationship to τὰ πάνυ παλαιά is not brought about via the material medium of the λόγος—the objective source—but by way of the ἀκοή,

[19] Macan (1908) II.lxviii.
[20] Baehr (1856) 640–41. Fowler (1996), esp. 76–80, has called Herodotus' constant talk about sources and how to assess them 'the most distinctive thing about him' (62).
[21] Thuc. 1.73 (Cf. Smith's translation, LCL).
[22] τῶν ἀκουσομένων: the middle future participle points, as subjective genitive governed by ὄψις, to the potential audience of the stories about the very distant past. Otherwise, Papantoniou (1958–9) 409.
[23] Classen–Steup (1892–1922) I.206: 'For the ἀκοαὶ λόγων are in an actual sense not μάρτυρες at all'. See also Poppo (1866) 145: 'ἀκοαὶ λόγων are λόγοι ἀκουσθέντες'.

which in essence only indicates the (subjective) *route* by which one is informed.[24]

This typical approach to the information problem could easily be further illustrated with numerous texts, in which the Greek historians describe their research in terms of ὄψις and ἀκοή.[25] We will confine ourselves, however, to a sample from Polybius, who in the course of his work repeatedly digresses on this matter.[26] His most explicit description of the methodological question at issue here is offered in 12.27. Apropos of his criticism of Timaeus he states the general rule

> that nature has given us two instruments, as it were, by the aid of which we inform ourselves and inquire about everything. These are hearing and sight... Now, Timaeus enters on his inquiries by the pleasanter of the two roads, but the inferior one. For he entirely avoids employing his eyes and prefers to employ his ears. Now the knowledge derived from hearing being of two sorts, Timaeus diligently pursued the one, the reading of books, ... but was very remiss in his use of the other, the interrogation of living witnesses'.[27]

It is difficult to think of a clearer formulation of the theory in which the entire information problem is reduced to a choice between various ways, or roads (ὁδοί), that enable the historian to establish contact with reality, *in casu* seeing, questioning, and hearing.

The passages from Herodotus, Thucydides, and Polybius hitherto discussed plainly reveal the chief characteristic of ancient source theory as compared with its modern counterpart: whereas modern theory aims at a description of the objective material that is assembled, the ancient historians dwell on the various subjective ways of assembling that material.[28]

---

[24] Compare e.g. Thuc. 3.38.4: οὐ τὸ δρασθὲν πιστότερον ὄψει λαβόντες ἢ τὸ ἀκουσθέν... {not using your powers of sight to give greater credibility to what has been done rather than what has been said}; 1.23.3: τά τε πρότερον ἀκοῇ μὲν λεγόμενα {the things formerly said in oral report}.

[25] By making the distinction between ὄψις and ἀκοή the ancient historians claim authority for their accounts: see Marincola (1997) 63–86.

[26] Apart from the passages in Book 12, which we intend to discuss here, see, e.g. Pol. 4.2.2–3; 20.12.8.

[27] Pol. 12.27.1–3. The translations of Polybius are those of Paton (LCL).

[28] The recognition of this fundamental difference is an important point of departure for the interpretation of the ancient historians' methodological statements, among them the controversial text Thuc. 1.22.2. There Thucydides names two ways

However, we must not content ourselves with having isolated this main trait. The difference between ancient and modern source theory is more than just a variance of viewpoint in the approach to an otherwise similarly defined methodological process. The pronouncements of the Greek historians on their sources frequently contain a number of what we are inclined to call 'heterogeneous' elements: terms that, unlike ὄψις, ἱστορίη, and ἀκοή, do not refer directly to the process of gathering information but to diverse activities or requirements that precede or follow the collecting of the evidence *stricto sensu*. Precisely because the objective material is not the point of departure for the Greek historians in their reflection on the foundations of historical knowledge, their statements on method can quite naturally include elements that have no direct bearing on the collection of evidence as such.

The passage from Herodotus discussed above is an early example hereof: to the modern historian it is strange that in 2.99 the *pater historiae*, in addition to ὄψις and ἱστορίη, also mentions γνώμη in the same breath. The 'judgement' (γνώμη) here referred to as a 'source' can only be interpreted as the subjective opinion formed by the historian on the basis of the data obtained through ὄψις and ἱστορίη. It cannot refer to any new *objective* material not already provided by ὄψις or ἱστορίη. As such the γνώμη is no longer part of the gathering of evidence in the strict sense, but an interpretation of sources or an instrument of criticism.[29]

The presence of the term γνώμη in the enumeration ὄψις τε ἐμὴ καὶ γνώμη καὶ ἱστορίη draws our attention to the fact that the

of active pursuit of data οἷς τε αὐτὸς παρῆν καὶ παρὰ τῶν ἄλλων ... ἐπεξελθών {going through ... both the events at which I myself was present and those from others}, linked by the τε ... καί connection and this should discourage an interpretation, according to which he got to know some events through his personal observation, while others—where he was not present—were narrated on the basis of eyewitness accounts. The idea that Thucydides would be making an 'objective' distinction between things seen by himself and [things] heard from others, has (mainly in the past) been forced upon the ἔργα-sentence with the help of the conjecture to be inserted before παρὰ τῶν ἄλλων. As I explained in Schepens (1980) 113–46, such manipulation of the *textus receptus* is unwarranted and runs counter to the idea that Thucydides, in accordance with the particular Greek approach to the information problem, merely singles out the two *ways* in which he acquired his knowledge of the events.

[29] Cf. Verdin (1971) 5–6.

description of method given in 2.99 may not be taken to relate strictly to the problem of historical information. Its proper meaning and the *forma mentis* of its author are undoubtedly more closely approached when we assume that Herodotus here intended to draw a distinction not simply between three sources, but, more generally, between three different methods of research.

The assembly and critical examination of the evidence—two phases of the working method of the historian kept carefully separated in modern handbooks—enter, in the Greek historians' viewpoint, into a very close relationship. A striking illustration hereof is Polybius' evaluation of the various methods of inquiry he distinguishes in 12.27.1–3. Citing Heraclitus' saying ὀφθαλμοὶ γὰρ τῶν ὤτων ἀκριβέστεροι μάρτυρες {'eyes are more accurate witnesses than ears'} he observes that in the search for historical truth the use of the eyes gives a much greater guarantee than the testimony of the ears. The various ways of collecting evidence are invested with a distinct critical value; in other words, the manner in which the historian gathers his material already implies an important critical act.

Focusing not on the material medium between the historian and past reality but on the subjective means—capabilities and activities of the researcher—the discussion of sources in Greek historiography is led to incorporate considerations on the personality of the historian, his living conditions, his intellectual or moral qualities. Just how deeply these ethical and biographical observations are involved in the argumentation Polybius develops in 12.27 is apparent from his discussion of the question why Timaeus confined his historical research almost exclusively to the study of written sources:

It is easy enough to perceive what caused him to make this choice. Inquiries from books may be made without any danger or hardship, provided only that one takes care to have access to a town rich in documents or to have a library near at hand. After that one has only to pursue one's researches in perfect repose and compare the accounts of different writers without exposing oneself to any hardship. Personal inquiry, on the contrary, requires severe labour and great expense, but is exceedingly valuable and is the most important part of history.'[30]

[30] Pol. 12.27.4–6.

The information problem here is not approached as a merely technical matter, but rather described in terms of a moral discipline:[31] in choosing a certain form of information the historian may not shrink from the dangers, the hardships and the expense historical research entails. Also, the historian is expected to lead such a life as to be able to fulfil his informatory mission in the best way possible; residence in a city offering a mass of written material is, in Polybius' opinion, not a valid starting point for historical inquiry.[32]

The historian who studies the distant past—Dionysius of Halicarnassus for example—can also frame his survey of the sources used to compose his work into a biographical notice. Dionysius concludes the relevant passage from his proem, which contains, in addition to a justification of his choice of subject, a description of the evidence (τῶν ἀφορμῶν), with the significant remark: 'So much, then, concerning myself' (ταῦτα μὲν οὖν ὑπὲρ ἐμαυτοῦ διείλεγμαι).[33] He specifically mentions his settling in Rome, where he applied himself for twenty-two years to the study of history. He obtained his information in part orally (διδαχῇ παραλαβών) through contacts with learned informants, in part by reading (ἀναλεξάμενος) historical literature.[34] The key words διδαχῇ παραλαβών and ἀναλεξάμενος indicate once again the way in which Dionysius acquired his data.

Diodorus' description of his sources provides yet another example of the strong ethical–subjective character of the ancient approach to the source problem. After mentioning his thirty years of laborious work and his travels—μετὰ δὲ πολλῆς κακοπαθείας καὶ κινδύνων {with many hardships and dangers}—so that he could see with his own eyes the most important regions of Asia and Europe,[35] Diodorus declares he was aided in the realization of his grand undertaking by two ἀφορμαί: 'They have been, first and foremost, that enthusiasm for the work which enables every man to bring to completion the task

---

[31] On this point, see Isnardi (1955) 102–10. Cf. Pédech (1961) xxxiv–xxxv; Roveri (1964) 59ff.

[32] In Polybius' Book 12, 'character' (αἵρεσις) and 'lifestyle' (βίος) appear as key concepts structuring his criticism of the historical method of Timaeus of Tauromenium: see Schepens (1990).

[33] D. Hal. *A.R.* 1.7.4.

[34] D. Hal. *A.R.* 1.7.1–3.

[35] Diod. 1.4.1.

which seems impossible, and, in the second place, the abundant supply which Rome affords of the materials pertaining to the proposed study.'[36] The mention of the ἐπιθυμία πρὸς τὴν πραγματείαν {enthusiasm for the undertaking} can only make sense in a declaration of method that is not simply intended to inform the reader about the sources, but, in a more general way, as the term ἀφορμαί indicates, about the *resources* the historian has to draw on for effectuating his research. The broad notion ἀφορμαί—means for undertaking the writing of history—covers both terms that refer to evidence proper and a variety of data that relate to the ἦθος {character} and external living conditions, such as, *in casu,* residence in a city offering good facilities.[37]

The insertion of the information problem into a more comprehensive theory, in which the discussion of the sources is linked to observations on the researcher's ἦθος and βίος {lifestyle} is the issue of an evolution that can be followed from the fifth century BC onwards. In Herodotus, whose historical method was to a large extent elaborated empirically, we find no information on the way an author can best organize his life for the purpose of historical inquiry. He does mention, for example, the voyages he undertook to obtain information on the most diverse matters; but nowhere does he offer a more general view on the necessity or the utility of such travels for the study of history.[38] Thucydides, who also does not seem to base himself on an already extant theory, emphasizes the fortunate coincidence of a number of circumstances that put him into a favourable position as an observer: his age, which enabled him to live through the entire war in full possession of his intellectual faculties; the attention (γνώμη) he devoted to the events; his exile, which enabled him to be present at events on both sides.[39] As far as we know, the first to offer an explicit coupling of the requirements of historical research to the idea of a life-task for the historian is Theopompus. He states that considerable preparations and financial sacrifices are necessary to allow the historian to gather his material as

---

[36] Diod. 1.4.2 (Oldfather's translation, LCL).
[37] Cf. Plut. *Mor.* 384c; *Dem.* 2.1–2.
[38] Cf. Verdin (1971) 46.
[39] Thuc. 5.26.5.

an eyewitness and by oral inquiry. To be successful the researcher may not regard the undertaking as a πάρεργον τοῦ βίου {secondary task in life} but he must earnestly devote his entire life to it: ἔργον τὸ πάντων ἀναγκαιότατον {a task most necessary of all}.[40] This very idea is, again, stressed by Polybius, when in 12.28 he describes his ideal of historiography, which can only come about 'either when men of action undertake to write history, not as now happens in a perfunctory manner, but when in the belief that this is a most necessary and most noble thing they apply themselves all through their life to it with undivided attention, or again when would-be authors regard a training in actual affairs as necessary for writing history.'[41] Polybius discusses the standards exacted by historiographical practice on the historian's way of life in greater detail in his comparison of pragmatic history and medicine.[42] In ascending order of importance he discerns three components in historical research, which can be summarily characterized as study, travel, and political activity.[43] With this hierarchy Polybius wishes to illustrate the one-sidedness and inadequacy of Timaeus' attitude toward writing history: 'having lived for nearly fifty years in Athens with access to the works of previous writers, he considered himself peculiarly qualified to write history' (ὑπέλαβε τὰς μεγίστας ἀφορμὰς ἔχειν πρὸς τὴν ἱστορίαν). But herein, according to Polybius, he is gravely mistaken.[44]

In a previous article I attempted to demonstrate that the tripartite division of πραγματικὴ ἱστορία {pragmatic history} in 12.25e.1

---

[40] *FGrHist* 115 T 20a.

[41] Pol. 12.28.3–5.

[42] Pol. 12.25d.2–e.

[43] Polybius breaks new ground by making travelling an ingredient of his theoretical considerations on pragmatic history writing. Cf. Zecchini (1991), who focuses in particular on chapters 57–9 of Book 3. In them Polybius expounds the need and usefulness of topographical knowledge for the study of history. He emphasizes the greatly improved opportunities for travel and research in his own period (see esp. 59.3–5), compared to the many obstacles which in ancient times 'made it not merely difficult but almost impossible to give a reliable description' (59.1) of the more remote parts of the world. For the views of the ancient Greek historians on the importance of travelling, see also Schepens (2006). In Greek historiographical literature, Odysseus—the man 'who saw the cities of many men and learned their mind' (Hom. *Od.* 1.4)—was frequently acknowledged—and emphatically so by Polybius—as a prototype historian; the best analysis is now Marincola (2007a).

[44] Pol. 12.25d.1.

relates to the fundamental preliminary requirements, and hence to the qualification of the historian to write contemporary political and military history.[45] Although it would be wrong to deny any link with the information problem—the ἀφορμαί study, travel, and political activity are indispensable prerequisites to the gathering of the evidence—it is clear that the μέρη {parts} discussed may not be equated with the sources *stricto sensu* and that, accordingly, there is no reason to suppose that in the subdivision made at 12.25e.1 certain sources are not mentioned, inadequately defined or overvalued.[46]

From here it is but a short step to the discussion of a few typical instances of classification of historical evidence. For, in accordance with the various viewpoints we have distinguished in the ancient approach to the information problem, different arrangements of the evidence are possible that supplement and, to a certain extent, correct each other. What follows here will be confined to a commentary on the three types of classification found in Polybius' methodologically important Book 12: the first at 4c.3–5, the second at 27.1–3, and the third at 28a.2–7. For the sake of clarity, it should be noted in advance that the shift in the hierarchical sequence of autopsy, oral inquiry, and the reading of books only affects the first two terms. In Polybius' view compiling information from written sources invariably ranks third. The main thrust of the comparison between history and medicine is to show 'that industry in the study of documents is only a third part of history and only stands in the third place' (τρίτον εἶναι μέρος τῆς ἱστορίας καὶ τρίτην ἔχειν τάξιν τὴν ἐκ τῶν ὑπομνημάτων πολυπραγμοσύνην).[47]

---

[45] Schepens (1974).

[46] Cf. Walbank (1972) 72: '. . . such studies are inadequate, not because these sources do not cover the period which the contemporary historian is concerned with—this is of course self-evident—but because contemporary history demands a kind of investigation which can not be learned in the library, any more than a painter can learn the technique of painting simply from the study of old masters.' See also Levene (2005).

[47] Pol. 12.25i.2. Polybius' tripartite comparison of history and medicine and his association of the incompetent 'bookish' historian with the 'logical' physicians, may well have been prompted by the so-called tripod in Hellenistic medicine (accurate observation, a well-stocked library, and an understanding of the virtues and limitations of similarity). On the 'tripod', see Nutton (2004) 140 ff., esp. 148–9. Polybius brings up the well known simile of the pilots steering ships by books in his comparison of history with medicine (25d.6); as Roselli (2002), esp. 44–6, suggests, this may not be merely accidental. Theopompus seems already to have delineated the specific

In his evaluation of the historical sources at the beginning of Book 12, Polybius quite straightforwardly calls oral inquiry the most important part of historical research (τὸ περὶ τὰς ἀνακρίσεις μέρος . . . ὅπερ ἐστι κυριώτατον τῆς ἱστορίας).[48] By way of explanation he advances that autopsy as a means of investigation about events and places is limited,

since many events occur at the same time at different places and one man cannot be in several places at one time; nor is it possible for a single man to have seen with his own eyes every place in the world and all the peculiar features of different places. Thus the only thing left for an historian is to enquire from as many people as possible.[49]

The temporal and spatial limits inherent in autopsy thus cause the historian to fall largely back, in assembling his data, upon the information he can obtain from other direct witnesses. This, clearly, is a quantitative evaluation of the role autopsy and oral inquiry can play in the collection of evidence: the latter source's share surpasses by far that of the former. This approach to the information problem in its purely 'heuristic' terms undoubtedly comes closest to our modern expectations. The classification at the beginning of Book 12 accordingly appears as the most realistic of the three found in Polybius.[50]

The most common disposition, however, in Polybius[51] as well as in other Greek historians, is the one in which the various ways of collecting evidence are arranged according to their critical value. Here autopsy appears as the preferred source of knowledge. Its priority is expressed in the proverbial saying ὦτα ἀπιστότερα ὀφθαλμῶν {ears are more untrustworthy than eyes}. This qualitative evaluation of the information problem, however, may not be simply equated, as one might conclude from the lapidary proverbial formulation, with an appreciation of the respective merits of the two sensory means by which the historian

competences of the historical profession by drawing parallels between history, on the one hand, and the τέχναι {skills} of medicine and navigation, on the other (*FGrHist* 115 F 342 = Pol. 12.27.8–9); cf. Vattuone (1997), esp. 101 and n. 24.

[48] Pol. 12.4c.3. It is perhaps preferable to take the term ἱστορία here as meaning 'historical research' rather than 'history'; otherwise, Mauersberger (1966) 1190–92 {= Mauersberger (2006) 1202–3}.

[49] Pol. 12.4c.4–5.

[50] Cf. Walbank (1972) 73.

[51] Pol. 12.27.1–4.

obtains his material.[52] As is apparent from Polybius' comments on the twofold character of the information διὰ τῆς ἀκοῆς {through oral report}, his critique of Timaeus boils down to the reproach that the latter confined himself mainly to the consultation of written sources, while almost completely neglecting the questioning of living informants. As is clear from other passages, the critical method in history is based essentially on the distinction between direct and indirect information. So the real distinction is one between autopsy and its extension, oral inquiry, on the one hand, and the reading of written materials on the other.[53]

The third classification of historical evidence will be found amid the observations with which for us Polybius' twelfth book now ends. In yet another critique Polybius says that Timaeus, having had no experience of personal participation in historical events and the deriving of information from it, 'naturally thinks that what is really of smallest importance and easiest is most important and difficult, I mean the collection of documents and inquiring from those personally acquainted with the facts'.[54] The division here presented is unquestionably the least clear of the three found in Polybius' work; this can be attributed in part to the deficient transmission of the passage at issue,[55] in part to the fact that Polybius—according to the most likely translation—seems to disavow somewhat the main conclusions from the two arrangements already discussed, in particular with regard to the role of oral inquiry.[56]

The surprising view expressed here can perhaps be made more understandable through a closer study of the context of 12.28a.7. Let us take as our point of departure the finding that Polybius' statement actually combines two views. The historian's personal participation, oral inquiry, and the consulting of written material are subjected to a twofold comparison: the first centres on the difficulty attending the several ways of collecting evidence, and is expressed in the

[52] Cf. Werner (1962); Schepens (1970).

[53] Cf. Pol. 4.2.2–3; 12.4c.3–5.

[54] Pol. 12.28a.7.

[55] In *Vaticanus Graecus* 73. Boissevain (1906) 165 reads: ἦν εἰς τέλος ἄπειρος ὢν εἰκότως ὑπελάβετο πάντων ἐλάχιστον καὶ ῥᾷστον εἶναι τοῖς πραγματευομένοις τὴν ἱστορίαν. See the crit. app. in Pédech (1961) ad loc.

[56] Cf. Walbank (1972) 73–4.

corresponding terms ῥᾷστον {easiest} and <χαλεπώτατον> {most difficult}; the relative weight or importance that can be attached to the methods of inquiry constitutes the second aspect conveyed in the terms ἐλάχιστον {least} and <μέγιστον> {greatest}. Now it is apparent from what goes before that the latter point must be regarded as an additional element in the train of thought that from 12.28a.2 is patently concerned with only the toil (μεῖζον ἔργον {a greater task}) and the accompanying expense and trouble (δαπάνη and κακοπάθεια) which the historian may not spare in assembling his material.[57] With Timaeus, who himself boasted of the incredible effort he made to gather his information,[58] Polybius enters into discussion on the question 'whether he thinks that to sit in town collecting notes and inquiring into the manners and customs of the Ligurians and the Celts involves more trouble and expense than an attempt to see the majority of places and peoples with one's own eyes'. 'Which again', he continues, 'is most troublesome, to inquire from those present at the engagements the details of battles by land and sea and of sieges, or to be present at the actual scene and experience oneself the dangers and vicissitudes of battle?'[59] The only conclusion that can follow from these premises is that Timaeus 'thinks that what is really easiest is most difficult', namely 'the collection of documents and inquiring from those personally acquainted with the facts'. In so far as Polybius' discussion focuses on the difficulties experienced by the practitioners of historiography, it is evident that this in no way detracts from his earlier utterances on the place of oral inquiry within the historical πολυπραγμοσύνη, and particularly on its role in the gathering of the material and its critical assessment. With the terms ἐλάχιστον and μέγιστον, however, the notion of the importance to be attached, respectively, to the two methods of inquiry also enters the picture.

Just how Polybius intends to demonstrate the greater importance of αὐτουργία {personal effort} and αὐτοπάθεια {personal experience} with regard to the other means of inquiry can perhaps be deduced from the continuation of his reasoning, which must indeed be seen as

[57] Pol. 12.28a.2–3.
[58] Cf. Lehmann (1974) 161 n. 2.
[59] Pol. 12.28a.4–5.

another objection (καίτοι γε {and yet}) to Timaeus' presumptions. 'And even in this task',[60] says Polybius,

men of no experience are sure to be frequently deceived. For how is it possible to examine a person properly about a battle, a siege, or a sea-fight, or to understand the details of his narrative, if one has no clear ideas about these matters? For the inquirer contributes to the narrative as much as his informant, since the suggestions of the person who follows the narrative guide the memory of the narrator to each incident, and these are matters in which a man of no experience is neither competent to question those who were present at an action, nor when present himself to understand what is going on, but even if present he is in a sense not present.[61]

In this passage Polybius emphasizes more clearly than anywhere else that the successful application of historical method is dependent on the historian's *experience*, i.e. the skill acquired from the practice of political and military life, a qualification (ἱκανός) that enables him to deal with his material authoritatively. In this sense the αὐτουργία and αὐτοπάθεια should not be regarded as a part of the historical method applied in the gathering and critical examination of the evidence, but as an essential prerequisite to historical πολυπραγμοσύνη. From this point of view Polybius' criticism of Timaeus becomes fully comprehensible: the part of historical method to which he attaches the greatest importance in fact becomes insignificant when the historian, due to a lack of experience, is not equipped to obtain good results.[62]

The twofold viewpoint—μέγιστον and χαλεπώτατον—from which Polybius advocates the superiority of αὐτουργία and αὐτοπάθεια, thus by no means encroaches upon the classifications in 12.4c.3 and 27.1–3. In 12.28a.7 the information problem is approached from the demands made upon the *practitioner of historiography*, as is clear from the clause τοῖς πραγματευομένοις <τὴν ἱστορίαν> {for

[60] Scil. τὸ συνάγειν ὑπομνήματα καὶ πυνθάνεσθαι παρὰ τῶν εἰδότων {putting together accounts and inquiring from those who know}. But Polybius seems to develop only the latter point. i.e. oral inquiry.

[61] Pol. 12.28a.8–10.

[62] As Walbank (2002) 10 rightly observes, in writing Book 12, Polybius did not 'set out to construct a consistent account of how historical research should be conducted', his primary purpose being 'that of demolishing all Timaeus' pretensions'. Cf. Schepens (2007) 51–2.

those composing history}.[63] The question of the effort the historian has to make in assembling his material and the observations on the skills he needs in guiding the memory of his informants both refer directly to the required qualifications of his ἦθος and βίος. If the connection between the two aspects of Polybius' argumentation in 12.28a thus becomes understandable, it must on the other hand be admitted that their combination in a single pronouncement (28a.7) has rather obscured matters. The fact that Polybius makes his findings on the difficulty of the various methods of inquiry into a point of departure for restating, once more, the importance of ἐμπειρία {experience} illustrates how in this historian associative thinking takes precedence over a strictly logical exposition.[64]

This brief description of the three types of classification in Polybius clearly reveals the three main concerns of ancient source theory: the problem of the assembly or of the amount of information that can be obtained by the various means; the problem of *criticism* or of the reliability of the various sources; and the problem of the *personal qualifications* or of the demands made upon the historian's ἦθος and βίος. Such a diversity of viewpoints is only possible in a fundamentally *open* definition of the information problem. Its peculiarities are ultimately rooted in the core of the Greek notion of ἱστορίη, in which the *person of the researcher*, with his various possibilities and activities, is central to the historiographical process.[65]

Ancient source theory thus not only draws attention to the essential role of the subjective element that is a co-constituent of all historical knowledge;[66] it should also be stressed that the ancient theory, precisely

---

[63] 12.28a.7.

[64] Cf. Petzold (1969) 181: 'The loose logical structure of his remarks shows itself, for example, in the omission of logical connections, in the combination of two theses'.

[65] See Snell (1924) 59–72, esp. 64 and 70–1; id. (1973), esp. 181. The evidence for the existence in Greek historiography of two distinct historiographical forms, ἱστορίη and συγγραφή, 'the one founded on personal research, the other on the elaboration of documents and of earlier writings' (Roveri 1963: 51) does not, from Thucydides onwards, stand up well to scrutiny.

[66] In Henz's opinion ((1974) 7ff.), the objective material becomes for historical purposes only a real source 'in the state of being subjected to a heuristic act'. Cf. Croce (1948) 14, who emphasizes the fallacious idea that our modern term 'source' is apt to evoke: 'And document and criticism, life and thought, are the true sources of history—that is to say, the two elements of historical synthesis; and as such they do not stand face-to-face with history, or face-to-face with the synthesis, in the same way as fountains are represented as being face-to-face with those who go to them with a pail...'

because it deals only with the various methods of acquiring evidence, as such in no way excludes any form of objective historical information. To be sure, the predominance of contemporary history in historiographical practice brought certain kinds of evidence to the fore to the detriment of others. In the present paper too the representatives of contemporary history have perhaps had the advantage. I realize that a richer and more qualified picture of ancient source theory can be drawn by involving historians such as Timaeus, Arrian, and Plutarch. On the other hand, it remains true that ancient, and particularly Greek, historiography is based on a scientific ideal not so much founded on the critical study of the transmitted sources, but on the historian's *immediate* contact with the *facts* themselves.[67] Consequently, the essential characteristics of the paradigm of ancient source theory were decisively established by the masters of contemporary history.

ADDENDUM

Except for some minor stylistic changes, this paper, first published in 1975, has not undergone any substantial rewriting. It has only been selectively and partially updated by some additional references to more recent scholarly literature in the footnotes as well as by the insertion of some new footnotes. For a more general update of the subject the reader may be referred to my contribution, Schepens (2007). In it the typical features of ancient Greek source theory are reiterated as part of the view of the Greek historians how historical research should be conducted and history written (see especially pp. 44–5). Within this larger framework some hints can be found as well for the study of closely related matters, such as, for instance, the gradual shift from mainly oral to mainly written sources in Greek historiography. Without affecting the paradigm for discussing source problems, important historians, at a given point in time, are going to claim superiority of ἀκοή over ὄψις.

---

[67] Cf. Verhaegen's definition ((1970), esp. 480–1) of the method of 'l'histoire immédiate', in which the term 'immédiate' stresses the fact 'that knowledge functions in an immediate manner—that is to say without the material mediation of the vestiges of the past—by observation and by direct contact between the inquirer and the object'. Cf. id. (1974), esp. 189ff.

5

The Tradition on Early Rome and Oral History*

Jürgen von Ungern-Sternberg
English translation by Mark Beck

The history of Rome began, for the Romans themselves, with the foundation of the city in the eighth century BC. For modern scholarship it begins in approximately the same time period with the problem of Rome's 'transformation into a city' ('*Stadtwerdung*').[1] Roman historiography first began around 200 BC with the work of Fabius Pictor. The accounts we have are from the middle (Cicero, *De republica*) and the end (Livy, Dionysius of Halicarnassus) of the first century BC.

In the face of this simple as well as fundamental fact, the question has been posed as to how Fabius could have possessed reliable information about the extensive periods of time prior to his own

---

* The first part of this article (Sections I–V) was given at the conference 'Übergänge von Mündlichkeit und Schriftlichkeit in der frühen römischen Literatur' at the University of Freiburg in December 1986, and a slightly modified version was published in the *Acta* of that meeting edited by Vogt-Spira (1989) 11–27. I thank the Fondation Hardt in Vandœuvres, the Schweizerisches Institut in Rome, the Deutsches Archäologisches Institut in Rome and Berlin, and the Kommission für Alte Geschichte in Munich for their friendly welcome while I was working on this topic.

[1] Traces of human settlement in the territory of the future city of Rome go back at any rate to a much earlier epoch. See the still fundamental treatment of Müller-Karpe (1962) on Rome's transformation into a city, a debate which is quite influenced by the Roman tradition and in the form it takes is, to my knowledge, unlike that for any other city. Cf. recently Ampolo (1982); Poucet (1985) 37f., 135ff. With regard to the influence of Greece the thoughtful and sober reflections of Dehl (1984) will hopefully not fail to achieve their intended effect.

epoch. This question first arose with the inception of critical historiographical thought in the seventeenth century and came under
more intense scrutiny beginning with Niebuhr. The second question—which is indeed much less recognized as a problem at all—asks
why his account as we have it, with all its interruptions and additions,
remained unchanged as the basis of Roman historical works up to the
time of Livy and Dionysius.[2]

I

Modern scholarship is primarily focused on the search for *written
sources*. This is justified to the extent that, since the eighth century BC
with the presence of the Greeks in Italy, the use of writing was basically
available as an option.[3] The first known Etruscan documents currently
go back as far as the beginning of the seventh century,[4] the first in
Roman territory are dated to the end of the seventh century.[5] In
principle, written documents may have existed already in the regal
period, at least in the second half of it; in any case, however, since the
beginnings of the Republic. A multiplicity of different kinds of documents of this type has been already considered up to now:

1. Archives of leading families[6] in which were found in particular the
   funeral orations (*laudatio funebris*) with a list of the deeds of the
   deceased and his forbears (Pol. 6.54),[7] and furthermore official

---

[2] On the beginnings of the discussion, Momigliano (1957); other early voices:
Ampolo (1983) 10ff.
[3] On literacy in the Greek sphere, see Heubeck (1979) 150ff.; specifically on
Pithecusae: Boardman (1999) 165–8; Heubeck (1986).
[4] Cristofani (1972) 468, 470; the iconographic evidence is discussed by Colonna
(1976) 187ff.
[5] See the survey by Poucet (1985) 63–4; according to Guarducci (1980), the *fibula
Praenestina* needs to be set aside for the time being; Wachter (1987) 55ff. recently
supported its authenticity.
[6] On this, see Gabba (1964) (with very justified scepticism).
[7] Kierdorf (1980a), who with good reason places the beginning of the genre in the
late fourth or early third century: 94ff. On the testimony of Cicero (*Brut.* 62) and,
following him, Livy (8.40.4–5) on the falsifying influence on the Roman tradition, see
now the fundamental study of Ridley (1983). In this context it is very noteworthy
that, on the one hand, some Roman families—indeed mostly quite late—strove to

records of former magistrates (*commentarii*).[8] The earliest extant *laudatio funebris* of indisputable authenticity, transmitted in fragmentary condition, is from the year 221.[9] Epitaphs, such as for the Scipios,[10] or the eulogies of the Etruscan *gens Spurinna* from the end of the fifth and the first half of the fourth century indirectly bear witness to this genre.[11]

2. References to inscriptions are frequently found already in the depiction of the regal period and then in the Republic: laws, treaties, and commemorative inscriptions.[12] The very controversial *Lapis Niger*[13] and the recently discovered inscription from Satricum for the *sodales* of Publius Valerius are both preserved.[14]

3. The list of the annual chief magistrates of Rome, the *Fasti*, from the beginning of the Republic on.[15]

4. The archive of senate decisions since the fifth century.[16]

5. The list of memorable events *ab initio rerum Romanarum* (Cic. *De Orat.* 2.52), collected by the Pontifex Maximus in eighty books.[17]

---

push back their origin into the distant past (Poucet (1985) 287ff.), but that practically no family, certainly not the great patrician ones, laid claim to historical deeds in the regal period: Momigliano (1984a) 411–12.

[8] Mommsen (1887) I.5, n. 2; III.1015–16.

[9] Plin. *HN* 7.139–40, on which Kierdorf (1980a) 10ff.

[10] *ILLRP* nos. 309–17; La Regina (1968).

[11] Torelli (1975), who, however, postulates unnecessarily rich family archives; the existence of a *laudatio funebris* completely covers the subject-matter; cf. Cornell (1976) 429 {= below, p. 193}.

[12] Cf. the list in Ampolo (1983) 15–16.

[13] Palmer (1969); Coarelli (1983a) 178ff.

[14] Stibbe et al. (1980); Versnel (1982); Ferenczy (1987).

[15] Fundamental survey of research in Werner (1963) 219ff.; cf. Ridley (1980); see also n. 7.

[16] Liv. 3.55.13; Ogilvie (1965) 503 upholds the credibility of the report. The basic problems are clearly discussed by Mommsen (1887) III.1010.

[17] Crake (1940); Frier (1979/99); cf. the survey of research in Timpe (1972) 928 n. 2. It is important to note the well-founded scepticism of Fraccaro (1957) 62–3; Rawson (1971) on the use of the priestly annals in Roman historiography. Cato's polemic (*HRR* F 77), however, presumes that the *tabula apud pontificem* had already been made literary use of (cf. Timpe (1972) 952–3). It is a completely different question as to how far back in time these lists extended, as well as whether they are authentic or not. Since Philippus Cluverius (Ampolo (1983) 10ff.), the well known passages on the outcome of the Gallic catastrophe have been culled (Clodius in Plut. *Num.* 1.2; Liv. 6.1.2), and scholars have wondered how widespread the catastrophe was—it is not even sufficiently clear whether or not the Capitol itself was captured (Skutsch (1985) 407–8; Cornell (1986c) 247–8 is sceptical)—and what was finally

The calendar (festivals, character of the days), cult rituals, and temple statues also fell into the domain of the priests. An Etruscan cult ritual is preserved for the most part in the Agramer mummy wrappings; others are attested in iconography.[18] The temple laws of the Imperial period make reference to the *lex sacra* of the Temple of Diana on the Aventine.[19]

6. Finally Roman events were also reported in Greek literature, above all in Greek historiography, probably also in (practically barely known) Etruscan historiography.[20] This applies to the time around 500 BC and then gradually increases for the fourth–third centuries (Timaeus).[21]

These sources were of very disparate quality, and even their authenticity in part is more than dubious. This cannot and need not be discussed here, however, as even in the case of an optimistic judgement it is clear that a coherent picture of the regal period could not be constituted under any circumstances and only a very sketchy one of the early Republic—that is unless one ascribes to the Pontifical Annals an abundance of material that they absolutely could not

saved. Hope was even derived from Livy's observation *pleraeque* [not *omnes*] *interiere* {many [*not* all] have perished}: Stuveras (1965) 51–2; this type of literary interpretation should at least take seriously Livy's own assessment of the tradition prior to the Gallic catastrophe (*paruae et rarae... litterae fuere* {written sources were... few and scattered}). If one adds Liv. 6.1.9–10, then it becomes clear that the Gallic catastrophe provided a reason for the *later* belief at Rome regarding the paucity and unreliability of historical reports from the first centuries of the city, and that the few that (supposedly) still existed were the result of an immediate search for remnants. Here it is noteworthy that the *tabulae apud ponificem* are not named (Fraccaro (1957) 62).

[18] Roncalli (1980) (I thank H. Rix for this reference); on its contents which possibly encompassed historical events see Cornell (1976) 432ff. {= below, pp. 196ff.}.

[19] *Lex arae numinis Augusti Narbonensis*: *ILS* 112, lines 21ff. (the inscription on the right side); in addition Laffi (1980); *Lex arae Salutis* in Ariminum: *CIL* XI.361.

[20] Cornell (1976) {= below, Ch. 7}; cf. the survey in Poucet (1985) 60–1 with n. 81.

[21] Hoffmann (1934); Gabba (1967); Cornell (1974); Frederiksen (1984) 95ff., 207ff. On Timaeus see also Timpe (1972) 929 n. 3. Greek influence on the Roman tradition is another problem, e.g. on the saga of Trojan origins that recently has been illuminated by discoveries in Lavinium: *Enea nel Lazio* (exhibition catalogue, Rome 1981); Galinsky (1983) 37ff.; Torelli (1984); Schefold (1989) 360–8; as is also the influence on the foundation saga of Rome: Strasburger (1968). In this regard one should remember how indifferent the Greeks were to local traditions: Bickerman (1952); Pearson (1975).

have possessed. Additionally the attempt was all too rarely made to imagine concretely Fabius Pictor's mode of composition. Is he supposed to have constructed a card catalogue from disparate material that he finally organized chronologically and fashioned into a narrative of events?

Alternately one should not by the same token conclude that Fabius entirely or even extensively invented his narratives. Modern research has therefore assumed, in its exhaustive search for written material pertaining to the time of the first kings in general and the following epochs in a subsidiary way, that Fabius' source was oral tradition.

II

Oral tradition as an important basis for the early history of Rome was first postulated by Perizonius and then, above all, by Niebuhr.[22] They based their speculation on the occasional remarks of Cato the Elder and Varro concerning the *carmina conuiualia de clarorum uirorum laudibus* {dinner-party songs on the praises of distinguished men}. This thesis continues to be resurrected today, although Niebuhr himself had already recognized that, according to Cicero's report, the 'heroic songs' (*Heldenlieder*) had disappeared long before Cato's time and that they therefore could not have had a significant impact on the Roman tradition.[23]

Theorizing the existence of a preliterate epic does not ameliorate the situation. In fact the great antiquity of the Saturnian can now—not least due to the papers presented at the colloquium in Freiburg—be regarded as proven. Because of the lack of distinctive formulae, however, the existence of developed oral poetry is unlikely. Moreover not the slightest would be known about its subject-matter nor thus also about the transmission of historical memories.[24]

---

[22] Cf. n. 2.

[23] Niebuhr (1969) 9ff.; cf. Fraccaro (1957) 59–60; Heurgon (1969a) 234 and Pöschl (1969) ix–x continue to maintain the influence of the heroic songs.

[24] Cf. the survey of research in Waszink (1972) 875ff.; Vogt-Spira (1989) and (1990).

In contrast, perusal of the first books of Livy and Dionysius of Halicarnassus brings to light a plethora of aetiological stories intended to explain strange places, monuments, religious rituals, and other customs. Individually they need not necessarily be old. They do, however, as a genre, coincide with a widespread oral storytelling tradition found throughout the world, as A. Schwegler, Th. Mommsen, and many others have already established.[25]

Schwegler makes the important observation, 'that the basic material of traditional history cannot be literary invention'.[26] The agreement in all essential aspects of the earliest annalists, who are independent of one another, Fabius Pictor, Cincius Alimentus, and Ennius, cannot be explained in any other way. This also applies to the fact, as Mommsen has previously indicated, that 'the basic structure of the narrative and namely its pseudo-chronology' occur 'even in the later tradition with unchangeable uniformity'.[27] Very recently J. Poucet also recognized this and coined the felicitous concept of '*motifs classés*', i.e. motifs that can indeed be elaborated, varied, or rationalistically reinterpreted (e.g. the *lupa* as prostitute), but that may remain unchanged in their essentials and cannot in any case be eliminated.[28] T. J. Cornell is of a similar opinion and for some time now has attempted to draw a distinction between 'structural facts' and 'narrative superstructure' in the Roman tradition; he recently has termed its entirety a 'living tradition' that predates Fabius Pictor and continued essentially unchanged until the end of the Republic.[29]

---

[25] Schwegler (1853–76) I.62, 69ff. Cf. Mommsen (1881) and (1886) on the Remus and the Tatius legends, respectively; further, Ogilvie (1965) *passim*.

[26] Schwegler (1853–76) I.64–5.

[27] Mommsen (1903) 463–4; cf. his unsurpassed case study of Coriolanus: Mommsen (1870); see in addition Münzer (1909) 1839–40.

[28] Poucet (1985) 54ff., 65ff., 237ff.

[29] On the distinction between 'structural facts' and 'narrative superstructure', Cornell (1982) 206, and Cornell (1986a) 52ff., esp. 61ff., with my objections: von Ungern-Sternberg (1986) 88–9. Cornell should not refer so much to Momigliano (1977) 484–5, who especially emphasizes the (relative) reliability of the statements on constitutional law in the tradition, thereby only following basically the old assumption of Rubino and Schwegler ((1853–76) I.62) as well as Mommsen (criticism voiced already by Meyer (1954) 473 n. 1). On the concept of the 'living tradition', see Cornell (1986b) 82ff.; on the delimitation of 'oral tradition', see n. 68.

Schwegler, Poucet, and Cornell have not considered why in fact the tradition, at the time of its first fixation in writing, remained so unsusceptible to change that it served as the basis of all subsequent ones, such that no competing traditions (of which we possess fragmentary traces from the Etruscans) could arise in Rome. Mommsen, however, perceived the problem,[30] and solved it by assuming the existence of written records of the Pontifical College in the first half of the fifth century, thus entering into the realm again of (purely hypothetical!) literacy; whereby, moreover, the absence of a divergent tradition would in no way be explained.

We may conclude that in the field of Roman history reference is frequently made to an oral tradition, and individual types of orality are considered and discussed, but no one to date has investigated in a general and fundamental way the nature of the oral tradition, to say nothing of utilizing the findings of relevant disciplines.

III

Prior to this we need to present a more detailed picture of the *structure of the early tradition*. To this end we will begin our discussion with an evaluation of Timpe's remarks.[31]

Dionysius[32] bears witness to a tripartite division in the works of Fabius and Cincius Alimentus. The narrative of the early period in brief compass follows the foundation ($\kappa\tau\iota\sigma\iota s$) of the city ($\dot{\alpha}\rho\chi\alpha\hat{\iota}\alpha$ $\tau\dot{\alpha}$ $\mu\epsilon\tau\dot{\alpha}$ $\tau\dot{\eta}\nu$ $\kappa\tau\iota\sigma\iota\nu$ $\tau\hat{\eta}s$ $\pi\delta\lambda\epsilon\omega s$ $\gamma\epsilon\nu\delta\mu\epsilon\nu\alpha$ $\kappa\epsilon\phi\alpha\lambda\alpha\iota\omega\delta\hat{\omega}s$ $\dot{\epsilon}\pi\dot{\epsilon}\delta\rho\alpha\mu\epsilon\nu$ {the early material, that which occurred after the founding of the city, he ran over in summary fashion}) and ultimately the author recounts events he himself has experienced ($o\hat{\iota}s$ $\mu\dot{\epsilon}\nu$ $\alpha\dot{\upsilon}\tau\dot{o}s$ $\ddot{\epsilon}\rho\gamma o\iota s$ $\pi\alpha\rho\epsilon\gamma\dot{\epsilon}\nu\epsilon\tau o$, $\delta\iota\dot{\alpha}$ $\tau\dot{\eta}\nu$ $\dot{\epsilon}\mu\pi\epsilon\iota\rho\iota\alpha\nu$ $\dot{\alpha}\kappa\rho\iota\beta\hat{\omega}s$ $\dot{\alpha}\nu\dot{\epsilon}\gamma\rho\alpha\psi\epsilon$ {because of his experience, he wrote up accurately those events at which he himself was present}).[33]

---

[30] See n. 27.

[31] Timpe (1972) 932 ff.; 930 nn. 5, 6 for the most important earlier literature. We would mention only Meyer (1882) 613ff.; Gelzer (1954); The criticism of Frier (1979) 255ff. does not disprove Timpe's hypotheses; see now also Raaflaub (1986) 1ff.

[32] D. Hal. *A. R.* 1.6.2 = *FGrHist* 809 T 4a.

[33] Timpe talks of 'contemporary history', because he, along with Gelzer, has Fabius' detailed account begin with the First Punic War; that cannot be regarded as

Of fundamental importance is Timpe's discovery that the *ktisis* (*origo*) encompassed not only the entire regal period, but even extended beyond the inception of the Republic to the Decemvirate. The origin and development of the Roman commonwealth was therefore depicted in broad strokes until it attained fully its characteristic form. This coincides entirely with the way Polybius later in Book 6 of his *Histories*[34] and Cicero in *De republica* Book 2 had the development of the Roman constitution conclude with the Decemvirate and afterwards took into account only a few additional improvements.[35] The subsequent time period was depicted in cursory fashion, while the respective author's own present was narrated in greater detail.

Of importance for us at present is the first part, the *ktisis*. Timpe emphasizes correctly its coherence, which bound legend and history indissolubly together.[36] Specifically the tendentious desire to represent Rome as great right from the beginning should be regarded as a core element of the narrative. This leads Timpe then back, following a reference in Plutarch, to Diocles of Peparethos (who is completely unknown to us), to categorize this tendency in the realm of Hellenistic *ktisis*-literature.[37] Fabius Pictor's achievement has thus consisted in connecting this *ktisis* with Rome's history. 'It had not yet occurred to anyone to give a detailed account of the she-wolf and Fabius Cunctator in *one* book.'[38] 'The additive procedure, whereby two

proven, according to Bung (1950), esp. 147ff. The only certain evidence for Fabius' lifetime testifies to his participation in the Celtic War (225–222 BC) and the embassy to Delphi in 216 (*FGrHist* 809 TT 2, 3).

[34] Pol. 6.11.1; 6.11a.

[35] Walbank, *HCP* I.674; Timpe (1970/71) 20–1, 29; Nicolet (1977) 29, 146; von Ungern-Sternberg (1990). Cicero (*Rep.* 2.1) indeed follows not only Polybius but also Cato; his remark at 2.21, however, refers to Plato: Büchner (1984) 188–9 (for a different interpretation, Walbank, *HCP* I.663–4). Noteworthy is Meyer's hypothesis ((1882) 618ff.) that the treaty after the fall of the Decemvirate in Diod. 12.25 reflects the same conception of the conclusion of the Roman constitution; see further Poma (1984) and the review of Staveley (1986).

[36] Timpe (1972) 945ff.

[37] Ibid. 940ff.; cf. Timpe (1970/1) 15–16; Strasburger (1968) 1030–1. It was thought that one could find a literary Greek *ktisis* in an inscription from Chios (*SEG* XXX 1073, lines 25ff.) dated to the beginning of the second century, but see Chaniotis (1988) 94ff.

[38] Timpe (1972) 960 with n. 80.

complexes that were so categorically different from one another as literary myth and contemporary history of the third century, were merged and connected by means of a chronological narrative' appears to Timpe to be original, but nevertheless unsatisfactory from either a literary or historical viewpoint; it is inorganic and in short not really successful. The conception of Fabius, according to Timpe, became binding for all time, but compelled later historians to develop it gradually into a continuous history of Rome by regular annalistic expansion.[39]

Undoubtedly Timpe has thus brilliantly analyzed the structure of Fabius' work and the subsequent development of Roman historiography. One problem in this regard is whether he also gave the correct explanation, or to put it differently, was Fabius really at such great liberty in the selection of his account? Was he its original creator, as Timpe presumes from the start?[40]

The above mentioned observations concerning the internal unity of Rome's early history warn against accepting this assumption—an early history that never knew alternate versions competing with the *motifs classés*. No individual, not even a Fabius, certainly not a Diocles of Peparethos, would have had the authority to construct the history of Rome once and for all conclusively.[41] Because of this,

---

[39] Timpe (1972) 962ff.

[40] Timpe (1972) 931; cf. now Timpe (1988), who adheres to his earlier theories and provides additional support for them. Probably more subtle distinctions should be made. For the narrative for the time period extending up to Rome's foundation by Romulus and Remus, many elements are found that are of Greek origin (Evander; Heracles; Aeneas; motifs in the Romulus–Remus saga) Anyone who wishes may insert Diocles of Peparethos as the (unknown) great figure in the equation and attribute to him the literary organization of material that nevertheless demonstrably had already found its way into the Roman tradition before him. For the subsequent period of Romulus' rule, for all the kings after him and the beginning of the Republic, i.e. for the actual phase of Rome's *ktisis* as the development of the community, it would be difficult to demonstrate that Greeks had to—or even could—'provide' for the Romans around 200 BC a 'preliminary model' for their conception of state and religion, and anchor it in the time of origins. In my opinion Timpe does not succeed in explaining why Fabius Pictor changed into the sober chronicle style after writing the *ktisis* which was (comparatively speaking) much more literarily challenging: anecdotes could have been found (in Greek) to spice up the narrative. The change was for him—as for his contemporaries—already present in his historical consciousness.

[41] Cf. Momigliano (1984a) 410; Cornell (1986b) 82ff. This is certainly the case for the theories of Alföldi (1965) 123ff.; id. (1976) 48ff.: but there is much of importance to be found there regarding the historicity of the tradition that is far too often casually overlooked.

Timpe's assumption is directly ruled out; the structure of Fabius' historical work does not possess uniqueness; rather, it shares common elements with all works of the earliest discernable stages of the tradition.[42] Dionysius attests to this for Cincius Alimentus (and the very sparse fragments confirm this),[43] but everything we know about the epics of Naevius and Ennius also points to this conclusion. Naevius[44] in his *Bellum Poenicum* combined myth with a contemporary history of the First Punic War. In Ennius' *Annales*,[45] the poet treated the regal period in two books, then followed with a narrative of Rome's wars up to the third century in three books, after which was a depiction of the war with Pyrrhus (one book), and then the remainder of the eighteen books treated events in his own lifetime (*c.* 235–169 BC).[46]

We may therefore conclude that the tradition of the early history of Rome not only had a firm compliment of *motifs classés* at the time of its first fixation in writing, but also that its structure as well was already predetermined.

IV

Now is the time to introduce into the discussion some of the results of research on oral tradition, as they have been utilized previously for

---

[42] Gabba (1967) 135ff.; cf. Peter, *HRR* I.LXXXIff.

[43] *FGrHist* 810. According to D. Hal. *A.R.* 1.79.4, Cincius 'followed' Fabius Pictor in one instance; cf. Timpe (1972) 932 n. 8. That could, however, have been concluded from the agreement of the narrative (in the few fragments of Cincius he is frequently mentioned in tandem with Fabius). But the not completely inconsequential circumstance that he set the foundation of Rome considerably later than Fabius (729/8 as opposed to 748/7) speaks for Cincius' independence. He faced the same problem of placing a timeless story into a chronological system. Later historians in the main followed Fabius.

[44] Waszink (1972); Timpe (1972) 929 n. 4. Unfortunately we know almost nothing about the subject-matter of the narrative (Waszink 1972: 915–6).

[45] Jocelyn (1972) 1005ff.; cf. Skutsch's commentary (1985) on the individual books. The depiction of the early Republic would be considerably abbreviated if, with Cornell (1986c: 249–50), we have Book 5 ending *c*.338 BC.

[46] Timpe (1970/71) 20–1, 30–1 and Kierdorf (1980b) 212–13 have shown that the first book of Cato's *Origines* went as far as the Decemvirate. Kierdorf (1980b) 213–14 has demonstrated furthermore that Cato, in Books 2 and 3, definitely depicted (even if in very abbreviated form) the history of Rome up to the First Punic War.

quite some time in the field of ethnology. The work of Jan Vansina provides a readily accessible overview.[47]

Of primary importance is the delineation of the concept 'oral history' which may be termed 'the history of those who are alive in the present': 'Oral traditions are no longer contemporary. They have passed from mouth to mouth, for a period beyond the lifetime of the informants.'[48] A typical tripartite structure of oral transmission is discernable: the recent past is reported in detail; there follows an epoch about which almost nothing is reported, 'the floating gap'; then once again copious information is given about origins.[49] The individual narrative unit is distinguished by great stability vis-à-vis 'setting, plot, episodes, and personages',[50] but this does not fundamentally exclude various versions resulting from the deep-seated opposing interests of the narrators.[51]

At the same time it also holds true that traditions about events continue to be told because the events are deemed important or significant. The selection process therefore is continuous. On the other hand it is by no means certain that an event will be transmitted, even if its importance is immediately clear.[52] In general the realm of actual 'historical narratives' proves to be quite limited: 'they may deal with origins, migrations, descent, wars (over land, women, other wealth), natural catastrophes, and not much more.'[53]

The selection of events, certainly the framework in which they are placed, depends entirely on the leaders of the élite in the respective community.[54] 'The repertoire is a blueprint of the political system, not as it is, but as it should be.'[55] At the same time the development of the community, of the political system, is not grasped as complex causality.

At some point in time something is initially introduced and then persists. Often in the beginning chaos reigns, until one or more individuals appear as 'culture heroes', while those who come later do not make changes but additions.[56]

---

[47] Vansina (1985); cf. Henige (1982). Much of importance already in Bernheim (1903) 317ff., 349ff., 457ff. and van Gennep (1910).

[48] Vansina (1985) 12–13.   [49] Ibid. 23, 168–9.

[50] Ibid. 79.   [51] Ibid. 65–6.   [52] Ibid. 118.

[53] Ibid. 120.   [54] Ibid. 114ff.   [55] Ibid. 120.

[56] Ibid. 131–2.

Even the tripartite nature of oral tradition can possibly be explained with reference to the social order (though this view is rejected by Vansina). The mythical beginnings then justify the basis of existing society; the middle period its functioning in a static model; the recent past is experienced as a disturbance of the legitimate order.[57]

In its entirety the corpus of the tradition serves to create the idealization of the community—'we-consciousness'—and it furnishes *exempla*: prototypes of tyrants, villains, and heroes to whom new anecdotes are continuously able to be attributed in a process of condensation[58] and also of increasing standardization.[59] 'Where versions are few and standardized, as in most traditions of genesis, the mnemonic process has gone a long way, especially when the tradition is widely known. The narrative has reached a point where stability betrays that structuring has achieved its purpose: to make the account most significant and most memorable.'[60]

From all of this it becomes clear that the problem of the historicity of oral tradition can only be handled with the greatest caution. Even a single tradition is only accessible to us in the written version; its prior stages or even original version cannot be reconstructed without independent material.[61] Certainly one should regard the entire corpus of a society's tradition as its self-representation at a given time, deriving from the interests of exactly this time period. These interests could differ radically from earlier time periods and have at any rate hardly anything in common with the (supposed) time of their origin.[62] It is generally true that no source simply wants to report the past. 'A message with this aim would only intend to convey

---

[57] Vansina (1985) 23 with the literature cited below, n. 58. The conspicuous fact that Fabius Pictor already knew the motif of decline can thus be readily explained. Cf. *FGrHist* 809 F 27, if one relates the fragment to the year 290 (on the motif of Sabine wealth see Alföldi (1965) 151–2). It is also found in the judgement of Polybius (about C. Flaminius, 2.21.8) that goes back to Fabius; on the motif of decline, see Bringmann (1977) 30ff., who wants to distinguish (incorrectly) Fabius in principle from the later Roman theorists of decline.

[58] Vansina (1985) 105ff.

[59] Ibid. 147ff.

[60] Ibid. 167–8. Cf. Henige (1982) 2: 'Strictly speaking, oral traditions are those recollections of the past that are commonly or universally known in a given culture.'

[61] Vansina (1985) 29.   [62] Ibid. 196.

information about events of the past in order to enrich our know-ledge of the past. This never occurs in any society', as Vansina observes and adds ironically: 'except perhaps among professional historians.'[63]

V

We can now draw a preliminary conclusion. The characteristic struc-ture of the early Roman tradition accords exactly with the laws of 'oral tradition'. Fabius Pictor is thus, contrary to what is generally assumed, not a beginning, either in terms of the content or the form of his work. On the contrary, he, along with Cincius Alimentus, Naevius, and Ennius, is the termination point of an oral tradition. This tradition was fixed by their works and henceforth could not be substantially changed or subject to continuous alteration. Because they portrayed Roman history in the way they did, as was valid for their generation(s), their version achieved canonical status instantly. There were simply no parallel *motifs classés* that still could or needed to be introduced later on.

In a certain way this epoch for Rome is comparable to the Homeric epoch for Greece,[64] with the important difference of course that the

---

[63] Ibid. 91.

[64] The comparison with Greece is revealing in many respects. The Greeks had practically no knowledge of the epoch after the heroic age (in later chronology, the eleventh to ninth century). They filled it with genealogies that can hardly be taken seriously (cf. Drews (1983), with certain exaggerations). As to the findings at Lef-kandi (see Blome (1984)) it is above all noteworthy that the Greeks had no recollec-tion of this place. Historical memories first begin in the eighth/seventh century, and they were never (not even in the special case of the *Atthis*) condensed into the annalistic portrayal of early Rome. The 'floating gap' was therefore too great, since, in polycentric Greece, only the appeal to a common age of origin was possible, and this had found an especially spectacular shape in the Homeric epics. Heubeck (1984) and Wickert-Micknat (1986) have stated what needs to be said about the Homeric epics' relations to a gradually discernable historical 'Mycenaean' time period; cf. Foxhall and Davies (1984). Switzerland offers a stunning modern parallel. The events of the Habsburg, Burgundian, and Swabian Wars, and the introduction of the Reformation as a constitutive epoch (*ktisis*) are embedded in the general conscious-ness—and kept alive through regular commemorative celebrations—even though

Roman tradition was shaped neither poetically (as far as it was poetically shaped at all) by a long rhapsodic tradition[65] nor could it satisfy the standards of Greek historiography. From a literary point of view there remained still much to do for the successors.

With regard to the subject-matter of the work we can initially determine that we have before us the predominant interpretation of the Roman tradition for the *entire* Roman ruling élite towards the end of the third century BC. It is hardly significant whether, for example, in the work of Fabius Pictor some Fabii are emphasized too much, some Claudii too little.[66] And yet it was in essence an oral tradition, not one composed from 'archives' and 'documents', even if the use of 'documents' of some type in a semi-literate society cannot be excluded *a limine*.[67] This conclusion is not insignificant for the third century. As far as the historical value of the tradition for the preceding time is concerned we can only state that we must evaluate it according to the criterion of 'oral tradition'.[68]

not all areas of present-day Switzerland took part in these events. Powerful vital myths (William Tell; Winkelried), the critical questioning of which meets with violent reactions, are also connected even today to the *ktisis*. Only specialists know about the subsequent time period until the Helvetian Republic (1798) and Napoleon with which modern times started.

[65] Latacz (1979) and (1989).

[66] This is the thesis of Alföldi (1965) 159ff.; id. (1976) 76ff. See now Wiseman (1979) 57ff.

[67] Certainly Fabius Pictor obtained the famous troop-list (Pol. 2.23–24, cf. Eutrop. 3.5; Oros. 4.13.6) from official records. It is equally certain that his count for the census of Servius Tullius is much too high and originates in 'a best case scenario' from a falsified source (Liv. 1.44.2, with Ogilvie (1965) 177–8), even though one may certainly ask with Alföldi (1965) 129ff. whether he did not invent it himself. Other written sources were hardly available for the regal period that interests us here (cf. nn. 7 and 17). The picture changes later on with *fasti*, the *tabulae apud pontificem*, and the *laudationes funebres*.

[68] This can be clarified by the concept of the 'living tradition' introduced into the discussion by Cornell (1986b); in describing it Cornell cites some essential characteristics that agree with the results of 'oral tradition' research: the attitude, exhibited by all members of the community, of taking things for granted; the stabilization of rule function; the portrayal of the present in the distant past. The difference, however, is not only a question of nomenclature (Cornell took it over from Plumb (1969), and thus from a completely different context). Cornell correctly perceives in fact that the Roman tradition from Fabius Pictor on remained unchanged in the 'structural facts', but he completely fails to recognize the decisive fact of fixation in writing, and therefore postulates incorrectly the same thing for the phase of oral tradition: 'To

VI

To follow up our presentation of structure, we will now delve more deeply into the first phase, the *ktisis*, by investigating closely the subject-matter of the Roman tradition of the regal period. We are able to restrict ourselves primarily to the first book of Livy in light of its correspondence with the *motifs classés*.[69]

Livy depicts the seven kings of Rome as a comprehensive spectrum of the possibilities of statesmen.[69a] Romulus, who as a typical culture hero is responsible for Rome's rise from next to nothing and its organization,[70] is followed by the priest-king Numa Pompilius, who in turn is followed by the warrior Tullus Hostilius, Ancus Marcius, Tarquinius Priscus, Servius Tullius, and finally by the tyrant Tarquinius Superbus. On the whole nearly everything that can be attributed to the pre-republican period concerning state and religious institutions and Roman greatness is attributed to them. What remains is then, as far as possible, localized in the first year of the Republic.[71]

my mind there is not the slightest doubt that the Romans of the last two centuries of the Republic were able to dispose of a great deal of authentic historical information, preserved and transmitted from the remote past in ways that we are not now able to reconstruct with any precision' ((1986b) 83). In the realm of pure 'oral tradition', according to all historical and ethnological analogies, it is possible that 'structural facts' (which may just lack the historical factuality maintained by Cornell) or *motifs classés* can have been inserted up to the third century. We have only their last stage and few possibilities for external control so as either to demonstrate or exclude this process. Cf. the observations of Wiseman (1983) 21.

[69] All the more so since there are some indications that Livy in the first book of his historical work in essence represents the state of the early Roman annalistic. Cf. the very noteworthy remarks of Poucet (1986). Livy (1.44.2) mentions as his very first source *scriptorum antiquissimus* {the oldest of writers} Fabius Pictor, then (58.8–9) only Fabius and Piso. Perhaps that is not simply 'name-dropping' in order to make an impression: Luce (1977) 158ff., *contra*, Ogilvie (1965) 6–7. On Livy's compositional method see also Mensching (1986); on Livy's own achievement in Book 1, see Haffter (1964).

[69a] Labruna (1984) provides a list of the relevant passages.

[70] On the concept of the culture hero, see Henige (1982) 86ff.; Vansina (1985) 251, Index, s.v. 'hero'. On Romulus, see the reflections of Piérart (1983) 57ff.

[71] Above all, the annually changing and collegial consulate (2.1.7–8); the supplementation of the senate by *conscripti* (2.1.10–11); the priestly office of the *rex sacrorum* (2.2.1); the protection of republican *libertas* (2.2.5; 2.8.2). Kornemann (1960) 71 correctly spoke of a *Sammeljahr* {catch-all year}.

Thus Romulus takes over the indispensable cults from Alba Longa and in addition the cult of the Greek Hercules (7.3) founded by Evander. He gives the informally assembled people (*concilium*) constitutional laws (8.1) and himself the official insignia of the monarchy (8.2). He establishes the senate and the patrician class (8.7). After unification with the Sabines, the organization of the people into thirty *curiae* and the creation of the three equestrian centuries becomes possible (13.6–8). The founding king thus establishes the entire state of Rome with its cults, and the fundamental divisions into magistracy, senate, and popular assembly. Interregnum (17.5–6) and *auctoritas patrum* (17.9) can arise only after the death of the first king. It remains then for the subsequent kings to further elaborate on the established form, for example, through the creation of official priesthoods by Numa (20), of new patrician families by Tullus Hostilius (30.2) and by Tarquinius Priscus (35.6), through the introduction of the census, the creation of the order of centuries (42.5), and the four city tribes (43.13) by Servius Tullius.[72]

The conception is not somehow a product of the Augustan classical period. In essence Fabius Pictor (*HRR* F 8), Polybius (6.11a) and Cicero in *De republica* Book 2 had already produced accounts prior to those of Livy, Dionysius of Halicarnassus, and Virgil (*Aen.* 6.781ff., 808 ff.), as would later on, for instance, a Florus (1.1–8).[73] Also Cato's famous dictum, that Rome was the work of many men over a long period of time (Cic. *Rep.* 2.2),[74] is correctly interpreted by Cicero to probably refer to the regal period (2.37). Every institution comes into existence and is henceforth timelessly present in Rome. Only a few, such as the senate, are modified in several phases, but even they in this process do not lose their original character.[75]

---

[72] It is also necessary to refer to the introduction of the *formulae*: thus, e.g. for the conclusion of a *foedus* (24.4ff.); for the *duumviri perduellionis* (26.6); for the beginning of a war (32.6ff.); for the *deditio* (38.2). Nevertheless we are dealing here with learned reconstructions from an antiquarian tradition. Cf. respectively Ogilvie (1965) and Luce (1977) 160.

[73] Schwegler (1853–76) II.71, who refers to Vico; Dumézil (1985) 16ff.

[74] Timpe (1970/1) 29.

[75] Cf. Vansina (1985) 131–2: 'So history becomes a sequence of greater or lesser culture heroes. These are responsible for classes of invention so that a later one never alters anything already invented by an earlier one, but merely adds.'

In addition to the establishment of state and religious institutions and often closely tied to them, the aetiological legends of localities, monuments, and customs form a constitutive element of the narrative.[76] Thus the introduction of the *consualia* for *Neptunus equestris* (9.6) and the marriage cry '*Thalassio*' (9.12) are associated with the rape of the Sabine women. The Temple of Jupiter Stator (12.6) and the *lacus Curtius* (13.5) are associated with the battle between the Romans and the Sabines (12.6). The *fossa Cluilia* (23.3), the graves of the Horatii and Curiatii (25.14), the *pila Horatia* (26.10), and the *sororium Tigillum* (26.14) are associated with the war against Alba Longa. Or, to mention a particularly scurrilous example, the formation of the island in the Tiber is attributed to the grain that had been dumped into the Tiber after the consecration of the Campus Martius (2.5.3–4). Coarelli and Ampolo have explained very impressively the assignments of the Volcanal/*Lapis Niger* to Romulus, Faustulus, and Hostus Hostilius as various aetiologies that all arose from the same visible monuments and the incomprehensible inscription.[77]

Hand in hand with its internal consolidation, Rome accomplished its external expansion without any setback or defeat. A. Alföldi has demonstrated convincingly the schematization of the narrative and its deficient historical basis: he was wrong, however, in wanting to show that it was primarily a conception of Fabius Pictor.[78] The tendency to describe Rome's greatness as a given from the outset was already present in the tradition.[79] Innumerable interchangeable motifs (*Wandermotive*) flowed into the narratives. In part these were of ancient and of hardly explicable origin (exposure and salvation of the king's children; fratricide),[80] in part they derive from Greek myth

---

[76] Cf. Ogilvie (1965) ad loc.

[77] Coarelli (1977), esp. 215ff., and (1983a) 161ff.; Ampolo (1983) 19ff.; subsequent interpretative attempts by Camassa (1984) and Robertson (1987). Poucet (1981) would like to attribute these and other aetiological stories to antiquarian erudition from the second half of the second century BC onwards. That may be true in certain cases; even then it would be necessary to inquire into the sources of the antiquarian tradition. See now also Fuhrmann (1987).

[78] Alföldi (1965) 101ff., 135ff.

[79] Timpe (1972) 946ff.

[80] The following provide a good survey: Cornell (1975); Binder (1964); Alföldi (1974) 108ff. On fratricide, see Classen (1963), esp. 454ff.; Piérart (1983) 107ff. The works of Ehrenzweig (1915) and (1919/20), although in many respects problematic, have nevertheless not yet been replaced.

(the Aeneas saga; Tarpeia)[81] and Greek literature (tyrant *topos*),[82] perhaps from the ancient Near East ('woman at the window').[83] It is very difficult or impossible to determine when and where they gained a foothold. We only have access to the phase of the first fixation in writing, whereas we can make a statement about the prior phases only in rare cases (see n. 92). Examples from other, better documented realms show how rapidly *Wandermotive* can be integrated into a tradition.[84] They also may have been told in Rome for a long time[85]—or even be partially of Hellenistic and thus of literary origin.[86]

'Oral tradition' in Rome does not thus form a realm that necessarily would have been far removed from all literacy. It therefore could have—to mention an extreme case—co-existed with Greek historiography on Rome. We employ the term more as a cipher for collective memory that changed continuously under all manner of influences in accordance with the exigencies of the prevailing present—until it received permanent 'textual fixation' in historical

[81] On the Aeneas saga cf. n. 21 und the interesting survey of scholarship in Schroeder (1971) 57ff.; cf. also Solmsen (1986). On Tarpeia, see Dumézil (1947) 279ff.; Poucet (1985) 193 and 228ff.

[82] Cf. Ogilvie (1965) 194–5, 205–6 on Liv. 1.53–54 (here D. Hal. himself notes the Greek model, *A.R.* 4.56.3); furthermore 1.56.1ff.; 57.1–2; 59.9: the tyrant oppresses the people by forced labour (this motif already in Cassius Hemina, *HRR* F 15). See also the supposed abdication plan of Servius Tullius, 1.48.9 with Ogilvie (1965) 194. The stories about Gabii are intended to refer to local oral traditions: Köves-Zulauf (1987) 131ff. I am only partially able to follow his far-flung combinations; I do, however, agree with him that one should not envision the process of the assimilation of Greek motifs as occurring too simply or late—they certainly could have become wandering motifs that at some point in time entered the Roman tradition. On the tyrant *topos*, see also Borzsák (1987).

[83] Liv. 1.41.4; cf. Winter (1983) 296ff., 585ff.

[84] Three examples chosen at random illustrate this: from the fourteenth/fifteenth centuries in Lucerne: Marchal (1984); from Bohemia in the nineteenth century: Palacky (1869) 111–12; from the South Seas in the twentieth century: Bühler (1952).

[85] This is in particular the assumption of Dumézil in numerous works since 1938 on *l'héritage indo-européen*; on this, see the overview in Poucet (1985) 171ff. and the critical appreciation of Momigliano (1984b); and the acceptance by Alföldi (1974) of the Eurasian legacy of Rome, on which, see the review of Poucet (1975), Werner (1976a) and (1976b). See in general Momigliano (1984a) 379ff.

[86] Cf. Alföldi (1965) 147ff.; Strasburger (1968); Timpe (1972) 944; Borgeaud (1987).

works and historical epics around 200 and was subject henceforth to the conditions of a literary tradition.

Finally, dual versions are conspicuous. The insignia of office are at one time attributed to Romulus, at another Tarquinius Priscus after his victory over the Etruscans.[87] The Temple of Jupiter Stator was, according to an alternate tradition, erected at the beginning of the third century.[88] The Etruscan '*condottiere*' Caeles and his allies[89] are supposed to have come to Rome either during the time of Romulus or the time of Tarquinius Priscus. There were in all three different traditions[90] for the origin of the *lacus Curtius*, just as there were for the Volcanal.[91] In each case events occurring later were retrojected into the past or also, more frequently, narratives that were originally timeless were subject to a different temporal fixation. The chronology imposed nearly insoluble difficulties upon every oral tradition.[92]

---

[87] Cf. Liv. 1.8.2–3 with D. Hal. *A.R.* 3.61–2 (dual tradition: Romulus or Tarquinius Priscus).

[88] Cf. Liv. 1.12.6 with 10.36.11; 10.37.15 on the year 294. The last passage is a report from Fabius Pictor (*HRR* F 16) and proves how easily in the third century the institutions of the recent past were retrojected. The weak attempt (Liv. 10.37.16) at equalization between the two dates cannot derive from Fabius because the temple was presumed to have already existed in the regal period (Liv. 1.41.4; Plin. *HN* 34.29). On the temple see Coarelli (1983a) 26ff.

[89] On this, see Alföldi (1965) 215ff.; (1976) 72ff., 176; Cornell (1976) 412ff. {= below, pp. 176ff.} Conspicuously Livy completely ignores the stories about Caelius, the brothers Vibenae, and Mastarna, perhaps because they were foreign to the oldest Roman annalistic: Poucet (1986) 212–13, 221. In this case was a piece of Etruscan oral tradition assimilated in Rome or were there also local traditions?

[90] Cf. Liv. 1.12.10, 13.5 with 7.6.1–5 on the year 362. Livy notices the difference (7.6.6), does not venture a decision, and designates the more recent history as the more widely disseminated. This is exactly what Varro, *LL* 5.148–50 attributes to a Proclus (completely unknown to us); the other he attributes to Piso, providing finally a third version for the year 445 according to a Cornelius and Lutatius Catulus.

[91] Cf. n. 77.

[92] The famous problem of the list of Alban kings, whose presence in Fabius Pictor has now been substantiated by the inscription in the gymnasium of Tauromenium (Manganaro (1974)), also belongs here. The list first became necessary when work on Roman history done in the third century in the scholarly spirit of the Greeks had uncovered the chronological difficulties of the juxtaposition of the Aeneas tradition with the Romulus tradition. We can still perceive here a late stage of the development of the canonical tradition because the poets Naevius and Ennius casually maintained that Romulus and Remus, by way of their mother Ilia, were the grandchildren of Aeneas. On this, see most recently Piérart (1983) 51–2; Cornell (1986c) 247. The

All of this constitutes a classical corpus of oral tradition in its *ktisis*-phase, whose intellectual spirit (based upon other premises) Timpe has characterized splendidly:

The Annalists had the experience of encountering their own essential nature in the legendary history; they lived in the illusion of an unbroken historical continuity. The heroes of antiquity reflected to them their own possibilities and their own will. A significant rupture was nowhere discernable.[93]

With the initial creation of a literary record of the oral tradition the portrait of early Rome was fixed in its essential characteristics. Later embellishments and rationalistic reinterpretations were thereby in no way excluded. Political *Tendenzen* and present-day problems, e.g. the conflicts between *optimates* and *populares*, could be brought in,[94] and the events could successively become incorporated into law.[95] Indeed, there is no lack of attempts to create an aetiological basis for innovations: this is still present in Caesar's introduction of a third group of *Luperci*.[96] True changes did not have a chance to become the

same is true for the connection between Numa and Pythagoras that was impossible once the 'timeless' list of Roman kings (although the Romans abandoned it only with great reluctance) had been fixed chronologically. See the discussion in Cic. *Rep.* 2.28–9, Liv. 1.18.2ff, with Klein (1962) 18–19, Ogilvie (1965) 9, Gabba (1967) 154ff.; Rosen (1985) (also methodologically instructive about the continued development of a tradition in the epoch of literacy).

[93] Timpe (1972) 967.

[94] A few examples: 1.15.8: Romulus 'was nevertheless more pleasing to the multitude than to the senate'; 17.7: during the first interregnum 'the plebs murmured that their servitude had been multiplied, that a hundred masters had been given them instead of one'; 35.2: Tarquinius Priscus 'is said to have been the first to canvass votes for the kingship and to deliver a speech designed to win the favour of the commons'; 41.6: 'Servius surrounded himself with a strong guard, and first ruled without the authorization of the people but with the consent of the senate.' The *primus* ('first') topos deserves special notice: see Alföldy (1980).

[95] This is especially clear in the transition from the monarchy to the Republic. The supposedly foolish (1.46.8) Brutus can as *tribunus celerum* lawfully convene an assembly of the people (59.7) and have the *imperium* of Tarquinius Superbus abrogated (59.11). It was a fortunate circumstance that Sp. Lucretius had already been installed as *praefectus urbis* by the king (59.12), so that he now, according to the *commentarii* of Servius Tullius, can have two consuls elected immediately by the *comitia centuriata* (60.4). On the problem of the incorporation into law (*Verrechtlichung*) of the tradition, see the (still fundamental) article of von Fritz (1950); cf. Ogilvie (1965) 228–9.

[96] D. Hal. *A.R.* 1.80.1–2 (according to Q. Aelius Tubero); cf. Poucet (1981/2) 183; Scholz (1984) 180 n. 16. A similar case: the justification of (some of) the politically disputed *collegia* by tracing them back to Numa: Gabba (1984); on the later annalists, see von Ungern-Sternberg (1986) 101ff.

common property of the tradition, whereby, admittedly, the historical tact of our source Livy (in comparison to Dionysius) may be involved.[97] The substance of the Roman *ktisis* always remained the same.[98]

VII

Once the homogeneity and coherence of the Roman tradition on the monarchy is recognized, it then also becomes clear that the extraction of individual elements of the tradition as simply 'historical' is out of the question. What right does one have—to mention a widely accepted extreme case—to treat the arrangement into centuries enacted by Servius Tullius differently from the attribution of state institutions to other kings, beginning with Romulus?[99] Or generally why should we set the boundary between the legendary and historical realms in the time of Ancus Marcius or Tarquinius Priscus?[100] The chronology of the last kings already confronted ancient historians and continues to confront modern historians with insurmountable problems: stories that originally were timeless and independent from one another prove to be all too unwieldy vis-à-vis those types of rationalizations.[101]

---

[97] Cf. n. 69.

[98] The comparison with *Genesis* is interesting. The written sources J and P, for example, could thus only have become incorporated together in the story of the flood because the *motifs classés* were common to both. The immense commentary of Westermann (1974–82) is a treasure trove for oral tradition research.

[99] See, e.g., Thomsen (1980) and the justified criticism of Werner (1982); cf. Richard (1983); Gabba ((1982) 809, with reff. cited in n. 26), at any rate, regards large sections of the ancient accounts as late invention.

[100] See, e.g., Dumézil (1985) 21 (on Ancus Marcius): 'despite some anachronisms... one cannot avoid the impression that it is with him that the authentic begins to have appreciable weight in the accounts' (cf., however, his analyses of the deeds of Tarquinius Superbus and of Sex. Tarquinius, 105ff.). The line of separation after Ancus Marcius forms the basis of the work of Poucet (1985); see further Cornell (1986b) 67: 'Admittedly the story of the origins of the city has the character of legend, but the narrative takes on a truly historical appearance with the arrival of the dynasty of the Tarquins...'.

[101] One need only read Schwegler (1853–76) I.47ff.

The existence of historically reliable elements in the tradition is thus not in general excluded. Their acceptance, however, must in each individual case be subjected to strict rules governing evidence, as have been formulated previously by Bernheim, and recently by Vansina or Finley.[102] The evidence alone of oral tradition cannot suffice; confirmation by other independent evidence is required.[102a]

Instructive here is the analogy of the *Nibelungenlied*, as we have it from the twelfth/thirteenth century.[103] It contains authentic names from the fifth and sixth centuries such as the kings of Burgundy, Attila the Hun, Theodoric, and the queen Brunhilde, and it preserves the memory of a catastrophic defeat of the Burgundians. At the same time, however, other names are associated with the myth and still other names belong to much later times. If the chronological as well as the spatial relations have shifted, if completely different social, political, and religious conditions obtain, then we learn nothing about the scope of the later Roman Empire. The availability of contemporary sources in this case enables modern research to separate

---

[102] Bernheim (1903) 457ff., esp. 464ff.; Vansina (1985) 159; Finley (1985) 16–17: 'With the passage of time, it becomes absolutely impossible to control anything that has been transmitted when there is nothing in writing against which to match statements about the past. Again we suspect the presence of the unexpressed view that the traditions of Greeks and Romans are somehow privileged, though no one has yet demonstrated a plausible mechanism for the oral transmission of accurate information over a period of centuries.'

[102a] Archaeology can, for example, provide such evidence. As important, however, as some of its discoveries are for the development of individual traditions (above, nn. 21, 77), it has up to now been able at most to contribute falsifications to the examination of the traditions of the regal period: Poucet (1985) 116ff. (for the eighth/seventh cent.); Raaflaub (1986) 11ff. Archaeology is naturally of extreme importance for *our* knowledge of Rome in the first half-millennium BC.

[103] Cf. the survey of scholarship by Reichert (1985), esp. 75ff. (on the mythical elements); 118ff. (on the historical bases); and Ehrismann (1987) 59ff. Reichert (1985) 119–20 correctly emphasizes that at least in monasteries works were available which could contradict the chronology of the *Nibelungenlied*. Fruotolf of Michelsberg had also already demonstrated the contradictions around 1100 with respect to the saga of Dietrich (*Monumenta Germaniae Historia* 6.130). 'That is to say, the bearers of heroic sagas lived as representatives of an unlettered majority under a tiny minority for whom a written tradition was accessible.' On the historical background see also Altheim (1962) 193ff. (his derivation of the heroic song from the Iranian–Hunn heroic song is rightly criticized by Werner (1966) 258–9; Stroheker (1965) 246ff.

out the elements: this could not be accomplished solely by analysing the *Nibelungenlied* itself.

This possibility does not exist for the narrative of the Roman regal period since we lack here contemporaneous traditions that would enable us to filter out historical names and memories. At any rate there are some grounds for the thesis that there is little reason for optimism. Specifically with regard to the last kings it is remarkable that the Roman tradition does not know anything about an Etruscan rule, rather it only knows about the immigration of Tarquinius Priscus from Etruria (ultimately, however, about his father Demaratus from Corinth)[103a] and about the battles with Etruscan kings, such as Porsenna. As soon as the Etruscan memories become tangible for us, even in scanty traces, a completely different view of things emerges. One should bear in mind the depictions in the François tomb in Vulci and the speech of the emperor Claudius before the Senate in the year 47. Some names recur more or less precisely but in different contexts; names alone thus imply here a 'historical core' as little as they do in the *Nibelungenlied*. The equating of Mastarna with Servius Tullius can only be judged as the desperate attempt to harmonize the canonical number of seven Roman kings with a completely different version.[104] Not one aspect of the account of the Roman tradition is paralleled in the other account! In this regard one must admit unquestionably with Cornell[104a] that the Etruscan memories do not *a priori* possess greater credibility than the Roman ones. Certainly, however, they are also not any less credible. Our concern here is with their divergence.

To an even greater extent have the Phoenicians disappeared from the horizon of the Roman tradition. In this context, close relations, at least with the neighbouring Etruscan realm, are well attested,[105] from which it is definitely possible to reckon with effects on the development

---

[103a] Musti (1987).

[104] Cf. nn. 89 and 99. Momigliano (1957) 114, id. (1984) 417–18 also repeatedly stressed the importance of the parallel Etruscan tradition. See further Heurgon (1969a) 240ff. (admittedly with the assertion that the Roman tradition drew on Etruscan works).

[104a] Cornell (1976) 417ff. {= below, pp. 181ff.}

[105] Cf. the survey in Boardman (1999) 210–16; Huss (1985) 65–6.

of early Rome.[106] But not even the first Roman–Carthaginian treaty[107] found its way into the original Roman tradition.[108]

The Greeks fared hardly any better. In fact, the Hercules cult was attributed to them, but this was probably wrong. Hercules was, moreover, incorrectly placed in the mythical primeval times of the Arcadian king Evander.[109] With respect to the actual regal period Livy and Dionysius knew something about the Greek influence on the inception of the *asylia* around the Temple of Diana on the Aventine.[110] In this regard the *lex arae Dianae in Auentino monte* (n. 19), which survived into the imperial period, may have provided some clues. By the same token the analogies to Greek legislation in the laws of the Twelve Tables were so evident that an aetiological explanation was suggested which told the story of an embassy to Athens or Magna Graecia.[111] In these cases we are dealing with learned combinations, not with old Roman tradition.[112]

---

[106] So there are arguments for the Phoenician origin of the Hercules cult at the *Ara Maxima*: van Berchem (1967); Rebuffat (1966); Bunnens (1979) 307–8. F. Coarelli in 1985 in Basel referred (in a still unpublished paper) to Phoenician elements in the cults at S. Omobono: 'L'area sacra di S. Omobono a Roma: Architettura e religione tra il sesto secolo e la fine della Repubblica'. See also n. 83.

[107] Pol. 3.26.2 says explicitly that the oldest men ($\pi\rho\epsilon\sigma\beta\acute{\upsilon}\tau\alpha\tau\sigma\iota$) of his time did not know of the treaties. On the dating, see Werner (1963) 299ff.; Musti (1972) 1137ff.; Bengtson and Werner (1975) 16ff. 339–40.

[108] Together with Schwegler (1853–76) I.18ff. one can ask oneself in general whether the oldest Roman historiography knew any document at all. Livy, in contrast to Dionysius of Halicarnassus, does not appear in the list for the regal period recently made up by Ampolo ((1983) 15–16)—which in view of the results of Poucet (1986) is indeed very significant. Livy *mentions* first the treaty of Sp. Cassius (2.33.9), presents no information on the contents of the XII Tables, and has the *lex uetusta* (7.3.5ff.) from antiquarian tradition. On this, see now the criticism of Heuss (1982) 450ff.

[109] Livy (1.7) represents it as being the only one of the cults taken over by Romulus that was of Greek origin.

[110] Livy (1.45.2) calls the Artemision of Ephesus the model for the Diana sanctuary on the Aventine in its function as the focal point for the surrounding populaces; D. Hal. (*A.R.* 4.26.3) attests to its function as an asylum. Van Berchem has, by comparing Ephesus and Naucratis, demonstrated the degree to which the Diana sanctuary corresponded to the temple foundations in frontier regions between Greece and foreign powers; cf. van Berchem (1960) and (1966). Another problem concerns the relationship between the Diana cult on the Aventine and the one from Aricia: on this, see Werner (1963) 397ff.; Alföldi (1965) 85ff., (1976) 123ff.

[111] Delz (1966); Wieacker (1967) 330ff. (343f. with n. 2 on Hermodorus); Siewert (1978); Eder (1986) 275–6; Toher (1986).

[112] For the sixth/fifth centuries it is necessary to reckon with Greek influence to a great extent on cultic and political spheres, of which the Romans were hardly aware:

Finally there is another very general consideration concerning the subject-matter of Livy's first book. Who in Rome could have been interested in transmitting orally for centuries political or social institutions of the regal period? And who, according to all the tenets of oral tradition research, would have even been able to do this? In particular, institutional change is not even perceptible at the moment of its occurrence, but instead is experienced as timelessly valid in its respective state and/or is based in a 'mythical past'! Of course in Rome—and this is a historical element—the foundation phase must have crossed over the border of the regal period, since certain institutions, such as the consulate and the plebeian tribunate, were absolutely incapable of being subsumed in it.[113]

Hardly any light at all can be shed on the individual stages of the formation of the tradition in the regal period. The early Greek testimonies concern only the actual foundation phase up to Romulus and Remus. Even there we often cannot be certain to what extent at all local traditions are represented. For the subsequent time period that is of more interest to us here we must take into consideration the impact of Etruscan and above all Greek motifs, methods of narration, and even the entire accounts of some time periods. In this respect we must also consider the reciprocal influence of orality and (externally derived) literacy. Even the entire conception of the *ktisis* of Rome, in the version we possess, may have been shaped by Greek thought, as it can be demonstrated that the reception of Greek political theory took place in Rome by the fifth century. It is, however, very difficult to be precise about this, since for us the state of the oral tradition is fixed around the year 200 once and for all.

VIII

In conclusion, we must ask about the transmitters and the modalities of oral tradition at Rome. First of all, it is significant that we always

cf. Frederiksen (1984) 160, 170 n. 21. The connection between ἡ γερούσια καὶ οἱ ἐπίκλητοι {the senate and the assembly} in Ephesus and *patres conscripti* {conscript fathers} in Rome could be an example of this: van Berchem (1980).

[113] Occasionally, as in the case of *prouocatio* {right of appeal}, there were indeed corresponding attempts: Cic. *Rep.* 2.54.

encounter a ruling class of great homogeneity in Rome as soon as we have any information at all. The problem of the origin and nature of the patrician class[114] need not concern us here, likewise the inception and the exact definition of the nobility.[115] It is certain that there existed, from the sixth/fifth centuries onward, a clearly delimited group which, in only slowly transforming and expanding itself, fulfilled in a nearly ideal way a basic precondition for the existence of a corpus of oral tradition. Authoritative in all areas of political and religious life, it ensured the continual exchange and thus ultimately the uniformity of the information about the past.

Within the ruling class (which we can equate approximately with the circle of members of the Senate at any given time, along with an encompassing institutional structure) we can discern specialists for the tradition, the *pontifices*. This priesthood was responsible, from time immemorial, for the calendar and the entire legal system that very gradually became differentiated into sacred and secular spheres.[116] During the tenure in office of the chief administrator, the *pontifex maximus*, the *tabula apud pontificem* was also posted, on which significant events were recorded annually. The scope and character of the recorded information have been the subject of intense scholarly debate, in particular the question as to how far back in time they went and in what form at what time they were collected, edited, and published.[117] At any rate it is certain that the Pontifical College did not possess any authentic (i.e. contemporaneous) notes on the regal period. It is likewise certain that it regarded itself as being responsible for Rome's entire past and for this reason, at some point in time, supplemented its records retrospectively back in time to the foundation of Rome and perhaps even anterior to this

---

[114] See on this the controversial contributions of Momigliano (1967a) and Alföldi (1967); see also Bickerman (1969); Ranouil (1975) with the review of Werner (1976a); Richard (1986); Mitchell (1986).

[115] Gelzer (1912). On the revisionism debate introduced by Brunt (1982) there are some correct observations in Ridley (1986), on which, see Simon (1988).

[116] The accounts in the histories of Roman religion of Wissowa (1912) 501ff. and Latte (1960) 195ff. do not sufficiently emphasize the full significance of the *pontifices* for early Rome. On the calendar, see Bergmann (1984); on the legal system, Pólay (1983); von Lübtow (1986).

[117] Cf. n. 17, with Kornemann (1911).

point in time.[118] Whatever type of literary activity this once was, it was not an ad hoc construction of Roman history—even when the momentary interests of the members may have flowed into it—but rather simply reproduced the heretofore orally transmitted version of Roman history of the *pontifices*. To what degree, however, this priesthood was connected, in the public eye, with Roman history, almost even identified with it, emerges from the simple fact that Ennius named his epic *Annales*, that Cato felt compelled to distinguish his work polemically from the subject matter of the *tabula ad pontificem*, and that Sempronius Asellio (*HRR* FF 1 and 2) still expressed his opposition to the *annales libri*.[119]

If the *pontifices*, however, were involved to a great extent in the formation and preservation of the Roman tradition, then their specific focus can be readily explained: the concentration on the foundation of the political and religious institutions of Rome. Then, however, a question can be answered that, as far as I know, has never even been asked: why historiography in Rome began so late, long centuries after the spread of literacy.

Up to now one has been implicitly content with the fact that Roman literature generally first began in the second half of the third century BC with Livius Andronicus. That would still, however, require explanation and would need to be thought about more deeply in the context of the problem posed by semi-literate societies, a topic that has recently come under discussion in ethnological circles.[120] In the meantime, a precise reason has been proposed for the late inception of historiography, i.e. the responsibility of the *pontifices* for the Roman past.[121]

---

[118] Cic. *de Orat.* 2.52; D. Hal. *A.R.* 1.74.3. Are we really supposed to take seriously *Or. Gent. Rom.* 17.3.5 as evidence for the Pontifical Annals?

[119] Timpe (1972) 964; Schäublin (1983) 147ff.

[120] On this see Elwert (1987); for the Greek sphere, Goody (1968).

[121] Nothing makes this clearer than the fact that the *pontifices* reported nothing at all about their own advancement in Rome's religious administration: cf. Latte (1960) 195: 'It is typical of the character of the pseudo-tradition about early Roman history that one of the most successful revolutions in the political–religious sphere, and the struggles associated with it, has disappeared without leaving the faintest trace: the revolution that had brought the Pontifex Maximus and the *collegium* attached to him to the summit of the Roman religious system.'

Through the end of the fourth century the Pontifical College knew how to protect its monopoly of knowledge in all areas of sacred and secular law, with regard to the character of the days as well as with regard to regulations governing ritual and legal formulae. Step by step it was forced to relinquish control:[122] a contributing factor in this process was the fact that, since the *Lex Ogulnia* (300 BC), plebeians could also become members of the College,[123] until finally the first plebeian *pontifex maximus*, Ti. Coruncanius, in the middle of the third century, established jurisprudence and the administration of justice in the public domain.[124] This led to an absence of the need to function eminently as 'caretakers' of the tradition, or more accurately as supervisors or regulators. The tradition was no longer an instrument of authority. It too was henceforth opened up to the public. Historical epic and historiography acquired their practitioners shortly thereafter.

The first historians of Rome, Q. Fabius Pictor and L. Cincius Alimentus, were themselves members of the ruling élite. Fabius came from a line of patrician Fabii, whose specific cultural ambitions are attested.[125] He was a senator and a member of the embassy that was sent to Delphi after the battle at Cannae in the year 216 BC (*FGrHist* 809 T 3). Cincius was a praetor in the year 210 (*FGrHist* 810 T 1, 2). If he later came into contact with Hannibal personally as a prisoner of the Carthaginians (F 5), then this may hinge entirely on his literary interests. Hannibal had Greek historians in his company who were charged with propagating his standpoint and simultaneously his fame. He himself had also composed a record of his achievements towards the end of his stay (205 BC) in Italy in Punic and Greek that was erected in the Temple of Hera on Cape Lacinium.[126] Why should he not try to influence even a Roman historian?

---

[122] Cf. n. 116; on this, see Wieacker (1970) 187ff.; Wolf (1980); Bauman (1983) 21ff. (with the review of d'Ippolito (1985b)).

[123] This is true even if the original intent of the law was supposed to have been a renewed strengthening of the priestly colleges; for this interpretation, see d'Ippolito (1985a).

[124] D'Ippolito (1978) 27ff., with the review of Nörr (1980).

[125] His ancestor received his cognomen by painting the Temple of Salus in 304 BC. One of his sons, N. Fabius Pictor (cos. 266), participated in the embassy to Ptolemy II in 273.

[126] Pol. 3.33.18; 3.56.4; Liv. 28.46.16.

Conditioned by this environment, Fabius and Cincius decided to write their works in Greek. The Carthaginian view of events for the First Punic War had been depicted repeatedly by Philinus of Acragas (*FGrHist* 174) and later by Silenus of Caleacte (*FGrHist* 175) and Sosylus of Lacedaemon (*FGrHist* 176), and finally by Hannibal himself. It was therefore important to correct the contemporary—in the broadest sense, Hellenistic—image of this war by relating the other side, the Roman side.[127] Simultaneously Carthaginians and Romans assumed their place in a developmental trend that had already been initiated some time ago in the eastern section of the Mediterranean, the self-fashioning of local history in Greek, the supra-nationally dominant literary language. One recalls in particular Berossus (*FGrHist* 680) who in 300 BC wrote his *Babyloniaka* and Manetho (*FGrHist* 609) who wrote his *Aigyptiaka* for Ptolemy II.

Naevius and Ennius had previously emigrated to Rome. We know, however, that Ennius was in contact with leading individuals, with Cato on the one hand and with M. Fulvius Nobilior (cos. 189) on the other.[128]

Generally it should be emphasized that Roman tradition was never in the hands of the *pontifices* alone. The situations in which history was employed as *argument*, as *legitimizing reason*, were too numerous in the traditional society of Rome. This was once true for the leading families. At the latest, with the change from patriciate to nobility, i.e. in the fourth century BC, an 'administrative aristocracy' arose in Rome. Its members had to find constituents to win election to the individual stages of their administrative careers up to the consulship. Whenever the opportunity presented itself, they made reference to their own achievements, and, to a great extent, to the achievements of their ancestors. Hölscher has shown to what extent historical representations found their way into Roman art as early as *c.* 300, above all in connection with the triumph, the most outstanding moment of a career.[129] The funeral, however, offered a special opportunity to put on display the contribution made by an entire family to Rome's

---

[127] Cf. Werner (1963) 119 n. 4 (with very full bibliographical survey).

[128] Jocelyn (1972) 993ff.

[129] Hölscher (1978). On the 'tomb of the Fabii', see now La Rocca (1984); his attribution of the tomb to an infantryman named Fannius is problematic, in view of the fact that this Fannius would not have been even a high-level officer; for the usual interpretation, see Colonna (1984b).

greatness. Polybius (6.53–4) has portrayed for us how in this ceremony the ancestors were represented with their official insignia and honours, how their deeds were verbalized in the *laudatio funebris.*[130] Nevertheless—one is again reminded of this—only for the time of the Republic. None of the great families endeavoured to connect themselves seriously with the *ktisis* of Rome, with the history of the regal period.

The past, however, was always present in Rome in other ways too. In all controversies one hardly referred to written laws or regulations, but rather to *mos maiorum* {ancestral custom}, to *exempla.*[131] That was true for arguments in the Senate as well as for speeches before the people, for trials as well as for the official conduct of censors or decisions on religious problems. Roman history was hardly ever narrated *in toto*—at any rate we know nothing about an established venue for that type of 'performance'; it was familiar, however, to all who were interested in its entirety.

ADDENDUM

In the last twenty years scholarly interest in the structure and modes of oral tradition has substantially increased: one need only refer to Hobsbawm and Ranger (1983), Assmann (1992), and Tonkin (1992). As regards Rome, Wiseman (1989) has made some observations both on the present article and the response of Timpe (1988). Referring to these works, scholars have more strongly considered 'oral tradition' as a factor in investigations of the credibility of early Roman history, for example, in the standard works of Cornell ((1995) 9–12), Poucet ((2000) 88–91) and Marincola ((1997) 99–101). Petzold (1993), Timpe (1996 {= below, Ch. 6}) and Kierdorf (2002) have critically engaged with the ideas expressed here, and extended their application, and the great survey laid out by Suerbaum ((2002) 345–56) on the topic accepts these ideas.

[130] Cf. n. 7.
[131] Bleicken (1975) 354ff. (with further literature cited, n. 50); see also Fabricius (1911); Kornhardt (1936).

I myself have undertaken to reveal, through concrete examples from Roman history, structures that can still be recognized as arising originally from oral tradition: e.g. on the figure of the founder-king Romulus (1993), on the famines of the fifth century BC (2006a), on the Gallic catastrophe (2000), and on the ancient problems of the periodization of the Struggle of the Orders (1990).

The interest of scholarship in latter years has rather concentrated on special aspects of the formation of the tradition, above all, on the noble *gentes* as bearers of tradition as well as of Roman ideas about the public realm. Prominent here is the monumental synthesis of Walter (2004) followed by the research on the *pompa funebris*, e.g. by Flower (1996) and Flaig (2003), which are important, but also additional articles in Eigler et al. (2003), as well as the contribution of Hölkeskamp (1996). On the other hand, the attempt of Horsfall (2003) to work out a specific plebeian tradition deserves attention. One can disregard Carandini ((1997) and much else besides) and Grandazzi (1991), which are scholarly fantasies that cannot be supported by the results of archaeological research.

For the question of whether in general we may reckon with a written tradition about the early period of the Republic, the problem surrounding the *Annales (Maximi)*, the *Pontifices*, and the consular *Fasti* is, now as before, decisive. To Rüpke ((1993), (1995))[132] and Mora (1999), who question the age and reliability of the tradition, the fundamentally optimistic view of, e.g., Cornell ((1995) 12–16) presents a glaring contrast.

---

[132] Very noteworthy is the proof by Manthe ((1993) 69–74) that the character of juridical thought comes through augural practice (and not through the pontiffs).

6

Memoria and Historiography in Rome

Dieter Timpe
English translation by Mark Beck

Memoria in Latin means 'memory', but also 'tradition' and 'historiography'.[1] The transition in meaning is easy to understand, but does not express identity in the subject. For the nature of the relationship between memory of a past and of an historical tradition is not such that, for example, memory of the tradition simply represents objectified memory and a tradition represents the mere fixation of memory, so that both would only be different aggregate conditions of the same substance. The relationship of memory to tradition, especially tradition fixed by writing, is rather ambivalent, complicated, and subject to change. Its definition is therefore a task of historical reflection. This process of reflection, however, may proceed from the assumption that historiography must always have recourse to memory in some form or other. It must also be conducted with the expectation that the way in which this occurs can provide information about the prevailing approach to the historical past. Accordingly, therefore, in reflecting on the relationship between memory and tradition, I will

---

[1] See the material in *TLL*, s.v. *memoria*, where, however, the substantive difference meant here naturally does not play any role, and tradition appears only under the rubric *res recordationem conservans*. The concept of *memoria* in rhetoric is entirely geared towards memory capacity: [Cic.] *Rhet. Her.* 3.28f.; Cic. *Inu.* 1.9; Quint. 11.2; cf. Lausberg (1998) 478–80; Martin (1974) 349–50. A differentiation of historical *memoria* is found in [Cic.] *Her.* 1.13: *historia est gesta res, sed ab aetatis nostrae memoria remota* {history is something that has been done, but distant from the memory of our age}.

sketch in outline form a history of Roman historiography.[2] This approach is based on the opinion that the history of Roman historiography is more than just history of literature, a rosary of biographies of authors accompanied by analyses of their works, or a history of the formal characteristics of the genre that represents phases of reception and productive misunderstandings. It is also more than a source-critical ancillary science for the purpose of reconstructing Roman history, or a superstructure of consciousness erected by a ruling class, a literary annex of the social history of the upper class. There still remains, however, much to be done with respect to the complex structure composed of history and consciousness, forms and traditions, constancy and change that the historiography of the Romans actually represents.

Memory is a function in the life of the individual and in social associations that is founded on human nature. It is adaptable, productive, and anchored in an interconnected system like other organ functions. Memory is therefore connected, on the one hand, with material supports (relics, local points of attachment, memoranda) and, on the other hand, with a symbolic superstructure that memory first produces (trophies, signs, concepts).[3] The forms and functions of memory are diverse. In the tribes and cities of the ancient Mediterranean world, memory focuses on two areas in particular: on the one hand it maintains the practice of rites, sacrifices, and cults that are necessary for life and thus serves to render life secure by preserving cult performances and events that recur uniformly and cyclically. On the other hand, memory is necessary for outstanding and singular facts, especially memorable deeds, and has therein the objective of illustrating normative behaviour, of conjuring up role models by appeal and exhortation, and also of arousing pleasure, e.g. in the presentation of a story-teller or singer.

---

[2] In this context I give a preliminary summary of my earlier work: Timpe (1972); (1979); (1987a); (1987b); (1988).

[3] The psychological research on memory appears to possess little that is conducive to our purposes: cf. e.g. Baddeley (1979); Jüttner (1979); Hobi (1988). Cultural anthropology has more of current relevance to offer in its consideration of the phenomenon, especially Assmann (1992), who refers to Halbwachs (1925) and Halbwachs (1950); further, Assmann et al. (1983); Assmann and Hölscher (1988); Cancik and Mohr (1990).

The forms and functions of memory also differ from the ways in which it is preserved. Recollected knowledge, however, relies on it in a decisive way. The original form of memory, (i.e. oral memory), is not weaker than the written one, but it has its own mechanisms of preservation and is subject to its own set of social conditions. An extensive supply of ritual forms (magic formulae, incantations, prayers, cult songs, etc., usually transmitted with scrupulous accuracy) preserves the primary form of memory. In this form of memory it is possible furthermore to draw a distinction between the secret knowledge of priests, as remembered subject-matter, and general knowledge; the one preserves the collective through authoritative instruction, the other helps to integrate everyone in correctly understood traditions and customs. Fame based on deeds, by contrast, lives at first in the collective memory of associations (clans, allegiances, dynasties, urban communities), but is much less well preserved. This type of memory can become detached, wander, be transferred, change stylistic level and genre, and is stabilized, if not through political and social authority, at best through art.[4]

Literacy serves here at first as an aid in the preservation of priestly knowledge and in the fixation of famous deeds in poetry. Then, however, as further use is made of it, it exceeds all previous boundaries through its enormously productive potentialities.[5] Chronicles and cultic systems arose from lists and sacred texts, comprehensive large-scale epics from songs, ethnographic and geographic syntheses from the records of sailors and merchants, and historiography perhaps from chronologically organized lists. Historiography is a late and particular refinement of memory.

But memory does not simply culminate in historiography, perhaps because historiography, for example, implements the most technically effective form of preserving memory. Republican authors at any rate see the decisive benefit of historiography not in the greater quantity or better quality of the knowledge supplied by memory, but rather in the way it aids in orienting one's life.[6] Memory reaching far

---

[4] Cf. Röhrich (1988) on wandering and the transmission of motifs; Bowra (1964) on the fixing of *res gestae* in epic.

[5] Goody and Watt (1968); Havelock (1982); Ong (1982).

[6] Cf. Cic. *Off.* 1.55, *de Orat.* 2.36; Liv. *praef.* 5, to name but a few.

back into the past permits thereafter a conscious adherence to that which has been preserved and a continuous measuring of oneself against what is old. Roman traditionalism and conservatism and the cultivation of historical memory are therefore interdependent. Appeal to the *mos maiorum* connects knowledge about (authentic or alleged) historical subjects with the claim to their normative validity. But it is clear that *memoria* is not such a natural organ as the Roman panegyrists maintain, rather it is guided by interests, is goal-oriented, selective or socially conditioned, and such interrelationships are capable of and require elucidation.

1. MEMORIA

At the beginning of our journey a well-known text may illustrate for us structural elements of Roman *memoria*: the account by Polybius (6.53) of the *pompa funebris*, the funeral service of the Roman *nobiles*:[7]

Whenever a member of the nobility dies, the deceased man is brought to the speakers' platform in the Forum decorated and in an upright position so that everyone can also see him. While the people stand there, an adult son or relative delivers a speech about the virtues and deeds of the deceased. This revivification allows the audience to experience this death as a loss for all. After the interment a wax mask of the dead man is erected in a wooden shrine in the atrium of his house. The shrines are opened during festivals and the masked are decorated. The dead are displayed in processions of mourning, during which living persons don the masks and put on their robes of office. In this manner they then accompany the procession, in which the dead members of a clan are transported on carts. When they arrive before the speakers' platform, the dead represented in this way sit in a row on ivory chairs [i.e. on the official chairs of magistrates]. All of this makes a deep impression. In the funeral oration the ancestors (who are envisioned as being present) are praised and the memory of their deeds is

---

[7] Walbank, *HCP* I.737ff.; Kierdorf (1980a) 1ff.; Hölkeskamp (1987) 222ff.; Wesch and Klein (1993). {The passage cited above is a summation, not an exact quotation, from Polybius.}

renewed in order. Thus their fame remains immortal and is transmitted from generation to generation to spur on the youth.

The Greek historian experienced in the middle of the second century BC the effect of this ancient ritual and conveyed his impressions. But he saw it only as an external observer and with the attitude of the admirer. He emphasized the visible act of mourning, which he certainly experienced repeatedly. By contrast he refrained from conducting an historical investigation of the legal and religious background. He also discovered a pedagogical impact that had in the first place nothing to do with the archaic magic of visualizing the dead. He also described a total impression—perhaps having become somewhat transfigured (such as the public enjoys today in a royal wedding as a televised spectacle)—wherein presumably the differences in detail were actually instructive for the down-to-earth Roman. Nevertheless the account is essential for understanding the relationship of the Roman nobility to the past.

Probably the custom of the *pompa funebris* is rooted in *ius gentium* {law of nations} (even if that is unclear and cannot be demonstrated with certainty).[8] The family performs the funeral service, the heir of the *paterfamilias* delivers the *laudatio funebris* {funeral oration}. The ceremony concludes with interment in the family tomb and preservation of the wax masks in the family home. At the same time, however, the general public participates in this ceremony. One experiences, according to Polybius, the loss as a general one. The entire event had characteristics of a state function with the use of the Forum, especially the Rostra, the use of magisterial insignia, and the presence of the entire populace, virtually like a family. A separation of private and public in our sense of the term is impossible. The *nobiles* unquestioningly regarded the state as the stage of their activities. This attitude on their part was not contested by anyone according to Polybius' idealizing depiction; on the contrary there was support for it.

Furthermore, when the sequence of generations of a clan was presented by its representatives in the *pompa* (it is unknown how that happened in detail), then that not only produced a continuously

---

[8] Cic. *Fam.* 9.21; Plin. *HN* 35.6. Cf. Mommsen (1887) I.442ff.; Meyer (1914); Hölkeskamp (1987); Wieacker (1988) 196f.

repeated spatio-temporal representation (since this type of thing can only have transpired on average every couple of months), but also served as a demonstration of the context of Roman history, like a tapestry composed of dozens of threads that were interwoven in a crisscross pattern. For the great families were all related to each other, connected by friendship or enmity, and whoever was aware of this had a personal network of Roman history before his eyes in graphic and incarnate vividness.

Finally, in the funeral orations, the ἀρεταί {virtues} and the πράξεις {deeds}, as Polybius says, *uirtutes* and *res gestae*, were praised. Deeds accomplished in an official capacity and personal character-istics (usually typical rather than individualized) were fluidly unified together in the person. Just as the *tituli*, the inscriptions under the wax masks in the house, combined data pertaining to offices held and formulae of praise, so also in like fashion public knowledge deriving from lists of magistrates and priests, calendars, and lists of triumphs was combined with the (more easily manipulable) family tradition and oral tradition. In pre-literary times the relative reliability of this complex of tradition was preserved, however, by the rivalry of the great clans. No one could thus check pronouncements of praise in an archive, no journalist could malign them; but competitors were intolerant of any wholly intentional distortions.

The circumstance of historical memory in the ruling class of the Middle Republic (the late fourth, the third, and the early second centuries BC) seems typically to evince the following characteristics: the public and private spheres partially permeated one another; the connection to Roman history appeared to the *nobiles* in the diachronic and synchronic intertwining of great clans and in the succession of their representatives. This information complex extended beyond the circle of active participants, but nevertheless could remain coherent, although there were no safeguards that guaranteed the authenticity of the tradition.

What is missing here is the conception of a development that changes. One is unaware of the uniqueness of epochs. That accords with what is known of aristocratic societies under conditions of oral tradition.[9] Just as the dead, represented by people wearing masks, can gather

---

[9] Schuster (1988) 64ff.; Vansina (1985).

together, in like manner that which is old or ancient is everywhere equally near and present. We have every reason to underline this, since the modern view of Roman history, the scholarly as well as the popular, suggests a decidedly different notion: namely, that of great transformation, of tremendous growth, of turbulent development towards something, towards fundamental quantitative change that turns into a different quality. Whether it is the Conflict of the Orders or the unification of Italy, whether it is a slave economy or a provincial conquest, it is always, according to modern opinion, the same: everything is subject to continuous change, people can hardly keep up and always limp breathlessly behind progress.

The opinion in any case of the classical Republic, of a semi-literate society, seems to have been completely different. According to it, one moved in familiar terrain when one thought about the past; constancy, not change, was decisive. It was precisely for this reason that the past could be exemplary and aid in decision making. The Fabii or Claudii considered themselves to be unified and to have a sense of community for generations. The inscription on the tomb of one Cornelius Scipio states:

I have added my way of life to the *uirtutes* of my family, left behind descendants, and emulated the deeds of my father. I have acquired for myself the praise of my ancestors; they were delighted to have me as their descendant...[10]

The recollection of the past that helped to orient one's life, and a naive identification with it, as expressed here, also hindered comprehension of what was historically foreign—of what became foreign or of what was different; apparently one cannot have both at the same time. Uninterrupted participation in the stream of life is not consistent with the distance that is required to perceive the past as an object, and where the past is *studied*, its life force is weakened. Thus it cannot be surprising that historical memory organizes the past, according to need and taste, into a treasure trove of types or a collection of examples, into a hall of fame or a storage cupboard. It

---

[10] *ILLRP* 6, Cn. Cornelius Scipio Hispanus, *praet.* 139 BC (Münzer (1901)). The approval of the *maiores* should be emphasized and may be connected to the fact that Scipio did not attain the consulship. This factor, however, does not affect the fundamental idea.

is surprising too that it also allows the strangest misunderstandings, errors in judgement, and areas of blindness to arise. Anachronistic retrojections, for example, are a source of errors that very frequently occur under such circumstances.

Historical memory of this type has an entirely different structure. The pontifical records, lists, and the calendar, funeral orations, commemorative inscriptions, public monuments and documents, statues, and temples supported it in the public sphere. In the private sphere the *tituli*, possibly the records of official activity, and the material memories of it such as, for example, items of booty, formed the real basis of memory among the élite. Added to this, however, is the fact that for everyone historical memories are attached to thousands of circumstances, to places, open fields, borders, graves, rights, habits, customs, cults, rites, ceremonies, relics, words, and names. Added to this, moreover, is the fact that in every situation of life examples may be called upon for which the *mos maiorum* serves as a universal regulatory authority that can be appealed to. And all of this enveloped people like the atmosphere without permitting fragmentation into special spheres and types. The *nobiles* had increasingly inclusive memories that were also more obligatory or binding, but not essentially different. All in all the greatest degrees of variation and the most colourful peculiarities should be presumed in knowledge derived from memory.

Yet it is an entirely different question as to whether even a senator could have known what we read in Mommsen's *Staatsrecht*, for example, about the history of the quaestorship or even what we know about the wars of the fifth century with the Volsci, and what historical knowledge in our sense of the term an average Roman would have possessed at all. Here too there might not have been any boundary between factual knowledge and richly imaginative saga. In dubious cases the authority was not an historical document or a rational argument; rather it was the authority of the socially superior individual. We should imagine an average southern Italian of today in order to be able to appreciate this: one can have an intimate relationship to the past without possessing precisely organized knowledge about the political course of history.

If this relationship to the past seems to be timeless, if it is destined for its part to be set in relief with respect to its developmental history, we can consequently begin with the question: where then is the historical memory of a political community as such located? Where does Roman history as the collective memory of the *populus Romanus* reside and how is this collective memory originally expressed prior to all historiography? With this consideration, the question of the composition and social organization of *memoria* must be pursued a bit further back than Polybius goes. And we must clearly establish first of all here what principle difficulties this mode of inquiry encounters. Contrary to naive opinion, Roman history of the early periods rests on a narrower and more insecure basis than later periods, but at least it rests on a basis formed by literature. Indeed, Livy and other historians produced accounts of the kings of the sixth century and patricians of the fifth century, but the threshold of literacy for Roman history in reality comes only in the fourth century. At that time Greek authors wrote for the first time about Rome. The state of consciousness of pre-literary time—to express it from a source-oriented viewpoint, a prehistoric time—is largely unavailable to us. We can only acquire information about it through cautious inferences drawn from later written sources and cautious interpretations of material remains, i.e. archaeological discoveries.

The hypothetical result of such investigative work is roughly the following: the political community of the archaic period preserved memory only in the form of lists of their officials and of the calendar on an officially kept tablet. Both were somehow connected with one another and were later both referred to by the same name (*Fasti*). This record-keeping served practical and sacred purposes. It was more a type of sacred bookkeeping and was therefore the responsibility of an association of priests (the *pontifices*). The recording of other occurrences followed this pattern, such as festivals, sacrifices, triumphs, omens, and dedications, since all such observances were likewise important from the viewpoint of sacred law. It is clear that historically relevant events were also considered since, for example, a solar eclipse can become a central point of chronology, or an act of foreign policy may be listed in the report of a triumph, or the personal success of a noble may be expressed in the dedication of booty that again can explain his political biography. Nevertheless the state's sacred lists originally have nothing to do with the memory of personal deeds as such, as praiseworthy *res gestae*.

This memory is located elsewhere, and it is seen in another conceptual horizon. In the François tomb of Vulci, for example, one wall displays representations of the Trojan and Theban cycle, another wall has representations of battles with Etruscan *condottieri*. A certain Tarquinius from Rome appears among them; Roman historical legend perhaps also knows him.[11] These aristocratic pirates thus styled their deeds according to the model of heroes, and the Roman aristocrats probably did not behave any differently from the Etruscans originally. Memory of this type possessed a different character and consistency than the pontifical variety. Its range was limited in pre-literate circumstances; but the vitality, binding force, and regulatory power of this memory for those whom it concerned cannot be imagined vividly enough. The member of a great family lived in it the way we live in our clothing and use our furniture. The *maiores* and their binding model will have been so present to him as though they all were sitting together on chairs in front of him and were looking at him.

Later, in historical times, it is fundamentally different. For all Roman historians it is a basic premise that the subject-matter of Roman history is the *res gestae populi Romani*. At first personal deeds had to be credited to the collective, or the individual had to identify himself with the community to the extent that this became possible. When the time was right, *publica memoria* preserved the memories of the *res gestae populi Romani*, the deeds and accomplishments of the collective of the Romans as such. That seems to us to be quite obvious, we who correspondingly also regard the deeds (and misdeeds) of the Germans as the subject-matter of German history. If, however, the community had no organ at all for such memories, and the *res gestae* on the other hand were not those of the *populus Romanus*, but rather of individuals, then an astonishing and important step is taken in thinking that the population as a whole is the actor of memorable deeds.

Naturally the increasing political integration of the patrician–plebeian community, an integration that was carried out in the fourth century, is reflected in this. We admittedly do not apprehend this political integration in historiography, because it did not yet

[11] Messerschmidt–von Gerkan (1930) 62ff.; Helbig (1972) 204ff., no. 3239.

exist. When it then did come into being, it could not hold a different view than that the state had existed as the agent of history and deeds from Romulus on. The monuments show, however, that, since the fourth century in Rome, public donations made by individuals could serve the political representation of the community. The great personalities thus step forward as representatives of the state and use the public as their audience and partner. A victorious general can therefore put his spoils of war on public display as a monument or have his victory publicly recorded in a portrait, and that corresponds precisely with the *pompa funebris* that uses the Forum and is unthinkable without reference to a public.[12] That is the first step on the way leading to the view that the *res gestae* of individuals add up to the total achievement of the *populus Romanus*.

We are thus in the world of the aristocratic state that blurs the distinctions between private and public, and where also the *priuata memoria* and the *publica memoria* supplement and mutually reinforce each other. For when the *res gestae* of the great Romans becomes the subject-matter of Roman history, they do not exactly enter into competition with an 'actual', legitimate, objective state history as well. That does not (yet) even exist. With all of the ambition and envy that fills to overflowing the aristocratic world in particular, there is indeed no alternative to it in general. When Cato the Censor, a *homo nouus* {new man, i.e. one without noble ancestors}, arrived at the idea, born of envy, of emphasizing the entire achievement of the Roman people instead of the fame of his noble rivals, at that point he could then only realize this in the amusing way of collectivizing (so to speak) *uirtus* by simply narrating the *res gestae* anonymously:[13] a late and eccentric, but logical consequence of the thought we have described.

What many erroneously regard as a congenital feature of the Romans was thus first achieved in the state of the Roman nobility of the classical Republic: what the *nobiles* achieve serves the political community, and this delivers the public sphere to the *nobiles* where their fame can appear as social authority. The deeds of great Romans

---

[12] Hölscher (1978) 315ff.

[13] Nep. 3.4; cf. Plin. *HN* 8. 11 (F 83). It is uncertain to what extent this ultimately impossible procedure was carried out.

become the most prestigious object of historical memory, and the *publica memoria* summarizes it as *res gestae populi Romani*, whatever laudable deeds the aristocrats accomplished. This situation is the one which Polybius illustrates with the description of the aristocratic funeral and ancestor cult. It demonstrates not social harmony, but a system whose stability was not called into question through conflicts in particular, but rather was promoted by them.

Once again the late Republic, the time of Cicero and Caesar, presents a completely different picture. There is here an enormous increase in historical material and historical knowledge: family archives and nearly museum-like collections, widespread written and material remains of official political activity, senate records, enormous amounts of booty, speeches published as literature, antiquarian research, and the activity of literary clients (including Greek ones). All of this distinguishes the basis of memory at this time fundamentally from the situation in the archaic world and the classical Republic. In addition the entire city of Rome, especially its political centres, the Capitol and the Forum, was an enormous museum full of monuments, memorials, and inscriptions. The minting of coins promulgated the fame and entitlement of the great families, because the aristocratic mint masters had the licence for self-representation on the coins. There was poetry and finally historical literature.

But still more important is the fact that now an opposition between *priuata* and *publica memoria* arises, after the history of deeds and events is claimed as the realm of *publica memoria*. Now critics are even of the opinion that *priuata memoria*, family traditions, and the thirst for glory of some individuals had falsified collective memories.[14] The ideational competition between the historical tradition of the population as a whole and the special requirements of individuals actually has its place here, because the preconditions for a literary civilization make it possible. (This can be disputed for the classical Republic, when there was very limited literacy.) The élite in fact even now still equate, in the most unembarrassed way, their advantage with the *bonum publicum*, but this attitude is occasionally hotly disputed and interpreted as arrogance and shameless *auaritia* {greed}.

---

[14] Cic. *Brut.* 62; Liv. 4.16.4, 7.9.5, 8.40.4; Plin. *HN* 35.8. Cf. Ridley (1983) 372ff.

How this came about and what this *publica memoria* really is, which allows it to be distinguished from private, is indicated by Livy when he laments the distortion of the historical tradition and adds that the only guarantee for the *memoria rerum gestarum* lies in literacy.[15] Livy wants to say: history is the location of *memoria publica*; it keeps watch over the undistorted knowledge of the *res gestae populi Romani* and protects it against interests from the private side that promote distortion. This confession has also often been repeated with conviction and without reflection in scholarly research because it strikes a powerful inclination that can hardly be shaken, a way of thinking accustomed to seeing in the biblical literary tradition a guarantee of its reliability and a source of truth. But what Livy's observation really implies is a question that leads us to the second part of these considerations, from one pole, memory, to the other, historiography. Prior to this, however, we should once again summarize what has been stated.

In Roman memory of the past, three epochs can be distinguished. The first, so to speak, prehistoric one is almost unknown to us with respect to its inner workings. What we call the state seems to have been more a religious than a political entity and its flourishing seems to have been ensured primarily through cyclical sacrifices and properly conducted rituals rather than through individual behaviour adapted to the situation. At that time the *res gestae* were rather the province of individuals, their families and clients. The state probably did not also maintain any historical memory encompassing events and deeds pertaining to the populace as a whole. In the second epoch, that of the classical Republic, the public and private spheres were reciprocally permeable, the deeds of the élite became the subject of Roman history and *publica memoria* was nourished and derived sustenance from *priuata memoria*. Private status and achievement, by contrast, acquired their scope and scale primarily through their public connection; there was no conflict between the two domains. The third phase was one of potential contrast between the objective *res publica* and the subjective ambition and demands of individuals in the Late Republic. In this phase the assumption of the *nobiles* that

---

[15] Liv. 6.1.2: *litterae... una custodia fidelis memoriae rerum* {letters... the single reliable guardian of the memory of events'}.

the state belongs to them, indeed that they are the state (as they think), first became so particular and ideological. Only at this point can their 'memory' be criticized as a private distortion of the public one, and it is just that too. Now the abstract general public, which is more than the sum of all that is individual, is juxtaposed with the naive and primitive egoism of the élite. It is in this context that historiography also belongs.

2. HISTORIOGRAPHY

Roman historiography arose late, during or after the war with Hannibal,[16] and it was not begun by scholars or historical specialists but rather by senators (i.e. politicians), for whom historiography was a continuation of politics by other means. The first among them, Fabius Pictor, obviously wanted to convey to the Greek-speaking world a more favourable view of the Roman state, because he wrote in Greek. He did not do that at any rate in a propaganda pamphlet, by means of speeches or in some other way. Instead he wrote an account of Roman history. Therein he combined a mythological foundation history and an early history (for which there were Greek literary models and guidelines furnished by genre) with a partisan treatment of contemporary and military history. He also somehow bridged the gap caused by the missing material of the middle period in summary fashion. Even if there were certain parallels in the western Greek local histories, it was on the whole a strange and bizarre compilation, saga narration, and tendentious war report all in one. It was vis-à-vis its language, form, objective, and time certainly nothing that would have arisen organically from Roman historical consciousness, as an expression of the memory Romans had of their own past; rather it was absolutely unthinkable without Greek political and literary impulses.[17]

---

[16] Perl (1964) 185–9, 213–18; Badian (1966); Flach (1985) 56ff.
[17] Cf. on this the different opinions of von Ungern-Sternberg (1988) {= above, Ch. 5); Timpe (1988).

Nevertheless all later Roman historians, including Livy, Tacitus, and Cassius Dio, understood themselves to be a continuation of this beginning. They expressed also therein the context of the genre's tradition in that they usually named their works *Annals*. With this title, their *libri annales* were linked to the *tabula annalis*, the annual notice-board of the pontiffs, those official lists that contained information about memorabilia, triumphs as well as (thunder)storms, or congenital deformities and which were stereotypically divided according to internal and external affairs. This organizational principle, attested for pre-literary sacred record-keeping, is also found in Livy and Tacitus, as a formal principle.

Based on this *formal* connection, earlier research concluded that there was a *substantive* relationship between the pre-literary pontifical chronicle and literary historiography, and regarded this in turn as an indication of credibility.[18] If, that is, the sparse but authentic chronicle continued in historiography, then its core may also have been credible. Then Livy would have been right in principle, when he complains about the distortion of *memoria publica*, while regarding literacy as a protective cloak for *memoria*. Certainly private embellishments of every kind would have proliferated around this basic objective material, but there would have been at any rate a narrow path of authentic information. There might be a difference of opinion about its width. Without discussing this question in detail, the conceptual model introduced in the first part above should permit the conclusion that the separation of a reliable core from unreliable constituents, of an objective framework from arbitrary private distortions, cannot be accurate. In the time when the fundamental principles of later historiography were established (in the fourth and third centuries), there was no such hard core whatsoever as opposed to an encasement in the subjective, the random, and the frivolous. There was no objective memory, no *publica memoria* that was dissoluble from the private. Historical literature hardly had anything to do with objective tradition.

Certainly it already seemed so to Late Republican authors. This impression originated in the perception that this literature laid claim

---

[18] Schwegler (1853–76) I.64; Mommsen (1920) 463ff.; Schanz–Hosius (1922–35) I.28–33.

to the authority of the *publica memoria*. The fact that this literature could do this is connected with the social position of the historians who enjoyed, as senators, the authority deriving from knowledge of politics and decision-making. For example, they were accustomed to be exact in dealing with questions of civil and sacred law; they therefore also regarded this exactitude in the chronological sphere as a sign of seriousness. Accordingly one expected it of them. They therefore incorporated these viewpoints into their description of the past. They bureaucratized and standardized the tradition in this direction. The regal period, for example, was subjected to extensive treatment by the literary annalists of the second century BC. Nearly nothing was known about this period and there were certainly no pontifical records from it, until eventually one could gather details from the historians about the individual years of Servius Tullius' reign. They thus wrote in the style of archival and priestly records so as to lend the stamp of authenticity, officialdom, and seriousness to what they had to say. And they did this certainly not with the conscious intent to distort; because who, if not they—to whom the *res publica* belonged, so to speak, like their own family's house—should know better what was right and what had happened!

Actually, however, a fantastic invention could be promulgated here. It was contingent first of all on the authoritative claim of the senators that they were in charge of the *memoria publica*; at the same time, however, it was a consequence of the innovation that private individuals could write books that had the *res gestae populi Romani* as their subject. Probably poets had begun to do this, but they were not taken seriously as members of society; with senators it was quite different.[19]

It has now been shown that it is not a strange peculiarity of the Romans that they took up literary historiography so late. It was rather, in the sense of its relationship to that which is historical, a critical and momentous change that finally placed the *publica memoria* at the disposal of the literary senators. The transformation to a literary culture was indeed a very coincidental one, an innovation engendered by external circumstances. It then, however, did succeed and had an enormous impact, as in fact literacy always does. Customarily it has

---

[19] Bömer (1952); Altheim (1961); Strzelecki (1963).

unforeseen and revolutionary consequences, since this wondrous thing is easy to use, is neutral as a medium, and reaches all who are capable and willing to read. Actually the Romans noticed this too very gradually. It took a long time until they too employed the discovery in a way that had an effect on their own realm, i.e. so as to appeal to readers of Latin.

When, however, the time was ripe, everything possible was introduced, especially the private tradition of great families, since there was little else with which the narrative chronicle of events (the formal principle of annalistic writing) could be so effortlessly filled in terms of content. It is therefore unsurprising that it happened, and that we therefore have the impression that the history of literary historiography was, so it seems, the history of the progressive distortion of its fundamental principles.

Many other disparate things, however, also entered into Republican historiography, for example, antiquarian subject-matter. This antiquarian component permitted the strangest kind of connections and combinations, for example, fantastic etymologies that derived things Italian from Greek roots, systematizations of Roman civil and sacred law, whose rubrics were ascribed to the old kings, or explanations of what was not understood in the spirit of the present or arising from the interests of the author. Also, political polemic, speeches, documentary material, or autobiographical reports are types of content that were present in the older annals and became incorporated in historiography only to be removed again from the first century BC on, and to become fixed in their own genres. Other endeavours too, such as the attempt by Cato and his successor Hemina, to break through the narrow city-state bounds and create the right of domicile for Italian traditions in Roman historiography, did not catch on at all. In these attempts it becomes clear to us that early Roman historiography was a medium whose form was not well established and was open to various types of enrichment.[20]

Therefore the influence of Greek historians in particular was not a peripheral and incidental phenomenon, but rather a perpetual constituent element of Roman historiography. It is unimaginable

---

[20] The extension (Badian (1966) 11) can be detected in the increasing scope of annalistic works, especially in Cn. Gellius (Schanz–Hosius (1922–35) I.197–8).

without its formal and subject-matter-related symbiosis with Greek models. The encounter, however, had from one generation to another a different character. The first influences of the superior literary culture led the Romans to imitate the means of representation, types of style, and themes of contemporary Hellenistic historians.[21] In the late second century BC Polybius became more important for Roman historians than any one of their own predecessors because he gave them an array of interpretative possibilities for their own historical situation, displayed the achievement of a historical method, and held out the promise of education through historical knowledge to those who were actively engaged. Via Polybius, Sallust discovered the way to Thucydides, the founding figure of political history, and thereby introduced exemplary analysis of historical contexts and moral absorption as historiographical dimensions.

These enrichments with ramifications extending in many directions show that early Roman historiography was not something uniform and more or less genre-like from the beginning, but was rather a complex that first developed with the possibilities of literary form, and brought together memory and reflection of various types together with changing intentions and methods.

Historiography thus narrates the idealized beginnings so as to reaffirm its own identity in a nearly timeless way. It reports deeds to keep alive examples with educational intent, or typifies past events to render them useful and applicable in this regard. It attaches meaningful explanations to circumstances and utilizes the intellectual instruments of Greek thought to organize and investigate the material. Finally it is able to avail itself of large-scale political and historical interpretive options (i.e. 'conceptions of history'), and it then far exceeds the function of memory whereby, however, precisly its political effect can be especially great. And as a general rule it does much of this simultaneously and concurrently. Roman historiography is neither determined by the structure of *memoria*, nor in general is it clearly fixed.

This openness coincided with an additional inclination. Thanks to the external and internal expansion of the Republic, the social basis of literature spread considerably in the first century. Now individuals

---

[21] Alföldi (1965) 147ff.

who were not senators also wrote about history. Their accounts were necessarily second-hand and they often were in the service of distinguished politicians, but they also had new intentions and a completely different relationship to the historical material than the tradition-oriented members of the ruling class. Considerably more readers read such productions. A public and a market arose for historiography that did not exist at all before. History was needed, for example, as instructional material and in the teaching of rhetoric, and for this reason historical works found consumers and interested parties. New forms such as collections of *exempla* or epitomes were created because of these new requirements.[22]

The socially expanded and modified engagement with history subjected this material—which was devoid of every scientific or other type of verification—to new phases of topicality. Finally, the Late Republic is a time in which intense debates are conducted about political objectives. There are factions and internal fronts that were long lasting and sometimes even inherited, which also influenced historiography, indeed often effectively stimulated it. This is because historiography could be related to current political interests and therefore was rendered useful from a propagandistic viewpoint. Sallust also shows us what was possible in terms of party hatred and demagogy.

The so-called Conflict of the Orders was described in light of the civil wars of the first century, and Romulus and the kings in the light of the experiences with commanders and dictators of this time. The typological mode of thinking permitted the demonization of Tarquinius Superbus with Sulla being meant, and so forth. Above all social questions, actions of the tribunes of the people, programmes for the distribution of arable land, and the like were rendered topical and modernized with an eye to viewpoints and alternatives that were of burning interest to the writers and readers of the first century, to such a point that it was not possible to recognize what had actually happened back then.[23] Behind all of this lies the general experience that change or competition with regard to social identity usually alters *memoria* also.

---

[22] E.g., Nepos' collection of *exempla*: Gell. 6.18.11; Plin. *HN praef.* 24; see further Timpe (1979) 115.

[23] Von Ungern-Sternberg (1990) 92ff.

Finally there is a connection between social changes and literary tendencies. For the senatorial representatives of tradition and all people with broadly rooted *memoria*, the literary element was a bonus. For newcomers (e.g. new citizens), the literature brought about the (possibly decisive) transmission of *memoria* and the orientation to historical memory. Moreover literacy, because it is efficient and compelling, possesses the characteristic of suppressing everything else. It thus came to pass that the opinion was held in the Late Republic, by Cicero for example, that *memoria*, historical memory, is first and foremost a written report in annalistic form.[24] Historiography now becomes the mainstream of memory: everything else is secondary. We have arrived at the point where *memoria* has the two meanings found in the dictionary.

All of these relationships that determined the internal development of Roman Republican historiography intersect for us in the author who collected the traditions and gave them their final form. Most importantly we can also still read this author, namely Livy, for the most part (in contrast to the majority of his predecessors). Livy can be used to illustrate most of what has been indicated here about the portrayal of history, about the social conditions of historical literature, and about the tendentious topicality of historical narrative.[25]

Livy was not a senator or active politician, but rather a *rhetor* and a literary figure, who followed no direct political objectives, but did indeed follow a type of intellectual programme, and one, moreover, that Augustus, under whom he wrote, welcomed, approved, and supported. Livy was also not a man from Rome or the regional centre of the Roman–Italian state, but from the upper Italian periphery. That made it easier for him to pay homage to a somewhat abstract and schematic patriotism, to identify himself with the Roman state generally without wanting to shape the politics of his day. Livy cultivates the gestures of clemency and neutrality. He sheds the subdued light of a noble classicism over the battlefields. It becomes still clearer, however, that for him the people in their entirety are the actual actors and representatives of meaning in Roman history. The people are conceived of as an organism that in fact grows or can

---

[24] Cic. *Brut.* 322; *de Orat.* 2.52; *Leg.* 1.5.
[25] Walsh (1961); Burck (1967); Luce (1977); Burck (1992).

also be threatened (namely through internal conflicts and external wars), but still actually remains constant in its essential and supra-historical nature, and is the same under Romulus and under Caesar; its habitat is Italy and its internal goal is the unity of this area. Livy thus produced a historical portrait: he wrote Roman history in the manner that German historians after 1870 wrote German history, with an eye to the *telos* of unification and peace. In this there was much that was correct, and it allowed him in a certain way to be in harmony with his time. For his conceptions harmonize in so far with the objectives of Augustus without compelling him to approve of Augustus' seizure of power and the construction of his rule.

Yet one still recognizes with amazement how this work that was compiled in substance from Late Republican predecessors is free of every attempt to verify the historical narrative critically and methodologically, even as its attempt to render a complete narrative of Roman history with great art has always been justly admired. It combines the dimensions of an encyclopaedia, the naivety of an anachronistic historical novel, and the political tendentiousness of a clever propagandist. The work as a whole was soon lost because only a few could cope with its size, but its author always maintained his reputation as a great historian. The fact that Livy did not have anything remotely to do with historical research did not mean that he objected to it. The structural form of *memoria* that played (and could play) the smallest part in the Roman sphere is memory in the form of historical science.

In the imperial period other problems asserted themselves. Now one man, the emperor, had a monopoly not only on power but also on information. Both together engendered the phenomenon of court historiography, that is works that were written with *adulatio*, that assiduously disseminated what was acceptable and glorified the em-peror. In some cases this incited enraged acts of vengeance directed at a fallen tyrant. Those historians in the tradition of senatorial annal-ists were occupied with the problem of freedom under the Principate, and this also included the defence of *memoria* that had not been falsified.[26] The topic betrays not so much the limitations of tradi-tionalists, but rather an attitude of meditation on the continuity of

[26] Tac. *Agr.* 1–3.

Roman history. But therein also lay a very one-sided worsening of the situation that coincided with the strange preservation of the annalistic form, that is the organizational structure of a city chronicle in the days of worldwide empire. The historiography of the imperial period thus expressed the historical thought of a small coterie of educated and tradition-conscious élite. It became sublimated and narrowly focused in the work of Tacitus; but the connection it had with reality became increasingly tenuous and problematic. Despite its increased readership, it deviated more than ever from representing the historical memory of the Romans altogether or even of the imperial relations in general at the time.

Roman history therefore is to be regarded, in sum, as the *publica memoria* absolutely. It owes this notion to its connection with the annalistic form, although it is something quite new as regards its subject-matter. The fact that representatives of the ruling class created and developed this genre and furnished it with authority and prestige obligated it also to the mode of thought of this class and its tradition, its horizon and its standards. But under this roof the impact of literacy on Roman society, the influx of Greek thought, the social changes and political experiences of the last centuries of the Republic and the shock to *memoria* that resulted from this had the effect that historiography became a framework for many different things. Only one thing was never stimulated by it: scientific research. In the imperial period historiography recedes and loses either its prestige or its impact in response to changes in the political significance of the senate and aristocratic freedom of information.

To be a treasury of memory of the past of the entire political population (the *populus Romanus*) *and* to treat as equivalent the past worthy of remembering with the memory of deeds (*res gestae*) represent the two conceptual preconditions for Roman historiography. They depend on the history of Rome itself and on the social history of the nobility in particular. The fact that they remained effective under completely different conditions indicates the impressive continuity and resiliency of the Roman consciousness. It also indicates, however, the clear limitations of the capacity for development in the imperial period. Roman historiography cannot be conceived of as preserving memory in the usual sense, because intention in Roman historiography was dependent on interest, selection was dependent on tradition, and its historically dependent consciousness of identity determined its relationship with the past to a much greater extent than the mechanical concept of storing something in memory would lead us to expect. The relationship to the past formulated in historiography is, however, just as little to be thought of as a construct, because the relationship of the Romans to their history and the access to the past that the expression 'construct' suggests, fall far short of doing justice to the vivid Roman connection with the past. In the cultural anthropological field that has arisen between such extreme conceptions, the relationship to the past in Roman historiography is characterized conspicuously on the one hand by the much discussed and socio-historically explicable conservatism of its value system, and the intensity of its historical orientation, and on the other hand by an especial relationship to literary forms, sources, and models that can only be explained culturally and historically. Both lead to the fact that not only does the literary tradition guarantee the history, but also that for the first time history explains the modes of literary tradition.

What then does historiography have to do with memory? It does not simply preserve memory by means of textual fixation. It forms, limits, and develops it under the influence of literary possibilities, political experiences, social changes, and intellectual stimuli. And it creates thereby a medium of orientation, understanding, and obligation that, objectified as literature, is capable of reception by those who come later.

ADDENDUM

The selective performance of human memory, and above all the recognition that memory is not the reliable and impartial witness of the past that a naive view would hold of it, stands at the centre of current historical reflection. Neurobiological and psychological research on the processes of memory (Tulving–Donaldson (1972); Fischer (1998); Markowitsch (2002)) and historical source-critical analysis of the development of oral tradition and collective memory increasingly converge in an effort at an interdisciplinary study of memory (Schmidt (1991/96); Schacter (1995), (1996); Fried (2004)).

Of special interest are on the one hand—in the works by J. and A. Assmann and others based on Halbwachs—the communicative structure of memory (Welzer (2008), and on the other hand the material and symbolic supports for memory, which compensate for the loss of a developed, coherent collective memory; P. Nora (1984), following F. Yates (1966), identifies it with the concept (borrowed from classical rhetoric) of *locus* as isolated 'places of memory' (*lieux de mémoire*).{26a}

One can speak of collective, social or cultural 'memory' only in a metaphorical sense. Collectives have no memory; the contents of memory, which exist intersubjectively in them, and are effective as establishers of identity, are socially conditioned traditions. They rest on traditions of specific bearers, traditions which have been differently formed, are selective, and driven by particular interests, and which were fed in Rome from both oral and written sources. A critical approach to them demands an understanding of the specifically social conditions of their development and importance rather than an explanation based on the general mechanisms of the psychology of memory. Nora describes the contrast between the modern and the traditional approach to the past, relying on his theory of 'places of memory': '*Lieux de mémoire* exist because there are no longer *milieux de mémoire*, settings in which memory is a real part of everyday experience' (Nora (1996) 1). He refers thereby to the opposition which Nietzsche recognized between a critically reconstructed but distanced 'history' and the unconscious, traditional 'memory' which is rooted in the relationships of life. But this opposition is not to be transferred to Roman conceptions, in which the 'places of memory' are always embedded in the developed culture of memory, and according to which *repraesentio* and *resurrectio* of the past are not at variance with each other.

In current scholarship Roman historiography is rightly viewed as a special and historically conditioned 'medium of memory' and as *one* element in a comprehensive relationship to the known and remembered past ('*Geschichtskultur*') (Walter (2004), with comprehensive bibliography). It stands in close connection with the system

---

26a {The standard English translation of Nora calls them 'realms of memory', but I have used 'places' in order to retain the connection with the Latin *locus*.}

of the stabilizing norms of the nobility, the *mos maiorum* that was orientated towards *exempla* (Hölkeskamp (1996); Linke–Stemmler (2000); Braun et al. (2000); Pina Polo (2004)), and it thereby shares with other forms of exhortative representations of the past—such as the maintenance of family memory (Flaig (1995); Flower (1996)), the public monument (Sehlmeyer (1999)), and historical drama (Flower (1995); Wiseman (1998); Manuwald (2001))—an intensive historical orientation, the continuous possibility for Roman *memoria* to be made topical, and the lack of a notion of historical development. Roman historiography too altered its function in the frame of memory culture: it was dependent on the authority of competing bearers of the tradition (Marincola (1997)), and on formal literary traditions, which it took over and developed.

7

Etruscan Historiography

T. J. Cornell

I

Direct evidence about Etruscan historical literature is very limited. The original works have entirely disappeared, and very little is known about the use which was made of them by Greek and Roman writers, because no coherent antiquarian or historical account of Etruscan history has come down to us. We know, however, that such works were written in Antiquity; it is sufficient to mention the *Res Etruscae* of Verrius Flaccus, and the emperor Claudius' *Tyrrhenica*. But we possess only a very few fragments of these accounts, and not many more of the works of those Roman writers such as Cato and Varro who endeavoured to examine local Italian traditions.

But there is little reason to doubt the contention that some sort of Etruscan historiography once existed. It seems to be confirmed by reliable evidence. The emperor Claudius, in a famous speech preserved on a bronze tablet from Lyon, contrasted the well-known Roman story of the origins of Servius Tullius with a tradition explicitly referred to in Etruscan sources. And Varro, in a discussion of the Etruscan theory of *saecula*, mentioned certain Etruscan histories (*Tuscae historiae*) which, he said, had been written in the eighth Etruscan *saeculum*. Claudius and Varro are trustworthy authorities, and their statements seem to add up to conclusive proof of the existence of an Etruscan historiography. J. Heurgon, for example, has written, 'The Etruscans certainly had an historical literature.'[1]

---

[1] Heurgon (1964b) 247.

This is a statement which very few scholars would call into question. But hardly any attempt has ever been made to consider its implications. Heurgon's little book contains the only competent survey known to me of the subject as a whole. Although I agree with most of what Heurgon says, it seems to me that a fuller treatment is both possible and desirable.[2] And even Heurgon fails, in my view, to distinguish clearly enough between the various forms in which Etruscan historical traditions could have been handed down.

II

When Claudius speaks of Etruscan authorities, what exactly does he mean? The relevant part of his speech is as follows:

Between this man [sc. Tarquinius Priscus] and his son or grandson (for even in this there is disagreement among writers) came Servius Tullius, who, if we follow our own authorities, was the son of Ocresia, a prisoner of war; if [we follow] the Etruscans he was once a faithful comrade of Caelius Vibenna, a friend in all his adventures. And being driven out after his luck had turned, he left Etruria with the remnants of Caelius' army, occupied the Caelian hill which he named after his former leader, and, changing his name (for in Etruscan his name was Mastarna), he took the name which I have mentioned (that is, Servius Tullius) and obtained the throne to the great benefit of the state.[3]

---

[2] An extensive treatment of 'the Historiography of Etruria' can be found in Harris (1971) 4–40. But it will be clear from what follows in the text that I cannot accept the majority of Harris's conclusions. In general his approach is too sceptical. He is doubtful about the *elogia Tarquiniensia*, and attaches little value to the Etruscan researches of Cato, Varro, Verrius Flaccus, and Claudius. On the other hand he places far too much trust in the testimony of Dionysius of Halicarnassus. Harris's discussion of these sources is the least satisfactory part of what is otherwise an admirable book.

[3] *Huic [sc. Tarquinio Prisco] quoque et filio nepotiue eius (nam et hoc inter auctores discrepat) insertus Seruius Tullius, si nostros sequimur, captiua natus Ocresia, si Tuscos, Caeli quondam Viuennae sodalis fidelissimus omnisque eius casus comes, postquam uaria fortuna exactus cum omnibus reliquis Caeliani exercitus Etruria excessit, montem Caelium occupauit et a duce suo Caelio ita appellauit, mutatoque (nam Tusce Mastarna ei nomen erat) ita appellatus est, ut dixi, et regnum summa cum rei publicae utilitate optinuit.* The text is taken from *ILS* 212. For a full commentary on the Table of Claudius see Fabia (1929).

The prima facie implication of this passage is that Claudius had found the Etruscan version of the origins of Servius Tullius in an Etruscan historical book. We know that Caeles Vibenna and Mastarna figured in a popular story which was genuinely Etruscan in origin because they are portrayed in the well-known painting of the François tomb at Vulci.[4] But what is not confirmed by any independent Etruscan evidence is the equation of Mastarna with the Roman king Servius Tullius.[5]

It is possible that Servius Tullius and Mastarna really were the same person, and conceivable that the memory of this fact had been preserved by an old and authentic Etruscan tradition; but it is extremely unlikely that Etruscan tradition should have remembered something of importance to Roman history which had been completely forgotten by the Romans themselves. The Roman annalistic tradition (Claudius' *nostri*) knew nothing of Mastarna, or of his supposed identity with Servius Tullius. It is much more likely that the Etruscan story had happened to record simply that Mastarna had ruled at Rome.[6] The identification of this Mastarna with Servius Tullius, whether true or not, is likely to have been a secondary

---

[4] The best photographs of the painting are still those published in Messerschmidt (1930) plates 14–26; see also Giglioli (1935) plates cclxvi–cclxx. For a masterly interpretation of the incident shown in the picture, see Alföldi (1965) 221–8, and plates viii–xii. For the date, see now Cristofani (1967).

[5] The bibliography on this question is very extensive. My own study is based on a reading of the following: Müller–Deecke (1877) 110ff.; Schwegler (1853–76) I.717ff.; Gardthausen (1882); Körte (1897); Petersen (1899); Münzer (1898); DeSanctis (1902); Cocchia (1924); Fabia (1929) 73ff.; Scott (1929) 75ff.; Pareti (1931a) = (1958) 283ff.; Pareti (1931b) = (1958) 305ff.; Momigliano (1961) 11ff.; Heurgon (1964b) 45ff.; Alföldi (1965) 212ff.; Gjerstad (1967) 272ff.; Scullard (1967) 122ff.; Hus (1971) 102 ff.

[6] That this was the hard core of authentic tradition around which everything else was constructed is shown by the fact that Mastarna, and not his leader, the more important Caeles Vibenna, became king. This can only be understood in the context of the actual historical situation in the late sixth century BC, when Rome was not yet of overriding importance as far as the Etruscans were concerned, and could safely be left in the hands of a subordinate. To later Romans and Etruscans, and even to some modern scholars, this was not only embarrassing, but incomprehensible. It must surely explain why Claudius (or, more likely, his source) was moved to imagine the defeat and premature death of Caeles Vibenna. There was certainly no evidence to suggest that Caeles had disappeared from the scene when Mastarna came to Rome; on the contrary, there was and old native tradition that Caeles Vibenna had in fact come to Rome in person (see below p. 179).

reconstruction.[7] 'No one doubts', writes A. Alfoldi, 'that the equation of the venerable old king of the Roman legend with the Etruscan intruder is an arbitrary contamination'.[8]

There are several ways in which this contamination can be explained. It is unlikely that Claudius himself tampered with the Etruscan story by inserting his own conjectures;[9] it is more probable that he found the tradition in an already contaminated form in his source.

This might mean that Claudius' source was the work of a Roman writer, and that his knowledge of Etruscan sources was indirect. Although one has the impression that Claudius was presenting evidence which he thought would be unfamiliar to his audience of senators, there is no good reason to suppose that he was the first Roman scholar to unearth it; indeed, there is perhaps some evidence to the contrary.

Varro knew of a tradition, which was probably ancient and indigenous, that connected Caeles Vibenna, and his brother Aulus, with Rome:

In Suburanae regionis parte princeps est Caelius Mons a Caele Vibenna, Tusco duce nobili, qui cum sua manu dicitur Romulo uenisse auxilio contra Tatium regem.[10]

---

[7] Momigliano (1961) 14.

[8] Alföldi (1965) 213. For Alfoldi arbitrary contamination automatically suggested the hand of his historical forger Fabius Pictor (133–4). But whatever view is taken of Alföldi's general interpretation of Fabius Pictor, it is clear that the identification of Mastarna with Servius Tullius cannot go back to him, since the main line of the Roman tradition (Claudius' *nostri*) knew nothing of Mastarna or of his alleged identity with Servius Tullius. Cf. Momigliano (1967b) 211. Alföldi argued that the tradition about Mastarna is reflected in D. Hal. *A.R.* 3.65.6, where Servius Tullius is described as ξένος καὶ ἄπολις {foreigner and exile} (cf. Harris (1971) 26). But this interpretation must be wrong. The description of Servius Tullius as a foreign exile is entirely compatible with the old Latin tradition (which Dionysius follows elsewhere: see 4.1.1, etc.) that he was the son of Tullius of Corniculum. Cf. Gjerstad (1967) 274.

[9] It would have been uncharacteristic of the honest and pedantic emperor who in the same sentence had observed the discrepancy between authorities on the relationship between the two Tarquins (cf. Momigliano (1961) 15). The introduction of Mastarna was not necessary for the validity of his argument that Roman history could show numerous examples of foreigners being admitted to high office; the Latin tradition of Servius Tullius as a foreign exile (see previous n.) was adequate on its own for this purpose. Cf. the speech of Canuleius in Livy 4.3–4, on which Claudius' speech is modelled.

[10] Varro *LL* 5.46; Serv. ad Verg. *Aen.* 5.560; D. Hal. *A.R.* 2.36.2, 2.37.2.

In the section of the Suburan region, the first shrine is located on the Caelian Hill, named from Caelius Vibenna, a noble Tuscan leader, who is said to have come with his followers to bring help to Romulus against King Tatius.

The interesting feature of this passage is the chronology. Varro's statement that Caeles Vibenna was a contemporary of Romulus obviously conflicts with the version of Claudius, who placed Caeles Vibenna and Mastarna in the time of the Tarquins and made Mastarna the successor of Tarquin the Elder. It appears that Varro either had no knowledge of the story given by Claudius or chose to reject it.

The earliest preserved reference to Mastarna in a Roman work is in a statement of Verrius Flaccus (ap. Festus p. 486L), and even this is based on a restoration of a missing part of the text:

Many writers say that the Tuscus Vicus was named after those Etruscans who remained in Rome after king Porsenna had abandoned his siege; and they [who remained] lived in a place which had been allotted to them. Or [it is so called] because it was occupied by the Volcentane brothers Caeles and Aulus Vibenna, who, they say, came to Rome with Maxtarna against king Tarquinius. (... *aut quod Volci]entes fratres Caeles et [A.] Vibenn[ae quos dicunt ad regem] Tarquinium Romam se cum Max[tarna contulisse eum incolue]rint*).[11]

Unfortunately we cannot be certain what the original text really said. But the reading Max[tarna...] seems to me to derive some support from the fact that Verrius Flaccus dated the arrival of the Vibennae in the reign of Tarquinius. The significance of this becomes evident when we consider the difficulties in which Verrius Flaccus found himself as a result of this chronology. We learn from another passage of Festus that Verrius was unwilling to reject altogether the opinion of Varro that the Mons Caelius was named after a contemporary of Romulus. For this man to have been the same Caeles Vibenna would have been chronologically impossible, so Verrius postulated the existence of two distinct persons, both named Caeles. Caeles Vibenna, he decided, was the man who came to Rome in the time of Tarquin the elder, while Romulus was helped by 'a certain Caeles from Etruria' (i.e. *not* the famous Vibenna):

---

[11] I have given the text as restored by Garrucci. But compare Muller's text: ... *regem] Tarquinium Romam secum max[ime adduxisse colue]rint.* (Festus, p. 356 M., 486 L.).

Caelius Mons dictus est a Caele quodam ex Etruria qui Romulo auxilium aduersum Sabinos praebuit eo quod in eo domicilium habuit. (Festus p. 38L)

The Mons Caelius is so-called from a certain Caeles from Etruria, who offered Romulus assistance against the Sabines, because he had his home on it.

If Verrius was prepared to go to such lengths to uphold the version of Varro, one wonders why he did not accept it *in toto*. The only possible explanation is that he had a very good reason to connect the brothers Vibenna with Tarquin. We must therefore assume that Verrius had access to new information about the Vibennae and their relations with Rome.[12] Verrius, we know, wrote a work on Etruscan matters—*Res Etruscae*[13]—and it seems reasonable to suppose that his new information about the Vibennae came from Etruscan sources, consulted while he was preparing his work on the Etruscans. This conclusion is supported by the independent evidence of the François tomb painting, which shows that the original Etruscan tradition synchronized these events with the age of the Tarquins, because one of the persons shown in the picture is Cneve Tarchunies Rumach.[14] Claudius' version of the story is rather different from that of Verrius Flaccus because the latter brought Caeles Vibenna to Rome, whereas in Claudius Mastarna arrived after the death of Caeles. This might have been the emperor's own conjecture, or possibly the interpretation of a writer intermediate between Verrius Flaccus and Claudius. If a Roman author was responsible for the equation of Mastarna and Servius Tullius, his purpose must have been to reconcile the Etruscan tradition with the Roman, and to admit Mastarna into the ranks of the Roman kings without causing too much of an upset to the traditional Roman picture of the monarchic age.[15]

[12] Cf. Münzer (1898) 605–6.

[13] *HRR* II.78–9; cf. Schanz–Hosius (1922–35) II.366–7 for discussion of Verrius Flaccus' *Res Etruscae*.

[14] That is, Cnaeus Tarquinius of Rome. The praenomen Cnaeus means that he is not to be identified with either of the Tarquins who were traditionally kings of Rome, and who were both called Lucius. But he must have been a member of the same family. Cf. Hus (1971) 104.

[15] Cf. Momigliano (1961) 14.

But it is equally possible that the identification of the two persons appeared for the first time in the work of an Etruscan historian. It cannot be denied that the result of the contamination was rather flattering to the Etruscans, and it could conceivably have originated because of the desire on the part of an Etruscan writer to 'etruscanize' important parts of Roman history, and in this case to claim as an Etruscan one of the best loved of the Roman kings, the creator of the most important Roman political institutions.[16]

It is worth mentioning that Claudius was in an exceptionally good position to consult Etruscan sources directly. This has been well argued by Heurgon.[17] By means of a prosopographical survey, Heurgon demonstrated that Claudius was closely connected by personal ties with the leading Etruscan aristocracy of his day; his first wife, Urgulanilla, came from a family which had maintained its national character by alliances of marriage with other families of Etruscan origin. The remarkable fact that these noble families had managed to survive for so long, and the tenacity with which they had held on to their Etruscan identity, might lead one to conjecture that they were a vehicle for the preservation and transmission of their national historical tradition. And it so happens that the conjecture can be confirmed. The *elogia Tarquiniensia*, which will be discussed more fully below (pp. 186–93), provide independent evidence of the fact that Etruscan noble families, even in the time of the Principate, kept alive the memory of their national history, and publicly paraded the achievements of their ancestors. In these circumstances, Claudius could hardly have ignored native sources when collecting material for his *Tyrrhenica*. Heurgon protested against the notion that Claudius relied solely on the reports of Roman antiquarian writers:

---

[16] Thus Münzer (1898) 610 ff.; Fabia (1929) 76. Of course, this interpretation cannot be considered anything more than a hypothesis; we do not have any certain knowledge of the motives which led to this manipulation. Perhaps the original Etruscan tradition recorded that Mastarna had replaced a king Tarquinius (the François tomb painting shows the death of Tarchunies Rumach), in which case he will have been identified with Servius Tullius simply because he could not have been identified with anyone else (cf. Momigliano (1961) 14). But this need not affect the basic argument unduly. Scullard remarks: 'it is sufficient to note the proud claim of Vulci to have imposed a king on Rome' ((1967) 123).

[17] Heurgon (1953a).

Indeed! Grandson-in-law, son-in-law, brother-in-law of some of the representatives of the Etruscan aristocracy of the time, whose scrupulous endogamy indicates their ethnic haughtiness and their loyalty to their memories, he had only to draw directly from their sources.[18]

But the precise character of the Etruscan sources, on which the equation Mastarna–Servius Tullius was based, is a matter for conjecture. It need not have been a written historical work. It could have been a book or document of some other kind; but it is equally likely that the original Etruscan source was nothing more than a firmly established and widely diffused oral tradition.

We know that the legend of the Vibennae was popular and widespread, since traces of it are found not only in the painting from the François tomb at Vulci and in the native Roman tradition,[19] but also on funerary urns from near Chiusi,[20] and on a bronze mirror from Bolsena.[21] The name *Aules V(i)pinas* appears on a fifth-century red-figure cup by an Etruscan artist who imitated an Attic cup of the school of Duris;[22] and in a temple at Veii a votive offering was found in the form of a bucchero vase bearing the inscription *Auile Vipiiennas*; this object is dated to the middle of the sixth century BC, and was perhaps offered by Aulus Vibenna in person.[23]

---

[18] Heurgon (1953a) 97. It is worth mentioning in this context that the Claudian *gens* had special connections with Etruria which went back a long way into the past. In the fourth century BC we hear of a certain C. Claudius, *Caere educatus apud hospites* (Liv. 9.36.3). Epigraphic evidence dating back as far as the fifth century BC has recently confirmed this. See Pallotino (1969), and especially Heurgon (1973) 551.

[19] The Roman legend emerges not only from the derivation of the name Caelius Mons from Caeles Vibenna, but also from the popular etymology of the word Capitolium, interpreted by the Romans as *caput Oli*; this derivation, which appeared already in Fabius Pictor (*HRR* F 12), refers to an indigenous Roman legend of a Vulcentane person named Olus, who is almost certainly to be identified with Aulus Vibenna. Cf. Alföldy (1965) 216ff.

[20] Giglioli (1935) plates ccxcviii, 1; ccciv, 3; Brunn–Körte (1870–1916) II.254ff.; Messerschmidt (1930) 79.

[21] *British Museum Catalogue:* Bronzes no. 633; Gerhard–Körte (1840–97) V, plate 127 and pp. 166ff.; Messerschmidt (1930) 77.

[22] *Corpus Vasorum Antiquorum* (France) n. 16 (Musée Rodin pl. 28–30); Beazley (1947) 25ff.

[23] Pallotino (1954) no. 35, and see Buonamici (1939); also Heurgon (1966). But notice the judicious remarks of Bickerman (1969) 397.

Thus, the presence of the brothers, or at least of traditions about them, is attested at Vulci, Rome, Clusium, Veii, and Volsinii. It could be fairly said that the legend of the brothers Vibenna is better attested in Etruria than any other native story. It has even been suggested that Caeles and Aulus Vibenna, and other *condottieri* of the same type, were celebrated in popular poetry;[24] that their exploits formed a widely known popular tradition can scarcely be doubted.

But it is likely that by the first century AD such Etruscan legends had been distorted by the influence of the Roman historical tradition. We might reasonably assume, *a priori*, that after the Roman conquest of Etruria the Etruscans' view of their own past developed a tendency to exaggerate the importance of events in the archaic period of their history which involved the Romans, and to stress the part they themselves had played in the formation and growth of Rome. This could explain the identification of Mastarna with Servius Tullius. There is no reason, therefore, why we should not take Claudius' phrase *si Tuscos (sequimur)* at its face value. But it does not necessarily furnish a prima facie argument for the existence of Etruscan historical literature.

III

The evidence of Varro, however, presents us with something more substantial. The passage in question derives from Censorinus (*De die natali* 17.6):

Quare in Tuscis historiis, quae octauo eorum saeculo scriptae sunt, ut Varro testatur, et quot numera saecula ei genti data sint et transactorum singula quanta fuerint quibusue ostentis eorum exitus designati sint continetur.

And so the Etruscan histories which, as Varro testifies, were written in the eighth *saeculum* of the Etruscans, contain how many *saecula* were given to that people, how long each of the *saecula* past lasted, and by what prodigies their end was marked.

---

[24] Heurgon (1964b) 46.

This passage cannot be treated in quite the same way as the extract of the Table of Claudius, who was probably referring to oral tradition,[25] because Varro stated explicitly that the *Tuscae historiae* were written (*scriptae sunt*). A consideration of the purely internal indications of the passage as it stands suggests the following observations:

The author of the *Tuscae historiae* is not named, which is odd if a literary composition is referred to. This implies one of two things:

(i) Varro was referring not to a single book but to a group of works by several authors. This explanation is advanced by Heurgon, who adds in its favour that Varro spoke of *Tuscae historiae* in the plural— which may not be a very compelling argument.[26] Niebuhr seems to have taken a similar view, for he postulated a series of Etruscan annalists, akin to the Roman.[27]

(ii) Alternatively, the absence of a writer's name might suggest that Varro was not in fact referring to a literary work in the normal sense, but rather to a non-literary document or group of documents, similar perhaps to the Roman *Fasti* or *Annales Maximi*.[28] Any difficulty there might be in Varro's statement that they were written in the eighth Etruscan *saeculum* can be overcome if we assume that the documents were first collected and published in the eighth *saeculum*, which was roughly equivalent to the second century BC.[29] This date, vague though it is, inevitably calls to mind the development of

---

[25] The fact that Claudius' story about Mastarna and Servius Tullius was independent of Varro might mean that it was not recorded in the *Tuscae historiae* which Varro had consulted. This cannot be certain, however, because we do not know whether Varro had read the *Tuscae historiae* right through for himself, or simply acquainted himself with that part of it which interested him. Cf. Heurgon (1964b) 248–9.

[26] Heurgon (1964b) 249. The use of the plural *historiae* to describe the contents of a single historical work was common in Hellenistic literature. But Heurgon's point is stronger when taken in combination with the fact that the *Tuscae historiae* are anonymous.

[27] Niebuhr (1853) I.384.

[28] Cf. Nogara (1933) 423.

[29] The eighth Etruscan *saeculum* ended in 88 BC (Plut. *Sull.* 7), but we do not know when it began. But if we take the average of the previous three *saecula* (the first four, one hundred years each, are clearly suspect), we arrive at a figure of *c.* one hundred and twenty years, which cannot be far wrong. The possibility of a connection between the beginning of the eighth *saeculum* and the disturbances in Etruria in 208–207 BC has been examined by van Son (1963). For practical purposes it will be sufficient to regard the eighth *saeculum* as roughly congruent with our second century BC. On the *saecula* in general see Thulin (1906–9) III.63ff.

Roman historiography, and especially the publication of the *Annales Maximi*, probably by the Pontifex Maximus Mucius Scaevola at the end of the second century.

The possibility of a connection between the *Annales Maximi* and the *Tuscae historiae* has sometimes been suggested, notably by Heurgon, who argues that the one might have given rise to the other—i.e. that the *Tuscae historiae* were produced in emulation of the Roman *Annales Maximi*.[30]

The historical consciousness of the Romans, which awoke at the beginning of the second century BC, and the concentration of attention by Roman historians on the history of their own city, might have impelled the other Italian peoples to undertake an examination of their own past; the possibility cannot be excluded that the Etruscans began to write local histories in order to impress on the Romans the fact that their achievements in early times were no less great than those of Rome. This kind of composition could have been inspired by Cato's *Origines*, written in the middle of the second century, a work which differed from its predecessors in that it dealt with the history of the Italian peoples as well as of Rome; Cato was the first to treat the early history of Italy as a subject worthy of independent study, regardless of whether or not it had a bearing on the doings of the Romans.[31]

The possibility that the *Tuscae historiae* were the work of a Roman, writing in Latin, who reconstructed the Etruscan past for Roman readers, seems to be ruled out by the absence of an author's name, which is surely evidence of their Etruscan origin.

But there is one further possibility. It is important to realize that the passage in question is not strictly speaking a 'fragment' of Varro at all, because it does not reproduce Varro's exact words. There must be a chance that Censorinus misunderstood what he had read in Varro. It is quite clear that Varro referred to a written composition,

---

[30] Heurgon (1964b) 249; Müller–Deecke (1877) II.298. Harris misses the point of the comparison with the *Annales Maximi* when he asserts 'there is not even any evidence or likelihood that the *Tuscae historiae* had an annalistic character' ((1971) 12).

[31] The most sensitive treatment of Cato's attitude to non-Roman Italy is probably that of De Sanctis (1953) 63ff.; also notice Klingner (1961), esp. 59. I know of no adequate discussion of the sources and methods of research employed by Cato in his account of early Italian history. Further bibliography on Cato's *Origines* in general can be found in Timpe's recent paper, Timpe (1970/71).

but it may be that he was actually speaking about some other kind of work; he may, for example, have written *libri Etrusci*—which Censorinus understood to be historical because of the nature of the passage quoted. Varro may have derived his knowledge of the Etruscan *saecula* from those books whose existence is well attested, namely the sacred books containing the body of doctrine known as the *Etrusca disciplina*.

Clearly none of these hypothetical reconstructions can be confirmed for the simple reason that no direct evidence exists whatsoever apart from the single passage under discussion. However, it seems to me that whatever view one takes of the *Tuscae historiae*—a publication of non-literary documents, a literary reconstruction of Etruscan history from a variety of sources, or a misquoted reference to the books of the *Etrusca disciplina*—one fundamental question is in any case bound to present itself.

Whatever may have been the precise nature of the *Tuscae historiae*, it is clearly necessary to ask what sort of primary historical evidence they were based on. An answer to this question might enable us to obtain a more precise idea of their character, because the form and content of a historical work are clearly dependent to some extent on the nature of the sources which the historian has at his disposal. The question can be put thus: if an Etruscan scholar were to try to write a local history, where would he be able to find the necessary raw materials? This question still has meaning even if we take the most sceptical view possible of Varro's mention of *Tuscae historiae*. Varro (and Claudius) may or may not mean that Etruscan history was established in a literary tradition; in any case we would want to know whether there existed in the Etruscan cities any systematic documentary records containing detailed and authentic historical information.

IV

Evidence for written records of an historical nature, going back to a very early date, is provided, in the first place, by the so-called *elogia Tarquiniensia*. These inscriptions were discovered shortly after the war during excavations at Tarquinia, and since then they have been discussed many times.[32] Written in Latin, they were at once recognized as *elogia*, set up in honour of famous persons from the past history of the city.

The style of lettering suggests that the inscriptions are of early imperial date, and this is supported by the fact that they are similar in character to the *elogia* set up at Rome in the Forum of Augustus in 2 BC.[33] *Elogia* of the same period have been found elsewhere in Italy, notably at Arezzo and Pompeii.

The distinctive feature of the *elogia Tarquiniensia* is that they celebrate persons and events of the history of Tarquinia, in contrast to the series of famous Romans, from Aeneas to the end of the Republic, honoured in Rome and other Italian cities. It is clear that at Tarquinia feelings of local patriotism were still strong even at the time of the early Roman Empire.

As far as we are concerned,[34] the significant implications of the *elogia* of Tarquinia can be summarized as follows: first, some of the inscriptions refer to events which took place at a very early date.[35] One of them[36] mentions a king of Caere, which indicates that the person who is the subject of the *elogium* must have lived at a time when there were still kings at Caere; the date of the fall of the monarchy at Caere is not known, but it is probably to be placed during the general constitutional crisis which affected the Etruscan

---

[32] First published by Romanelli (1948) 260ff.; discussion in Heurgon (1950) and (1951); Pallotino (1950–51); Kahrstedt (1953); Vetter (1955) 59ff.; Della Corte (1955–6); Lamprechts (1955) 102 ff.; Heurgon (1964b) 256ff.; Alföldi (1965) 212ff.; Scullard (1967) 91ff.; Torelli (1968); Heurgon (1969b); Harris (1971) 28ff. Cf. below, n. 34.

[33] Degrassi (1937) 1ff.

[34] This is not the place for a full discussion of these texts. For epigraphic details, see Pallottino (1950–1); Vetter (1955); Heurgon (1969b). Prof. M. Torelli has discovered some more material which will increase our knowledge considerably. A full treatment is promised in his book *Elogia Tarquiniensia* {see Addendum}. For the present, see Torelli (1974–5) 53ff.

[35] The idea that one of the *elogia* (Romanelli no. 44) concerned Tarchon the founder of the city, cannot be maintained. As Heurgon (1969b) has shown, the letters '…CHO…', on which this interpretation is based, could equally well form part of one of several known Etruscan names, for example Holchonius. The Tarchon theory is finally condemned by the presence in the inscription of a word beginning with the letters 'HAM…'. This can hardly be anything other that the beginning of the name Hamilcar.

[36] Romanelli (1948) 266, no. 77.

cities at the end of the sixth century BC, and which is symbolized in our tradition by the expulsion of the Tarquins from Rome.[37] At any rate we know that most of the Etruscan cities were governed by republican constitutions by the end of the fifth century, because Livy says that their hatred of monarchy was one of the reasons why the other Etruscan cities did not send aid to Veii, where the monarchy had been restored in 403 BC.[38] Another *elogium*[39] concerns a Tarquinian magistrate who *primus... Etruscorum mare... traiecit* {first crossed the sea of the Etruscans}. However this sentence is to be restored,[40] and whatever may be the historical implications of *primus*,[41] this maritime expedition must surely have taken place at a relatively early date, perhaps in the late fifth or fourth century BC.[42]

[37] Mazzarino (1945) 95ff.

[38] Liv. 5.1.3.

[39] Romanelli, no. 48.

[40] Pallottino's version ((1950–1) 160–3) retains the simple sense of what is already preserved; taking *traiecit* in its transitive sense, he restores: *primus [trans] Etruscorum mare c[lassem] traiecit* {he first brought a fleet across the sea of the Etruscans}. The difficulty is that *Etruscorum mare* is an odd way of describing the Tyrrhenian Sea (normally *Mare Tuscum*). Heurgon ((1951) 130) proposes: *primus [ducum] Etruscorum mare c[um milite] traiecit* {Of Etruscan commanders, he first crossed the sea with infantry}, so that the originality of the enterprise is expressed in the words *primus cum milite*, rather than by *primus mare traiecit*. He thus avoids the chronological difficulty of *primus*, which, if taken literally, would date the expedition to prehistoric times (see below, n. 41).

[41] The Etruscans are recorded in Greek sources as being active as 'pirates' around Sicily as early as the eighth century BC (Str. 6.2.2; Ephorus *FGrHist* 70 F 137). Thus *primus... Etruscorum mare... traiecit* can scarcely be taken at its face value, especially in view of the fact that the subject of the *elogium* was *praetor*—i.e. a republican magistrate. Hence Heurgon's suggested reading *primus c[um milite]*. More satisfactory, it seems to me, is the view of Pallottino (1950–51), followed by Della Corte ((1955–6) 75) that *primus* is little more than a commonplace, often found in *elogia*, and is not to be taken very seriously.

[42] Heurgon ((1951a) 132ff.), following a suggestion of J. Bayet, proposed that the praetor was the leader of a band of mercenaries; we find Etruscan mercenaries fighting in Sicily for Hamilcar (cf. above, n. 35) against the forces of Agathocles in 311 BC (Diod. 19.106.2); and Agathocles himself employed Etruscan mercenaries in 310 (Diod. 20.64.1), and again in 296 (20.64.3). F. Miltner (cited by Vetter (1955) 62) refers the expedition to the year 307, when eighteen Etruscan warships went to the aid of Agathocles (Diod. 20.61.6–8). Della Corte ((1955–6) 76ff.) favours the events of 414–413 BC, when an Etruscan contingent was present at Syracuse on the Athenian side (Thuc. 6.88.6, 7.53.2, 7.57.11). A full list of occasions on which the Etruscans intervened in Sicily is given by Heurgon (1951) 130ff.

Second, the *elogia* contain detailed information about the careers of the persons they honour; let us consider first the career of the subject of no. 77, which we know to be early; the person or persons who composed the text in the first century AD knew not only that this man had had dealings with the king of Caere and had fought a war against Arretium; they also knew the number of fortresses he had captured from the Latins (or Arretines).[43] The last line, where the restorations must be essentially correct, reads:

[de Arre]tinis nouem o[ppida cepit]

He captured nine towns from the Arretines

or

[de La]tinis nouem o[ppida cepit]

He captured nine towns from the Latins

Detailed information of this kind can hardly be attributed solely to oral tradition, and the general character of the *elogia* seems to suggest that they were based on written sources. This impression emerges even more strongly from the best preserved and most informative of the *elogia*—no. 48.[44] This concerns a man who had twice held the office of *praetor*,[45] who had led an expedition to Sicily, and who had been awarded a golden crown. The interesting point about this text, as Pallottino has emphasized,[46] is that the *praetor* is not credited with

---

[43] The restoration *de La]tinis* is more probable than *de Arre]tinis* because the city of Arretium is referred to in the previous line of the text, and would be unlikely to be repeated. See Heurgon (1964b) 258; Alföldi (1965) 208.

[44] The text reads:

V.....R SPUR....
      LARTIS F.
PR. II.. MAGISTRATU AL.....
EXERCITUM HABUIT ALTE.....
SICILIAM DUXIT PRIMUS.....   5
ETRUSCORUM MARE C......
TRAIECIT A QU.........
AUREA OB VI.........
        (Romanelli, no. 48).

[45] The *interpretatio Latina* of the Etruscan title *zilath*. Kahrstedt's arguments against this are not convincing ((1953) 68ff.).

[46] Pallottino (1950–1) 161, 164.

any positive achievement. We are told simply that he commanded an army and led an expedition to Sicily. No battle is mentioned, nor is there room in the lacunae for such a mention to be restored.[47] It is extremely unlikely, for that reason, that a victory was referred to in the last line of the text.[48] It seems, then, that the *elogium* is dealing with a *praetor* who did nothing in his first, and little of any real significance in his second period of office. And yet, despite the passage of several centuries,[49] the compilers of the *elogium* in the first century AD were able to enumerate the details of his career. The inevitable conclusion is that this information was recorded in a written document or collection of documents, as there is no other way in which such unmemorable events could have been handed down. Moreover, the relative insignificance of the achievements attributed to this Etruscan magistrate constitutes a telling argument against the only possible alternative—that the *elogia* were simply the product of free invention.

It can be said, therefore, that the *elogia Tarquiniensia* must imply the existence of written documents surviving from a very early period. These documents must have recorded the names of magistrates and at least something about what they did. It is tempting to think in terms of a local chronicle originally in the form of a list of magistrates with additional notes attached to the names, comparable to the Roman *Fasti* (perhaps later to be established in a literary form, as the *Tuscae historiae*?). A chronicle of this type could undoubtedly have furnished the necessary material for the compilers of the *elogia Tarquiniensia*. We shall see, moreover, that there is some independent evidence from Tarquinia for a list of eponymous magistrates, the necessary precondition of any type of yearly chronicle.

There is, however, a second possibility. Some evidence has recently come to light which suggests that the major sources of the *elogia*

---

[47] Heurgon's restoration...*a[d Caere?] exercitum habuit*...in lines 3–4 is now refuted by the fragment identified by Torelli (see below, n. 50) which shows traces of the top of a vertical stroke after the A at the end of line 3. Whatever this letter was (L?), it cannot have been a D.

[48] *ob ui[rtutem*...is better than *ob ui[ctoriam*...

[49] The date of the events must at any rate be earlier than the incorporation of the Etruscan cities in the Roman confederacy; cf. above, n. 42.

Tarquiniensia may have been private archives of individual aristocratic families rather than an official public record. This conclusion is based on what is now known of the motives which led the citizens of Tarquinia to set up the *elogia* in the first place.

In a recent article,[50] M. Torelli published a new fragment of the most important of the *elogia* (no. 48). This fragment revealed part of the name of the person who was the subject of the *elogium*; it is now beyond doubt that he was a member of the *gens* Spurinnia.

Pallottino had already observed[51] that several of the fragments published by Romanelli bore the name of members of this *gens*,[52] and he had suggested that they too might have been fragments of *elogia*. Torelli's discovery seems to confirm this hypothesis, and one is led on to imagine a series of *elogia* enumerating the achievements of members of this family.[53] The significance of the Spurinnae is that they were an important family at the time of the early empire: one of them, Vestricius Spurinna, was a man of consular rank whose career is relatively well known.[54] If we add to this the fact that another *elogium* from Tarquinia bears the name of a Caesennius,[55] another influential family during the Principate, several members of which reached the consulship,[56] we can begin to see the emergence of a pattern. For this evidence implies that the publication of the *elogia* was not simply the product of sentimental recollections of past glories by the people of Tarquinia,[57] nor merely the result of research undertaken by antiquarian scholars;[58] rather, it seems that the *elogia* were set up in honour of the ancestors of the leading Tarquinian *gentes* of the time—more specifically, of those families which formed part of the new senatorial aristocracy of the early Roman Empire.

These Etruscan senators, who were relatively new arrivals on the Roman scene, clearly felt a desire to distinguish themselves from other new men who owed their position to promotion from a more humble level; it seems not unreasonable to suppose that the *elogia Tarquiniensia* were set up by men who wanted to show the Romans that they were not

---

[50] Torelli (1968).   [51] Pallottino (1951) 149.
[52] Romanelli, nos. 45, 46, 47.   [53] Torelli (1968) 467.
[54] Schuster (1958); cf. Torelli (1968) 468.   [55] Romanelli, no. 43.
[56] Cf. *PIR*² II.32ff., s. v. *Caesennius*.
[57] Cf. Kahrstedt (1953) 69; Pallottino (1951) 164.
[58] Cf. Heurgon (1951) 126; Heurgon (1953a) 92; Pallottino (1951) 151.

'new men' in the ordinary sense: they wished to emphasize their ancient and noble family origins, and to show that their ancestors were no less illustrious than those of the old Roman nobility.[59]

The possibility that the leading Tarquinian aristocrats of the day undertook the publication of the *elogia* strongly suggests that the information they contain came from the private archives of those families. In Rome, family archives consisted of portraits of a nobleman's ancestors which were regularly produced at family funerals.[60] Accompanying these portraits were documents in which a record was kept of their magistracies and achievements, as Pliny tells us (*HN* 35.6–7):

tabulina codicibus implebantur, et monimentis rerum magistratu gestarum.

the rooms were filled with documents and with records of the things accomplished in his magistracy.

Aulus Gellius also tells us that he himself was able to consult the records of the *gens Porcia* when he was checking up on the ramifications of the family of Cato the Censor:

. . . cum et laudationes funebres et librum commentarium de familia Porcia legeremus.[61]

. . . when we were reading the funeral eulogies and the *commentarius* on the Porcian family.

The *laudatio funebris* was an encomiastic speech delivered at a family funeral—a ceremony which Polybius describes for us.[62] The speech contained an account, according to Polybius, of τὰς ἀρετὰς καὶ τὰς ἐπιτετευγμένας ἐν τῷ ζῆν πράξεις {the virtues and successful

---

[59] It is surely relevant to observe that the same sort of efforts were made by Maecenas, a new name in the highest circles at Rome, but a proud descendant of the most important family in his native Etruscan city of Arretium. Horace (*Sat.* 1.6.1–4) writes: *Non quia, Maecenas, Lydorum quidquid Etruscos / incoluit finis, nemo generosior est te / nec quod auus tibi maternus fuit atque paternus / olim qui magnis legionibus imperitarent*, etc. {of all the Lydians settled in Tuscan lands, none is of nobler birth than you, Maecenas, and your grandfathers on both mother's and father's side once commanded great legions, etc.} (cf. Hor. *Odes* 3.29.1; Prop. 3.9.1).

[60] The practice of setting up *elogia* is normally thought to have originated with the *imagines* and the *tituli* that went with them, which were placed in the *atria* of noble houses. See Mommsen, *CIL* I 282; C. Hülsen, *CIL* I² 189; von Premerstein (1905) 2443; Degrassi (1937) ix; Beloch (1926) 97.

[61] Gell. 13.20.17.

[62] Pol. 6.53–4; see Marquardt (1886) I.357–60; Schanz–Hosius (1922–35) I.38–40.

achievements of his life} of the deceased. This is borne out by a papyrus fragment, recently published by L. Koenen,[63] which contains a Greek translation of the *laudatio funebris* delivered by Augustus at the funeral of Agrippa. This document is important for the student of historiography because it shows that a *laudatio funebris* gave an account of the public career of the dead man with very much more chronological and substantial detail than Polybius' ἀρετὰς καὶ πράξεις might suggest. A family archive, therefore, consisted mainly of a series of former *laudationes*, as Gellius informs us, whose contents must have provided a major historical source.

Obviously, records of this type could have provided the necessary material for the *elogia Tarquiniensia*; there is no reason why the noble families in the Etruscan cities should not have kept records similar to the Roman. The *elogia* in themselves show that a desire to glorify one's ancestors was characteristic of the aristocratic *gentes*, and they can surely be considered strong evidence for the preservation of substantial family archives.

V

I have already mentioned the possibility of local chronicles in the Etruscan cities, and it will be well to consider this subject further. Here again we have no direct evidence, but if we postulate, *a priori*, the existence of local Etruscan chronicles on the Greek pattern, it is necessary to examine the evidence for signs of conditions which the writing of local chronicles inevitably presupposes; this means, above all, a systematic method of recording the passage of time. The fundamental basis of a Greek local chronicle is a documentary list of eponymous officials, together with brief annotations of annual events, usually of a perfunctory character, which concern the office whose representatives are enumerated as eponyms—an activity which develops into the recording of annual events on an increasing scale until a regular chronicle is formed.[64]

[63] Koenen (1970).   [64] Cf. Laqueur (1926).

Unhappily we know very little about the method of measuring time in Etruria, and the evidence we have is not conclusive. But there are two important pieces of evidence which show that eponymous dating was probably used in at least some of the Etruscan cities. This has been argued by E. Vetter,[65] on the evidence of inscriptions from the tomba degli Scudi at Tarquinia, and has since been generally accepted.[66] A painting from the tomb shows a demon writing on a diptych (two tablets joined together), and the text which appears on it reads:

zilci Velus Hulchniesi Larth Velchas Velthurs Aprthnalc clan sacnisa thui eith suthith acazr.[67]

The meaning of this text is well enough established as:

In the magistracy of Vel Hulchnie, Larth son of Velthur and Aprthni received in this tomb the funeral honours.[68]

This is undoubtedly a clear instance of dating by means of an eponymous magistrate. It may be objected that this could be an isolated case which does not necessarily imply the widespread use—even in the city of Tarquinii—of eponymous dating. But it must be realized that the eponymous method cannot allow of isolated usage, because dating by the name of a magistrate is meaningless in chronological terms if that magistrate cannot readily be related to a yearly list of magistrates. Mere names on their own cannot indicate duration of time or relative chronology. In other words, the text quoted above must surely indicate that a list of annual eponymous magistrates existed in Tarquinia.

Further evidence of the use of eponymous dating by the Etruscans is furnished by the now famous Pyrgi inscription. The text, which is a temple dedication, mentions the ruler of Caere, Thefarie Velianas,[69] and states that the temple was dedicated in his third year. It seems to

[65] Vetter (1940) 168.

[66] Pallottino (1940); id. (1955/6) 50ff.; Heurgon (1957) 85; id. (1961) 273–4; Lambrechts (1955) 97ff.

[67] Pallottino (1954) no. 98.

[68] Heurgon (1964b) 219.

[69] It is uncertain whether he was king or magistrate. The Phoenician text says that he was king (*melek*), but the original Etruscan has *zilath*. He had been in power for three years, which means either that he had been elected for three years in succession, or that he was a long-term magistrate, analogous to the ten-year archons at Athens.

indicate, therefore, that at Caere during this period (the early fifth century BC), events were dated by regnal (or magisterial) years. This method, if continued, inevitably develops into normal eponymous dating with the introduction of annual magistrates in place of kings (or long-term magistrates). Again, if there is evidence at Caere for the use of eponymous dating, the inevitable conclusion is that there existed a list of eponymous magistrates. The existence of a list might also suggest the existence of a chronicle, although this cannot yet be confirmed by any evidence. Nevertheless, a list of magistrates is a vitally important historical document and is in itself a primitive form of chronicle.

Equally interesting, however, are certain indications that the Etruscans had a system of dating other than the use of eponyms. The only possible alternative to the eponymous method is the use of an *era*— that is to say, the dating of events by the number of years before or after an epochal event. In Etruria, the era is to be connected with the system of *saecula*. In simple terms, the *saeculum* was conceived of as being concurrent with the lifetime of a person; a *saeculum* was reckoned to end with the death of the last surviving person to have been alive at the time when the *saeculum* began. The Etruscan nation was thought to have been destined to last for ten *saecula*.

Such a system obviously required the recording of the passage of time, and, in view of the religious character of the concept of *saecula*, it would seem that the business of recording time was supervised by priests. But the most interesting fact about the *saecula* is that the majority of our knowledge is derived from Varro, and from the very same passage in which he refers to *Tuscae historiae*. This obviously suggests that the *Tuscae historiae* were arranged within a 'saecular' framework: that is to say, their chronology took the form of an indication of which year of which *saeculum* saw the occurrence of a given event. Exactly comparable in this respect is the Greek system of Olympiads; and, as with the Greeks, it is quite possible that the Etruscans used two chronological systems—the 'saecular' and the eponymous—side by side.

The supposition that the *Tuscae historiae* were arranged according to *saecula* cannot be certain because the passage of Varro cannot be said to imply it directly; but the possibility is nevertheless strong. Moreover, the passage is bound to suggest that the *Tuscae historiae* were connected in some way with the Etruscan religion in general, and it raises the question, to be discussed below, of whether or not the recording of time by means of *saecula* also involved the recording of events—i.e. the keeping of a priestly chronicle.

VI

The content of the 'fragment' of Varro inevitably suggests a connection between the *Tuscae historiae*, whatever they were, and the *Etrusca disciplina*. The relationship is strongly emphasized by Heurgon, whose opinion of the *Tuscae historiae*, as far as I understand it, is that they were so closely dependent on the *Etrusca disciplina* that they can be regarded as part of the sacred literature of the Etruscans, along with the *libri rituales*. He writes:

The anonymous *Tuscae historiae* which we know of through Varro also enter into the category of sacred literature . . . Everything gives us to understand that the original text was in Etruscan, like the other *libri rituales*.

and again:

The Etruscan histories which had come to the notice of Varro . . . [were] . . . closely dependent on the *Etrusca disciplina*.[70]

Whether or not Heurgon's remarks are valid, the question they imply is an important one. One wants to know if the *Etrusca disciplina*, which incorporated a body of sacred texts, some of which undoubtedly contained archaic material, was instrumental in preserving historical tradition.

If the *Tuscae historiae* are in any sense a true parallel of the Roman *Annales Maximi*,[71] then we must presume that the priests in the Etruscan cities kept an annual record. At Rome the pontifical *tabulae* were connected with the calendar, which was supervised by the pontiffs; the most plausible reconstruction of their character is that the *tabula apud pontificem maximum* was a publication of the calendar—divided into months and days—on which the festivals and

<hr/>

[70] Heurgon (1964b) 249, 251.
[71] See above, p. 185 and n. 30.

ceremonies were entered, together with a record of events of a
religious significance, such as eclipses and famines,[72] which required
the performance of a specific religious ceremony.[73]

We have no evidence that annual calendar tables were set up in Etruria,
and day-by-day events recorded as at Rome.[74] But one wonders whether
the priests in the Etruscan cities kept any kind of record of their activities.
The books of the *disciplina*, especially the *libri haruspicini* and the *libri
fulgurales*, must have contained information about the interpretation of
omens, signs and portents of various kinds, and this in itself suggests that
they may also have recorded past observations of this nature. Haruspical
divination was based on a tradition recorded in sacred books and
instruction passed on from father to son among the noble families.[75]
What we would like to know is whether this tradition was based on
precedent—i.e. whether it was a 'science' depending on empirical observation and evolving out of the recording of signs and the noting of
subsequent events. Cicero seems to suggest that this was the case:

Quae uero aut coniectura explicantur aut euentis animaduersa ac notata sunt,
ea genera diuinandi, ut supra dixi, non naturalia, sed artificiosa dicuntur; in
quo haruspices, augures coniectoresque numerantur.... Quorum alia sunt
posita in monumentis et disciplina, quod Etruscorum declarant et haruspicini
et fulgurales et rituales libri, uestri etiam augurales.[76]

Those methods of divination dependent on conjecture or on deductions
from events observed and recorded are, as I said above, not natural but
artificial; they include haruspices, augurs, and interpreters...Some are
based on records and usage, as is evident from the Etruscan books on
divination by inspection of entrails, divination by thunder and lightning,
and from the ritual books, the books of your augural college.

The possibility that the *Etrusca disciplina* included a corpus of recorded
and classified observations makes it likely that the sacred texts also
contained historical allusions. This likelihood is increased by the fact
that historical traditions are known to have been preserved in this way in
ancient Mesopotamia. The Babylonian omen texts, which survive in late

---

[72] Cato, *HRR* F 77.
[73] Cf. Cichorius (1894) 2249–50.
[74] Cic. *de Orat.* 2.52. N.B. the phrase *per singulos dies* {day-by-day}.
[75] Cic. *Fam.* 6.6.3; cf. Thulin (1912) 2437.
[76] Cic. *Div.* 1.33.72.

copies, have been shown by A. Goetze[77] to contain authentic traditions which go back to the time of the events themselves. This conclusion is confirmed by the findings of J. J. Finkelstein,[78] whose analysis of the traditions of the Akkadian dynasty shows that the omen texts are a more reliable source of genuine information than the legends and popular traditions about the same events. The omen texts were used for the purpose of instruction, i.e. they were intended to show what kind of events could be expected if certain signs were observed.[79]

The similarities between the religions of Etruria and the Ancient Near East have been discussed many times; and especially the matter of divination by means of extispicy seems to indicate a connection between them.[80] The comparison has naturally been thought to have a bearing on the controversial question of Etruscan origins, and to suggest that the antecedents of the Etruscan religion are to be sought in the East.[81] It is not necessary, however, to discuss this vexed problem; it will be quite sufficient to mention the Babylonian and Assyrian omen texts as a parallel case, because it is obvious that a method of divination which claims for itself a rational or scientific basis must inevitably rest on a foundation of recorded precedent.

It would therefore seem likely, *a priori*, that the books of the *Etrusca disciplina* contained allusions to past events, and this assumption is borne out by the available evidence.

Pliny the Elder, in a discussion of thunder and lightning, tells us that the Etruscan city of Volsinii was once completely burned down by a thunderbolt.[82] A few sentences later, he writes:

Exstat annalium memoria sacris quibusdam et precationibus uel cogi fulmina uel inpetrari. uetus fama Etruriae est inpetratum Volsinios urbem depopulatis agris subeunte monstro quod uocauere Oltam, euocatum a Porsina suo rege.[83]

---

[77] Goetze (1947).
[78] Finkelstein (1963).
[79] Goetze (1947).
[80] See e.g. Nougayrol (1955) 509ff..
[81] On this question in general, see Thulin (1906–9) Introduction, x–xv; Ducati (1938), esp. 154ff.; Pareti (1926) 182ff.; Pallottino (1947) 135ff.; Altheim (1950) *passim*; Altheim (1938) 46ff.; etc.
[82] Plin. *HN* 2.53.139.
[83] Plin. *HN* 2.54.140.

Historical record also exists of thunderbolts being either caused by or granted in answer to certain rites or prayers. There is an old story of the latter in Tuscany, when the portent which they called Olta came to the city of Volsinii, when its territory had been devastated; it was sent in answer to the prayer of its king Porsina.

This passage gives us a glimpse of Etruscan history preserved by native tradition, and its survival is clearly due to the religious significance of the events, so that the ultimate source is likely to have been a priestly tradition. Pliny's immediate source is not in doubt. Among the authors listed in the index of the second book of the *Natural History*, Pliny mentions 'Caecina de Etrusca disciplina, Tarquitius qui item, Julius Aquila qui item {Caecina, *On the Etruscan Discipline*; Tarquitius, the same; Julius Aquila, the same}'. And at the beginning of 2.53 (the chapter on the origins of thunderbolts) Pliny names as his source 'Tuscorum litterae' {Etruscan literature}, and again 'Etruria . . . arbitratur' {the judgement of Etruria}.

We know nothing about Julius Aquila, but Caecina and Tarquitius Priscus were well known Etruscan experts of the late Roman Republic who introduced the *Etrusca disciplina* to the Romans by translating the books into Latin. Tarquitius Priscus, moreover, translated into Latin a collection of supernatural events (*ostentaria Tusca*), which were undoubtedly based on some sort of documentary record probably going back a long way into the past.[84] It seems to me that Pliny's phrases *Tuscorum litterae* and *Etruria . . . arbitratur* refer to authentic documents in Etruscan which recorded observations of supernatural signs. We know, again on the authority of Pliny, that the sacred books of the *disciplina* did contain historical events, and that newly observed phenomena continued to be added until a relatively late date:

Factum est semel, quod equidem in Etruscae disciplinae uoluminibus inuenio, ingens terrarum portentum, L. Marcia Sexto Iulio coss. in agra Mutinensi.[85]

I find in the books of the *Etrusca disciplina* that the enormous portent of an earthquake once occurred in the district of Mutina during the consulship of Lucius Marcius and Sextus Julius [= 91 BC].

---

[84] On Tarquitius Priscus, see Heurgon (1953b).
[85] Plin. *HN* 2.85.199.

But what is otherwise known of the sacred books might seem at first sight to conflict with this interpretation. We read in Cicero[86] that the *libri haruspicini* originated from a speech made by the semi-divine Tages, who sprang one day from the soil of Tarquinia and revealed to the Etruscans the art of extispicy; again, the *libri fulgurales* were thought to have contained the teachings of the nymph Vegoia. These stories, together with other evidence,[87] suggest that the books were of a purely prescriptive character and can hardly have contained a catalogue of recorded precedent, which increased with the passage of time.

It is necessary, however, to take into account the nature of our surviving sources; writers who refer to the Etruscan discipline, such as Cicero, Seneca, Pliny, and John Lydus, were interested in the religious significance of what was recorded in the books, and not in any historical information they may have contained. And the fact that the *Etrusca disciplina* was held to be derived ultimately from the revelations of mythical figures such as Tages and Vegoia does not preclude the possibility that the texts also contained a record of observed happenings which bore out the validity of the original doctrine. Indeed, Cicero himself confirms this assumption, when he says that the original Tagetic text was continually added to in the light of new knowledge:

Tum illum [sc. Tages] plura locutum multis audientibus, qui omnia uerba eius exceperint litterisque mandarint; omnem autem orationem fuisse eam, qua haruspicinae disciplina contineretur; eam postea creuisse rebus nouis cognoscendis et ad eadem illa principia referendis.[88]

Then Tages spoke at length to his numerous hearers, who received with eagerness all that he had to say and committed it to writing. His whole address was devoted to an exposition of the science of soothsaying. Later, as new facts were learned and tested by reference to the principles imparted by Tages, they were added to the original fund of knowledge.

That these additions included a recording of events is proved, as we have seen, by the evidence of Pliny. There can be no doubt, in fact, that many of the local Etruscan traditions known to us, including the theory of *saecula* attributed by Varro to *Tuscae historiae*, are closely

[86] Cic. *Div.* 2.23.50.
[87] E.g. Sen. *QN* 2.32ff.
[88] Cic. *Div.* 2.23.50; cf. 1.25, and Thulin (1906–9) III.76 and n. 1.

connected by their strong religious emphasis with the tradition of the *Etrusca disciplina*.

Cicero's source for the story of Tages was almost certainly the *de Etrusca disciplina* of A. Caecina, a man with whom Cicero was personally acquainted.[89] Caecina's *de Etrusca disciplina* certainly contained historical and legendary traditions, as is shown by a fragment of it fortunately preserved by a scholiast on Virgil:

Caecina...Archon, inquit, cum exercitu Appenninum transgressus primum oppidum constituit quod tum Mantuam nominauit uocatumque Tusca lingua a Dite patre est nomen. Deinde undecim dedicauit Diti patri...ibi constituit annum et item locum consecrauit, quo duodecim oppida condere...nem.[90]

Caecina...Archon, he says, having crossed the Apennines with an army, established the first town, which he named at that time Mantua, and the name was so called from father Dis in the Etruscan language. Then he dedicated eleven to father Dis...there he established the year and similarly he consecrated the place, where twelve towns found[...

Heurgon supposes that this fragment was taken from a historical work by Caecina, written in Latin but derived from native sources.[91] However, as Heurgon himself observes, Caecina emphasized the religious aspects of Tarchon's activities, and it seems to me that this points in the direction of the *de Etrusca disciplina* rather than a hypothetical historical work for which there is no supporting evidence. This conclusion is supported by the description, by Verrius Flaccus, who himself used Caecina,[92] of the *libri rituales*:

Rituales nominantur Etruscorum libri in quibus perscribtum est quo ritu condantur urbes, arae aedes sacrentur, qua sanctitate muri, quo iure portae, quomodo tribus curiae centuriae distribuantur, exercitus constituantur ordinentur, ceteraque eiusmodi ad bellum ac pacem pertinentia.[93]

The books of the Etruscans are called 'Ritual' in which is set out the rite with which cities are to be founded and altars and temples made sacred, with

---

[89] Cicero corresponded with Caecina (*Fam.* 6.5ff.), and in 69 BC defended his father in the speech *Pro Caecina*.

[90] Schol. Veron. ad Verg. *Aen.* 10.200. The end of the sentence is obscure.

[91] Heurgon (1961) 306; cf. Münzer (1898) 606.

[92] Münzer (1898) 606.

[93] Festus, s.v. *rituales libri* (358 L).

what sanctity walls, with what legal procedure gates [sc. are to be made sacred]; in what manner tribes, *curiae*, and centuries should be distributed, how armies should be established and arranged, and other things of this sort that concern war and peace.

It seems to me that the fragment of Caecina corresponds fairly precisely to the content of the *libri rituales* as defined by Verrius Flaccus. The story of Tarchon's foundations in Etruria Padana could have been recorded in the *libri rituales* themselves, but it could equally well have been recounted in Caecina's commentary on the books.

What all this evidence amounts to is that Etruscan legends and history were preserved in a religious tradition which must have relied to a great extent on the recording of events which were thought to be a consequence of signs and prophetic utterances. Whether these events were recorded for the most part in the sacred books themselves, or whether they were recorded in a comprehensive catalogue in the form of a priestly chronicle which lay outside the central body of the *Etrusca disciplina* cannot be known. It is also uncertain whether the *Tuscae historiae* mentioned by Varro were based entirely on a systematic priestly chronicle, or whether they were a literary reconstruction using a variety of sources, including religious documents. In any case, it seems fairly certain that the *Tuscae historiae* and the books of the *Etrusca disciplina* were closely linked.

VII

To sum up, it may be said that we still know nothing certain about the *Tuscae historiae* apart from what Varro tells us. Claudius probably never came into direct contact with historical works written in Etruscan. From Varro we can infer that they were genuinely Etruscan in origin, that they were written in the eighth *saeculum*, and that they contained a discussion of the *saecula*. Any further conclusions we might form about the *Tuscae historiae* must be based on what we know of the available primary sources.

In Etruria, as well as in Rome, we may presume that primary historical evidence could have survived in texts of laws, treaties and other official documents, paintings and sculptured monuments, popular poetry, accounts of Greek historians, and of course, a rich oral tradition. But apart from these rather haphazard sources, we have been able to indicate three areas in which an Etruscan historian could have found systematic records containing authentic historical material.

(1) The evidence of the *elogia Tarquiniensia* implies that an ample tradition was preserved in private family archives which still survived at the time of the Principate. (2) A list of magistrates existed at Tarquinia and perhaps also at Caere; these will have formed an important historical source in themselves, but they also open up the intriguing possibility of local city chronicles. (3) The Etruscans seem to have kept records of events of a religious significance. This conclusion is based on the assumption, which I think is reasonable, that the profoundly serious business of divination required a systematic body of recorded precedent, in the form not only of a record of the observed signs, but also of the events which were thought to be a consequence of the signs. Clearly, these events would often have been historically important.

ADDENDUM

This juvenile piece, actually written in 1971, formed part of my PhD thesis (Cornell (1972) 178–214). Since its publication in 1976 the article has been frequently cited whenever the subject of Etruscan historiography has come into question (e.g. Poucet (1985) 60 n. 81; Bandelli (1988) 507 n. 17; Vernole (2002) 183–6; Forsythe (2005) 102 n. 10), and as far as I am aware it has not been superseded by any comparable study. But some aspects of the topic have been transformed by subsequent scholarship. Our understanding of the Etruscan tradition of Mastarna–Servius Tullius has been substantially advanced by Coarelli's brilliant reading of the frescoes of the François tomb (Coarelli (1983b)), and by the complete publication of all the data connected with the tomb in Buranelli ed. (1987), which is now the starting point for any serious research. Other important studies include Pallottino (1977), (1987), and (1993), 237–58; Thomsen (1980); Ampolo (1988) 203–10; Briquel (1988a), (1988b), (1990), and (1997) 57–116; Capdeville (1992), (1995) 7–39; Fraschetti (1994); Martínez-Pinna (1996) 273–89, Poucet (2000) 192–212; Vernole (2002) 187–98. My own (revised) view of the matter is presented in Cornell (1995) 130–41.

Any discussion of the *elogia Tarquiniensia* must now start from Mario Torelli's full edition of the texts, with extensive historical commentary (Torelli (1975)). Torelli's reconstruction of the texts, of the monumental complex, and of the events referred to, remains conjectural; my own doubts were set out in a review article (Cornell (1978), rejected by Torelli (1983) 7–8). Alternative readings and attempts to identify the events can be found in Gabba (1979) and Colonna (1984a), (1989). But the real importance of the book in the present context lies elsewhere, namely in its demonstration of the existence of historical records in the Etruscan cities. First, it confirms the suggestion that the *elogia* commemorate members of the gens Spurinnia, and reveals the importance of family records as a vehicle for the preservation of historical traditions in Etruria (an aspect further developed in Torelli (1996)). The second important element is Torelli's re-publication of inscriptions recording the achievements of *haruspices* of Tarquinii who were active in the Late Republic and early Empire (Torelli (1975) 103–35). These texts, whether or not they form a systematic record of local members of the *ordo LX haruspicum*, as Torelli thinks (for some doubts, Rawson (1978) 140; North (1990) 67), appear to confirm the existence of Etruscan priestly records.

Other aspects of my case have not aroused much attention. The idea that the *Tuscae historiae* were contemporary with the publication of the *Annales Maximi* at Rome would have to be revised if Frier was right to date the latter event to the time of Augustus (Frier (1999) 179–200), and if Turcan was right to date the eighth Etruscan *saeculum* (when the *Tuscae historiae* were produced) to the period 284–164 BC (Turcan (1976)). The question of whether the Etruscan cities maintained lists of eponymous officials remains open; but experts continue to assume the widespread use of eponymous dating. The latest word on Etruscan magistrates known to me is Maggiani (1996).

Part II

Rhetoric, Truth, and Falsehood

8

Cicero and Historiography*

P. A. Brunt

There is a general consensus of scholarly opinion that with few exceptions Hellenistic historians sought primarily to 'charm, divert, and edify' and paid at most 'lip-service to truth'; 'if they deal with events already narrated by others, their overriding aim is not to outdo their predecessors in accuracy or balanced judgement, but to outshine them in splendid and dramatic description. Often the theme is chosen on artistic criteria, being a self-contained whole like a plot for tragedy', and mere fables or irrelevant digressions are introduced 'to alleviate the tedium of continuous narrative'.[1] This practice is often traced to rhetorical theory, deriving ultimately or

---

* This paper defends a conception of Cicero's views on history rather like those of Boissier (1903) 54f.; Laistner (1947) ch. 1 and 29–35; Leeman (1963) I.168–74, cf. 329ff.; Rambaud (1953) ch. l, but seeks to provide a fuller analysis. Not only the views of Cicero but the general notions in antiquity of what history should be are, to my mind, in various degrees misrepresented in e.g. von Christ (1920–34) I.204–6; 303f.; Norden (1909) I.81–95; Peter (1897) I.10f.; Pippidi (1944) 14ff., and more recently by Kennedy (1972) 207, 292–4, 421, 524. Misconceptions also infect d'Alton (1931) 491–523; Walsh (1961) ch. II and Flach (1973) 13ff., though they are more balanced. Much dogma on 'the Hellenistic tradition' rests on Scheller (1911) (useful but for its conclusions). Henze (1899) was inaccessible to me. I have learned much from Walbank (1972) and especially from Avenarius (1956). The only extant ancient work on the theory of historiography, Lucian's *How to Write History*, satirizes the faults that modern scholars ascribe to the influence of theory. Note also his remark that others thought that they needed no rules in writing history (*h.c.* 5). I am indebted for some observations on this paper to Michael Winterbottom.

[1] Walsh (1961) 27ff.

directly from Isocrates; many suppose that the assimilation of history to tragedy was inspired by Theophrastus and the Peripatetics. Such rhetorical and sensationalist models, it is contended, were to be adopted at Rome, for instance by Livy and Tacitus. Cicero's sparse references to the writing of history are held to show that while he formally recognized that it was the first duty of the historian to tell the truth, in reality he regarded literary effects as all-important. Whether or not his dicta are thought to have had any actual influence on later historical writing at Rome, they are taken to be important evidence that truth was almost wholly subordinated to rhetoric. It is my purpose to show that when interpreted in their context they prove nothing of the sort. I also doubt if any theory ever justified the kind of bad historical writing which is held to be typical of the Hellenistic age or indeed whether we know enough to be sure that it was typical.

Cicero, as will be seen, had a low opinion of Latin historical writing. His views on historiography, whether or not they owed anything to putative Hellenistic theory, were formed by critical appreciation of the accepted masterpieces of classical and Hellenistic historical works composed in Greek.

No writer has ever appeared to set a higher value on history than Cicero. In his words it is *testis temporum, lux ueritatis, uita memoriae, magistra uitae, nuntia uetustatis* {witness of the ages, light of truth, life of memory, guide for life, messenger of antiquity} (*de Orat.* 2.36). Perhaps echoing Plato (*Tim.* 22b), he declares *nescire quid ante quam natus sis acciderit, id est semper esse puerum* {not to know what happened before you were born is to remain always a child}; knowledge of the past, especially of the history of Rome and of imperial peoples and famous kings, was valuable to the orator. The reason was not merely that it supplied him with a store of impressive *exempla*; indeed, as Cicero's own practice too often showed, it hardly mattered for the effects at which the orator aimed whether the *exempla* were true or not.[2] It was also essential to the truly cultivated man and to the statesman, to the 'perfect orator', as delineated by 'Crassus' in his *de Oratore*, who in some degree prefigures the humanistic ideal of the

---

[2] *Orat.* 120; *Exempla: de Orat.* 1.18; 60; *Part. Orat.* 96; Rambaud (1953) ch. II.

Renaissance. For his practice in the courts, the advocate should be familiar with the civil law, but quite apart from that consideration, *mira quaedam in cognoscendo suauitas et delectatio* {there's a marvellous charm and pleasure in learning}; *plurima est et in omni iure ciuili et in pontificum libris et in duodecim tabulis antiquitatis effigies, quod et uerborum prisca uetustas cognoscitur et actionum genera quaedam maiorum consuetudinem uitamque declarant* {there is a complete image of antiquity in the common law and in the books of the priests and in the Twelve Tables, since ancient archaic language can be learnt there and certain types of legal formulas reveal the custom and way of life of our ancestors}; with some extravagance 'Crassus' affirms that the Twelve Tables (which Cicero often cites) were to be preferred to all philosophical works, as they were the source of the law of Rome, the fatherland that was the *domus uirtutis, imperii, dignitatis* {home of bravery, empire, honour} and whose *mens, mos, disciplina* {spirit, custom, orderly conduct}, it was the first duty of a patriotic Roman to learn.[3] Cicero continually appealed to *mos maiorum* {ancestral custom}; in particular in a speech in which he was demonstrably uttering his own political convictions, he characterized the Roman political system as *discriptionem ciuitatis a maioribus nostris sapientissime constitutam* {an arrangement of the state, most wisely constituted by our ancestors} (*Sest.* 137), and in the *de Republica* he traces the evolution of that system, which he regards as the best actually attainable, to the wise expedients adopted by successive generations in Rome's remoter past. A senator should know *exempla maiorum* {the precedents of our ancestors} (*Leg.* 3.41); tradition and precedents were in fact the fabric of the Republican constitution. In the *Hortensius* Cicero also represented Lucullus (implausibly enough) as having taught himself the art of warfare from history, and claimed that *omnis rei publicae disciplina* {every branch of study for the state} was to be acquired from the annalistic records (frr. 11–14 Grilli). Thus he adopted the view common in antiquity that history furnished lessons indispensable to the general and statesman.

If history was indeed to supply such guidance, if it was to be *magistra uitae* because it was *testis temporum* and *nuntia uetustatis,*

---

[3] *de. Orat.* 1.193–6, cf. 18; 159; for importance of constitutional precedents, 201. Cf. n. 35.

it was necessary that it should also be *lux ueritatis*; as a mendacious witness, it would serve no useful end. It was then natural for Cicero to emphasize that the historian must be truthful.

Nam quis nescit primam esse historiae legem, ne quid falsi dicere audeat? Deinde ne quid ueri non audeat? Ne quae suspicio gratiae sit in scribendo? Ne quae simultatis? Haec scilicet fundamenta nota sunt omnibus

For who does not know that the first law of history is not to dare to say anything false? And then not to dare not to say anything true? That there be no suspicion of favour in the writing? And no suspicion of animosity? These foundations, of course, are known to all. ('Antonius' in *de Orat.* 2.62)

This was the accepted view in antiquity, as Cicero indicates,[4] even if practice too often departed from theory. History was thus to be differentiated both from poetry, though the historian could at times properly use poetic diction,[5] and as we shall see later, from epideictic oratory, to which it was closely related in style. The first of these distinctions is made by Cicero, when he excludes from history such fictions as he himself had introduced into his epic on Marius, *cum in illa* [history] *omnia ad ueritatem referentur, in hoc* [poetry] *ad delectationem pleraque* {although in history everything must be guided by truth, in poetry much is guided by pleasure}; he has even made the antithesis too sharp, since it was certainly his opinion that the historian should write in a manner that gave pleasure, though without deviating from the truth (*infra*). By adding that Herodotus and Theopompus had admitted countless *fabulae {mythical stories}* in their histories, he implies that they had fallen short of the standard to be required.[6]

---

[4] Lucian, *h.c.* 7, cf. Avenarius (1956) 40–55 (truth): 22–6 (utility). Scheller (1911) 72–8 distinguishes the various ways in which history was thought useful; cf. n. 14.

[5] Avenarius (1956) 63–7. Quintilian's remark that history is *proxima poetis* {very close to the poets} refers in the context to diction (10.1.31), cf. Leeman (1963) 329. The style of Thucydides was especially poetical (e.g. D. Hal. *Thuc.* 51f.). The orator too is like the poet and may benefit from study of poetry, *de Orat.* 1.70; 154; 158; 3.27.

[6] *Leg.* 1.4f.; *de Fin.* 5.64; *Rep.* 2.18f. (Cicero has his tongue in his cheek, cf. 4); *Offic.* 3.99; *Div.* 2.115f. Like Thucydides and modern scholars, Cicero of course knew that poets may furnish historical evidence, cf. *Brut.* 57 f. Fictions: Kroll (1924) 369: 'In theoretical writings it had long been expressed that the historian had the same aims as the poet'; Norden (1909) I.91–5, whose views are refuted by the texts he transcribes; Flach (1973) 44. See Avenarius (1956) 16–22, 163f.

In the very context of the passage quoted, 'Antonius' discerns some affinity between the historian and the orator. Yet since truth is the first requirement of history, there is again a fundamental difference that divides them. The forensic orator has a duty *non numquam ueri simile, etiam si minus sit uerum, defendere* {sometimes to defend the plausible even if it is less true} (*Offic.* 2.51). 'Antonius', who does not represent Cicero's ideal orator but who none the less is undoubtedly the exponent of much that he thinks required of the successful advocate,[7] observes that his activity is concerned with opinion, not knowledge; he addresses the ignorant on matters that he may himself know nothing of, and on identical issues he expresses different views in different speeches, to suit the interests of his clients (*de Orat.* 2.30). Though he has to instruct ('docere') the court, verdicts depend more on passions than on the relevant facts or law (178), and his chief aim must be to win the favour and play on the emotions of the jurors; it is the means by which he can best achieve this end to which 'Antonius' devotes most of his discourse; it will indeed be harmful to the orator's case if he says anything *patently* false or self-contradictory (306). As for deliberative speeches, 'Antonius' again lays great weight on conciliating a popular audience and working on its passions, and it is perhaps only out of tact that Cicero does not let it appear that the same arts are useful in the supposedly grave and wise debates in the senate (333–40). Thus in Cicero's view the forensic and deliberative orator aims at persuasion, the historian at truth.[8] The epideictic orator, as we shall see, could neglect not only truth but plausibility too (n. 57).

According to Cicero then, the historian is to tell the truth, and the whole truth, without rancour or fear. It is bias, however caused, that he sees as the great obstacle to veracity. He says nothing of the historian's problems in investigating and ascertaining the truth. His

[7] Cicero's spokesman, Crassus, endorses his discourse in Book 2 (*de Orat.* 3.37).

[8] See also *de Orat.* 1.17 (Cicero); 53; 143 ('Crassus'); 2.178–216 ('Antonius'); *Orat.* 24, 51, 69, 122, 131; *Brut.* 89, 199, 276, 184f., 188; *Part. Orat.* 8–11. In narration the orator aims only at credibility (*de Orat.* 2.80; *Orat.* 124; *Part. Orat.* 32); the writer followed by Cicero, *de Inu.* 1.29 and in *Rhet. Herenn.* 1.16 made it clear that this was not the same as truth, cf. Quint. 4.2.34f. In deliberative speeches to the people he would appeal to men's beliefs, however ill-founded, and to their emotions, *de Orat.* 2.337; *Part. Orat.* 90. For epideictic speeches cf. pp. 228–33; narrative, *Part. Orat.* 71. Cf. Quint. 8.3.70 falsely referred by Flach (1973) 46 to history.

silence can easily be explained. He is concerned with history as a
literary genre, and therefore with the way in which it should be
written, not with the work preliminary to writing. What his views
on this subject were must be a matter for surmise.

The younger Pliny, a conventional man, took it for granted that if a
historian were to traverse *uetera et scripta aliis* {ancient matters
written by others}, he would not need to do any research of his
own, but he would be bound to collate existing accounts (*parata
inquisitio, sed onerosa collatio* {the inquiry is to hand but the collation
is burdensome}). By implication, where no such accounts were
available, he would have to undertake his own investigations, as
Pliny expected Tacitus to undertake them for his *Histories*; in such
cases some ancient historians undertook, or professed to have undertaken, extensive enquiries, involving the examination of eyewitnesses, consultation of documents and travel to distant scenes.
Collation would be 'burdensome', only if it were thorough; probably
Pliny had his uncle's practice in mind. Of course there were some
historians in antiquity who were content to write out, abbreviate, or
embellish the work of a single predecessor. But others claimed to
have done what Pliny assumes to be normal, and I see no reason to
believe that all these claims are to be treated as false.[9] Nor would they
have been made at all, unless collation of existing accounts was at
least expected of a historian. Furthermore, some writers professed to
have done more, or actually did more, referring to documents and
other material contemporary with the events they were describing.[10]
This is not to say that any ancient historians undertook the comprehensive research into transactions earlier than their own times that is
now demanded; whether those who wrote contemporary history,
resting in large part on the examination of witnesses, were more or
less thorough than the rare modern historians who attempt this kind
of investigation we have no means of telling. Again, perhaps no one
in antiquity employed, or had any conception of, thorough historical
research or of all the critical methods required, the complexity of

  [9] *Ep.* 5.8.5 and 5.8.12, cf. 3.5 (elder Pliny); 7.33.3 (Tacitus).
  [10] Polybius 12.25.e and 12.25.i, cf. 3.33, 3.21ff. (but see Walbank (1972) 82f.);
Avenarius (1956) 71–85; unfortunately (like others) he injects Isocrates 10.149f. into
the discussion; it is not concerned with history writing, cf. nn. 14, 56. Philochorus
and Timaeus (Pol. 12.9; 11; 27) *inter alios* used documents.

which it is in any case easy to overstate. Experience in affairs and natural good sense seemed to qualify anyone with the necessary leisure and industry to discover historical facts, though for their exposition he also needed a mastery of style.[11] In relation to Cicero, we have to ask not whether he had any notion of historical investigation that would satisfy a scholar today but only whether his standards would have been the best accepted in antiquity.[12]

There is no doubt that for the limited purposes of his analytic sketch of the early development of Roman institutions in *de Republica* 2, and for the *mise-en-scène* of certain dialogues or for historical allusions which he inserted in them Cicero consulted various historical and antiquarian works and made careful enquiries on quite minute points. He would then surely have regarded as necessary extensive collation of earlier accounts and even reference to documentary material, like the Twelve Tables or for a later period contemporary poems, speeches, and memoirs, of which he shows such wide knowledge particularly in his *Brutus*, if he had embarked on a history of events before his own day; for instance, since Scaurus was plainly no stylist, his memoirs 'which no one reads' can only have been *sane utiles* {very useful} (*Brut.* 112) to anyone interested in the transactions of his time. It is significant that in 59 BC, when still deeply engaged in politics, he abandoned the project of composing a geographical treatise, because of the labour involved in the examination of discordant sources (*Att.* 2.6.1), and that at a time when his forensic practice was still exacting, he claims that he had insufficient time to spare to compose a history either of early Rome or of contemporary events (*Leg.* 1.8–10).

After 48 indeed Cicero had ample leisure to comply with the appeals of his friends to take up the writing of history, yet he never did so. Instead he devoted his time to philosophy, which (unlike history) was already recognized as a hard discipline in its own right. Cicero had long been engaged in philosophical study, however intermittently, and was adequately prepared for the task he undertook, of popularizing Greek doctrines for a Latin-reading public; and to a considerable extent, he could, if he chose, take a series of Greek

---

[11] Avenarius (1956) 30–40.
[12] For the next three paragraphs, see Rambaud (1953) ch. III; Rawson (1972).

treatises and adapt each in turn; I do not mean that he exercised no judgement of his own in the work. In the last resort philosophy offered him more consolation and seemed more important for the instruction and improvement of others. But given his pre-existing familiarity with the subject, it also demanded less effort than would have been required for the investigations preparatory to historical composition.

Of course mere collation of evidence was not enough. Conflicts of testimony had to be resolved, and truth disentangled from fable or fiction. It is certain that Cicero was aware of this, and that he had some feeling for the value of documentary material. But we cannot be sure how successful he would have been by ancient standards as a critical historian, since he never made the attempt. The historical sketch in the *de Republica* manifests the 'rationalism' that Rambaud detected, but his omission of legends may in part be ascribed to the fact that he is exhibiting only Rome's constitutional evolution, and that in mere outline.

For Cicero veracity is the basis on which the historian must build a more elaborate structure: *haec scilicet fundamenta nota sunt omnibus, ipsa autem exaedificatio posita est in rebus et uerbis* {these foundations are of course known to all, but the completion of the structure is in the substance and language}. So far as substance (*rebus*) is concerned, 'Antonius' requires *ordinem temporum, regionum descriptionem* {chronological arrangement, geographical description}.

With the diversity of eras and fluctuations in calendars in the ancient world, chronological exactitude was not easy to attain or to present clearly, especially if the historian, like Thucydides or Polybius, often had to transfer the reader's attention from one part of the world to another and perhaps to show how transactions in different parts reacted on each other. Elsewhere Cicero goes out of his way to commend Atticus' chronological handbook (*Orat.* 120) and evinces a special interest in dating events (n. 12). But he probably had in mind not only the importance of accuracy but the problem of arranging the narrative artistically and clearly.

Geographical discourses were often introduced in order to impart an agreeable variety and colour, and like battle scenes tempted historians to free inventions to amuse or thrill their readers. Cicero implies in the *Orator* (66) that these were occasions for an 'ornate' style. We shall see, however, that the 'ornamentation' he approved can be restricted to the careful choice of words and rhythms, and that he was by no means lending his authority to fictions that might heighten the effect. That would contradict his basic principles. And in any case, 'Antonius' is here not discussing literary effects at all (*uerbis*) but the content of a history. It was a patent truth that in the absence of maps, military operations, which formed a large part of history as Cicero and the ancients in general conceived it, would be unintelligible, at least if they took place in unfamiliar lands, unless the scenes were carefully described. Polybius, who inveighed against fictitious descriptions, also insisted on the need for accurate and relevant topographical explanation.[13] By the same token it was desirable to depict the life and customs of remote peoples.

Nor was it sufficient for Cicero that the historian should tell what had happened: he must also explain causes and consequences, and show just how events took place. He was also to express his own judgement on the conduct of the actors and give particulars of the lives and characters of the more notable among them. These words do not imply that the judgements should be entirely or chiefly moralistic, still less that they should take the form of encomium or invective. Cicero is not expressly advocating a type of historical exposition different from that commonly employed by modern political historians, who also think it necessary to give biographical particulars of individuals who appear to have influenced the course of events, when such particulars seem relevant to explaining their conduct, and who do not refrain from interpreting their motives and attempting a general assessment of their personalities.

Cicero then turns to style, but it is apparent that it is not style alone that determines the quality of a history. It must also be accurate, intelligible and 'pragmatic'. Cicero's conceptions of the purpose and substance of history agree well with those of Polybius.[14]

---

[13] Pol. 1.41.7, 3.36, 3.47f., 5.21, 10.9.8 and 10.9.27, 12.25e, 29.12; Avenarius (1956) 144–9.

[14] Walbank (1972) chs. II–IV. Pol. 10.21 defends biographical excursuses and distinguishes them from panegyrics (at 8.10): see Walbank *HCP* ad loc. and n. 55. Herodotus *praef.* had already held that famous deeds should be explained as well as commemorated. D. Hal. *Thuc.* 8 says that virtually all philosophers and rhetoricians approved the views on history in Thuc. 1.21f. From this time history was thought to

Historical style in the view of 'Antonius' was to be flowing and ornate; this will be considered later. Cicero's comments on both Greek and Roman historians give us further indications of the literary qualities he admired. Among the former 'Antonius' praises the 'eloquence' of Herodotus, Thucydides, Philistus, Theopompus, Ephorus, Xenophon, Callisthenes, and Timaeus (2.55–8). In the *Orator* Cicero ignores Philistus, Callisthenes, and Timaeus, and classes Xenophon partly as a philosopher (32 and 62). It is significant that he did not include in the canon Polybius, whom he regarded as an exceptionally reliable historian (*Offic.* 3.113), unsurpassed in chronological accuracy (*Rep.* 2.27), and whose account of early Rome he certainly drew on (n. 12), nor Duris, although in his eyes that writer was *in historia diligens* {careful in history} (*Att.* 6.1.18). Dionysius of Halicarnassus names both with other Hellenistic writers among the countless historians whose *diction* is so ugly that no one can bear to read them through (*Comp. uerb.* 4). Their style did not find favour with the Atticizing fashion of the first century. For Dionysius, who also ignored Callisthenes, the best literary models were Herodotus, Thucydides, Xenophon, and Theopompus (*Pomp.* 3–6). The writer *On the Sublime* thought Callisthenes' style absurdly elevated (3.2). Timaeus, the only Hellenistic author listed by 'Antonius', whom Cicero elsewhere treats as a follower of the Asian style, marked by clever and pleasing but shallow *sententiae* (*Brut.* 325), apparently of the kind favoured by epideictic orators (*Orat.* 65), was ranked by Dionysius among those would-be imitators of Isocrates who were 'flat, frigid, prolix, and tasteless' (*Dinarch.* 8) and censured by the writer *On the Sublime* for frigidity and a childish predilection for strange 'conceits' (4). Cicero's early indebtedness to Asian rhetoric may have made him partial to Timaeus, perhaps more so when writing his *de Oratore* than in his later years. In general his judgement on the style of Greek historians reflects what was to

be useful, inculcating political or moral lessons—for this purpose it had to be true (Lucian *h.c.* 9). Cf. Avenarius (1956) 22–6, who ascribes 'the moralizing tendency' to the school of Isocrates, but whatever view be taken of Herodotus and Thucydides in this regard, Xenophon was explicit in moral judgements (e.g. *Hell.* 5.4.1). Perhaps no history can be written, in which they are not inherent, however covert.

be the orthodox opinion;[15] much may go back to Theophrastus.[16] But the silence on Polybius in particular proves that 'Antonius' is concerned only with their literary qualities, and Cicero's allusions to historians in the *Orator* are even more patently restricted in the same way. We are not to infer that he thought no other qualities important for a complete assessment of their worth.

In what follows, I shall conflate the views ascribed to 'Antonius' with those Cicero expresses elsewhere on the historians named. He adopted Theophrastus' opinion that Herodotus and Thucydides were the first to write history *uberius et ornatius* {more richly and with more adornment}, earlier historians having aimed only at clearness and brevity.[17] Herodotus 'flows along like a tranquil stream without any rough water', while Thucydides has more impetus and sounds like the trumpet of war; Cicero admired the abundance, terseness and pungency of his *sententiae*, and thought his exposition of events sagacious and weighty, and his diction appropriate and grand, but at least in the speeches too obscure.[18] Philistus was almost a diminutive Thucydides, dense, acute, and concise.[19] Both Herodotus and Thucydides did well to avoid the extravagances of the early

---

[15] Cf. Quint. 10.1.73–5, and nn. 17–19, 23, 27, 37. D. Hal. *Pomp.* 3–6; despite his criticisms of Thucydides Dionysius accepts the 'universal' view that he was the greatest of historians (*Thuc.* 2). For Lucian, Herodotus and Thucydides are the best historians (54), especially the latter, who was the general model for often feeble emulation (5, 15, 25f., 42, 57); admiration for the old Attic style could have absurd effects (21). On the literary merits of both, see e.g. D. Hal. *comp. uerb.* 3f., 7, 10, 18; Thucydides was master of the austere style (22), for Demetrius, who quotes him often, on a par with Plato, of the magnificent style (*Eloc.* 39f.), cf. [Long.] *Subl.* 14. Luschnat's account of his *Nachleben* ((1978) 1266–1311) for all its length is defective on his enormous literary reputation from the first century BC.

[16] *Orat.* 39 on Herodotus and Thucydides. Theophrastus cannot have assessed Timaeus. Works on *Historia* are ascribed to him (Diog. Laert. 5.47) and his pupil, Praxiphanes (Aly (1954); Marcell. *Vita Thuc.* 29), but whatever their subject and content (Avenarius (1956) 165–78), it may be that Cicero consulted only Theophrastus' treatise *On Diction*, whence also *Orat.* 79, 172, 218, 228.

[17] *Orat.* 39; *de Orat.* 2.53; D. Hal. *Thuc.* 5 and 23, though more favourable to the predecessors of Herodotus, roughly agrees; cf. also n. 15.

[18] *De Orat.* 2.55f.; *Orat.* 39. On Thuc., see also *de Orat.* 2.93; *Orat.* 30–32; *Brut.* 27–9; 66; 287f.; *Opt. Gen.* 15f.; he names no other historian so often. Impetus: D. Hal. *Pomp.* 3 (772). Obscurity and other faults: *Amm. II, passim*; of the speeches, *Thuc.* 49.

[19] *De Orat.* 2.57; *Brut.* 66; *Q. fr.* 2.12(11).4; *Diuin.* 1.39 (*doctum . . . et diligentem* {learned . . . and careful}. Cf. D. Hal. *Pomp.* 5; Quint. 10.1.74. The alleged similarity with Thucydides is stylistic.

rhetoricians like Gorgias (*Orat.* 39), but there was a welcome new development when Isocrates perfected the periodic structure and the verbal melodies that Herodotus and Thucydides had obtained only by chance; it was these stylistic qualities that Ephorus and Theopompus imported into historiography; they were his pupils, and Cicero supposed, perhaps without foundation, that they became historians at his prompting.[20] Despite his manifest approval of this innovation, we may perhaps detect a certain irony when Cicero says that Theopompus eclipsed Thucydides in the lofty exaltation of his language,[21] and a hint of disapproval when he remarks that Callisthenes wrote almost in the rhetorical fashion: of Demochares he says that his account of Athens in his own time was in an oratorical rather than a historical style:[22] in a letter to Quintus (*Q.f.* 2.12(11).4) he depreciates Callisthenes, and 'Antonius' perhaps prefers Xenophon's sweeter style, devoid of the orator's vehemence.[23] Timaeus is *longe eruditissimus et rerum copia et sententiarum uarietate abundantissimus et ipsa compositione uerborum non impolitus; magnam eloquentiam ad scribendum attulit* {far and away the most eloquent and most abounding in wealth of material and range of thought, and not unpolished in the very arrangement of words; he brought great eloquence to his writing}.[24]

---

[20] *De Orat.* 2.57, 2.94, 3.36; *Orat.* 40–42 (on Isocrates); *Brut.* 66; D. Hal. *Isaeo* 19; *Comp. uerb.* 23; he is encomiastic of Theopompus partly on strictly historical grounds (*Pomp.* 6), but omits Ephorus from his canon (n. 15). Quint. 10.1.74 also seems to prefer the former, and Dio Chrys. 18.10 condemns Ephorus' diffuse and flat style. Cf. also n. 67.

[21] *Brut.* 66: [*Thucydidi*] *officit Theopompus elatione atque altitudine orationis suae* {Theopompus eclipsed [Thucydides] with his high-flown and elevated style}, yet Thucydides was by others regarded as a master of the grand style (n. 15) and in *Leg.* 1.7, if we adopt Vahlen's emendation of a corrupt text, Cicero says of Macer's speeches [*habet*] *elatio* (*datio* codd) *summam impudentiam* {his magniloquence has the greatest effrontery}; 'magniloquence' might be the sense in both passages. Demetr. / *Eloc.* 75 and 247 censured him for this fault.

[22] *De Orat.* 2.58; *Q. fr.* 2.12(11).4, cf. [Long.] *Subl.* 3.2. Demochares: *Brut.* 286, cf. *de Orat.* 2.95. See n. 34.

[23] *De Orat.* 2.58, cf. *Orat.* 32, 62 (where he is treated as a philosopher); *Brut.* 132. Xenophon, but not Callisthenes, was to remain a literary model. Cf. D. Hal. *Comp. uerb.* 10; *Pomp.* 4.

[24] *De Orat.* 2.58, cf. p. 216. *Eruditissimus* {most learned} seems to refer to his learning as a historian, of *rerum copia* {abundance of material}; here then Cicero introduces non-literary criteria.

As for the Roman historians Cicero's comments are curious in two respects. (1) 'Antonius' says that at first *monumenta solum temporum, hominum, locorum gestarumque rerum reliquerunt* {they left behind only bare records of dates, names, places and events} (*de Orat.* 2.53); they were following the manner of the pontifical annals. Yet Cato expressly despised the kind of information found in these annals on such matters as the price of grain or on lunar and solar eclipses (*HRR*, F 77); like Cicero he evidently thought that the historian should restrict himself to *rebus magnis memoriaque dignis* {events great and worthy of memory} (*de Orat.* 2.63). Cicero perhaps suggests that the Roman writers had not understood the 'pragmatic' function of history. But Asellio had proclaimed that unlike the annalist, the historian must show *quo consilio quaque ratione gesta essent* {;with what intention and for what reason things were done}; (*HRR*, F 1). In all probability Fabius Pictor had already adopted this principle in his Greek history and had been generally followed by his successors writing in Latin.[25] In his very criticisms of the Roman historians, Cicero seems to concede that they were at least truthful. He makes 'Catulus' say that they thought it enough if a historian were not a liar (*de Orat.* 2.51). Yet, when he wrote the *Brutus* he was aware that the Roman historical tradition had been distorted by family laudations (*Brut.* 62), and in his own analytic summary of early Roman history he admits that very little was known of the regal period, which Fabius and others had certainly treated at some length; he pretty clearly has his tongue in his cheek in narrating some of the fables, and on the whole he provides a far more rationalistic account than Livy was to cull from the earlier annalists.[26]

Whatever Cicero really thought of the substance of the Roman annalists, he makes 'Antonius' censure them, as he praises the Greek historians, on the purely literary grounds which are most relevant to his discourse. Comparing them to Herodotus' predecessors, he says that at any rate down to Coelius Antipater they aimed stylistically at mere conciseness: *non exornatores rerum, sed tantummodo narratores fuerunt* {they were not embellishers of events but merely narrators}. Even Coelius who had naively aimed at some verbal effects was

---

[25] Gelzer (1933); (1934); (1954).
[26] *Rep.* 2.33, cf. Rambaud (1953) ch. III.

defective in *uarietate locorum* {diversity of reflections} as in *uerborum collocatione et tractu orationis leni et aequabili* {arrangement of words and a smooth and unvarying flow of style}. 'Atticus' too is made to depreciate the earlier writers as thin and meagre, stigmatizing even Cato, for whom Cicero was later to claim an antique 'eloquence' in his *Origines*. Atticus will allow Coelius only a rustic vigour, and of his successors, Asellio and Clodius relapsed into the older manner, Macer was prolix and magniloquent (cf. n. 21); the best was Sisenna, but he had taken a poor Greek model in Cleitarchus. The context indicates that Cicero was not thinking of Cleitarchus' mendacity, to which he alludes elsewhere (n. 58), but rather of some literary defect, probably that absurd showiness for which he was castigated by other writers on style, sometimes along with Callisthenes and Hegesias, whom Cicero too expressly disparages.[27]

Thus Roman historical writings gave no pleasure such as 'Antonius' found in reading the Greek masters and such as history could afford even to humble people, who could not expect to avail themselves of the lessons that it taught.[28] This evaluation of historical writing does not show that Cicero prized it only for literary merits. That conclusion would patently contradict his own explicit statement of its distinctness from poetry (*supra*). But in his rhetorical treatises he was naturally concerned with the relevance of history to oratory. Philosophy too is considered from the same standpoint: we need only ask which system is most closely connected with oratory, not which is nearest to the truth (*de Orat.* 3.64). Plato, Democritus, Aristotle, Theophrastus, and Carneades are also commended for their eloquence.[29] But it would be manifestly wrong to think that

---

[27] *De Orat.* 2.53f.; *Leg.* 1.6. Cleitarchus: *Brut.* 42; for style Demetr. *Eloc.* 303; [Long.] *Subl.* 3.2. Hegesias: *Orat.* 226, 230; D. Hal. *Comp. uerb.* 4 and 18, and Philod. *Rhet.* 1.180.15 Sudhaus, link him with Cleitarchus in common censure. Sisenna as orator, *Brut.* 228, cf. 66 and 294 on Cato's *Origines*, 106 on Piso's jejune annalistic style, 238 on Macer's speeches: *Orat.* 230 on Coelius.

[28] *De Orat.* 2.59; *Fin.* 5.51. Parallels in Avenarius (1956) 26–9. Even Polybius conceded that stylistic elegance was desirable, 16.17.9, cf. 12.28.10. The proposition that history, like poetry (n. 6) and epideictic oratory (e.g. *de Orat.* 2.341), ought to give delight does not entail that it is like them in all respects, or that truth is a subordinate purpose.

[29] *Orat.* 62, cf. *de Orat.* 1.47 on Plato as *summus orator* {utmost orator}, with 3.67, 3.139, and 3.60 and 129 on the eloquence of the Platonic Socrates; *Brut.* 120f.; *Tusc.*

this was the chief quality for which in Cicero's view they were to be prized. There is then as little reason to suppose that he admired Herodotus or Timaeus solely for their 'eloquence'.

Moreover, though it was Cicero's fundamental conception that history was to provide essential instruction on the past, that instruction would be ineffective if it found no pupils. The annals of early Rome were so badly written that no one would read them (*Leg.* 2.8). *Historia quoquo modo scripta delectat* {History gives pleasure in whatever style it is written} (Plin. *Ep.* 5.8.4): that was certainly not Cicero's opinion. Unlike dry-as-dust scholars of modern times, he had no patience with the most learned books 'which do not make easy reading'. It was of philosophical works in Latin that he wrote:

fieri autem potest, ut recte quis sentiat et id, quod sentit, polite eloqui non possit; sed mandare quemquam litteris cogitationes suas, qui eas nec disponere nec inlustrare possit nec delectatione aliqua adlicere lectorem, hominis est intemperanter abutentis et otio et litteris. Itaque suos libros ipsi legunt cum suis, nec quisquam attingit praeter eos, qui eandem licentiam scribendi sibi permitti uolunt

It is possible for someone to hold right views and yet be unable to express them in a polished style; but to commit one's thoughts to writing without being able to arrange or express them clearly or attract the reader by some sort of charm, indicates a man who makes an unpardonable misuse of leisure and literature. And so such men read their own books with their disciples, and none of them reaches a wider public than that which wishes to have the same privilege of scribbling extended to itself. (*Tusc. Disp.* 1.6)

In the same spirit, Lucretius, whose passion for truth cannot be impeached, sought *suauiloquenti / carmine Pierio rationem exponere nostram / et quasi musaeo dulci contingere melle* {to set forth my reasoning in the sweet-tongued Pierian song and as though to touch it with the sweet honey of the Muses} (4.20–21).

In Cicero's usage 'eloquence' may often be, as he described it in an early work, *artificiosa eloquentia, quam rhetoricam uocant* {artificial

---

1.24. For most later literary critics Plato was of course a supreme master of style. Democritus etc.: *de Orat.* 1.49, 2.161, 3.141; *Orat.* 62. In *Fin.* 1.15 and *de Orat.* 3.143 he allows that eloquence is not essential to a philosopher, though lucidity is. The orator can out-debate the philosopher unskilled in exposition (*de Orat.* 3.78f.).

eloquence, which they call rhetoric}.[30] But it can also have a much
wider connotation: *nihil enim est aliud eloquentia nisi copiose loquens
sapientia* {eloquence is nothing other than wisdom speaking pro-
fusely' (*Part. Orat.* 79). As such it is *ingeni lumen* {the light of the
intellect} (*Brut.* 59), whereby we can communicate knowledge that
might otherwise be hidden in our own minds (*Off.* 1.156). It is
therefore not confined to oratory; dialectic too can be regarded as
one of its species, *quasi contracta et astricta* {as if contracted or
compressed} (*Brut.* 309, cf. 119). In the *de Oratore* 'Crassus' maintains that:

una est enim . . . eloquentia, quascumque in oras disputationis regionesue
delata est; nam siue de caeli natura loquitur siue de terrae, siue de diuina ui
siue de humana, siue ex inferiore loco siue ex aequo siue ex superiore, siue ut
impellat homines siue ut doceat siue ut deterreat siue ut concitet siue ut
reflectat siue ut incendat siue ut leniat, siue ad paucos siue ad multos, siue
inter alienos siue cum suis siue secum, riuis est diducta oratio, non fontibus,
et quocumque ingreditur eodem est instructu ornatuque comitata.

eloquence is one, into whatever shores or realms of discourse it ranges.
Whether its subject is the nature of the heavens, of the earth, the power of
gods or men, whether it speaks before the judges or before senators or before
the people, whether its purpose is to move men to action, instruct them,
deter them, excite them or curb them, fire them or calm them down,
whether spoken to few or many, among strangers or with one's own or by
oneself, the flow of language, though running in different channels, does not
spring from different sources, and wherever it goes, it is accompanied by the
same matter and adornment.[31]

Similarly, while the term 'orator' normally designates the man
skilled in forensic and deliberative speaking, it can also connote the
master of eloquence in its wider sense, the man who has the gift for

---

[30] *Inv.* 1.6, cf. *de Orat.* 3.70, 72. So in *Orat.* 63f. he distinguishes from philosophical *sermo* the *eloquentia de qua nunc agitur* {eloquence we are here discussing}, cf. 13
(*eloquentia forensis* {forensic eloquence}); see *Offic.* 2.48f. and *Orat.* 113 and 117 on
the differences of oratorical and philosophic style.

[31] 3.22f., cf. 55; 76 ('Crassus'); 1.94; 2.66 ('Antonius'). Cf. 'Antonius' on Greek
historians: 'eloquentissimi homines, remoti a causis forensibus' {most eloquent men,
strangers to forensic oratory} (2.55) Tacitus could credit poets with 'eloquence' (*Dial.*
10.4); hence, when he praises the eloquence of previous historians (Dial. 23.2; *Agr.*
10.3; *Hist.* 1.1.1), he is not necessarily referring to their mastery of rhetoric in a
narrow sense. Cf. D. Hal. *Comp. uerb.* 11.

expounding any subject, however technical, not excluding mathematics, architecture, or medicine (1.61–3). Thus Plato, when ridiculing orators (in the ordinary acceptation of the term) in the *Gorgias*, seemed to 'Crassus' to be *summus orator* (1.47, cf. n. 29), and anyone may, if he chooses, designate the eloquent philosopher as an orator, or the professional orator who possesses wisdom as a philosopher (3.142). 'Antonius' had at first taken a much lower view of the orator, as no more than a clever speaker, who knows the tricks of the trade, but in the second book he too proposes to discourse *de tota eloquentia* {on eloquence as a whole} (2.26), and he too exalts the ideal of the perfect orator as one who can illuminate any subject with the splendour of language (33f.); 'Crassus' intervenes to remark that 'Antonius' has now adopted his own thesis that the orator must be a truly cultivated man (40), and later claims that 'Antonius' had accepted his own view of the range of eloquence (3.22).

It is from this standpoint that 'Antonius' asks *historia . . . qua uoce alia, nisi oratoris, immortalitati commendatur?* {whose voice but the orator's can entrust history to immortality?}; here the orator is the expert in the choice and invention of words and in the orderly and attractive treatment of any subject to which he applies his art (2.36). 'Antonius' endorses the thesis of 'Crassus' that the expert in any other art is an orator in so far as he expounds his knowledge with verbal skill (37f.). History too is then necessarily a *munus oratoris* {task for the orator} and indeed, according to Catulus, if it is to be written up to the standard set by the Greeks, it requires the *summus orator*, that is to say, the ideal master of language.[32] 'Antonius' actually emphasizes that the Greek historians whom he praises for their style were not themselves forensic orators, even though some were trained in rhetoric (55–8). It is surely the same conception that underlies the encouragement 'Atticus' is made to give Cicero in *de Legibus* (1.5) that he should remedy the deficiency of Latin literature in history, *quippe cum sit opus . . . unum hoc oratorium maxime* {seeing as this is

---

[32] *de Orat.* 2.51; 62: note the sequence: *Videtisne quantum munus sit oratoris historia? Haud scio an flumine orationis et uarietate maximum.* {Do you see how great a task history is for the orator? It may be the greatest in terms of fluency in speech and variety.}

a task more than any other fit for an orator}. He also says that this is Cicero's own opinion: *ut tibi quidem uideri solet* {as indeed it always seems to you}. I take these words, put in the form suitable to the dialogue, to be an allusion to the views which, as readers could be expected to recall, Cicero had set out in the *de Oratore.*

Cicero is indeed claiming rather more than that the writing of history requires the literary skill of the 'orator'. How can we explain *opus oratorium maxime*?[33] Why is history more suited to the 'orator' than law or philosophy?

Like the historian, the practical orator had often to tell a story, and even though his aim was verisimilitude and not truth (n. 8), one might think that the orator and historian could learn something of technique from each other. But that is not a point that Cicero makes. On the contrary, he says expressly that the orator must use in his narrative almost the language of daily speech; by implication that of the historian should be more elevated.[34] Though he approved of Thucydides' narrative, he thought it no more useful to the orator than his speeches, which had never been taken as a model by teachers of rhetoric (n. 8) Similarly Pliny was to reflect: *habet quidem oratio et historia multa communia, sed plura diuersa in his ipsis, quae communia uidentur* {indeed oratory and history have much in common but they differ in many points where they seem alike}: each had its own proper style for narrative (*Ep.* 5.8.9f.).

The past was of course a storehouse of *exempla* which the orator could often cite with great effect—but also with little regard for truth. In adverting to the value of *exempla*, Cicero makes the different claim that knowledge of the past is essential to the humane education of the perfect orator (n. 2). Eloquence actually derives from studies in philosophy, law and history (*Brut.* 322). But in the most elaborate

---

[33] Perhaps *maxime* should not be taken too seriously: strictly it implies that history is more oratorical than oratory itself.

[34] *Orat.* 124: *narrationes credibiles* (cf. n. 8) *nec historico sed prope cotidiano sermone explicatae dilucide* {credible narratives are clearly expressed, not in historical style but almost in everyday speech}, cf. *de Orat.* 2.329: *uerbis usitatis* {ordinary language}. The precepts for oratorical narrative in 2.323–9 are in various ways inapplicable to history, though in 3.211 'historia' seems to refer to such narrative. Differences are implied by Cicero elsewhere (*infra*) and e.g. in Quint. 10.1.31 (n. 5) and Pliny, *Ep.* 5.8.9f., cf. Avenarius (1956) 55ff. and n. 22 on Demochares and Callisthenes.

exposition of this ideal, which Cicero puts into the mouth of 'Crassus', and again in the *Orator*, Cicero puts law before history—and whatever the value of historical *exempla*, the utility of jurisprudence for forensic practice was more manifest[35]—and he lays supreme emphasis on the value of philosophy as the source of clarity in ideas and arguments and of richness in diction.[36] On his view knowledge of history was less essential to the orator than that of law and philosophy.

In any case, Cicero seems to assert not that the orator has to learn chiefly from history but that he is best equipped to write it. This contention was hardly connected in his mind with the ancient convention of inserting speeches in histories, which were the composition of the historian even when they had a basis in what had actually been said. Cicero alludes only once to the convention, differentiating the style required from that of forensic oratory. Speeches do not appear as essential to a good history in the discourse of 'Antonius', while the only speeches in the histories that Cicero admired, which he chooses to mention, are those of Thucydides, and then to find faults in them.[37]

So it seems to me probable that we must find another explanation for Cicero's view of history as *oratorium maxime*. Both law and philosophy were recognized as hard disciplines only to be mastered by prolonged application. By contrast, the collation or investigation

[35] *Orat.* 120, 322; cf. n. 3, and see generally the rival views on the importance of juristic knowledge to the orator in *de Orat.* 1.165–201 ('Crassus'), 212, 216, 234–55; 2.142–5 ('Antonius'). Cicero continually refers in *Brutus* to speakers, not all eloquent, who possessed juristic knowledge, see 78, 81, 98 (with *de Orat.* 1.216), 102, 108, 113f., 127, 129, 175, 178f., 214, 264; *de Orat.* 3.135 on Cato, and above all *Brut.* 143–57, 194–8 for comparisons between Crassus and Scaevola, and himself and Servius Sulpicius. The number and length of these passages indicate the importance that the subject had in his eyes. He naturally thought eloquence more valuable than knowledge of the law (*Orat.* 141f.), but clearly suggests that such knowledge could in some degree supply a want of rhetorical skill, and that the more the orator possessed, the nearer he came to the ideal.
[36] The long discussions of the relationship between oratory and philosophy between 'Crassus' and 'Antonius' in *de Orat.* are inconclusive, but 3.82 ('Catulus') represents the view proclaimed by Cicero in *Orat.* 11–16, 113–19; *Brut.* 44; 120f.; *Part. Orat.* 139. The ideal orator was to store his mind and enrich his style by reading in history, law, and philosophy (*de Orat.* 1.158, 256; 2.85; *Brut.* 161, 322, 331f.), as well as poetry (n. 5) but philosophy is most important. Cf. also nn. 29–30.
[37] *Orat.* 66, cf. 31–3 on Thucydides, with D. Hal. *Thuc.* 49.

of historical evidence, though time-consuming, required no technical preparation. Cicero might almost have said of the subject-matter of history as of that of a speech: *ipsae quidem res in perfacili cognitione uersantur* {the facts themselves are easily acquired} (*Orat.* 122). A work on history was more easily composed than one on law or philosophy by the orator in his capacity as the master of language.[38]

From this it did not follow that the historian was to use, in Cicero's own ironic description of his grand manner, all the colours of the orator's paint-pot (*Att.* 1.14.3f.). 'Antonius' remarks that history was not furnished with any specific rules by the teachers of rhetoric: *neque eam . . . usquam separatim instructam rhetorum praeceptis* {it is nowhere taught separately in the precepts of rhetoricians}.[39] This does not indeed mean that they had uttered no dicta on historical writing; we know that Theophrastus had commented on the style of Herodotus and Thucydides, and the parallels between Cicero's own observations on particular historians or on the style suitable to history and those of other writers no doubt derive from a common source or reflect an earlier consensus of opinion.[40] Still the statement is proof that Cicero knew of no systematic treatment of history in rhetorical treatises; what was to be found in them were perhaps observations as scattered and marginal as his own.[41] In his view, and probably in that of previous theorists, history is a separate genre with its own appropriate style, differing even from the narrative of the orator with none of the acerbity of the courts and the stinging epigrams of the advocate, therein resembling that of philosophical exposition.[42]

---

[38] *De Orat.* 1.212 ('Antonius'); minute investigations in philosophy required life-long application, of which indeed Cicero disapproves, 3.57 ('Crassus'). But Cicero no doubt deemed himself to know more philosophy than 'Crassus' desiderates (3.77–9, 86–9).

[39] 2.62. 'Antonius' also says that no rules are *needed* for panegyrics (2.45), a different matter; they certainly *existed* (2.341 ff.; *Orat.* 37ff.; *Part. Orat.* 70ff.).

[40] Cf. n. 16. The numerous parallels between Lucian's precepts and those found elsewhere proved the consensus, if not the existence of a treatise on which Lucian drew; cf. Avenarius (1956) 165–78.

[41] *De Orat.* 2.64, cf. *Orat.* 62 (philosophy cf. n. 54), 66; Luc. *h.c.* 49; Pliny, *Ep.* 1.16.4, 5.8.9f. Different genres: *Leg.* 1.5; *Brut.* 286 (n. 22); *Orat.* 68.

[42] E.g. *de Orat.* 1.144, 3.37; *Orat.* 79 (Theophrastus).

Of the four qualities in oratorical style which he approves, correctness, clarity, appropriateness, and ornamentation,[43] we can certainly assume that the first three were required of the historian; Thucydides is censured for occasional obscurity (n. 18). The first two virtues are easily intelligible. But what is appropriateness? In general terms, and in the commendations of some individual writers, he indicates that the historian should maintain, even in speeches (n. 37), a smooth, gentle, even flow, though Thucydides' manner was more impetuous (n. 44); again one is reminded of the *aequabile et temperatum orationis genus* {unimpassioned and restrained style of speech} which he claims for his own philosophical writing (*Offic.* 1.3). We have seen that the diction should also be elevated (n. 34) and, we may add, copious; the early Greek and Roman historians were meagre, and Herodotus and Thucydides 'fuller'. But Cicero also demands ornamentation; this can be connected with his reference to the *uarietas* of *loci* or *sententiae* and the *collocatio* or *compositio* of words (*de Orat.* 2.54, 56, 58).[44] It will appear that euphony and rhythm are all-important. It was on this account that Ephorus and Theopompus were much admired; they were the best exemplars among historians of the smooth style (D. Hal. *Comp. uerb.* 23). We can readily understand that these were qualities that exercised a natural appeal to the audience of a speaker (cf. *de Orat.* 3.181, 195–7). But histories too and other prose works were written perhaps as much to be heard as to be read, and it was necessary that they should sound well.

In oratory itself Cicero distinguishes three styles, the grand and plain, and one intermediate between them,[45] each of which was appropriate to different occasions, or to different parts of the same speech and each of which was accordingly employed by Demosthenes and by himself.[46] The plain style admitted of very little ornamentation except for a judicious profusion of *sententiae*, and it was not periodic and rhythmical.[47] Cicero commends the *Commentaries* of Caesar as 'bare, correct, and full of charm, though divested of all

[43] *Offic.* 1.3.
[44] *De Orat.* 2.54, 56, 58, 64; *Orat.* 39; parallels in Avenarius (1956) 55ff.
[45] E.g. *de Orat.* 3.177, 199, 210–12; *Orat.* 20ff., 69ff.
[46] *Orat.* 100–4, 110f., 123–5.
[47] Ibid. 76–90.

ornamentation', but these works professed to be no more than the raw material for history, and it is clear that Cicero's admiration for them does not mean that he thought such a style normally suitable for the historian.[48] Ornamentation was to be used most abundantly in the grand style, but the vehemence and sharpness which that style also comprised must have made it inappropriate to history, nor was it necessarily periodic.[49] There remains then the middle style, in which the orator interspersed ornaments more moderately. According to Cicero this style, characterized by *suauitas, uno tenore, ut aiunt in dicendo* fluit *nihil afferens praeter facultatem et aequalitatem* {*flows*, as they say, in an even tenor, carrying nothing but ease and uniformity}; it is apparently its exponents who *elaborant in* lenitate et aequabilitate *et puro quasi quodam et candido genere dicendi* {labour in *smoothness* and *uniformity*, and as it were a pure and clear style of speaking}. Among them Cicero singles out Demetrius of Phalerum *cuius oratio ... sedate placideque liquitur* (or *labitur*)' {whose speech flows (*or* glides) calmly and peacefully}. The similarity with the style he recommends for histories is manifest.[50]

It was, he says, the philosophic and sophistic schools that commonly produced practitioners of the middle style (*Orat.* 95f.).[51] We have already seen that philosophic and historical discourse have a certain likeness. By sophists he means the adepts of epideictic oratory in the manner of Isocrates, the stylistic master of Ephorus and Theopompus. Their works of course included panegyrics, and Cicero cites as a specimen of his own use of the middle style his laudation of Pompey in his speech for the Manilian law (*Orat.* 102). In epideictic oratory a very free use of 'ornament' was allowed (*Orat.* 38), more apparently than would be appropriate when the middle style was adopted in the forum, and (though Cicero does not say this), perhaps more than was considered tasteful in history.[52] But the epideictic

---

[48] *Brut.* 262; cf. Hirtius, *BG* 8 *pr.* Caesar, however, also said *uerborum dilectum originem esse eloquentiae* {choice of words is the foundation of eloquence} (253). Cicero's own *commentarii* (*Att.* 1.19.10; 2.1.2, cf. *Fam.* 5.12.10) were more ornate. Cf. Avenarius (1956) 85–104.

[49] *Orat.* 20, 97–9.

[50] Ibid. 91–6, cf. 21, 53. *Suauitas*: 91f., 99; *Part. Orat.* 72; *de Orat.* 3.28 (Isocrates).

[51] *Orat.* 207.

[52] Ibid. 37–42, 65–8; *de Orat.* 2.341–50; *Part. Orat.* 69–82; cf. Avenarius (1956), on Lucian *h.c.* 44.

style is described as *dulce et solutum et* fluens, *sententiis argutum, uerbis sonans* {sweet and easily flowing and *smooth*, clever in thoughts and with sounding phrases} (*Orat.* 42), which again reminds us of what Cicero thinks a good historical style. He expressly says that the periodic structure should always be employed both in epideixis and in history (*Orat.* 207). It is in a stylistic context that Cicero remarks of epideixis: *huic generi historia finitima est. In qua et narratur ornate et regio saepe aut pugna describitur; interponuntur etiam contiones et hortationes* {history is near to this genre. In it there is an ornate narrative and often a place or battle is described; harangues and speeches are also inserted} (*Orat.* 66). Narration took the foremost place in a panegyric (*Part. Orat.* 71). Indeed the sophists themselves wrote histories (*Orat.* 37). Here Cicero may have in mind the exercises in narrative, which might be concerned either with fables or with actual events, recommended by the manual on which his early treatise *de Inuentione* (1.27) and the work addressed to Herennius (1.12f.) had both drawn. We are not to infer that he conceived true histories as mere epideictic displays. He himself contrasts the practical orator with both sophist and historian (*Orat.* 68), and can claim of his own writings on his consulship that they are not 'encomiastic' but 'historical' (*Att.* 1.19.10); thus the genres were distinct.[53]

It is true that Hermogenes, a theorist of rhetoric in the second century AD, was to class historians among panegyrists, i.e. epideictic orators, among them Herodotus, Thucydides (though his writing is held to belong partly to the forensic or symbouleutic genres), Hecataeus and a medley of other great names; the greatest master of the genre was Plato.[54] This farrago of undiscriminating absurdity has sometimes been cited as reputable evidence that the ancients made no distinction between history and panegyric. Yet the distinction is emphatic in Lucian, who in general reflects traditional views, and is made among earlier writers not only by Polybius, who might be treated as exceptional, but by Ephorus and Timaeus, who had both received a rhetorical training. Immersed as he was in ancient rhetoric, Dionysius of Halicarnassus differentiates among the writings of

---

[53] Demetrius distinguished rhetorical, historical and philosophical periods (*Eloc.* 19).

[54] *Rhet. Gr.* II.403–25 (Spengel), esp. 417, cf. Marcell. *Vit. Thuc.* 41f.

Isocrates' pupil, Theopompus, between his panegyrical and historical works (*Pomp.* 6.1).[55] They belonged to different genres. We should not even suppose that Isocrates himself conceived that historians should model their narratives on those which he had inserted in his epideictic orations.[56]

Still, if much the same style was employed in epideictic and historical narrative, wherein did the difference lie? It must be found in purpose and function. Epideictic orators sought simply to give pleasure. They did not even aim, like the speaker in the courts, at persuasion; hence *concinnas magis sententias exquirunt quam probabilis* {they seek out elegant rather than persuasive ideas}. Cicero's Epicurean contemporary, Philodemus, said that panegyrists disregarded not only truth but even verisimilitude, and Cicero himself noted that *a re saepe discedunt, intexunt fabulas* {they often wander from the subject, they weave in tall tales}.[57] So they were to be aligned with poets rather than historians; truth was not even their objective. Cicero knew how Roman history had actually been falsified by the funeral laudations of the nobility (p. 219); since many of these are likely to have been artless enough (*de Orat.* 2.341), the mendacity of panegyrics was not so much the product of sophisticated instruction as a quality inherent in their very nature. We can now correctly interpret the remark that Cicero puts into the mouth of Atticus: *concessum est* rhetoribus *ementiri in historiis, ut aliquid dicere possint argutius* {it is permitted *to rhetors* to lie in history, so that they can express themselves more pointedly}; to illustrate this, he contrasts the inventions of Cleitarchus and Stratocles, characteristic of 'rhetorical and tragic embellishments', on the death of Themistocles with the sober account of Thucydides. So far from showing his approval of such embellishments, Cicero is mocking his own resort to them.[58] In any event, they are only a conventionally permitted device in histories written by rhetors, or sophists. Such works belong to the epideictic

---

[55] Luc. *h.c.* 7, cf. Pol. 10.21.8, 12.28.11; Avenarius (1956) 13–16. The distinction is blurred by Norden (1909), and by Woodman (1977) 28ff., in a vain effort to show that Velleius did not fall below the canons of ancient historical writing.

[56] No proof has ever been given that Isocrates taught anything but style to Ephorus, Theopompus etc., cf. n. 10. *Contra* Flach (1973) 17f.

[57] *Orat.* 65; cf. *Part. Orat.* 12 and 71–3; Philod. 1.285–7 (Sudhaus).

[58] Cf. Boyancé (1940). But Cicero relapses into error in *de Amic.* 42.

and not to the historical genre.[59] We may perhaps recall Cicero's ambiguous comments on historians who wrote in a rather rhetorical manner (nn. 21–3 and 27).

To prove that history was commonly regarded as a branch of rhetoric, some scholars have adduced the statement of a second century sophist, Rufus of Perinthus (Philost. *Vit. Soph.* 2.17), that 'there are four kinds of rhetoric, forensic, symbouleutic, encomiastic, and historical' and that the historical kind is 'that in which we give an ornate account of certain actions as having happened' (*Rhet. Gr.* I.399 Sp.). This specification seems quite isolated; Cicero, in particular, recognized only Rufus' first three species of oratory. The definition of history does not differentiate between true events and mere fables, which of course the rhetorician would recount 'as having happened'. Like the more extreme statement of Hermogenes, it shows only how far rhetoricians in the second century had distanced themselves from the orthodox theory of historiography, as we find it in the contemporary essay by Lucian. It would never have been accepted in principle by any historian. Nor does it correspond to the practice of such late writers as Arrian, Appian, and Cassius Dio. Cicero would certainly have never countenanced it.

Cicero did assume that historians would include accounts of the life and character of those *qui fama ac nomine excellent* {who are pre-eminent in reputation and name} (*de Orat.* 2.63), he certainly expected them to mete out praise and blame, and makes 'Atticus' suggest to him that if he were to write a history of contemporary events he would praise the deeds of Pompey and his own (*Leg.* 1.8). It might seem that history could thus after all turn into a panegyric. Modern as well as ancient instances will come to mind. But the modern historian who glorifies a Napoleon or a Bismarck may write in perfectly good faith. He is not necessarily departing from the truth as he sees it. Mommsen thought that Caesar merited his encomia, and Cicero surely believed that the truth justified anyone extolling Pompey's victories or his own preservation of the Republic. He would not have dissented from Polybius' view that it was not

[59] Metrodorus' work (*FGrHist* 184) may be of this category; see Avenarius (1956) 171. Likewise Hegesias' work on Alexander; no one describes him as a historian, only as a *rhetor* (*FGrHist* 142).

proper for the historian to indulge in unqualified panegyrics (8.8), or in bitter and extravagant denunciations (8.9.1–10.2): a balanced and rational assessment was required. Accounts of a great man's life and character were not necessarily encomiastic even in the works of a pupil of Isocrates. Philip II was certainly the hero of the history that Theopompus called the *Philippica*, but Polybius complained that he libelled the king and his friends after calling him the greatest man Europe had produced.[60]

Of all rhetorical devices Cicero lays perhaps the chief emphasis on *amplificatio: summa laus eloquentiae est amplificare rem ornando, quod ualet non solum ad augendum aliquid et tollendum altius dicendo sed etiam ad extenuandum atque abiciendum* {the highest distinction of eloquence consists in amplification by means of ornament, which can be used not only for increasing something and raising it higher by speaking, but also for diminishing and disparaging it} (*de Orat.* 3.104f.). It could be employed not only in the courts but in epideictic oratory in praise of virtue and condemnation of vice when *ea quae certa aut* pro certis posita sunt *augentur* {it amplifies statements that are certain or that are *advanced as being certain*} (*Part. Orat.* 71). It can be described as *augendi minuendiue causa ueritatis supralatio atque traiectio* {an exaggeration and crossing-over of truth for the sake of increasing or diminishing} (*de Orat.* 3.203).[61] Clearly this should not have been regarded as an 'ornament' appropriate to history. None the less, Cicero in urging Lucceius to write a monograph on his own consulship and its aftermath, down to his return from exile, begs him *ut ornes ea uehementius etiam quam* fortasse *sentis* {that you adorn those things rather more strongly than *perhaps* you feel}, just as he had earlier hoped that Posidonius would on the basis of his own *commentarium* treat the subject *ornatius* {with more adornment} (*Att.* 2.1.2). However he admits that his request to Lucceius is rather shameless and that he is inviting him to transgress the laws of history. Probably his conscience was hardly troubled. He might not have admitted to himself that any magnification of his own merits could

---

[60] D. Hal. *Pomp.* 6. Luc. *h.c.* 59 reflects Polybius' opinion.

[61] Cf. *de Orat.* 1.221 (building on what men believe); 3.104 (working up emotions); *Part. Orat.* 53–8 (listing various devices, some only available to an orator), 71 (use in *epideixis*); 27, 52; *Orat.* 126f.

go much, if at all, beyond the truth, though he would be painfully aware that others, Lucceius *perhaps* included, did not esteem them quite so highly.[62] Nor of course would all *amplificatio* necessarily involve the historian (or indeed the orator) in conscious falsehood. It might be no more than the employment of stylistic devices (to which we all resort) to convince the reader of the truth and importance of what the writer believes. Exaggeration could be the result. I give one familiar example, which too many modern scholars have taken literally. Thucydides' assertion that Pericles' influence at Athens was so great that in his time the system 'was coming to be a democracy only in name, but in reality government by the leading man' is disproved by the facts that he has just related (2.65.9 with 2). A real difference between Pericles and his successors is overstated for effect.

Some of the other 'ornaments' discussed at length by 'Crassus' in the *de Oratore* and by Cicero *in propria persona* in the *Orator* are plainly available only to the practical speaker and are as irrelevant to the historian as the advice given on pronunciation and delivery.[63] The demand that history should be 'ornate' cannot be equivalent to one that the historian should adopt all the devices appropriate to the orator. However, the ornamentation on which most emphasis is placed concerns diction and rhythm. The orator is to vary and embellish his language with archaisms, used sparingly, with newly coined words, and with metaphors; his vocabulary should be abundant, and the words chosen not commonplace but full and sonorous. All this could apply to history; indeed the diction of the historian should be more exalted than that sometimes proper to the orator (*supra*). Cicero enlarges still more on balance, rhythm, euphony, which is attained by *uerborum collocatio* {arrangement of words}; a

---

[62] *Fam.* 5.12.2f. The proposal was a delicate compliment to Lucceius; perhaps that was why Cicero thought his letter 'very pretty' (*Att.* 4.6.4). So too Pliny would have Tacitus immortalize him in his history (*Ep.* 8.33.1), though he is more discreet: *haec, utcumque se habent, notiora clariora* maiora *tu facies; quamquam non exigo ut excedas actae rei modum nam nec historia debet egredi ueritatem, et honeste factis ueritas sufficit* {these things, such as they are, you will make better known, more distinguished, *greater*; although I do not ask that you exceed the measure of what was actually done, for history should not transgress the truth, and truth suffices for honest deeds} (8.33.10).

[63] *de Orat.* 3.202–12; *Orat.* 135–9. Some devices for pungency, emphasis, or assonance were of course available to a writer of any kind.

subject to which Dionysius devoted a whole treatise.[64] It is precisely in discussing it that Cicero (like Dionysius) comments on the effects that Greek historians, and Plato too, had obtained or failed to obtain; it was here that Herodotus and Thucydides were wanting, whereas under the influence of Isocrates, both Ephorus and Theopompus introduced the periodic structure which he expressly declares necessary in history.[65] Yet Cicero also admired the style of Herodotus and Thucydides, partly no doubt for their choice of words. Another reason, especially in the case of Thucydides, can be found in the *sententiae* that abounded in his work (n. 18). *Varietas locorum* {variety of locales} was also a proper way of 'adorning' a history.[66]

Whatever we may think of these desiderata for historical writing, some of which were not acceptable to Sallust and Tacitus, none was incompatible with veracity. *Sententiae* could be not only applicable to the facts but illuminating. A flowing, euphonious and rhythmical style, an elevated and even poetic diction, could serve facts as well as fiction. For some all this was not enough. Duris censured Ephorus and Theopompus for not rising to the height of events they described, since they made no attempt at *mimesis*, i.e. vivid representation, or at evoking the pleasure this would give, but paid attention only to the actual writing,[67] presumably to those qualities of diction and rhythm which Cicero admired in them. Dionysius of Halicarnassus, whose judgements on historians often resembled those of Cicero, and who especially approved of Theopompus (n. 60), counted Duris with Phylarchus, Polybius, and many other Hellenistic historians among those whose inattention to the beauty of language produced by the euphonious combination of words made it impossible

---

[64] *De Orat.* 3.147–208; *Orat.* 80, 134, 149–end.

[65] *Orat.* 151, 172, 175f., 186, 191f., 207, 219, 230, 234f. Demetrius, *Eloc.*, draws on the historians for similar purposes (12, 17, 27, 39f. etc.).

[66] See e.g. *de Orat.* 3.96; *Orat.* 136 (oratory); *de Orat.* 2.54, 56, 58 (history).

[67] *FGrHist* 76 F 1, which does not imply that Duris propounded or had in mind any theory of history more elaborate than that of Polybius, or indeed any theory equally elaborate. The fact that he had been a pupil of Theophrastus (T 1) does not show that he remained a Peripatetic or followed the teaching of Theophrastus (n. 16) on history. The character of Duris' history can hardly be determined, despite the efforts of Kebric (1978), from hostile comments and sparse, probably unrepresentative, fragments, very many from Athenaeus. Some moderns condemn it as anecdotal: Athenaeus' quotations impart that appearance to every history from which he culls, e.g. that of Herodotus, who (like most historians) did include anecdotes. Cf. n. 79.

to read their works through,[68] yet he shared Duris' opinion that historical writing should 'represent' men's characters and sufferings.[69] Cicero barely mentions vividness among the ornaments of oratorical style,[70] but perhaps if he had been more than incidentally concerned with history, he would have made the same point. But, if we believe Duris, it was not a quality that distinguished the writing of the pupils of Isocrates. It could be employed, we may suppose, for merely pictorial effect, but it could also be the means of communicating pathos and evoking emotion. Instead of soberly recording and analyzing actual transactions, the historian might set out to titillate his public with lurid descriptions and strange and exciting incidents, embroidering the facts with a free use of his imagination.

Some Hellenistic historians, including Duris and Phylarchus, were accused of these malpractices by Polybius and later writers. Phylarchus, in particular, so Polybius alleges, did not see that it was the function of the historian to recount faithfully what had been said and done, however commonplace, not to thrill his readers or seek the effects of a tragic poet. In other criticisms of rival historians it is, however, not 'tragic history' precisely of this kind that Polybius condemns, but simply the invention of vivid details for their own sake, or the intrusion of 'marvels', a characteristic of Theopompus among others.[71] The calumnious treatment of Herodotus in Plutarch's

[68] *Comp. uerb.* 4: the common vice (as he sees it) of these writers is merely in their diction.

[69] *Pomp.* 3 (776) on Herodotus and Thucydides, cf. n. 73. So too Plut. *Moral.* 347A thinks that the best historian is one whose vivid representation of emotions and characters makes his narrative like a painting, as Thucydides always sought to do, e.g. in 4.10–12, 7.71; he praises Xenophon for similar effects (*Artax.* 8.1). Cf. Avenarius (1956) 130–40; [Long.] *Subl.* 25f.

[70] *de Orat.* 3.202; *Orat.* 139.

[71] Pol. 2.56–61 (Phylarchus); 7.7, cf. 2.16 (tragic fables in Timaeus); 3.47f. (absurd introduction of the supernatural by unnamed writers); 58 (travellers' tales credulously retailed); 16.16–20 (incorrect topography and incoherent narrative); 15.34 (miraculous embellishments); 29.12 (invented descriptions). Cf. for Duris *FGrHist* 76 TT 7–8; Plut. (*Per.* 28) charges him with 'exaggerating for tragic effect'; D. Hal. *Thuc.* 28 uses the same term in censure of Thuc. 3.82f.; Plutarch who approves of vividness (n. 69) also condemns other historians for seeking false tragic effects (*Artax.* 6.9, 18.7; *Them.* 32; *Alex.* 75). Some modern scholars seem to assume that any dramatic and vivid account must be false (except in Thucydides!). Why? Polybius had more sense: he reproached Timaeus and others for lack of clear and accurate details and pictorial vividness, 12.25g and 25h.

essay on his malignity should make us wary of accepting criticisms of authors whose works cannot be read in their own defence (cf. n. 67). Ancient historians were given to censuring each other for reasons not always sound or even creditable. Still, we can well believe that some Greek historians, in default of evidence, invented details to make their narratives vivid, thrilling or pathetic; certainly this was the practice of Livy, or his predecessors.[72] No one ever surpassed Thucydides in those qualities, or indeed in pathos, in which Dionysius noted his supremacy; of his account of the last sea-battle at Syracuse he observed that 'every man's heart is carried away by such language'.[73] Here was the fount of tragic as well as of scientific history in the ancient world, nor was there any inevitable discordance between them. The historian does well to bring out the tragedy that may be inherent in events, and to depict them as they are with all the graphic power at his command. Whether this was the teaching of the rhetorical schools I do not know, for lack of clear testimony: it was certainly the teaching of good sense, commended by the example of the greatest historian in antiquity. In principle Duris' conception of narrative history was right, whether or not he and others adopted meretricious means to give it effect.

Cicero writes to Lucceius:

nihil est aptius ad delectationem lectoris quam temporum uarietates fortunaeque uicissitudines.... Viri saepe excellentis ancipites variique casus habent admirationem, exspectationem, laetitiam, molestiam, spem, timorem; si uero exitu notabili concluduntur, expletur animus iucundissima lectionis uoluptate;

nothing tends more to the reader's pleasure than varieties of circumstance and vicissitudes of fortune.... the doubtful and various fortunes of an exceptional individual afford surprise, suspense, joy, distress, hope, fear; if indeed they end in a memorable outcome, the mind in reading is filled with the liveliest gratification;

and again, the subject he proposes *habet uarios actus mutationesque et consiliorum et temporum* {contains many 'acts' and changes of plan and circumstance}. This is held to reflect a Hellenistic theory

[72] But Kroll (1924) 351–69, with wonderful self-confidence, could infallibly detect Livy's personal touches. With equal certitude others discern what Tacitus did not derive from his lost sources but himself invented in writing the *Annals*.

[73] *Thuc* 15, 23f. and 27, cf. *Pomp.* 3 (776); *Comp. uerb.* 7; n. 69. Thuc. 2.4 is a good instance.

of what all history should be, modelled on a tragedy—'quasi fabulam' {as if a play}.[74] Cicero is also suggesting a monograph with an organic unity but of modest proportions, *modicum quoddam corpus*. It might as well be inferred that on Hellenistic theory all history should take the form of relatively small monographs, unlike the works of (say) Duris, Phylarchus, Agatharchides, Timaeus, and Posidonius, to say nothing of Polybius. Cicero is not laying down what every history should be, but is simply urging that the particular subject he proposes to treat is exceptionally attractive because the events to be described are as exciting as those of a drama. There is nothing strange or reprehensible in this. Some scholarly accounts of the French Revolution which end with the fall of Robespierre and exclude the less colourful events that ensued conform precisely to Cicero's pattern. Nor again, in asking Lucceius to magnify his own deeds in violation of the *leges historiae* (which therefore applied as much to a monograph as to any other historical work) was he suggesting that in any other respect his narrative should be untruthful: there is no call for a sensationalism unwarranted by the facts.

It is perhaps rather curious that only here does Cicero suggest that history should have some artistic unity, which of course need not be in conflict with truth; he does not complain of the annalistic structure of the early Roman historians. Yet Polybius had claimed that his own history had an organic form, and Ephorus in a work of vast compass had apparently sought some kind of unity for his several books. But this again was nothing new. Artistic unity can be claimed for the design of Thucydides and even of Herodotus. If any theorists required it, they were (as usual) drawing on the best examples, furnished by writers too early to have been influenced by any theory.[75]

All this is not to exculpate ancient historians from charges to which many of them are vulnerable.

According to P. Scheller: 'there existed from the Hellenistic age a certain fixed way of writing history which . . . was taken in its entirety

---

[74] *Fam.* 5.12.4–6. Walbank's remarks on 'tragic history' ((1972) 34–40 with bibliography) have made too little impact on Flach (1973). Cf. nn. 16, 40, 67.

[75] Pol. 1.3.4, cf. Walbank (1972) 66–8; Avenarius (1956) 107–13. Diod. 5.1.4, 16.1.1 suggests Ephorus' practice. The influence of e.g. Gorgias on Thucydides' diction has of course nothing to do with any rhetorical theory of history.

from rhetoric'. It went back, so he and others think, to Isocrates, though Theophrastus is supposed to have imported the conception that history should be in some sense tragic (cf. n. 67). The influence of Isocrates on the *style* of some historians is beyond question, and Theophrastus too certainly expressed judgements, which others like Cicero were to repeat, on *style* (n. 16). That is really all we know of their teaching, as it affected history. Everything else is speculative combination. We know also that some Hellenistic historians like Polybius (who was not necessarily unique) were little affected by this teaching, and that Duris at least thought that more was needed than the smooth language that others copied from Isocrates. It is also clear, meagre though the remains of Hellenistic historians are (save for Polybius), that they had very different manners. The only generalization that we can safely make is that from the end of the first century none of them was regarded as a literary model. By contrast, the ancient historian who is most admired today, Thucydides, was according to Dionysius by general consent of *rhetoricians* and philosophers supreme, not least for the attention to truth which Dionysius, rhetorician as he was, commends, but also for his literary qualities; thus he is much cited by the writer *On the Sublime*, and for Demetrius he was *par excellence* the master of the grand style; Dionysius has to apologize for arguing that he was not faultless. It is pretty clear that Cicero, though not uncritical, held a similar opinion. It persisted; his most remarkable imitator known to us was Cassius Dio. Though Thucydides was himself indebted to the early rhetoricians—hence his predilection for antitheses, sometimes contrived, and perhaps his occasional tendency to overstate for effect what he sees as the truth—it would be absurd to suggest that their influence (which did not please later taste) distorted his history as distinct from his phraseology. This long-lasting admiration of his work in Roman times is a curious commentary on the modern dogma that historiography had later been corrupted by the schools of rhetoric.[76]

Ancient historians could certainly be variously negligent in collecting material, careless in reporting what they found in their sources, credulous in accepting marvels, anecdotes and ill-authenticated reports,

[76] See nn. 14–19, 37, 69, 73.

given to sheer inventions, adulatory, or malignant, and ready to conceal or misrepresent the facts which did not suit their interests or prejudices. But these faults were not inculcated by the precepts of rhetoric, or any sort of theory.[77] Myths and marvels had figured largely in the work of Herodotus. Thucydides censured the *logographoi* for using such material to delight their readers at the expense of truth and implied that his own care in investigation of the facts was unprecedented (1.21.1). Yet these early writers were not moulded by rhetoric. But the charm or power of their narratives supplied models for later historians who sought to please their readers. And if rhetoric did encourage some of those historians to neglect or distort the truth, it was not the sole cause of such defects. Carelessness enough can be found in stylistically unpretentious epitomators, like the author of the *Periochae* of Livy. The Roman annalists, artless as they were on Cicero's showing, had yet accepted as historical a mass of legend (already to be found in Fabius Pictor), and of falsehoods put about in funeral laudations (*Brut.* 62): the very dimensions of the history of Cn. Gellius, which ran to at least ninety-seven books and reached the same point in Book 15 as Livy in Book 6, also prove that the meagre traditions of early Roman history had been augmented by fiction on the large scale, long before so rhetorical a writer as Livy set to work. Some such fictions lent vividness to the story, and we have Polybius' testimony that there were Hellenistic historians who simply invented details for that purpose. But it is precisely the historians, whose debt to the rhetorical precepts of Isocrates is most certain, who were accused of failing in vividness, Ephorus and Theopompus by Duris, Timaeus by Polybius himself, while Phylarchus, whose 'tragic writing' was deprecated by Polybius and others, and Duris stand condemned along with Polybius by a critic so immersed in the rhetorical tradition as Dionysius. And 'tragic history' itself had a classic exemplar in Thucydides.[78] As for bias, it is not always (if ever) absent from the productions of modern scholarship, however devoid they may be of vehemence, elegance or charm. Polybius, for all his depreciation of literary graces, was not impartial.[79]

---

[77] Norden (1909) I.81ff. lumps together all Polybius' criticisms of other historians, even for mere bias (1.14), as polemics against rhetoric in history: others regard the most diverse faults as marks of tragic history. This is modern 'rhetoric'.

[78] Cf. Brunt (1967) and (1969).

[79] Coelius, Macer and Sisenna had indeed learned something from rhetoric (Flach (1973) 26–30).

No doubt the rhetorical schools helped to form the taste of the reading public, and they set so high a value on style that some historians whom they had trained cared too little for the work of ascertaining and accurately stating the truth. Rhetoric also supplied them with the arts of distortion when it suited their purpose. But it was also the instrument by which, if they chose, they could induce the public to read, or to hear, 'what had really happened' and make it convincing. It could be the handmaiden either of truth or of falsehood. In principle Cicero thought that it should be the handmaiden of truth. In so far as he wished to sacrifice this ideal to his own glorification, he was prompted by vanity, self-delusion or political interest, not corrupted by rhetorical teaching. By describing history as *opus oratorium maxime*, he was making a demand, adjusted to the taste of his age, that the historian should write well. *Nihil est aliud pulchre et oratorie dicere nisi optimis sententiis uerbisque lectissimis dicere* {delivering a beautiful speech is nothing other than speaking with the best thoughts and the choicest language} (*Orat.* 227).[80]

[80] In Brunt (1980b) I have argued that we can seldom pronounce with certainty on the character of lost histories on the basis either of so-called fragments, which may be inaccurate and unrepresentative, or of epitomes, which may be garbled, or of the censures of other writers, which may be unfair. It was not my intention in this essay to express any judgement on the merits or demerits of such histories as those of Duris or Phylarchus.

9

Cicero and the Writing of History

A. J. Woodman

INTRODUCTION: THE LETTER TO LUCCEIUS AND THE *DE ORATORE*

Though Cicero's friends repeatedly expressed the hope that he would embark on a major work of history,[1] any such project remained unwritten by the time of his murder in December 43 BC. Cornelius Nepos, the dedicatee of Catullus' poetry book and himself a historian, had no doubt that a unique opportunity had thereby been missed.[2]

This is the one branch of Latin literature which not only fails to match Greece but was left crude and inchoate by the death of Cicero. He was the one man who could and should have fashioned historical discourse in a worthy rhetorical manner [*historiam digna uoce pronuntiare*] ... I am uncertain whether the country or historiography lost more by his death.

Yet despite Cicero's omission, the great orator was nevertheless responsible for various statements concerning historiography to which modern scholars have attached considerable importance.[3]

---

[1] See Kelley (1969) 143–54 with references.

[2] F 3 (OCT).

[3] For a representative sample of the most important during the past thirty years or so, see the works of Rambaud (1953); Leeman (1955) 188–91 = (1963) 168–74; Trencsényi-Waldapfel (1960); Walsh (1961) Ch. 2; Kelley (1969); Petzold (1972); Rawson (1972); and Brunt (1980a) {= above, Ch. 8}. The arguments of the last named scholar deserve particularly careful treatment, since, despite his wish to appear as a lone voice, his is the most recent and detailed expression of views which are in fact standard amongst modern students of ancient history.

The two most substantial and famous of these statements both belong to the year 55 BC.

In the middle of April Cicero wrote a letter to his friend L. Lucceius, advising him how to approach the work of history on which he was engaged (*Fam.* 5.12):

Dear Lucceius,

I have often tried to raise the following matter with you in person, only to be prevented by an embarrassment which is uncharacteristic of my metropolitan temperament. However, now that we're apart, I feel bold enough to broach the subject. After all, a letter can't blush.

You won't believe how much I want you to celebrate my name in your writings—a quite justifiable desire, in my opinion. I know you've often indicated that this was your intention, but please excuse my impatience. You see, I always had high hopes of your particular kind of writing, but it has now exceeded my expectations and taken me by storm: I've a burning desire for my achievements to be entrusted to your monumental works as quickly as possible. It's not just that I can hope for immortality by being remembered by posterity: I also want to enjoy while I'm still alive the authority which only your work can provide—your seal of approval coupled with your literary distinction.

2   It's true that even as I write I am only too well aware of the pressure you're under from the material which you have embarked upon and already arranged. But as I see that you've almost finished your account of the Italian and Civil Wars, and you told me yourself that you've made a start on the remaining period, I don't want to miss the opportunity of asking you to consider this question. Would you prefer to incorporate my story into that remaining period or . . . deal with the Catilinarian conspiracy separately from the wars with foreign enemies? As far as my reputation is concerned, I don't see that it makes much difference either way; but I'm frankly impatient and don't want you to wait till you reach the appropriate point in your continuous narrative: I'd much rather you got down to the period of the *cause célèbre* straight away and on its own terms. In addition, if you give your undivided attention to a single theme and a single personality, I can envisage even now the greater scope for rich elaboration [*ornatiora*].

Of course I'm well aware how disgracefully I'm behaving: having first landed you with this considerable responsibility (though you can always plead other engagements and turn me down), I'm now demanding elaborate treatment [*ornes*]. What if you don't think my achievements deserve
3   elaboration [*ornanda*]? Still, once the limits of decency have been passed, one should be well and truly shameless. So I repeat—elaborate [*ornes*] my

activities even against your better judgement, and in the process disregard the laws of historiography [*et in eo leges historiae neglegas*]: that prejudice [*gratiam*], which you discussed quite beautifully in one or other of your prefaces and which, you revealed, could no more influence you than Pleasure could influence Hercules in Xenophon's book, well, please don't suppress it if it nudges you strongly in my favour, but simply let your affection [*amori*] for me take a degree of precedence over the truth [*ueritas*].

If I can persuade you to take on the responsibility, I'm sure you'll find that
4 the material will bring out the best in your fluent artistry. For it seems to me that a modest volume could be compiled if you start with the beginning of the conspiracy and end with my return from exile. On the one hand, you'll be able to capitalize on your knowledge of the civil disturbances by explaining the causes of the revolutionary movement or suggesting remedies for political crises, at the same time criticizing whatever in your opinion requires criticism [*uituperanda*] and giving full and reasoned approval [*exponendis rationibus comprobabis*] to whatever you approve of. On the other hand, if you think a more outspoken [*liberius*] treatment is called for, as you often do, you can denounce the disloyalty, plotting, and treachery which many people displayed towards me. For my experiences will provide you with plenty of variety [*uarietatem*] when you come to write—variety mixed with the kind of pleasure [*uoluptatis*] which can hold the attention of your readers. For nothing is more calculated to entertain a reader [*delectationem lectoris*] than changes of circumstance and the vicissitudes of fortune [*temporum uarietates fortunaeque uicissitudines*]. I didn't welcome them at the time, of course, but to read about them will be sheer delight [*iucundae*]: it's a pleasure [*delectationem*] to recall past misfortune in the safety of your own
5 home. When people who haven't undergone any troubles of their own look on [*intuentibus*] other people's misfortunes without suffering themselves, they experience pleasure [*iucunda*] even as they take pity on them. After all, which of us does not derive pleasure [*delectat*] as well as a kind of pity from the scene of Epaminondas dying at Mantinea? Remember, he did not order the spear to be removed until he had received a satisfactory answer to his question whether his shield was safe, so that despite the pain of his wound he could die honourably with his mind at rest. Whose attention is not alerted and held [*retinetur*] by reading about Themistocles' exile and death? The monotonous regularity of the *Annales* has as much effect on us as if we were reading through official calendars; but the unpredictable and fluctuating circumstances [*ancipites uariique casus*] surrounding a great figure induce admiration, anticipation, delight, misery, hope, and fear [*admirationem, exspectationem, laetitiam, molestiam, spem, timorem*]. And if they have a

memorable outcome [*exitu notabili*], the reader feels a warm glow of pleasure [*iucundissima uoluptate*].

6   So I'll be all the more gratified if you do decide to separate the drama (so to speak) of my experiences from the on-going narrative in which you deal with the continuous history of events. You'll find that it has its various 'acts' and numerous examples of dramatic reversal [*multasque mutationes et consiliorum et temporum*].

Though this letter is recognized by scholars as important, it is usually for different reasons from that on which I wish to focus.[4]

It will be seen from section 3 of the letter that Cicero contrasts truth (*ueritas*) with prejudice (*gratia, amor*), from which it appears to follow that Cicero saw the truth in terms of impartiality. As modern readers and critics we have been conditioned, both by a mistaken view of Thucydides and by the conventions of modern historiography, to expect ancient historical writers to be concerned with historical truth in our sense of the term; but if we look closely at what the ancients actually say, instead of what we think they ought to be saying, we shall see that Cicero's view of the truth is by no means peculiar to him.[5] On the contrary, the view is also that of the three major historians of the classical period. Here are Sallust's words at the start of the *Bellum Catilinae* (4.2–3):

statui res gestas populi Romani carptim . . . perscribere, eo magis quod mihi a spe metu partibus rei publicae animus liber erat. igitur de Catilinae coniuratione quam uerissume potero paucis absoluam.

I decided to write an historical monograph on a Roman theme, especially since I was *unaffected by ambition, fear, or partisan politics*. And *for that*

---

[4] It is usually taken as a kind of blue-print for Hellenistic or 'tragic' historiography (on which see below, n. 151). The importance of the letter should not, however, be allowed to obscure its humour, which I have tried to bring out in my translation. Some further points: Cicero describes his embarrassment as *subrusticus* (1), yet he wrote to Lucceius from the country; he professes to forget which of Lucceius' prefaces contained the beautiful discussion of prejudice he is now urging him to discount (3); *modicum uolumen* (4) is false modesty; *enumeratio fastorum* (5) perhaps playfully recalls Plat. *Hipp. Mai.* 285E. In addition, Ullman (1942) 53 points to various colloquial touches which 'were deliberately introduced to give an air of informality'. On the other hand, Shackleton Bailey (1980) 139 says that the letter is written in Cicero's most ornate style, which he naturally (but in my opinion quite wrongly) represents in his Penguin translation.

[5] See Herkommer (1968) 140–4.

reason I will compose my brief account of the Catilinarian conspiracy *as truthfully as possible.*

In the *Histories* Sallust says that during the civil wars partisan politics did not cloud his view of 'the truth' (1.6: *neque me diuersa pars in ciuilibus armis mouit a uero* {nor has a different side in the civil wars shifted me from the truth}), words which are later echoed by Livy in his preface (5: see Woodman (1988) 131). Later still, Tacitus never even mentions 'truth', which, in the limited sense under discussion, has to be inferred from his coded references to *neque amore ... et sine odio* {neither with favouritism ... and without animosity} in the *Histories* (1.1.3)[6] and to *sine ira et studio* {without anger and parti- ality} in the *Annals* (1.1.3). Finally we should note that even Lucian, whose book on historiography is the only one to have survived from the ancient world and who is always appealed to by scholars as the ultimate authority on 'truth', in fact takes exactly the same view as Cicero and the other historians.[7]

If we can rid ourselves of the mistaken notion that the ancients' view of historical truth was the same as ours, we will be able readily to appreciate why truth and falsehood were seen in terms of prejudice and bias.[8] In both Greek and Roman society, political life was based

---

[6] For the use of *amor* in particular, cf. Cicero's letter to Lucceius.

[7] Brunt (1980a) 313 {= above, p. 210} appeals to Luc. *h.c.* 7 as illustrating truth in our modern sense, but it is quite clear that here and elsewhere Lucian is referring to (im)partiality: see, e.g., 7 τοῖς ἐπαίνοις, ἐπαινέσαι, 8 ἐπαινέσαι, κολακείαν, τὸ ἐγκώμιον, 9 ἐπαινετέον, τὸ ἐγκώμιον, 10 τῶν ἐπαίνων, ἐπαίνοις, 11 οἱ ἔπαινοι κτλ. The same is true of Polybius: see Herkommer (1968) 138, who also remarks (145–6) that Ammianus is the only Roman historian who professes 'truth' in what he (Herkommer) regards as the 'Thucydidean' sense. It is worth remembering the parody of an historian's preface at Sen. *Apoc.* 1.1 *nihil nec* offensae *nec* gratiae *dabitur: haec ita<que> uera* {no concession will be made to offense taken or favour given: these things are therefore true}. [*itaque,* my easy suggestion for an awkward *ita* (on which see Eden (1984) ad loc.) would, if correct, make the point even clearer: *itaque* is postponed roughly 300 times elsewhere in Seneca, though he prefers it in first place, cf. *TLL* 7.2.521.73ff.] Wiseman (1981) 387 has rightly seen the limitations of Lucian's words.

[8] We should not forget the phenomenon which Veyne (1984) 222, for example, spotlights when he remarks that 'in the seventeenth century preachers and moralists spoke a great deal about favourites [sc. at court] ... but did not describe the system, for everyone was steeped in it'. Just so in the ancient world they took for granted and referred regularly to a concept of impartiality which, since they had no reason to explain it further, requires a considerable amount of mental adjustment on the part of readers today.

on a code of honour, with each man pursuing his own τιμή or *gloria*.⁹
Now 'envy is characteristic . . . of all honour societies, since the man
of honour is anxious to promote his own honour at the expense of
the honour of others. There is only a limited amount of honour at
hand, and one resents and envies the possession of it by other
people'.¹⁰ In classical terms, one man's τιμή or *gloria* provoked the
φθόνος or *inuidia* {jealousy} of others;¹¹ and since the historian
was responsible for recording and perpetuating men's honour in as
elaborate a medium as possible, he found himself in a particularly
awkward position. On the one hand he could not risk alienating one
group of readers or another by appearing to be either too prejudiced
in favour of someone to whom they were opposed, or too biased
against someone of whom they approved.¹² This is the risk to which
Tacitus testifies in his *Annals*.¹³ On the other hand, the historian
would not wish to appear invidious on his own part, as both Sallust
and Pliny testify.¹⁴ It was therefore quite natural for the historian
to disclaim prejudice and bias by means of prefatory statements such
as those quoted in the preceding paragraph. Indeed there was all the
more reason for such statements if, as I have suggested (Woodman
(1988) 41–3), ancient historiography itself could be seen in terms of
praise and blame.¹⁵

Thus Cicero's letter to Lucceius is important for illustrating what
he meant by 'the truth' in historiography; but it is of course considerably less important than the work which he published seven

---

⁹ For Greek society, see e.g. Adkins (1972) 14ff.; for Roman, Earl (1967) and
Wiseman (1985a) 1–13.

¹⁰ Walcot (1973) 117, with references in n. 1.

¹¹ See, e.g., Walcot (1978); Woodman (1983a) 63–4.

¹² I say 'too' because all historians are of course biased and prejudiced to some
extent. Realization of this fact may have been at the back of Cicero's mind when he
chose the metaphor of *fundamenta* to designate the laws of historiography (see
p. 256): just as foundations (being below ground) are generally invisible, so the
laws of historiography (being frequently broken) are also often invisible.

¹³ *Ann.* 4.33.4. For an extended case-study, see Wiseman (1979) 57–139.

¹⁴ For Sallust, see Woodman (1988) 43 and n. 266; for Pliny cf. *Ep.* 5.8.13 'if you
praise you're said to have been grudging, if you criticize you're said to have been
excessive'.

¹⁵ Note that the eighteenth-century theologian Chladenius drew a distinction
between 'point of view' (i.e. Dionysius' διάθεσις) and bias as such (see Gossman
(1978) 6).

months later. In November 55 BC he published the *De Oratore*, a treatise on oratory which contains a two-part discussion of historiography (2.51–64). This discussion, consisting of a critique of the early Roman historians (51–61) and an account of how history should be written (62–4), can fairly be described as the most valuable treatment of its subject to have come down to us from ancient Rome.[16] Yet despite the attention which has been paid to it, its key section on the theory of historiography has been consistently and fundamentally misunderstood. It is therefore this section on which I shall be concentrating in the present chapter.

The *De Oratore* is a dialogue, set thirty-six years earlier in 91 BC, between various orators and politicians who were prominent at the time. In the part of Book 2 which concerns us, the conversation is between M. Antonius, who was the most famous orator of his day and is the principal speaker, and L. Licinius Crassus and Q. Lutatius Catulus. After some preliminary paragraphs, which in part recapitulate points made during the previous day's discussion in Book 1, Antonius at length promises to give his view of the whole field of oratory (29).[17] The first stage of his exposition falls into three main parts (30–50, 51–64, 65–73),[18] of which the second is our principal concern; yet historiography itself has already been introduced in the first part, and from the viewpoint of the modern reader it is instructive to see how this introduction is made.

In attempting to describe the province of the orator, Antonius says that nothing at all lies outside his field, provided that it requires elaborate and impressive treatment (34 *neque ulla non propria oratoris est res, quae quidem ornate dici grauiterque debet*). He then lists some examples (35–6): giving advice (*in dando consilio*), arousing (*incitatio*), calming (*moderatio*), prosecution, defence,

---

[16] If Cicero is reflecting Hellenistic material which is now lost (see below, nn. 77, 146), this only serves to increase its value.

[17] All references are to Book 2 of the *De Oratore* unless otherwise stated.

[18] A break after 73 is generally accepted: see e.g. Wilkins (1881) 221 and O'Mara (1971) 74 (but the latter's detailed analysis of the dialogue as a whole is most unhelpful: she is concerned almost entirely with its mathematical proportions and ignores the verbal correspondences by which much of the argument is signposted). I have resisted the temptation to provide full analyses of 30–50 and 65–73, despite the complex and at times paradoxical nature of the arguments (see e.g. n. 35 below; also p. 280 and n. 130).

encouragement (*cohortari*), criticism (*uituperare*), eulogy (*laudare*), accusation (*accusando*), consolation (*consolando*) and historiography (*historia*)—the last of which is climactically described in a series of laudatory phrases: 'the witness of crises, the illumination of reality, the life of memory, the mentor of life, the messenger of antiquity'. That historiography should feature at all in a list of such rhetorical modes strikes the modern reader as very strange, especially since Antonius has earlier stated that rhetoric 'depends upon falsehood' (30 *mendacio nixa*);[19] but, like Cornelius Nepos already quoted, Antonius takes it for granted that it is an orator who should write history. The full implications of this assumption become clear in the second part of Antonius' exposition,[20] where historiography is exclusively the subject under discussion.[21]

THE DEFICIENCIES OF THE EARLY
ROMAN HISTORIANS

As I have already said (above, p. 247), Antonius' discussion of historiography falls into two complementary sections, the first of which (51–61) he begins with a question: 'What kind of an orator,

[19] His point is (30) that in any kind of rhetorical debate speakers discuss matters of which they are ignorant, and they maintain different opinions on an identical issue (so one of them cannot be true). Hence rhetoric 'depends upon falsehood'.

[20] It is a commonplace of classical scholarship that ancient historiography was 'rhetorical' and that its theoretical background can be seen in Antonius' speech (cf. e.g. McDonald (1957) 159–61 and (1968) 467); my contention is that, with the distinguished exception of T. P. Wiseman, most scholars have failed to realize the implications of this nomenclature (see below, pp. 264–6). (Some scholars prefer the label 'Isocratean' historiography, on the grounds that it was instigated by the historians Ephorus and Theopompus, who (cf. *de Orat.* 2.57) were pupils of Isocrates.)

[21] We cannot now know whether or to what extent Antonius' words reflect his own or Cicero's views. For my purposes the question does not really matter, since I am more concerned with the views themselves than with whoever was responsible for them. However, as will become clear (pp. 283–6), I think we can at least infer that Antonius' words reflect the views of Cicero himself. Most scholars would agree with this inference, which explains why I use the names 'Cicero' and 'Antonius' interchangeably.

how great a speaker, do you think should write history)' (*Qualis oratoris et quanti hominis in dicendo putas esse historiam scribere?*). In the light of the praise heaped on historiography at 36 above, this question clearly invites the answer 'Very great indeed'. Yet Catulus' reply comes in two parts, of which only the first meets our expectations: 'Very great indeed, if you're talking about Greek historiography, but not if you're talking about ours, which doesn't require an orator at all. The sole criterion is not to be a liar'. This reply provides Antonius with the cue for a comparative critique of the early Roman historians and their Greek predecessors.

The critique begins as follows (51–4):

'Atqui, ne nostros contemnas,' inquit Antonius, 'Graeci quoque ipsi sic
52 initio scriptitarunt ut noster Cato, ut Pictor, ut Piso: erat enim historia nihil
    aliud nisi annalium confectio, cuius rei memoriaeque publicae retinendae
    causa ab initio rerum Romanarum usque ad P. Mucium pontificem max-
    imum res omnis singulorum annorum mandabat litteris pontifex maximus
    referebatque[22] in album et proponebat tabulam domi, potestas ut
    esset populo cognoscendi, eique etiam nunc annales maximi nominantur.
53 hanc similitudinem scribendi multi secuti sunt, qui sine ullis ornamentis
    monumenta solum temporum, hominum, locorum gestarumque rerum
    reliquerunt; itaque qualis apud Graecos Pherecydes, Hellanicus, Acusilas
    fuit aliique permulti, talis noster Cato et Pictor et Piso, qui neque tenent
    quibus rebus ornetur oratio—modo enim huc ista sunt importata—et, dum
    intellegatur quid dicant, unam dicendi laudem putant esse breuitatem.
54 paulum se erexit et addidit maiorem historiae sonum uocis uir optimus,
    Crassi familiaris, Antipater; ceteri non exornatores rerum, sed tantum modo
    narratores fuerunt.' 'Est,' inquit Catulus, 'ut dicis; sed iste ipse Caelius neque
    distinxit historiam uarietate colorum[23] neque uerborum conlocatione et
    tractu orationis leni et aequabili perpoliuit illud opus; sed ut homo neque
    doctus neque maxime aptus ad dicendum, sicut potuit, dolauit; uicit tamen,
    ut dicis, superiores.'

'But you mustn't be too hard on our historians: after all, in the beginning
52 the Greeks too wrote just like Cato, Pictor, and Piso. For historiography was
    simply an aggregate of the annals. Indeed, it was with this in mind,[24] and

---

[22] Lambinus' emendation of the MSS's *efferebat*. The latter could still be right: see *OLD* s.v. 7, 8.

[23] Jacobs' correction of the MSS's *locorum*: see below, n. 26.

[24] i.e. with historiography in mind. The phrase is obscure, but I take it that *rei* refers back to *historia*.

also to preserve some kind of public record, that each high priest from the beginning of Roman history down to the pontificate of P. Mucius entrusted all the events of each year to literary form, transposed them onto a whiteboard, and displayed the board at his official residence in the interests of

53 public information. The *Annales Maximi* are still so called even today, and it was this kind of writing which many historians followed: they transmitted, without any elaboration, only plain notices of dates, persons, places, and events. So, just as the Greeks had their Pherecydes, Hellanicus, Acusilaus etc., we had their equivalents in Cato, Pictor, and Piso, who did not possess the subjects required to produce elaborate discourse, which have been imported here only recently. Provided their reports were intelligible, they

54 thought brevity was the sole criterion of praise. It's true that Crassus' friend Antipater, an admirable man, gave a better account of himself and employed a more rhetorical form of historiography; but all the others only recorded their subjects without elaborating them.'

'You're right, of course', said Catulus. 'But even Crassus' friend Coelius failed to highlight his history with chiaroscuro, nor did he smooth his work by the arrangement of words or the slow and regular movement of his discourse: rather, he hacked away like the man of limited ability that he was, neither a scholar nor even particularly suited to rhetoric. Still, as you say, he was better than his predecessors.'

This passage is of vital importance since it specifies the precise areas to which Antonius will pay attention at 62–4 in his discussion of how historiography should be written. Thus 51–4 and 62–4 are complementary, the former providing the necessary background to the latter (see further below, pp. 266–9).

Here at 51–4 two points require emphasis. First, Antonius twice draws a distinction between the 'hard core', on which historiography is based, and its elaboration, of which the art of historiography consists. At 53 he calls the former *monumenta*, which he subdivides into the four elements of time, person, place, and event; the latter he describes as *ornamenta*. Then at 54 he uses the generic term *res* ('subjects') for the former, and *exornatores* for would-be elaborators. Second, the elaboration which Antonius has in mind has *nothing to do with style*. Just as the core elements (53) are *res* (54), so the items required to produce elaborate discourse are also *res* (53 *quibus rebus ornetur oratio*). In other words, Antonius is talking about the elaboration of *content by means of content*, a concept which is puzzling for us but fully explained in the sections which follow (pp. 260–75). That this is Antonius' meaning is confirmed by his exchange with Catulus over Coelius Antipater (54). It is to be inferred from *ceteri non exornatores rerum* that Coelius himself was an *exornator rerum*, as Catulus readily grants (*Est... ut dicis*):[25] where he fell down, in Catulus' opinion, was style (*neque distinxit... dolauit*), which is therefore a different matter from the *exornatio* about which Antonius has been talking. And indeed Catulus' reservations about Coelius' style are clearly signalled as an interruption of Antonius' main argument, since he concludes his little speech by returning to his initial agreement with what Antonius said (*uicit tamen*, ut dicis, *superiores*).[26]

In the remainder of this section, Antonius first (55–8) provides a potted history of Greek historiography in order to contrast its rhetorical nature with the unrhetorical nature of Roman historiography just described in 51–4. Then, after some further exchanges with Catulus (59) and other discursive remarks (60–1), Antonius at last says 'But I return to my point', by which he means the question to which Catulus gave a two-part answer at 51 above (p. 249).

---

[25] This assessment seems to be confirmed by the surviving fragments: Coelius is likely to have been the first Roman historian to have put fictitious speeches into the mouths of his characters (D'Alton (1931) 515), and he also described a storm at sea (Badian (1966) 16). Cf. *HRR*, FF 6, 26, 47 (speeches), 40 (storm: doubted by Livy, cf. n. 84 below).

[26] Brunt (1980a) 322 {= above, p. 219} gets the argument of 53–4 doubly wrong. First, he says that Antonius censures the early Roman historians 'on the purely literary grounds which are most relevant to his discourse'. It is clear from the rest of his paragraph that by 'literary' Brunt means 'stylistic', although it is clear from Antonius' actual words, as I have demonstrated, that content is being referred to. Second, Brunt says that 'even Coelius who had naively aimed at some verbal effects was defective in *uarietate locorum*', evidently thinking that *loci* refers to a stylistic phenomenon. Yet if *locorum* is what Cicero wrote, the word would refer to general reflections or commonplaces, not style; but in any case it seems certain from the metaphorical use of *distinxit* that Cicero wrote *colorum* (cf. *Rhet. Herenn.* 4.16 *distinctam... coloribus*, *Orat.* 65), which here refers to style (see Fantham (1972) 170 and n. 31).

HOW HISTORY SHOULD BE WRITTEN

In the second part of his discussion of historiography (62–4) Antonius gives his own extended answer to the question which he raised at 51 and which he now begins by repeating in a slightly different form:[27]

```
          1          2                    3         4
62  Videtisne  quantum munus sit   oratoris  historia? Haud scio an
          5         (3)            6       (2)                    4
    flumine   orationis et uarietate   maximum, neque tamen   eam
       7         8                       9          10
    reperio usquam  separatim  instructam  rhetorum  praeceptis
                                  (1)
    (<s>ita  sunt  enim  ante     oculos).
```

```
                 ┌──11──┐
    nam     quis nescit  primam  esse  historiae  legem, ne  quid  falsi

    dicere  audeat?  deinde  ne  quid  ueri  non  audeat?  ne   qua

63  suspicio  gratiae  sit  in  scribendo,  ne  qua  simultatis?  haec
                           ┌────(11)────┐
    scilicet  fundamenta  nota sunt omnibus,  ipsa   autem   exae-
                            12      13      12     14
    dificatio posita est in  rebus et  uerbis.  rerum  ratio ordinem
```

[27] In the Latin text I use superimposed numbers to indicate verbal repetitions or (when bracketed) correspondences. Note that these numbers, while illustrating the articulation of the argument, obscure certain implications of what is being said. For example, the distinction between '*rerum* [12] ratio' and 'in *rebus* [15] magnis', though valid in differentiating elaboration from hard core, obscures the point I made on p. 250, namely that both are *res*. Again, the sequence *acta–euentus*, in which *acta* is evidently equivalent to 'in *rebus* [15] magnis', suggests that the *euentus* is the elaboration of some hard core; yet in the case of a battle whose *euentus* is a triumph, it is the triumph about which there is likely to be hard core information (see pp. 266–7).

As for my translation, I would like to think it is more accurate than existing versions. That of the Loeb editor, who is followed by Rambaud (1953) 13–14 and Kelley (1969) 45, seems to me simply wrong; that of Fornara (1983) 138–9 is a gross distortion (see below, n. 36).

┌────────(6)────────┐
temporum   desiderat,   regionum descriptionem;   uult   etiam—
            15   16
quoniam   in   rebus   magnis   memoriaque   dignis   consilia
                    (15)   17
primum,   deinde   acta,   postea   euentus   exspectentur—et   de
          16   ┌──15──┐
consiliis   significari   quid   scriptor   probet,   et   in   rebus gestis

declarari   non   solum   quid   actum   aut   dictum   sit   sed   etiam
                                  17
quo   modo,   et   cum   de   euentu   dicatur,   ut   causae   explicentur

omnes,   uel   casus   uel   sapientiae   uel   temeritatis,   hominumque
                              ┌──15──┐
ipsorum   non   solum   res gestae   sed   etiam,   qui   fama   ac
                                                                    13
64   nomine   excellant,   de   cuiusque   uita   atque   natura.   uerborum
                  14   (3)
autem   ratio   et   genus   orationis   fusum   atque   tractum   et
                                              (5)
cum   lenitate   quadam   aequabili   profluens,   sine   hac   iudiciali

asperitate   et   sine   sententiarum   forensium   aculeis   persequen-

dum   est.

                    (2)   1   (8)   10
Harum   tot   tantarumque   rerum   uidetisne   ulla   esse   praecepta
                    9   7
quae   in   artibus   rhetorum   reperiantur?

62   Don't you see how great a task history is for an orator? In terms of fluency of
discourse and variety it is probably his greatest task, yet I can't find a
separate treatment of the subject anywhere in the rules of rhetoric (and
they're easily available for inspection).

Everyone of course knows that the first law of historiography is not daring
to say anything false, and the second is not refraining from saying
anything true: there should be no suggestion of prejudice for, or bias
63   against, when you write. These foundations are of course recognized by

everyone, but the actual superstructure consists of content and style. It is in the nature of content, on the one hand, that you require a chronological order of events and topographical descriptions; and also that you need—since in the treatment of important and memorable achievements the reader expects (i) intentions, (ii) the events themselves, and (iii) consequences—in the case of (i) to indicate whether you approve of the intentions, of (ii) to reveal not only what was said or done but also in what manner, and of (iii) to explain all the reasons, whether they be of chance or intelligence or impetuousness, and also to give not only the achievements of any famous protagonist but also his life and character.

64   The nature of style and type of discourse, on the other hand, require amplitude and mobility, with a slow and regular fluency and without any of the roughness and prickliness associated with the law-courts.

These points are both numerous and important, but do you see them covered by any of the rules to be found in books entitled *Art of Rhetoric*?

This passage is impressive because much of it sounds very like what a modern historian would expect to hear. Indeed P. A. Brunt observes: 'Cicero is not expressly advocating a type of historical exposition different from that commonly employed by modern political historians.'[28] Brunt is talking about Cicero's remarks on individuals and their characters, but we may also compare the central section with the following extract from a modern manual on historiography:[29]

The historian must achieve a balance between narrative and analysis [cf. *declarari non solum quid actum aut dictum sit sed etiam quo modo*], between a chronological approach [cf. *ordinem temporum*] and an approach by topic,...and, as necessary, passages of pure description [cf. *regionum descriptionem*].

The two are indeed very similar, as we see. It is therefore perhaps not surprising that modern commentators, as we shall observe more fully below, interpret Cicero's words as if he were one of themselves.

---

[28] Brunt (1980a) 318 {= above, p. 215}.
[29] Marwick (1976) 144, cf. Atkinson (1978) 22, 'It is the essence of history...that it should locate events in space and time'.

The Foundations of Historiography

Of the opening of the above passage P. G. Walsh has written as follows:[30]

The basic canons of history are ably propounded by Antonius in the *De Oratore*. 'For surely everyone knows', he says, 'that the first law of history is to dare to say nothing false, and again to omit nothing which is true. And in writing there should be no suspicion of either partiality or hatred.'

A. P. Kelley expresses a similar point thus:[31]

Truthfulness is the essential quality... Accuracy is the very essence of history. It was laid down as a fundamental law by Antonius in the *De Oratore* that the historian must be, above all else, truthful in recounting the facts... Cicero had a great interest in historical accuracy.

And again P. A. Brunt, whose contribution to the subject is intended to promote a general thesis different from that of Walsh, has written:[32]

It was natural for Cicero to emphasise that the historian must be truthful. *Nam quis nescit primam esse historiae legem... haec scilicet fundamenta nota sunt omnibus.*

Yet for two reasons these comments entirely misrepresent what Cicero has in fact written.

In the first place it should be clear from the numbered words (above) that the passage is a unified whole and that Cicero returns at the end to the point which he made at the beginning. The passage, in other words, exemplifies ring composition, and within its outer frame (emphasized by edentation) there is a clearly articulated argument which must be taken as a whole. To extract a sentence or two and say 'this is what Cicero believed', as scholars have done, is to distort Cicero's meaning.[33]

---

[30] Walsh (1961) 32.
[31] Kelley (1969) 42, 101. Cf. also Petzold (1972) 259–60; Leeman (1955) 188 = (1963) 171.
[32] Brunt (1980a) 313 {= above, p. 210}.
[33] Ibid. 312 {= above, p. 208} makes much of the claim that he has interpreted Cicero's key statements 'in their context'.

The implication of Antonius' opening question is that his listeners, like the early historians already mentioned at 51–3, do *not* see how great a task history is for an orator.[34] It is precisely for this reason that he proceeds to rectify matters in the course of the present paragraph. *But he does not do so immediately.* Historiography is seen in metaphorical terms as a building consisting of foundations (*fundamenta*) and superstructure (*exaedificatio*), which are expressly contrasted with each other (*scilicet... autem*). The foundations are disposed of in sentences which begin with the words *nam quis nescit* and end *nota sunt omnibus*, and which, being a further example of ring composition, constitute an interpolation into Antonius' main argument.[35]

[34] Like most other scholars I accept the vulgate correction [*s*]*ita*. Since this word can only refer to *praeceptis*, it seems that Antonius is drawing a contrast (cf. *tamen*) between *praecepta rhetorum* and *munus oratoris* in terms of familiarity.

[35] The interpolation is exactly like that of 54, already noted (p. 251), except that in the present case it also acts as a 'foil' for what follows (cf. *scilicet... autem*). If this interpretation of the passage is correct, it means that *nam* is not here being used as an explanatory or causal particle but, as often in Cicero, has an elliptical sense (see Pease on *N.D.* 1.27). Failure to realise this, which seems universal, leads to travesties such as Kelley's, where Antonius is made to say the exact opposite of what he in fact does say: 'Antonius, while affirming that the orator's skill is perhaps called into play more in history than in any other genre, says that this art is not "supplied with any independent directions from the rhetoricians". He suggests that *the reason for this is that* the laws of historical composition are known to all' (87 [my italics, and also note that Kelley mistakenly refers *eam* to *munus*, not to *historia*], cf. also 45). The objection to versions such as this has already been hinted at in n. 34 above. Given the near synonymity of *sita sunt enim ante oculos* and *nam quis nescit...*, the obvious function of an explanatory *nam* would be to suggest that the latter sentences are an illustration of the former; but this is impossible since truth, which is the subject of the latter sentences, is not a *praeceptum rhetorum*, and it is the *praecepta rhetorum* which is the only familiar element in the former (n. 34).

It follows from the above that Antonius' argument in 62–4 is different from that employed in 44–6 for eulogy, the only other subject which he treats at any length in this part of the dialogue. There the obviousness of eulogistic techniques (45 *quis est qui nesciat quae sint in homine laudanda?*) {everyone knows what qualities are praiseworthy in a human being} is both given as a reason why the rules for eulogy should not be codified (*neque illa elementa desiderare* {nor do they require those elements}, cf. 49 *num... propriis praeceptis instruenda?* {surely... they do not need to be fitted out with their own precepts?}, 50 *sed ex artificio res istae praecepta non quaerunt* {those matters do not need precepts coming from theory}) and is also used to introduce a *praeteritio* whereby Antonius proceeds to list (45–6) precisely the rules for eulogy which were in fact codified in e.g. *Rhet. Herenn.* 3.10–15. Despite the element of unintended paradox in this argument, which Catulus naturally seizes upon (47 *Cur igitur dubitas... facere hoc tertium genus, quoniam est in ratione rerum?* {Why then do you hesitate... to make this a third type, since it is one in the nature of

Since Antonius is concerned only with what is *not* familiar to his listeners, as we have just seen, and since he twice explicitly says that the 'first and second laws of historiography' *are* familiar, as we have also seen,[36] it follows that the foundations are not his principal concern at all. Thus the laws of historiography are subordinate to what is said in the rest of the paragraph, which is exactly the opposite of what scholars have thought.[37] This interpretation is confirmed by its exact correspondence with sections 51–3 above. There the truth-fulness of the historian is taken for granted and is therefore a familiar notion, but the rhetorical techniques required for historiography are said to have been imported into Italy only recently: this is given as the reason why they were unfamiliar to the early Roman historians and presumably explains why they are still unfamiliar to Antonius' lis-teners. Antonius himself, however, is in a privileged position, as his acquaintance with Greek historiography and its techniques, amply demonstrated in the intervening sections (55–9), makes clear.[38]

its content?}), Antonius nevertheless concludes that eulogy should not be given a rhetorical classification of its own (47–50). At 62–4, on the other hand, Antonius is capitalizing on an intentional paradox: namely, that despite the (to himself) obvi-ously rhetorical nature of historiography (62 *haud scio an ... maximum,* 63 *ipsa autem exaedificatio ...*), the genre has not been given separate treatment in the rules of rhetoric (62 *neque tamen ... rhetorum praeceptis*) and its rhetorical nature has escaped the notice of his interlocutors (*Videtisne ... ?*). Thus, despite some similarity of phrasing, there is a different point at issue in each case: at 44–6 the rules for eulogy do not require the codification which they have in fact been given; at 62–4 the rules for historiography have not received the codification which might naturally have been expected. Such variation not only avoids monotony but also fits the view of eulogy as trivial (47 *exigua*) and of historiography as important (36).

[36] Fornara (1983) 138 not only makes Antonius say the exact opposite of this ('Obviously, these foundations are known to everyone, *and also that* its edifice consists of events and speeches'), but prints his mistranslation, which I have itali-cized, in bold type to indicate its presumed importance. As a result, he too, like Kelley (above, n. 35), completely misinterprets the rest of the passage (139). (It will also be noticed that he renders *uerbis* as 'speeches', a fantasy which the repetition and explanation of the word at 64 ought to have dispelled.)

[37] In addition to the quotations already given on p. 255 see, e.g., Piderit–Har-necker (1886–90) ad loc. (*Grundgesetze* {basic laws}), North (1956) 237 ('the first rule of history' etc.), Herkommer (1968) 149 (truth is history's 'very first law'), Brunt (1980a) 314 {= above, p. 211} ('truth is the first requirement of history', cf. 317 {= above, p. 214}). No doubt the derivation of such words as 'fundamental' from *fundamentum* has contributed to the misunderstanding.

[38] It is clear from the exchanges of conversation in 59–60 that Antonius' familiar-ity with Greek historiography is regarded as something unusual; his interlocutors' ignorance of its rhetorical nature and technique is therefore dramatically realistic.

In the second place it should be clear from the context that by the 'laws of historiography' Cicero does not mean what scholars think he means. Antonius' first pair of rhetorical questions, dealing with *falsum* and *uerum*, are explained by his second pair, which deal with *gratia* and *simultas*.³⁹ Thus Cicero here sees truth only in terms of impartiality (the historian should not show prejudice for or bias against anyone); and though this interpretation will undoubtedly seem contentious to some readers, Cicero's meaning is confirmed by his letter to Lucceius, written only a few months earlier, in which he wrote: 'Elaborate my activities even against your better judgement, and in the process disregard the laws of historiography [*et in eo leges historiae neglegas*]: that prejudice [*gratiam*], which you discussed..., well, please don't suppress it if it nudges you strongly in my favour, but simply let your affection [*amori*] for me take a degree of precedence over the truth [*ueritas*]'. Here the wording is virtually identical to that in the *De Oratore*, and the context of the letter makes it plain, as we have already observed, that Cicero resembles the major Roman historians in seeing truth in terms of impartiality (above, pp. 244–6).⁴⁰ Thus, contrary to what scholars have generally believed, Cicero in the *De Oratore* does not present truth as the opposite of what we would call fiction.⁴¹

---

³⁹ That is, there are only two laws of history, expressed by *prima* and *deinde* (for which, cf. e.g. *Off.* 1.20, *Rep.* 1.38, *Leg.* 3.19, *Verr.* 5.90).

⁴⁰ Though the similarity of wording explains what is meant by the *leges historiae*, Cicero is of course contradicting in the letter what he was soon to publish in the *De Oratore*. Scholars have sought to explain (away) the contradiction along four lines (see Herkommer (1968) 149 n. 3, Kelley (1969) 22–32). (1) There is no contradiction since in the letter Cicero is talking about a monograph, the rules for which were different from those for a continuous history. (2) There is no real contradiction since Cicero's words in such theoretical works as the *de Orat.* are merely fine-sounding sentiments: his true opinions are revealed in the letter. (3) The letter does indeed contradict *de Orat.* but it is a special case deriving from Cicero's particular circumstances and his personal wish to feature in a work of propaganda. (4) The contradiction is only apparent, since Cicero's letter is plainly a joke. While I do not accept (1), for which (despite Puccioni (1981)) there is simply no evidence, or (2), I think there is some truth in (3) and (4). Cicero clearly knew that his request to Lucceius contradicted *de Orat.* 2.62, on which he was engaged at the same time; he hoped that his delightful and captivating style (above, n. 4) would enable him to get away with it; if not, he could always pass it off as a joke.

⁴¹ So too Wiseman (1981) 387. Brunt (1980a) 315 {= above, p. 211} also acknowledges that 'it is bias, however caused, that he [Cicero] sees as the great obstacle to

I hope that in this section I have succeeded in demonstrating, first, that Antonius' remarks on the laws of historiography are relatively unimportant in the context of his argument, and, second, that the truth required by those laws is quite different from what we today might call 'historical truth'.[42] If these conclusions are correct, it follows that we may legitimately concentrate our attention on the superstructure (*exaedificatio*), which is Antonius' principal concern, and that we should not be prevented by modern misconceptions from explaining that superstructure in terms of the rules of rhetoric to which Antonius refers at both the beginning and the end of the passage.

The Superstructure of Historiography: Content and Style

Antonius explicitly states that the superstructure of historiography consists of *res* and *uerba*, content and style: it is therefore precisely these two items which might naturally have been mentioned in the rhetorical handbooks but which, since they are not mentioned there, Antonius now proceeds to discuss here. This line of argument is confirmed by the very division of the *exaedificatio* into content and style, *res* and *uerba*, since this division is itself one of the most basic in rhetorical theory and practice. As Quintilian says, 'every speech consists of content and style [*rebus et uerbis*]'.[43]

---

veracity', but he is unaware of the implications of his statement, since he continues: 'He says nothing of the historian's problems in investigating and ascertaining the truth. His silence can easily be explained. He is concerned with history as a literary genre, and therefore with the way it should be written, not with the work preliminary to writing. What his views on this matter were must be a matter for surmise.' Brunt fails to realize that there was no alternative to history 'as a literary genre' in the ancient world; and when he proceeds to surmise Cicero's allegedly scientific historio-graphical technique from Plin. *Ep.* 5.8.12, he seems to be misusing the letter (see below, n. 137).

[42] The second conclusion explains the first: it is because the ancients lacked our concept of 'historical truth' that Antonius was able to dismiss his own limited concept of impartiality which was so often disregarded in practice (above, n. 12).

[43] Quint. 8 *pref.* 6 'orationem porro omnem constare rebus et uerbis: in rebus intuendam inuentionem, in uerbis elocutionem' {every speech consists of content and style; for content one must study invention, for style elocution}. The structural

Content. The requirements which Antonius lists under the heading of *rerum ratio* ('nature of content') are introduced by the two verbs *desiderat* ('requires') and *uult* ('needs'), the first of which tells us that a writer of history requires *ordinem temporum* and *regionum descriptionem*. Now according to the usual interpretation of this sentence, Cicero is here referring to accurate dating and scientific topography. Thus Brunt writes:[44]

With the diversity of eras and fluctuations in calendars in the ancient world, chronological exactitude was not easy to attain or to present clearly, especially if the historian, like Thucydides or Polybius, often had to transfer the reader's attention from one part of the world to another and perhaps to show how transactions in different parts reacted on each other. Elsewhere Cicero goes out of his way to commend Atticus' chronological handbook (*Orat.* 120) and evinces a special interest in dating events … It was a patent truth that, in the absence of maps, military operations, which form a large part of history as Cicero and the ancients in general conceived it, would be unintelligible, at least if they took place in unfamiliar lands, unless the scenes were carefully described. Polybius, who inveighed against fictitious descriptions, also insisted on the need for accurate and relevant topographical explanation.

And Walsh writes that Cicero

is at pains to distinguish clearly between the functions of history and oratory, showing that history is different both in its material and in its treatment, for chronological order and geographical clarification are essential.[45]

similarity of this to our passage of Cicero suggests a standard manner of expression which no doubt derives from some earlier common source. For content and style cf. also Quint. 3.3.1, 5.1; Lausberg (1998) 26 §45, 113, 149.

[44] Brunt (1980a) 318 {= above, p. 215}. He rightly says of *regionum descriptionem* that 'at this point "Antonius" is not discussing literary effects at all … but the content of a history', but mistakenly precedes this remark by saying that the ornamentation of which Cicero approves 'can be restricted to the careful choice of words and rhythms', a topic on which Cicero does not in fact embark until 64 below. It is indeed a feature of scholarship on our passage that writers anxiously slide over the matter of *res* in their haste to reach *uerba*. This is true also of e.g. Leeman (1963) 171–3, and see North (1956) 237: 'The perfection of history depends on *res* and *uerba*. It was to the second of these elements that most of Cicero's comments were directed'—an observation which simply flies in the face of the evidence of the passage.

[45] Walsh (1961) 32. See too Leeman (1955) 188–9 = (1963) 171.

Yet by failing to allow for the contrast between the first and second parts of Antonius' speech these scholars have been entirely misrepresented what Antonius is saying.

The contrast between *haec* **scilicet** *fundamenta* and *ipsa* **autem** *exaedificatio* clearly indicates that the *exaedificatio* or superstructure of historiography is to be explained in terms of the rules of rhetoric to which Antonius refers at the start of the passage (see above, pp. 255 and 259). Now speeches were conventionally divided into six sections, one of which was the *narratio* or 'statement of the case';[46] and if we look at the rules for the *narratio* as expressed by (among others) Cicero himself, we shall see that Antonius has simply transferred their requirements to historiography. Thus Cicero said (*Inu.* 1.29) that 'The *narratio* will be clear if we explain first that which happened first, and keep to the order of events and times [*temporum ordo*]', repeated at *Rhet. Herenn.* 1.15 'Our *narratio* will be clear if we set out first whatever happened first, and preserve the order of events and times [*temporum ordinem*]'.[47] Similarly, as Cicero himself again said, the *narratio* required a demonstration that 'the place was suitable for the events about to be related' (*Inu.* 1.29):[48] this in its turn might give rise to a digression,[49] which could be 'of various kinds…, for example, the praise of…places or the description of regions [*descriptio regionum*]'.[50] Thus Antonius is not recommending any sophisticated techniques such as those suggested by the scholars above; since identical phraseology to his occurs in the other passages I have quoted, it is clear that he is offering standard rhetorical advice to the effect that the historian, like the forensic orator, should not invert the natural order of events and should enliven his work with topographical digressions.[51]

---

[46] The six sections are: *exordium* (introduction), *narratio* (statement of the case), *diuisio* (division), *argumentatio* or *confirmatio* (proof), *confutatio* (refutation), and *peroratio* (conclusion). See Lausberg (1998) 122–3.

[47] See further Lausberg (1998) 149 §317.

[48] See also *Rhet. Herenn.* 1.16, Quint. 4.2.36, 52.

[49] Cf. Quint. 4.3.12–13; Lausberg (1998) 158 §340.

[50] Quint. 4.3.12. See Lausberg (1998) 365 §819.

[51] Digressions were a recognized method of entertaining one's audience (Cic. *Inu.* 1.27 *delectationis…causa* {for the sake of pleasure}, *Brut.* 322, cf. *de Orat.* 2.311), and this was particularly true of those dealing with topography (see below, n. 78). For this reason I have suggested by my superimposed number 6 in the Latin text above that

We have just seen that the two requirements which Antonius introduced by the verb *desiderat* derive from the requirements of the *narratio*, and it is important to note that exactly the same is true of those which he introduces by the verb *uult*. Antonius says that historiography requires mention of the 'intentions, events and consequences' associated with any important and memorable issue (*consilia, acta, euentus*), and also the elaboration thereof (the manner in which things were done or said; the reasons for things, whether they result from acts of god, a person's innate qualities or temporary emotions like impetuousness; and a person's life and character). And again it is Cicero himself who makes it clear that most of these elements are also those of the *narratio*. In *Part. Or.* 31–2 he says:

> Our *narratio* must be clear and convincing [*probabiliter*], but it can also be entertaining [*suauitatem*] . . . It will be convincing if the events correspond to the individuals, times and places involved [*personis, temporibus, locis*], and if we set out the reason [*causa*] for each event [*facti*] and consequence [*euenti*] . . . It will be entertaining if it induces surprise [*admirationes*] and suspense [*exspectationes*], and if it involves unexpected outcomes [*exitus inopinatos*], conflicting emotions [*interpositos motus animorum*], dialogues between individuals [*colloquia personarum*], grief, anger, fear [*metus*], delight [*laetitias*], and passion [*cupiditates*].

And in *Inu.* 1.29 he says:

> The *narratio* will be convincing [*probabilis*] if it appears to contain elements which customarily appear in real life [*in ueritate*]: if the proper qualities of the individuals are maintained, if reasons for their actions [*causae factorum*] are plain, . . . and if the subject-matter fits in with the character [*naturam*] of those involved.[52]

---

regionum descriptionem here corresponds to *uarietate* in Antonius' opening remarks (for variety as a source of *delectatio* see Lausberg (1989) 114, 115–16). It is however possible that *orationis . . . uarietate* refers merely to variety of style (cf. *Rhet. Herenn.* 4.18 *dignitas est quae reddit ornatam orationem uarietate distinguens* {distinction is that which renders a speech ornate, embellishing it by variety}), which is of course how Brunt (1980a) 325 n. {= above, p. 220 n. 27} takes it; yet since topographical digressions were themselves an opportunity for a heightened and varied style (cf. Plin. *Ep.* 2.5.5, Quint. 9.2.44, 10.1.33; Lausberg (1998) 365 §819), it may be that my suggestion should not be excluded.

[52] See further Quintilian (n. 48 above); Lausberg (1998) 153 §328.

When Quintilian deals with the same points, but at greater length, he illustrates Cicero's last statement here by saying that you must make a murderer appear impetuous (*temerarium*) or the opposite, depending upon your point of view.[53] Quintilian also notes that the fourth part of a speech, the *argumentatio*, is really no more than a mirror image of the *narratio*[54] and that on this basis it is legitimate to introduce *argumenta* into the *narratio*.[55] The standard *argumenta*, as Cicero himself tells us, covered the individual concerned and his character (*personis*), the place, time, occasion, manner, and conditions of the relevant event (*Inu.* 1.34–8)—a list which makes the similarity to the *narratio* abundantly clear.[56] Thus one could deal with a person's intentions (*consilia*, cf. *Inu.* 1.36)[57] or argue *ab euentu*, i.e. 'from the result of some action, when we enquire what resulted from each activity' (*Inu.* 1.42), a matter to which Cicero devotes more attention elsewhere (*Top.* 67): 'The topics of cause and effect are closely related: just as the cause reveals what results, so the result reveals the cause'.[58] Again, Cicero says that 'one can always introduce the element of chance [*casus*] . . . when it can be shown that some supernatural force [*aliqua fortunae uis*] interfered with a man's intentions' (*Inu.* 2.96).[59]

The correspondence between these prescriptions for the *narratio* and those which Antonius introduces by the verb *uult* will, I hope, be obvious enough: the precise items with which orators were trained to deal were also those recommended by him for treatment in historiography. The correspondence is, of course, hardly fortuitous.

[53] Quint. 4.2.52, cf. also 3.7.25.

[54] Quint. 4.2.79 *quid inter probationem et narrationem interest, nisi quod narratio est probationis continua propositio, rursus probatio narrationi congruens confirmatio?* {what is the difference between the proof and the narrative except that the narrative is a preliminary statement of the proof while the proof in turn is a confirmation which conforms to the narrative?}

[55] Quint. 4.2.54–5. Cf. Atkinson (1978) 21 on a 'method of presentation recommended and apparently practised' by G. R. Elton, namely 'to weave in the analytical material, thus producing "thickened" narrative'.

[56] Compare Cicero's topics for the *argumenta* (*persona, locus, tempus, occasio, modus, facultas*) with Quintilian's for the *narratio* (4.2.55 *persona, causa, locus, tempus, instrumentum, occasio*), to which Quintilian's own *loci argumentorum* are naturally even closer (5.10.23 *persona, causa, tempus, locus, occasio, instrumentum, modus*).

[57] Cf. also Quint. 5.10.28–9; Lausberg (1998) 68–9, 175, 177–8.

[58] Cf. also Quint. 5.10.86; Lausberg (1998) 179 §381.

[59] Cf. also Quint. 7.4.15; Lausberg (1998) 79 §189.

Like others, Cicero defines the *narratio* as 'an exposition of events that have occurred or are supposed to have occurred' (*rerum gestarum aut ut gestarum expositio*),[60] which accords exactly with the definition of historiography as 'the exposition of events which have occurred' (*historias ... esse ... rerum gestarum ... expositionem*).[61] Given the affinity between the two types of writing, therefore, it is hardly surprising that Lucian should say that 'the body of a work of history [i.e. everything apart from the preface] is simply an extended *narratio*'.[62] Since Lucian makes this remark immediately after he has been discussing prefaces, his words are extremely suggestive. The preface was where a historian was expected to profess impartiality,[63] exactly the topic to which Antonius refers in his opening sentences about the laws of historiography; the body of the work was where the historian was expected to deal with the narrative of events, paying due attention to their antecedents, attendant circumstances and consequences, exactly as Antonius recommends in his following sentences. Thus the lay-out of Antonius' historiographical theory corresponds precisely to that of an actual work of history.

Now it is of the greatest importance to note that each of Antonius' prescriptions, even the most specific (e.g. the role of chance, *casus*), falls under the heading of *inuentio*,[64] one of the five techniques in which rhetoricians were supposed to be expert.[65] As Quintilian said, 'Every speech consists of content and style [*rebus et uerbis*]; with reference to content [*in rebus*] we must study *inuentio*' (8 *pref.* 6). It is therefore equally important to realize that none of Antonius' prescriptions is expected to deal with data which are necessarily true; on the contrary, *inuentio* is defined by Cicero himself as 'the devising of matter true or lifelike which will make a case appear convincing' (*Inu.* 1.9),[66] and what is convincing is 'that which for the most part

---

[60] *Inu.* 1.27, also at *Rhet. Herenn.* 1.4.
[61] Gell. 5.18.6. Cf. Atkinson (1978) 32 'narrating is basic to history'.
[62] Lucian *h.c.* 55.
[63] See pp. 244–5.
[64] See Lausberg (1998) 119–208. My remarks in this paragraph are close to those of Wiseman (1981) 388–9.
[65] The five techniques are: *inuentio, dispositio* (arrangement), *elocutio* (style), *memoria* (memory), and *pronuntiatio* (delivery). Cf. e.g. Cic. *Inu.* 1.9, *Rhet. Herenn.* 1.3.
[66] Cf. also *Rhet. Herenn.* 1.3.

happens or which does not strain credibility or which contains within itself an approximation to either of these, whether it be true or false'.[67] And since *inuentio* makes no distinction between the true and the probable, but accords the same status to the latter as to the former (and sometimes even more),[68] its prescriptions share no common ground at all with modern historiography. Antonius and P. A. Brunt are simply talking a different language.[69]

When Antonius requires that a historian should reveal 'how something was done or said', his requirement is quite different from that which a modern narrative historian imposes on himself. A modern historian would try to satisfy the requirement by investigating the primary sources and familiarizing himself with the appropriate terrain; naturally some questions would still remain, which he would try to answer in terms of probability, with himself in the role of impartial judge.[70] Antonius' historian, however, would have automatic recourse to the rules of rhetoric in which he had been trained; he too would deal with matters of probability, as we have seen, but he would be unlikely to be responding to any unanswered questions: he would see himself in the role of advocate and would know in advance, as it were, the case which he would have to make. The reason for this is that his recourse to rhetoric necessarily involved

---

[67] *Inu.* 1.46.

[68] Cf. *Rhet. Herenn.* 1.16 *si uera res erit, nihilominus haec omnia narrando conseruanda sunt, nam saepe ueritas, nisi haec seruata sint, fidem non potest facere* {if the matter is true, all these precautions must nonetheless be observed in the *narratio*, for often truth cannot gain credence if these things are not observed}, Quint. 4.2.34, 56. Wiseman (1981) 390 quotes Tac. *Ann.* 11.27 as an example of an episode which was implausible but demonstrably true, 'a paradox with which the historians of the ancient world were ill-equipped to deal'. Herkommer (1968) 150 n. 5 seems to me quite mistaken in saying that 'the aim of "narratio probabilis"... is nevertheless quite different from the pursuit of historical "ueritas"'.

[69] Cf. Brunt (1980a) 318 {= above, p. 215}, quoted above, p. 260.

[70] Wiseman (1979) 47–8 remarks on 'how far the ancient historiographical tradition was from the modern concept of the historian as judge, weighing up the evidence'; Atkinson (1978) 75 enlarges on this by saying that the 'historian is legislator, judge, jury, counsel, witnesses, all in one', but the point remains basically the same. It is true that the historian as 'impartial judge' is mentioned by Lucian *h.c.* 41, but the context is not that of weighing evidence but the standard one of disavowing malice. Herkommer (1968) 140 n. 1 says that Dionysius (*Pomp.* 6 = 2.394–5 Usher) describes Theopompus as 'the judge who examines scrupulously', but there the context is the same as that in Lucian, just mentioned (see further Woodman (1988) 43).

inuentio, which, as D. A. Russell has remarked, 'is simply the "discovery" of what requires to be said in a given situation, the implied theory being that this is somehow already "there" though latent'.[71]

Thus when Cicero says that historiography is 'oratorical', we should remember that *orator* is the Latin word for 'advocate'. Cicero is referring to the processes which have just been described and which are different from those in which modern narrative historians are engaged. On the other hand, it is interesting to note that modern economic or sociological historians, if they are concerned with investigating aspects of a society for which there is little or no hard evidence, will often appeal to certain 'models' which are partly based on the evidence of other known societies and are partly theoretical. There is thus a sense in which ancient historiography resembles certain forms of modern historiography, since the ancients had their rhetorical models which were based partly on existing cases in historical and other writing (see Woodman (1988) 27) and partly on the theoretical works of authors such as Cicero himself. Yet because the ancients applied their rhetorical models to *narrative* history, and because narrative history is still recognizable and indeed flourishing today, modern scholars tend to assimilate the ancient (and in fact unfamiliar) genre to the modern (and familiar), and thus fail to appreciate how different is the one from the other. It is for this reason that modern scholars, though they may often apply the word 'rhetorical' to classical historiography, do not mean by it what Cicero meant.[72]

How does the theory of *inuentio* work in practice? At 53 above (pp. 248–51) Antonius complained that the early Roman historians did little more than reproduce the techniques and conventions of the annals: they transmitted merely plain notices (*monumenta*) of times, persons, places, and events, without any attempt at elaborating them (*sine ullis ornamentis*). What Antonius has in mind, as is made clear by one of the early historians themselves,[73] is presumably the kind of triumphal notice which Livy reproduces in his work (e.g. 36.40.11

[71] Russell (1967) 133, quoted by Wiseman (1981) 389. Compare the way in which heroic poetry is composed, as described by Hainsworth (1984) 113–17.

[72] See above, n. 20. A good example is provided by Momigliano (1981).

[73] Sempronius Asellio, *HRR* F 2 '[early annalists wrote down] in whose consulship a war started and in whose it finished, and who celebrated a triumph because of it'.

'P. Cornelius consul triumphauit de Bois', 'The consul P. Cornelius celebrated a triumph over the Boi'). While such notices correspond fairly closely in general format to the *fasti triumphales* (triumphal records) which were set up in the late first century BC by Augustus,[74] modern scholars are uncertain about their precise relationship with, and dependence on, any of the earlier categories of record, such as the annals, which are known or thought to have existed.[75] Whatever the truth of this complicated problem might be, it is at least quite likely that these earlier records transmitted the four vital elements which occur in the example from Livy: namely, time (the consulship),[76] person (P. Cornelius), place (the Boi were a Gallic tribe), and event (the triumph presupposes a victory in battle). This was evidently Cicero's view: the annals-like work of the early historians contained precisely the four elements with which Antonius' rhetorical require-ments at 62–4 were equipped to deal (see above, pp. 261–3).[77] I shall therefore take the 'Livian' type of triumphal notice as my hypothet-ical example in what follows.

The qualifications for a triumph were a victory over a foreign enemy and the slaughter of 5,000 of them—qualifications which bring to mind Cicero's definition of historiography as the genre in which 'regions or battles are regularly described' (below, p. 279).

---

[74] See Phillips (1974), esp. 269–70.

[75] For the *Annales Maximi* themselves, see Frier (1979); for the *Fasti* and con-nected problems see Ridley (1980); for aristocratic epitaphs (*elogia*) and other forms of monument or inscription, both of which were liable to contain the kind of bare information to which Antonius refers, see respectively Earl (1967) 21–3, 27, and Wiseman (1986). There is a good general discussion of these and other possible sources in Wiseman (1979) 12ff.

[76] Magistracies were of course a traditional method of dating events.

[77] The four elements of time, person, place, and event were regarded as the four essential components of historiography by Cicero's contemporary, the obscure Ascle-piades of Myrleia (ap. Sext. Emp. *Math.* 1.253), by Sex. Empiricus himself (ib. 1.257) and by Eustathius (*GGM* II.215.14, though he in fact substitutes genealogy for persons): see Scheller (1911) 17–19. The same four elements also constituted stand-ard topics to be elaborated in rhetorical descriptions: see Lausberg (1998) 359–60; also below, n. 105. All this suggests that the views which Cicero attributes to Antonius had already been given expression considerably earlier—perhaps in the lost works *On Historiography* by Theophrastus and Praxiphanes (see p. 247 and n. 16, p. 285 and n. 146). Professor D. A. Russell has suggested to me that these lost works in their turn may have been a reaction to Aristotle's 'debunking' of historiography in the *Poetics* ('what Alcibiades did or what happened to him'): see Woodman (1988) 62 n. 163.

Thus a triumphal notice inevitably invited the writer to compose a *descriptio regionis* and a *descriptio pugnae*, both of which were standard issue in rhetorical training.[78] Let us consider the second of these in more detail. A rhetorical theorist in the second century AD writes as follows:

> We describe events if we take into account their antecedents, their attendant circumstances, and their consequences. For example, if we are describing a war, we shall first of all mention the preliminaries such as the generals' speeches, the outlay on both sides, and their fears; next, the attacks, the slaughter, and the dead; finally, the victory trophy, the triumphal songs of the victors, the tears, and enslavement of the victims.[79]

Naturally one could always introduce refinements. Perhaps the key battle is envisaged as having taken place at night, in which case a 'mixed description' is called for, since 'night' was also a standard topic of the *descriptio*.[80] Perhaps the victory involved the besieging of a city, in which case there are full instructions in Quintilian 8.3.67–70.[81] Indeed these instructions constitute an example in miniature of precisely the process which I am describing here:

> The plain statement 'the city was stormed' no doubt includes everything which attends such a calamity, but in its similarity to an official communiqué it has no emotional effect. But if you make explicit everything which the single word 'stormed' implies, you will see houses and temples drowned in flames, hear the crash of falling roofs ... [etc.] Provided it is all lifelike, we shall achieve the vividness we are after.

The vividness to which Quintilian refers is the familiar technique of 'expressing a matter in such a way that it seems to be taking place before our very eyes'—exactly the technique which Thucydides in my

---

[78] For the former, see Woodman (1977) 107, Brink (1971) on Hor. *AP* 16–18 and (1982) on *Ep.* 2.1.252, Lausberg (1998) 365–6 §819; for the latter, see Aphthon. 46.21, 47.1, Hermog. 16.17 (quoted), Liban. 8.460–64; Kroll (1913) on Cic. *Orat.* 66.

[79] Hermog. 16.22ff. The sequence antecedents–attendant circumstances–consequences, exactly as Antonius had recommended, is absolutely standard: cf. Theon. 119.14ff., Aphthon. 46.27ff., Nicol. 492.18–19.

[80] Hermog. 16.20–22.

[81] See further Paul (1982).

opinion was aiming for and which Cicero implicitly urged on his friend Lucceius (see Woodman (1988) 25–6 and above, p. 243).[82]

There is thus a distinction between a 'singular factual statement about the past', which will normally be one of the 'public facts' of history (in our case the triumphal notice) and will constitute the hard core,[83] and the *exaedificatio* or superstructure which required to be built up around it. This distinction may seem artificial to our way of thinking, but that is simply because our preconceptions about historiography are so different.[84] In fact the distinction is exactly that which Thucydides himself voiced about the speeches in his work, namely that there is a substratum of truth buried (so to speak) under a superstructure of rhetorical elaboration.[85] The same distinction can be found elsewhere in Cicero, and in Pliny. At *Brutus* 262 Cicero describes Caesar's *commentarii* as 'ready material from which would-be writers of history could select', and the context makes it clear that any material so selected would then be subject to rhetorical elaboration. In AD 107 Pliny sent Tacitus an account of an incident in which he had been personally involved and which he hoped Tacitus would include in his *Histories*. Pliny ends his letter, which is clearly inspired by that of Cicero to Lucceius, with these words (7.33.10): 'This sequence of events, such as it is, you will be able to make more notable, more distinguished and more important, though I'm not asking you to go beyond the norm for an incident of this type:

---

[82] Quint. 8.3.70. ἐνάργεια {vividness} was at home in the *narratio*, cf. Quint. 4.2.63–5. Brunt (1980a) 336 {= above, p. 236} says that 'we can well believe that Greek historians, in default of evidence, invented details to make their narratives vivid, thrilling or pathetic: certainly this was the practice of Livy', a statement which seems to contradict one of the principal theses of his essay, since elsewhere (311–12 {= above, pp. 207–8}) he implies that Livy did *not* adopt the 'rhetorical and sensationalist models' of Hellenistic historiography.

[83] The former is Atkinson's phrase ((1978) 39) to describe statements like 'Caesar was killed on the steps of the Capitol', the latter Kitson Clark's (in McCullagh (1984) 26) to describe those such as 'the battle of Waterloo was fought on Sunday, 18 June 1815'.

[84] For various examples from Greek, Roman, and medieval times see e.g. Wiseman (1979) 12–25 and 149, Fleischman (1983) 291–5. See also the general remarks of Fornara (1983) 134–5.

[85] See Woodman (1988) 11–13. Leeman (1955) 188 = (1963) 171 attributes to common opinion the (to him) erroneous view of Roman historiography as 'truth being submerged under floods of rhetorical commonplaces', quoting as example Boissier (1903), whom Brunt (1980a) 311 {= above, p. 207} invokes as a supporter!

history oughtn't to exceed the truth, and truth is quite adequate for honourable deeds.' Here Pliny is drawing a clear distinction between the hard core, with which he has supplied Tacitus, and the *exaedificatio*, which Tacitus is expected to provide.⁸⁶

It is also worth remembering that an analogous distinction lay at the very heart of Greek and Roman rhetoric. Much rhetorical training consisted in learning to elaborate *quaestiones* or *causae*, to which the Greek equivalents are θέσεις and ὑποθέσεις.⁸⁷ Indeed when Cicero wrote to his brother Quintus in 54 BC, he said this:⁸⁸

I was delighted to get your letter from Britain. I'd been afraid just thinking of the Ocean and the coastline. That's not to deny the other factors, of course, but they engender hope [*spei*] rather than fear [*timoris*] and I'm exercised by suspense [*exspectatione*] more than by fright [*metu*]. As for yourself, I see that you've got a marvellous topic [ὑπόθεσιν] to write about—those places [*situs*], those strange events and localities [*quas naturas rerum et locorum*], those customs [*mores*] and races [*gentes*], those battles [*pugnas*]! And what a general!

⁸⁶ The same distinction is also found in a letter of the emperor Verus to his teacher and historian, Fronto: *meae res gestae tantae sunt quantae sunt scilicet, quoiquoimodi sunt; tantae autem uidebuntur, quantas tu eas uideri uoles* {my achievements, such as they are, are of course no grater than they actually are, but they can be made to seem as great as you would have them seem} (II.196 Loeb edn.). It is clear from the examples I have quoted that the whole trend of ancient historiography was towards bigger (and therefore better) narratives: size was equivalent to definitiveness (see Luce (1977) 144–7 and 173–4), and it is noticeable that Livy, for example, even gives versions of events about which he has doubts (thus poisoning at 8.18.1–11 and a sea-storm at 29.27.14–15, both items being stock rhetorical commonplaces). It is mainly for this reason that we rarely find the converse, viz. an historian 'deconstructing' an account to lay bare the hard core, although in practice it would be an almost impossible procedure anyway (for the reasons given on pp. 273–4). The obvious exceptions are rationalizations of myths and *fabulae* (see e.g. Schultze (1986) 126 and Wiseman (1985b) 196–7, with references), for which the critical criteria are those standard in rhetoric, viz. plausibility and credibility. See also Woodman (1988) 49 n. 24 and 60 n. 150.

⁸⁷ See Bonner (1949) 2–11 and (1977) ch. 18; Fairweather (1981) 104–31. The terms are difficult to reproduce in English, but *quaestiones* refer basically to abstract propositions, *causae* to more concrete topics.

⁸⁸ *Q. fr.* 2.16.4, rightly referred to by Norden (1909) in the context of topographical digressions (*Nachträge* 19). Allen (1955) 158 rightly connects the letter with Cicero's remarks in *Part. Or.* 34 on the standard rhetorical topics of person, place, time, event, etc. (though Cicero is there discussing, not the *narratio*, but the *argumentatio*).

Here Cicero uses precisely the word ὑπόθεσις to describe what I have hitherto been calling the hard core. Its singular form suggests a distinction between Quintus' projected topic and the listed items which will constitute his *exaedificatio* and which, as we may infer from their familiar and conventional nature, he is expected to elaborate according to the rhetorical rules of probability and the rest.

If we now return to our example of the hard core of historiography, namely the triumphal notice, we find that Cicero himself complains that many such notices are simply false. In the course of a discussion of funeral eulogies, by which aristocrats commemorated the achievements of their families for posterity, he says:[89]

Yet the writing of Roman history has been falsified by these eulogies, since they contain many instances of events which never took place: false triumphs, extra consulships, false genealogies, and transfers to the people...

Livy too makes a similar complaint,[90] yet it may well be asked how these authors can complain that history has been falsified while at the same time they were promoting a method of writing history which depended so heavily on rhetorical *inuentio*. The explanation of the paradox would seem to be that the Romans required the hard core of history to be true and its elaboration to be plausible, and further that they saw no contradiction between these two requirements but rather regarded them as complementary. Thus if a historian had reason to believe that his hard core was false, it seems that he was debarred from using it for the purposes of *exaedificatio*. If, on the other hand, an historian was faced with an awkward but true hard core, he was under an obligation not to omit it:[91] on the contrary, he should

---

[89] *Brut.* 62. For some early examples, see Wiseman (1986); for an Augustan example, see Woodman (1983a) 192–6.

[90] Liv. 8.40.4–5. It is significant (cf. n. 91 below) that both authors attribute the falsification to *gloria* (see p. 246): Cicero refers to *laus*, Livy to *fama* (both = 'praise').

[91] It will be clear that here I am simply repeating in different words the first and second laws of historiography which Antonius expressed in *de Orat.* 2.62. It is therefore perhaps possible to conclude that when Cicero wrote that passage he had in mind the hard core elements of historiography. Indeed this may be another reason why his choice of metaphor (*fundamenta*, from building) so strongly resembles the metaphor he used at 53 to describe the hard core (*monumenta*, also from building). If this is so, then Cicero's advice to Lucceius that he should ignore the laws of historiography is all the more outrageous (see n. 40). Brunt (1980a) 337 {= above, p. 237} says that 'in asking Lucceius to magnify his own deeds in violation of the

employ all his rhetorical skill to put a good interpretation upon it. Such a challenge was indeed the very essence of rhetoric.[92]

To our modern way of thinking it seems very strange to insist that the hard core should be true when the elaboration of that hard core is by definition (in our terms) false. Yet clearly matters did not present themselves this way to the ancients.[93] On the contrary, the concept of a true hard core seems to have been the very thing which distinguished historiography from other types of literature. In 60 BC Cicero sent to Atticus a sketch of his consulship (*commentarium consulatus mei*) in Greek, with the remark that its contents were 'not encomiastic but historical'.[94] Since a *commentarius* was by definition supposed to be a factual account,[95] Cicero's choice of words suggests that he was sending merely a list of hard core elements; but we happen to know from a later letter that the sketch was in fact an elaborate rhetorical composition:[96] Atticus might therefore have been forgiven for wondering in which genre Cicero had been operating—eulogy, where a basis in truth was not required, or historiography, where it

"leges historiae"... [Cicero was not] suggesting that in any other respect his narrative should be untruthful: there is no call for a sensationalism unwarranted by the facts'— a comment which, in so far as I understand it, seems contradicted by everything which Cicero wrote in the letter and which Brunt himself has adequately summarized earlier in his paragraph. For a case in which an historian (Timaeus) evidently did omit some awkward but true hard core material see Pol. 12.15.9–11.

[92] See Jerome (1923) 370–2, who quotes e.g. Quint. 4.2.66–7, 76–8, 5.13.7–8.

[93] I find it particularly interesting that Fornara (1983) 136 has arrived at the same conclusion ('If you develop the inherent possibilities of a true datum, *ornare* is legitimate; if from a fiction..., the practice is culpable') by a different route (viz. Cic. *Leg.* 1.1–5, *de Orat.* 2.54 [*not* 63], and *Brut.* 43 *mortem rhetorice et tragice ornare potuerunt* {they were able to elaborate [sc. Themistocles'] death in a rhetorical and tragic manner}). Yet with reference to the last of these passages Fornara comments: 'It is vital to note... that only the imaginative reenactment is covered by the term *ornare*; the false and contrived nature of the scene is expressed adverbially by *tragice et rhetorice* [*sic*]. *Ornare* in itself is to take a fact and from it to set a scene, developing its latent potentialities. But in a historical work *ornare* subserves the laws of history and is tested by the standard of truth. Otherwise how could Cicero declare that the law of history was truth and yet condemn the Roman writers for the absence of *ornare*?'. It will be clear that with much of this comment I disagree; and his concluding question is one which I hope I have been able to answer in the present discussion.

[94] *Att.* 1.19.10 'non ἐγκωμιαστικὰ sunt haec sed ἱστορικὰ quae scribimus'.

[95] See Bömer (1952) and Eden (1962). An example is the letter of Ser. Sulpicius Galba to Cicero describing the battle of Forum Gallorum in 43 BC (*Fam.*10.30), which has all the hallmarks of the *commentarius*-style.

[96] *Att.* 2.1.1.

was.[97] Cicero's reassurance is designed to forestall Atticus' puzzlement, and also to enhance his own reputation, since an historiographical account, being based in truth, would presumably carry
more authority.[98]

This convention raises the whole question of what constitutes a
hard core element. Since the hard core is a matter of content, as
Antonius said at 54 above (pp. 249–50), and since the *exaedificatio*
also involves matters of content, as Antonius makes clear at both 53
and 63, there is no intrinsic means of distinguishing the one from
the other.[99] A time-honoured and seemingly fundamental datum
of Roman history could be the product of *exaedificatio* and hence
false; a neglected and apparently trivial detail could be a core element
and hence (but by no means necessarily) true.[100] Given the rhetorical
nature of ancient historiography, the relative significance of such
data is no guide, since it was the essence of rhetoric to inflate
the less significant and deflate the more. It is true that we, with our
modern conception of historiography and our research expertise in
such areas as archaeology and topography, can on a limited number
of occasions isolate the (to us) fictional elements in a particular
account.[101] But the ancients themselves, with their different

[97] For epideictic not requiring truth Brunt (1980a) 331 {= above, p. 228} n. 52
quotes Philod. 1.285–7 Sudhaus (his other quotations from Cicero do not seem to me
relevant).

[98] For some good remarks on this general topic, see e.g. Balfour (1979) 424 ('The
skilful propagandist tries to give his argument the appearance of an objective
statement' etc.).

[99] Cf. Finley (1985) 18 'I am unaware of any stigmata that automatically distinguish fiction from fact'; Fornara (1983) 137 'The approach leaves us almost helpless
when we attempt to extricate fact from fancy'.

[100] I say 'not necessarily' because of course the ancients themselves realized that
many hard core elements were false: see p. 271. On the other hand, they no doubt also
accepted as true many that they should have considered false, since for them, as for
the historians of the Middle Ages, 'history was what was willingly believed' (Fleischman (1983) 305, and see also Ray's excellent account (1980) of the phrase *uera lex
historiae* in Jerome and Bede).

[101] See, for example, the splendid analysis (and demolition) by Horsfall (1982) of
Livy's description of the battle of the Caudine Forks; also his more general discussion
(1985) of topographical techniques in Latin authors. In referring to topography and
archaeology I do not wish to give the impression that I am dismissing or underesti-
mating the value of modern literary analysis (on the contrary, see Woodman (1988)
176–9). But it is in the nature of the case that literary analysis will not always produce

conception of historiography and no criterion of judgement except that of plausibility, had neither the instinct nor the capability to do so.[102] The implications for the modern study of the ancient world are of course momentous, but scholars do not yet seem to have come to terms with them.

Thus the ancients saw a theoretical distinction between the core element and the superstructure of historiography in terms of truth, although in practice the distinction was usually impossible for them to make. If we, with our superior knowledge, were to say to them that a given core element was false, I imagine they would be glad of the information: particularly in the Augustan age, when intellectual life was inspired by the example of Alexandrian scholarship, there was a general desire for increasingly exact knowledge, and historians, like poets, were always on the alert to correct their predecessors.[103] This was simply an aspect of literary *aemulatio*.[104] If, on the other hand, we were to say to an ancient historian that a given example of *exaedificatio* was untrue, he would no doubt reply, with some indignation, 'It *must* have been like that'.[105] To use the language of

conclusions which modern historians might regard as certain. Some conclusions thus reached will, however, be very likely; and we ought to be far more prepared than we are at present to extrapolate from them.

[102] 'The ancients...would have repudiated any such analytical exercise, for they wrote in the expectation that their histories in fact established the record in a final and conclusive sense' (Fornara (1983) 137). Luce (1977) 161 rightly says that 'antiquarian research could give only limited help to an historian seeking to narrate *res gestae*. Antiquarianism was not history, but the stuff of which digressions were made'. See also Rawson (1985) 200 and, on antiquarian research in general, 233ff.

[103] Thus Pollio criticized Caesar's *commentarii*, nominally a collection of hard core elements (p. 272) but in fact an elaborately completed work of history (cf. Cic. *Brut.* 262; Eden (1962) 75–8): *parum diligenter parumque integra ueritate compositos putat, cum Caesar pleraque et quae per alios erant gesta temere crediderit et quae per se... perperam ediderit* {he thinks they were written with too little diligence and too little regard for truth, since Caesar often rashly believed what was done by others and gave a wrong account of his own} (Suet. *Iul.* 56.4).

[104] See Woodman (1988) 49 and n. 24.

[105] Wiseman (1981) 389. Very revealing is Ti. Donatus' comment (197.6–9) on *Aen.* 9.80–3: 'He [Virgil] provided the time [*tempus*], place [*locum*], characters [*personas*], and event [*rem*], by means of which he gave his narrative as much credibility [*fidem*] as possible: for it is precisely when we are told when an event took place, and where, and on whose initiative, that it is shown to be true [*uerum*]'. Here the same four key elements of *inuentio* as Cicero mentions (and see also above, n. 77) are said to produce credibility, which is expressly stated to be equivalent to truth.

Antonius at 53, the *monumenta* and *ornamenta* of historiography
were both important, but each had its own terms of reference.[106] It is
in acknowledgement of this that Livy wrote in his preface: 'New
historians always think either that they have some more exact knowledge to impart to the subject-matter or that their literary skill will
improve on the inferior standards of their predecessors'.[107]

Since Antonius' remarks on truth and falsehood at 62 are to be
seen in terms of impartiality and prejudice (above, p. 258), he does
not contradict himself when at 63 he requires that content be elaborated by means of *inuentio*.[108] Yet Brunt, quoting Antonius' praise
of historiography at 36 (above, p. 248), has argued that since 'history
furnished lessons indispensable to the general and statesman', it was
necessary that it should also be true: 'as a mendacious witness, it
would serve no useful end'.[109] Yet Brunt fails to complete the quotation, which goes on: 'Whose voice but the orator's can entrust her
[sc. historiography] to immortality?'. And in the complete sentence,
as Wiseman has remarked, the dilemma in which we moderns find
ourselves recurs: 'the orator provides a style worthy of the material,
but also a technique that cannot help but distort it'.[110] Brunt has
simply imputed to the ancients a way of thinking which is prevalent
today, a practice which he elsewhere rightly criticizes.[111] The ancient
evidence is actually different from that which Brunt supposes. Deliberative oratory often aimed to impart moral advice, yet it did not

---

[106] If I may literalize the metaphor and introduce a parallel from building, the
fourth-century Arch of Constantine (= *monumentum*) was decorated with re-used
reliefs and sculptures (= *ornamenta*) from the second century. Whatever the reason(s)
for this practice (see Bianchi Bandinelli (1971) 83), it well illustrates the ancients'
unhistorical (in our view) way of thinking. (Interestingly enough, this same parallel
had also occurred to Peter (1897) I.287.) See also Woodman (1988) 14 on speeches.

[107] *Praef.* 2. Livy's statement, while disproving the allegation of Fornara (1983) 56
that 'the concept of research finds no place in the Latin prefaces', is not strictly at
variance with my remarks on pp. 273–4 since the evidence suggests that such research
was always the exception rather than the rule. For *aemulatio* in *exaedificatio* (Livy's
ars scribendi) see Peter (1897) II.190ff.

[108] 'When Homer's account of Achilles is accepted as essentially reliable because he
was not writing of him in his lifetime and therefore had no motive for lying, we
realise how limited this criterion [of truth] is as an index of historical inaccuracy'
(Wiseman (1981) 387–8, referring to Lucian *h.c.* 40).

[109] Brunt (1980a) 313 {= above, p. 210}. A similar point in Rawson (1985) 215.
[110] Wiseman (1979) 38.
[111] Brunt (1980a) 316 {= above, p. 213}. See further Woodman (1988) 201.

eschew the quintessentially rhetorical technique of *amplificatio*
which is at the opposite end of the scale from truth.[112] Indeed Cicero
recognized that Xenophon's portrait of Cyrus was beneficial precisely
because it was written 'not according to historical truth but as the
image of a just ruler'.[113] It has been shown that in practice Livy did
not fail to distort 'the truth' in order to enhance the moral aspects of
his work;[114] his contemporary Diodorus expressly stated that fictitious myths had moral value, and a similar point was discussed at
considerable length by another contemporary, Strabo.[115] Finally
Quintilian, in a passage which seems to echo a well known sentence
of Cicero's *Brutus*, says that rhetoric is criticized because 'it deals in
falsehood and excites the passions. Yet neither of these is disgraceful
when the motive is good... Even philosophers are sometimes permitted to tell lies [*mendacium dicere etiam sapienti aliquando concessum est*], while the orator has no option but to rouse passions if
that is the only way he can lead the judge to justice. For judges are not
always enlightened: often they need to be deceived in case they make
a mistake.'[116] It seems from these examples, therefore, that the moral
aspect of Roman historiography should not be used to argue that
ancient historiography was not written according to the principles
and practice of *inuentio*.

Style. At 64 Antonius at last turns to discuss the nature of historical
style (*uerborum ratio*), this being the other element of which the
exaedificatio of historiography consists (above, pp. 252–4, 259). His
statement that the style of historical writing should be ample, mobile
and fluent reappears in the work which Cicero published nine years
later, the *Orator*, where the same river or stream metaphor is used
(66): 'the style should be mobile and fluent, without the contortions

[112] Deliberative oratory demanded proof and refutation (*Rhet. Herenn.* 3.8);
argument involved *exornatio* (2.28), which in turn employed *amplificatio* (2.46, cf.
47 *fin.*).
[113] *Q. fr.* 1.1.23; cf. Trencsényi-Waldapfel (1960) 9. Cicero was presumably referring to core elements of the portrait.
[114] Walsh (1955), referred to by Herkommer (1968) 137, who is altogether more
realistic than Brunt on this topic.
[115] Diod. 1.1.2; Str. 1.2.8–9.
[116] Quint. 2.17.26–8, cf. *Brut.* 42 *concessum est rhetoribus ementiri in historiis* (on
which sèe below, n. 151). Jerome (1923) 363 remarks that Quintilian 'finds frequent
occasion to treat of lying as a fine art', quoting 4.2.89–94, 123–4, 12.1.1–14, 34–5.

and bitterness of the law-courts' ('*tracta* quaedam et *fluens* expetitur, non haec contorta et acris oratio'). Earlier in the same work Cicero gave a more detailed account of the style which, by implication, was best suited to historiography (37–8): it demanded a fullness of vocabulary, freer rhythms than forensic oratory, symmetry of sentences, rounded periods, and above all a feeling for balance and corresponsion.[117] Since in the same work he also describes the style of Herodotus as 'flowing along like a calm stream without any choppiness' (*sine ullis salebris quasi sedatus amnis fluit*), whereas that of Thucydides 'is carried headlong in a violent rush' (*incitatior fertur*), it would appear that Herodotus was Cicero's ideal historical stylist.[118] And since Seneca many years later described Cicero's own style as 'moving gradually to its conclusion, landing gently and unhurriedly, and unvaryingly true to its customary rhythm',[119] it is

---

[117] *uerborum copia alitur et . . . numerus liberiore quadam fruitur licentia. datur etiam uenia concinnitati sententiarum . . . certique et circumscripti uerborum ambitus conceduntur, de industriaque non ex insidiis sed aperte et palam elaboratur ut uerba uerbis quasi demensa et paria respondeant, ut crebro conferantur pugnantia comparenturque contraria et ut pariter extrema terminentur eundemque referant in cadendo sonum.* The supply of words is rhythm encouraged and . . . the symmetry of sentences enjoys a certain more liberal license. Concessions are also made to, and well-defined and rounded periods are allowed; the ornamentation is done of set purpose, with no attempt at concealment, but openly and avowedly so that words correspond to words as if measured off in equal phrases, frequently things inconsistent are placed side by side, and things contrasted are paired; clauses are made to end in the same way and with similar sound.}

[118] *Orat.* 39, and see further Woodman (1988) 45–7. It is usually suggested that the Herodotean style was taken up by Isocrates and his pupils Ephorus and Theopompus and mediated through to the works of Cicero and Dionysius, who also advocates it, by Theophrastus: see e.g. Avenarius (1956) 55–9, Leeman (1963) 173. Scheller (1911) 64 seems to argue that the Herodotean style was not that advocated by the Isocrateans; but Cicero and others describe Herodotus, Isocrates and the others in the same terms (cf. *Orat.* 39, above, with 207 *in historia . . . placet omnia dici Isocrateo Theopompeoque more illa circumscriptione ambituque* {in history it is desirable that everything be said in the manner of Isocrates and Theopompus with that rounded and balanced periodic style}), and it is this which is significant for our purposes. There are full comments on Cicero and the smooth style in Brunt (1980a) 320–1 {= above, pp. 215–16} and 328–30 {= above, pp. 227–9}, who identifies it with the *genus medium* (cf. also Quint. 12.10.60).

[119] *Ep.* 114.16 *illa in exitu lenta, qualis Ciceronis est, deuexa et molliter detinens nec aliter quam solet ad morem suum pedemque respondens.* Lucian's comment on the *narratio* that it should progress αὐτῇ ὁμοίως {uniformly} (55) is very like Seneca's remark; but I think it refers to the transitions between topics rather than to style (*contra* Leeman (1963) 173).

also clear that Cicero was recommending for historiography the very style which he had himself perfected during his long oratorical career.

After his brief remarks on style at 64,[120] Antonius at length returns to the point which he made at the beginning of his speech at 62, the ring composition (see above, p. 255) bringing to an end his discussion of how historiography should be written.[121]

ALTERNATIVE DEFINITIONS

Historiography and Epideictic

Though Antonius' discussion is recognized by scholars as being of great importance, this assessment is based, as I have tried to argue, on a complete misunderstanding of what Antonius actually says. It is therefore worth asking whether, on this new interpretation, his words are representative of Roman historiography in general.

It is clear, both from the parallels with which I have illustrated his argument (pp. 260–4) and from the articulation of the argument itself,[122] that Antonius sees historiography in terms of *judicial* oratory, of which the *narratio* was an integral part. Yet there were of course two other types of oratory, deliberative and epideictic (or

---

[120] I too have been brief, but I return to the subject in Woodman (1988) 117–20.

[121] Since the following sentences in 64 (*cohortationes, consolationes, praecepta, admonita, quae tractanda sunt omnia disertissime sed locum suum in his artibus, quae traditae sunt, habent nullum* {exhortation, consolation, instruction, and admonition should all be treated with the utmost oratorical skill, but none has its own place in the systems that have been handed down}) echo those which Cicero wrote in 50 (*illa, quae saepe diserte agenda sunt... neque habent suum locum ullum in diuisione partium neque certum praeceptorum genus, et agenda sunt non minus diserte quam quae in lite dicuntur, obiurgatio, cohortatio, consolatio* {those things, which often must be handled with oratorical skill... do not have their own place in any division of the subject into parts, nor their own particular type of precepts, and they must be treated with no less skill than those matters in the courtroom, i.e. rebuke, exhortation, and consolation}) it is clear that Cicero's whole discussion of historiography in 51–64 is included within an outer frame of ring composition. And both passages in their turn look back to 34–6 (quoted on pp. 247–8).

[122] The sequence *uerborum autem ratio... sine hac iudiciali asperitate et sine sententiarum forensium aculeis* suggests that everything under the heading of *rerum ratio* is to be seen in terms of judicial oratory.

'display') oratory,[123] and it is well known that Cicero himself else-where sees historiography in terms of *epideictic*.[124] At *Orat.* 37 he brackets together historiography and panegyrics under the heading of epideictic,[125] and later in the same work (66) he says that 'closest to this type of oratory [i.e. epideictic] is historiography, in which the narrative is elaborate and regions or battles are regularly described [*in qua et narratur ornate et regio saepe aut pugna describitur*]'. Part of the reason for the close relationship between the two types of writing is implicit in the second of these quotations, since epideictic was recognized as a branch of oratory in which elaborate narrative was particularly at home;[126] but part of the reason was also that epideictic was the branch of oratory in which persons, places, cities, and buildings were praised or (in the case of persons) blamed,[127] and such material naturally figured prominently also in historiography. Indeed I have argued elsewhere {= Woodman (1988) 41–4} that classical historiography falls into two types, based on praise and blame respectively, and so the connection between historiography and epideictic is established at a fundamental level. Does this asso-ciation with epideictic therefore invalidate Antonius' view of histori-ography as analogous to judicial oratory?

[123] See e.g. Lausberg (1998) 1ff. Together the three make up the *tria genera causarum*, the three types of oratory.

[124] This is even implied in *de Orat.* 2.35–6 (see below, n. 128).

[125] Since he makes only selective reference to *Orat.* 37, Brunt (1980a) 330 {= above, p. 229} is able falsely to state that Hermog. 417–25, which he describes as 'a farrago of indiscriminating absurdity', is the only evidence that the ancients made no distinction between historiography and panegyric. Brunt's restriction of *Orat.* 66 to 'a stylistic content' (330 {= above, p. 229}) is questionable in view of the way the sentence develops (*sed in his tracta quaedam ... oratio*), and his distinction between the two genres on grounds of pleasure (331 {= above, p. 230}) is implausible, as he himself is inclined to recognize (cf. 313–14 {= above, p. 210}), since historiog-raphy also sought to give pleasure (see, e.g., Woodman (1983b) 111–12, Fornara (1983) 120–34: see also below, n. 136. As the above evidence clearly shows, there *was* a close affinity between the two genres. Yet there was also a difference (pp. 272–3); but this difference does not of course invalidate the case which I have been making. It was entirely characteristic of the ancients to debate the relationship of one genre to another (see below, pp. 286–7), recognizing that no one genre was absolutely iden-tical with another. For an analogous distinction in the Middle Ages, see Fleischman (1983) 305.

[126] Cf. Cic. *Part. Or.* 71, 75, Quint. 3.7.15, and Adamietz (1966) ad loc.; Lausberg (1998) 106–7.

[127] Quint 3.7.6–28.

At first sight, the answer to this question might appear to be affirmative. We have already seen that the first stage of Antonius' general exposition (30–73) falls into three parts, of which historiography is only one (above, p. 247). In the first of these parts (30–50) his argument is essentially reductive. The rhetorical modes he lists at 35–6 (above, pp. 247–8) almost beg to be divided into deliberative, judicial and epideictic respectively;[128] yet Antonius himself (41) prefers to use an alternative classification consisting of only two types, the so-called 'open-ended' (*infinitum*) and 'specific' (*certum*).[129] By insisting on this classification he is thus able to eliminate a third type (*laudationes* or eulogy, which Crassus had mentioned earlier in the dialogue), on the grounds that it is trivial and does not need rules of its own (43–7).[130] With this dismissal out of the way, Antonius in the third part of his exposition (65–73) attempts to dismiss open-ended topics similarly, on the grounds that they do not constitute a separate branch of rhetoric since their treatment can be subsumed under that of specific topics. By specific topics Antonius in fact means judicial topics,[131] from which it is clear that in the first and third parts of the exposition Antonius is anxious to assert the primacy of judicial oratory.[132] Sandwiched between these two

---

[128] See Wilkins (1881) 219: 'Cicero keeps in view here the three main *genera* of eloquence: (1) *genus deliberatiuum*, (a) in the senate, (b) in the *contio*; (2) *genus iudiciale*; (3) *genus demonstratiuum*, which includes panegyrics, exhortations, censures, consolations, etc. History was added by some, and Cicero inclines to agree with them'.

[129] For these see e.g. Lausberg (1998) 39–41.

[130] See further above, n. 35. Despite the present elimination of eulogy, O'Mara (1971) 151–2 rightly notes that the structure of Antonius' discussion 'affirms the threefold division' (see above, n. 128) and that he does in fact acknowledge its generic nature later at 341–9, where he repeats at more length the rules which he professed to deny at 45–6. This is just a further example of the paradoxicality which characterizes Antonius' arguments in the dialogue.

[131] Cf. 42–3 *certum autem . . . quae in foro atque in ciuium causis disceptationibusque uersantur. ea mihi uidentur aut in lite oranda . . . esse posita* {The specific, however, . . . are those things which are dealt with in the forum and in judicial cases and disputes involving citizens. These things, it seems to me, are classified either in the pleading of cases . . . }, 70–1; Fantham (1979) 443, though she is of course wrong to add that 'history is distinguished from oratory'.

[132] There is a similar emphasis on judicial oratory at Cic. *Inu.* 2.13–154 (only 155–76 on deliberative, and 176–7 on epideictic). This emphasis on judicial oratory has a 'primitivist' aspect to it, since it alone was the subject of the earliest rhetorical handbooks (see Hinks (1936)).

parts is his discussion of historiography, which he sees in terms of judicial oratory. Has he therefore tailored his account of historiography to suit his general position? Or has he supported his general position by appealing to a neutral genre which happens to suit it?

Cicero's remarks on historiography and epideictic, quoted above, no doubt suggest that the first of these alternatives is correct; but the matter is not quite so straightforward: the ancients recognized that the three types of judicial, epideictic and deliberative oratory were in no way mutually exclusive (see e.g. Quint. 3.7.28), and the essential characteristics of one type could surface in either of the other two in a different form. I shall provide three examples of what I mean.

First, Antonius recommends that the historian should 'indicate what he approves of', something which Cicero expanded in the letter to Lucceius (above, p. 243) by recommending that his friend should indicate also what he disapproved of (*uituperanda*). The background of these recommendations is of course the moral aspect of ancient historiography, according to which advice was to be given to readers on how they should conduct their lives;[133] and the kind of oratory which was principally concerned with giving advice was deliberative, which was actually called *hortatiuum genus* by Quintilian (5.10.83). Yet some remarks of Cicero make it clear that advising was also an implicit function of epideictic (*Part. Or.* 69–71): 'There is no type of oratory capable . . . of doing more service to the state,[134] nor any in which the speaker is more occupied in recognizing virtue and vice . . . I will give a brief account of the principles of praising and blaming [*uituperandi*], since they are a valuable guide . . . to a moral life [*ad honeste uiuendum*] . . . Naturally, everything associated with virtue deserves praise, while everything associated with vice deserves blame [*uituperanda*]'.

Second, Antonius requires that the historian should emphasize the role played by the individual protagonists and their characters. Now we have already noted that a judicial *narratio* might include a digression, for which the traditional topics were 'praise of men or

---

[133] Leeman (1963) 172 recognizes this, but chooses to repeat his earlier statement of (1955) 189 that this is the only subjective element in the whole of Antonius' discussion!

[134] Compare esp. Sempronius Asellio, *HRR* F 2, Sall. *Jug.* 4.4.

localities' (Quint. 4.3.12 *laus hominum locorumque*). Yet the 'praise of men or localities' would naturally follow the rules for precisely these topics which were laid down in epideictic oratory and which, at least in the case of 'praise of men', Cicero dramatized as follows *(Part. Or. 72–3)*:

Because the whole *raison d'être* of these compositions is the pleasure and entertainment of the listener [*ad uoluptatem auditoris et ad delectationem*] ... we must regularly elaborate our material [*ornamenta rerum*] with surprising or unexpected events [*admirabilia et necopinata*] or ... with what will appear to be occurrences sent by heaven or fate to the person under discussion. For the listener's sense of anticipation [*exspectatio*], the element of surprise [*admiratio*] and unexpected outcomes [*improuisi exitus*] all induce a kind of pleasure [*uoluptatem*].

This passage in its turn is strikingly similar to Cicero's own description of the practice *narrationes* on which young orators trained (*Inu.* 1.27):[135]

In this type of *narratio* the key-note should be liveliness resulting from variety of material [*rerum uarietate*], contrast of characters, seriousness, gentleness, hope [*spe*], fear [*metu*], ... pity [*misericordia*], reversals of fortune [*fortunae commutatione*], unexpected disasters [*insperato incommodo*], sudden delight [*subita laetitia*] and a happy outcome [*iucundo exitu*].

And of course both passages are highly reminiscent of the *historiographical* advice which Cicero gave to Lucceius (above pp. 243–4).[136]

Third, Antonius' tripartite scheme of *consilia–acta–euentus* presupposes argument and inference, a methodology which we more normally associate with judicial oratory; yet Quintilian makes it clear that such a procedure could also be employed in epideictic oratory too (3.4.8, 5.3, 7.3–6).

There is therefore much less difference between the three types of oratory than their individual labels might suggest; and Cicero's own ascription of historiography to epideictic in no way invalidates

---

[135] Repeated almost verbatim in *Rhet. Herenn.* 1.13; and see also Ullman (1942) 33.

[136] These similarities seem to disprove Brunt's statement ((1980a) 330 {= above, p. 229}) that 'we are not to infer that he [Cicero] conceived true histories as such epideictic displays [as *Inu.* 1.27]'.

Antonius' subsuming it under judicial oratory. Historiography could be defined equally well in terms of either type; and we must remember that Lucian, who had no axe to grind, described a work of history as 'an extended *narratio*' (above, p. 264). I thus conclude that, on this score at least, there is nothing unrepresentative about Antonius' account of how to write history.

Historiography and Poetry

During the last ten years of his life Cicero was at work on the *De Legibus*, towards the beginning of which there is a well known passage of dialogue where Atticus tries to persuade Cicero to write history (1.5):

potes autem tu profecto satis facere in ea, quippe cum sit opus, ut tibi quidem uideri solet, unum hoc oratorium maxime.

You will of course do justice to the genre, since it's a task which is singularly well suited to an orator—or so it has always seemed to you at least.

In the light of *De Oratore* 2.62–4 it is of course hardly surprising that Atticus should impute this view to Cicero himself;[137] but from the reservation 'tibi *quidem*' ('to you *at least*') it might be inferred that, more than forty years after Antonius 'spoke' the words which Cicero there attributed to him, most men were still not accustomed to seeing historiography as 'a task which is singularly well suited to an orator'.

---

[137] Atticus' statement (particularly *maxime*) is naturally an embarrassment to Brunt. On the one hand he suggests that 'perhaps "maxime" should not be taken too seriously: strictly it implies that history is more oratorical than oratory itself' ((1980a) 325 {= above, p. 224} n. 33); alternatively he suggests that *maxime* distinguishes historiography from law and philosophy because these 'were recognised as hard disciplines only to be mastered by prolonged application', whereas 'the collation and investigation of historical evidence, though time-consuming, required no technical preparation' (327 {= above, pp. 225–6}). Yet this seems inconsistent with his earlier contention that ancient historians undertook 'extensive enquiries, involving the examination of eyewitnesses, consultation of documents and travel to distant scenes' (315 {= above, p. 212}), a contention for which he offers no real evidence. The drawback of contemporary historiography at Plin. *Ep.* 5.8.12 is *not* that it required personal research but that it was dangerous (*graues offensae, leuis gratia* {offenses are serious, thanks are small}, omitted by Brunt); and when he says that 'others claimed to have done what Pliny assumes to be normal', his reference to Walbank (1972) 82–3 demonstrates only that such claims are to be regarded with the greatest scepticism.

Such an inference would, however, be mistaken, as a glance at the evidence reveals.

T. P. Wiseman has recently emphasized that there is a massive difference in scale between the history of Cn. Gellius, the early historian who was contemporary with the dramatic date of the *De Oratore*, and those of his predecessors, such as L. Piso and L. Cassius Hemina.[138] Gellius, for example, was treating in his *fifteenth* book an incident which Hemina had treated in his *second*; and historians writing later in the first half of the first century BC wrote at even greater length than Gellius.[139] This difference in scale can only be accounted for by the wholesale employment of rhetorical *inuentio*.[140] It therefore follows not only that Antonius' depreciatory critique of the earlier Roman historians is correct, but also that later historians *did* write history according to the rhetorical principles which he enunciated. Yet, if this is so, how is Atticus' reservation in the *De Legibus* to be explained?

It is, I think, significant that Atticus' remark arises immediately out of a comparison between historiography and poetry.[141] When we recall the close connections between Homer and both Herodotus and

---

[138] Wiseman (1979) 9–12.
[139] Ibid. 11; Woodman (1975) 286.
[140] Wiseman (1979) 21–6.
[141] The comparison concludes with the following exchange between Cicero and his brother Quintus (1.5): Q. 'I understand that in your opinion different laws obtain in historiography and poetry'. M. 'Yes. In history most things have their basis in *ueritas*, whereas in poetry they have it in pleasure, although in both Herodotus, the father of history, and Theopompus there are countless *fabulae*.' Cicero's reply here has naturally been used by those scholars who wish to assert that his views on historiography are similar to our own (e.g. Brunt (1980a) 313–14 {= above, pp. 209–10}, Fornara (1983) 128 n. 5, Kelley (1969) 105–6); yet I am certain that they are misinterpreting the word *ueritas* here. The context, and in particular the reference to *fabulae*, suggests that *ueritas* = 'real life', as it does at *Inu.* 1.29 (quoted on p. 262), *de Orat.* 2.34, 36 (p. 248), 94 (see below); other examples in *OLD* s.v. 2a. That is: *ueritas* embraces the *uerisimile* and is contrasted with *fabula*, as at *Inu.* 1.27 *fabula est in qua nec uerae nec ueri similes res continentur* {*fabula* contains material neither true nor realistic}, *Rhet. Herenn.* 1.13, and see further my interpretation of Thuc. 1.22.4 at Woodman (1988) 23–4. Cicero is drawing a comparison between 'credible' texts on the one hand, a category into which historiography normally falls, and the far-fetched Roman stories of §§3–4 on the other, with which the *fabulae* of Herodotus and Theopompus have everything in common.

Thucydides (see Woodman (1988), 1–9, 28–31, 35, 38), it can be inferred that historiography was originally seen in terms of poetry and that there was a continuing debate as to their precise relationship and proximity.[142] Thus Aristotle in the fourth century BC and Polybius in the second each maintained that there were differences between historiography and poetry,[143] while much later Quintilian stated the opposite, that 'historiography is very close to poetry and is rather like a poem in prose'.[144] Yet by Aristotle's time the historian Ephorus had also begun to compare historiography and oratory, something in which he was followed by the historian Timaeus.[145] What impetus was given to this debate by Theophrastus and Praxiphanes, whose works *On Historiography* have both been lost, is impossible to say;[146] but Dionysius in the first century BC was followed by Pliny the younger and Hermogenes in the second century AD in seeing historiography as closely allied to oratory.[147]

The text of Cicero's reply to Quintus is also problematical. Above I have translated my own version: *Quippe, cum in illa ad ueritatem* [*pleraque*], *Quinte, referantur, in hoc ad delectationem* [*pleraque*], the assumption being that *pleraque* was mistakenly omitted from the first colon, where it is needed, and added on at the end. Others prefer versions which include *omnia* or *cuncta* in the first colon. It is immaterial to my interpretation whether *pleraque* or *omnia/cuncta* is read; but I think it is more realistic if Cicero is made to say *pleraque*, since it was well known that histories almost inevitably contained *some* 'fables', and on this view the word *innumerabiles* will have some point.

[142] See e.g. Peter (1897) II.203–4; Norden (1909) 91–3; Avenarius (1956) 16–22; Wiseman (1979) 143–53.

[143] Arist. *Poetics* 1451b1ff. (on which, see Woodman (1988) 62 n. 163), Pol. 2.56.11.

[144] Quint. 10.1.31.

[145] See Pol. 12.28.8–28a.2 (the comparison is with epideictic).

[146] Norden (1909) 84 suggests that Cic. *Orat.* 66 (above, p. 279) derives from Theophrastus, which is no doubt quite likely (see above, n. 77). The existence of these works does not of course necessarily disprove Antonius' repeated statements that there were no separate instructions for historiography in *rhetorical* handbooks: see Walbank (1957) 418–19 and (1972) 36 n. 20 (*contra* Fornara (1983) 137–9 and n. 59, who has however completely misinterpreted Cicero's remarks: see above, n. 36).

[147] D. Hal. *Thuc.* 9 refers to histories as ῥητορικαὶ ὑποθέσεις {rhetorical topics}, an extremely interesting combination of words (see pp. 270–1), though he elsewhere (*Pomp.* 3 = 2.384 Usher) refers to the works of Herodotus and Thucydides as ποιήσεις {poetical works}! Pliny (*Ep.* 5.8.9) says that 'historiography and oratory have, of course, much in common'; Hermog. *De Ideis* 417.28–418.1 says that 'historians should be set alongside panegyrists, as is in fact the case, I think: their aims are amplification and entertainment', etc.

There were thus two main alternative ways of defining historiography, and it is hardly surprising that Cicero, the outstanding Roman orator, should prefer the latter definition to the former. After all, it is clear from numerous passages that he seriously contemplated writing history himself.[148] But since the earlier discussion in the *De Legibus* concerned the relationship between historiography and poetry, *quidem* ('at least') at 1.5 is merely Atticus' acknowledgement that Cicero belongs with those who prefer the alternative definition of historiography as oratory.[149]

Lest it be imagined that there is some essential contradiction between these two definitions, two passages of the *De Oratore*, where *oratory* is seen in terms of *poetry*, show that this is not so.[150] Though we today see poetry, oratory, and historiography as three separate genres, the ancients saw them as three different species of the same genus—rhetoric. All three types of activity aimed to elaborate certain data in such a way as to affect or persuade an audience or readership. So when in Cicero's *Brutus* (43) Atticus says that the historians Cleitarchus and Stratocles 'were able to elaborate Themistocles' death in a rhetorical and tragic manner [*rhetorice et tragice*]', the two terms represent, not a contradiction, but alternative ways of describing the same phenomenon.[151]

---

[148] See above, n. 1.

[149] The only passage which casts doubt on this, so far as I am aware, is *Brut.* 286: *Demochares . . . et orationes scripsit aliquot et earum rerum historiam quae erant Athenis ipsius aetate gestae* non tam *historico* quam *oratorio genere perscripsit* {Demochares wrote several speeches and a history of events at Athens in his own lifetime in a made not so much historical as oratorical} (not really capitalized on by Brunt (1980a) 321 {= above, p. 218} and n. 20). Fantham (1979) 447 explains the contrast, to which she is in general sympathetic (above, n. 131), by suggesting that the reference is to style rather than content. But I doubt this. There is a passage of Diodorus, roughly contemporary with the *Brutus*, in which the historian complains that some other historians put too many (and too long) speeches into their histories, thus almost turning them into works of pure oratory (20.1.1–3). Since Cicero tells us that Demochares wrote speeches as well as histories, I suspect that his contrast between *historico* and *oratorio* may be intended to make a similar point to that of Diodorus.

[150] 1.70 'The poet is a very close relative of the orator', 3.27 'poets have the closest relationship with orators'; further examples in Kroll (1913) on *Orat.* 66.

[151] Modern scholars (cf. McDonald (1968) 467–8) tend to see a distinction between what they call 'rhetorical' historiography (above, n. 20) and so-called 'tragic' historiography, such as that outlined in the letter to Lucceius (see, e.g., Ullman (1942) and Walbank (1960) {= below, Ch. 14}). But for two reasons I believe this distinction

Moreover, the Roman system of education encouraged young men to study and emulate the works of famous orators, historians, and poets, with the result that future orators, historians and poets were all reared in the same system.[152] Indeed the sixth-century AD historian Agathias claimed that in his youth he had concentrated exclusively on poetry but that a friend encouraged him to write history by saying that 'there is no great gulf between poetry and historiography: they are close relatives from the same tribe and separated from each other only by metre'.[153] And in exactly the same way Quintilian was able to say that when an orator retires from his profession, he can devote himself to the writing of history.[154] It was thus perhaps the educational system as much as anything which ensured that the debate on the real nature of historiography continued.[155] Aristides in the second century AD maintained that historians 'fall between orators and poets', while four centuries later the biographer of Thucydides, Marcellinus, said that 'some people have ventured to demonstrate that the genre of historiography is not rhetorical but poetic'.[156]

---

to be mistaken: (a) scholars have not realized what is meant when they describe Antonius' words as rhetorical (see above, pp. 264–6); (b) Cicero's account of historiography in the letter (above, pp. 243–4) is strikingly similar to that of rhetorical *narrationes* in *Inv.* 1.27 (above, p. 252) and *Part. Or.* 31–2 (above, p. 262).

Brut. 42–3 is also the notorious occasion on which Atticus is made to say: *concessum est rhetoribus ementiri in historiis, ut aliquid dicere possint argutius* {it is permitted to rhetors to lie in history, so that they can say something more pointedly}. I agree with those who believe this is a reference to historical *exempla* in oratory, not to historiography itself: so Walbank (1955) 13 n. 58, Wiseman (1979) 32, Brunt (1980a) 331–2 {= above, pp. 230–1}, Fornara (1983) 136 n. 57.

[152] See Bonner (1977) Chs. 16–19.

[153] Agathias, pref. 7–13 (the quotation from 12), quoted by Norden (1909) 92. See Cameron (1970) 58–9, who (n. 5) compares Menand. Protect. F 1 Μουσῶν ἐραστὴς ποιημάτων τε καὶ ἱστορίας ἐπαΐων {a lover of the Muses, enthusiastic for poetry and history} and contrasts Procop. 1.1.4, where a strong distinction is made between oratory, poetry, and historiography.

[154] Quint. 12.11.4. Cf. Theon 70, who says that training in rhetoric is required by an historian.

[155] Cf. e.g. Quint. 3.8.49 on *prosopopoeia* (impersonation): it 'is of the greatest use to future *poets* and *historians*, while for *orators* of course it is absolutely essential' (Adamietz (1966) ad loc. compares Theon 60.22, where a similar point is made). See in general Jerome (1923) 360, whose quotations (n. 1) include Quint. 2.17.26–7, 39, 5.12.22, 9.2.81.

[156] Aristid. *Orat.* 49; Marc. *Vit. Thuc.* 41.

Modern historians from time to time try to argue that their own genre is also poetic: thus Marc Bloch urged, 'Let us guard against stripping our science of its share of poetry'.[157] But the fact that modern historiography is indeed seen principally as a science, as Bloch's words indicate, means that no amount of such exhortation will help to narrow the gap between the ancient genre and its modern namesake. When Bloch talks of poetry, he is referring to the presentation of historiography and he means that works of history should be readable. But when Quintilian or Agathias talk about poetry, they mean the same as those who define historiography in terms of oratory: underlying both definitions is the assumption, which the ancients took for granted, that historiography depends very largely upon rhetorical *inuentio*. It is because Cicero spells this out so systematically in the *De Oratore*, and not for any other reason, that Antonius' words there are so important.[158]

ADDENDUM

Rhetoric in Classical Historiography, the book from which this chapter is taken, was rejected by several publishers (by return of post, in the case of Colin Haycraft at Duckworth), before being accepted by Richard Stoneman at Croom Helm, which was then a small publishing house supportive of classical scholarship (it was subsequently absorbed into Routledge). When published, the book had a mixed reception from reviewers ('no major insights here', concluded one), but its chapter on Cicero provoked specific responses from Leeman (1989); Blockley (2001); Damon (2007); Northwood (2008); and Lendon (2009).

---

[157] Bloch (1979) 8. See further, e.g., Marwick (1976) 14.

[158] The statement by the second-century AD Rufus of Perinthus (399) to the effect that historiography is a branch of rhetoric is described by Brunt (1980a) 332 {= above, p. 231} as an 'isolated' piece of evidence which 'would never have been accepted in principle by any historian' and which 'Cicero would certainly have never countenanced'. In view of the evidence accumulated in the present chapter, I find this description beyond belief; yet it well illustrates the gulf which exists between historical and literary interpretations of ancient historiography in modern times.

Northwood's recent paper so completely misrepresents my views that I have felt obliged to reply in detail elsewhere (Woodman (2008)), but, since one of his misunderstandings is not unique to him and relates to a fundamental issue, I shall recapitulate briefly the relevant part of my argument. (a) In *De Oratore* 2.62–3 Cicero mentions only two laws of historiography: each of them concerns bias and prejudice and neither of them has anything to do with truth-as-opposed-to-fiction. (b) These laws are described metaphorically as the foundations of historiography (*fundamenta*) and, like the foundations of a real building, apply to the *whole edifice* of a work of history: nowhere in his narrative must the historian be biased against or prejudiced in favour of anyone. (c) These foundations are *not* equivalent to the 'hard core', to which Cicero makes *no reference at all* in this passage; 'hard core' was my own way of referring to what Cicero describes as *monumenta* in an earlier passage (2.53) and by the term ὑπόθεσις in a letter to his brother (*Q. fr.* 2.16.4). (d) I suggested tentatively that the hard core was required to be true (as opposed to false or fictional); the minimum criterion for *inuentio* (i.e. for the elaboration of the hard core as outlined at 2.63) was plausibility, as standardly prescribed by rhetorical theorists including Cicero (but not in this passage, where, given that the subject is historiography, plausibility is taken for granted).

It is impossible to deal appropriately with all the other responses here; but, since Lendon has been able to take into account points made by them, some brief comments on his contribution may be in order. Lendon quotes against me *Brut.* 42, a joke (though he seems not to realize it) about fictive synchronisms which constituted a special category of *miracula* in ancient historiography (e.g. Tac. *Ann.* 1.9.1; see Feeney (2007) 43–4). 'The joke . . . has nothing to do with rhetorical historians' (Reinhardt–Winterbottom on Quint. 2.4.19). Lendon ascribes to me a mistranslation of *de Orat.* 2.62 which I did not commit and alleges that my interpretation of the passage has been 'gracefully corrected' by John Marincola, by whom it was in fact described as a 'convincing demonstration' (Marincola (1997) 160 n. 139). Lendon says that I read into *de Orat.* 2.62 a definition of *historiae leges* 'where none was intended'; but this takes no account either of the presence (to which I drew attention) of *primam* and *deinde* or of the interpretation of the same expression as given by Cicero himself in *Fam.* 5.12.3 (quoted by me but conveniently omitted by Lendon). Lendon, like others, quotes *Leg.* 1.5 (*cum in illa* [sc. *historia*] [*omnia*] *ad ueritatem ... referantur*) to prove that 'truth is fundamental to history'; but that passage is dealing with the categories of narrative known as *fabula* and *historia* and is quite irrelevant to the argument: *ueritas* there means 'real life', a usage 'much favoured by Cicero' (Brink (1989), 476 n. 24), as opposed to the supernatural elements found in prose or poetic *fabulae* (Cicero's poem *Marius* is the topic of discussion; in general see e.g. Martin–Woodman on Tac. *Ann.* 4.11.3). Lendon believes it significant that according to *de Orat.* 2.55 Greek historians 'had nothing to do with speaking in the courts', as if anyone ever maintained that history could not be written except by a practising lawyer. Cicero's point is that the Greek historians were *eloquentissimi*: when he says that Thucydides was supreme in 'dicendi artificio', it is clear from his use of the same phrase elsewhere (1.93, 2.29, *Orat.* 140) that he means the whole panoply of rhetoric. Lendon says that a 'defence of parts' of my position will be found in Oakley, who in fact concludes from my 'clear interpretation' of the passage that 'rhetorical elaboration affects content as well as style' and says, with reference to my interpretation, that this conclusion is 'self-evident' from *de Orat.* 2.62–4 and is 'confirmed' by *de Orat.* 2.53–4 (Oakley (1997–2005) I.8 nn. 20–1).—These remarks will give some indication of Lendon's own accuracy and methods and of whether his attack has any force.

I have re-stated my views more recently in Woodman (2001), and, from a rather different perspective, Woodman (2007). In both of these I have emphasized the point, which is commonly made in modern discussions of historical texts, that in practice it is often very difficult to separate the 'content' of a narrative from the 'style' in which it is written. (In 1988 I was principally concerned to analyse and explain Cicero's discussion, in which *res* and *uerba* are treated separately, as was conventional in ancient rhetorical theory.) Other post-1988 contributions include Fleck (1993), Feldherr (2003), and Fantham (2004) 146–60. Fox (2007) 134–41 misquotes and mistranslates Cicero, and contributes nothing.

10

Ancient Views on the Causes of Bias in Historical Writing

T. J. Luce

I. THE CAUSES OF BIAS

Tacitus' phrase *sine ira et studio* ('without anger and partiality') at the start of the *Annals* (1.1.3) is the most memorable claim by an ancient historian that he is free from bias. The same assertion had appeared at the start of his *Histories* (1.1.3), and we find other ancient historians claiming this impartiality for themselves and decrying the lack of it in their predecessors.[1] The claim is not as widespread as is sometimes stated or implied; but that it was a commonplace by the early Empire is assured when we read, at the start of Seneca's *Apocolocyntosis* (1.1), *nihil nec offensae nec gratiae dabitur* (there'll be no indulging in denunciation or flattery). Polybius is the first extant historian to address the problem of bias directly; it was noted most frequently by those who wrote of the Late Republic (e.g. Lucceius, Sallust) and the Empire (e.g. Josephus, Tacitus). Cicero's friend L. Lucceius appears to have made the claim most elaborately: he

---

[1] Pol. 1.14, 8.8.5–9, 10.21.8, 38.4; Cic. *Fam.* 5.12 (on the historian Lucceius); Sall. *Cat.* 4.2, *Hist.* 1.6M; Jos. *B.J.* 1.1–2, *A.J.* 20.154–7; cf. *Vit.* 336–9; for criticism of predecessors, see below and n. 31. General statements enjoining impartiality are frequent: e.g., D. Hal. *Thuc.* 8; Luc. *h.c.* 38–42. Avenarius (1956) 13–16, 40–54, 157–63 usefully reviews much of the ancient evidence. Fornara (1983) 99–104, 169–93 has a challenging discussion of several aspects of the topic. I wish to thank the following for their comments on an earlier draft of this paper: W. R. Connor, E. Fantham, K. Raaflaub, K. Sacks, and G. Verbrugghe.

imagined that he had been tempted by *Gratia*, just as Hercules had been enticed by *Voluptas*, and had rejected the temptation, as had the great hero (*Fam.* 5.12.3).[2]

Most discussed are the two passages in Tacitus; Joseph Vogt's article 'Tacitus und die Unparteilichkeit des Historikers' is perhaps the best known.[3] Vogt and other commentators are chiefly concerned to account for the disparity between Tacitus' claim and his failure to fulfil it. The sentiment itself has received scant analysis, evidently because it is assumed that the classical historians meant what we mean when we speak of the historian's impartiality and objectivity. In this study I will argue that they took a narrower and more particularized view of the problem, especially as it concerns the reasons why a historian might let prejudice distort his presentation. I will focus throughout on what the men of antiquity said and thought, not on modern discoveries of bias in the ancient historians, most instances of which are not noticed or mentioned by ancient writers. It is hoped that this study will explain, at least in part, why they went unnoticed.

One should first remark the way in which the idea is expressed. The Greeks and Romans usually spoke of the absence of favouritism or hatred.[4] Today the desideratum is often given as a positive and

---

[2] Cicero says Lucceius made the claim *quodam in prohoemio* (in some preface or other), almost certainly in reference to a historical subject. Yet the phrase does not suggest the main preface to Lucceius' history, although this is where we would expect to find such a claim; possibly, then, in some later book of the *Italici belli et ciuilis historiam iam ... paene ... perfectam* (a history, now nearly complete, of the Italian and Civil War, *Fam.* 5.12.2), which Cicero asks Lucceius to abandon temporarily to take up the project he now proposes. The 'choice of Heracles' refers to Prodicus' allegory recorded at Xen. *Mem.* 2.1.21–34 (cf. Cic. *Off.* 1.118).

[3] Vogt (1936).

[4] E.g., Pol. 38.4.8 παράδοσιν ἀμιγῆ παντὸς ψεύδους (an account free of all falsehood); Sall. *Hist.* F 1.6M, *neque me diuersa pars in ciuilibus armis mouit a uero* (nor do partisan feelings in the civil war dissuade me from [speaking] the truth; Jos. *B.J.* 1.2: περιέχει δὲ αὐτοῖς ὅπου μὲν κατηγορίαν ὅπου δὲ ἐγκώμιον τὰ συγγράμματα, τὸ δ' ἀκριβὲς τῆς ἱστορίας οὐδαμοῦ (their writings contain accusations at one moment and praise at another, but nowhere historical truth); *A.J.* 20.154–6: τῆς ἀληθείας ἀμέλησαν ..., μηδὲ ... τὴν ἀλήθειαν τῆς ἱστορίας τετηρήκασιν (they are careless of the truth ... and they do not ... have regard for historical truth); cf. Lucian's manner of describing the ideal historian at, e.g., *h.c.* 41: ξένοις ἐν τοῖς βιβλίοις καὶ ἄπολις, αὐτόνομος, ἀβασίλευτος (in his writings he is a foreigner and without a country, independent, ruled by no king). Examples couched positively are less common: e.g., Pol. 10.21.8: κοινὸς ὢν ἐπαίνου καὶ ψόγου ζητεῖ τὸν ἀληθῆ [sc. ἀπολογισμόν] (distributing praise and blame impartially, it [sc. an historical account] demands a true

particularized virtue, 'objectivity' or 'impartiality', for which the ancients had no special vocabulary, speaking simply of the 'truth', which could be compromised in ways other than through bias. What historical truth was, and how it could be attained, were questions seldom addressed (Polybius is the chief exception), partly because, no doubt, the concept of historical truth seemed obvious, and partly because the concept was so often couched in negative terms: when favouritism and hostility are removed, truth is the residuum. I will return to this idea at the end of the paper.

The claim to be free from partiality, hatred, and the like appears in historians who wrote contemporary or nearly contemporary history; those who wrote of the distant past, such as Livy, Dionysius of Halicarnassus, Diodorus, and Cassius Dio, do not make it.[5] Plutarch, in his *Life of Pericles* (13.12), distinguishes clearly between the two types of history: the passing of time, he asserts, hinders historians of past events from attaining sure knowledge of what happened,[6] whereas in contemporary history it is envy and enmity, favour-seeking and flattery that distort the picture and impair the truth. Why this difference exists is explained when we look at the under-lying causes of bias.

Tacitus' two prefaces present a clear picture. In the introduction to the *Histories* (1.1) he declares that after Actium one could no longer find historians of talent like those of the Republic, who wrote with eloquence and freedom.[7] The truth, Tacitus says, was doubly

account); yet even this describes history by saying what it is not. On truth as the highest desideratum in history, see, e.g., Pol. 2.56.11, 34.4.2; Cic. *de Orat.* 2.62. Cf. Avenarius (1956) 40–46. See also Woodman's incisive comments in his recent book (1988) 73–4, 82–3 {= above, pp. 244–6, 256–9}.

[5] When Livy writes (*praef.* 5) that he is *omnis expers curae, quae scribentis animum etsi non flectere a uero, sollicitum tamen efficere potest* (wholly free from the anxiety that may assail a writer's mind, although it cannot deflect him from the truth), he is speaking of the anxiety that he will feel much later, when he comes to write of his own times. On Dionysius' statement at *A.R.* 1.6.5, see below at n. 29.

[6] Cf. Livy 6.1.2: knowing events far in the past is as difficult as making out objects seen from a great distance.

[7] At *Agr.* 1.2 he had also stressed the contrast between earlier and contemporary writers; of the earlier he says *celeberrimus quisque ingenium ad prodendam uirtutis memoriam sine gratia aut ambitione bonae tantum conscientiae pretio ducebatur* {the most distinguished men of ability were led to publish a memory of their virtue, without partisanship or ambition, and with the reward only of a good conscience}.

compromised: first, by ignorance of statecraft, which was now the preserve of one man (*inscitia rei publicae ut alienae*); second, by the desire either to write what the powerful wished to hear (*libido adsentandi*) or to express one's hatred for them (*odium aduersus dominantes*). Although Tacitus does not say so, the implication clearly is that adulatory histories are written for a living emperor to see, hostile accounts after a monarch's demise. In an aside he notes that readers more readily discern and despise the ambitious flatterer than the traducer, since the latter puts on a false front of speaking freely (*malignitati falsa species libertatis inest*). Tacitus then turns to himself:

mihi Galba Otho Vitellius nec beneficio nec iniuria cogniti. dignitatem nostram a Vespasiano inchoatam, a Tito auctam, a Domitiano longius prouectam non abnuerim: sed incorruptam fidem professis neque amore quisquam et sine odio dicendus est.

I received neither favours nor injury from Galba, Otho, or Vitellius. I would not deny that my career was begun under Vespasian, continued under Titus, and carried still further under Domitian; on the other hand, those who promise the unvarnished truth must speak of no one out of affection or hatred.

The conclusion is clear: recipients of favours will be prone to give flattering portraits of powerful patrons, those who have been injured, to malign them. Tacitus himself, therefore, has no cause to speak falsely about Galba, Otho, or Vitellius, because he did not know them; he will have to be on his guard, however, when speaking of their Flavian successors, since he was the conspicuous recipient of their favours and (the implication is clear) would therefore be inclined to give a rosier picture of them than the facts might warrant.

When we turn to the *Annals* the same or analogous sentiments reappear: historians of talent, who had flourished under the Republic, were deterred from writing in the midst of growing adulation (1.1.2). While emperors lived, their actions were falsified out of fear; when they were dead, their deeds were written up under the stimulus of recent hatred: *inde consilium mihi pauca de Augusto et extrema tradere, mox Tiberii principatum et cetera, sine ira et studio, quorum causas procul habeo* (my plan henceforth is to say a few things about Augustus and his last days, and then to relate the principate of

Tiberius and what followed without anger and partiality, the reasons for which do not affect me). The *causae* (reasons) are clearly *iniuria* (injury) in the case of *ira* (anger) and *beneficium* (favours) in the case of *studium*.[8] As in the instances of Galba, Otho, and Vitellius (*mihi nec beneficio nec iniuria cogniti*), Tacitus had had no experience of Tiberius and his three successors. Hence the causes that might have led to a biased account are absent. Note that it is not simply time that guarantees Tacitus' objectivity at *Annals* 1.1.2 (although it is an important factor) but also the absence of favours or harm done to himself, to his family and ancestors, and even to his close friends (on these extensions, see below).

The more immediate causes of bias, therefore, are emotions felt by the historian: hope and fear, favouritism and hatred. The causes of the emotions, in turn, are benefits one has enjoyed or hopes to enjoy and injuries one has received or fears to receive.[9] The objects of bias are most often autocrats, which explains the prominence of the disclaimer of bias by those who wrote in Hellenistic Greece and imperial Rome.[10]

The disclaimer does not appear in Herodotus, Thucydides, or Xenophon. Thucydides 1.22 is sometimes cited as an example of the general sentiment; yet this passage is immediately concerned not with bias on the historian's part but with carelessness about the facts and with the prejudice (εὔνοια) and faulty memory of eyewitnesses, whose testimony the historian must gather and evaluate. That Thucydides thinks of himself as free from bias, however, is implicit throughout, and the same may be said of Herodotus.[11] The disclaimer may have had its origin in the later fourth century with

---

[8] See Avenarius (1956) 48 n. 33—Syme (1958) 420, n. 1, and Goodyear (1972) 100–1—who also remarks on the unusual meaning of *procul habeo* here ('are far removed from me', not 'I keep at a distance, avoid').

[9] See Avenarius (1956) 46–54, for numerous passages; his division of the discussion into φόβος (fear) vs. ἐλπίς (hope) and χάρις (favouritism) vs. ἐπάχθεια (hatred), however, creates a dichotomy that the ancient texts sometimes belie (contrast the full text of Dio 53.19.2 with the selective quotation on p. 54).

[10] On Pol. 8.8.3 (concerning Philip V) Walbank, *HCP* II.79 notes that the passage is 'the first expression of a sentiment later to become a commonplace, that fear of rulers affects historical impartiality'.

[11] See Avenarius (1956) 52; Fornara (1983) 99–105.

historians who recorded the careers of Philip II and Alexander.[12] Another influence may have been the oath of the fourth-century juror, in which he swore to be free from hatred and partiality.[13] Certainly a common analogy to the ideal historian in antiquity was the ideal juryman.[14] The connection is apt, in that both juror and historian were to sit in judgement of the persons appearing before them and render a verdict on their behaviour; the historian, like the juror, was not to allow personal feelings to influence his final judgement. But the analogy does not go very deep. Jurors were excused for having personal ties to the defendant, whereas the historian was faced with no such disqualification: he was self-appointed. The juryman was presented with the evidence gathered by others; the historian was himself in charge of the collecting. Above all, the juryman was himself judged competent or incompetent on the basis of the simple vote that he cast, guilty or not guilty; the historian was judged on the basis of a huge verbal construct in which a reader expected to find ample evidence of the writer's accuracy and moral sensibility.

In the disclaimer of bias by Tacitus and other historians the personal element is pre-eminent: each refers to the treatment that he has received from prominent individuals, whether rulers or acquaintances, who will appear in his pages. Did they recognize that the bias historians feel toward individuals could be extended to institutions, general historical conditions, and the like? Vogt and others believe that they did, since Tacitus, like other ancient writers, connected such general states with particular individuals.[15] Now, though individuals loom large in ancient explanations of causation, I see no basis for such an extension of meaning in this connection. We today may be pleased to seek Tacitus' antipathy to Tiberius in that monarch's shaping of an institution—the principate—by promoting *delatores* (informers) and trials for *maiestas* (treason). But this was not the way Tacitus thought, or the way the ancients thought

[12] Fornara (1983) 64 selects Callisthenes as a detectable turning point, following Pearson (1960) 22–49, esp. 33, 46.

[13] The first examples occur in Dem. 8.1, 23.97, 57.63; see Weyman (1908), who collects other passages on the theme.

[14] The analogy is everywhere present, for instance, in Lucian's *h.c.* (e.g., 38, 41, 47). Ἵστωρ, the cognate of ἱστορία and ἱστορέω, occurs already in Homer (*Il.* 18.501, 23.486), where it means a 'judge' or 'witness.'

[15] See Vogt (1936) 5.

generally. The idea is now so familiar that we assume they must have shared it; but Tacitus makes his own thinking clear. Personal benefits and injury are what engender bias; and since he received none from such as Tiberius or Nero, he cannot be prejudiced for or against them. This, then, is the reason why the disclaimer appears in the works of historians who wrote contemporary or nearly contemporary history; for those who wrote of the distant past, such as Livy, the disclaimer would be silly, since it would occur to no one that Livy could have been helped or harmed by the individuals who appear in his pages.

Reflection will show, however, that the causes of bias extend somewhat beyond the personal and contemporary, narrowly interpreted, in two areas. The first concerns patriotic history. Alone of ancient writers, Lucian and Polybius insist that the historian must be objective in matters pertaining to his native city.[16] Yet even Polybius concedes that the historian could show partiality, provided that he does not contradict the facts (16.14.6). Livy is more representative of the general attitude: in his preface (11) he cheerfully admits to his love for Rome, and he makes his attitude explicit in a number of other passages (e.g. 9.16.11–19.17; 22.54.7–11; 27.8.4–10). Once again we see a wide gulf between the sensibilities of fifth-century historians and their successors, a gulf of which the ancients were keenly aware. Plutarch, for example, severely criticizes Herodotus for being a 'barbarian lover' (*Her. mal.* 857A). In the case of Thucydides, his failure to favour his native Athens brings down the harsh and uncompromising condemnation of Dionysius of Halicarnassus in his *Letter to Pompeius* (3). The cause of Thucydides' hostility was his exile, says Dionysius: he bore his city a grudge thereafter. He consequently found her partly to blame for the outbreak of the Peloponnesian War, whereas he ought to have shifted the blame wholly onto Sparta; Dionysius then proceeds to show how Thucydides could have written the first book of his history with this aim in mind. Bias could therefore be expected in the matter of patriotic feeling and, by extension, could be displayed against the enemies of one's country.[17] One need not be apologetic or write disclaimers about patriotic bias;

[16] For Lucian, see *h.c.* 40–1 and Avenarius (1956) 49–54. For Polybius, see 1.14, with the demonstration of his credo at 38.4.

[17] Josephus, for example, speaks of those who wrote biased accounts of the Jewish War either to flatter the Romans or out of hatred of the Jews (*B.J.* 1.1–2).

on the contrary, it was something that one might even proudly admit, as does Livy (*praef.* 11): *aut me amor negotii suscepti fallit aut nulla umquam res publica nec maior nec sanctior nec bonis exemplis ditior fuit* (either the love of the task I have set myself deceives me or there has never been any state grander, purer, or richer in good examples). In addition to a historian's *patria*, friends and members of his family might produce bias in his work. So Livy catches Licinius Macer inventing noble deeds for an early Licinius (7.9.5): *quaesita ea propriae familiae laus leuiorem auctorem Licinium facit* (the glory he seeks to heap upon his family makes Licinius an unreliable authority).[18] Tacitus recognizes that injuries done to kinsmen can be remembered and may hurt long after the fact.[19] Josephus cites the gratification of those who will appear in the narrative (*A.J.* 1.2) as one of four motives that prompt men to write history, while Polybius couples friends with country when speaking of the historian's duty to preserve objectivity (1.14). When the historian and his friends are part of a political faction, bias might extend to the group.[20]

According to the ancient view, then, a historian could be biased for personal reasons, the favours and injuries that he himself may have received from the men who populate his work; and when country, family, and friends affect a historian's objectivity, the reasons are no less personal. This is because country, family, and friends confer benefits upon the individual, in return for which he is expected to exhibit proper gratitude. Failure to acknowledge these debts in his life and writings is the sign of moral defect, as Dionysius' indictment of Thucydides demonstrates. Similarly, the historian is expected to

[18] On the general problem of distortion caused by family considerations, see Cic. *Brut.* 62, Livy 8.40.

[19] Cf. *Ann.* 16.28.1, *Paconium Agrippinum, paterni in principes odii heredem* (Paconius Agrippinus, who inherited his father's hatred of the emperors); 4.33.4, *at multorum, qui Tiberio regente poenam uel infamias subiere, posteri manent* (but the descendants survive of many who suffered punishment or infamy under Tiberius, although here Tacitus strictly is speaking of the readers of history rather than of historians themselves). It would be interesting to know how Tacitus treated his father-in-law, Agricola, in the lost portion of the *Histories*.

[20] So Sallust at *Cat.* 4 (*partibus rei publicae*, 'political partisanship') and *Hist.* 1.6M (*diuersa pars in ciuilibus armis*, 'partisan feelings in the civil war'). Could this bias extend to members of one's social class as a group? I doubt it: although it is often claimed, for example, that Tacitus shows significant partiality for the senatorial order, there are too many negative descriptions of that body at work to sustain such a claim.

make suitable pronouncements on the goodness and badness of the people appearing in his pages.[21] Again, failure to do so pointed to a serious imperfection in character. Polybius criticizes some of his predecessors for just this flaw. Phylarchus, for example, is to be condemned as much for his failure to praise noble actions as for his love of sensationalism (2.61); and among Timaeus' many shortcomings is his unwillingness to praise the good qualities of his bête noire Agathocles (12.15.9).

Such strictures show that in his writing the historian's own character is as important as the character of the personages appearing in his pages, perhaps more so. As the historian is to judge the moral worth of his subjects, so the reader judges the moral worth of the historian.[22] Hence the historian must be centrally concerned with his own persona: he must endeavour to demonstrate his own ethical sensibility through the judgements he makes on others. Almost the entire force of Plutarch's attack on Herodotus centres on this point: despite a certain surface attractiveness, declares Plutarch, Herodotus possessed a captious and malicious nature, in consequence of which he either could not appreciate goodness or, if he did appreciate it, was unable to express that appreciation without undercutting and devaluing it. Κακοήθεια is Plutarch's term for this failing: the historian erred not out of carelessness or arrogance but because he was wilfully ill-disposed and unjust: 'He does not know how to give praise without finding fault.'[23] Plutarch is at pains to emphasize that he is concerned throughout his essay not with Herodotus' lies in general, but with his deliberate lies.[24] By contrast, a good historian was expected to be not merely impartial but even generous: in matters

---

[21] See Cic. *Fam.* 5.12.4, *de Orat.* 2.63; D. Hal. *Pomp.* 3. Cf. Avenarius (1956) 159–63; Sacks (1981) 132–44, 166–70, 190–3; Woodman (1988) 40–4.

[22] Here again the wide gulf that separates historians of the fifth and early fourth centuries from those who came later is especially marked.

[23] *Her. mal.* 866D, 869A; Dionysius had argued the exact opposite in his *Letter to Pompeius* (3): ἡ μὲν Ἡροδότου διάθεσις ἐν ἅπασιν ἐπιεικὴς καὶ τοῖς μὲν ἀγαθοῖς συνηδομένη τοῖς δὲ κακοῖς συναλγοῦσα (Herodotus is fair to all, delighting in the good and distressed by the bad).

[24] *Her. mal.* 870A: the distinction between deliberate and inadvertent falsehoods was important in evaluating a historian's character: see Avenarius (1956) 44 n. 23. Polybius, for example, does not think that Philinus and Fabius told deliberate lies, στοχαζόμενος ἐκ τοῦ βίου καὶ τῆς αἱρέσεως αὐτῶν (judging by their lives and principles, 1.14.2).

of doubt he should adopt the more favourable, more creditable interpretation. This is Plutarch's injunction (*Her. mal.* 855F). Josephus in his autobiography offers an illustration: he concedes that in the *Jewish War* he omitted to mention certain things: but he did so, he maintains, because a historian should refrain from harshly scrutinizing the bad behaviour of others, 'not out of favouritism to the people involved but out of his own moderation'.[25]

Such remarks touch on a central incongruity in ancient historiography from the late fourth century BC on. The historian was not, on the one hand, to let emotions arising from personal experience intrude into the narrative;[26] on the other, he was to pronounce judgement in such a manner that his appreciation of goodness, his patriotism, and his feeling of gratitude for benefits received were on display for the reader's approval. To claim that there existed a line, however fine, between the two attitudes would be overly optimistic: a no-man's land of considerable extent stretched between them. And since it was commendable both to claim to be objective and to advertise one's moral sensibility, a historian might venture to do both in the same breath. Josephus, for example, admits that because he cannot help feeling great pity for the Jews when he describes their terrible misfortunes, he must ask the reader to pardon him for indulging his emotions contrary to the law of history; but if anyone should be immune to pity, he requests that the facts be chalked up to history, the grief to the author.[27] Similarly, Polybius would concede

---

[25] *Vit.* 339. The dominant ἦθος {character} of a historian could become the commonly accepted way of characterizing him: thus, e.g., Theopompus' overly critical nature (see D. Hal. *Pomp.* 6, Luc. *h.c.* 59, Plut. *Her. mal.* 855A, and, in general, Meister (1975) 59–60), or, on the other hand, Livy's *mira iucunditas clarissimusque candor* (marvellous pleasantness and splendid lucidity) his treatment of *adfectus dulciores* (the gentler emotions, Quint. *Inst.* 10.1.101–2), and his being *candidissimus omnium magnorum ingeniorum aestimator* (an outstanding judge of all men of great talent, Sen. *Suas.* 6.22).

[26] Cf. the general criticism at Marcellin. *Vit. Thuc.* 27: οἱ πολλοὶ τοῖς ἰδίοις πάθεσι συνέθεσαν τὰς ἱστορίας, ἥκιστα μελῆσαν αὐτοῖς τῆς ἀληθείας (many write their histories in response to what they themselves have suffered, and pay little heed to telling the truth), followed by examples from Herodotus, Timaeus, Philistus, and Xenophon.

[27] *B.J.* 1.11–12; at 5.20 he restrains himself from displaying his emotions to the reader. Cf. Plut. *Per.* 28.3 (Duris' emotions when describing Athenian atrocities against his native Samos).

(συγχωρήσαιμ' ἄν) that the historian may give preference to his native land, but not that he may make pronouncements that contradict what has happened (16.14.6).[28] Dionysius, in the introduction to his *Roman Antiquities*, declares that he is writing not out of a desire to flatter (οὐχὶ κολακείας χάριν) but for the sake of truth and justice, and in order to thank his adopted city for the many good things it has bestowed upon him.[29]

So attractive was it for a historian to show partiality of which readers would approve that the claim of impartiality could assume a decidedly secondary place. This is the thrust of Cicero's request that Lucceius set aside the laws of history by writing up Cicero's exploits 'a bit more sympathetically even than the truth might permit' (*Fam.* 5.12.3).[30] In doing so, says Cicero, Lucceius can display his finely honed sense of right and wrong (5.12.4): Cicero implies that it will be clear where the historian stands on touchy issues, and right-thinking men will approve. He alleges that he makes his request by letter rather than face-to-face 'because a letter does not blush' (5.12.1). Yet clearly neither Cicero nor his friends thought the request excessive: after all, when the great man urged Atticus to borrow the letter to read, he did so with considerable satisfaction, pronouncing it *ualde bella* (*Att.* 4.6.4).

II. DISCOVERY AND EXPLANATION OF BIAS IN PREDECESSORS

Authors who used writers of contemporary history as sources were sensitive to the question of how bias may have affected these sources. We encounter more comments on this problem than we do declarations by historians of their own impartiality or general proscriptions

---

[28] Meister (1975) 174 and 181 emphasizes the force of συγχωρήσαιμ' ἄν as a potential optative and denies that Polybius regarded this concession as applying to his own work.

[29] *A.R.* 1.6.5. The κολακεία that Dionysius denies is presumably flattery of his adopted city, in which elements of falsity and self-seeking would coexist.

[30] Both Fornara (1983) 101–2, and Woodman (1988) 70–4 have some excellent remarks on this much-discussed letter.

of bias. This sensitivity was heightened by the venerable practice of criticizing one's predecessors, a tradition begun by Hecataeus when in his opening words he scoffed at the 'silly tales' told by the Greeks (*FGrHist* 1 F 1a). Bias is prominent among such criticisms, which came into their own with the historians of Alexander and his successors and thereafter were most often made with reference to a historian's treatment of an autocrat, whatever his title, whether he was a Sicilian tyrant, a Jewish king, or a Roman emperor.[31]

Separate monographs by non-historians, such as Plutarch's *On the Malice of Herodotus*, could be devoted to an attack; so could large portions of a narrative history (though this was somewhat exceptional), such as the twelfth book of Polybius, which is directed at the failings of Timaeus and certain other historians. Attacking Timaeus, in fact, became something of a cottage industry. Ister of Cyrene ('the Callimachean'), who coined the epithet ἐπιτίμαιος (faultfinder), composed a critique that ran, it seems, to more than one volume (Athen. 6.272B). Polemon of Troy ('the Exegete') followed by writing *Against Timaeus* in at least twelve volumes (Athen. 15.698B), in the course of which he seems to have included criticisms of Ister. Polybius, the last of the trio, is brief by comparison.[32]

Criticism of one's sources could be not only extensive but intricate. For example, Timaeus censured Aristotle for his version of the founding of Locri, and Polybius in turn censures Timaeus (12.8): if Aristotle is to be properly discredited, says Polybius, he must be shown to have acted 'either to curry favour (χάριτος ... ἕνεκεν) or

---

[31] On Alexander, see, e.g., Arr. *Anab.* 7.14.2 (writers for or against Alexander and Hephaestion); on Alexander's successors, Paus. 1.9.8, 1.13.9 (Hieronymus of Cardia on the Diadochi, esp. Antigonus and Lysimachus); on Sicilian tyrants, Diod. 21.17 (Timaeus and Callias of Syracuse on Agathocles) and Paus. 1.13.9 (Philistus on Dionysius of Syracuse); on Herod, Jos. *A.J.* 16.184 (the portrait by Nicolaus of Damascus); on Roman emperors, Tac. *Hist.* 2.101 (contemporary historians of the Flavians), *Ann.* 16.6 (detractors of Nero on Poppaea's death), Herodian 2.15.7 (contemporary historians of Severus).

[32] Polybius himself did not escape criticism: Posidonius accused him of trying to curry favour with Ti. Gracchus by calling the three hundred πύργοι (defence towers) that Gracchus had destroyed in Spain three hundred πόλεις (cities). Strabo, who reports the criticism (3.4.13 = *FGrHist* 87 F 51), finds it plausible, because both generals and historians like to puff up the deeds that were done (καλλωπίζοντες τὰς πράξεις).

to receive a reward or out of personal enmity'.[33] If one of these motives is not apparent, we should rather believe that Timaeus made his attack on Aristotle 'out of ill will and malice.' Two points are of interest here. First, if one looks at the ancient evidence, the motives for explaining bias do not extend much beyond those that Polybius notes here. Second, when the obvious explanations do not satisfy, there frequently was a fallback: the historian had a naturally malicious character. Thus Polybius says that Timaeus attacked Aristotle out of 'enmity and malice.' Bad character might also be embraced as the primary cause, although more normal explanations could be found. Plutarch, for example, selects κακοήθεια as the chief cause of Herodotus' falsehoods, even though other, more 'regular' causes are at hand, such as his giving unwarranted prominence to his native Halicarnassus and its citizens (*Her. mal.* 868A, 869F) while favouring barbarian races over the Greeks generally (857A), or currying favour with individuals by featuring them (Hipponicus son of Callias: 863B), or taking money for praising its donors (the Athenians: 862A), or, when the request for money was rejected, attacking those who withheld it (the Thebans: 864D).

If the usual motives do not seem operative and if bad character cannot be adduced, puzzlement is evident. Polybius, for example, in criticizing Theopompus for his hostility to Philip II, can only darkly invoke some 'advantage' derived by Theopompus (8.11.6, τὸ σύμφερον), but he specifies nothing; a few lines earlier (8.11.2) he had suggested that by reviling Philip, Theopompus perhaps was hoping to gain credit for impartiality, because at the start of his history he had praised the king! Josephus speaks of those contemporary historians who wrote of Nero out of either favouritism or hatred; and yet, he continues (*A.J.* 20.154–5), these writers also wrote biased accounts of Nero's predecessors, for whom they had no hatred, since they lived much later. Josephus exaggerates somewhat in writing πολλῷ χρόνῳ (much later); Tacitus was nearer the mark when he spoke of *recentibus odiis* (recent hatred, *Ann.* 1.1.2) in describing the same phenomenon. But the point here is that Josephus

---

[33] Walbank, *HCP* II.342, suggests that χάριτος ἕνεκεν may mean 'to curry favour' (which I prefer) rather than 'prompted by partiality' (Shuckburgh); on the passage as a whole, see Meister (1975) 13–29.

is at a loss: he simply cannot explain why later writers would be prejudiced against someone already dead.

Though some of its practitioners championed contemporary history,[34] many of the ancients believed non-contemporary history to be more objective and hence a better thing. Contemporaries were too likely to be the recipients, or the prospective recipients, of benefits and injuries, whereas those who lived later would be exempt from such influences. A passage in Lucian's *How to Write History* (40) illustrates this belief: because Homer did not live when Achilles did, some people maintain that he could not have been biased in his favour, 'for they can discover no reason why he would lie'. Likewise Arrian (*Anab.* 1.1.2) prefers as sources Ptolemy and Aristobulus, who, since they wrote after Alexander's death, felt neither compulsion nor hope of reward from that monarch.

On the other hand, contemporary historians often faced an unpleasant dilemma. If they published a favourable picture of an autocrat during his lifetime, they laid themselves open to charges of flattery and self-promotion; if the account was critical, they risked punishment. A common solution was to withhold publication until after the autocrat had died. Ammianus, having arrived in his history at his own age (26.1.1–2, *ad usque memoriae confinia proprioris*), also encounters *pericula...ueritati saepe contigua* (dangers...closely connected with the truth); some older writers, he observes, had chosen not to publish in their lifetimes, in order to avoid the dangers that might impair the truth, including the complaints of critics and the importunities of friends. Pliny the Elder wrote a history of his own times in thirty-one books but refused to publish it while he was alive, lest he expose himself to the charge of self-seeking (*ambitio*); publication, he assures Titus, will fall to his heir (*HN praef.* 20). The motive of the outspoken T. Labienus was different, his solution similar. The elder Seneca recalls (*Contr.* 10 *praef.* 8) that at a recitation Labienus rolled up a large part of a book of his histories, declaring: 'what I omit now will be read after my death' (Seneca adds: *Quanta in illis libertas fuit quam etiam Labienus extimuit!* How much free speaking was in them, which even Labienus feared!).

---

[34] E.g., Pol. 4.2.3, 9.2; Jos. *B.J.* 1.13–16.

In a slight variation of this pattern, Livy's last twenty-two books, covering the years 43–9 BC, appeared only after Augustus' death.[35] A particularly noteworthy example is given by Procopius. In the introduction to his *Persian Wars* (1.1.4–5, a heady mix of Herodotean and Thucydidean reminiscences) Procopius declares his allegiance to historical truth, eschewing the clever display of rhetoric or the improbabilities of poetry; he will venture, he says, to write negative things about even his closest friends, frankly revealing everything that they did, good and bad. This noble declaration was in fact untrue, as he concedes later in the introduction to his *Secret History*: it simply was not possible to say everything in his earlier works on Justinian's wars while the participants were still living. Now that they are dead, he can tell all (*Arc.* 1.1–2).

Josephus and his rival historian of the Jewish War, Justus, illustrate a further twist (*Vit.* 357–67). Justus composed his history shortly after the event but delayed publication for some twenty years; in it he had many critical things to say of Josephus' work in respect to both content and *Tendenz*. Nettled, Josephus attributes the delay to Justus' fear that if he had published it earlier, he would have been contradicted by the participants who were still alive: Vespasian, Titus, King Agrippa, and members of King Agrippa's family. Josephus, we now learn, had submitted his work to these monarchs for advance approval; Titus even inscribed the work with his own hand, ordering that it be published, while from Agrippa Josephus had received no fewer than sixty-two letters acknowledging the truth of the narrative (he quotes a few specimens for Justus' edification). In light of this confession, Josephus' earlier professions of impartiality (*B.J.* 1.1.1–2; cf. *A.J.* 20.154), and especially his criticisms of historians who displayed χάρις to powerful patrons (e.g., *A.J.* 16.184, on Nicolaus of Damascus and Herod), have a distinctly hollow ring. Josephus is on the horns of a dilemma: he must choose between refuting Justus' criticisms of his veracity and protecting himself from charges that he

---

[35] The superscription to the *periocha* of Book 121 reads *qui editus post excessum Augusti dicitur* (which is said to have been published after the death of Augustus); cf. Luce (1977) 8 n. 17. I do not find convincing L. Canfora's arguments (Canfora (1969)) against accepting the superscription; cf. below, n. 38.

had written to please the participants. He elects to risk a charge of toadyism in order to rebut the charge of inaccuracy.³⁶

Hence the common and accepted belief that those historians who had no personal experience of prominent persons, especially rulers, were likely to give the most accurate accounts. Three responses naturally followed from this attitude. First is the tendency to believe that praise of a monarch after his death is likely to be true, since there can be no hope of reward. One illustration is Arrian's preference for Ptolemy and Aristobulus, mentioned above (Arrian does not acknowledge that they were contemporaries who had benefited from Alexander). Another is found at *Histories* 4.81, where Tacitus recounts how Vespasian at Alexandria miraculously cured two people of their afflictions: 'Those who were present attest even now to both events, when nothing can be gained from telling such a falsehood'.³⁷ Second, where a historian was plainly independent of a living monarch's likes and dislikes, praise was due: so Tacitus has Cremutius Cordus praise Livy's independence from Augustus despite the friendship that existed between the two (*Ann.* 4.34.3, *Titus Liuius, eloquentiae ac fidei praeclarus in primis*, Titus Livius, distinguished especially for his eloquence and truthfulness). Livy deserves to be believed because he cannot be thought to have written as Augustus wished.³⁸

³⁶ If Domitian was still on the throne when the *Vita* was written, it would help to explain Josephus' somewhat curious stance; see Cohen (1979) 170–80. Earlier in the *Vita* (336) he had included Justus among those historians who wrote δι' ἔχθραν ἢ χάριν (out of hatred or favour).
³⁷ Heubner (1963–82) IV.182, cites as a parallel Ov. *Tr.* 3.10.35–6: *cum sint praemia falsi / nulla, ratam debet testis habere fidem* (since there would be no reward for playing false, the witness ought to win unquestioned trustworthiness). Ovid is himself the 'witness' here; contrast Quintilian's remarks at *Inst.* 10.1.34, quoted below at n. 39. In a remarkable passage at *Ben.* 4.11.4–6, Seneca declares that in deciding to whom to leave our money we as testators are concerned about matters that will be of no benefit to us; motives of self-interest have no influence (*remotis utilitatibus*), among which are *spes ac metus et inertissimum uitium, uoluptas* (hope and fear, and that utterly worthless vice, pleasure). Seneca likens the *testator* to an *incorruptus iudex* (incorruptable judge), whose only motive is to seek the best person to whom to leave his money.
³⁸ Koestermann (1963–8) II.120, takes *fides* to refer less to Livy's reliability than to his reputation for high principles and a generous disposition (cf. above, n. 25), Fornara (1983) 74 argues persuasively that it refers to Livy's independence. Cordus'

Third, the judgement of posterity will be free from the bias that affects contemporaries. Here is Cicero's exhortation to Julius Caesar in his speech on behalf of M. Marcellus (29):

serui igitur iis etiam iudicibus, qui multis post saeculis de te iudicabunt, et quidem haud scio an incorruptius quam nos; nam et sine amore et sine cupiditate et rursus sine odio et sine inuidia iudicabunt.

Have regard, too, for those judges who many ages hence will judge you, and perhaps more honestly than we do; for they will judge without love and without desire, and, on the other hand, without hatred and without envy.

The writer of the panegyric to Julian recalls this passage (*Pan. Lat.* 3.31.1): *te ... sciam ... his maxime seruire iudicibus qui de rebus gestis tuis sine odio et gratia uenturis saeculis iudicabunt* (I know ... that you ... will have regard for those judges who will judge your deeds in the coming ages without hatred and favour-seeking). Tacitus puts the same sentiment in the mouth of Aper in the *Dialogue on Orators* (23.6). Indeed, Quintilian declares (*Inst.* 10.1.34) that in the courtroom historical examples have 'a significant advantage [over the testimony of witnesses] in that they alone are immune to the suspicion of hatred and of favouritism'.[39] And Ammianus, in giving an appraisal of Valentinian I, discusses that emperor's virtues separately from his vices: only posterity, 'unconstrained by fear or base flattery', will be able to come to an unbiased synthesis (30.8.1), for which Ammianus sees himself as supplying the raw material.

assertion that Augustus knew how Livy portrayed Cassius and Brutus does not disprove the statement of the superscription to the *periocha* of Book 121 (see above, n. 35) that the book was published after Augustus' death, *pace* Canfora (1969): we do not need to suppose that the argument Tacitus assigns to Cordus must be wholly correct in the facts it deploys; and since Book 120 brought the narrative at least to the death of Cicero in December 43, Augustus would have known how Livy described the bulk of Cassius' and Brutus' careers.

[39] Cf. the same idea at *Inst.* 5.11.37 (*liberis odio et gratia mentibus*, minds free of hatred or favour-seeking). Ullman (1943) traces the derivation of Tacitus' phrase from Cic. *Marcell.* 29 through Quintilian; on Ullman's suggestion, see Goodyear (1972) 100 n. 23.

III. POSTERITY'S RELATION TO THE PAST

For the contemporary historian, therefore, freedom to express one's beliefs (παρρησία, *libertas*) does not have quite the same meaning as it does for the historian of the remoter past. For the former it signifies fearlessness in speaking out, whatever the effects upon the feelings of contemporaries: this is often an unpopular undertaking, and one difficult to achieve in any event.[40] But for the historian of the distant past it is an ideal that could be fully realized, because freedom—like its product, 'truth'—is essentially a negative concept, made possible by the absence of fear and favour. Hence the frequent assurances by writers like Diodorus and Dionysius that they write the truth.[41] 'History's customary freedom of speech' enables Diodorus to fulfil his obligation to bestow praise and blame as he sees fit.[42]

Thus the past, when viewed from this perspective, is wholly dead. The passions that animated the participants have passed away along with those who felt them: no one in the present is personally affected by the issues that were then so alive, no one cares about them. This view sometimes clashes with the obligation to write patriotic history, and it can be presented as the dominant view when it serves the historian's rhetorical purpose. For example, when contrasting histories of bygone days with the sensitive material that is his own subject, Tacitus writes (*Ann.* 4.33.4): 'Few are moved to criticize the writers of ancient history; it is a matter of indifference whether you give greater

[40] Thus παρρησία was especially characteristic of Theopompus: D. Hal. *Pomp.* 6, *De imit.* 3,209.13 U–R. Polybius concedes that personalities and circumstances sometimes prevent the contemporary historian from recording what really happened (8.8.8): ἀλλ' ἴσως τοῦτ' [i.e. the objective bestowal of praise and blame on monarchs] εἰπεῖν μὲν εὐμαρές, πρᾶξαι δὲ καὶ λίαν δυσχερὲς διὰ τὸ πολλὰς καὶ ποικίλας διαθέσεις καὶ περιστάσεις, αἷς εἴκοντες ἄνθρωποι κατὰ τὸν βίον οὔτε λέγειν οὔτε γράφειν δύνανται τὸ φαινόμενον (but this is perhaps easy to say yet quite difficult to achieve because of many and varied conditions and circumstances, yielding to which men in their lifetimes cannot say or write what happened). Cf. Hor. *Carm.* 2.1.6–8.

[41] E.g., Diod. 1.2.2, 21.17.4; D. Hal. *A.R.* 1.1.2, 1.6.5, 9.22.5; *Thuc.* 8.

[42] See Diod. 15.1.1 (τῇ συνήθει τῆς ἱστορίας παρρησίᾳ, with the customary free-spokenness of history), 31.15.1 (τῇ τῆς ἱστορίας παρρησίᾳ, with the free-spokenness of history); cf. 14.1.2 (τὴν ἀλήθειαν μετὰ παρρησίας κηρύττουσαν τὰ πάλαι σιωπώμενα, proclaiming with the free-spokenness of history things long kept silent).

praise to the armies of Carthage or of Rome.' And Juvenal observes (10.147–8) that the only persons who care about the great Hannibal are boys in their schoolroom declamations. On the other hand, Cicero declares (*Amic.* 28) that Rome will always hate the Carthaginian because of his cruelty, whereas the honourable conduct of Pyrrhus elicits 'feelings not overly hostile' (*non nimis alienos animos*).

Is there any evidence for the ancients' acknowledging that someone, especially a historian, was biased against a deceased figure with whom he had not been personally involved? I know of none.[43] Naturally, a writer is not without feelings—admiration, antipathy, and the like—when he judges the goodness or badness of men, past or present. But when such feelings were independent of personal experience, a balanced assessment, compounded both of intellect and emotion, was thought possible: an unprejudiced, therefore true appraisal was the result. Hatred, love, and partisanship were emotions one usually felt for people one had known or whose acts had in some way touched one directly. The dead were rarely objects of these stronger, more 'personal' feelings.[44]

Consider, for example, Cicero's remarks to the jury in his defence of A. Cluentius in 66 BC. After describing the villainous, but now deceased, Oppianicus and the crimes for which he was tried eight years before, Cicero says that he perceives how shocked the present jury is to hear of Oppianicus' misdeeds. What must the earlier jurors have felt, he asks, if the present jury is so moved? His answer: the

---

[43] Tacitus says (*Ann.* 4.33.4) that a reader of bad character can resent historical personages in whom he sees his own bad traits, fancying that a charge against them is also a charge against himself; he may also resent those with good qualities because the contrast is obvious. Presumably a historian of bad character could also have the same reactions.

[44] Cicero (*Amic.* 28) says that we sometimes love or hate historical personages because of their uprightness or their bad character: *etiam eos, quos numquam uidimus, quodam modo diligamus. quis est qui C. Fabrici, M'. Curi non cum caritate aliqua beniuolam memoriam usurpet, quos numquam uiderit? quis autem est qui Tarquinium Superbum, qui Sp. Cassium, Sp. Maelium non oderit?* (We esteem even people whom we have never seen. Who is there who does not have a favourable opinion of Gaius Fabricius and Manius Curius not without a certain degree of affection—men whom one has never seen? And who is there who does not detest Tarquinius Superbus, Spurius Cassius, or Spurius Maelius?) Tacitus at *Ann.* 16.16.2 denies that he hates those who died so tamely under Nero. On this difficult passage, see Luce (1991).

jurors then hated Oppianicus because of the enormity of his crimes; but—and this is the point—the present jury cannot hate him. The dead Oppianicus is past hating. Cicero's vocabulary is instructive (*Clu.* 29):

> sentio, iudices, uos pro uestra humanitate his tantis sceleribus breuiter a me demonstratis uehementer esse commotos.... uos auditis de eo in quem iudices non estis, de eo quem non uidetis, de eo quem odisse iam non potestis.... illi audiebant de eo de quo iurati sententias ferre debebant, de eo cuius praesentis nefarium et consceleratum uoltum intuebantur, de eo quem omnes oderant propter audaciam.

> I perceive, gentlemen of the jury, that because of your humane feelings you have been moved by my brief account of these terrible crimes.... You are hearing about a man whom you are not sitting in judgement upon, whom you do not see, whom you cannot now hate.... Those [jurymen] were hearing about a man in whose trial they were bound to cast their vote, a man whose wicked and criminal countenance they were looking at, a man whom everyone hated because of his shamelessness.

The earlier jurors saw Oppianicus face to face and had to deliver a verdict upon him; everyone eight years ago hated the man, Cicero affirms. But the present jurors—though they are agitated (*commotos*) in accordance with the feelings that all men share (*pro uestra humanitate*)—cannot now hate Oppianicus (*odisse iam non potestis*), because they have had no personal experience of him. Hence, when Tacitus declares that he will write of Tiberius and his successors *sine ira et studio*, he can be taken to speak with full conviction; his declaration conforms wholly to the view on the causes of bias that the men of his time accepted.

Some remarks of Benedetto Croce on this subject illustrate the gap that separates the attitude of antiquity from that of our world.[45] On the one hand, Croce fully agrees with the ancient view that the past is wholly dead: 'They are men of the past who belong to the peace of the past and as such can only be the subjects of history.' He also argues that freedom from the emotions that engender bias is essential: 'Only historical judgement liberates the spirit from the pressures of the past; it is pure and extraneous to conflicting parties, and

---

[45] The quotations that follow are taken from Croce (1955) 44–7.

guarding itself against their fury, their lures, and their insidiousness, it maintains its neutrality.' On the other hand, Croce wholly rejects the notion that history should set up tribunals to judge the goodness and badness of the dead: 'They... can suffer no other judgement than that which penetrates and understands the spirit of their work.... They now stand beyond severity or indulgence, beyond censure and praise.' What he terms 'historical judgement' is the opposite of what he calls 'value-judgements' or 'affective expressions', since the latter really aim at bridging the gap between the past and the present: 'Our tribunals (whether juridical or moral) are present-day tribunals designed for living, active and dangerous men, while these other men have already appeared before the tribunals of their day, and cannot be condemned or absolved twice.' This is plainly opposed to the ancient point of view, since the ancients viewed 'contemporary tribunals' as subject to the bias that most contemporaries feel; the final verdict must be reserved for the tribunal of posterity, over which historians of a later day will preside. Croce concedes that the historian cannot help but betray some value-judgements when he treats personalities of the past who are the 'symbols of that which is loved and hated in the present', such as Socrates, Alexander, or Judas: 'We need not feel guilty at having thereby revealed something in our minds that it was impossible to hide, something which we need not be ashamed of unless with shame for ignominious affections or for unworthy aversions. But these are not historical judgements, still less are they the object of historiography, as the judge-like historians imagined that they were, the imitators of Tacitus.'

I return to Tacitus for a final question: what happens when the truism is contradicted, when the past is not a matter of indifference to those in the present? Cremutius Cordus, on trial in the reign of Tiberius for having praised Brutus and having called Cassius the last of the Romans in his histories, argues in his defence that Julius Caesar and Augustus not only allowed contemporary writers to praise their enemies but even suffered false and scurrilous remarks about themselves to pass as if unnoticed (*Ann.* 4.34); but above all, Cordus continues, criticism of men who were dead was completely open: the dead were not subject to the hatred or love of the living (*Ann.* 4.35.1, *sed maxime solutum et sine obtrectatore fuit prodere de iis, quos mors odio aut gratiae exemisset*). To convict him as if this principle were not true, he argues, is senseless. Nor can it be maintained that through his narrative he somehow is creating present dissension. All that happened is long past; there are no 'passions which yet survive':

> Are Cassius and Brutus now in arms on the field of Philippi, or am I inciting the people to civil war by my harangues? Did they not die more than seventy years ago? Do we not know how they looked in life by their statues, which even the victor did not destroy, just as we know something of what they did through what men have written? To each man posterity gives his due. If I should be condemned, there will be those who will remember me, just as they do Cassius and Brutus.

It is Cordus' rhetorical strategy (doubtless Tacitus' invention)[46] to pretend that the real issue of the trial does not exist. Cassius and Brutus, though dead more than seventy years, are clearly very much the 'symbols of that which is loved and hated in the present', to use Croce's words. Everyone knows this, including the defendant. Yet Cordus adopts as his main argument the widely accepted belief that the dead cannot be the objects of the love or hatred of the living. In effect, he is challenging his listeners and opponents to articulate what Cassius and Brutus do stand for in the political climate of AD 25—something that no one, understandably, is so foolhardy as to do out loud.[47]

Cordus is using a literary technique especially characteristic of the first century AD: the introduction into history and tragedy of persons of the past, including figures from mythology, who are made to represent the issues of the present. Tacitus tells us, for example, that toward the end of Tiberius' reign Macro, the praetorian prefect, accused Mam. Aemilius Scaurus of writing a tragedy in which certain verses could be taken to be critical of Tiberius (*Ann.* 6.29.3, *detuleratque*

---

[46] See Syme (1958) 337 n. 10; Koestermann (1963–8) II.119.

[47] Cf. *Ann.* 3.76, where Tacitus ends the book with the funeral of Junia, niece of Cato, wife of Cassius, and sister of Brutus: *sexagesimo quarto post Philippensem aciem anno supremum diem expleuit. . . . uiginti clarissimarum familiarum imagines antelatae sunt, Manilii, Quinctii aliaque eiusdem nobilitatis nomina. sed praefulgebant Cassius atque Brutus, eo ipso quod effigies eorum non uisebantur* (She died sixty-four years after the battle of Philippi. . . . Twenty images of her distinguished family were carried in front, Manlii, Quinctii, and other names of high nobility. But Cassius and Brutus outshone them all, precisely because their portraits were not on view). See the excellent article by Suerbaum (1971), esp. 86–91.

argumentum tragoediae a Scauro scriptae, additis uersibus qui in Tiberium flecterentur {he had denounced the plot of a tragedy that had been written by Scaurus, adding verses that could be adapted to Tiberius}).[48] One thinks also of Curiatius Maternus in Tacitus' *Dialogue*: when we meet him in the year 75, he has written a *Cato* that has offended those in power (2.1) and is at the very moment finishing a *Thyestes*, which will make clear whatever he had left unsaid in the *Cato* (3.3).

This essay has been concerned with the ancients' declarations about the nature of bias in historical writing. When viewed from our modern perspective, their notions often seem puzzlingly narrow and incomplete. The episode of Cremutius Cordus represents a major problem that has only been touched on here: the extent to which figures of the past could stand as symbols of present concerns. And even if, for the sake of argument, we should agree that bias may be restricted to individuals of whom one has had personal experience, what of those emotions that the historian feels toward men of the past upon whom he is obligated to pass judgement? Cannot these emotions colour and distort in some degree? This in turn raises the twin questions of what the ancients conceived historical truth to be and how they thought it could be achieved—two large questions indeed.[49]

[48] The tragedy was an *Atreus* according to Cass. Dio 58.24.4, an *Agamemnon* according to Suet. *Tib.* 61.3.

[49] Woodman (1988) has a brilliant and provocative discussion of a number of basic issues involved in these two questions.

11

Lying Historians: Seven Types of Mendacity

T. P. Wiseman

I

For Seneca, in the first century AD, it was axiomatic that historians are liars. There is a passage in his *Quaestiones Naturales* (7.16.1–2) where, discussing comets, he brushes aside the theory offered by Ephorus with a damning remark: 'It takes no great effort to refute him—he's a historian.' And yet history, of all genres, was supposed to tell the truth. In the only theoretical discussion of historiography that survives from antiquity, Lucian's essay *How to Write History*,[1] that principle is stated without irony or embarrassment (39): 'The historian's one task is to tell it as it happened . . . the one particular characteristic of history is this, that if you are going to write it you must sacrifice to Truth alone.'

Seneca justifies his paradox with a sardonic little digression on the practice of history as mere entertainment:

Some historians win approval by telling incredible tales; an everyday narra-tive would make the reader go and do something else, so they excite him with marvels. Some of them are credulous, and lies take them unawares; others are careless, and lies are what they like; the former don't avoid them, the latter seek them out. What the whole tribe have in common is this: they

---

[1] Text, translation and short commentary in MacLeod (1991) 198–247, 283–302. Detailed commentary in Avenarius (1956) and Homeyer (1965).

think their work can only achieve approval and popularity if they sprinkle it with lies.

Writing in a different genre, as the narrator of the 'pumpkinifica-tion of Claudius', Seneca gives a brilliant impersonation of the irresponsible historian:[2]

I want to put on record the business transacted in heaven on 13 October... No concession will be made to umbrage taken or favour granted. This is the authentic truth. If anyone inquires about the source of my information, first, I shan't reply if I don't want to. Who's going to compel me? ... If I *do* choose to reply, I'll say whatever trips off my tongue. Who ever demanded sworn referees from a historian? But if it is obligatory to produce the originator of the account, let the inquirer ask the man who saw Drusilla on her way to heaven.

In the first passage, Seneca has in mind the telling of marvel-stories more appropriate to poetry, and that idea is present in the *Apocolo-cyntosis* too: the contrast with sworn testimony was usually applied to poets, and Seneca makes one of his characters describe the events as an appendix to Ovid's *Metamorphoses*.[3] However, the reference to Drusilla's apotheosis shows that in the second passage he is thinking mainly of flattery and panegyric.[4]

Those two perversions of history are, in fact, the only items in the 'what not to do' section of Lucian's essay (7–13): if you avoid 'poetic stories' (*muthoi*) and 'praise of rulers and generals', it seems that you have done enough to satisfy truth. But it would be premature to infer that tall tales and flattery of the powerful were the only types of 'lying' that historians were thought to indulge in.

Let us move on to the fourth century AD, and listen to a performer every bit as sophisticated as Seneca and Lucian. The author of the *Historia Augusta* presented his thirty imperial biographies under six different pseudonyms, and was unmasked only in 1889.[5] As Sir Ronald Syme put it,[6] 'the *HA* is a genuine hoax... the text discloses a rogue scholar, delighting in deceit and making a mock of historians.

[2] *Apoc.* 1.1–2: tr. (slightly adapted) from Eden (1984) 29.
[3] Testimony: Cic. *Leg.* 1.4, Ovid *Amor.* 3.12.19, etc.; Feeney (1991) 40. Meta-morphoses: Sen. *Apoc.* 9.5.
[4] See Moles (1993) 94 on encomium.
[5] Dessau (1889).
[6] Syme (1983) 221, cf. 62, 128–9; see also Syme's earlier books, Syme (1968), esp. ch. 26, and Syme (1971), esp. ch. 17. For the psychology, cf. Grafton (1990).

Perhaps a professor on the loose, a librarian seeking recreation, a civil servant repelled by pedestrian routine.' Such a man's view on history and lies should be worth having.

It comes in the preface to the *Life of Aurelian* (1.1–2), and the setting is perfect:

> On the day of the Hilaria, when, as we know, all deeds and words should be festive, his excellency Junius Tiberianus, Prefect of the City, invited me into his official carriage after the ceremony.

The Hilaria festival was a day of masquerade and disguise; according to Herodian (1.10.5), 'anyone can play the fool by concealing his true identity, making it difficult to tell the real person from the impersonator.' Just as Plato presents his account of Atlantis as a story told at the *Apatouria*,[7] as Virgil's underworld narrative ends with Aeneas emerging through the ivory gate,[8] as (perhaps) Apuleius specifies the first watch of the night for his witch's metamorphosis,[9] so too the author of the *Historia Augusta* leaves a delicate hint, flattering the reader who is alert enough to appreciate it.

The man in the City Prefect's carriage is 'Flavius Vopiscus', one of the *HA* author's aliases.[10] On the way from the Palatine to the Varian Gardens, he engages the Prefect in conversation about imperial biography. Why, asks the Prefect, doesn't he write a Life of Aurelian? 'I'll even get his Linen Books brought out of Trajan's Library for you.' Linen books (*libri lintei*) were documents appropriate to the fourth century BC, six hundred years before Aurelian's time;[11] but 'Vopiscus' blandly urges his readers to consult them in the Library themselves if they aren't satisfied (1.7–10).

The conversation in the carriage now resumes with a discussion of the work of Trebellius Pollio—who is in fact another of the *HA* author's aliases (2.1–2):

> Tiberianus maintained that much of Pollio's work was brief and careless. I protested that as far as history was concerned there was no author who had

---

[7] Plat. *Tim.* 21b; Gill (1980) 40.

[8] Virg. *Aen.* 6.893–8; West (1987) 7–14 = Harrison (1990) 230–8.

[9] Apul. *Met.* 3.21.3; Laird (1993) 164. Cf. Gill (1993) 58–9; Morgan (1993) 216–17 on hints of fictionality.

[10] The dramatic date is either 291–2 or 303–4: see Syme (1968) 192; (1983) 120.

[11] Liv. 4.7.12, 4.20.8, etc.; Roncalli (1978–80).

not lied about something. I went so far as to cite the places where Livy, Sallust, Cornelius Tacitus, and even Trogus were refuted by clear evidence, at which he yielded to my argument and jokingly held up his hand. 'All right then', he said, 'write what you want. You can safely say whatever you like, and you'll have those admired masters of historical style as your companions in mendacity.'

Here again is the Senecan assumption that all historians lie, but evidently not restricted to Lucian's two categories of panegyric and myth. What sort of examples are we to suppose 'Vopiscus' cited?

The paradox of lying historians needs a wider enquiry. What I hope to do in this chapter is to identify the different definitions of 'lying' that are implied by the various criticisms of historians in the Hellenistic and Roman world.

I shall be emphasizing the influence on ancient historiography of rhetorical and imaginative forms of discourse, and from time to time, as a contrast, I shall use phrases like 'history in our sense'. I realize, of course, that modern historians too necessarily use their imaginations and write to persuade their readers. Rather than invoke literary–critical theory,[12] I cite the experience of a practitioner: 'to become intelligible, history has to aspire to the coherence of fiction, while eschewing most of its methods. There is no choice, no escape.' Historians are like novelists to this extent, that 'they too are fabricators and creators of illusion'.[13] That is the mature judgment of a great modern historian of Rome (a connoisseur of Proust and Flaubert), whose own works could not conceivably be read as novels.

Is the inevitable overlap of the genres the same in modern historiography as it was in the ancient world? I think not, and it is the differences that are interesting. I hope that concentrating on allegations of lying will help us to identify some of them.

II

The first and most obvious type of falsehood—tendentiousness— finds its classic statement in the prefaces to the *Histories* and the

---

[12] For instance LaCapra (1985) ch. 5, 'History and the Novel'; or (in wholly abstract terms) White (1987). Cf. Gill (1993) 85.

[13] Syme (1982) 19 and (1984) 164—*obiter dicta* from public lectures given in 1982 and 1984.

Annals of Tacitus. The twin vices of adulation and malice—flattery of a living emperor, execration of a dead one—militate equally against the truth.[14] Tacitus regards the phenomenon as peculiar to the Principate, originating in the time of Augustus; the elder Seneca, according to his son,[15] put it a little earlier, at the beginning of the civil wars, the point at which 'truth first retreated'. But of course political tendentiousness in historians was familiar long before that. Sallust insisted that his freedom from 'hope, fear, and partisanship' enabled him to narrate Catiline's conspiracy 'as truthfully as possible', and a surviving fragment of his *Histories* shows that this work contained a similar declaration.[16] A. J. Woodman has very convincingly argued that Cicero's definition of the fundamental laws of history—never dare to say anything false, never fear to say anything true—refers precisely and exclusively to truth in the sense of impartiality and freedom from prejudice.[17]

As it happens, none of these authors uses the word 'lie' in this context, though Tacitus does refer to the 'falsification' of history (*res...falsae*). It would be interesting to know if that was deliberate. Polybius, in his polemic against Timaeus, whom he accuses of gross political partiality, distinguishes between pardonable 'lies from ignorance' and culpable 'lies from choice' (12.12.4–5), and undertakes to show that Timaeus' work is an example of the latter. The distinction is reminiscent of Seneca's analysis in the passage with which we began (*QN* 7.16.2). A Late Republican scholar even tried to apply it to the synonyms *mentiri* (to lie) and *mendacium dicere* (to tell a lie): only the former, he said, referred to deliberate lying; the latter he wanted to restrict to the sense of 'telling a falsehood unawares'.[18]

Are we to infer that for some authors, at least, 'lying' was too crude a term for what historians were tempted to do? If so, it was certainly not a general reluctance. Lucian (*h. c.* 7) had no inhibitions about

---

[14] Tac. *Hist.* 1.1.1–2; *Ann.* 1.1.2; Goodyear (1972) 96–101.

[15] Peter, *HRR* II.98 (Seneca, *De vita patris*); Fairweather (1981) 15–17.

[16] Sall. *Cat.* 4.2–3; *Hist.* 1.6M.

[17] Woodman (1988) 80–3 {= pp. 254–9, above} on Cic. *de Orat.* 2.62; 72–4 {= pp. 243–6, above} on *Fam.* 5.12.3. See in general Luce (1988) {= above, Ch. 10}; and cf. Moles (1993) 115.

[18] Nigidius Figulus in Gell. *NA* 11.11; Holford-Strevens (1988) 129 n. 17 {= (2003) 175 n. 17}.

describing panegyric in history as a lie (*pseudos*). Nor, conversely, had Josephus (*A.J.* 20.154–5), in his criticism of historians' malice:

Many have written the history of Nero. Some have been favourable to him, careless of the truth because he benefited them. Others, out of hatred and hostility towards him, have behaved like shameless drunkards in their lies, and deserve condemnation for it. I am not surprised at those who have lied about Nero, since even in their accounts of events before his time they have not preserved the truth of history.

Naturally, Josephus distances himself from such authors. 'Let them write as they like, since that is what gives them pleasure. As for me, I am aiming at the truth' (20.156)—by which he means impartiality.

Lucian specified only two things that the truthful historian had to avoid—panegyric and *muthoi*. The latter category is our second type; for Roman authors, it provided evident proof that the Greeks were liars.

Valerius Maximus, for instance, in his chapter on friendship (4.7.4), contrasted a true story of Roman loyalty at the battle of Philippi with the tale of Theseus and Pirithous:

Let Greece talk of Theseus entrusting himself to the kingdom of Father Dis in support of the base loves of Pirithous. Only a knave would write such stuff, only a fool would believe it. . . . These are the monstrous lies of a race given to deceit.

'Monstrous', literally—*monstro similia mendacia*. A similar phrase occurred to the elder Pliny (*HN* 5.3–4), describing the town of Lixus on the Atlantic coast of Mauretania, where Claudius had founded a Roman colony: according to the 'portentous falsehoods of the Greeks' (*portentosa Graeciae mendacia*), it was the site of Hercules' wrestling match with Antaeus, and of the grove of the Hesperides where dragon–snakes guarded the golden apples.

The objection to such stories was that they involved miracles (*monstra, portenta*). Men do not go alive to the Underworld, trees do not bear golden fruit. The Greeks themselves had two answers to this criticism. First, the historian might include such stories 'not in ignorance of the facts, but inventing impossibilities for the sake of wonder and pleasure'; but he should make it clear that he was doing

so, as Theopompus evidently did.[19] Alternatively, he could rationalize the marvellous into the credible, like Dicaearchus in his *Bios
Hellados*:[20] 'by eliminating the excessively fabulous one reduces it,
by reasoning, to a natural meaning.'

The two approaches could easily be combined, as by Dionysius
of Halicarnassus in his account of Hercules in Italy and at the site
of Rome. The historian carefully distinguishes the mythical story of
Cacus and the cattle of Geryon—which he tells at length—from the
'more truthful' version, that Hercules was the leader of an invading
army, and Cacus a brigand chieftain.[21]

Both strategies were of course familiar to Hellenized Romans. The
first, avowed myth for the sake of entertainment, is clearly the
historia fabularis with which Tiberius used to torment the professors
at his dinner table. The second, rationalizing in the manner of
Euhemerus, was evidently basic to Varro's *De gente populi Romani*,
the fragments of which are full of schematic contrasts between
fabulosa mendacia and *historica ueritas*—respectively the traditional
and the rationalized versions of myths.[22]

What lies behind all this is the Hellenistic grammarians' tripartite
division of narrative.[23] Our sources, which date from the first century
BC, define the three categories in varying terms, as follows:[24]

	1	2	3
Asclepiades:	true history	false history	quasi-true history
Cicero and *Rhet. Herenn.*:	history	myth (*fabula*)	plot (*argumentum*)

The criterion for the second category was the familiar one of physical
impossibility: Cicero's example is Medea's dragon-drawn chariot;
Asclepiades evidently cited the poisonous creatures born from the

---

[19] Str. 1.2.35 *ad fin.*, C43: Theopompus, *FGrHist* 115 F 381.

[20] F 49 (Wehrli (1944) 24.10). Cf. Feeney (1991) 31–2 on Palaephatus and
Euhemerus, 76 n. 62 on Diodorus.

[21] *A.R.* 1.39–40 (*muthikos logos*), 41–4 (*alêthesteros logos*).

[22] Suet. *Tib.* 70.3; Peter, *HRR* II.10–24, esp. FF 3, 6, 7b, 8, 13, 14, 17. Cf. Rawson
(1985) 244–5.

[23] See Meijering (1987) 76–90; Feeney (1991) 42–4; Morgan (1993) 189.

[24] Asclepiades of Myrlea, quoted in Sext. Emp. *Math.* 1.252–3; Cic. *Inv.* 1.27; *Rhet.
Herenn.* 1.13.

blood of the Titans, and various stories of metamorphosis.[25] Legends (in our sense) which did not involve such marvels were accommodated in the first category, which included the deeds of gods and heroes as well as men.

Notoriously,[26] the grammarians never mention the novel; perhaps the genre did not yet exist when their schema was first devised. Nevertheless, the third category approximates to our idea of fiction. For the ancient theorists, its function was to account for comedy and mime, where realistic characters and action were invented by the playwright. Tragedy on the other hand, with its traditional plots and characters, and indeed the whole of what we think of as mythology, was divided between categories 1 and 2, according to the absence or presence of the miraculous.

That was the distinction that mattered. It gave rise also to a simpler schema which we know from Servius' commentary on the *Aeneid*:[27]

The difference between myth (*fabula*) and . . . history (*historia*) is that myth is the report of something against nature, whether or not it happened, as about Pasiphae, and history is whatever is reported according to nature, whether or not it happened, as about Phaedra.

In this version, the truth-value of both categories is explicitly immaterial. Trying to seduce your stepson is according to nature; being impregnated by a bull is not. So Phaedra's story is *historia* and Pasiphae's is *fabula*; whether or not either of them was (in our sense) historical is not at issue.

However, such austere suspension of judgement was not for everyone. Plutarch is a better guide. In his *Life of Theseus*, where he is explicitly rationalizing poetic myths ('purifying the mythical, making it submit to reason and take on the appearance of history'), he has this to say about Phaedra and Hippolytus:

---

[25] Sext. Emp. *Math.* 1.264; Meijering (1987) 78–9; Morgan (1993) 190, 227–8.

[26] The issue is a recurring them in Gill and Wiseman (1993): see Gill (1993) 41, 79–80; Laird (1993) 154; Morgan (1993) 176–7, 232 n. 6. Detailed discussion of the problem in Kuch (1989) 11–51.

[27] Servius on *Aen.* 1.235—confusingly giving *argumentum* as a synonym for *historia*. Cf. Feeney (1991) 255.

As for the calamities that befell Phaedra and the son of Theseus, since there is no conflict between the historians and the tragic poets, we must suppose that they happened as all the poets represent them.

For his purposes, and in the absence of any 'more truthful' version, he takes the tragedians' plot as (in our sense) historical.[28]

It was an episode in the life of Theseus (p. 319 above) that prompted Valerius Maximus to brand all Greeks as liars. Plutarch's version of it shows how easily 'false history' could be turned into 'true'. Theseus, Plutarch blandly reports (31.4), was imprisoned by Aidoneus, a king of the Molossians who happened to call his wife Persephone, his daughter Kore, and his dog Cerberus.[29]

Type three consists of travellers' tales.[30] From the very beginning, historiography had been concerned with distant and exotic lands. Herodotus, like his predecessor Hecataeus, was a great collector of stories about far-away places (not all of which he believed); a generation later, Ctesias of Cnidus exploited his position as the Persian court doctor to produce a farrago of tall tales about the Persian empire; two generations later again, when that empire fell to Alexander, historians were able to offer eyewitness accounts of the very ends of the known world.

'For the most part,' wrote Strabo in the first century BC (2.1.9, C70), 'those who have written about India have all been liars [*pseudologoi*]'. The Alexander-historians were writing first-hand accounts of contemporary events—about as far from mythography as it is possible to get. But their travellers' tales were as liable as the myths of the distant past to be dismissed as fabulous and incredible. Indeed, the whole story of Alexander, including the wonders he saw in India, was soon converted into pure fiction.[31]

[28] Plut. *Thes.* 1.3, 28.2 (cf. 16.3 for Plutarch's rejection of the tragedians' view of Minos). For the important concept of 'true *enough*' in Plutarch, see Pelling (1990), esp. 49.

[29] On the general theme of this section, see Veyne (1988); also Gill (1993) 57 n. 45.

[30] For thrills, wonders, and 'the marvellous', see Moles (1993) 93; Morgan (1993) 195–6, and Romm (1992), esp. ch. 5, 'Geography and Fiction'.

[31] Romm (1992) ch. 3, 'Wonders of the East'; Stoneman (1991); and Dowden (1989). For the related genres of paradoxography and utopian writing, see Gabba (1981) {= below, Ch. 12}.

The *locus classicus* for this most elementary category of lies in history is Lucian's preface to his *True History* (1.3):[32]

> Ctesias of Cnidus in his work on India and its characteristics gives details for which he had neither the evidence of his eyes nor of hearsay. . . . Many other writers have adopted the same plan, professing to relate their own travels, and describing monstrous beasts, savages, and strange ways of life. The fount and inspiration of their buffoonery is the Homeric Odysseus, entertaining Alcinous' court with his prisoned winds, his men one-eyed or wild or cannibal, his beasts with many heads and his metamorphosed comrades; the Phaeacians were simple folk, and he fooled them totally.

Like these distinguished predecessors,[33] Lucian is going to tell lies. The difference is that he admits it at the start, in the one true statement of the work: 'My subject is, then, what I have neither seen, experienced, nor been told, what neither exists nor could conceivably do so. I humbly solicit my readers' incredulity.'

The first three categories of lies have been straightforward enough. Now we approach something more complex—the effect of rhetoric and drama. In his dialogue *Brutus*, Cicero represents himself as conversing with his friend Atticus, the author of an outline history of Rome, about Themistocles and Coriolanus. He asserts that the parallels between the two men's careers extend to the nature—suicide, he says—of their respective deaths. He then continues (42–3):[34]

> 'You have a different account of Coriolanus, Atticus; but you must allow me to acquiesce in this manner of his dying rather than yours.' Atticus laughed and said: 'It's your choice. It's granted that orators may tell lies in historical matters in order to make a point more neatly. Just as you made up a story about Coriolanus, so Cleitarchus and Stratocles produced their fictions about Themistocles.

As Atticus goes on to point out, we know from Thucydides (1.138.4) that Themistocles died a natural death.

---

[32] Tr. Fowler and Fowler (1905), slightly adapted; cf. Romm (1992) 211–14. Syme, following Lucian, picked Ctesias as the originator of 'fictional history': Syme (1971) 263; (1991) 157, 319.

[33] For Homer's Odysseus as the lying story-teller *par excellence,* see Juvenal 15.13–26; Romm (1992) 183–96.

[34] Tr. M. Winterbottom, in Russell and Winterbottom (1972) 222. Discussion in Wiseman (1979) 31–4.

'But the other two say that he sacrificed a bull, caught the blood in a bowl, drank it, and dropped dead. That, of course, was the sort of death they could give a rhetorical and tragic gloss; the other ordinary kind left no scope for decoration. So since it suits you that everything was parallel in the cases of Themistocles and Coriolanus, you can take the bowl from me too, and I'll give you the victim as well!'

Although Atticus is talking specifically about orators ('concessum est *rhetoribus* ementiri in historiis'), one of the false authorities he quotes on Themistocles was a very well-known historian.[35] So one cannot pretend that this passage is relevant only to the practice of oratory, or to 'histories written by rhetors or sophists' as if they somehow didn't count as historiography.[36] The techniques of history writing, oratory, and poetry (especially tragic drama) overlapped and affected each other in various ways:[37]

> Though we today see poetry, oratory, and historiography as three separate genres, the ancients saw them as three different species of the same genus— rhetoric. All three types of activity aimed to elaborate certain data in such a way as to affect or persuade an audience or readership.

Elaborating the data was what Cicero's Atticus meant by 'giving a rhetorical and tragic gloss' (*rhetorice et tragice ornare*)—like providing Coriolanus and Themistocles with deaths more dramatically satisfying than the banal reality. All right for an orator or a tragic poet, but permissible to a historian only with a laugh, to show that he was going beyond his proper function—lying, in fact, for dramatic effect.[38]

There is a famous passage in Polybius (2.56.10–12), where the historian attacks his predecessor Phylarchus for failing to distinguish between history and tragedy:[39]

[35] Cleitarchus: *FGrHist* 137; cf. Pearson (1960) ch. 9. Stratocles was an orator and politician.

[36] Brunt (1980a) 330–3 {= above, pp. 229–34}; quotation from 331 {= above, p. 230}.

[37] Woodman (1988) 95–101 {= above, pp. 283–8}, quotation from 100 {= above, p. 286}.

[38] Others did not make this distinction: see p. 331 below for vivid elaboration as historical truth.

[39] Tr. from Scott–Kilvert (1979). For what Phylarchus was doing, see Walbank (1960) {= below, Ch. 14} and Moles (1993) 112–13; Morgan (1993) 185–6.

It is not a historian's business to startle his readers with sensational descriptions, nor should he try, as the tragic poets do, to represent speeches which might have been delivered, or to enumerate all the possible consequences of the events under consideration; it is his task first and foremost to record with fidelity what actually happened and was said, however commonplace that may be. For the aim of tragedy is by no means the same as that of history, but rather the opposite. The tragic poet seeks to thrill and charm his audience for the moment by expressing through his characters the most plausible words possible, but the historian's task is to instruct and persuade serious students by means of the truth of the words and actions he presents, and this effect must be permanent, not temporary.

Polybius' standards, however, were unusually austere. He calls Phylarchus a liar (2.56.2); but I think most people in the ancient world would not describe as 'lying' the use in history of such oratorical and dramatic techniques as vivid and imaginative presentation, composition of appropriate speeches, the invention of circumstantial detail *ad libitum*. What Cicero's Atticus calls lying (*ementiri*) is when you know the facts but deliberately substitute a more dramatically effective version.

It is important to remember that episodes of Roman history were regularly represented in the theatre, and that Roman drama was older than Roman historiography. The historians themselves were sometimes conscious of the danger of taking as historical something that had been invented for the stage. Livy, for instance (5.21.8–9), dismisses an episode from the capture of Veii as unworthy of belief; it was 'more suited to a stage show, for the stage delights in marvels'. Ovid (*Fasti* 4.326) neatly confirms Livy's point as he tells a miracle-story about Quinta Claudia in 204 BC: 'it is astonishing, but attested by the stage.' Even Plutarch and Dionysius occasionally suspect the presence of dramatic fiction (*plasma*) in some item of the tradition, though not nearly often enough for modern tastes.[40]

As the Ovid passage shows, this type of dramatic influence was not restricted to the very early period, where it would simply count as 'myth'. Polybius offers a startling example from historians of the Second Punic War, who had Hannibal guided over the Alps by

---

[40] E.g. Plut. *Rom.* 8.7 (*dramatikon kai plasmatôdes*); D. Hal. *A.R.* 9.22.3 (*plasmata theatrika, muthoi*).

supernatural apparitions:[41] 'they fall into the same difficulties as the tragic dramatists, who all need a *deus ex machina* to resolve their plots, because they are based on false (*pseudeis*) or improbable assumptions.'

Seneca, as we saw at the beginning, was no great admirer of historians. Another passage of his *Quaestiones Naturales* (4.3.1) leads us into a more fundamental definition of lies in history:

> [This is] what historians do: when they've told numerous lies of their own choice, they pick out one thing they don't want to guarantee, and add the phrase 'my authorities must take responsibility for this'.

Ever since Herodotus (7.152.3), it was a commonplace of historical writing to annotate certain items with the plea that 'I'm reporting what I was told, I don't necessarily believe it'.[42] But according to Seneca, historians make this virtuous declaration at random, to give the illusion that the rest of what they say is guaranteed.

What lies behind his complaint is best illustrated in the preface of Arrian's history of Alexander the Great (*Anab. praef.* 1, 3):[43]

> Everything concerning Alexander which Ptolemy and Aristobulus have both described in the same way I have reproduced as being true in every respect; when they have not given the same account, I have chosen the version which seemed to me more worthy of belief and also more worthy of telling.... Other incidents recorded by other writers, because they seemed to me in themselves worthy of telling and not altogether unworthy of belief, I have reproduced as being merely 'reported' about Alexander.

Arrian has two criteria for what to include—essentially, credibility, and interest, what's worth believing and what's worth telling.

The word Arrian uses for 'more worthy of telling' (*axiaphêgêto-tera*) is constructed out of *aphêgêsis*, which means narrative, the act of relating. Like its synonym *diêgêsis* (which is now a technical term in modern literary theory),[44] *aphêgêsis* is derived from the verb 'to

---

[41] Pol. 3.48.8, taken by Feeney (1991) 261 as an example of the common ground of history and epic.

[42] *Fides penes auctores*: e.g. Sall. *Jug.* 17.7 (on Africa); Val. Max. 1.8.7 (on the migrating Penates); Plin. *HN* 17.93 (on olive yields). Cf. Curt. Rufus 9.1.3 ('I report more than I believe'), and Moles (1993) 95, 120.

[43] Tr. Pearson (1960) 2.

[44] Four distinct meanings are identified by Booth (1983) 438 n. 16.

lead': the narrator, as it were, 'conducts' the listener 'through' the story, or 'from' one event to the next. The origin and truth-status of the events—whether they were discovered or invented—is neither here nor there. *Aphêgêsis* is simply 'story'.

History, as we understand it, originated in the intellectual climate of Ionian rationalism, with Herodotus' 'publication of his research' (*historiês apodeixis*) into the origins of the conflict between Greeks and Persians.[45] His *historiê* meant not just reporting the stories that were told, but *finding out* by his own enquiries and taking responsibility for the result. Never mind the tales about the rapes of Io and Europa; he will start from Croesus, the man whom he knows, from his enquiries, to have originated the enmity (Hdt. 1.1–5).

Historia as enquiry is what sets apart the great historians of classical antiquity (Thucydides, Polybius, Tacitus); but it always had to coexist with *aphêgêsis*,[46] and in many historical authors *aphêgêsis* ruled alone. See, for instance, the preface to Diodorus Siculus' universal history in the first century BC. For him, history is a branch of the art of words: 'there is a harmony between the facts and their literary expression',[47] and it does not occur to him to ask how the facts are achieved. Similarly Lucian,[48] in the second century AD, thought of the historian's mind as like a mirror, reflecting what is already there, and his craft as like that of a sculptor, creating a work of art from material that was already provided for him.

Arrian's two criteria ('worthy of belief, worthy of telling') correspond precisely to these two concepts. The question 'is it true?' addresses *historia*, enquiry, or research, what we regard as the historian's proper business; the question 'is it worth telling?' addresses *aphêgêsis*, narration, the business of the story-teller. And to keep them separate, as Arrian very properly does, implies that some credible things are not worth relating, and some incredible ones are.

---

[45] See Moles (1993) 92.

[46] See Gould (1989) 47–8, who points out that enquiry does not necessarily entail narrative. What made Herodotus 'the father of history' was his brilliant combination of *historia* and *aphêgêsis*.

[47] Diod. 1.2.7: tr. Toynbee (1924) 32.

[48] *H.c.* 51: 'what historians have to relate is fact and will speak for itself, for it has already happened' (tr. K. Kilburn, LCL). Cf. Moles (1993) 89.

We are now better placed, I think, to see what Seneca was getting at. His sardonic assumption is that all historiography is irresponsible *aphêgêsis*; the historian is merely a story-teller, and story-tellers are liars. Remember Odysseus at the court of Alcinous:[49]

Alcinous answered: 'Odysseus, as we look at you we cannot think you to be a deceiver and a cheat, though the dark earth breeds a great crop of such, forgers of lies drawn from places beyond our ken.'

Seneca would have agreed with Lucian that the Phaeacians were simple folk.

The most revealing part of his indictment is that historians tell lies 'of their own choice' (*ad arbitrium suum*). Cicero's Atticus used a similar phrase—'it's your choice' (*tuo arbitratu*). 'Write what you want,' said the City Prefect to the imperial biographer; 'you can safely say whatever you like.' Josephus said the same about the historians of Nero. Seneca himself, in his guise as narrator, will say 'whatever trips off his tongue'—a proverbial phrase used also by Lucian to describe what bad historians do.[50]

Historia takes the responsibility for what it tells; *aphêgêsis* has a free and irresponsible choice. The conflict is well expressed by the historian of Zuleika Dobson, describing his heroine's conjuring act:[51]

Was there ever, I wonder, an historian so pure as not to have wished just once to fob off on his readers just one bright fable for effect? I find myself sorely tempted to tell you that on Zuleika, as her entertainment drew to a close, the spirit of the higher thaumaturgy descended like a flame and found in her a worthy agent. Specious Apollyon whispers to me: 'Where would be the harm?... Why not? Your readers would be excited, gratified. And you would never be found out.' But the grave eyes of Clio are bent on me, her servant. Oh pardon, madam: I did but waver for an instant.

---

[49] Hom. *Od.* 11.362–6: tr. W. Shewring (World's Classics).
[50] Cic. *Brut.* 42; *SHA Aurelian* 2.2; Jos. *A.J.* 20.156; Sen. *Apoc.* 1.2; Luc. *h.c.* 32.
[51] Max Beerbohm, *Zuleika Dobson* (London 1911) 165; cf. 293 for a composite messenger-speech and 'indirect narration'—'Credibility is not enough for Clio's servant. I aim at truth.'

III

'You would never be found out.' 'Who ever demanded sworn referees (*iuratores*) from a historian?'[52] But sometimes it does happen.

The disastrous fire at the Bradford City stadium in May 1985 came at a time when the British public was very concerned about the anarchic violence of soccer fans. So when the *Daily Star* reporter linked the tragedy with hooliganism, readers were probably not surprised. Under the headline 'I saw killer smoke bomb', Ian Trueman reported: 'I saw everything, every horrifying second. I saw a smoke bomb thrown by hooligans from a stand adjoining the main building.' The following month, a judicial enquiry into the disaster was set up under Mr Justice Popplewell, and the reporter was called to give evidence and questioned by the counsel for the enquiry:[53]

Under questioning by Mr Collins yesterday, Mr Trueman agreed that he had not seen anything being thrown but after noticing the trail of smoke in the stand had assumed it to have been caused by a smoke bomb. He added that he stood by his story.

He stood by the standards of *aphêgêsis* against the demands of *historia*.

Journalism is relevant to our subject simply because it did not exist in the ancient world. It is essential to remember, as A. J. Woodman has rightly insisted,[54] that much of what happens in Greek and Roman historiography happens for us in 'the media'. A professional journalist who systematically monitored a full year of Fleet Street reporting summed up his results as follows, in terms which could apply equally to ancient historiography:[55]

Newspapers had lied to entertain, to compete with each other, to propagate their political convictions, and to persecute those with whom they disagreed. And when there was no other obvious reason, journalists continued to lie simply out of habit.

[52] Sen. *Apoc.* 1.2 (n. 2 above).
[53] *The Times* (8 June 1985) 3.
[54] Woodman (1988) 207–15; id. (1983b) and (1979) 155. Cf. also Veyne (1988) 5, 9–10, 110.
[55] Porter (1984) 142.

To entertain: *delectatio* (enjoyment) was accepted as one of the legitimate aims of history.[56] To compete: Josephus (on Greek historians) and Livy and Justin (on Roman ones) make it clear that rivalry with predecessors and contemporaries was a common motive.[57] To propagate political convictions: tendentiousness was endemic in ancient historiography; to the items mentioned above (pp. 317–18), add the 'democratic' and 'oligarchic' treatments of Athenian history that were imperfectly reconciled in the Aristotelian *Constitution of Athens*.[58] To persecute: malice too was often complained of in historians, as with Timaeus on Demochares and Agathocles, Theophanes on Rutilius Rufus.[59] Out of habit: that, essentially, was Seneca's charge against all historians.

Then there are the visual media, which achieve what the Greek and Roman historians always strove for, the vividness (*enargeia*, p. 335 below) which could bring a scene to life in the imagination of the audience, or the reader. Consider Polybius' attack on Phylarchus' 'lying' account of the fall of Mantinea:[60]

Since it was his purpose to emphasize the cruelty of Antigonus and the Macedonians, . . . he introduces graphic scenes of women clinging to one another, tearing their hair and baring their breasts, and in addition he describes the tears and lamentations of men and women accompanied by their children and aged parents as they are led away into captivity. Phylarchus reproduces this kind of effect again and again in his history, striving on each occasion to recreate the horrors before our eyes.

This is what we call nowadays 'good television'.

The other great difference between their literary world and ours is the present-day ubiquity of the novel. The origins of the modern genre were marked by problems and ambiguities about its truth status which are remarkably similar to ancient views of historiography.[61] And before we smile at the naivety of those who thought Defoe's fictions were genuine documents, we should remember a

[56] See Fornara (1983) 120–34; Morgan (1993) 184–6.
[57] Jos. *Ap.* 1.24–7; Liv. *praef.* 2–3; Justin *praef.* 1 (*aemulatio gloriae* {rivalry for renown}); cf. Moles (1993) 99–100.
[58] See Rhodes (1981) 15–30, esp. 21–3.
[59] Pol. 12.13–15; Plut. *Pomp.* 37.3.
[60] Pol. 2.56.6–8 (n. 39 above).
[61] Davis (1983); cf. Nelson (1973) and Day (1987).

scene from only thirty years ago, in the House of Lords debate on
Lady Chatterley's Lover:[62]

'The story he tells is pure invention!' Lord Teviot said in a tone of outraged
wonder at the end of his lashing of Lawrence. 'It never actually happened!'
That, Lord Boothby hastened to inform him, is the thing about fiction.

The ancient genre too overlapped with history, as other contributors
to this volume demonstrate at length.[63]

It may be helpful to recapitulate the five types of mendacity
identified so far, and see where they would be in *our* generic structure. The first is easy: deliberately false historiography is still all too
familiar, exemplified in its extreme form by Soviet histories of the
Soviet Union.[64] The second and third types, marked as they are by
fantasy and 'events against nature', correspond respectively to 'sword
and sorcery' novels in the Tolkien tradition, and to science fiction.
The fourth is clearly 'docu-drama' or 'faction', that hybrid genre that
intermittently exercises media consciences.[65] As for the fifth, most
people, then and now, are content with *aphêgêsis* and have no notion
of *historia*; we all have in our heads an amalgam of information and
misinformation from all kinds of sources which passes for a view of
the past.[66]

And yet, beyond all that, there is the sheer intellectual achievement
of *historia* as enquiry. Herodotus, Thucydides, Polybius, and Tacitus
were great historians by any standard. So my two final types of
historical mendacity, deliberately antithetical, mark the extremes of
the familiar and the alien in ancient attitudes to historiography. They
are, respectively, lies defined as too much detail, and lies defined as
not enough.

Discussing the size of Hannibal's forces in the invasion of Italy,
Polybius contrasts his own accurate information, drawn from contemporary documents, with that of other historians who merely

---

[62] N. Shrapnel, *The Guardian* (15 December 1960) 1; cf. *Hansard* (Lords, 14
December 1960) 530, 561. Cf. Morgan (1993) 179: Solon evidently took Lord Teviot's
View.

[63] See Gill (1993) 79–81; Morgan (1993) 186–7, 197–8, 205–6.

[64] Now of course discredited: see Davies (1989).

[65] See for instance Fiddick (1990); O'Kelly (1991).

[66] See Lowenthal (1985) ch. 5.

invent details to add verisimilitude (3.33.17); they are, he says, 'plausible liars' (*axiopistôs pseudomenoi*).

That is a very modern type of judgement. It depends on a clear distinction between the historian's type of narration and that which practically all educated men had been trained in at their rhetorical schools. The orator's type of narration depended on *inuentio*, which the handbooks defined as 'the devising of matter true or probable [*uerum* or *ueri simile*] which will make a case appear convincing.'[67] That was what the historians Polybius complained about were doing, and what I imagine most authors and readers would take for granted as acceptable technique; as Christopher Pelling puts it (discussing Plutarch), 'this is not fiction or invention, but creative reconstruction'.[68]

I know of no other passage in ancient literature where that sort of elaboration is explicitly condemned, as Polybius condemns it. The nearest is a quotation that happens to survive from the first book of Ephorus' universal history:[69]

On contemporary events, we regard as most believable those who give the most detailed account; on events in the distant past, however, we consider such an account wholly implausible, on the grounds that it is unlikely that all actions and most speeches would be remembered over so long a period of time.

The sort of thing Ephorus probably had in mind was his contemporary Cleidemus' detailed account of Theseus' battle with the Amazons. Plutarch calls Cleidemus' technique 'excessive' (*perittos*)—the word Polybius used to describe a taste for the kind of history he himself did *not* write.[70] No doubt Ephorus, like Plutarch, raised his eyebrows only at such extreme examples as Cleidemus. Polybius' uncompromising critical standards, though sympathetic to us, were a rarity in the ancient world.

[67] Cic. *Inu.* 1.9; *Rhet. Herenn.* 1.3; effects on historiography discussed by Wiseman (1979) ch. 3, and id. (1981). See also Morgan (1993) 187–8.
[68] Pelling (1990) 38.
[69] *FGrHist* 70 F 9, quoted in Harpocration's *Lexicon*.
[70] Plut. *Thes.* 27.3–4, 19.4 (Cleidemus, *FGrHist* 323 FF 17–18); Pol. 9.1.4. See Wiseman (1979) 151–2.

Paradoxically, those whom Polybius castigated as 'plausible liars' could retort that their accumulation of circumstantial detail was not a mere literary device, but actually a way of reaching the truth.

Polybius himself (3.32.6) and Cicero after him (*de Orat.* 2.63), both serious and responsible critics, declare that the truth of history,[71] and thus its value for the understanding of public affairs, depends on the detailed analysis of events according to their causes, their accompanying circumstances, and their consequences. It follows

> ... that neither writers nor readers of history should confine their attention to the narrative of events, but must also take account of what preceded, accompanied and followed them. For if we remove from history the analysis of why, how and for what purpose each thing was done and whether the result was what we should reasonably have expected, what is left is a mere display of descriptive virtuosity, but not a lesson, and this, though it may please for the moment, is of no enduring value for the future.

Polybius' concluding remarks here put him explicitly in the tradition of Thucydidean historiography.[72] Like Thucydides, he demands *akribeia*, accurate detail, and that includes the reporting of significant speeches; Polybius insists that 'the historian must devote his whole energy to finding out what was actually said, and repeating the most important and appropriate parts of it' (36.1.7).

Naturally, both Thucydides and Polybius took it for granted that it was only for very recent history that such detailed information could be discovered. They were practitioners of *historia* as enquiry, which meant by personal interview.[73] But their ideal of detailed analysis was taken over by historians concerned with the distant past, who ignored Ephorus' warning about the worthlessness of detail in such contexts.

The best example is Dionysius of Halicarnassus, an honest man with a serious view of the value of history,[74] but who had little or no conception of *historia* as enquiry. He prides himself on *akribeia*, and insists that what makes history valuable—both for practical politics

---

[71] Truth: Pol. 3.31.7–8; Cic. *de Orat.* 2.62.
[72] Pol. 3.31.11–13; cf. Thuc. 1.22.4.
[73] Thuc. 1.22.1; Pol. 12.28a.8–10.
[74] See now Gabba (1991).

and for 'philosophical contemplation'—is a detailed account of the causes of events and the manner in which they took place, including, of course, the speeches made at the time.[75] The trouble is, he applies these Polybian precepts to a wholly un-Polybian subject—the early Roman Republic, four to five hundred years before his own time.

Though his sources may have had *some* genuine information about that period (how much, is controversial), all modern historians would agree that the details they supplied were mere elaboration.[76] Dionysius, of course, accepted them in good faith, and used them to provide examples to guide the judgement of statesmen, an aim for which only the truth would suffice.[77]

The conceptual nexus of truth, detail, and the value of history is pure Polybius (3.31–2), but detaching it from *historia* as enquiry— the investigation of recent events—brings about the exact opposite of Polybius' view of history and its methods. For Dionysius never asked himself 'how do my sources *know* this?'; he was a professor of rhetoric as well as a historian, and his type of *akribeia*, applied to previous writers' accounts of the distant past, was essentially a rhetorical technique.

Polybius' tripartite analysis of 'what preceded, accompanied, and followed' the events was a standard item in rhetorical handbooks, as a guide to the elaboration of narrative:[78]

For example, if we are describing a war, we shall first of all mention the preliminaries such as the generals' speeches, the outlay on both sides, and their fears; next, the attacks, the slaughter, and the dead; finally, the victory trophy, the triumphal songs of the victors, the tears, and enslavement of the victims.

Dionysius confirms that historians elaborated military narrative in precisely this way, and criticizes them for not doing the same with accounts of political unrest; his own treatment of the conflict of

---

[75] D. Hal. *A.R.* 1.5.4, 1.8.2–3, 3.18.1, 5.56.1, 5.75.1, 7.66.1–5, 11.1.1–6; Gabba (1991) 80–5.

[76] See for instance Ogilvie–Drummond (1989).

[77] *Paradeigmata*: D. Hal. *A.R.* 5.75.1, 11.1.5. Truth: 1.1.2 (the source of both practical and philosophical wisdom), 1.5.1–2, etc.

[78] Hermogenes 16.22: tr. Woodman (1988) 89 {above, p. 268}; cf. 108 n. 79 {above, p. 268 n. 79} for other references.

patricians and plebeians, 'characterized by precise detail [*akribeia*] rather than brevity', shows what should be done.[79]

For the rhetoricians, this technique was a means of achieving *enargeia*, the vividness that compels belief. Quintilian explains in his *Institutio Oratoria* (6.2.31–2):[80]

> I am complaining that a man has been murdered. Shall I not bring before my eyes all the circumstances which it is reasonable to imagine must have occurred in such a connection? Shall I not see the assassin burst suddenly from his hiding-place, the victim tremble, cry for help, beg for mercy, or turn to run? Shall I not see the fatal blow delivered and the stricken body fall? Will not the blood, the deathly pallor, the groan of agony, the death-rattle, be indelibly impressed on my mind?
>
> From such impressions arises that *enargeia* which Cicero calls *illustratio* and *euidentia*, which makes us seem not so much to narrate as to exhibit the actual scene, while our emotions will be no less actively stirred than if we were present at the actual occurrence.

Don't tell, show! As we shall see in the next two chapters,[80a] the technique Quintilian describes was of great importance for writers of fiction. Certainly it was not confined to oratory: the examples he goes on to give are from Virgil's *Aeneid*, and we know from Polybius' attack on Phylarchus, as well as from many extant examples, that historians used it too.[81]

The Latin for *enargeia* was *euidentia*. For a modern critical historian, what matters above all is the quality of the evidence. A Roman might well agree, but he would not mean the same. In rhetoric, *euidentia* meant 'vivid illustration'; in philosophical discourse, it meant 'self-evidence'.[82] With *euidentia*, there was no need for argument: you could simply *see* the thing was true. And you achieved

[79] D. Hal. *A.R.* 7.66.3 and 7.66.5. Cf. Gabba (1991) 83: 'Such a procedure is fundamentally analogous to that followed by the late Roman annalists, who, in all seriousness and with a wholehearted belief in a substantial continuity of both problems and institutions, reconstructed the ill-known archaic phase of the city by following the political and ideological pattern of contemporary life.'

[80] Tr. H. E. Butler (LCL). On *enargeia*, see Meijering (1987) 29–52.

[80a] {Wiseman here refers to chs. 5 and 6 in Gill–Wiseman (1993).}

[81] Fiction: see Morgan (1993) 185–6, 211. History: Woodman (1988) 84–92 {= above, pp. 261–75}.

[82] Cic. *Acad.* 2.17; Quint. 4.2.63, 8.3.61, 9.2.40.

that end by making explicit 'all the circumstances which it is reasonable to imagine must have occurred'. That is, the invention of circumstantial detail was a way to reach the truth.

And so at last we find our seventh type of mendacity, precisely antithetical to the sixth. On this way of looking at things, lying is the *absence* of elaboration—a view detectable in Cato's account of the unlettered Ligurians' oral traditions, or in the attitude of the cultured world of Lactantius' time to the simple literature and unsophisticated doctrine of the Christians.[83]

I suspect we may be blind to this concept in the ancient texts simply because it is so utterly at variance with our notion of 'the plain unvarnished truth'. One place where it seems to be implied is in that conversation in the City Prefect's carriage (p. 316 above). The Prefect complains about 'Trebellius Pollio' for writing too often in a brief and careless manner (*breuiter, incuriose*).[84] But all historians lie about *something*, the pseudo-biographer protests. Lying was brevity and carelessness, because truthful narrative consisted of elaborate detail—what for us the historical novelist supplies.

Our rogue scholar was *perittos*, like Cleidemus and the readers of non-Polybian histories (p. 332 above). He and Seneca both affected to believe that all historians were liars;[85] but it turns out that they were complaining about diametrically opposite things.

---

[83] Cato, *Origines*, HRR F 31 (*inliterati mendacesque sunt* {they are unlettered and liars}); Lact. *Inst.* 5.1.15–18.

[84] *SHA Aurelian* 2.1. Thucydides (1.97.2) makes the same complaint about Hellanicus: brevity and lack of *akribeia* (cf. D. Hal. *A.R.* 7.66.5).

[85] For Seneca, see above, pp. 214–15, 326.

12

True History and False History
in Classical Antiquity*

Emilio Gabba

Like all works of literature, works of history end up sooner or later
with a readership quite different from that envisaged or hoped for by
their authors. A subtle and polemical work such as the *Gallic War* of
Caesar has become a standard text for teaching Latin in the early
years of secondary education, as have the tender and sophisticated
elegies of Tibullus and Propertius. In Italy, the unpopularity of *The
Betrothed* by A. Manzoni, a finely ironical and difficult but rewarding
novel, is the result of the distaste or boredom experienced by children
forced to read it at school.

A similar fate has dogged Thucydides. As T. P. Wiseman has
recently emphasized,[1] Thucydides and Polybius, precisely because
their historical method is close to our own, are regarded as the
paradigms against which to judge ancient historical writing—quite
wrongly. In fact they are untypical and exceptional; and one has
moreover to ask to what extent they were even properly understood
in antiquity. In a famous chapter near the beginning of his work
(1.22.4), Thucydides proudly distances it from that of Herodotus,

---

* This paper was read as a Lady Margaret Lecture at Christ's College, Cambridge
and to Professor Millar's seminar. I should like to thank the Master of Christ's College
and Professor Millar for their invitations, Michael Crawford for the translation and
the audiences on both occasions for their comments. I have added some indispensable annotation. In general, I owe an enormous debt to A. Momigliano and in
particular to the reflections in Momigliano (1972) and (1978).

[1] Wiseman (1979) 149ff. and *passim*.

though without naming him: his own history is not designed for passing appreciation, but is to be of permanent value. Because human nature is always the same, a critical record of past events will present analogies and resemblances when compared with future developments. Knowledge of the past is thus useful, because it improves one's judgement and understanding and even suggests how to behave in situations in which one may find oneself.

Nowadays, we tend to be sceptical of the capacity of history or historical knowledge to teach us anything; but Thucydides, proud of his historical method, shared with many others in antiquity the view that knowledge of historical events was of practical educational value; he also believed, of course, that the narrative of these events should be innocent of any trace of the spectacular, designed to entertain the reader.

It is clear enough that Thucydides, a politician before he was a historian, regarded himself as writing for politicians like himself— men with their roots in the compact and integrated world of the Greek *polis*, within which the whole of their activity belonged: practical, economic, intellectual. The history of Thucydides, like the comedy of Aristophanes, is a product of the civilization of the *polis* of the late fifth century BC and its *raison d'être* disappeared with that civilization. With few exceptions, the methodological lessons of Thucydides were ignored in antiquity, to be picked up only in the modern world. In fact, the *History* of Thucydides is at once a narrative of certain historical events and a critical evaluation of those events. I do not know how many of the politicians of his day were in a position to follow Thucydides through the thickets of his analysis. Even when the work was read and studied with the intention of imitating its literary style and of learning from its moral outlook, the sheer difficulties of understanding were enormous. In the Age of Classicism, Dionysius of Halicarnassus, literary critic and historian, remarks in his treatise on Thucydides that 'the number of those who can understand Thucydides fully is limited, and even these cannot understand some passages without the help of a linguistic commentary' (*Thuc.* 51).

In the end, the struggle for conceptual clarity and the concern for brevity succeeded in making the text of Thucydides obscure. More seriously, the decline and collapse of the political and cultural world of the *polis* in the course of the fourth century finally made it impossible, or almost impossible, to understand the political significance of the work—precisely the aspect to which Thucydides attached most importance. A marvellous piece of committed history writing soon became a simple example of historical narrative, more difficult than earlier or later examples, but not different in kind. Yet in fact their methodologies and aims were quite different.

The *History* of Thucydides became one of a sequence of historical works, on the analogy of the Epic Cycle.[2] For, in order to provide a background for the Peloponnesian War, Thucydides outlined historical developments after the Persian Wars, in the course of which the Hellenic alliance led by Athens emerged as an Athenian empire. Thucydides hardly did this in order to provide a link with the *History* of Herodotus, for which he could have had no sympathy. Nonetheless, Thucydides was considered a continuator of Herodotus, with a change of style and of cultural context. In the same way, fourth century historians like Xenophon and Theopompus and even the author of the so-called *Hellenica* of Oxyrhynchus wrote histories which began where Thucydides broke off. Xenophon was an honest man, but an abyss lay between his historical understanding and that of Thucydides, whose work he set out to edit. Theopompus was an historian whose interests were predominantly cultural and who catered for tastes and interests which were close to those of the Hellenistic world. Put in position in such a sequence, Thucydides became a classic, with all that this implies in terms of use for educational purposes and as a model for the recovery of classical norms, moral as well as literary. Such a use was of course essentially an élite phenomenon, characteristic of conservative circles and not of 'popular' culture. Thucydides became part of a 'canon' of historians, the definition of which is attributed by H. I. Marrou to the School of Pergamum in the second century BC.[3] The problem, for whom a literary 'canon' was designed, in whose interests an author became a classic, involves the whole problem of the diffusion of culture in antiquity. It is enough in this context to say that the intention in creating a 'canon' of historians was to provide a continuous

[2] Canfora (1971a) {= below, Ch. 13).
[3] Marrou (1965) 245 ff., 405–6. Further bibliography in Virgilio (1979) 133 n. 5.

exposition of Greek history, while at the same time providing a sequence of literary models.

The presence of an author in the 'canon' does not mean that he was widely used in schools or read in general, any more than does his presence in a library catalogue; the same argument applies to modern bibliographies, where many authors are more cited than read. In fact there is an example of a library catalogue from antiquity, from the Gymnasium of Tauromenium in the second century BC, where it is clear that the historians listed—Callisthenes, Philistus, Fabius Pictor—are the result of a political choice and provide no evidence for literary taste.[4]

The point that must be emphasized, in any case, is that Thucydides was read in a political sense for a very short period and by very few people, in the latter case as the author himself expected. Thereafter, the work had few readers, as Dionysius remarked, though they seem to have been widely scattered, including some Greeks in Egypt—where, as M. P. Nilsson observed, people seem to have read a bit of everything.[5]

The same fate overtook Polybius, whose *History*, politically committed, grew from a reaction to the Roman acquisition of the hegemony of the Mediterranean in the second century BC. The fate of the work of Polybius has always seemed to me even sadder than that of Thucydides. Polybius set out to analyse, with a historical method and a critical approach close to those of Thucydides, the causes of the Roman rise to power. He dealt with military and political institutions, he described land and sea battles using his own tactical and strategical experience, he was aware to a certain extent of economic factors; he criticized on good methodological grounds contemporary and earlier historians; above all, he understood, despite doubts and uncertainties, the lack of any real legitimation for Roman hegemony. But for whom was he committing to writing all these fundamental points? At the stage of the final redaction of the work, after 146 BC, Carthage had disappeared from the face of the earth; the Hellenistic monarchies had been defeated or destroyed altogether; the *poleis* of classical Greece had been razed to the ground, like Corinth, or deprived of political importance, like Athens. Who was left in the

---

[4] Manganaro (1974).   [5] Nilsson (1955) 96.

Greek world to appreciate the historical and political lessons of Polybius? No one. Polybius himself said that his type of history writing was aimed at specialist readers, hence few readers, while other genres—genealogy, myth, foundations of cities—found greater favour, as being of greater interest and amusement (9.1).

Precisely because committed history writing is in the first instance the result of an urge of the historian himself, he is often aware that he is writing something at odds with the temper of the time. Livy, in his Preface, turned to an idealized past of Rome to find strength to face the tragedy of the present; but he knew that the interest or the curiosity of his contemporaries was directed towards the dramatic events of the Civil Wars (*praef.* 4).

Polybius found a few readers at Rome, his friend Scipio Aemilianus and his friends; then in the first century BC Cicero, whom he greatly influenced. He then served as a source or a model for other historians—Posidonius, Livy, Josephus, Zosimus—but their aims were radically different.

One could multiply examples, but the conclusion would, I think, always be the same. We are always inclined to exaggerate the cultural significance of 'elevated' history writing in antiquity, not only in the cases of Thucydides and Polybius. For we are still influenced by the importance for Western culture of the rediscovery of classical Greek historiography in the fifteenth century, when it was translated into Latin and entered into European consciousness.[6] As a result, we are inclined to suppose that it had a similar influence in antiquity, whether because of the fact of its survival, even if only in part, or because its interests are relatively close to our own and our methods are derived in large measure from it or because it has served (and to a certain extent still serves) as a foundation for our own culture. Classical Greek historiography did have some influence in antiquity, but in very restricted circles (even if these were of some political and historical importance) and in a way which was quite different from that envisaged by the authors themselves.

The fact is that political history, varying in skill and value, but always principally interested in political, constitutional, and military affairs, always co-existed with other forms of history writing, aimed

---

[6] Momigliano (1974).

at a somewhat different public. I have already mentioned Polybius' sharp and proud awareness of his isolated position in relation to more popular and less committed historical genres. But the practice of reading a work in public probably goes back to Herodotus, whose *History* was also characterized by narrative description and was full of interesting facts about strange or unknown places, about customs alien to those of the Greeks. At the end of the fifth century BC, a historian such as the court doctor Ctesias, who worked in and wrote on Persia, had lived outside the traditional political and cultural world of the Greek *polis* and catered for a taste for exotic and fantastic tales. The decline of the *polis* in the course of the fourth century BC meant the end of a culture which was centripetal and *dirigiste*, whose concern was the life and liberty of an exclusive city-state, which absorbed all the energy and interest of its citizens. Already in the second half of the fourth century, the history of Ephorus and Theopompus, who were followed in the next century by Timaeus, although it started from the same point of view as classical Greek historiography, went beyond mere political and military history. It picked up the wider interests of Herodotus, concerned itself with barbarian culture and became universal history.

The widening of geographical and cultural horizons which followed the Asiatic conquests of Alexander produced a profound shift in cultural interest, not least because new levels of society were now involved in political and historical processes; their influence was not only economic and social, but cultural also. And the cultural milieu which resulted was a far cry from the all-embracing culture of the classical *polis*. As a result, even Polybius, despite his methodological debt to Thucydides, has cultural interests which are much wider than those of his model, has a much more 'modern' approach, as E. A. Freeman correctly observed.[7]

In the Hellenistic period, changing cultural interests and the responses thereto of historians meant that historical research lost much of its political element and returned to traditional narrative forms, which had lost ground in the face of a developing historical criticism. The relationship between history and poetry goes back to earliest times and the origin of historical narrative is in a sense unintelligible

---

[7] Freeman (1893) 175ff.

without it; the poetry of Homer was always regarded as an historical text. At the end of the classical period and in the Hellenistic period, the mythical and legendary phases of Greek prehistory and proto-history, with their store of divine and heroic genealogies, which had been eliminated from Thucydides' history or used as evidence for purely human history, recovered a role and function in works of history. History writing turned once more to these elements in the Greek cultural heritage not in order to rationalize them, but in order to make use of anything which could be regarded as plausible or possible.[8] The change must reflect a change in the tastes and interests of readers who belong to levels of society not previously of social or cultural significance.

We are in a world which is far removed from that of Thucydides or even Polybius. But only so can we understand why there now flourished a dramatic approach to history, which sought to involve the emotions of the reader; Polybius found it dangerous and insidious, and resisted it.

It is in this context that the novel develops, with its close links with local history and its proliferation of fantastic and exciting episodes. The subject-matter of the earliest novels was historical or pseudo-historical persons, sometimes national heroes of the distant past, around whom myths and legends had clustered.[9] The novel is thus a lesser form of history writing, which attracts its readers by its emphasis on the fantastic or the erotic, both elements which are present in so-called dramatic history. It has been remarked that the novel is a democratic genre.[10] Rightly, and for two reasons: the protagonist is always a private individual and the genre caters for the taste of levels of society other than the élite of the classical *polis*.

In addition, an enormous paradoxographical literature reflects one of the central concerns of middle-brow culture in the Hellenistic and Roman periods.[11] An awareness of the miraculous and the fantastic were of course already present in Greek epic poetry, in part because the strange and the portentous were regarded as a way of introducing

[8] Wiseman (1979) 143ff.
[9] Plut. *Is. et Osir.* 24 (*Mor.* 360B); Braun (1938).
[10] Perry (1967) 63.
[11] The texts are collected by Giannini (1967); see also id. (1963) and (1964). Ziegler (1949) remains fundamental.

the divine into the world of men. Miracles and portents occur in Herodotus and Ctesias and figure largely in Theopompus, in the context of descriptions of foreign peoples. The scientific interests of Aristotle and Theophrastus necessarily involved the study of freaks and remarkable phenomena in the world of nature.

But it was only later that people took to noting for its own sake anything extraordinary or abnormal and hence interesting in the world of men. The extension of geographical knowledge after Alexander encouraged contact with distant peoples, to whom strange customs could be attributed, and with previously unknown countries, where stories of the most fantastic kind could be located. The result was the emergence of a literature which was specifically and explicitly paradoxographical; in some cases, for instance that of Callimachus, learned research was involved; but the result for the most part was a pseudo-historical literature, popular and escapist.

Its unifying characteristic was its acceptance without question of any available information; the problem of the truth or credibility of the phenomena or facts, which were presented, was simply not raised, since the question of truth was not present in the minds of readers.

The genre of literature which resulted, along with the exotic, the portentous, the abnormal, jumbled up myths, heroic legends, genuine historical and geographical data, scientific information. The result was a fascinating mosaic, which could always be further elaborated. The search for novelty encouraged ever more daring ventures: it was not for nothing that the first century AD mythographer and paradoxographer Ptolemy Chennos called his work 'A New History'.[12] It was even possible to resort to serious works of history in order to excerpt strange and fantastic details.

None of our normal critical yardsticks is appropriate to such literature. Indeed, it already presented a problem to ancient writers on historiography. Its concern was not to distinguish the true from the false or to establish the cause, but to provide lively and highly coloured pictures of milieux and situations, whose historicity was already accepted. Pseudo-historical or paradoxographical narrative was enriched with learned trivia, intended to ensure greater verisimilitude

[12] Tomberg (1968).

and hence win greater acceptance; such trivia also reflected the
ever greater role played by antiquarian learning in education, as
Marrou has pointed out.[13] Antiquarian learning was understood
as covering mythology, genealogical, and heroic legends, geography
and the material necessary for an understanding of Greek poetry.
The 'history as fable' (*historia fabularis*), which diverted the emperor
Tiberius (Suet. *Tib.* 70.3), was linked to this kind of educational
interest. The emperor was at his most serious when he was debating
with his grammarian friends and discussing the name of the mother
of Hecuba.

Sophisticated antiquarian learning and the citation of recondite
sources conveyed to the reader an impression of scholarship, which
was in many cases simply a further element of fantasy. The so-called
Lesser Parallel Lives, handed down among the works of Plutarch, are a
paradoxographical work, which cites sources existing only in the
imagination of the author, along with the material actually presented;[14] the same technique is liberally employed by the author
(or authors) of the *Historia Augusta*. This is the principal factor
which distinguishes the work from the *Lives of the Caesars* of Sueto-
nius, a learned work composed in imitation of precise literary
models.

Writers on historiography in the Hellenistic and Roman periods
found that within the vast field of historical literature they had to
distinguish between true history and 'false' history, the latter constructed out of myths and genealogies, and finally 'history resembling true history', under which they classified comedy and mime.[15]
The problem was further complicated because it was an open question whether history was the province of grammarians or of rhetoricians, a distinction which was important in an educational context.
What is relevant for our present purposes is that the tripartite
division of historical literature reveals that there was in widespread
circulation 'false' history; it must have had many adherents, if the
necessity was felt in the course of a theoretical discussion to explain

---

[13] Marrou (1965) 254; 409.
[14] Jacoby (1940).
[15] Sex. Emp. *Math.* 1.253–5; 258–61 (reproducing arguments of Asclepiades of
Myrleia): Mazzarino (1966) I.486–94; for a different view, Slater (1972). Cf. also *Rhet.
Herenn.* 1.12–16.

the approaches and characteristics of true history and 'false' history. It is also worth remarking that the theory I have outlined went on to assign to true history not only human actions located in time and space, but also the biographies of gods and heroes alongside those of famous men. In other words, divine history was accepted as a narrative of events.

Other texts confirm the extent of the diffusion of 'false' history. In the middle of the second century AD, Lucian gave the title of 'A True History' to a utopian fantasy involving a journey to the moon; he found it necessary to remark ironically in his preface that he was going to tell stories, albeit possessed of verisimilitude and credibility; earlier poets, historians, philosophers, from Homer to Ctesias and Iambulus, had propounded similar falsehoods and been taken seriously.[16] At about the same time, Aulus Gellius, browsing in the bookstalls in the harbour of Brindisi, found works of paradoxography, not works of history (9.4). In the middle of the fourth century AD, the emperor Julian intended to lay down for his new pagan clergy a curriculum of reading of history of real events; by way of contrast he intended to ban the type of history which was full of fantasy and eroticism, what we should call novels.[17]

It is worth pausing to reflect on the scientific dress with which the historical literature I have been discussing often invested itself, specially at the beginning of the Hellenistic period. It is not simply a question of erudite citation of sources, but of the actual content of the narrative, closely concerned with the world of nature, animals, minerals, physics, geography. It seems clear that we have here something which reflects the scientific and technical progress made in the Hellenistic period between the fourth and the second centuries BC. The effect of this progress may be seen in a remarkable flowering of scientific literature covering every field of human knowledge, including ethnography and anthropology. For whatever reason, the advent of Roman rule saw the end of the phenomenon.

The Hellenistic period is an age of contradictions. Initially science and reason co-existed with unreason and the love of the fantastic; in the end, the latter prevailed. In his justly famous book, *The Greeks and the Irrational*, E. R. Dodds posed the problem of the contrast

---

[16] *Ver. Hist.* 1.1–4.   [17] *Epist.* 89.301b–c.

between reason and unreason in the third century BC.[18] His attention was directed above all to philosophical problems and to the decline of traditional religiosity; but an analogous approach is possible in the field of historiography. Elements of unreason are present not only in paradoxography, but also in history. Dodds rightly noted that the great age of Greek rationalism, between the fourth and third centuries, was not a period characterized by the widespread enjoyment of political liberty and that therefore one cannot attribute any check or discouragement to intellectual development to loss of liberty. It is rather a fear of the liberty which did exist in the open society of the Hellenistic period that provoked the irrational urges which we can observe and finally called in Fate as arbiter. It seems to me that this explanation captures important elements of the truth and can be linked to some further reflections. The end of the regime of the *polis* and of its integrated culture favoured the development of the rationalism of the fourth and third centuries. History understood as cultural history, as in the case of Theopompus, presupposes the passing of earlier schemata and an interest in a larger public with wider interests. The social basis of unreason is even wider, new levels of society outside the traditional governing classes. Rationalism and unreason are two aspects of freedom, cultural freedom from the trammels of the *polis*.

The novel, paradoxography, history as fable—all are different ways of dealing with reality, of describing it and explaining it, regarding it as essentially miraculous, but allowing it a scholarly aspect; in other words, they deliberately reject the intellectual methods which had been created to investigate it critically. Similarly with the decline of traditional religiosity; in both cases the move came from levels of society only recently absorbed and in both cases the change had far-reaching implications.

The classical revival of the Augustan period, which aimed to recover the classical aspect of Greek culture and rejected Hellenistic culture *en bloc*, can be regarded as in a certain sense a rationalist revival also; Dionysius of Halicarnassus was quite right to suppose that it was limited to the upper classes.[19] The movement was an important one in terms of the history of culture and influenced the

---

[18] Dodds (1951) 245ff.   [19] *Ant. Orat.* 1.3.1.

ruling class of the Roman Empire down to the fourth century AD, but its impact outside that class was limited. It was Christianity which played the larger role in revitalizing the literary content and form of classical culture.

But at the same time Christianity admitted a substantial romantic and miraculous element into its hagiographical texts, particularly those of a popular nature aimed at a general public.[20] Miracles, of course, were intended to convince simple minds to follow the way of salvation and were an obvious form of propaganda;[21] at the same time, as Marrou has observed, the dimension of the invisible is a prominent motif in late antiquity.[22] But it must also be remarked that the presence of the miraculous in the lives of Saints and in the Acts of the Martyrs provides further confirmation of the taste and the public attracted by this kind of material in pagan times.

After these general reflections, I should like to turn to two specific examples, which show how easy it was to pass from an ostensibly scientific approach to the fantastic and the miraculous and how shifting are the boundaries between high learning and popular forms of historical literature.

*

A typical field for the display of Hellenistic erudition was the writing of works on islands and their settlements. Even the great Callimachus wrote a work of this kind.[23] The reasons for the practice are complex. Basically, an island was always considered as a privileged location for the occurrence of natural phenomena, the emergence of unusual human situations, the development of the exotic and the miraculous. An example of this 'island' literature survives in the fifth book of the *Historical Library* of Diodorus Siculus, a compiler of the age of Caesar, to whom we shall return; the book is entirely composed of histories of islands.

One can distinguish without too much difficulty the various components, or rather levels, of the ancient interest in islands. Observations of natural phenomena had from the beginning provoked

[20] Söder (1932).
[21] Cracco Ruggini (1980) 186 n. 51.
[22] Marrou (1977).
[23] Pfeiffer (1949) I.339 and F 580.

scientific reflection, along with an interest in practical matters of navigation and geography. A logical consequence of this was that large-scale natural phenomena were regarded as factors in human history, not only because they conditioned human behaviour, but also because they were one of the elements which were associated with human behaviour, in curious and significant coincidence. They often marked the beginning of new phases of human existence. These concepts are even present in Thucydides (1.23.3), who noted the concatenation of great natural disasters in the period of the Peloponnesian War and their political effect. Sometimes an earthquake appears as a sign of war (2.8.3; 3.89.2–5).

Polybius, under the influence of Stoic philosophy, noted how great natural disasters, such as floods, epidemics, dearths, can bring about the destruction of the human race and its achievements; this had actually happened in the past; and the result for the survivors was the beginning of a new historical cycle, with the development of civilization and hence of constitutional forms.[24] Plato had already expressed analogous ideas in the *Critias* (109d–110b), involving consideration of the cultural consequences of cataclysms: the few survivors lose their memory of earlier history and remember at the most their names, occupied as they are with the rebuilding of society. Reflection and historical reconstruction occur only later, at a time of repose and contentment, when the necessities of life have been obtained.

Above all, great natural disasters on land and at sea were a reality with which the Greeks had to live. Numerous and elaborate theories in the field of seismology were early elaborated, linked of course to ideas of geography. The two principal theories were the pneumatic and the Neptunic. Aristotle actually regarded the origin of earthquakes as lying in the weather. Popular beliefs linked these strange phenomena with the world of the gods and used them to interpret myths and legends.[25]

Within the field of Hellenistic historiography, historians and antiquarians such as Demetrius of Callatis and Demetrius of Scepsis drew up lists of all earthquakes which had occurred in Greek lands

---

[24] Pol. 6.5.5–6.   [25] Capelle (1924).

and changes which had resulted from volcanic activity.[26] The geographer Strabo, our principal source for Greek geographical science, is careful to note that among the consequences of volcanic activity on land and at sea is the emergence of islands in the sea and the submersion of continents, of which some elements remain as islands. Even Attica was what remained of a submerged continent, according to Plato (*Crit.* 111a–b). In other cases, the separation of portions of land from a continent forms islands; or, on the other hand, islands have become promontories.[27] The Lipari Islands, in particular, lent themselves to accounts of this kind, which often went far beyond what was credible (Str. 5.4.9 = Timaeus, *FGrHist* 566 F 58).

The most remarkable cases of volcanic activity in historical times were the brief emergence in 197 BC of an island in the Aegean Sea between Thera and Therasia (Str. 1.3.17) and in 46 BC of the island Theia (Plin. *HN* 2.202). But the most celebrated cases of all were the supposed emergences of the islands of Delos and Rhodes. The birth of Rhodes was already the theme of some famous verses in the Seventh Olympian Ode of Pindar (7.50ff.).

Simply for scientific reasons, then, an island was something worthy of particular attention. The transition to the field of human history was easy. It was supposed that on an island it was easier to realize a *rapport* between man and nature; and I should like to remind you that Rousseau, in his 'Discours sur l'origine et les fondamens de l'inégalité parmi les hommes',[28] echoing remarks made in antiquity, held that it was precisely on islands, formed as a result of great natural disasters, that languages had been born, as a result of the compulsion on the survivors to create a life in common in a restricted space; the development of human societies followed. I remind you also that Caesar placed the origin of the religion of the Druids in the British Isles, whence it passed to the continent.[29]

Furthermore, in the history of archaic Greece, centred on the Aegean Sea, the islands had had an obvious practical significance: routes across the sea passed by them, and they were, with their

[26] Str. 1.3.17 (Demetrius of Scepsis); 1.3.20 (Demetrius Call. = *FGrHist* 85 F 6).
[27] E.g. Str. 1.3.10, 3.16 ff.; 6.1.6, 6.2.10–11. Strabo adopts the views of Posidonius.
[28] *Oeuvres complètes* III.168–9 (Éd. Pleiade).
[29] Caes. *B.G.* 6.13, 6.11–12.

harbours and springs of fresh water, indispensable stages in any voyage. In a geo-political context, the control of the islands is the fundamental aspect of any thalassocracy, whether it is that of Minos, Agamemnon, or the Athenians, or that of the Etruscans in the west.[30] Plato held that the expansion of the state of Atlantis occurred via the control of the islands of the Mediterranean, from Egypt to Etruria (*Crit.* 114c). The theme became a cliché: in the second century AD, the Alexandrian historian Appian used Roman control over the islands of the Mediterranean to prove the superiority of the Roman Empire over all earlier empires.[31]

In the context of the political history of Athens, her resemblance to an island became an essential characteristic of her imperialism, discussed in connection with the problem of the food supply and the grain trade. Athens was at the centre of the world and at the point where all routes by land and sea met, by reason of her geographical position as isolated as if she were an island. These concepts are to be found expressed with great clarity in the pamphlet on the Constitution of Athens by the so-called Old Oligarch, in the *Critias* of Plato, and by Xenophon in his account of the finances of Athens. For Plato, the island of Atlantis combined self-sufficiency with a position at the centre of the trade routes of the world (*Crit.* 114d–e). Being in the centre of the world and of its climatic structure of course also affected the character of a people and its constitutional arrangements.[32]

As far as islands are concerned, it is worth remembering that the Old Oligarch based an entire argument on the advantage for a *polis* in being an island.[33] It can dominate the sea and at the same time be secure from enemy attack; betrayal is impossible because one would not know to what enemy one could open the gates; civil war was thus impossible. The tragic civil strife on Corcyra of course disproved this line of reasoning; but political and military analysis of the advantages of a *polis* on an island remained important. Such a *polis* is regarded as politically independent and naturally protected, a centre of imperial activity, which can get what it wants from where it wants. On this

---

[30] Thuc. 1.4, 1.7.2, 1.9.3–4, 1.15.1; Diod. 5.13.4.
[31] *Praef.* 16–18.
[32] Xen. *Poroi* 1.6–7.
[33] [Xen]. *Ath. Pol.* 2.14–16.

view, to be an island in the sea was regarded as providing a source of wealth and power and as conducing to correct relations with other states.

Plato, on the other hand, and later Cicero (*Leg.* 4.705a; *Rep.* 2.4, respectively) held the opposite view, that contact with the sea led to moral decline and racial mixture: with foreign goods come foreign ideas, which corrupt and confuse. But even in this context, the sea is still the means of contact; this view is as old as travel by sea and maritime trade, as old as attempts at maritime hegemony.

The view of the sea as a divisive factor is equally old.[34] It has its roots in the primitive idea of water as an element which serves to divide one thing from another, a religious notion which developed into a juridical concept. Implicit in this view is the concept of an island as something apart, untouched by corruption. It was characteristic of Greek historical and geographical thought at all stages to concern itself with ideal races far from our world; to such races, both in the past and in the present, were attributed experiments in approaches to the problems of human existence, of society, of government. It made little difference whether the accounts of such experiments were wholly utopian or had a basis in reality. It is not surprising that strange phenomena, whether natural or human, tended to be located on islands, distant, inaccessible, apart. The island is the characteristic element in paradoxographical literature; in this, human action is linked with the occurrence of natural phenomena; together, they become objects of speculation and subjects of fantasizing narrative. Here again, rational and scientific discourse become embroiled with the fantastic, the novelistic, the strange, the miraculous. To see this, one only has to consider how many of the episodes in the pseudo-Aristotelian essay, *On Marvellous Things Heard*, are set on islands.

Let us look again for a moment at utopias. A utopia can be regarded as the result of the assertion of spontaneity as against reason. Thus nature, which renders up its fruits without the necessity of human labour, allows men to live in a state of nature, without any particular social organization, and makes trade unnecessary. Alternatively, a utopia can be regarded as the result of a social organization

---

[34] Von Scheliha (1931).

perfected by reason, as opposed to the normal world, which is corrupted by contact between communities. An island as home of a utopia is in both cases outside history and anti-historical.

An idealized and fantasized construct of this kind picks up and gives prominence to the idealistic constitutional arrangements propounded by philosophers. Naturally, utopias imagined in various periods reflect the concerns of those periods. The island of Scheria in the *Odyssey*, with its peaceful and well-ordered government, can be regarded as the first Greek utopia: 'We live isolated in the stormy sea; no mortal is in contact with us' (*Od.* 6.204ff.). It is significant that the generous welcome accorded to the shipwrecked Odysseus brought misfortune to the Phaeacians. The Platonic myth of Atlantis projects into a distant past a model derived from historical Greek and Athenian society, with some admixture of Persian and oriental elements.[35] Attempts to locate the island, supposed to have disappeared in a cataclysm along with the early *polis* of Athens, are one example of the close links between myth and scientific thought in the Hellenistic period.

That period, indeed, saw a proliferation of utopias, in which primitivist longings, already present in fourth century history writing, are combined with philosophical theories and egalitarian leanings.[36] It seems reasonable to argue that they arise in response to social crises of the period; and they offer an account of a Golden Age, located on distant islands, dressed up to suit contemporary taste.

At the beginning of the third century BC, Euhemerus located on the island of Panchaia in the Indian Ocean a society which was highly structured into three classes and under the control of priests.[37] There may be some reference to contemporary Egyptian society; but it is more important to observe that the island is self-sufficient and that there is no private property. Elements of reality are furnished by the fact that the inhabitants were in part Cretan by origin, a fact allegedly demonstrated by an inscription recording the story of Ouranos and Zeus.

---

[35] Vidal-Naquet (1964).
[36] Mossé (1969); Ferguson (1975) 73ff., 104ff., 122ff.; Bertelli (1977).
[37] Diod. 6.1 (*FGrHist* 63 F 2), 6.41–6 (*FGrHist* 63 F 3). Braunert (1965).

The utopia of Iambulus belongs to the middle of the third century BC; it is localized on the round island of the Sun, on the equator and one of an archipelago of seven. Full of scientific allusions, the utopia insists on life in a state of nature and on the importance of education; the organization of society and the distribution of land are based on egalitarian principles. In consequence, life on the island is one of bliss, surrounded by strange and symbolic animals. The inhabitants of the island are completely isolated from the rest of the world, but welcome strangers, only driving them away if they turn out to be incapable of reaching their own level of perfection.[38]

Perhaps in the middle of the second century BC, Dionysius Skytobrachion, following in the traces of Plato and Euhemerus, described in the course of a mythographical and romantic work two utopias—one in the west, an island called Hesperia in the lake of Tritonis, beyond the Columns of Hercules, inhabited and ruled by the Amazons; the other Nysa, a city on an island in a river, where Dionysus was supposed to have been brought up.[39]

In works of this kind, it is not only that the highly coloured narrative catered to the tastes and cultural interests of readers; the construction of ideal societies was a response to ambitions of the same readers, although it remains uncertain whether it was the utopia of Iambulus which provided ideological backing for the insurrection of Aristonicus, at Pergamum in 132 BC.[40]

All these Hellenistic utopian narratives, embellished with the highlights and purple patches of paradoxography, were regarded as historical texts. Euhemerus, Iambulus, and Dionysius Skytobrachion are all known to us because their works were used in the *Historical Library* of Diodorus Siculus. This work further included a utopian account of the Hyperboreans who lived on a large island off Gaul, as compiled by Hecataeus of Abdera at the end of the fourth century BC.[41] It is precisely works of this kind to which Lucian referred when he criticized the extravagant fantasies which were regarded as 'true history'.

---

[38] Diod. 2.55–60.
[39] Diod. 3.53.4–6 (*FGrHist* 32 F 7); 3.68.5–69.4 (*FGrHist* 32 F 8).
[40] For a discussion, see Bömer (1961) 396–415.
[41] Diod. 2.47 (*FGrHist* 264 F 7); cf. Ael. *NA* 2.1 (*FGrHist* 264 F 12).

The inclusion of utopias as if they were real societies by Diodorus, in the middle of the first century BC, is significant. Wholly detached from the real world, these utopias were just as plausible and possible for the vast majority of their readers, who read novels as if they were history and who longed to escape from the present to an egalitarian dreamworld. Diodorus is right to insist on the fact that such narratives deserve to be called history (5.41.4, 5.42.4).

Accounts of island utopias in Diodorus stand side by side with social and political observations on some of the historical islands described in Book 5.[42] Thus, once upon a time, a communist regime existed on the Lipari Islands (5.9–10); the inhabitants of Corsica are praised for their civilization and humanity (5.14), the Sardinians for their love of liberty; the inhabitants of the Balearic islands for their rejection of gold and silver in order not to be corrupted and for their peculiar marriage rites (5.17–18).

Through Ennius, the philosophy and political outlook of Euhemerus had penetrated Roman society. It is not surprising, then, that a learned senator of the period before Sulla, Manilius (?), the author of the first Roman work of paradoxography, managed to speak quite seriously of the city of the Sun on the island of Panchaia and of Phoenice in Araby.[43] I should like to remind you in this context of another famous Roman politician, who was the author of a substantial work of antiquarian curiosity with a scientific bent, probably called *Admiranda*. The man is C. Licinius Mucianus, thrice consul, who acted as king-maker for Vespasian.[44]

Returning to the first century BC, the Roman general Sertorius, a younger contemporary of the senator who wrote on paradoxography, apparently hoped to escape from the tyranny of his enemies and from the horrors of civil war by fleeing to the Isles of the Blest, beyond the Columns of Hercules. Some sailors had actually described them to him, with their gentle and healthy climate and their luxuriant growth of edible fruits.[45] The desperate desire to escape from the tragic reality of the present and to recover a Golden Age recurs in Horace's

---

[42] Von Pohlmann (1925) I.36ff.
[43] Plin. *HN* 10.4; Mommsen (1861) 72–6.
[44] Peter, *HRR* II.cxxx–cxxxii, 101–17; Kappelmacher (1926) 440–5.
[45] Plut. *Sert.* 8.2–5, 9.1.

famous Sixteenth Epode: written in the spring of 38 BC, during the wars of the age of revolution, it comes only shortly after the Fourth Eclogue of Virgil, which belongs to 40 BC and is likewise dominated by longing to return to a Golden Age.[46]

Escapism in the face of civil war may have replaced the egalitarian aspirations of the Hellenistic utopias, which Diodorus was including in his work as Virgil and Horace were writing; but we are evidently in the same spiritual and cultural milieu.

The idealization of human societies, perfect in their internal organization and their relationship with nature, was not limited to the construction of utopias. During the reign of Claudius, an embassy came to Rome from the King of Ceylon, where a Roman had by chance arrived.[47] Pliny, who records the event (*HN* 6.84–91), was probably a witness. The forms of a utopia are presented anchored to a historical reality, which is distant, but nonetheless concrete; into the historical account there are insinuated implausible notices on the longevity of the inhabitants. The absence of slavery goes along—alas—with the fact that even in Ceylon gold and silver are valued, despite their being contrary to nature; and there are riches in the form of jewels and marbles. But there are no lawsuits and hence justice reigns without the presence of judicial organization. Some scholars have supposed that the elective nature of the monarchy and the absence of dynastic continuity feature in intentional opposition to the Roman Empire. But it is more likely that the whole portrayal of the island and its society, featuring prominently the exotic and the isolated, is in opposition to Roman society. It is easy to think of other examples of peoples more directly in contact with the Roman Empire whose portrayal serves to highlight in a negative and hostile sense the Roman world; Germany as described by Tacitus is a case in point.

I should like to turn now to my second example. The materials of which paradoxographies were composed derive for the most part from local histories. The principal aim of these was to note and record the peculiarities and characteristic features of particular places and individuals. The origin of much of the content of Greek novels has been rightly seen as lying in the raw material of local history. In the light of what I have said, it is readily intelligible that the

---

[46] Fraenkel (1957) 52ff.   [47] Starr (1956).

Hellenistic period saw an enormous development of local history. This observation on the development of local history leads one to consider another type of historical literature, which serves to demonstrate once again just how vague the boundaries were between the erudition which was real and was the preserve of a cultivated élite, and a popular version, full of legendary material.

Much Greek (and to a lesser extent Roman) historical tradition was always tied to cults and places of cult. Transmission of knowledge in such cases was ensured by priests and temple attendants, in the Greco-Roman world as well as in the east. It has long been observed that the priests cited by Herodotus as his informants for anecdotes and other material on Egyptian history were more likely temple attendants or temple guides—one thinks of the guide who translated for Herodotus a hieroglyphic inscription; the translation had, however, clearly been invented (2.125). Temple traditions in Egypt are related to statues, monuments, inscriptions, cult places in general, ritual. Historical information as such tends to be anecdotal and often scandalous, particularly if it refers to the private life of the kings. Priests, who give the appearance of being learned, in fact retail fables, oddities, and portents. Sacerdotal tradition in fact is really popularizing, and its market is popular.

From the little we know of the Greeks who wrote on religious matters, the situation was not different in Greece.[48] Originally, sacred literature must have had a practical function and a limited circulation: information on ceremonies and rites was collected in order to be handed on within the priestly circle; archives of often secret documents were created. Later, such archives acquired a literary form: accounts of religious law were published; the historical origin of rituals and ceremonies, oblations and mysteries, was expounded; professional exegetes produced works with a religious content. In the Hellenistic period, the tendency to publish arcane knowledge became stronger and the resulting literature often had a paradoxographical character. There was a growing interest in local cults; specialized works were compiled on cults, temples, rituals, including any relevant legends or myths. Local patriotism fostered rivalry between

---

[48] Tresp (1914).

cities—their mysteries, their oracles, the names of their gods all forming subjects for monographs.

In all this, along with temple archives, inscriptions, monuments, statues, literary texts were all used as sources. The material collected was used heavily by the Alexandrian poets and then by the compilers of guidebooks. The greatest guidebook writer of the Hellenistic age, Polemon of Ilion, wrote dozens of books of this kind, on Greek cities, Italian cities, Sicilian cities, and on Carthage. We can form some idea of the form and content of his work from the guidebook of Pausanias, who in the second century AD wrote a guidebook to Greece:[49] we are accustomed to read it as a text-book on ancient art history, but it is in fact a guidebook for tourists.

In works of this kind, obscure learning, the interpretation of an inscription or the minute description of a monument, co-exists with records of miracles and portents, with legends and myths. Pausanias often refers to local expounders of sacred lore, usually to local histories or accounts of particular monuments, but sometimes to temple attendants and to guide-books deliberately prepared for visitors.[50]

This kind of literature, directly linked with temples, priests and temple-attendants, seems not to have existed in the Roman world. The reason is presumably the lack of any kind of separate priestly class and the different role of the temple in the civic structure of the Roman world. Nonetheless, attendants will certainly have provided information to visitors, factual and legendary. The attendant of the Temple of Tellus at Rome, who was the host to Varro and his friends during the dialogue which forms the *de Re Rustica*, was no doubt a person of education.[51]

Already in the Republican period, there were guidebooks of Rome, not to mention the descriptions of Rome and her monuments contained in the works of Varro. It was J. Heurgon who identified the Cincius cited by Livy, for the custom of marking the passage of the year by hammering a nail into the wall of the Capitoline temple, with the author of a guidebook of Rome, or at least of the Capitol, called

---

Pasquali (1913).
[50] E.g., 1.41.2 and 5.10.7. Cf. Reinach (1892) 885–6.
[51] *De re rust.* 1.2.1, 2.12, 2.69.2–3.

Mystagogica.[52] Cincius, like Polemon, explained the meaning of inscriptions and probably compared them with analogous Etruscan examples. He will also no doubt have described ancient monuments and retailed legends and anecdotes relating to them. It also looks as if some kind of description of the monuments to be seen along the Tiber has been used for the dictionary of the Augustan scholar Verrius Flaccus, whose work survives in that of Festus.[53]

It is more to the point to observe how material of this kind infiltrated into history proper. In the first two books of Livy, legendary or historical events are in a certain sense validated by reference to monuments, in particular statues, still visible in the time of Livy or his sources.[54] Such references were intended to guarantee the historicity or at least the credibility of the legend or event in question. The problem is instructive from a methodological point of view. It seems clear that monuments, statues, toponyms, whose significance was for various reasons unclear, were at first invested with fantastic meanings of different kinds, but always related to legendary episodes or episodes of earliest Roman history; this took place in the context of an antiquarian and guidebook tradition aiming to explain and expound the monuments involved. In a complete reversal of roles, the monuments then became the documents which guaranteed the historicity or credibility of the legends or stories which had grown up.

Even better examples of this kind of literary product, a mixture of antiquarianism and the legendary or miraculous, may be found in the guidebooks to Rome of the Christian period.[55] The guidebooks were mostly for pilgrims and, then as now, were regularly altered and up-dated. They constitute an entire literary genre of substantial proportions.[56] In principle, the Christian pilgrim took the guidebooks with him as he visited the great basilicas and the places sanctified by the blood of the martyrs. But as time went on, things changed and

[52] Liv. 7.3.5–7: Heurgon (1964a).
[53] Bona (1964) 125.
[54] E.g., 1.25.14, 1.26.13–15, 1.36.5, 1.48.6–7, 2.10.12, 2.13.5, 2.13.11, 2.14.9, 2.40.12, 2.41.10–11.
[55] The principal texts are in Valentini and Zuchetti (1940–53) II–III, III.93ff. contains the earliest edition of the *Mirabilia*.
[56] For the development of this literature in the sixteenth and seventeenth centuries: Hay (1977) 135.

interest in earlier pagan monuments grew. The best-known and most widely used of these texts was the *Mirabilia Vrbis Romae*, of which a number of editions are known. The original text probably goes back to the middle of the twelfth century, but it is based on a complex series of earlier sources and pagan models.[57] Accounts of episodes in pagan history, attached to Christian monuments, are clear evidence of admiration for antiquity, even if pagan Rome derives its *raison d'être* from the new Christian Rome. There is a powerful feeling of continuity: pagan historical tradition is invoked, naturally in a much altered form, to explain monuments, statues, tombs. Events of Roman history make their appearance. Monuments and buildings attributed to Octavianus Augustus have a special place. It seems clear that behind the work lies an unbroken tradition of local history and of topographical guide-books. Here again, we find the combination of antiquarian tone with mythological content.

Outside Rome, also, there was a local literature, dealing with churches or monasteries and their traditions or with the famous tombs of saints or kings. This literature again combined accounts of real events and people with stories of miracles which had taken place at the sites in question. We are still in the middle of an essentially pagan tradition.

If local literature of this kind is subsumed into mainstream history, the miraculous becomes an essential element of the historical narrative. There is, I think, no better example than the *Ecclesiastical History of the English People* of the Venerable Bede. It is explicitly based on native chronicles of churches and monasteries and on lives of saints. There has been much discussion of the role of the miraculous in the work of Bede;[58] but in my view it is to be explained in terms of the Greek and Roman cultural traditions which I have attempted to characterize. It is not a question of historical method or of the credulity of Bede. Traditional models explain the function which this element had in his narrative: it attested to a genuine faith, linked to places of cult and to the tombs of saints; and it showed the diffusion of belief among the people, as evidenced by hundreds of

---

[57] Schramm (1929) II.45–6, 105–11; Valentini–Zucchetti (1940–53) III.3ff.; Weisthanner (1954).

[58] Rosenthal (1975); Ward (1976); Colgrave (1979) xxxiv–xxxvi.

works of local history and spiritual edification. It was in fact Bede's duty to record this material, as it had been recorded by the works which were his models. All he is doing is to transfer it from its local setting and include it within the general historical and religious patrimony of his people and bring it to the attention of a much larger public. Its function in support of belief is the same. It was certainly not Bede's duty to subject the material to an analysis such as Thucydides would have undertaken, and nor should we use on Bede critical approaches which are irrelevant to his work.

Part III

History and Poetry

13

The Historical 'Cycle'

Luciano Canfora
English translation by Gail Trimble

In a famous passage of the *Poetics*, Aristotle denies that the only difference between poetry and history consists in the metrical form which is typical of one but not of the other. 'Even if we were to put Herodotus into verse', he adds, 'it would nevertheless remain a work of history' (1451b1–4). The opinion that Aristotle argues against would appear to be that which Strabo, for example, sets out in very general form at the beginning of his work: prose, he says, is nothing other than the imitation of poetry, and the first prose writers (he cites Hecataeus, among others) 'abandoned the metre of poetry but preserved the rest' (1.2.6). Both Aristotle and Strabo seem to refer above all to epic; both of them have before them the image of an historical work as epic without metrical form.

I

1. 'They abandoned the metrical form but preserved the rest.' And before anything else they kept the cornerstone of the epic form, the thing that seemed to Plato one of its more reprehensible characteristics: the constant alternation between narration and characters' speeches (*Rep.* 393–4). Plato criticizes Homer because, by making his characters speak in direct discourse, 'he aims to make us believe that it is not he who is speaking, but Chryses' (the example which he

is considering is Book I of the *Iliad*), while, on the other hand, it is always he who narrates, 'both when he reports the speeches (*tas rheseis*) and when he reports the events between one speech and another (*ta metaxu rheseôn*)' (393b). Moreover, Plato continues, in composing the speeches, Homer adapts 'his own style to that of those whose speeches he from time to time introduces', and it is exactly this which is one of the 'mimetic' aspects of epic that Plato deprecates (393c). Plato immediately tries his hand at rewriting ('without metre') the Chryses episode, replacing the direct speech with an equal amount of paraphrase (393e–4a). It is a pointless and monstrous attempt, since the archaic mentality puts word and action on the same level and perceives speech as a form of action.[1]

Thucydides, therefore, in his famous 'methodological' chapter, divides the material he has to deal with into ὅσα μέν λόγῳ εἶπον ἕκαστοι {as many things as each said in speech} and τὰ δὲ ἔργα τῶν πραχθέντων {the deeds of the things done}, 1.22.1–2). If one does not clearly understand that for Thucydides, as for Homer, *logoi* and *erga* are, on the same level, *ta prachthenta* {the things done}, the second of these two expressions can especially appear somewhat obscure. And in fact the most varied translations of that expression have been proposed: 'what really happened, not just what was said to have happened';[2] 'the reality of events';[3] 'the sum total of the actions';[4] 'for reasons of symmetry he expresses himself pleonastically'[5] is Haacke's and Poppo's explanation. K. W. Krüger imagined a distinction between *erga* = the events of the war and *ta prachthenta* = 'not only the events of the war, but also—and particularly—the political debates and the diplomatic negotiations; and even [!] the speeches, in so far as they are the instrument of these negotiations.'[6] Stahl found

---

[1] Cf. e.g. Pagliaro (1953) 143–4, who refers to *Il.* 11.703 ('the old man, angry about such actions and words', in a context in which there is no sign of any words).

[2] *id quod vere factum est, non tantum dicitur factum esse* (Goeller (1836) 118, referring to Hermann on Soph. *Trach.* 229).

[3] Reisig (1823) CXCIII: 'die Wirklichkeit des Herganges'; Classen–Steup (1892–1922) I.407–8.

[4] Bernhardy (1829) 54: 'die Thatensumme'.

[5] Haacke (1831) 12: 'concinnitatis causa [with reference to λόγῳ εἶπον] pleonastice dixit'.

[6] Krüger (1851) 215: 'nicht bloß die Kriegstaten sondern namentlich auch politische und diplomatische Verhandlungen; ja selbst [!] die Reden insofern sie die Organe derselben sind.'

Krüger's proposal unfounded but conceded, 'even the speeches, in so far as they related to the deeds that were to be done, were in a certain way part of the action'.[7] Lobeck referred to Antiphon, *Tetralogy* 2.4.10 ἡ πρᾶξις τῶν ἔργων {the accomplishment of the action}, 'which is to say, τὰ ἔργα τὰ πραχθέντα {the deeds that were done}' (Lobeck (1838) 526), but the passage should be understood ἡ πρᾶξις τῶν ἔργων *sc.* αἰτία ἐγένετο {the accomplishment of the action … was responsible}; cf. the *Index Antiphonteus* of Van Cleef. Unique is Wilhelm Schmid: 'the Thucydidean division of ἔργα {deeds} into λεχθέντα {things spoken} and πραχθέντα {things done}.[8]

Thucydides adopts such a difficult and almost untranslatable combination of words because he is reflecting a tradition for which it is obvious that every action consists, like the Homeric poems in Plato's analysis, of *rheseis* and *ta metaxu rheseôn*. And in fact Polybius understood the Thucydidean passage in this way when, echoing it, he divided τὸ γεγονός {what has happened} into τὸ πραχθὲν ἢ ῥηθέν {what was done or said} (12.25b.1–2). Naturally the Thucydidean terminology is not rigorous (in 1.23.1 ἔργα = τὰ πραχθέντα), nor does it seem to coincide with the Herodotean one (ἔργα = 'Bauwerken' {buildings} in the Herodotean proem: cf. Jacoby (1913) 333–4). In short, it does not reflect a technical vocabulary: Polybius too expresses the same thought in other terms.

The Thucydidean formula for referring to the speeches (ὅσα λόγῳ εἶπον ἕκαστοι) has also caused embarrassment. Solutions have been various: from Reiske ('in fact said')[9] to Classen–Steup ('λόγῳ is used here of a more extended speech'[10]) to Bothe, who proposed ὅσα λόγων (= ὅσους λόγους) {as many things of speech (= as many speeches)}. All these arise out of difficulty with the tautological λόγῳ. But if one considers that, according to the epic (and general archaic) conception, every action is realized in 'actions and words' (*Il.* 11.703), even when there is no sign of words in the context, the

---

[7] Poppo–Stahl (1875–83) 115: *etiam orationes, cum ad res agendas pertinerent, rerum actarum quodammodo partes erant.*

[8] Schmid–Stählin (1929–48) II.587 n. 2: 'Th.' (1.22) Teilung der ἔργα in λεχθέντα und πραχθέντα'.

[9] *reapse dixerunt*: in his commentary on D. Hal. *Thuc.* 20.5–6, where the Thucydidean chapter is transcribed in full.

[10] Classen–Steup (1892–1922) I.75: 'λόγῳ ist hier von längerer Rede gesagt'.

apparent tautology will not seem awkward (Krüger well comments: 'what they said in speeches').[11] And it is no coincidence that, throughout this chapter, Thucydides describes how he has reported the thoughts of his characters approximately as, according to Plato, Homer did with his ('as it was suitable for each one to have spoken on various occasions'; cf. *Rep.* 393c).[12]

Ancient critics already found a contradiction between the Thucydidean aim for rigorous truthfulness and the evidently fictional character of many of the speeches which he attributes to his characters (D. Hal. *Thuc.* 41 [I.395.11–22 UR], referring to the dialogue between the Melians and the Athenians). On the other hand, Thucydides himself recognized immediately that he obviously did not have the ability to reflect 'the exact words', even if he assures us that he will keep 'as much as possible to the general concept' (1.22.1).[13]

It is therefore allowable to ask why, although conscious of this inevitable 'imprecision', he has nevertheless constantly introduced direct speeches of the characters themselves, without contenting himself with paraphrasing the 'general concept', of whose truthfulness he assures us. Evidently this second solution was not even conceivable: the schema was that of epic narration, as had already been the case for Herodotus, and Thucydides conformed to it. But he is in a hurry to make clear that the speeches which he reports *are not truthful,* and so he ostentatiously introduces every speech with the formula τοιάδε (*not* τάδε!) ἔλεξεν {he spoke some such things (*not* the following things)} *uel sim.* to reaffirm the approximation, the *non-truthfulness* of the speeches he reports. Herodotus, on the other hand, like Homer, reports the speeches as if they were 'the very

---

[11] Krüger (1823) 121: 'quae orationibus habitis dixerunt'. Naturally there is little use in signalling the *concinnitas* between λόγῳ εἶπον and ἔργα τῶν πραχθέντων without pointing out the apparent tautology of both expressions.

[12] For Thucydides a clarification of this kind is much more appropriate, inasmuch as his is contemporary history.

[13] The first speech of Pericles (1.140–4) seems to reflect authentic thoughts. This has been observed by, e.g., Kalinka ((1913) 233) in his commentary on the pseudo-Xenophontine *Athenian Constitution*, where he points out precise agreement between Thuc. 1.143.5 and *Ath. Pol.* 2.14–16. Aristophanes attributes this same thought to Aeschylus when he is asked for good advice for the city (*Frogs* 1463–5). Thucydides confirms at 2.65.7 that what Pericles expresses in 1.144.1 is Pericles' own thought.

words' (Gomme (1954) 142) of the protagonists: 'said this' or simply 'said'.[14] There is therefore a rule, the epic one, however unwelcome it is to Plato. Thucydides does not think of departing from it, even if he is constrained, in 1.22 and then each time a speech appears, to reassert the fictitious character of the speeches of his historical actors.

This constituted a decisive literary precedent for successive Greek and Roman (and Byzantine and humanistic) historiography, through the canonical position which Thucydides' work had already assumed in the fourth century. In accordance with it even Polybius, though he certainly lacked any enthusiasm for the practice, saw himself as constrained to introduce direct speeches every so often, sometimes even long ones (e.g., 9.28–39).[15] It was the historiographical 'genre' that by this time imposed this. The exception that proves the rule is that *commentarii* escape this norm, as they do others (although from antiquity we have only the Caesarian commentaries and perhaps in a certain sense also the *Monumentum Ancyranum*); these are in fact understood not as historical works but as 'material for a historical work', ὕλη ἱστορίας (Nicephorus Bryennius, *Patrologia Graeca* 127, p. 37 D). Cicero says this of Caesar ('He wanted other people, such as might intend to write a history, to have material at their disposal').[16]

It is unlikely that the authors of the *Genealogies* (Hecataeus, for example) had already assumed this narrative scheme from epic. The later tradition is decisive on this topic (Marcell. *Vit. Thuc.* 38):

The historians before him [Thucydides] composed works which were, so to speak, soulless and made up only of narration; to their characters (*prosopois*) they did not attribute speeches, nor did they compose political speeches (*dêmêgorias*). Herodotus did attempt this, but without great capacity; his speeches are short, more a characterization of the personages than true political speeches. Only Thucydides devised and composed them excellently, etc.

Here Marcellinus' tone—it is, as usual, polemically directed against the opposite stance of Dionysius of Halicarnassus—is pro-Thucydidean

---

[14] Thucydides' caution is not usual in Xenophon (cf. *Hell.* 2.3.35 but also 3.5.7); it is so, however, in Polybius (9.31.7, 9.32.1, etc.). Later the prudent τοιάδε/τοιαῦτα {such things} is perhaps only a traditional formula.
[15] Ziegler (1952) 1524–7.
[16] *Brut.* 262: *uoluit alios habere parata unde sumerent qui uellent scribere historiam.*

and anti-Herodotean; this explains the restrictive[17] way in which the comparison with Herodotus is made.

All the same, the attestation is explicit: the use of direct speeches 'for characterization of personages' (as in epic, according to Plato) is a Herodotean innovation. The preceding generation (Hecataeus; the *Genealogies*) gave uniform and 'soulless' narration. That Herodotean innovation was for Thucydides already the tradition, to which he obviously had to submit (1.22.1).[18]

2. This being the case, *for whom* was Thucydides writing? One answer seems to be suggested by Thucydides himself, already in 1.22: ἐς μὲν ἀκρόασιν ἴσως τὸ μὴ μυθῶδες ... ἀτερπέστερον φανεῖται ... κτῆμά τε ἐς αἰεὶ ἢ ἀγώνισμα ἐς τὸ παραχρῆμα ἀκούειν ξύγκειται {in the hearing perhaps the lack of a mythical element ... will appear less pleasurable ... it has been set up as a possession for all time rather than as a display-piece to be heard for the moment}. Both these well-known declarations seem to signify that Thucydides

---

[17] Unjustly restrictive: he ignores very long speeches such as 5.92.

[18] On opposing speeches in Herodotus' work see Jacoby (1913) 494 (esp. lines 28ff.). Paired speeches in Homer: Lohmann (1970) 231–76. Even Polybius resigns himself to adopting this stylistic method (cf. Ziegler (1952) 1526.49–54). The opportunity for an analysis of the speeches in Herodotus' work was pointed out by Jacoby (1913) 429.39. The higher standard, on the oratorical level, of the Thucydidean speeches is obviously connected to political and cultural factors (the sophistic movement, etc.): cf., in general, Deffner (1933). The Thucydidean superiority in this field is even recognized by the anti-Thucydidean Dionysius (*Thuc.* 23 [I.360.22–4 UR]). So opinions like those of a Cratippus—according to whom Thucydides would have done well to decide to stop having his characters speak directly because their political speeches turned out to be difficult for the public (D. Hal. *Thuc.* 16)— appeared more than ever to be the grotesque speculations of a later age. In the Thucydidean age, it could occur to no historian to break what was a canon, even a pillar, of the *forma storiografica*. In reality, as Schwartz, Meyer and Jacoby first observed, Cratippus' opinion was an 'autoschediasma' {ill-advised remark} based on the condition of the text in the actual eighth book of Thucydides. (If Cratippus had really been a 'contemporary' of Thucydides, he would have noted that political speeches are entirely lacking in the eighteenth year of the war also.) Nevertheless, Cratippus has found some adherents every so often: most recently Pédech (1970). This is on the grounds that according to Dionysius he was a 'contemporary' of Thucydides (συνακμάσας αὐτῷ): but would this term not signify that, in his work, the good Cratippus 'competed' with Thucydides? (Cf. Pol. 16.28.1 and the related explanation in Dimitrakou (1936–51) VIII.6863). And in fact the only fragment of Cratippus is a fatuous alternative version of the Thucydidean account of the mutilation of the Herms; and perhaps the work of Cratippus was a collection of similar Thucydidean 'omissions' (cf. Canfora (1970) 206).

does not entirely exclude *akroaseis* {recitals} even of his own work. He says φανεῖται {will appear} and not, for example, φανείην ἄν {would appear} or the like;[19] that μᾶλλον...ἤ {rather...than} then indicates here the 'complete negation of the second member' (Classen–Steup) cannot be definitely affirmed, since 'this is not the case in other places'.[20] That is not all. These two phrases also testify that *akroasis* is, for Thucydides, the natural destination of a historical work, and that normally a historical work is something that matters less to Thucydides: a piece destined for public and agonistic reading, ἀγώνισμα ἐς τὸ παραχρῆμα ἀκούειν, 'a display piece, so called because through such one enters into competition with other performers'.[21] And it is not clear why Thucydides could have conceived of, for his own work, a destination different from this usual one.

Certainly, he did not cherish the illusion of obtaining an easy and immediate success. Not even Euripides, so little favoured by the Athenian public, would have cultivated such an illusion, yet he was regularly represented in dramatic competitions. It is true that a passage such as 1.22.4 could not have been designed for an *akroasis*. But it could be a testimony, appropriate for the harsh and 'arrogant' tone (as Dionysius defines it, *Comp. uerb.* 22), for a succession of *akroaseis* that have already taken place.[22] So much the more so when we are very probably dealing with one of the latest passages, as is clear

[19] Haacke translates correctly: *Ac fortasse, quod fabulis caret haec scriptio mea, audientibus minus voluptatis praebebit* (and perhaps, since this work of mine lacks a story-telling element, it will be found less pleasing to its hearers). On the other hand, the force of the future gets a little lost in this paraphrase by Jacoby ((1926) 17 = (1956) 88): 'Mein Werk mag ja vielleicht beim festlichen Vortrag [...] weniger ergötzlich wirken' (indeed my work might perhaps... in a ceremonial recitation be less pleasurable).

[20] Classen–Steup I.206. One can see, in fact, how Lucian (*h.c.* 42) paraphrases the passage.

[21] Krüger (1860) ad loc; cf. Classen–Steup ad loc.: 'any performance in an *agôn*'. Lucian paraphrases correctly: ἐς τὸ παρὸν ἀγώνισμα (the translation of Homeyer (1965) 149 is incorrect; and so does Quintilian: *opus non ad actum rei pugnamque praesentem sed ad memoriam posteritatis... componitur* {the work is composed not for practical effect and the present contest but for the memory of posterity}' (10.1.31). The Thucydidean expression implies reading of an agonistic nature. The scholiasts appropriately refer to 'the poetic contests of the comedians or tragedians' (p. 25 Hude).

[22] A piece such as the Melian Dialogue is evidently destined for a dramatic *akroasis*; on the dramatic presentation of the dialogue and on its placement within its actual context, see Canfora (1971b) 410, 424.

from, among other things, the logical break that occurs between 1.21.2 and 1.23.1 (Krüger (1846) ad loc. noted this).

The inadequacy for public readings (*panêgyris*) of a work like that of Thucydides was due, according to Dionysius, to a style that was in no way 'popular', but on the contrary 'archaic and arrogant'; and he adds: 'Thucydides himself recognized that his writing is ill suited to an *akroasis, κτῆμα δ'εἰσαιεὶ μᾶλλον ἢ ἀγώνισμα (ἐστίν)* {[it is] a possession for all time rather than a display-piece}' (D. Hal. *Comp. uerb.* 22 [II.108.5–12 UR]). This is a style in the aristocratic (one might say 'Heraclitean') tradition, which does not aim at popularization among the masses 'deceived by *μῦθοι δεδαιδαλμένοι ψεύδεσι ποικίλοις* {stories embellished with elaborate lies}' (Pind. *Olymp.* 1.28–30).[23]

This failure was probably 'discounted' by the author, since he was assured of written survival by the efforts of a younger element of his circle (Xenophon), 'a cultured, intelligent young man, coming from the aristocratic atmosphere very favourable to Sparta, to which Thucydides also belonged'.[24] (Heraclitus had deposited his difficult book in the temple of Artemis: Diog. Laert. 9.6). This is a better explanation of the well-known declaration, which Dionysius already found 'arrogant', by which Thucydides defines his own work as a *κτῆμα ἐς αἰεί*. The author's retreat in favour of a restricted (socially homogeneous with himself) circle of readers, including future readers, is already clear from the immediately preceding phrase, where he declares that he will be satisfied if he continues to be read by politicians 'who wish to know with clarity the events of the past, which will be repeated in the same or similar ways, given human nature'. The renunciation of a wider public can be noted in the words *ἀρκούντως ἕξει* ('it will be enough for me').

3. On the other hand, the Thucydidean testimony on the oral dissemination of historical works is in agreement with internal evidence provided by Herodotus' work.

There is a famous example. Before narrating the debate 'on constitutions', which is supposed to have taken place at the Persian court

---

[23] The pairing of this passage with Thucydides 1.22.4 is that of Ernst Friedrich Poppo, in his *editio maior* of Thucydides (Poppo (1831) 187). The disdainful taunts about the 'ignorance' and incoherence of the 'mass of Athenians' are also part of this 'arrogance', and are evidently not meant for *akroaseis*.

[24] Delebecque (1957) 53.

on the occasion of the political crisis preceding the accession of Darius, Herodotus informs us that 'to some Greeks' it seemed incredible that such a debate could actually have taken place (3.80.1); but he insists: 'and nevertheless they really did occur'. It seems to be an attestation of the 'discussions that took place after his readings' (Jacoby (1913) 242.33–4). Again in 6.43 Herodotus records the disagreement of 'some Greeks' with his account of this episode 'And now I will tell something which will appear incredible to those Greeks who did not believe that Otanes [one of the Persian dignitaries who spoke at 3.80] proposed a democratic government to the Persians'. Jacoby observes that a different interpretation of these passages could also be given, but he does not suggest it. On the contrary, after some hundred columns, he finds that this is the most convincing ((1913) 353.58–68).

The attestations of Lucian concerning the readings held by Herodotus in Olympia (*Her.* 1) are certainly modelled on the analogous custom of the sophists (Jacoby (1913) 242.47–8). Nevertheless Marcellinus reflects a tradition concerning Herodotean readings, evidently in Athens (*Vit. Thuc.* 54; cf. also Phot. *Bibl.* 60 and the Suda, s.v. 'Thucydides').[25] And Jacoby himself demonstrated ((1913) 379–80) the determining importance of the readings held by Herodotus in Athens as the turning-point in his work: from the historical–geographical *logoi* along the lines of the *Periodos* of Hecataeus (which could be made to achieve exterior unity within the scope of a single 'Persian History', *Persika*) to the history of the Greek–barbarian conflict, *Ta Mêdika*, truly and properly *Hellenika* as it already appeared to Thucydides (1.97.2). For this reason it is incomprehensible that Jacoby then categorically denies that Thucydides had heard Herodotus in Athens[26] and prefers to imagine that he must have waited for 'the publication of Herodotus' work shortly after 428'[27] to become acquainted with it.

[25] The anecdote was more favourably appraised by Jacoby (1926) 16. On historiographical and Herodotean readings, see Schmid–Stählin (1929–48) II.590 n. 5.

[26] Jacoby (1913) 242.42–3. Herodotus was in Athens until 444–443, then at Thurii. Nothing rules out the idea—and indeed the tormented political life which already characterized the colony immediately after its foundation would lead one to suppose—that he returned to Athens (cf. Schmid–Stählin (1929–48) II.589, with n. 7). Marcell. *Vit. Thuc.* 17 even seems to know that he was buried in Athens.

[27] Jacoby (1913) 506.29–30.

Wilamowitz also expressed himself in the same modernistic terms[28] and Wilhelm Schmid again seems to connect the Aristophanic parody of Herodotus' work[29] to its diffusion between the death of Herodotus and the year 425 (when the *Acharnians* was performed).[30] But it is more realistic to think that the Aristophanic allusions could be grasped by the public not because copies of the 'recently published bulk' had been selling like hotcakes but because the public was familiar with Herodotean *akroaseis*.[31] It is no coincidence that the passages where the parody is unquestionable, for example, that of the exordium in *Acharnians* 524–9, are among the most famous and most popular of Herodotus' work. At least until the end of the fifth century 'listening was commoner than reading in all kinds of literature and ἀκούειν {hear} tended everywhere to be used in this connexion in the place of γράφειν {write} and ἀναγιγνώσκειν {read}'; and a term like ἀγώνισμα in Thucydides 1.22.4 could not fail to refer 'to public recitations such as Herodotos is said to have given'.[32]

Diffusion by recitation allows for works to become known while they are being worked on. It is difficult to imagine a Herodotus and a Thucydides who worked for their whole lives on their one work (true *Lebenswerke*) with a view to dissemination only of a complete work,[33] remaining silent during their lifetimes in expectation of the completion of their work.[34] The opposite is obviously to be imagined: a continuous provisional diffusion, accompanied by revisions, second thoughts etc. concerning the parts already made public (for which reason—among others—any analysis or reconstruction of the strata of composition is often impossible).[35]

---

[28] Wilamowitz (1893) I.27: 'the recently published bulk of Herodotus' work presented itself, in its imposing size, before his [sc. Thucydides'] mind'.

[29] Nestle (1911) 245–6; Stein (1893–1908) I.lii, n. 4; Schmid–Stählin (1929–48) II.591; Riemann (1967) 9–11.

[30] Schmid–Stählin (1929–48) II.590–91.

[31] The public was always like that. Significant here is the 'defensive' clarification of Thucydides 1.21, where the historian claims to have treated subjects shared with epic and the logographers but in a less attractive manner.

[32] Gomme, *HCT* I.139. Polybius often speaks of 'readers' proper (cf., e.g., 3.31.11).

[33] And, what is more, to diffusion which in both cases was actually posthumous.

[34] Nor, in general, have modern writers worked in this way. On the contrary, they have 'tried out' their work, at least in their own circle.

[35] A list of more or less extended passages 'which according to their content and form have come to be recognized as late and incidental supplementary additions' in Stein (1893–1908) I.lii.

In this picture—oral and performative diffusion of historical works too (ἀγωνίσματα)—it is entirely comprehensible that Thucydides *obviously* conformed to the narrative form (ῥήσεις καὶ τὰ μεταξὺ ῥήσεων {speeches and the events between speeches}) which his predecessors, and Herodotus above all, had taken over from epic.

II

1. The contests of rhapsodes of the Homeric poems (Ὁμηρείων ἐπέων εἵνεκα) were already taking place in Sicyon when Cleisthenes became tyrant there around 600 BC (Hdt. 5.67.1). The expression that Herodotus uses implies a general diffusion of such contests. In the contest of the rhapsodes is the genesis of Homeric epic; a rhapsodic song follows the preceding one and continues it, resuming the discourse (ἀναβάλλεσθαι ἀείδειν {to begin to sing}: *Od.* 1.155, etc.).[36] And this, for epic, is the first and fundamental form of continuation.

The other is the 'chain' of poems, the so-called 'cycle'. Even if the cycle in its entirety is not mentioned before the second century (West (1970) 388; (1996) 531), and the term κύκλος {cycle, *lit.* circle} came into being between Aristotle and Callimachus (Wilamowitz (1894) 359), Herodotus already knew *Epigoni* and *Cypriae* and discussed their attribution (or non-attribution) to Homer. The *Thebaid* (Theban cycle) was known to Callinus (Paus. 9.9.5), and already for the author of the *Odyssey* the *nostoi* {returns} were a theme of rhapsodic songs (1.326).

The shared character of these poems composed 'around the *Iliad*'[37] is their explicit connection to the preceding narrative, that is, their continuation of it. The first line of the *Epigoni* (νῦν αὖθ᾽ ὁπλοτέρων ἀνδρῶν ἀρχώμεθα Μοῦσαι {Now, Muses, let us begin to sing of younger men}: *Contest of Homer and Hesiod* 259, p. 235 Allen)

---

[36] More than plentiful bibliography on this topic in Broccia (1967) 12–18.
[37] Schol. to Clement, *Protreptic* II.30 (I.305–6 Stählin): κυκλικοὶ δὲ καλοῦνται ποιηταὶ οἱ τὰ κύκλῳ τῆς Ἰλιάδος ἢ τὰ πρῶτα ἢ τὰ μεταγενέστερα ἔξω [ἐξ codices] αὐτῶν τῶν Ὁμηρικῶν συγγράψαντες {Those poets are called 'cyclic' who wrote up events around the *Iliad* or events before or after the *Iliad*, aside from the Homeric poems themselves}. Cf. Bethe (1929) 204.

presupposes a preceding poem. Aristoxenus knew a different opening of the *Iliad* (ἔσπετε νῦν μοι Μοῦσαι Ὀλύμπια δώματ᾽ ἔχουσαι {Tell me now, Muses, who have your homes on Olympus}), which evidently aimed to connect the *Iliad* to the chain of the cycle. It is in fact a typical connection/opening: the 'Catalogue of Ships', for example, begins in this way (*Il.* 2.484). For the same reason, there was also an alternative redaction of the end of the *Iliad* (Sch. T on 24.804). Aristophanes of Byzantium and Aristarchus placed the end of the *Odyssey* at 23.296, probably because they considered what follows to be part of the *Telegony* (so West).

The formula of continuation in epic will then have been roughly that which featured at the beginning of the *Epigoni* and that with which the 'Catalogue of Ships' begins: in fact, the 'Catalogue of Women' continues the Hesiodic *Theogony* with an analogous formula (*Theog.* 1019–20 → *Cat.* 1–2).[38]

Now Herodotus begins his narrative by informing us that he will not speak of the more remote phases of the historical conflict between Greeks and barbarians, since others have already done that: περὶ μὲν τούτων οὐκ ἔρχομαι ἐρέων ὡς οὕτως ἢ ἄλλως κως ταῦτα ἐγένετο . . . προβήσομαι ἐς τὸ πρόσω τοῦ λόγου {concerning these things I am not going to say that they happened in this way or in some other way . . . I shall go forward into my account} (1.5.3). It is the first formulation, Jacoby observed, of the concept of the *spatium historicum*: Herodotus formally refers to genealogical literature and understands himself as its continuator.[39] 'This has been said, now we are saying something else': ἔσπετε νῦν μοι Μοῦσαι. It is difficult to escape from the impression that with ὡς οὕτως ἢ ἄλλως κως Herodotus is alluding[40] to the peremptory exordium of Hecataeus' *Genealogies* (FGrHist 1 F 1a): τάδε γράφω ὥς μοι δοκεῖ ἀληθέα εἶναι. οἱ γὰρ Ἑλλήνων λόγοι πολλοί τε καὶ γελοῖοι ὡς ἐμοὶ φαίνονται εἰσίν {I write what follows as it seems to me to be true; for the stories of the Greeks are many and, as is manifest to me, laughable}. Herodotus also declares himself to be a continuator of the *Genealogies* at 6.54–5.[41]

---

[38] Cf. the apparatus of Merkelbach–West (1990) 113.

[39] Jacoby (1909) 99.

[40] Not without irony: as when he mentions the 'historiographical misadventure' that befell Hecataeus with the Egyptian priests (2.143).

[41] For Hecataeus' continuation of the epic *Periegesis*, cf. Jacoby (1912) 2687–8.

The Thucydidean *Pentecontaetia*, that is, the history of the years 479–431 BC (1.89–117), has as its point of departure a not particularly significant event: the Athenian conquest of Sestos. To this point did Herodotus' narrative reach. Such an exordium can be satisfactorily explained only as an intentional and explicit continuation.[42] Now Thucydides explains his own decision to pick up the narrative from where Herodotus had left it with the consideration that 'no one had treated' the following period and it was therefore a χωρίον ἐκλιπές {omitted period} (1.97.2).

2. A defect of some of the poems of the cycle (*Cypria*, *Little Iliad*), according to Aristotle, was the lack of a unitary theme (*Poet.* 1459a–b): in short, these poems merely aimed to cover a certain *spatium* of events (West). The later imitation by Quintus of Smyrna perhaps gives us an idea of how these poems filled a χωρίον: with the first lines of his *Posthomerica* he picks up the narration of the funeral rites of Hector (with which the *Iliad* ends) and with the last he connects himself to the *Nostoi*.[43]

Proclus, in his *Chrestomathia* (cf. Phot. *Bibl.* ch. 239), one of the richest testimonies for the epic cycle, observed that 'many were interested in the cycle not so much for its literary value as *for the continuation of the narrative* (διὰ τὴν ἀκολουθίαν τῶν ἐν αὐτῷ πραγμάτων)'.[44] Among the first admirers and imitators, in their own field, of *akolouthia tôn pragmatôn* were, therefore, the historians: Herodotus, who joins his work to the *Genealogies* with the formula of epic continuation, and Thucydides, for whom the most natural opening is *a fine Herodoti* {from the end of Herodotus}.

III

1. Thucydides was immediately felt to be, already by his own continuators, a continuator of Herodotus. Theopompus, for

---

[42] Of the moderns it was Wilamowitz ((1893) I.26–7) who first recognized this. The clearest formulation is that of Jacoby (1909) 100 with n. 2).

[43] On the lack of doublets in the Trojan cycle, cf. Bethe (1929) II.212–20.

[44] Procl. *Chrest.* 319a32–3. Cf. Wilamowitz (1894) 358: 'This continuity does not need to be conscious and complete: it is not necessary for the individual poems to fit together line to line; the continuity is that of content'.

378 *History and Poetry*

example, having compiled an *Epitome of Herodotus* (*FGrHist* 115 FF 1–4), picked up the narrative, with his *Hellenica*, 'from where Thucydides stops' (T 19), and this, Jacoby observed, was apparently within the scope of a project of Greek history from its origins.[45] To Theopompus, that is, the narrative continuity between Herodotus and Thucydides was clear, notwithstanding the order (or disorder) of Thucydides' exposition.[46] And so, after the *Epitome of Herodotus*, he could at once continue *a fine Thucydidis* because the Thucydidean narration covered the entire intervening χωρίον {period}. Xenophon, on the other hand, after having brought out the unpublished Thucydidean text (Diog. Laert. 2.57) together with his own *Paralipomena*, writes his own *History of Greece*, and begins it from the point where his own 'completed Thucydides' concluded.{46a} And he ends this with an invitation to a further continuation (7.5.27).

Those critics who, according to Dionysius (*Thuc.* 11), found the order of the material in the first book of Thucydides unnatural, and who would have preferred that the *Pentecontaetia* had been placed at the beginning of the narrative, evidently also understood the work of Thucydides as a (not too well-ordered) continuation of Herodotus' work. And again Aelius Aristides, in the *Panathenaicus*, when he comes to recount Athenian history after Herodotus, paraphrases the *Pentecontaetia* (cf. Dindorf (1829) I.252).[47]

2. These critics were not entirely wrong. The first Thucydidean book really does appear somewhat 'disordered'.[48] And certainly, if

[45] Jacoby (1909) 104 n. 2.

[46] The *continuatio Herodoti* begins from 1.89. After having reported the Spartan decision to declare war on Athens, Thucydides observes that the important decision was taken 'not so much because of the entreaties of the allies, as through fear that the Athenians, who already dominated a large part of Greece, might increase their power further' (1.88). Here, with a rather feeble join, there follows a narration *a fine Herodoti* (1.89–117).

[46a] {Canfora has repeatedly argued that Xenophon edited the unfinished text of Thucydides and that Xenophon, not Thucydides, is the 'I myself' referred to in Thuc. 5.26.1, but this has won little scholarly support.}

[47] Cf. also von Fritz (1969) 585.

[48] Quite apart from its dimensions, which are very much greater than those of its successors: ninety small Teubner pages, against the normal fifteen to twenty-five (in extraordinary cases, forty to sixty) for the years of the war, each one corresponding to a book of the original subdivision.

Thucydides had intended from the first to write a history *a fine Herodoti*, he would very probably have followed the chronological succession of events, and the *Pentecontaetia* would have been situated at the beginning of the work, as the critics known to Dionysius would have preferred.

It is clear, on the other hand, from various indications that the 'digression' (it is Thucydides who defines it as such in 1.97.2) on the years 479–431 was inserted at a later point into a pre-existing narrative which concentrated exclusively on the conflict which began in 431. Naturally Thucydides inserted the digression (as he also did the other minor ones, on Cylon, Pausanias, and Themistocles) according to the only possible model, the Herodotean one. The *Pentecontaetia* interrupts the narrative, to which it is connected by an external link (which is repeated at the end according to the stylistic model of ring composition); so, similarly, Herodotus in Book 5, for example, used analogous links to insert into the account of Aristagoras' arrival in Athens, with the Ionian revolt imminent, a lengthy *logos* on Athenian history from the expulsion of the Peisistratids (5.55–96).

As a consequence, the narrative in the first book of Thucydides seems to proceed on two levels which are somewhat incongruous with one another: in one respect an analytical narrative of the events immediately preceding the conflict (the 'pretexts': Corcyra, Potidaea), in another the *Pentecontaetia* with its introductory chapter (1.88) in which the 'pretexts' are devalued and the 'real cause', that is the Spartan decision to put a stop to the growing power of Athens even at the cost of a war (1.23.6 and 1.88), is contrasted with them. A real friction, so to speak, exists between these two narrative levels: while in the account of Corcyra and Potidaea Sparta appears unwilling to get itself dragged into a war at the insistence of the Corinthians (and the Corinthians in 1.68 lament Spartan inertia), in 1.88 we learn—at the end of the debate in which the Corinthians have expressed themselves in this way!—that Sparta has decided on war 'not so much because of the insistence of the allies, but because it was preoccupied by the growing power of Athens'.

On the other hand, that Thucydides in one phase of his redaction considered only the 'pretexts' as causes of the conflict could also be deduced from the very solemn advance announcement of 1.23.5: 'I have written up the causes and the disagreements[49] in the first place so that no one ever in the future should need to investigate anew the reasons which caused so serious a war to break out'.

I do not presume to get involved with the analysis of the layers of Thucydides' work (that is, in the Thucydidean 'question'), but certainly one deduction appears obvious: the passages relating to the 'real cause' of the conflict (1.23.6 and 1.88 which brings 1.89–117 along with it) were inserted in the text at a later point, evidently when Thucydides had become convinced that, beyond the 'pretexts' (to which at an earlier stage he had dedicated such an analytical narrative), there was a deeper cause to the origin of the 'greatest conflict in Greek history' (1.1).

3. When was this? Unlike his contemporaries, still less the historians and politicians of the following century, Thucydides shows (already in the progressive numeration of the years of the war) that he considers the Ten Years' War, the Sicilian campaign and the Decelean war as phases of a single conflict. It is not superfluous to insist on the originality and on the apparently arbitrary character of such a conception.

Moreover, in 446–445, after a serious conflict (Coronea, the defection of Euboea, a Spartan invasion), a thirty-year peace was concluded, which in turn was already broken in 431; similarly the fifty-year peace of 421 had been violated in 414–13 (beginning of the Decelean war). Nevertheless, for Thucydides (and to moderns this now seems obvious) it was in 431 that there began a single long conflict which, interrupted by unreliable peaces or by distractions (Syracuse), would end in the collapse of one of the two powers. This being the case, at a certain point the conviction matured in him that deeper cause, which was not the clash over Corcyra and Potidaea, had unleashed the conflict: the Spartan determination to resolve once and for all and in the most radical manner the clash with Athens that had already begun during the Persian wars (Hdt. 8.3). From such a perspective—but *a posteriori!*—the peace of Nicias (very much more than the peace of 445) could not fail to appear to him to be a 'truce'.

---

[49] I.e., the so-called pretexts, as is clear from a comparison with 1.146 (cf. Classen–Steup).

At the point, that is, at which Thucydides became convinced of the unity of the entire conflict—not, therefore, before the Spartan intervention in Syracuse, and by the time the history of the Ten Years' War had already been written—there formed in him the conviction of a 'real cause'. The unity of the entire conflict and the 'true cause' are two aspects of the same thought, evidently developed by the time the peace of Nicias had been definitively compromised.

Of the durability of the peace no one at first could have had doubts, and it was in substance a success for Athens. And in fact in Thucydides' first draft, as has been said, the image of Sparta fixed on a war to resolve the situation appears to be absent, and thus on the first level we find the 'pretexts' as the only causes of the conflict (cf. 1.23.5).

Naturally this does not mean that the entire excursus on the *Pentecontaetia* was therefore *composed* late. It is certainly true that the citation of the *Attic History* of Hellanicus (1.97.2) will be later than the diffusion of that work (i.e. at least later than 407, since Hellanicus reached at least that year), but only the immediate context in which Hellanicus is named can be considered late.[50] Therefore the reference to Hellanicus can give no evidence for the time of composition of the *Pentecontaetia*.

4. But the *Pentecontaetia is not necessary to the narrative.*

An observation like that of 1.88 is characterized by self-sufficient rigour: 'the Spartans decided on war in fear of the growth of the Athenians' power, seeing that they already dominated a large part of Greece'; it does not need to be supported by an *excursus* which describes the rise of Athens step by step. And in fact Thucydides himself offers no excuse, except in a completely subordinate line, for the *excursus* as something necessary to the narrative;[51] instead he affirms explicitly that he has made the 'digression' because no historian up until that time had treated that period: τὴν ἐκβολὴν τοῦ λόγου ἐποιησάμην[52] διὰ τοῦτο ὅτι τοῖς πρὸ ἐμοῦ ἅπασιν ἐκλιπές τοῦτο

---

[50] Ziegler (1929) 66 n. 2; Adcock (1963) 122–3; Jacoby, *FGrHist* 323a, *Komm.* n. 47.

[51] 1.97.2: ἅμα δὲ καὶ τῆς ἀρχῆς ἀπόδειξιν ἔχει τῶν Ἀθηναίων ἐν οἵῳ τρόπῳ κατέστη {and simultaneously it contains a demonstration of the manner in which the empire of the Athenians was established}.

[52] That Thucydides here defines as a 'digression' only the chapters which follow (98–117) is maintained by Wilamowitz ((1883) I.27) and Jacoby ((1909) 100 n. 2). But τὴν ἐκβολὴν τοῦ λόγου ἐποιησάμην could also refer to the interior *excursus*, nor is

ἦν τὸ χωρίον καὶ ἢ τὰ πρὸ τῶν Μηδικῶν Ἑλληνικὰ ξυνετίθεσαν ἢ αὐτὰ
τὰ Μηδικά {I made this digression from my account because all those
before me omitted this period and they recounted either Greek affairs
before the Persian Wars or the Persian Wars themselves} (1.97.2).

This is perhaps Thucydides' most 'generous' confession about the
formation of his work. It forces a question: why has he inserted into
his monograph on the Peloponnesian War, this lengthy 'digression',
which, on the contrary, aims only to fill the *spatium historicum* left
empty by the *Hellenikas* of his predecessors?[53] Apparently because his
work—which by now included the unity of the entire conflict, and
looked as if it would have to narrate the history of over a quarter of a
century[54]—*could no longer have appeared to him as the original
monograph on the Ten Years' War, but as a true and proper Hellenika.*
And in fact anyone with a correct understanding of the phrase which
I cited above could not fail to recognize that there already Thucydides
clearly defines his own work too, as well as that of his predecessors, as
a *Hellenika.* And the *excursus* is also defined as a *Hellenika* in its
concluding phrase (1.118.2: ταῦτα...ὅσα ἔπραξαν οἱ Ἕλληνες πρός τε
ἀλλήλους καὶ τὸν βάρβαρον {these things . . . as many as the Greeks did
against one another and against the barbarian}).

Not only was the prospect already that of narrating almost thirty
years of history, but the narrative was becoming ever more analytical,
the years of the war ever longer (the seventeenth and nineteenth years
are about sixty small Teubner pages, the summer alone of the twenty-
first year is thirty-five, as against the normal fifteen to twenty-five
pages of the years of the Ten Years' War, with high points of forty for
the fifth and eighth years each). As Thucydides proceeded he did not
have before him only the history of the conflict between Sparta and
Athens; by this point the real great power was Persia (Demosth.
10.51), while the war by now also included Syracuse, and the theatre
of operations was becoming ever vaster, the threads of the military,

it necessarily equivalent to ἔγραψα δὲ αὐτά. Moreover 89–96 also are a 'digression'
(one only has to consider the exordium); and a stage of the text in which there was
only 1.89–96 after 1.88 is not imaginable (cf. *infra*).

[53] This is the first attestation of the term Ἑλληνικά {Greek affairs} (Jacoby (1909)
96 n.1).

[54] A much lengthier period than that covered by the Herodotean Μηδικά {Persian
affairs}!

political and diplomatic actions ever more intricate. (It is, in fact, highly improbable that Thucydides, no longer young, hoped at this stage to bring to an end a narrative which was assuming ever vaster proportions.)

Once this turning point had been determined and the original monograph had been changed into a *Hellenika* proper (as is said in 1.97.2), this *Hellenika* now had to be linked to the historiographical 'chain' which Thucydides outlines in 1.97 (τὰ πρὸ τῶν Μηδικῶν Ἑλληνικά—αὐτὰ τὰ Μηδικά {events before the Persian Wars–the Persian Wars themselves}). *Hence the necessity of continuing* μετὰ τὰ Μηδικά {after the Persian Wars}, *the necessity, that is, of the* Pente-contaetia.[55] By this time, however, it was not reasonable to plan a lengthy and analytical narrative starting from 479, to precede what was already written: hence the compromise of the inserted 'digression', in the Herodotean manner, at the point where it seemed least unjustified. Naturally, this was a compromise which did not satisfy the pedants: for Dionysius (*Pomp.* II.235.8–10 UR) the *Pentecontaetia* is 'out of place and slipshod'.

5. Constrained now to write a *Hellenika*—and it was as such that Xenophon and Theopompus understood his work, since they continued it with *Hellenikas*—Thucydides decided to start *a fine Herodoti.*

The *excursus* which connects *ta Mêdika* to the Ten Years' War is divided into two parts: 89–96 (from the capture of Sestos to the formation of the maritime league) and 98–117 (Athenian expansion from 477 onwards); chapter 97 is a sort of 'second proem'.

The first part completes *ta Mêdika* (for Aristotle too (*Ath. Pol.* 25.1) it is with 478–7 that *ta Mêdika* end). On this issue:

a. It is, as Jacoby wrote,[56] undoubtedly irrelevant to establish whether the break—within the scope of the *Pentecontaetia*—on the occasion of the formation of the league does or does not signify that for Thucydides the Herodotean work was incomplete. But a chronological indication such as that which concludes Herodotus' work

---

[55] *Ta Mêdika* is a Herodotean term. Before Thucydides 1.97, it occurs only at Hdt. 9.64.2. And it is the *new* term to indicate 'the Persian wars' (*Persika* meant something else). So, in declaring his own *Anschluss* to *Ta Mêdika*, Thucydides explicitly declares that he is himself continuing the Herodotean work.

[56] Jacoby (1909) 100 n. 2.

(9.121: 'in the course of that year nothing else happened') is a clear advance announcement of further narrative, on the same level as 6.42–43, 9.41, and 9.107.[57] And this will also have been how it appeared to Thucydides: a further stimulus and a precise hook for continuation (as the last phrase of the Thucydidean text, 8.109.2, is for Xenophon).

b. Since the allusion to Hellanicus is not a chronological indication of the time of composition of the *Pentecontaetia*, there is no evidence to sustain the idea that 1.89–96 (the Herodotean *Paralipomena*) is earlier than or even originally autonomous with respect to 1.97–117.[58] On the contrary, the strict syntactic connection between 1.88 (advance announcement *of the entire Pentecontaetia*) and 89 confirms the compositional unity of 89–117. Besides all this it is difficult to imagine a stage of the Thucydidean text in which the presupposition of 1.88 ('seeing that already [in 431] Athens dominated a great part of Greece') was followed up with nothing apart from the description of what were merely the first steps of Athenian power (89–96).[59]

6. When Herodotus' work already had the form of a *Hellenika* (Books 6–9), Herodotus adopted a chronology typical of *Hellenikas*, by years and seasons (6.42–3, 7.37.1, 8.113.1, 9.121). This was a chronology, as Thucydides defined it (5.20), that was universally valid and not tied to the magistrates of this or that city (the Thucydidean character of expressions such as 6.43 is recognized by How and Wells (1928) II.79).

The last words of the Herodotean narrative (9.121) definitely suggest an annalistic chronology, and so in this respect too the annalistic Thucydides connects himself closely to his predecessor. Taking on the predecessor's chronological system is a characteristic of continuation: Xenophon in the *Paralipomena* adopts the Thucydidean system; Polybius adopts the chronology of Timaeus by Olympiads; Tacitus continues Livy with that of the *Annales*.

---

[57] *Contra*, Schmid–Stählin ((1929–48) II.596 with n. 5); cf. Legrand (1954) 77 with n. 2 and Jacoby (1913) 375.30–2.

[58] For Wilamowitz ((1893) I.27), on the other hand, 89–96 were written under the impression made by the 'publication' of the Herodotean work, 97–117 as a polemic against Hellanicus.

[59] Gomme's assertion (*HCT* I.363 n. 1) that the two prefaces of the *Pentecontaetia* (1.89 and 97) 'cover all the ground' is unfounded.

7. With the *Pentecontaetia* Thucydides wanted to fill a χωρίον ἐκλιπές. This must perhaps have dissuaded others from turning back to it: 'There was no better narrative of this period and so successive authors were constrained, whether they liked it or not, to base themselves on Thucydides'.[60] If Diodorus, on the subject of the construction of the walls (9.39–40), has direct verbal echoes with the Thucydidean account (1.90–1), this will signify that Ephorus had not found anything better than to repeat what Thucydides had said (Cf. also Jacoby (1909) 98 n. 5). As in the cycle, no doublets.

IV

Von Fritz has written:

Through the continuators of Thucydides the peculiar idea of a *historia perpetua* was formed, according to which every time death took the pen from a historian's hand, a younger man had to pick it up to continue the historical narrative: an idea that lasted until Posidonius.[61]

After Thucydides, Xenophon, and Theopompus, the continuation was now the natural form of historiography:[62] Polybius, whose 'universal' history develops in two theatres, the West and Greece, declares his own relationship of continuation both in the first (with Timaeus: 1.5.1) and in the second (with Aratus: 1.3.2), and in addition, when he sets himself to speak of Greek history, he finds a way of alluding to the final words of the *Hellenica* of Xenophon (2.39.8; cf. *Hell.* 7.5.27).

His work will then have been continued by Posidonius and by Strabo. For the continuators of Ephorus (Demophilus and Diyllus) and for Psaon, the continuer of Diyllus, cf. *FGrHist* 70 T 9a–b; 73 T 1; 78. Not only does the phenomenon manifest itself regularly in historiography of the Hellenistic, Roman, Imperial Greek, and Byzantine periods, but it becomes, with the continuators of Eusebius,

---

[60] Beloch (1916) 8.   [61] Von Fritz (1969) 585.
[62] The alternative was, naturally, to start again from the beginning (Ephorus).

the natural form of ecclesiastical history.[63] In the sixth century
Evagrius was justly able to entitle an important 'historiographical'
chapter of his continuation of the continuators of Eusebius περὶ τῆς
καθ' εἱρμὸν ἱστορίας μέχρι ἡμῶν σωζομένης {concerning the history
in sequence preserved up to our time} (5.24), that is, 'On the
historiographical chain'. The image of the historiographical chain
already exists in the proem of Justin: *quae historici Graecorum prout
commodum cuique fuit inter se gregata occupaverunt* {all that the
historians of Greece had undertaken separately, according to what
was suitable to each}. And again in the years following the Turkish
conquests of Constantinople Michael Critobulus, in the dedication
of his historical work to Mehmed II, laments that the deeds of the
Persians, of the Greeks and of the Romans have been immortalized τῇ
διαδοχῇ τοῦ χρόνου παραδοθέντα ταῖς Ἑλληνικαῖς ἱστορίαις {things
handed down in the succession of time by Greek histories} while the
same is not true of those of Mehmed II (*FHG* V.52).

Other factors went into contributing to the 'chain' beyond the
centrality of the Herodotus/Thucydides/Xenophon triad and the
resulting literary tradition. In the late empire and then in the Byzantine age, for example, it was the norm not to write the history of the
reigning sovereign. When he reaches that point, the historian stops,
declaring that to speak of the reigning sovereign he needs a 'higher
style', and exhorts others, more skilful, to proceed with the narrative
(so Jerome, Eutropius, Ammianus, some of the *Scriptores Historiae
Augustae*, Paul the Deacon, etc.).[64]

Meanwhile there is another constant factor. Historical works from
antiquity to the Byzantines are principally contemporary history: the
example of Thucydides was in this sense decisive. Even someone who
begins with the remotest antiquity aims towards the history of the
present: so Ephorus,[65] so Livy, so Zosimus, to give only a few
examples. Moreover, historiographical activity is normally a life's
work (*Lebenswerk*). It is a consequence of this that someone who
succeeds in bringing his narrative to the point he had proposed may
decide to carry on, continuing to narrate contemporary history (this
is the case, for example, with Polybius). And so it happens that quite

[63] An analytical exposition, with other chapters, in a continuous work.
[64] Straub (1952) 133–4.   [65] Jacoby (1909) 103–4.

often historiographical works remain incomplete (this is already the case for Thucydides: he started to write again after having concluded the Ten Years' War, but he left his new narrative, that of the Decelean war, incomplete).

In this way, carrying on previous incomplete works (as Thucydides does for Herodotus, Xenophon for Thucydides, etc.) becomes a natural stimulus to continuation. And this, the connection of one's history to a previous incomplete work, is the easiest way of resolving one of the principal problems of historiographical activity: the choice of a starting-point.

Polybius already reflects on this point and observes that, in setting about a historical work, it is important to establish the 'starting point', otherwise one ends up always going back further from cause to cause 'and the beginning of the entire work becomes unstable' (1.5.3). Dionysius, who records (and shares) the criticisms of others on the starting point of the Thucydidean work (*Thuc.* 10), attempts to define in general terms how the starting point should be chosen: 'something that is preceded by nothing else' (I.338.7–8 U–R). Not a very clear definition, certainly (Krüger (1823) 83), but one that seems to reflect the same Polybian preoccupation with being constrained to go back from cause to cause into infinity.

Polybius found that, in his own case, the best solution was to pick up the narrative 'from where Timaeus stops' (1.5.1). To Dionysius the beginning of Xenophon's *Hellenica* seemed excellent (*Pomp.* 4.1): it was a continuation.

ADDENDUM

The manuscript tradition itself seems, in certain cases, to be governed by the intent to construct a narrative chain: historians who continued one another are transmitted in the same manuscripts. They are collections constructed with the available (or selected) works.

J. E. Powell (1937) has identified the 'twin' manuscripts of Herodotus and Thucydides, both from the hand of George the Cretan (middle of the fifteenth century). At least three witnesses bring together the work of Thucydides and Xenophon's *Hellenika* (for which they are amongst the oldest witnesses): Vaticanus Graecus 1293; Ambrosianus A 4 inf. (from the fourteenth century); and Parisinus Coislin 317 (fifteenth century). In classical historiography there are no other surviving cases—apart from Herodotus, Thucydides, Xenophon—of narrators who continued one another; for the Caesarian *commentarii*, however, one part of the tradition brings together the books of the Gallic War and those of the Civil War using a single numeration; for the *Annals* and *Histories* of Tacitus, it seems that a single numeration of books came into use at a certain point: Jerome (*Comm. in Zach.* 3.14) indicates that there were thirty books *in toto*.

The phenomenon can be observed much more clearly when there are consistently surviving clusters from the historiographical chain: in the tradition of ecclesiastical histories and of Byzantine historians and chronographers.

14

History and Tragedy

F. W. Walbank

Two centuries divide Xenophon's *floruit* from that of Polybius, and no Greek history of any substance survives from this period. Discussion about the character of Hellenistic history writing depends therefore in the main on fragments preserved in later authors, along with the occasional remarks of critics whose assumptions may be very different from ours. It seems clear that much of the history written at this time aimed at stirring the reader's emotions. Phylarchus, for example, was obviously not unique in his pathetic accounts of captured cities, clinging women, with hair dishevelled and breasts bare, and crowds of children and aged parents weeping and lamenting as they were led off into slavery.[1] This style of writing Polybius calls 'tragic', and it certainly shared many of the characteristics of tragedy, though indeed it contained several other ingredients, for instance the marvellous and the monstrous ($\tau\grave{o}\ \tau\epsilon\rho\alpha\tau\hat{\omega}\delta\epsilon s$), which Aristotle specifically excluded from tragedy,[2] as well as the trivial, the meretricious, and the sentimental—night scenes, detailed descriptions of clothing, love-interest, and the almost human behaviour of animals.

If there was a Hellenistic theory behind all this it has not survived, and modern attempts to discover one have enjoyed limited success. Perhaps the most popular hypothesis, and one which still holds the field, is that propounded fifty years ago in a series of articles by Ed. Schwartz, and later developed in an important pamphlet by Scheller,

---

[1] Pol. 2.56.7–12.   [2] Arist. *Poet.* 14.2, 1453b8.

which derives tragic history from the Peripatetics as a result of a curious reversal of Aristotle's own teaching.[3] In the *Poetics*,[4] as is well known, Aristotle draws a clear line between poetry and history. But someone within Aristotle's school, it was supposed, blurred this distinction and diverted those features characteristic of poetry, and in particular of tragedy, to the field of history. About fifteen years ago this view was challenged by B. L. Ullman,[5] who tried to establish the origins of tragic history in the school of Isocrates, but not I think with success. Ullman's thesis revived interest in the problem and was followed by a good deal of discussion;[6] and on the whole opinion was tending to the view that 'tragic history' was perhaps being rather too rigidly defined and that its origins were to be sought over a wider area and at an earlier date than had hitherto appeared. However, any further consideration of the matter now has to take account of an extremely stimulating paper read by Professor Kurt von Fritz to a meeting of the Fondation Hardt in August 1956, and recently published in the fourth volume of the *Entretiens sur l'antiquité classique* under the title of 'The Importance of Aristotle for Historiography'.[7] In this paper I propose first of all to, consider von Fritz's new arguments in favour of a Peripatetic origin for 'tragic history', and then to give reasons why I still believe that this problem has to be approached in a rather different way.

I

Concerning poetry, Aristotle[8] remarks that it is more philosophical and a higher thing than history; ἡ μὲν γὰρ ποίησις μᾶλλον τὰ καθ᾽ ὅλου, ἡ δ᾽ ἱστορία τὰ καθ᾽ ἕκαστον λέγει—poetry tends to express the universal, history the particular. And by the particular Aristotle

[3] Schwartz (1943) 123–5; (1897) 560ff., (1900) 107ff., (1909) 491; Scheller (1911).
[4] *Poet.* 9.2–9, 1451b1–32.
[5] Ullman (1942).
[6] Cf. Laistner (1947) 14ff.; Wehrli (1946) and (1947); Giovannini (1943); Walbank (1955).
[7] von Fritz (1958).   [8] *Poet.* 9.3, 1451b5–7.

means τὰ γενόμενα, by the universal, οἷα ἂν γένοιτο, 'what a certain type of person on a certain occasion will do or say according to the law of probability or necessity'. μᾶλλον, as von Fritz rightly insists, goes with both halves of the sentence: poetry is *more* concerned with the universal, history *more* concerned with the particular—for clearly it would be absurd to argue that there is no element of τὰ καθ' ἕκαστον in tragedy, which deals with the fate of individual men, just as it would be absurd to deny to history any concern with τὰ καθ' ὅλου, inasmuch as historical situations can be repeated and the lessons of one apply quite often to another. This is, I think, true and was worth saying; though it is perhaps not so novel as von Fritz suggests, for Butcher's translation, 'poetry *tends* to stress the universal, history the particular', had already accurately rendered the Greek, and given μᾶλλον its force in both clauses.

It is this μᾶλλον which, according to von Fritz, leaves the door open for the supposed Peripatetic theory of tragic history. If history was less philosophical (and so less meritorious) than poetry, this was because poetry dealt with the universal. The conclusion was clear: to raise the status of history, it too must be made more universal, and so more like poetry. Aristotle, von Fritz rightly points out, had not said that history *ought* to be more concerned with the particular, but merely that it *tended* to be so, as compared with poetry; but he was, after all, not discussing history, and had only made reference to it incidentally. There was nothing in what he had said to prevent anyone propounding and developing the view that history would be improved by becoming more universal and hence more like poetry.

As an *a priori* argument this is plausible; and von Fritz would appear to be right in claiming that if it was put forward, it is more likely than not to have come from a follower of Aristotle, since obviously the compulsion to take the master's definition into account would be felt by a Peripatetic rather than by someone without his affiliations. Such a Peripatetic, it is suggested, was Duris of Samos, who is known not only as a writer of emotional and sensational scenes,[9] but also as the author of a famous criticism of two eminent historians of Isocrates' school. 'Ephorus and Theopompus', he

---

[9] Cf. *FGrHist* 76 T 12, FF 5, 7, 14, 18, 52.

wrote,[10] 'proved for the most part unequal to the events they described, τῶν γενομένων ἀπελείφθησαν; for in their presentation they made no attempt at dramatic *mimesis* with its associated pleasure in the narrative, and concerned themselves only with the formal aspects of writing: οὔτε γὰρ μιμήσεως μετέλαβον οὐδεμίας οὔτε ἡδονῆς ἐν τῷ φράσαι, αὐτοῦ δὲ τοῦ γράφειν μόνον ἐπεμελήθησαν.' Clearly this implies that Duris believed μίμησις to be an integral part of the historian's task; but before he can link Duris with his hypothetical theorist inside the Peripatos, von Fritz has to trace a connection between μίμησις and τὰ καθ' ὅλου, since although Aristotle has a good deal to say about μίμησις in various art forms it is in terms of τὰ καθ' ὅλου and τὰ καθ' ἔκαστον, the universal and the particular, and not by virtue of the presence or absence of μίμησις, that he distinguishes history from tragedy.

What is μίμησις? Bywater thought it was 'imitation' in the straightforward sense of producing a copy; but Gomme very properly corrected this.[11] μίμησις, he argued in his Sather lectures on poetry and history, is rather to be rendered by 'representation'. Von Fritz quotes Gomme with approval, but in fact he reads very much more than Gomme into μίμησις. μίμησις in tragedy, he argues,[12] μίμησις which inspires fear and pity in the spectator, is to be defined as a 'concentrated representation' of what in real life is much less concentrated; and it is in this 'concentrated representation' that the universality emerges. 'The universality of tragedy', he goes on, 'consists of the fact that it represents what stands as an extreme possibility behind every life and perhaps also in a less extreme form becomes reality in every life.' Now I am not quarrelling with this as a description of what happens in tragedy. But it does seem extremely unlikely that the word μίμησις can be stretched to mean 'concentrated representation' in this sense, and still more unlikely that 'the special tragic form of concentration [i.e. of μίμησις] consists of the presentation of the extreme case'. In the first chapter of the *Poetics* Aristotle in fact discusses the different forms of μίμησις exhibited by

---

[10] *FGrHist* 76 F 1 = Phot. *Bibl.* p. 121 a41; the passage came from Book 1 of the *Histories* and almost certainly from the prologue, the traditional place for polemic and the discussion of general principles.

[11] Gomme (1954) 53ff.   [12] Von Fritz (1958) 120ff.

epic, tragedy, comedy, dithyramb, and instrumental music.¹³ All these, he says, are forms of μίμησις; but they differ from each other in their medium, their subjects, and their mode of representation. What then is the form of μίμησις peculiar to tragedy? Is it 'representation of the extreme case'? Aristotle does not say so. When he seeks to establish the mode in which the μίμησις of tragedy differs from other forms of μίμησις he simply says that the poet may represent by narration, like Homer, or 'he may present all his characters as living and moving before us'. In short, the special tragic form of μίμησις consists of putting people on the stage.

Now if Aristotle had meant to define μίμησις as '*concentrated* representation' with 'concentrated representation of the extreme case' as the specific aspect peculiar to tragedy, here was his opportunity to make that distinction. Since he does not, we are hardly justified in reading such an idea into the word, and then asserting that this concentrated representation of the extreme case is in fact τὰ καθ' ὅλου of tragedy. The reason von Fritz tries to read all this into μίμησις is of course that he has to bridge the gap between Aristotle's distinction between poetry and history in terms of the particular and the universal, and Duris' remark about the need for μίμησις and ἡδονή in the writing of history. If von Fritz is right, Duris was here demanding that history should depict the extreme case, οἷα ἂν γένοιτο. It seems far more likely that the μίμησις which he desiderates is simply a vivid presentation of events, emotive writing, as we might say; this would certainly fit what is known of his technique, for judging from the extant fragments anything capable of moving and titillating his readers finds a place in his pages—wonder-stories and travel-tales, prodigious births, and scandalous customs, love-intrigue, the robes of Demetrius Poliorcetes, the dolphin that fell in love with a boy—all is grist to his mill. But little of this is tragic in the true sense or can in any way be regarded as depicting the universal; nor does Duris ever define the μίμησις which he requires as specifically tragic.

It is true that Duris was a pupil of Theophrastus; and I have no doubt that he used the word μίμησις in relation to history—for the first time (as far as we know)—because he was familiar with it from

---

¹³ *Poet.* 1.2–3, 1447a13–18; cf. 3.1, 1448a19–23.

the Peripatos. But we are not therefore justified in describing the vivid and melodramatic history which he composed as Peripatetic history. Both Theophrastus and Praxiphanes, another Peripatetic, are known to have written works entitled Περὶ ἱστορίας; and it can be reasonably assumed that these were concerned with the theory of historiography.[14] But *what* they wrote is a question which we are in no position to answer. There is however one scrap—and it is only a scrap—of evidence which perhaps militates against the view that Theophrastus' theory was the counterpart to Duris' practice. In a passage in Cicero's *Orator*,[15] Theophrastus praises Thucydides and Herodotus for their rich and ornate diction which, however, avoided the *deliciae uel potius ineptiae* {mannerisms or rather the absurdities} of Gorgias. It is not unreasonable to think that Theophrastus' treatise on history paid some attention to the appropriate style; and if he approved of Thucydides it is on the whole unlikely that he approved of Duris, who, according to Dionysius of Halicarnassus,[16] was one of those whose neglect of stylistic principles ensured that no one ever read their books to the end. Not perhaps a point to press hard; but, for what it is worth, against the view that Theophrastus provided the theoretical blueprint for Duris and Phylarchus.

There is a case for making Duris an important link in the development of sensational historiography, and also for thinking that he had a theory of sorts, to the extent at least that he knew what he wanted to do, and that his aims were something quite other than those of Theopompus and Ephorus. But there is no evidence that his theory is the Peripatetic theory, or that Theophrastus would have endorsed history as he wrote it. Further there is no evidence that his μίμησις has anything at all to do with universality in the Aristotelian sense, or with the presentation of the extreme case as von Fritz argues that it is presented in tragedy. Finally, Schwartz's hypothesis that some

[14] It has recently been argued by Avenarius ((1956) 171–2) that these cannot be treatises on the theory of history because Cicero, *de Orat.* 2.62, puts into the mouth of M. Antonius the explicit declaration *neque eam* [sc. *historiam*] *reperio usquam separatim instructam rhetorum praeceptis* {nor do I find it [history] treated separately anywhere in the teachings of the *rhetors*}. But this means only that in the rhetorical handbooks history is not given special treatment distinct from the general precepts of the *ars*. See my comments in Walbank, *HCP* I.418–19.

[15] Cic. *Orat.* 39.   [16] *FGrHist* 76 T 10 = D. Hal. *Comp verb.* 4.

successor of Aristotle applied the master's definition of tragedy to history remains just as hypothetical as it was before. Though ingenious and illuminating, von Fritz's thesis fails to make its main point.

Perhaps the whole problem of 'tragic history' has suffered from a concentration on theory, on what Aristotle said, and how far the practice of later historians conformed with it. In the discussion which followed von Fritz's paper several scholars expressed reasonable doubts whether historians are very much moved by writers on the theory of history;[17] and there was widespread agreement that many other factors, political and social, the climate of the time and the example of predecessors, counted far more in shaping a tradition of writing. Among such factors are the presuppositions which a historian will inherit; and in the second half of this paper I want to examine certain factors which taken together were likely to predispose a Hellenistic historian, despite the dicta of Aristotle, and the kind of criticisms familiar to us from Polybius and Lucian, to confuse the categories of history and tragedy.

II

A good reason why tragedy and history were from their beginnings regarded as akin was their employment of the same subject-matter. Thucydides, for example, in his review of early Greek history in Book 1[18] is dealing up to a point with precisely the same facts as Homer or Euripides. His purpose is of course different; but it does not occur to him, any more than it occurs to them, to question the historicity of Hellen, the son of Deucalion, of Minos and his thalassocracy, of Achilles, Pelops, Tyndareus, Atreus, Agamemnon, and the rest. He does of course distinguish between the traditions surrounding these characters and the element which he calls τὸ μυθῶδες and regards as inappropriate to history.[19] τὸ μυθῶδες Gomme[20] took to mean 'the

[17] Von Fritz (1958) 131ff.; observations of Latte, Syme, Hanell, de Romilly, Momigliano.
[18] Thuc. 1.1–23.
[19] Cf. Thuc. 1.21.1, 22.4; cf. Luc. *h.c.* 42, 55.
[20] *HCT* I.149; cf. Gomme (1954) 117.

story-telling aspect', 'for example Candaules and Gyges, Croesus and
Adrestus, Polycrates and his ring, Xerxes' dream before the sailing of
the armada, and Hippias' dream before Marathon, Themistocles and
the allied admirals before Salamis, i.e. historical romance. It has nothing', he goes on, 'to do with belief or disbelief in the main traditions of
what we call the "mythical" period of Greek history (the Theban and
Trojan wars, the migrations and so forth, which Thucydides accepted).'
One might perhaps add to this explanation that τὸ μυθῶδες also
includes the 'mythical' or miraculous aspects of the legends. Achilles,
Minos, and Agamemnon are discussed as ordinary human beings in a
world free from miracles, and any supernatural incidents attached by
tradition to their names, such as Achilles' descent from a goddess, or
Minos' possession of the Minotaur, are simply omitted from the
discussion. This element of rational scepticism is not however peculiar
to the historian; it can be detected under a flimsy disguise in Euripides,
who, Aristophanes alleged,[21] 'by representing the gods, persuaded men
that they did not exist'. It constitutes no fundamental distinction
between the historian and the tragic writer.

The relationship between the two can be further illustrated from
the character of the first Greek historians. Thucydides' treatment of
early legend in Book 1 is of course outstanding in its clarity and in its
firm grasp of the nature of historical evidence; but it also follows a
tradition going back to Hecataeus, which can be summed up in
Jacoby's remark that the main source for the early history of the
Greek people was the panhellenic epic.[22]

Both the panhellenic historians of Ionia and such local historians as
the Atthidographers who built on their work dealt with legendary
times and derived their narrative from a critical analysis of the
subject-matter of epic. Some were more credulous, some less; but it
is interesting to find Dionysius of Halicarnassus[23] using the same kind
of language to criticize early Ionian history as Polybius uses concerning Phylarchus. 'It contained', he writes, 'myths which had been
believed from time immemorial and many theatrical reversals of
fortune which seem very naive to the modern reader'—ἐν αἷς καὶ

[21] *Thesm.* 450–51.   [22] Jacoby (1949) 202; cf. d'Alton (1931) 491–2.
[23] *Thuc.* 5.

μῦθοί τινες ἐνῆσαν ἀπὸ τοῦ πολλοῦ πεπιστευμένοι χρόνου καὶ θεατρικαί
τινες περιπέτειαι πολὺ τὸ ἠλίθιον ἔχειν τοῖς νῦν δοκοῦσαι.

It was perhaps this naivety and theatricality to which Thucydides
was objecting when he asserted[24] that his own observations about
early Greek history 'will not be disturbed either by the lays of a poet
displaying the exaggeration of his craft, or by the compositions of
prose-writers whose attraction is gained at the expense of truth, the
subjects they treat of being out of the reach of evidence, and time
having robbed most of them of historical value by enthroning them
in the region of legend'. Similarly Hecataeus of Miletus opened his
work with his famous expression of incredulity[25] about the 'stories of
the Hellenes' which were 'many and ridiculous'.

It is these same 'stories of the Hellenes' which form the material of
Attic tragedy; for, as Jacoby has pointed out,[26] despite the fact that
tragedy was a local Athenian product, it took the bulk of its subject-
matter from panhellenic myths, only rarely introducing specifically
Athenian material. As Aeschylus remarked about his own plays,[27]
they were 'slices from the great feast of Homer'. In short, as far as
subject-matter went, tragedy and history were both derived from a
single source—epic.

The historian had a good deal of work to do on this material before
he could reduce it to a form suited to his purpose. Many legends were
so interwoven with impossibilities that only a radical process of rationalization or 'historicizing' would make them literally credible. There is
plenty of evidence for this, especially among the Atthidographers.
Plutarch, for instance,[28] in his *Life if Theseus* contrasts the rationalized
versions of the Minotaur story, such as the Cretan one which turns the
Minotaur into an arrogant general called Bull (Tauros), with the
τραγικώτατος μῦθος {very tragic *mythos*} of the hybrid monster and
the victims in the labyrinth. This kind of treatment was forced on the
Atthidographers, who were compelled to use legendary material if they
were to write the early history of Athens at all.[29] They had to take their
subject-matter where they could find it, and they were in fact as ready

[24] Thuc. 1.21.1.   [25] *FGrHist* 1 F 1a.   [26] Jacoby (1949) 220.
[27] Athen. 8.39, 347e.   [28] Plut. *Thes.* 15.2.
[29] So, rightly, Jacoby (1949) 136; for the various forms of the Minotaur legend in
the various Atthidographers, see his comments on Philochorus, *FGrHist* 328 F 17.

to draw on tragedy as on epic—certainly from the fourth century
onwards;[30] and indeed Jacoby has suggested that even in the fifth
century Hellanicus may have let his discussion of the founding of the
Areopagus be influenced by the version in the *Oresteia*.[31]

These facts are not of course new. Most of the details I have
mentioned can be found in the well-known handbooks. But it
seemed worth while to recall this background before returning to
what is probably the most famous ancient statement on the question,
Aristotle's discussion of the nature of history and tragedy in the
Poetics.[32] In that passage, as we saw, Aristotle distinguishes poetry
as a more philosophical and higher thing than history, because it
tends to express the universal, and history the particular. The universal, τὰ καθ᾽ ὅλου, is how a person of a certain type will on occasion
speak or act, according to the law of probability or necessity; and it is
this universality at which poetry aims, just adding proper names to
the characters.[33] The particular, τὰ καθ᾽ ἕκαστον, is what Alcibiades
did or what happened to him. At this point comes a significant
statement: ἐπὶ μὲν οὖν τῆς κωμῳδίας ἤδη τοῦτο δῆλον γέγονεν—
which I take, with Gomme,[34] to mean 'in the case of comedy this is
at once apparent'. For in comedy, Aristotle continues, the plot is
invented on lines of probability (διὰ τῶν εἰκότων) and names
assigned to the characters; hence it is clearly universal on his definition. Tragic writers on the contrary keep to real names (τῶν
γενομένων ὀνομάτων ἀντέχονται). By real names he means of course
the names of real people like Agamemnon and Orestes; and what
they did has been defined as history. That is why the claim of tragedy
to be accounted universal has to be specially argued.

[30] Jacoby (1949) 220 argues that Hellanicus felt an antipathy for Euripides which
prevented his use of him as a source.

[31] Commentary on *FGrHist* 323a F 1 (Hellanicus).

[32] See above, n. 4.

[33] I agree with Gomme (1954) 71 that the adding of the proper names is mentioned as something which does not really hinder the universality of tragedy. Butcher
translates 'it is this universality at which poetry aims in the names she attaches to the
personages'; but though the proper names may constitute no serious obstacle, they
can hardly *help* to make tragedy more universal. Bywater agrees with Gomme.

[34] Gomme (1954) 72 n. 6. Alternatively Gudeman's rendering makes good sense:
'It is now agreed by all for comedy, but not for tragedy'; for in the case of comedy it is
easily apparent.

In this chapter Aristotle takes it for granted that his readers will immediately appreciate the distinction between comedy (which is universal) and history (which deals with the particular); but he expects the difference between tragedy and history to need special argumentation. This contrast between the two dramatic forms is widely made, and its echoes appear in both earlier and later critics. In the fourth century the comic writer Antiphanes,[35] for example, asserted that the tragic poet merely reminds his audience of what they all know whereas the comic poet has to make it all up, πάντα δεῖ εὑρεῖν. This view might appear at first sight to contradict Aristotle's insistence[36] that the tragic poet is the creator of plots rather than verses (μᾶλλον τῶν μύθων εἶναι δεῖ ποιητὴν ἢ τῶν μέτρων), since he is a poet because he represents (κατὰ τὴν μίμησιν) and what he represents are actions. Certainly this statement of Aristotle implies—as both Gomme[37] and Baldry[38] have recently insisted—that the poet had a considerable freedom of invention in relation to the traditional themes; but the limits of such freedom are indicated in another passage[39] in which Aristotle states that 'the poet may not destroy the framework of the received legends, the fact for instance that Clytemnestra was slain by Orestes and Eriphyle by Alcmaeon', and goes on to show by examples that what he means when he calls the poet a creator of plots is that he ought to show skill in the manipulation of the traditional material (τοῖς παραδεδομένοις χρῆσθαι καλῶς). Hence, despite the difference of nuance between one play on the Orestes legend and another, the main outlines of the story would be preserved, and would confirm the average Athenian theatre-goer in his belief that the tragedies he saw represented the fortunes of real people, just as Elizabethan audiences by and large must have taken *Richard II* to be a representation of what had happened to a real English king.

But if to the fifth- and fourth-century spectator tragedies dealt with traditional stories and real people, to that extent they came very close to history. Consequently when Aristotle goes on to establish the universality of tragedy—its concern with οἷα ἂν γένοιτο rather than

[35] *CAF* II.90–91, F 191 {= *PCG* F 189} = Athen. 6.222.a–c; see Giovannini (1943) 308.
[36] *Poet.* 9.9, 1451b27–30.   [37] Gomme (1954) 5–6, 54–5.
[38] Baldry (1954) 156 n. 1.   [39] *Poet.* 14.5, 1453b22–6.

with τὰ γενόμενα—this superficial closeness to history causes him
some embarrassment. The poet, he argues, is to relate οἷα ἂν γένοιτο,
what is possible according to the laws of probability or necessity; and
the poet includes the writer of tragedy for these reasons. Tragedians
keep to real names, because the use of real names (like Orestes and
Clytemnestra) is as it were a guarantee of credibility. We feel a certain
natural doubt as to whether something that has not happened could
have happened at all; whereas what *has* happened is clearly possible.
On the other hand, tragedies may contain some fictitious characters,
as well as real ones (one thinks for instance of the watchman in the
Antigone), or even nothing but fictitious ones, like Agathon's
Antheus, in which both the incidents and names are alike made
up. In any case, he adds, since most of the audience are ignorant of
the traditional stories, they are as good as fictitious: τὰ γνώριμα
ὀλίγοις γνώριμά ἐστιν ἀλλ᾽ ὅμως εὐφραίνει πάντας {the known stories
are known to a few but nevertheless they delight all}—which seems
to imply that what is fictitious can make a more immediately obvious
claim to universality than what is based on the literally true legends.

   This argument might, however, lead to the conclusion that tragedies like the *Antheus* were in fact superior to those based on the
traditional panhellenic legends; and this would be paradoxical, since
the majority of the tragedies and virtually all the most famous ones
fell into the second category. So Aristotle concludes by saying that in
any case if a poet happens to take real events as the subject of his
poetry, γενόμενα ποιεῖν—which must mean actual happenings, the
received legends as opposed to the fictional events in tragedies like
the *Antheus*, and not, as some have believed, specifically historical
tragedies like the *Persae*—there is no reason why *some* actual events
should not also conform to the law of the probable and the possible,
and it is by virtue of that quality in the events that the author is
a poet.

   The amount that has been written about this argument clearly
indicates its difficulties;[40] and these, I suggest, arise to a large extent

----

[40] It has even been argued recently, by Grayeff (1955–6) 110–18, that *Poetics* 9 is a
composite production incorporating the arguments of a series of Peripatetic lecturers
who have tried, each in turn, to add his comments to a rather abortive discussion
without great success. This argument, which takes no account of Baldry's discussion
(1954), does not convince me.

from the embarrassment Aristotle experiences in the face of the firmly established belief that the subject-matter of almost all Greek tragedies was also the subject-matter of history. The Greeks, it has been said, had only historical tragedies. This is true for almost the whole range of tragedy, and it means that the only difference between a play like the *Persae* and the *Troades* lies in the fact that one conforms to the custom of going back to the old traditional stories, while the other does not; but both alike are regarded as based on historical material.[41]

III

This view of the matter long continued to be the usual one. As an American scholar, Giovannini,[42] has recently pointed out, it can be well illustrated from the way in which the later grammarians divided up their material for classification. In his second book Quintilian[43] divides the field of *narrationes* (excluding those used in law-court speeches) into three categories, which he calls *fabulae, argumenta,* and *historiae.* The Greek equivalents are given in Sextus Empiricus,[44] for *fabula* μῦθος, for *argumentum* πλάσμα, while ἱστορία serves in both languages. The same divisions appear with slightly different names in Asclepiades of Myrleia,[45] in the *ad Herennium,* in Cicero's *de Inuentione,* and in the Byzantine *scholia* to Dionysius Thrax.[46]

---

[41] Isoc. *Euag.* 36 has been adduced (by Gudeman on Arist. *Poet.* 9) in support of this view, but wrongly. Its meaning is that 'of all the poets who have told of returning exiles, both real and of their own imagining (παρ' αὐτῶν καινὰς συντιθέασιν), none has told a story (of anyone) who returned home after enduring such dreadful and fearful dangers (as Euagoras)'. It does not mean that no tragedian ever told a μῦθος, as indeed the previous sentence makes clear. In the context of the *Euagoras,* however, Isocrates is led to stress the differences between the poet and the prose panegyrist (cf. §§8–11).

[42] Giovannini (1943).

[43] 2.42.

[44] *Math.* 1.263–4.

[45] Viz. ἀληθὴς ἱστορία (= ἱστορία), ψευδὴς ἱστορία (= μῦθος, fabula), and ὡς ἀληθὴς ἱστορία (= πλάσμα, argumentum). On Asclepiades, see Reitzenstein (1906) 90ff.; Barwick (1928) 270. The relevant text is from Sext. Emp. *Math.* 1.252, where both Reitzenstein and Barwick are agreed in accepting Kaibel's emendation, so as to include τὴν περὶ πλάσματα under ὡς ἀληθῆ.

[46] See *Rhet. Herenn.* 1.12f.; Cic. *Inu.* 1.27; Barwick (1928) 261ff.

These three types of *narratio* are sharply distinguished. 'History', says Sextus,[47] 'ἱστορία, is the recording of certain things which are true and have happened, as for example that Alexander died at Babylon through having been poisoned by conspirators [perhaps an unfortunate example!]; fiction (πλάσμα, *argumentum*) is the narrating of things which are not real events but are similar to real events in the telling, such as the hypothetical situations in comedies and mimes; and legend (μῦθος, *fabula*) is the narrating of events which have never happened and are false, like the story that the species of venomous spiders and snakes were born alive from the blood of the Titans, that Pegasus sprang from the Gorgon's head when her throat was cut, and that Diomedes' companions were changed into sea-birds, Odysseus into a horse and Hecuba into a dog.' Quintilian likewise defines *fabula* as what has neither truth nor verisimilitude.

Asclepiades discusses the subject-matter of tragedy in relation to these categories and differentiates what is ἱστορία and so true from what is μῦθος (or ψευδὴς ἱστορία) and so false. But remarkably little falls into the latter category; indeed he mentions only one heading, τὸ γενεαλογικόν, which probably includes the fabulous origins of living creatures mentioned by Sextus under μῦθος—the spiders springing from the Titans' blood, Pegasus from the Gorgon's head, and so on. Indeed it seems[48] as though the ancient grammarians, Greek and Roman, reserved the name μῦθος or *fabula* for what was impossible κατὰ φύσιν {according to nature}, while all the subject-matter of legend, as well as what we should call history, fell under ἱστορία, provided that it was physically possible.

Now it is precisely the residuary 'mythical' element in the early legends which hinders the full identification of this traditional material with history. Thucydides, as we saw, excluded τὸ μυθῶδες from his history; and later Polybius,[49] in his account of Cisalpine Gaul and the

47 *Math.* 1.263–4.

48 For example, Theon in his *Progymnasmata* reckons the story of Medea's murder of her children as πραγματική {pragmatic}, not μυθική {mythical} (cf. Barwick (1928) 271 n. 1, quoting a point made by Heinze).

49 Pol. 2.16.13–15. Whom Polybius is attacking is not clear. He says that to take issue with these stories is not suitable at this point in his work (presumably because it is in one of the introductory books), but he promises to do so later, 'especially as Timaeus has shown much ignorance concerning the district'. This sounds as if the object of criticism was Timaeus, and this view, accepted by Müllenhoff, has been

course of the river Po, criticizes the legends told of this area—of Phaethon and his fall, the transformation of his sisters into weeping poplars,
and 'the black clothing of the inhabitants near the river who, they say,
still dress thus in mourning for Phaethon, καὶ πᾶσαν δὴ τὴν τραγικὴν
καὶ ταύτῃ προσεοικυῖαν ὕλην—and all similar matter for tragedy'.

These stories are of the kind Sextus quotes to illustrate the nature
of μῦθος, and Asclepiades reckons under τὸ γενεαλογικόν, if this can
be stretched to include metamorphoses; certainly the transformation
of Phaethon's sisters into poplars is exactly parallel to Hecuba's
metamorphosis into a dog, or that of Diomedes' companions into
sea-birds. Such stories must be excluded from history; but by a
careful process of rationalization the amount sacrificed could be
reduced to a minimum. For example, Polybius himself finds it
possible by this method to accept almost the whole of Homer against
the more sceptical attitude of Eratosthenes, who had remarked that
we might perhaps find out where Odysseus travelled when we found
the cobbler who sewed up the bag of the winds. Polybius admits that
some mythical elements have been added but, he says, 'Homer's main
statements about Sicily correspond to those of other writers who
treat the local history of Italy and Sicily.'[50] Even the account of Scylla
ravening after dolphins, dog-fish, and the like can be directly compared with the methods used by natives of the Straits of Messina in
catching sword-fish.[51]

recently argued afresh by Stiehl (1955), who thinks Polybius took most of his account
of Lombardy from Timaeus. But Polybius attacks Timaeus, not for the myths, but for
general ignorance, a very different matter (cf. Pédech (1956) 19 n. 58); and if Diod.
5.23.5, dealing with the same stories, derives from Timaeus (as seems likely), Timaeus
also regarded such myths as out of place in history.

[50] Pol. 34.2.9–10.

[51] The same tendency to rationalize Homer also appears in the Stoic Strabo, who in
a discussion of the place of the false, mythical, element in the poet explains (1.2.9, C20)
that his work fell within the province of education, τὸ παιδευτικὸν εἶδος, but that he
mingled therein a false element to give sanction to the truth, and to win popular
favour—adding myth to real events (ταῖς ἀληθέσι περιπετείαις προσετίθει μῦθον) 'as
when some skilful man overlays gold on silver', and so aiming at the same purpose as
the historian or the person who relates facts. This emphasis on the paideutic function
of myth to control and out-manoeuvre the masses (δημαγωγῶν καὶ στρατηγῶν τὰ
πλήθη) links up with Plato; but the distinction between the true legends and the small
admixture of the false is not restricted to any one school. Some of the most striking
examples of the rationalizing of myth are to be found in Palaephatus, a Peripatetic.

In this way the amount of μῦθος or *fabula* in the epics and tragedies
was minimized, and the amount falling under the heading ἱστορία
extended. The third category, fiction (*argumentum* or πλάσμα),
hardly concerns us here, since it is proper to mime and comedy.
Originally all three categories seem to have applied only to poetry;[52]
but by the second century at the latest some critics, such as Asclepiades, were employing them in relation to narratives throughout the
whole field of literature. Where they originated is uncertain. Barwick
suggests that they arose in the Peripatetic school, but his arguments
are not very strong.[53] On the other hand, Asclepiades' version at least
seems to imply a fairly advanced stage of the theory, since he refers the
three categories to a field which has been extended from that of poetry
to the whole of literature. It therefore looks as though one might safely
take the original, limited form of the theory back to an earlier date
than Asclepiades, and it *may* derive from the Peripatos.

The grammarians, it is true, like Aristotle are concerned with the
relationship between history and legend from the point of view of
poetry. They postulate that such parts of tragedy as are not specifically ἀδύνατα {impossibilities} shall be accounted *historia* (as well as
tragedy based on recent events, like the *Persae*); but they are not
interested in the historian's conception of history. On the other hand,
although the grammatical categories may originally have referred
only to poetry, their influence will obviously have been felt by anyone
who came within the range of rhetorical education, and with the
early extension outside the narrow field of poetry they must have
affected the historian too. The very use of the word ἱστορία to
describe the bulk of the traditional subject-matter of epic and tragedy
will have contributed to a blurring of the distinction which Aristotle
had tried to draw, and so to a confusion about where precisely the
historian was to set up the frontier between his own craft and
tragedy.

[52] Cf. Barwick (1928) 282, who points to their appearance in the scholia to
Dionysius Thrax, and notes too that the examples of them quoted by Cicero and in
the *ad Herennium* are all taken from poetry.

[53] His argument rests on association of Palaephatus' rationalization of myth with
the tripartite division into history, myth and *argumentum*; but Palaephatus makes no
reference to this division, and seems merely concerned to explain away apparent
improbabilities in the traditional stories.

IV

To this factor making for confusion can be added yet another.
Aristotle's definition of tragedy was not universally accepted. The
grammarians, and the scholiasts on whom we have often to rely for
their views, believed that it was the main function of tragedy to
provide examples of virtue and so to point a moral. 'Tragedy', we
read in the scholia on Dionysius Thrax,[54] 'is the name given to the
poems of the tragic writers, for example those of Euripides, Sophocles, and Aeschylus, and similar authors. These men lived in Athenian
times (ἐπὶ τῶν χρόνων τῶν Ἀθηναίων). Being tragic writers, and
wishing to help the people of the city as a body, they took certain
ancient stories of heroes, containing certain sufferings, sometimes
deaths and lamentations, and exhibited these in the theatre to the
eyes and ears of the spectators, demonstrating that they should be on
their guard against sin. For if heroes such as these suffered such
things, clearly because of the sins they had committed, how much
more shall we or our contemporaries suffer if we sin? Therefore... we
ought as far as possible to lead lives that are free from sin and devoted
to philosophy (ἀναμάρτητον καὶ φιλοσοφώτατον). Hence the poetry
of the tragic writers was produced with a view to helping the citizens.'
    This is obviously both a narrower and a more naïve view of the
function of tragedy than Aristotle's; but it is remarkably similar to
the Isocratean—and Polybian—view of the purpose of history, which
regarded it as a store-house of examples calculated to help the reader
either morally or practically according to the bent of the particular
writer. Moreover, it is not simply a late view of the purpose of
tragedy; on the contrary it is recognized as early as Aristotle's own
time, for his contemporary, the dramatist Timocles—a practitioner,
no mere theoretician—according to Athenaeus[55] attributed the
moral benefits of tragedy to the realism with which it displayed
events which were clearly to be regarded as historical. 'Man', he
says, 'is a creature born to labour, and many are the distresses
which his life carries with it. Therefore he has contrived... respites

---

[54] See Kaibel, *CGF* I.11, scholia ad Dion. Thrac. p. 746.1.
[55] Athen. 6.223b–d {= *PCG* VII.758–9, F 6}; cf. Giovannini (1943) 314 n. 33.

from his cares. . . . Look . . . at the tragedians and see what benefit they
are to everybody. The poor man, for instance, learns that Telephus
was more beggarly than himself, and from that time on he bears his
poverty more easily. . . . One has lost his son in death: Niobe is a
comfort. Another is lame: he sees Philoctetes. . . . Thus he is reminded
that all his calamities . . . have happened to others, and so he bears his
own trials more readily.'

As the counterpart to this, tragedy and its stories may likewise act
as a moral deterrent. 'If', writes Diodorus in his prologue,[56] 'myths
about Hades (μυθολογία), containing fictional material, conduce
greatly to inspiring men to piety and justice, how much more must
we suppose history, the interpreter of truth and the source of all
philosophy, capable of shaping men's characters in honourable ways!'
Myths about Hades are of course a traditional ingredient of tragedy,
as we know from the *Poetics*,[57] where Aristotle refers to 'the spectacular element exemplified by . . . the *Prometheus* and scenes laid in
Hades' and it seems likely that in this passage Diodorus (or whatever
the source from whom he derives the substance of his prologue)[58] is
tendentiously selecting one of those features of tragedy which, while
being morally efficacious, nevertheless fall traditionally under the
heading of μῦθος rather than ἱστορία, in order to demonstrate the
superiority of history, the προφῆτις τῆς ἀληθείας {the prophetess of
truth} as an instrument of ethical instruction. But the fact that he
institutes the comparison at all illustrates yet again how closely the
two fields are associated in the popular mind.

V

History and tragedy are thus linked together in their common origin
in epic, in their use of comparable and often identical material, and
in their moral purpose. It is therefore not very surprising that the

[56] Diod. 1.2.2.   [57] *Poet.* 18.3, 1456a1–3.
[58] Barber (1935) 103 makes the source Ephorus; but it looks post-Polybian and
may be from Posidonius. Kunz (1935) 101, however, claims it for Diodorus himself;
cf. also Nock (1959) on Posidonius; Palm (1955) 140 n. 1.

treatment proper to one genre should fairly frequently be applied to the other, and that the historian who seeks to play upon his reader's emotions should be attacked as a would-be tragedian. There is, however, yet a further point which is not wholly without relevance to this question. The reaction to any particular dramatic performance will obviously vary greatly according to the character of the audience. 'In our London theatres', writes George Thomson,[59] 'the members of the audience usually keep their emotional reactions (other than laughter) to themselves; but in the cinemas of the west of Ireland, where the spectators are peasants, the atmosphere is far more intense. At the critical moments of the plot almost every face wears a terrified look and continuous sobbing may be heard. In this respect, an Athenian would undoubtedly have felt more at home in the west of Ireland than in the West End of London.' In support of this view Thomson quotes the famous passage from Plato's *Ion* in which the sophist describes his own effect upon his audience.[60] 'From the platform I see the audience weeping, and with looks of horror on their face, as they respond emotionally to what I am saying.'

There is, I think, reason to believe that this high degree of Athenian sensibility, this naivety one might almost say, is perceptible in the Greek reaction to narrative descriptions as well as to dramatic representations. This point can be illustrated if one considers some of the comments by Greek critics on passages in surviving historians and observes their apparent exaggeration. It is of course perfectly true that Thucydides contains some highly dramatic elements. It has often been pointed out[61] that the juxtaposition of the Melian Dialogue and the start of the Sicilian Expedition creates some of the tension of tragedy; and even if the main thesis of *Thucydides Mythistoricus* has to be rejected, the fact that Cornford ever wrote it is in itself a significant comment on the effect the historian can produce. But despite these dramatic elements, the picture which ancient critics draw of Thucydides, and even of Xenophon, is hardly recognizable when set up beside the authors themselves.

---

[59] Thomson (1941) 380–1.   [60] Plat. *Ion* 535c.
[61] Cf. Laistner (1947) 14. For other dramatic elements in Thucydides, see Finley (1942) 321–4.

'Sometimes', writes Dionysius,[62] 'Thucydides makes the sufferings [sc. in conquered cities] so cruel, so terrible, and so deserving of pity, that he leaves nothing worse for either historians or poets to describe.' The examples he quotes are Plataea, Mytilene, and Melos; in all three a modern critic would be inclined to regard Thucydides' treatment as vivid, but emotionally restrained. Plutarch, however, shares the views of Dionysius. Xenophon, he tells us,[63] by his moving and lifelike account of the battle of Cunaxa creates in the reader the impression of actually taking part in the events and of sharing in the perils of the battle. Similarly[64] Thucydides constantly strives after a high degree of vividness (ἐνάργεια) in his passion to convert the listener into a spectator (οἷον θεατὴν ποιῆσαι τὸν ἀκροατήν ... λιχνευόμενος) and to engender in his readers the consternation and emotional disturbance actually experienced by those who saw the events (τὰ γινόμενα περὶ τοὺς ὁρῶντας ἐκπληκτικὰ καὶ ταρακτικὰ πάθη τοῖς ἀναγινώσκουσιν ἐνεργάσασθαι). This recalls a remark of Isocrates,[65] who spoke of tragedians who introduced myths into their plays, ὥστε μὴ μόνον ἀκουστοὺς ἡμῖν ἀλλὰ καὶ θεατοὺς γενέσθαι {so as to make us not only listeners but also spectators}. In short, Plutarch is criticizing Thucydides in precisely the same kind of terms as are elsewhere used of Duris and Phylarchus.

This suggests one of two conclusions. Either later critics such as Plutarch and Dionysius described the effects of Thucydides and Xenophon on their readers in terms that were obviously exaggerated, and could be seen to be exaggerated by anyone who took the trouble to read the account of Cunaxa or the siege of Plataea for himself. Or alternatively the Greeks—I suppose one must say of Plutarch's and Dionysius' age, though it would probably be true of ancient Greeks at all times—reacted more directly and emotionally to both the written and spoken word than we normally do. As between the two explanations a choice is not difficult. The history of Greek literature suggests beyond doubt that the Greeks were especially sensitive to the effects of language. The intense interest shown in verbal devices from the time of Gorgias, the wide and persistent influence of Isocrates and his school, the receptivity of the Greek audience to rhapsode and

---

[62] D. Hal. *Thuc.* 15.			[63] Plut. *Artax.* 8.1.

[64] Plut. *De glor. Ath.* 347A.			[65] Isoc. *In Nicocl.* 49.

declaimer—all point in the same direction; and this furnishes yet a further reason why the reaction to tragedy should so frequently be confused with the reaction to a historical narrative constructed with all the resources of ἐνάργεια and designed to play upon the emotions of the reader or listener. When finally one bears in mind that history like other compositions would normally be read aloud, often in public gatherings, with the additional attractions with which the skilful declaimer can invest a narrative, it is easy to see why the confusion between tragedy and history should have been of such long standing.

VI

In discussing this question von Fritz made Aristotle's influence his starting point. But, as he admits, many of the characteristics of so-called tragic history appear in Callisthenes, though Callisthenes' work was written long before the *Poetics*.[66] One need only recall the story of the ravens rounding up Alexander's stragglers by cawing during the famous visit to the oracle of Ammon,[67] that of the *proskynêsis* {prostration} of the sea when Alexander passed the Climax after leaving Phaselis,[68] an anecdote designed, says Plutarch,[69] to provide historians with material for a bombastic and terrifying description—ὑπόθεσις γραφικὴ πρὸς ἔκπληξιν καὶ ὄγκον—or the sudden reanimation of the oracle of Branchidae, the transition to which from the story of the visit to Ammon is referred to by Strabo[70] with the phrase: προστραγῳδεῖ τούτοις ὁ Καλλισθένης {Callisthenes tragically adds to this}. This does not of course mean that Callisthenes was the originator of this kind of history, any more than Duris. For, long before Callisthenes, Ctesias of Cnidus, writing with an Ionian background,[71] was composing Persian and Indian histories in a sensational and credulous manner which does no credit to his scientific training as a doctor. In later critics at any rate, his work

---

[66] von Fritz (1956) 130. [67] Plut. *Alex.* 27 = *FGrHist* 124 F 14(b).
[68] *FGrHist* 124 F 31. [69] Plut. *Alex.* 17.3.
[70] *FGrHist* 124 F 14(a) = Str. 17.1.43, C814. [71] Cf. Wehrli (1947) 68.

inspired much the same feelings as Phylarchus' histories inspired in
Polybius. 'The charm of his history', writes Photius,[72] 'springs above
all from his manner of constructing narrative passages which arouse
emotion (τὸ παθητικόν), and afford many examples of the unexpected and of various embellishments which bring them close to the
confines of the mythical.' To Plutarch,[73] who used him in his *Arta-
xerxes*, his work 'often turns aside from the truth into fable and
romance (πρὸς τὸ μυθῶδες καὶ δραματικόν)'; and in his account of
the bringing of the news of Cunaxa to the queen mother Parysatis, he
conceals the news of Cyrus' death until the very end of the speech for
dramatic effect, as if it were a messenger's speech in a tragedy.[74] In
such ways as these, remarks Demetrius in his treatise *On Style*, he
aims at pathetic and vivid effects precisely as if he were a poet.

It is tempting to bring Gorgias too into the picture. Gorgias
developed a theory and a style which drew no clear distinction
between poetry and prose,[75] and probably set up ψυχαγωγία {pleas-
ure/entertainment} as the common goal of works of art, literature,
and oratory.[76] But despite his stylistic influence on Thucydides who,
as Bury remarked,[77] would occasionally write 'crooked passages
which produced upon a Greek ear almost the effect of dithyrambs
released from the bonds of metre', there is no evidence to show that
Gorgias concerned himself with the writing of history or influenced
views concerning its purpose. But even without Gorgias there is no
difficulty in reaching the fifth century. Lucian links Herodotus himself with Ctesias[78] as a composer of 'monstrous little fables', τεράστια
μυθίδια. To Aristotle he was a μυθόλογος {fable-monger};[79] and
Diodorus[80] accuses him of inventing wonder-stories and myths at
the expense of truth in order to entertain (τὸ παραδοξολογεῖν καὶ
μύθους πλάττειν ψυχαγωγίας ἕνεκα). Here again, significantly, there
is no division between the fifth century and later writers: the line
of development is continuous. There is then sufficient indication
that the main features of 'tragic history' go back well beyond the

---

[72] *FGrHist* 688 T 13 = Phot. *Bibl.* 72 p. 45a12ff.
[73] Plut. *Artax.* 6.9.
[74] *FGrHist* 688 F 24 = Demetr. *Eloc.* 216.
[75] Arist. *Rhet.* 3.1, 1404a29.   [76] Cf. Avenarius (1956) 140.
[77] Bury (1909) 111.   [78] Luc. *Philops.* 2.
[79] Arist. *Gen. Anim.* 3, 75b5.   [80] Diod. 1.69.7.

Hellenistic period, and Aristotle, who is supposed to have played so
vital if involuntary a part in their formulation.

VII

In the discussion which followed von Fritz's paper, and which is
printed after it, there was a general and it would seem wholly justified
reluctance to accept the Peripatos in the important role to which the
speaker had assigned it. It appeared improbable that theory had so
decisive a part to play in the shaping of practice. Were there not more
likely to be predisposing causes for this form of historiography, it was
asked, in the climate of the times, in the demands of the reading
public, in the nature of the historical material available, in itself often
violent and sensational, and even in the political sympathies of the
historians?[81] As factors likely to accentuate a trend towards vivid and
sensational historiography these are all possibilities worth bearing in
mind. But it is perhaps no less important to recognize that the sharp
isolation of 'tragic history' as a separate school in need of explanation
and of a definite and immediate ancestry is very largely a figment and
a distortion. Duris may have borrowed a vogue-word $\mu\acute{\iota}\mu\eta\sigma\iota\varsigma$ from
the Peripatos. That is not important. What matters is that the link
between tragedy and history, which constituted the main feature of
the supposed tragic–historical school and was felt to need special
elucidation, is in fact a fundamental affinity going back to the earliest
days of both history and tragedy, and insisted upon throughout
almost the whole of the classical and later periods down to the
Byzantine scholiasts. It was there by virtue of descent and of analogous literary techniques, it was encouraged by a common moral aim
and by the sharpness of Greek emotional sensibility, and it was taught
in the rhetorical schools to generations of Greek students.

What should have been a patent fact staring us in the face has been
obscured through the prestige of Aristotle's name and his analysis of
the *difference* between tragedy and history. And because two of his
successors, Polybius and Lucian, whose interests lay in history, both

[81] Von Fritz (1956) 129–45.

to some extent accepted his distinction, it has tended to be regarded as the normal belief of educated Greeks. As a result we have had to invent the expression 'tragic history' in order to reunite what few Greek writers were interested in dividing. To ignore this is not merely to misunderstand Hellenistic history: it is also to underestimate the character of Polybius' protest. For the reasons indicated most of his predecessors and contemporaries aimed at stirring the emotions by the vivid representation of scenes sensational in themselves, and at titillating their readers' palates by serving up the wonder-stories which went back originally to the Ionians including Herodotus, but for which there was a growing taste, stimulated of course by the Alexander historians, and such figures as Pytheas of Marseilles. Polybius' criticism is not therefore to be regarded as simply polemic against a single limited school with a specific and clearly defined theory and practice of recent origin. On the contrary, it is to be taken seriously as a demand for new standards and canons in Greek historiography. Perhaps it will make for a more sympathetic understanding both of him and of his opponents, if the term 'tragic history' is discarded from subsequent discussion.[82]

[82] This paper was read at a meeting of the Hellenic Society in London on 24 April 1959.

15

Poetry and Historiography: A Study in the Use of Sources

Hermann Funke

At the end of the sixth century AD, Evagrius Scholasticus wrote an
ecclesiastical history, the fifth book of which he finished with a survey
of the historical works available at his time, regarding himself as their
continuator:[1]

> Thank God a good ecclesiastical history exists which we owe to the assiduity
> of the best writers: Eusebius who covers the early centuries including the
> time of Constantine; Theodorus, Sozomen, and Socrates describing the
> century from Constantine to Theodosius. Many scholars wrote the older
> history, both ecclesiastical and secular. Moses, in fact, who wrote history for
> the first time, has noted down the events that happened from the beginning
> of the world according to the truth as he had learned it from God who had
> talked to him on Sinai. His successors paved the way for our faith, compos-
> ing the later events in the Holy Scriptures. Josephus also wrote a large and
> useful history. Charax, Theopompus, Ephorus, and many others have
> recorded the events of mythical times and what has happened since. The
> history of Rome we read in the books of Dionysius of Halicarnassus. His
> work is continued by Polybius, Diodorus Siculus, and Cassius Dio. Hero-
> dian, Nicostratus of Trapezunt, and Dexippus are followed by Eusebius
> whose subject is also dealt with by Arrian and Asinius Quadratus. Finally,
> there are Zosimus, Priscus, Eustathius of Epiphania, Procopius, Agathias,
> and my relative and compatriot John Malalas.

---

[1] 5.24, *PG* 86.2, 2840ff. (Migne).

There are various things we learn from Evagrius' survey of Greek historiography: (1) Moses is the first historiographer; (2) God dictated to him what he writes and therefore he writes the truth, word for word; (3) Apparently there was already a tradition before Evagrius regarding Moses as a historiographer among others; (4) The enumeration of his predecessors offers an undiscriminating jumble with regard both to subject and quality; (5) It is striking that Herodotus and Thucydides are missing.

These points raise a couple of questions. The first is: how is it possible that a historiographer at the end of antiquity—and that means after more than a thousand years of reflection on historical methods—can treat Moses and Diodorus Siculus alike and state that Moses has transmitted truthfully the history from the beginning of the world? Let us take an example from this beginning of the world and consider its implications. According to the historical understanding on which Evagrius' reading of the Mosaic Genesis is based, God in Paradise has planted trees like a gardener (*Gen.* 2:9) and sewed clothes out of skins like a shoemaker for Adam and Eve after the Fall (*Gen.* 3:21).

To answer this question we shall turn first to the ecclesiastical historiography which precedes his age and is considered by him. At first sight it appears to be, in its estimation of the Old Testament and especially the Mosaic books as historical sources, rather homogeneous.

It is not surprising that John Malalas, whose *Chronicle* is full of anecdotes and curiosities, is using at the same time the Old Testament and secular and ecclesiastical history as sources; so we find, besides Moses, Homer as a witness for a fact of the early history of Egypt, 'concerning which Homer the poet provides a poetic narrative (περὶ οὗ ἱστορεῖ ποιητικῶς Ὅμηρος ὁ ποιητής)'.[2] But Sozomen, who knows how to use documentary material in writing history, also shows, like his predecessor Socrates, the same fundamentalist understanding of the Bible—not to speak of a soteriological understanding of secular history.

At the beginning of his work he puts the question why men believe in God and he gives the answer 'because Christ has been predicted in

---

[2] P. 24 Dindorf {= 2.1, pp. 17–8 Thurn}.

the Old Testament and because everything has happened according to it. But also Josephus, esteemed by both Jews and Romans', he continues, 'is an important witness of the truth of Jesus'.[3] The fact that the historiography of a Josephus is put on an equal footing with the message of salvation of the Old Testament shows how little the categories of criticism are distinguished, but it also emphasizes the fact that someone can recommend himself as a witness for the truth of Christ by the reputation which he enjoys with Jews and Romans as well.

On the other hand we find an example of the symbolical understanding of the Scriptures in the ecclesiastical history of Theodoret of Cyrrhus[4] where he mentions a heretic named Audianus who understands *Genesis* 1:26 'Let us make man in our image' literally, as if God had a human shape and human limbs. Audianus is said to have misunderstood the Scriptures; for they often attach names of human organs to divine activities, because in this way those who are incapable of a more spiritual understanding can come easier to the knowledge of divine providence.

This is not to say that this knowledge of the double, the literal, and the spiritual meaning of the Scriptures is the invention of the historian Theodoret; it can easily be a quotation from a church decree against that heretic. What is important is that this distinction is known to an ecclesiastical historiographer, a distinction which leads us into the field of Alexandrian theology and its understanding of the Scriptures.

But first let us have a look at Eusebius, the 'archegetes', the founder, of ecclesiastical history. In his work, which sets out to describe the history of the church of Christ from its beginnings until its triumph under Constantine, Eusebius writes in accordance with the literary form of secular historiography. Even if his intention, to present a whole out of scattered materials—that is a genetic development of history— has not been achieved in reality, he does qualify as a master of his craft, who knows its methodological principles. His historiography is based

³ *HE* 1.1.1 (*GCS* L, p. 7): καὶ Ἰώσηπος … ἀνὴρ παρά τε Ἰουδαίους ἐπιδοξότατος γενόμενος, ἔτι δὲ καὶ παρὰ Ῥωμαίοις, ἀξιοχρέως ἂν εἴη μάρτυς τῆς περὶ Χριστοῦ ἀληθείας.
⁴ *HE* 4.10 (*GCS* XIX, p. 228).

on: (1) a study of sources, which also includes extra-canonical books (Josephus, Philo); (2) a critical interpretation of historical material which is partly interspersed with legendary and apocalyptical materials; and (3) quotations from documents such as registers of bishops, deeds, letters.

As to the problem of his understanding of the Scriptures as the foundation of his historiography, Eusebius declares in the introduction to his work that it is not that he regards the Old Testament as the historical description of a time preceding the epoch that he describes himself, but as a self-revealing of God in human shape, ἐν ἀνθρώπου μορφῇ καὶ σχήματι {in the shape and form of man}.[5] Eusebius' intention is to understand the activities of the pre-existent Logos in the course of history but not to describe this history or even to give its chronology. In the introductory chapters of his work he shows by his treatment of the Scriptures how inadequate such an enterprise would be.[6] The passages of the Old Testament which he quotes here are all of a prophetic and apocalyptical nature, and are also understood and interpreted by him as such. His remarks on scriptural texts which point to the founder of the church whose history he is about to write are something that Eusebius wants to be taken as lying before, i.e. outside, his historiography, ταῦτα μὲν οὖν ἀναγκαίως πρὸ τῆς ἱστορίας ἐνθαῦτά μοι κείσθω {these things then, of necessity, I have placed before my history}.[7]

If we try now to figure out the focal point of these thoughts about literal and spiritual understanding of the Scriptures which are so differently expressed, we have to look for them, as already indicated, in the sphere of the Alexandrian exegesis of the Scriptures. Inside this sphere we are referred, as regards our special question concerning the relationship of Scriptures and historical authenticity, to a figure for whose identification we are given definite hints by Eusebius himself. It is Origen, whose pupil Eusebius calls himself, though he lived more than two generations separated from him. To Origen he has dedicated almost the whole sixth book of his historical work, and for him he has written a defence to save him from the reproach of heresy.

---

[5] *HE* 1.2.11 (*GCS* IX.1, p. 16).   [6] *HE* 1.1.1–2.16 (*GCS* IX.1, pp. 6–20).
[7] *HE* 1.4.1 (*GCS* IX.1, p. 38).

It is obvious that in the context of this essay we cannot develop Origen's understanding of the Scriptures in all its depth and many-sidedness. So I would only draw attention to the following: certainly Origen distinguishes three levels of meaning of the Scriptures—a somatic, a psychic, and a pneumatic one—but he always emphasizes that the last one, the secret sense of the Scriptures, is the true goal of anyone who devotes his energies to their study. In the fourth book of his *On Beginnings* (περὶ ἀρχῶν) where he explains his theory of exegesis he says: 'The modest believer will be edified by the body of the Scriptures, so to speak; this is how we call the most obvious meaning; the advanced, by the soul of the Scriptures; the perfect, finally, by the spiritual law that contains a foreshadowing of future goods.'[8] We also find this gradation of values in the fifth homily on Leviticus where Origen actually calls the lowest meaning of the Scriptures the historical one; there he says (in Rufinus' translation): 'As we said, one can find three modes of divine understanding in the Scriptures, the historical, the moral and the mystical; hence we understand it to have a body, a soul and a spirit—*triplicem in scripturis diuinis intelligentiae inueniri saepe diximus modum, historicum, moralem et mysticum, unde et corpus inesse ei et animam ac spiritum intelleximus*.'[9] In most of the passages of his work, however, Origen completely denies the literal meaning. So he says in *On Beginnings* 4.15: in the Scriptures scandals and impossible things happen (σκάνδαλα καὶ προσκόμματα καὶ ἀδύνατα {scandals, obstacles, and impossibilities}; this is God's will, so that the intelligent should know how not to get stuck in the words—in this context we also find the examples mentioned above of God as a shoemaker or gardener in Paradise—and when Origen says this, he is rejecting principally the literal or historical meaning of the Scriptures. Add to this—as we know it also from Homeric epic—the existence of contradictions in the subject-matter which leads him in the same way to the realization that the truth of such stories does not lie in their historical reading but points towards a hidden goal, the μυστικὸς

---

[8] *De princ.* 4.11. This pedagogic aspect also in *hom. Jer.* 5.15 (*GCS* VI.44); cf. Koch (1932) 60.

[9] *5. hom. in Lev.* 5 (*PG* 12.455C).

25

σκόπος {mystical goal} which is found out by allegorical interpretation.

Philo, on the one hand, could resolve his problem as to how to provide an understanding of the Old Testament to his contemporaries by the same method by which the Alexandrians explained the Homeric epics—that is, the allegorical method—whereas Origen, on the other hand, was forced in addition to this to explain the inconsistencies between the Old Testament and the New Testament which were pointed out especially by the Gnostics.[10] It goes without saying that this problem could not allow him to take the Scriptures as historiography.

In the fourth book of *On Beginnings* we also read: 'Viewed historically, most of the passages in the Holy Scriptures have no sense; they gain it only by spiritual understanding (*plurima sacris scripturis inserta esse...*, *quae historia quidem non recipiat, spiritualis autem teneat intellectus*)'.[11] So we understand Jerome, who translated many works of Origen, when he states about him: 'He never touched history, but was occupied with allegorical interpretation after his own fashion (*historiam omnino non tetigit et more suo totus in allegoriae interpretatione uersatus est*)'.[12]

This is the school of exegesis in which the historian Eusebius was brought up. But Eusebius himself was not only a historian but also a scholar and a critic of the Bible. In his commentaries on Isaiah and the Psalms as well as in his work περὶ τῶν ἐν εὐαγγελίοις ζητημάτων καὶ λύσεων {*On Problems and Solutions in the Gospels*} we see him following the ideas of Origen. Eusebius not only started his literary activities with critical studies on the Bible, he also dedicated his whole life to exegetical studies. In doing so he could rely upon the voluminous work of Origen as we learn from Jerome. This would also lead us to expect that he should follow in his historical work, as far as it concerns biblical matters, the standards established by Origen.

So we are all the more astonished, when we see Eusebius in his *Chronicle* going back to the level of the literal, historical understanding

---

[10] Cf. Preuschen (1903) LXXXIV.
[11] *De princ.* 4.16 (*GCS* XX, pp. 322–3)
[12] *Comm. in Mal. Prol.* 6.941f. (Vallarsi²).

of the Bible. In this work which he regards as a precursor of his *Ecclesiastical History*[13] and in which he tries mainly to depict the earlier age of Jewish history, Eusebius uses the Old Testament beside Josephus and Clement of Alexandria as a source for the history of the Hebrews in the same way as he uses Castor, Porphyrius, and Diodorus as sources for Greek history and, beside these, Dionysius of Halicarnassus for Roman, and Abydenus, Cephalion, and Manetho for Egyptian and Assyrian history. The question as to how Eusebius could use such a procedure seems to be legitimized by the fact that he is by no means a second- or third-rate ecclesiastical historiographer (like Evagrius or Malalas); on the other hand, this question could be answered by considerations which are based on the fact that Eusebius is the first who applied the method of ancient secular historiography to the field of ecclesiastical history.

Before turning to ancient secular historiography and the problem of its sources, a conjecture should be offered: the contradiction we have just mentioned might be explained by the fact that Eusebius, in the programmatic introduction to his work, that is, in a place where a writer is reflecting consciously on the principles of his profession, formulates and observes a rule of historiography, whereas, in another place, in the course of his narrative, where he is not explicitly dealing with questions of principle, he easily happens to succumb unconsciously to an uncritical attitude.

We find this supposition confirmed if we turn to Procopius, whom Evagrius mentioned among his immediate predecessors.[14] In his introduction to his *Gothic War*, Procopius gives a definition of his profession in contradistinction to others: 'As power of words befits rhetoric and fantasy befits poetry, so truth is suitable for historiography.'[15] Neither this programmatic statement, nor the reassurance reiterated at the beginning of his Book 8[16] that a line of demarcation has to be drawn between myth and history and their literary manifestations poetry and historiography, nor hints that already Herodotus and Thucydides had doubted the authority of Homer, have saved Procopius from taking poetry as a historical source. Thus Aeschylus is for him a witness for the location of the river Phasis,

---

[13] *HE* 1.1.6 (*GCS* IX.1, p. 8).   [14] Cf. also Veh (1951).
[15] Procop. *Bell.* 1.1.4.   [16] Procop. *Bell.* 8.1.12.

and he takes the evidence of Homer for facts relating to geography and the history of civilization, and what is more, for the authenticity of the wanderings of Odysseus. That is to say that Procopius, in practice, does not distinguish between myth and history; for him, myth is merely an unreliable thing, to be used with caution, 'for on account of the length of time complete certainty cannot be reached,' says Procopius.[17] 'I do not write about the remote past, since on account of the length of time it is impossible to explore it exactly'— says Thucydides.[18] Here we have, so to speak, earliest and latest instances of the ancient debate over whether poetry can be regarded as a historical source.

The most decisive contribution to that discussion has been made by Thucydides, to whom we shall turn first. Thucydides could refer to the works of two predecessors, to Hecataeus and Herodotus, who had already in their historiography doubted the authority of poetry. When Hecataeus, for instance, says: 'Aegyptus had, as Hesiod relates, fifty sons; but I say twenty,'[19] he is doing two things: (1) he corrects, so to speak, his poetical source according to rational considerations, that is, according to the critical methods of the Ionian sciences—and to have twenty children is for him the maximum possible for one man; but (2) while criticizing poetry, Hecataeus still remains dominated by it; he regards it as a historical work and sees fundamentally a historical truth in the events told there—for him, too, Aegyptus is a historical figure.

Herodotus, on the contrary, does not start his historical criticism from poetry; for him that which can be explored, that which can be grasped empirically is true, and on the basis of conclusions obtained in this manner he criticizes poetry. He concludes the preface of his work as follows: 'I do not regard it as my task to decide about the mythical tradition of Io, Medea, and Helen; I myself will mention the man whom I know to have started hostilities against the Greeks.'[20] But it is significant that he puts the statements of poets he quotes behind the reports based on his own researches. For instance the priestesses of Dodona testify for him that the Pelasgi have the oldest names of the gods whereas Homer and Hesiod are told that their

---

[17] Procop. *Bell.* 8.22.22.   [18] Thuc. 1.1.3.
[19] *FGrHist* 1 F 19.   [20] Hdt. 1.5.3.

testimony on the matter is more recent.²¹ In the same way he compares the stories Homer tells about Helen's trip to Egypt with the information he gets from an Egyptian priest.²² In another passage he tries to figure out the reason for the rising of the Nile. Among the numerous explanations he rejects, there is one which speaks of a river Oceanus; he rejects it, 'because it starts from something mythical which does not admit examination (οὐκ ἔχει ἔλεγχον)'; in his opinion Oceanus is an invention of Homer.²³ On the other hand, he appreciates poetry as a testimony if it confirms his own empiric research, as, for instance, a Homeric verse containing the observation that no horns sprout on cattle in cold Scythia (4.29).

It is only Thucydides who disengages himself fundamentally from poetry. In the so-called 'Archaeology' of his work, in which he describes the origins of the conflict between Athens and Sparta which exploded into the Peloponnesian War, he deals with remote times and events. As for the Trojan War, nothing would have been easier than to refer to Homer.

Concerning the number of the boats sailing to Troy under Agamemnon's command—later historiographers are never tired of finding them out by reckoning in accordance with Homer—he only says: 'These are Homer's statements if anybody wants to rely on him as a witness (εἴ τῳ ἱκανὸς τεκμηριῶσαι)'²⁴ and 'as far as you wish to trust the poetry of Homer who as a poet embellished and magnified the Trojan War (τῇ Ὁμήρου αὖ ποιήσει εἴ τι χρὴ κἀνταῦθα πιστεύειν, ἣν εἰκὸς ἐπὶ τὸ μεῖζον μὲν ποιητὴν ὄντα κοσμῆσαι)';²⁵ ποιητὴν ὄντα— 'Homer who as a poet': here it is evident that for Thucydides the significance of poetry is of a completely different quality from that of scientific historiography as he understands it.

Certainly for him also the Trojan War is a historical fact; for him however the proof does not come from poetry; he obtains it either by testimonies or by his own logical combinations κατὰ τὸ ἀνθρώπινον {in accordance with human nature}, as he says in 1.22.3.

By testimonies: Agamemnon, he says in 1.9, rallied the troops because he was the highest authority of his time and not because Helen's wooers had sworn

---

²¹ Hdt. 2.52–3.   ²² Hdt. 2.116–7.   ²³ Hdt. 2.23.
²⁴ Thuc. 1.9.3.   ²⁵ Thuc. 1.10.3.

military service to Tyndareus. We are also told this by the Peloponnesians, where the most reliable traditions of remote antiquity can be found.²⁶

By combinations κατὰ τὸ ἀνθρώπινον: circumstances like the scarcity of material goods, the geographical location of Troy and the resulting difficulties of obtaining provisions prove that the Greek campaign was only a small enterprise. In consequence, as the facts show, this campaign was much smaller than the myth that is propagated about it by the poets.²⁷

Add to this a criterion which is not related to the Trojan War itself, but which nevertheless contributes to the process of finding the historical truth independently from poetry, and this is archaeology. To prove that the Carians as a race of pirates endangered the Aegean Sea in ancient times Thucydides points to the tombs excavated by the Athenians during the Peloponnesian War on the occasion of the purification of the island of Delos. Half of the dead could be identified as Carians by the arms buried alongside their bodies.²⁸

In the course of supplying information about the most ancient period of Greek history as verified by scientific methods, and in the course of the methodological statements Thucydides makes concerning the irrelevance of poetry for historiography, the few scattered remarks like 'as Homer says,' 'as it can be seen in the old poets' appear like mere literary reminiscences. Add to this that Thucydides only quotes poets to illustrate facts which already have been established by appropriate reasons. So, for instance, he explains the growing wealth in Greece by the fact that kingship with its legal privileges was exchanged for tyranny which was followed in turn by growing trade. Special circumstances caused the ascendancy of Corinth over other towns; then follows an allusion to poets who call Corinth 'wealthy'.²⁹

Thucydides has been blamed for an unclear, wavering attitude towards Homer which little harmonizes with the energy of thought, the sureness of expression, and the consistency of his work.³⁰ This reproach might seem obvious at first sight, but it is far from being so if looked at more closely. Besides the passages quoted above in which the citation of a poet as useless for historical argumentation has to

²⁶ Thuc. 1.9.2.   ²⁷ Thuc. 1.11.   ²⁸ Thuc. 1.8.1.
²⁹ Thuc. 1.13.1–5.   ³⁰ So Täubler (1927) 24.

yield to other methods, there are those that apparently prove the opposite.

In the third chapter of the 'Archaeology' Thucydides doubts somewhat whether the Greeks had attempted anything in common before the Trojan War. As evidence he says (1.3.2–3):

At that time, Hellas as a whole did not yet have this name; on the contrary, this name did not exist at all before Hellen, son of Deucalion, and only single tribes, in particular the Pelasgian one, spread their names as far as possible. When Hellen and his sons came to power in Phthiotis and other tribes joined him, those communities sometimes were called Hellenes. But this development is very recent, as *Homer* testifies, who, after all, lived much later than the Trojan war; for he nowhere calls the community this way, except for the fellows of Achilles exclusively who in fact were the first Hellenes; in his epic, however, he speaks of Danaans, Argives, and Achaeans.

By emphasizing the fact 'that Homer, after all, lived much later than the Trojan War', Thucydides already shows that he is far from regarding Homer as a war correspondent. What is more important is the fact that Thucydides, when dealing with the names of the Hellenes and tracing them back to the epic is regarding this epic from a different angle than, for instance, in passages where he labels Homer's remark that the Greek navy consisted of about 1,200 ships as the product of a poet's fantasy. Here Thucydides distinguishes between two levels of understanding; that is to say, he distinguishes between certain historical circumstances under which poetry originated and which are reflected in it, and statements that were merely invented by the individual poet and cannot be verified elsewhere. In doing so, he develops a scientific standard that even nowadays is observed by scholars applying themselves to the study of early Greek history. Thucydides does see Homer as an exponent of his time, and this Homer could not have spoken of Hellenes as a unity if this classification did not yet exist in his time. Hence this phenomenon as such is historical. Here Thucydides infers, so to speak, a historical condition under which Homer composed his poetry, the contents of which, on the other hand, are for Thucydides a poetical product. This kind of argumentation is indeed in no way affected by the fact that the concrete, negative result—that in the times of Homer a common people of Greeks did not exist—is much less substantial and certain than the precise statement deduced by others from the *Iliad* that the Greek navy at Troy consisted of 1,200 ships.

Let us conclude this part with a last example from Thucydides. In connection with the purification of the island of Delos we mentioned already the archaeological excavations by which the prehistory of this place could be clarified. To the historical knowledge gained in this manner, one can add that there is a tradition concerning games that took place on this island in honour of Apollo and that go back beyond Polycrates into earliest times, and these games are re-established by the Athenians now during the Peloponnesian war. To illustrate these old games Thucydides quotes verses from the *Homeric Hymn to Apollo*.[31] Here we see the application of another category of poetical statements different from those mentioned above. In the cult-song, i.e. the invocation of a god and the description of a festival or a rite, we find a manifestation of an event that recurs year after year, something static, therefore, and not subject to historical change.

Thus we find in Thucydides different kinds of passages from poets both quoted and distinguished with regard to their historical significance. He constantly tries to disengage himself from the authority of the Homeric poems. No doubt, Thucydides has hereby laid down standards for later historiography, but this debate also proves what an important and unquestioned authority Homer was in those times.

Turning to historiography after Thucydides, we learn what effects this criticism of poetry has produced. As representative for many I would like to present a brief outline of the attitude of Polybius and Diodorus to the same problem. Polybius has inserted several reflections on the relation of poetry and historiography, both generally and as regards his estimation of Homer in particular. Since we are asking whether and to what extent a historiographer evaluates poetry as a source, we can omit Polybius' intense polemic against so-called 'tragic historiography' because there it is only the form of representation that is being discussed.[32]

As a historian, Polybius sets the highest value on his own experience and on the perspicuity of his narrative. The best historical works for him are those whose readers instinctively exclaim: the author must have been a political man himself, must have joined

[31] Thuc. 3.104.   [32] Cf. von Scala (1890); Pédech (1964) 582–6.

the campaigns, and so on. Considering himself to have met all
these demands extensively, he sees their realization especially in the
works of Homer whose liveliness he praises again and again: ἱκανὸν
ὑπόδειγμα πρὸς πίστιν ὁ ποιητής, παρ᾽ ᾧ τὸ τῆς τοιαύτης ἐμφάσεως
ἴδοι τις ἂν ὑπάρχον {the poet is a convincing instance; for in him one
might see the existence of such vividness}.³³ Thus, the description of
towns in the Homeric 'Catalogue of Ships' (in Polybius' hometown,
Megalopolis, Cercidas had made it compulsory to learn this by heart)
is for Polybius historic, because (!) it is so vivid.³⁴

During a trip around Greece with Aemilius Paulus, Polybius not
only points out the curiosities of landscape, religion, and art; in the
bay of Aulis he also has the following historical reminiscence: 'The
journey proceeded through the famous port of Aulis, the place where
once the thousand boats of Agamemnon were lying and where the
king, thanks to the sacrifice of his daughter, obtained the departure
of the navy.'³⁵ Here Polybius, by his enthusiasm for his native country, procures us such an insight into his confidence in the authenticity of the epic that we are consequently able to judge by it his
theoretical statements on the relation of epic and historiography.

For Polybius, the aim of historical reports must be the truth (τῆς
μὲν οὖν ἱστορίας ἀλήθειαν εἶναι τέλος). That sounds as evident as the
following is significant. Polybius continues:

In his 'Catalogue of Ships' Homer gives exact information on the particu-
larities of each town; one of them he calls 'rocky', another one 'remote', a
third one 'rich in pigeons', the fourth 'near the coast'. Certainly, not everything in poetry is authentic; history is mixed up in it with rhetorical
ornament and legend (ἱστορία καὶ διάθεσις καὶ μῦθος).

When Polybius assures us that changes that happened in the meantime, simple error or poetic license (ποιητικὴ ἐξουσία) are responsible for the occasional discrepancy between poetry and reality, he
shows that he puts the ἱστορικόν of poetry above all else. On the other
hand, he protects Homer from the reproach that his stories were
mere inventions and that one should not look for anything authentic

³³ Pol. 12.25h–i.1.
³⁴ Pol. 34.4.2; cf. von Scala (1890) 68–9; cf. 12.27–8 for Homer as 'war correspondent'.
³⁵ Pol. ap. Livy 45.27.9.

in his works.[36] Here, it must be admitted, the question of the mere authenticity of Homer or the intermingling of his reports with his own inventions is still open; but seeing the regular and unreflective approach of Polybius to Homer we get the impression as above.

In spite of the incidental affirmation that Homer added quite a lot of fiction to his report of the wanderings of Odysseus, it is not only the wanderings themselves but also their details that are authentic for Polybius.[37] For him, it is inadmissible to take Aeolus, who showed the way to Odysseus through dangerous straits, for a figure of myth, or in general to take the wanderings of Odysseus for a mere tale, because the essential information about Sicily had been given by other authors who wrote the local history of Italy and Sicily in the same way as Homer had.[38]

It follows that from the consistency of geographical information in the Homeric epic Polybius deduces the authenticity of the Trojan War and the wanderings of Odysseus in the sense of history of events and, in his words, 'except for some inventions, just as Homer reports it.' Even Eratosthenes' satirical remark—'when the shoemaker will be found who sewed the sack of the winds, only then will one know the itinerary of Odysseus' wanderings'[39] (we remember Origen's similar remark concerning the literal conception of the Genesis passage about God as a shoemaker who sews clothes for Adam and Eve)—could not weaken Polybius in his belief in the authenticity of Homer's tales; on the contrary, he is able to believe, with the utmost composure, that Scylla catches her fish in the same was as fishermen do nowadays in the Straits of Messina; what he tells us about Charybdis is also in accordance with the proceedings in the straits today; and while Homer says that three times a day she made the floods flow up (τρὶς μὲν γὰρ ἀνίησιν, *Od.* 12.105), instead of 'twice' (as the geographic reality would be), that is either an error in writing or a factual error (γραφικὸν εἶναι ἁμάρτημα ἢ ἱστορικόν). That Homer makes the floods rise three times to illustrate the atrocity of the scene[40] is rejected by those who are looking for the ἱστορικόν in it.

---

[36] Pol. 34.4.1–4.　　[37] Pol. 34.2.1.　　[38] Pol. 34.2.9.
[39] Pol. 34.2.11 (Eratosth. F 1 A 16, Berger); cf. Fraser (1970) 190 n. 2.
[40] Cf. Fränkel (1962) 591ff.

If it can be admitted that Polybius still shows traces of a discussion as to what historical constructions can be founded on poetical statements, Diodorus of Sicily a hundred years later offers us an example of how poetry is used as a source among others without reflection. Referring to Ephorus, Diodorus says that the better historiographers do not follow mythological accounts because the different versions are contradictory in themselves and that therefore, because of the difficulties inherent in the subject, it is almost impossible to go back to the old times, τῆς μὲν ἀρχαίας μυθολογίας ἀπέστησαν διὰ τὴν δυσχέρειαν {they kept away from ancient mythological accounts because of the difficulty}.[41] For a moment, one could imagine that one was listening to Thucydides, who, in the first chapter of his work, gave the reason why he restricts himself to the present: τὰ ἔτι παλαίτερα σαφῶς μὲν εὑρεῖν διὰ χρόνου πλῆθος ἀδύνατα ἦν {it was impossible to discover clearly things still older because of the amount of time}; but Diodorus proceeds to disillusion the reader by stating that he himself will include the ἀρχαία μυθολογία in his work, not because this would seem to him uncontradictory and trustworthy, but because 'most of the greatest exploits have been achieved by heroes and demi-gods and other super-human beings', and for them he generally takes the old poets as witnesses. Thus the fourth book of his work begins with the history of Dionysus who provided the human race with the greatest benefits;[42] he uses as his source the *Homeric Hymn to Apollo*. In connection with the benefactor Dionysus he deals with the Muses, and if contradictions occur in the tradition, Diodorus has recourse to the authority of 'the most famous men', i.e. of Homer and Hesiod.[43] The question whether Heracles on the campaign against Troy took with him eighteen boats or, as Homer says, only six, is also one which Diodorus cannot answer.[44] But what Diodorus says about Hebe and Heracles Homer has 'established' (τεθεικέναι) in the 'Nekyia'.[45] In Homer, Diodorus also finds confirmation for the occasional tradition concerning Heracles' fight at Troy, that the hero conquered the town not with the support of the Argonauts but with his own six

[41] Diod. 4.1.2–4 (= Ephorus, *FGrHist* 70 T 8).   [42] Diod. 4.1.6.

[43] Diod. 4.7.2.   [44] Diod. 4.32.2; Hom. *Il.* 5.638–42.

[45] Diod. 4.39.3; Hom. *Od.* 11.602–3.

boats.[46] Philomelus founds the Phocians' claim to Delphi on the fact
that in the old days they already had had the control and charge of
the oracle; Homer is his witness for it. On the early history of Sicily
he comments: 'The best authorities among the historiographers
testify (φασὶν οἱ νομιμώτατοι τῶν συγγραφέων) that the Sicanioi
have been the first inhabitants of this island.' After all that, it is not
surprising to find Homer among these συγγραφεῖς: περὶ ὧν καὶ τὸν
ἐπιφανέστατον τῶν ποιητῶν μαρτυρεῖν λέγοντα {concerning them the
most renowned of poets speaks in witness} (this sentence is followed
by a description of the Cyclopes' country with verses from *Odyssey* 9).[47]
Here, Diodorus could have learned from Thucydides, who says about
the early history of Sicily: 'Whether and under what conditions the
Cyclopes and Laestrygonians inhabited this country first, I do not
know; let everyone think about the matter what he wants or believe
what the poets tell him about it.'[48]

In another passage of his early Greek history Diodorus says: 'About
the gods various stories have been transmitted by the historians and
mythographers (παρὰ τοῖς ἱστορικοῖς τε καὶ μυθογράφοις); Euhemerus as a historian wrote the *Sacred History*; Homer, Hesiod,
Orpheus, and others as mythographers invented fantastic legends
about the gods. We, however, will try to pass in review briefly the
writings of both groups and not to lose sight of the symmetry of our
work.' Thus Diodorus makes use of both kinds of sources, historians
and poets, without indicating a difference of quality; the only aspect
for him is that both sides are equally represented in his work.[49]

It was not without intention that we have represented the manner
of Diodorus in utilizing the old poets and in abusing them as
historical authorities in all its stupidity and dullness. This should
make it easier for us to realize how exceptional are his occasional
remarks as opposed to his general practice of stereotyped and unreflective quotations from the poets.

We have already mentioned the ironic remark of Eratosthenes
concerning the attempts to reconstruct the route of Odysseus from

---

[46] Diod. 4.49.7: (προσμαρτυρεῖν δὲ τούτοις καὶ Ὅμηρον ἐν τοῖσδε τοῖς ἔπεσι {and
Homer also gives witness to these things in his poems}).
[47] Diod. 5.2.4; Hom. *Od.* 9.109–11.
[48] Thuc. 6.2.1.   [49] Diod. 6.1.3.

the words of Homer. In serious and most general terms, Eratosthenes addresses himself to those who do not distinguish between poetry and historiography: poetry is not to be measured with the intellect, i.e. not to be judged by its literal meaning, nor should one seek history in it (κελεύων μὴ κρίνειν πρὸς τὴν διάνοιαν τὰ ποιήματα μηδ' ἱστορίαν ἀπ' αὐτῶν ζητεῖν {he directs us not to judge the poems by their meaning, or look for history from them}).[50]

Lucian also offers his advice regarding scepticism in principle, directed against mythical elements, as it appears in the discussion which took place in historiography between the rejection of poetry and reliance on it. In his work *How to write History*, the ideas of which follow closely those of Thucydides whom he calls a νομοθέτης τῆς ἱστοριογραφίας {law-giver of history}[51] he mocks 'people who take the stories of Homer about Achilles that are, after all, more or less fictions as true.'[52] In other words, surely the Homeric epic does not lack a historical background, but most of it is myth, and it is impossible to separate these two ingredients. Therefore the historiographer, Lucian continues,[53] should call the myth a myth if he reports it at all, should not hide his suspicion, and should leave its credibility to the judgement of the reader.

If finally we read Lucian's statement that different principles and rules apply to poetry and historiography (ἄλλοι ὑποσχέσεις καὶ κάνονες ἴδιοι),[54] we remember the definition Aristotle gives in the ninth chapter of his *Poetics* about the substantial difference between poetry and historiography, and at the same time we observe that even his statement had no influence on the practice of ancient historiography.

But then rhetoric, which, for Lucian, is the main enemy of historiography, had obliterated the limits between itself and poetry more and more since the fourth century BC. At the end of this development Quintilian can say: 'Historiography is the most similar to poetry and is somewhat of a poem in prose.'[55]

Let us illustrate this development with two examples. Callisthenes, more a panegyrist than a historian, regarded himself as the 'Homer of

[50] Pol. 34.4.1–4 (Eratosth. F 1 A 17, Berger).   [51] Luc. *h.c.* 42.
[52] Luc. *h.c.* 40.   [53] Luc. *h.c.* 60.
[54] Luc. *h.c.* 8.   [55] Quint. 10.1.31.

Achilles Alexander' (and consequently he regarded Homer as the biographer of Achilles and the historian of the Trojan War). When Alexander had the oracle of Zeus Ammon announce to him his divine origin, according to Callisthenes,[56] he got the answer not in words but by a nodding, just as in Homer Zeus promised to Thetis compensation for Achilles by nodding (there follows the quotation ἦ καὶ κυανέῃσιν ἐπ' ὀφρύσι νεῦσε Κρονίων {and the son of Cronos nodded assent with his dark brows}).

Cicero in his *De Diuinatione* (2.166) points out that no less credibility is due to Ennius than to a Herodotus. That this is not simply an isolated remark becomes apparent from his request to the historian Lucceius to write the history of his (Cicero's) consulate and thereby to go beyond the historical truth (*Fam.* 5.12.3): *itaque te plane etiam atque etiam rogo, ut et ornes ea uehementius etiam quam fortasse sentis, et in eo leges historiae neglegas* {and so I ask you again to adorn those events rather more enthusiastically than you perhaps feel and in doing so neglect the laws of history}. When reflecting on the theory of this subject he certainly makes distinctions; thus, in the *de Oratore* (2.61–2), he establishes the *leges historiae*, outlining them as against rhetoric and poetry 'which after all has a different goal (*poetas omnino quasi alia lingua locutos* {it's as if poets speak a different language entirely}).' But when a practical occasion arises, theory is forgotten and the true *leges historiae* come to light, and Cicero wishes to have Lucceius as a panegyrist of his exploits—and an even more dignified one than Themistocles found in Herodotus, Timoleon in Timaeus—and Achilles in Homer.[57]

Here, both in Callisthenes and in Cicero, we have an example of how historiography, in consequence of the influence of rhetoric, has been turned into apologetic and panegyric. Historiography is put on an equal footing with poetry by claiming for it the same goals and rules, and by obliterating the literary lines of demarcation between them.

We have tried to draw a rough picture of ancient historiography in its relation to poetry as a historical source. We have seen that the distinction between these two literary genres, foreshadowed by Hecataeus and Herodotus and consciously realized by Thucydides was always known to historiographers, but that in practice the authority of the poets, especially of Homer, proved itself to be more resilient.

A historiography conditioned by this practice lay before Eusebius when, for the first time, he represented the events of the church in this literary form. At the same time Eusebius, as we have seen, had passed through Origen's school of exegesis of the Bible. Consequently, he was as little allowed to regard and interpret the Bible as a historical source as a pagan ancient historian after Thucydides was allowed to deal with Homer in that way. But since Eusebius, as his *Chronicle* shows, approaches the Old Testament with an understanding of the Bible that apparently has not been influenced by Origen, but regards it as a mere book of history in the manner of Hippolytus of Rome and Sextus Julius Africanus, this only proves that in his field he succumbed to the authority of the 'Holy Scriptures' as secular historiography did to the authority 'Homer'. It goes without saying that for his exegetical studies the Bible was the highest authority for Eusebius; when he started writing history the Bible became a historical authority for him as well; and the methodological distinction between the reading of the Scriptures and their theological, not historical, meaning which he had learned from Origen was overshadowed by the greater influence of secular historiography, the literary form and methods which Eusebius took over, an influence which continued in spite of many a counter-movement until the end of antiquity, and under which Evagrius could still call Moses the first historiographer.

ADDENDUM

The inconsistency in the ancient attitude towards the relationship between poetry and historiography can be shown using Plutarch as an example: he is rightly considered a transmitter and representative of Greek popular philosophy, and he accurately reflects the contradiction.

As the Pythia once gave her oracle responses in verse, then later in prose, 'so also history descended from verse as from a carriage, and through the form of prose the true was especially distinguished from the mythic. Like philosophy historiography welcomed clarity and teachability in preference to creating amazement and pursued its investigations through the medium of everyday language' (*Pyth. orac.* 24, 406E). A little before this, however, he says that in regard to truth there is no difference between verse and prose (18, 402E–F). What had been written in verse—from which historiography is descended—was myth, especially Homer and Hesiod, but Plutarch reckons this indirectly as historiography; for Greek history had never been written in verse (from which historiography could have descended).

In his essay, 'On the Fame of the Athenians' (4, 348A) we read: 'Poetry manufactures myths; these, however, are nothing other than invented tales that resemble truth. Thus myths are far removed from events since a tale (*logos*) is a picture of reality, while myth is an image (*eidôlon*) of a tale, and thus those who write of imaginative exploits lag as far behind historians as those who tell of deeds come short of those who do them.' Even without Plutarch's reference to Plato (*Phaed.* 61b) it is obvious that the wish here is to establish a gradation of *Seinswirklichkeit* {actuality of being}. As (real) deeds are to historiography, so (invented) deeds are to poetry. This is thus thrice removed from truth, and historiography takes evident precedence over poetry.

But Plutarch would not be himself if he could not speak differently when required, especially when the theme is pedagogy and it is a matter of opinions not proofs. So in his essay, 'How a Young Man Should Read Poetry' (11, 30C–D), he remarks, 'just as the bee seeks the flower, the goat the tender shoot, the swine the root, so in the reading of poetry one person culls the historical flowers, another prizes artistic expressions, and another is concerned with what is useful for the building of character'. Here too the desire for an evaluative gradation is evident, although it does not harmonize with the similes used. If one reflects that these remarks are framed with and enforced by citations of Homer, so it is clear that for Plutarch the stories that are narrated by Homer are simultaneously history.

Bibliography

Adamietz, J. (1966) *M. F. Quintiliani Institutionis Oratoriae Liber III* (Munich)

Adcock, F. E. (1963) *Thucydides and his History* (Cambridge)

Adkins, A. W. H. (1972) *Moral Values and Political Behaviour in Ancient Greece* (London and New York)

Alföldi, A. (1965) *Early Rome and the Latins* (Ann Arbor)

—— (1967) 'Zur Struktur des Römerstaates im V. Jh. v. Chr.', in *Les origines de la république romaine* (Entretiens sur l'antiquité classique 13; Vandœuvres-Genève) 223–90

—— (1974) *Die Struktur des voretruskischen Römerstaates* (Heidelberg)

—— (1976) *Römische Frühgeschichte* (Heidelberg)

Alföldy, G. (1980) *Die Rolle des Einzelnen in der Gesellschaft des römischen Kaiserreichs* (*SHAW* Jahrg. 1980, Ber. 8; Heidelberg); repr. in id., *Die römische Gesellschaft: Ausgewählte Beiträge* (Stuttgart 1986) 349ff.

Allen, W. (1955) 'The British Epics of Quintus and Marcus Cicero', *TAPhA* 86: 143–59

Alonso-Núñez, J. M., ed. (1991) *Geschichtsbild und Geschichtsdenken im Altertum* (*Wege der Forschung* 631; Darmstadt)

Altheim, F. (1938) *A History of Roman Religion*, trans. H. Mattingly (London)

—— (1950) *Der Ursprung der Etrusker* (Baden-Baden)

—— (1961) 'Naevius und die Annalistik', *Romanitas* 3: 86–110

—— (1962) *Geschichte der Hunnen* IV (Berlin)

Altheim-Stiehl, R. and M. Rosenbach, edd. (1986) *Beiträge zur altitalischen Geistesgeschichte: Festschrift . . . G. Radke* (Münster)

Aly, W. (1954) 'Praxiphanes', *RE* XX.2: 1769–84

Ampolo, C. (1982) 'Die endgültige Stadtwerdung Roms im 7. und 6. Jh. v. Chr.: Wann enstand die civitas?', in D. Papenfuss and V. M. Strocka, edd., *Palast und Hütte: Beiträge zum Bauen und Wohnen im Altertum* (Mainz) 319–24

—— (1983) 'La storiografia su Roma arcaica e i documenti', in Gabba (1983) 9–26

—— (1988) 'La città riformata e l'organizzazione centuriata: lo spazio, il tempo, il sacro nella nuova realtà urbana', in Momigliano–Schiavone (1988) 203–39

—— ed. (2006) *Aspetti dell'opera di Felix Jacoby* (Pisa)

Andronikos, M. (1981) 'The Royal Tombs at Aegae (Vergina)', in M. B. Hatzopoulos and L. D. Loukopoulos, edd., *Philip of Macedon* (London) 188–231

Antonetti, C. (1990) *Les Étoliens: image et religion* (Besançon)

Assmann, A., J. Assmann, and Chr. Hardmeier, edd. (1983) *Schrift und Gedächtnis: Beiträge zur Archäologie der literarischen Kommunikation* (Munich)

Assmann, J. (1992) *Das kulturelle Gedächtnis: Schrift, Erinnerung und politische Identität in frühen Hochkulturen* (Munich)

—— and T. Hölscher, edd. (1988) *Kultur und Gedächtnis* (Frankfurt)

Atkinson, R. F. (1978) *Knowledge and Explanation in History* (Ithaca, NY)

Aujac, G. (1991) *Denys d'Halicarnasse: Opuscules Rhétoriques IV: Thucydide, Seconde Lettre à Ammée* (Budé; Paris)

—— (1992) *Denys d'Halicarnasse: Opuscules Rhétoriques V: L'Imitation, Première lettre à Ammée, Lettre à Pompée Géminos, Dinarque* (Budé; Paris)

Avenarius, G. (1956) *Lukians Schrift zur Geschichtsschreibung* (Meisenheim am Glan)

Baddeley, A. D. (1979) *Die Psychologie des Gedächtnisses* (Stuttgart)

Badian, E. (1966) 'The Early Historians', in T. A. Dorey, ed., *Latin Historians* (London and New York) 1–38.

Baehr, J. C. F. (1856) *Herodotus* I (Leipzig)

Baldry, H. C. (1954) 'Aristotle and the Dramatization of Legend', *CQ* 4: 151–7

Balfour, M. (1979) *Propaganda in War 1939–1945* (London)

Bandelli, G. (1988) 'La frontiera settentrionale: l'ondata celtica e il nuovo sistema di alleanze', in Momigliano–Schiavone (1988) 505–25

Barber, E. L. (1935) *The Historian Ephorus* (Cambridge)

Bardon, H. (1952–6) *La littérature latine inconnue*, 2 vols (Paris)

Barnes, J. A. (1967) 'Genealogies', in A. L. Epstein, ed., *The Craft of Social Anthropology* (London) 101–28

Barwick, K. (1928) 'Die Gliederung der Narratio in der rhetorischen Theorie und ihre Bedeutung für die Geschichte des antiken Romans', *Hermes* 63: 261–88

Batstone, W. W. (2009) 'Postmodern Historiographical Theory and the Roman Historians', in Feldherr (2009) 24–40

Bauman, R. A. (1983) *Lawyers in Roman Republican Politics: a Study of the Roman Jurists in their Political Setting, 316–82 BC* (Münchener Beiträge zur Papyrusforschung und antiken Rechtsgeschichte 75; Munich)

Beazley, J. D. (1947) *Etruscan Vase Painting* (Oxford)

Beloch, K. J. (1912–27) *Griechische Geschichte*², 4 vols in 8 (Strasbourg)

—— (1926) *Römische Geschichte bis zum Beginn der punischen Kriege* (Berlin)

Bibliography

Bengtson, H. and R. Werner (1975) *Die Staatsverträge des Altertums* II² (Munich)

Bentley, M. (1999) *Modern Historiography: An Introduction* (London and New York)

—— ed. (1997) *Companion to Historiography* (London and New York)

Bergmann, W. (1984) 'Der römische Kalender: zur sozialen Konstruktion der Zeitrechnung. Ein Beitrag zur Soziologie der Zeit', *Saeculum* 35: 1–15

Bernhardy, G. (1829) *Wissenschaftliche Syntax der griechischen Sprache* (Berlin)

Bernheim, E. (1903) *Lehrbuch der historischen Methode*³ (Leipzig)

Bertelli, L. (1977) 'Il modello della società rurale nell'utopia greca', in L. Firpo, ed., *Studi sull'utopia* (Florence) 5–30

Bethe, E. (1929) *Homer: Dichtung und Sage* II² (Leipzig and Berlin)

—— (1935) *Ahnenbild und Familiengeschichte bei Römern und Griechen* (Munich)

Bianchi Bandinelli, R. (1971) *Rome: The Late Empire (Roman Art AD 200–400)* (London and New York)

Bickerman, E. J. (1952) 'Origines Gentium', *CPh* 47: 65–81; repr. in id. (1985) 401–17

—— (1969) 'Some Reflections on Early Roman History', *RFIC* 97: 393–408; repr. in id. (1985) 523–40

—— (1985) *Religion and Politics in the Hellenistic and Roman Periods*, edd. E. Gabba and M. Smith (Bibliotheca di Athenaeum 5; Como)

Binder, G. (1964) *Die Aussetzung des Königskindes: Kyros und Romulus* (Meisenheim am Glan)

Biraschi A. M. et al., edd. (2003) *L'uso dei documenti nella storiografia antica: Incontri Perugini di Storia della Storiografia XII. Centro Servizi S. Spirito, Gubbio, 22–24 maggio 2001* (Naples)

Bleicken, J. (1975) *Lex Publica: Gesetz und Recht in der römischen Republik* (Berlin)

Bloch, M. (1979) *The Historian's Craft* (Manchester repr. of 1954 original)

Blockley, R. C. (2001) 'Ammianus and Cicero on Truth in Historiography', *AHB* 15: 14–24

Blome, P. (1984) 'Lefkandi und Homer', *WJA* 10: 9–22

Boardman, J. (1999) *The Greeks Overseas: Their Early Colonies and Trade*⁴ (London)

Bohannan, L. A. (1952) 'A Genealogical Charter', *Africa* 22: 301–15

Boissevain, U. Ph. (1906) *Excerpta Historica iussu Imperatoris Constantini Porphyrogeniti confecta, IV: Excerpta de Sententiis* (Berlin)

Boissier, G. (1903) *Tacite* (Paris)

Bollack, J. (1975) 'Ulysse chez les philologues', *Actes de la récherche en sciences sociales* 5–6: 9–35

Bömer, F. (1952) 'Naevius und Fabius Pictor', *SO* 29: 34–53

—— (1960) *Untersuchungen über die Religion der Sklaven in Griechenland und Rom III: Die wichtigsten Kulte der griechischen Welt* (Ak. Wiss. Mainz, Geistes und Sozialwiss. Kl., 4; Wiesbaden)

Bona, F. (1964) *Contributo allo studio della composizione del 'de verborum significatu' de Verrio Flacco* (Milan)

Bonner, S. F. (1949) *Roman Declamation* (Liverpool)

—— (1977) *Education in Ancient Rome* (London–Berkeley)

Booth, W. C. (1983) *The Rhetoric of Fiction*² (Chicago)

Borgeaud, Ph. (1987) 'Du mythe à l'idéologie: la tête du Capitole', *MH* 44: 86–100

Borza, E. N. (1990) *In the Shadow of Olympus: The Emergence of Macedon* (Princeton)

Borzsák, St. (1987) 'Persertum und griechisch-römische Antike: zur Ausgestaltung des klassischen Tyrannenbildes', *Gymnasium* 94: 289–97

Bousquet, J. (1988) 'La stele des Kyténiens au Létôon de Xanthos', *REG* 101: 12–53

Bowen, A. J. (1993) *Plutarch: The Malice of Herodotus* (Warminster)

Bowie, E. (1986) 'Early Greek Elegy, Symposium and Public Festival', *JHS* 106: 13–35

Bowra, C. M. (1952) *Heroic Poetry* (London)

Boyancé, P. (1940) 'Sur Cicéron et l'histoire', *REA* 42: 388–92; repr. in id., *Études sur l'humanisme cicéronien* (Collection Latomus 121; Brussels) 135–40

Braun, Martin (1938) *History and Romance in Graeco-Oriental Literature* (Oxford)

Braun, Maximilian, A. Haltenhoff and F.-H. Mutschler, edd. (2000) *Moribus antiquis res stat Romana: römische Werte und römische Literatur im 3. und 2. Jh. v. Chr.* (Munich)

Braunert, H. (1965) 'Die heilige Insel des Euhemerus in der Diodor-Überlieferung', *Rh. Mus.* 108: 255–68

Bringmann, K. (1977) 'Weltherrschaft und innere Krise Roms im Spiegel der Geschichtsschreibung des Zweiten und ersten Jh.s. v. Chr.', *A&A* 23: 28–49

Brink, C. O. (1971) *Horace on Poetry Vol. II: The 'Ars Poetica'* (Cambridge)

—— (1982) *Horace on Poetry Vol. III: Epistles Book II. The Letters to Augustus and Florus* (Cambridge)

—— (1989) 'Quintilian's *De Causis Corruptae Eloquentiae* and Tacitus' *Dialogus de Oratoribus*', *CQ* 39: 472–503.

Briquel, D. (1988a) 'Claude, érudit et empereur', *CRAI* 217–32

—— (1988b) 'Que savons-nous des *Tyrrhenika* de l'empereur Claude?' *RFIC* 116: 448–70

—— (1990) 'Le témoignage de Claude sur Mastarna-Servius Tullius', *RBPh* 68: 86–108

—— (1997) *Le regard des autres: les origines de Rome vues par ses ennemis* (Besançon)

Broccia, G. (1967) *La forma poetica dell'Iliade e la genesi dell'epos omerico* (Messina)

Brunn, E. and G. Körte (1870–1916) *I Rilievi delle urne etrusche*, 3 vols (Rome, Berlin)

Brunt, P. A. (1967) Review of Stahl (1966), *CR* 17: 278–80; repr. in id. (1993) 394–8

—— (1969) Review of von Fritz (1967), *CR* 20: 198–201, repr. in id. (1993) 398–403

—— (1980a) 'Cicero and Historiography', in *ΦΙΛΙΑΣ ΧΑΡΙΝ: Miscellanea di studi classici in onore di Eugenio Manni* (Rome) I.311–40; repr. in id. (1993) 181–209 (= this volume, Ch. 8)

—— (1980b) 'On Historical Fragments and Epitomes', *CQ* 30: 477–94; repr. in Alonso-Núñez (1991) 334–62

—— (1982) '*Nobilitas* and *Novitas*', *JRS* 72: 1–17

—— (1993) *Studies in Greek History and Literature* (Oxford)

Büchner, K. (1984) *M. Tullius Cicero: De re publica, Kommentar* (Heidelberg)

Bühler, A. (1952) 'Kritische Bemerkungen zur Verwendung ethnographischer Quellen in der Psychologie', *Schweizerische Archiv für Neurologie und Psychiatrie* 68: 415ff.

Bung, P. (1950) *Q. Fabius Pictor, der erste römische Annalist* (diss. Cologne)

Bunnens, G. (1979) *L'expansion phénicienne en Méditerranée: Essai d'interprétation fondé sur une analyse des traditions littéraires* (Brussels)

Buonamici, G. (1939) 'Rivista di Epigrafia Etrusca, Anno 1938–9', *SE* 13: 455–79

Buranelli, F., ed. (1987) *La tomba François di Vulci* (Rome)

Burck, E. (1992) *Das Geschichtswerk des Titus Livius* (Heidelberg)

—— ed. (1967) *Wege zu Livius* (*Wege der Forschung* 132; Darmstadt)

Burn, A. R. (1935) 'Dates in Early Greek History', *JHS* 55: 130–46

Bury, J. B. (1909) *The Ancient Greek Historians* (London/New York)

Butti di Lima, P. (1996) *L'inchiesta e la prova: immagine storiografica, pratica giuridica e retorica nella Grecia classica* (Turin)

Calame, C. (1987) 'Le récit généalogique Spartiate: la répresentation mythologique d'une organisation Spartiate', *QS* 13: 43–91

Camassa, G. (1984) 'Sull'origine e le funzioni del culto di Volcanus a Roma', *RSI* 96: 811–54

Cameron, A. (1970) *Agathias* (Oxford)

Cameron, A. (1989a) 'Introduction: the Writing of History', in ead. (1989b) 1–10

—— ed. (1989b) *History as Text: The Writing of Ancient History* (London and Chapel Hill)

Cancik, H. and H. Mohr (1990) 'Erinnerung/Gedächtnis', in H. Cancik, ed., *Handbuch der religionswissenschaftlichen Grundbegriffe* (Stuttgart) II.299–323

Canfora, L. (1969) 'Su Augusto e gli ultimi libri liviani', *Belfagor* 24: 41–3

—— (1970) *Tucidide continuato* (Padua)

—— (1971a) 'Il "ciclo" storico', *Belfagor* 26: 653–70; repr. in id., *La storiografia antica* (Milan 1969) 61–91 (= this volume, Ch. 13)

—— (1971b) 'Per una storia del dialogo dei Melii e degli Ateniesi', *Belfagor* 26: 409–26

—— (1977) 'La préface de Thucydide et la critique de la raison historique', *REG* 90: 455–61

Capdeville, G. (1992) 'Le nom de Servius Tullius', in *La Rome des premiers siècles: légende et histoire: Table-ronde en l'honneur de M. Pallottino* (Florence) 47–68

—— (1995) *Volcanus* (Rome)

Capelle, W. (1924) 'Erdbebenforschung', *RE Suppl.* IV: 344–74

Carandini, A. (1997) *La nascita di Roma* (Turin)

Cartledge, P. (1979) *Sparta and Lakonia: A Regional History, 1300–362 B.C.* (London and Boston)

—— (1993) *The Greeks: A Portrait of Self and Other*[2] (Oxford–New York)

Chambers, M. (1990) 'Felix Jacoby', in W. W. Briggs and W. M. Calder III, edd. *Classical Scholarship: A Biographical Encyclopedia* (New York) 205–10

Chaniotis, A. (1988) *Historie und Historiker in den griechischen Inschriften: Epigraphische Beiträge zur griechischen Historiographie* (Stuttgart)

Cichorius, C. (1894) '*Annales*', *RE* I.2: 2248–55

Clark, E. (2004) *History, Theory, Text: Historians and the Linguistic Turn* (Cambridge, Mass.–London)

Clarke, K. (2008) *Making Time for the Past: Local History and the* Polis (Oxford)

Classen, C. J. (1963) 'Zur Herkunft der Sage von Romulus und Remus', *Historia* 12: 447–57

Classen, J. and J. Steup (1892–1922) *Thukydides*[3–5], 8 vols (Berlin)

Clinton, K. (1974) *The Sacred Officials of the Eleusinian Mysteries* (Philadelphia)

Coarelli, F. (1977) 'Il comizio dalle origini alla fine della Repubblica', *PP* 32: 166–238

—— (1983a) *Il Foro Romano: Periodo arcaico* (Rome)

—— (1983b) 'Le pitture della tomba François de Vulci: una proposta di lettura', *Dialoghi di Archeologia*³ 3: 43–69 = id., *Revixit Ars* (Rome 1996) 138–78

Cocchia, E. (1924) 'La leggenda di Servio Tullio', *AAN* n.s. 8: 209–29

Cohen, S. J. D. (1979) *Josephus in Galilee and Rome* (Leiden)

Colgrave, B. (1979) 'Historical Introduction', in id. and R. A. B. Mynors, edd., *Bede's Ecclesiastical History of the English People* (Oxford) xvii–xxxviii

Colonna, G. (1976) 'Scriba cum rege sedens', in *L'Italie préromaine et la Rome républicaine: Mélanges offerts à Jacques Heurgon* (Paris) 187–95

—— (1984a) 'Apollon, les Étrusques et Lipara', *MEFR* 96: 557–78; repr. in id. (2005) I.213–29

—— (1984b) 'Un "trofeo" di Novio Fannio, commandante sannita', in M. G. Marzi Costagli and L. Tamagno Perna, edd., *Studi di Antichità in onore di G. Maetzke* (Rome) 229–41

—— (1989) 'Nuove prospettive sulla storia etrusca tra Alalia e Cuma', in *Secondo congresso internazionale etrusco, Firenze 26 maggio–2 giugno 1985: atti* (Rome 1989) 361–74; repr. in id. (2005) I.313–25

—— (2005) *Italia ante Romanum Imperium*, edd. C. Ampolo and G. Sassatelli, 4 vols in 6 (Pisa–Rome)

Cornell, T. J. (1972) 'Cato's *Origines* and the non-Roman Historical Tradition about Ancient Italy' (unpublished PhD thesis; London)

—— (1974) 'Notes on the Sources for Campanian History in the Fifth Century BC', *MH* 31: 193–208

—— (1975) 'Aeneas and the Twins: The Development of the Roman Foundation Legend', *PCPhS* 21: 1–32

—— (1976) 'Etruscan Historiography', *ANSP* 6: 411–439 (= this volume, Ch. 7)

—— (1978) 'Principes of Tarquinia', *JRS* 68: 167–73

—— (1982) Review of Wiseman (1979), *JRS* 72: 203–6

—— (1986a) 'The Value of the Literary Tradition Concerning Archaic Rome', in Raaflaub (1986b) 52–76

—— (1986b) 'The Formation of the Historical Tradition of Early Rome', in Moxon–Smart–Woodman (1986) 67–86

—— (1986c) Review of Skutsch (1985), *JRS* 76: 244–50

—— (1995) *The Beginnings of Rome: Italy and Rome from the Bronze Age to the Punic Wars (c.1000–264 BC)* (London–New York)

Cracco Ruggini, L. (1980) 'Università e campanilismo, centro e periferia, città e deserto nelle storie ecclesiastiche' in *La Storiografia ecclesiastica nella tarda antichità: atti del convegno tenuto in Erice (3–8 XII 1978)* (Messina) 159–94

Crake, J. E. A. (1940) 'The Annals of the Pontifex Maximus', *CPh* 35: 375–86.

Cristofani, M. (1967) 'Ricerche sulle pitture della tomba François di Vulci: i fregi decorativi', *DArch* 1: 186–219

—— (1972) 'Sull'origine e la diffusione dell'alfabeto etrusco', *ANRW* I.2: 466–89

—— ed. (1987) *Etruria e Lazio arcaico: atti dell'incontro di studio (10–11 novembre 1986)* (Rome)

Croce, B. (1948) *Teoria e storia della storiografia* [6] (Bari)

—— (1955) *History as the Story of Liberty*, trans. S. Sprigge (New York)

Curty, O. (1995) *Les parentés légendaires entre cités grecques: catalogue raisonné des inscriptions contenant le terme syngeneia et analyse critique* (Geneva)

D'Alton, J. F. (1931) *Roman Literary Theory and Criticism: A Study in Tendencies* (London–New York)

D'Ippolito, F. (1978) *I giuristi e la città: sulla giurisprudenza romana della repubblica* (Naples)

—— (1985a) 'Das ius Flavianum und die lex Ogulnia', *ZRG* 102: 91–128

—— (1985b) 'Review of Bauman (1983)', *Labeo* 31: 324ff.

Damon, C. (2007) 'Rhetoric and Historiography', in W. Dominik and J. Hall, edd., *A Companion to Roman Rhetoric* (Oxford–Malden, Mass.) 439–50

Davies, J. K. (1971) *Athenian Propertied Families, 600–300 B.C.* (Oxford)

Davies, R. W. (1989) *Soviet History in the Gorbachev Revolution* (London)

Davis, L. J. (1983) *Factual Fictions: the Origins of the English Novel* (New York)

Day, G. (1987) *From Fiction to the Novel* (London)

Day, J. and M. Chambers (1962) *Aristotle's History of Athenian Democracy* (Berkeley–Los Angeles)

De Sanctis, G. (1902) 'Mastarna' *Klio* 2: 96–104

—— (1953) *Storia dei Romani* IV.2.1 (Florence)

Deffner, A. (1933) *Die Rede bei Herodot und ihre Weiterbildung bei Thukydides* (Munich)

Degrassi, A. (1937) *Inscriptiones Italiae XIII, fasc. III: Elogia* (Rome)

Dehl, Chr. (1984) 'Die korinthische Keramik des 8. und frühen 7. Jh.s v. Chr. in Italien: Untersuchungen zu ihrer Chronologie und Ausbreitung', *MDAI(A)* Heft 11 (Berlin)

Delebecque, E. (1957) *Essai sur la vie de Xénophon* (Paris)

Della Corte, F. (1955/56) 'Su un elogium tarquiniense', *SE* 24: 73–78

Delz, J. (1966) 'Der griechische Einfluβ auf die Zwölftafelgesetzgebung', *MH* 23: 69–83

Dessau, H. (1889) 'Über Zeit und Personlichkeit der Scriptores Historiae Augustae', *Hermes* 24: 337–92

Dimitrakou, D. (1936–1951) *ΜΕΓΑ ΛΕΞΙΚΟΝ ΤΗΣ ΕΛΛΗΝΙΚΗΣ ΓΛΩΣΣΗΣ*, 9 vols (Athens–Thessaloniki)

Dindorf, W. (1829) *Aristides*, 3 vols (Leipzig)

Dionisotti, C. (1989) *Ricordo di Arnaldo Momigliano* (Bologna)

Dodds, E. R. (1951) *The Greeks and the Irrational* (Berkeley; London)

Dowden, K. (1989) 'Pseudo-Callisthenes: The Alexander Romance', in B. P. Reardon, ed., *Collected Ancient Greek Novels* (Berkeley–Los Angeles London) 650–715

Drews, R. (1983) *Basileus: the Evidence for Kingship in Geometric Greece* (New Haven)

Droysen, J. G. (1877) *Geschichte des Hellenismus* I².1 (Gotha)

—— (1920) *Geschichte Alexanders des Grossen*, ed. H. Berve (Leipzig)

Ducati, P. (1938) *Le problème étrusque* (Paris)

Dumézil, G. (1947) *Tarpeia: essais de philologie comparative indo-européenne* (Paris)

—— (1985) *Heur et Malheur du guerrier: aspects mythiques de la fonction guerrière chez les Indo-Européens*² (Paris)

Dumville, D. N. (1977) 'Kingship, Genealogies and Regnal Lists', in P. H. Sawyer and I. N. Wood, edd., *Early Medieval Kingship* (Leeds) 72–104

Earl, D. C. (1967) *The Moral and Political Tradition of Rome* (London and Ithaca)

Ebert, J. (1982) 'Zur Stiftungsurkunde der Λευκοφρυηνά in Magnesia am Maänder (Inschr. v. Magnesia 16)', *Philologus* 126: 198–216

Eden, P. T. (1962) 'Caesar's Style: Inheritance versus Intelligence', *Glotta* 40: 74–117

—— (1984) *Seneca: Apocolocyntosis* (Cambridge)

Eder, W. (1986) 'The Political Significance of the Codification of Law in Archaic Societies', in Raaflaub (1986b) 262–300

Ehrenberg, V. (1962) *The People of Aristophanes: a Sociology of Old Attic Comedy*³ (New York)

Ehrenzweig, A. (1915) 'Kain und Lamech', *Zeitschrift für alttestamentliches Wissenschaft* 35: 1–11

—— (1919/20) 'Biblische und klassische Urgeschichte', *Zeitschrift für alttestamentliches Wissenschaft* 38: 65–86

Ehrismann, O. (1987) *Niebelungenlied: Epoche–Werk–Wirkung* (Munich)

Eigler, U., U. Gotter, N. Luraghi, and U. Walter, edd. (2003) *Formen römischer Geschichtsschreibung von den Anfängen bis Livius* (Darmstadt)

Elwert, G. (1987) 'Die gesellschaftliche Einbettung von Schriftgebrauch', in D. Baecker et al., edd., *Theorie als Passion: Niklas Luhmann z. 60. Geburtstag* (Frankfurt am Main) 238–68

Ernst, F. (1957) 'Zeitgeschehen und Geschichtsschreibung', *Die Welt als Geschichte* 17: 137–89

Fabia, P. (1929) *La table claudienne de Lyon* (Lyons)

Fabricius, E. (1911) 'Über die Entwicklung der römischen Verfassung in republikanischer Zeit', *Prog. Univ. Freiburg i. Br.*, 21ff.

Fairweather, J. (1974) 'Fiction in the Biographies of Ancient Writers', *AncSoc* 5: 231–75

—— (1981) *Seneca the Elder* (Cambridge)

Fantham, E. (1972) *Comparative Studies in Republican Latin Imagery* (Toronto)

—— (2004) *The Roman World of Cicero's De Oratore* (Oxford)

Feder, A. (1924) *Lehrbuch der geschichtlichen Methode*³ (Regensburg)

Feeney, D. C. (1991) *The Gods in Epic: Poets and Critics of the Classical Tradition* (Oxford)

—— (2007) *Caesar's Calendar: Ancient Time and the Beginnings of History* (Berkeley–Los Angeles)

Feldherr, A. (2003) 'Cicero and the Invention of "Literary History"', in Eigler et al. (2003) 196–212

——, ed. (2009) *Cambridge Companion to the Roman Historians* (Cambridge)

Ferenczy, E. (1987) 'Über das Problem der Inschrift von Satricum', *Gymnasium* 94: 97–108

Ferguson, J. (1975) *Utopias of the Classical World* (London; Ithaca)

Fiddick, P. (1990) 'Facts do Furnish a Story...', *The Listener* 124 (25 October 1990) 4–6

Finkelstein, J. J. (1963) 'Mesopotamian Historiography', *PAPhS* 107: 461–72

Finley, J. H. (1942) *Thucydides* (Cambridge, Mass.; London)

Finley, M. I. (1975) 'Myth, Memory and History', in id., *The Use and Abuse of History* (London and New York) 11–33

—— (1978) *Monde d'Ulysse*² (Paris); French trans. of *The World of Odysseus*² (London; New York, 1977)

—— (1985) 'The Ancient Historian and His Sources', in id., *Ancient History: Evidence and Models* (London; New York) 7–26; orig. in Gabba (1983) 201–14

Finnegan, R. (1970) 'A Note on Oral Tradition and Historical Evidence', *H&T* 9: 195–201

—— (1977) *Oral Poetry: Its Nature, Significance and Social Content* (Cambridge)

Fischer, E. P., ed., (1998) *Gedächtnis und Erinnerung* (Munich)

Flach, D. (1973) *Tacitus in der Tradition der antiken Geschichtsschreibung* (*Hypomnemata* 39; Göttingen)

—— (1985) *Einführung in die römische Geschichtsschreibung* (Darmstadt)

Flaig, E. (1995) 'Die *pompa funebris*: adlige Konkurrenz und annalistische Erinnerung', in O. G. Oexle, ed., *Memoria als Kultur* (Göttingen) 115–48

—— (2003) *Ritualisierte Politik: Zeichen, Gesten und Herrschaft im alten Rom* (Göttingen)

Fleck, M. (1993) *Cicero als Historiker* (Stuttgart–Leipzig)

Fleischman, S. (1983) 'On the Representation of History and Fiction in the Middle Ages', *H&T* 22: 278–310

Flower, H. I. (1995) '"*Fabulae praetextae*" in Context: When Were Plays on Contemporary Subjects Performed in Rome?', *CQ* 45: 170–90

—— (1996) *Ancestor Masks and Aristocratic Power in Roman Culture* (Oxford)

Fornara, C. W. (1983) *The Nature of History in Ancient Greece and Rome* (Berkeley; Los Angeles; London)

Fornaro, S. (1997) *Dionisio di Alicarnasso Epistola a Pompeo Gemino: introduzione e commento* (*Beiträge zur Altertumskunde* 95; Stuttgart)

Forsythe, G. (2005) *A Critical History of Early Rome* (Berkeley–Los Angeles)

Foucault, M. (1969) *Archéologie du savoir* (Paris)

Fowler, H. W. and F. G. Fowler (1905) *Lucian*, vol. 1 (LCL; London–Cambridge, Mass.)

Fowler, R. L. (1996) 'Herodotos and his Contemporaries', *JHS* 116: 62–87

—— (1998) 'Genealogical Thinking, Hesiod's *Catalogue* and the Creation of the Hellenes', *PCPS* 44: 1–19

Fox, M. (2007) *Cicero's Philosophy of History* (Oxford)

Foxhall, L. and J. K. Davies, edd. (1984) *The Trojan War: Its Historicity and Context* (Bristol)

Fraccaro, P. (1957) 'The History of Rome in the Regal Period', *JRS* 47: 59–65.

Fraenkel, E. (1957) *Horace* (Oxford)

Fränkel, H. (1962) *Dichtung und Philosophie des frühen Griechentums: eine Geschichte der griechischen Epik, Lyrik und Prosa bis zur Mitte des fünften Jahrhunderts*[2] (Munich)

—— (1975) *Early Greek Philosophy and Poetry* (Oxford–New York); trans. M. Hadas and J. Willis of Fränkel (1962)

Fraschetti, A. (1994) 'Servio Tullio e la partizione del corpo civico', *Mètis* 9: 129–41

Fraser, P. M. (1970) 'Eratosthenes of Cyrene', *PBA* 56: 175–207

—— (2003) 'Agathon and Kassandra (*IG* IX.1 (2) 4.1750)', *JHS* 123: 26–40

Frederiksen, M. (1984) *Campania* (Rome)

Freeman, E. A. (1893) *History of Federal Government in Greece and Italy* (London–New York)

Fried, J. (2004) *Der Schleier der Erinnerung: Grundzüge einer historischen Memorik* (Munich)

Frier, B. W. (1979/1999) *Libri Annales Ponificorum Maximorum: The Origins of the Annalistic Tradition* (Rome); repr. with new Introduction (Ann Arbor)

Frost, F. J. (1980) *Plutarch's Themistocles: A Historical Commentary* (Princeton)

Fuhrmann, M. (1987) 'Erneuerung als Wiederherstellung des Alten: zur Tradition antiquarischer Forschung im spätrepublikanischen Rom', in R. Herzog and R. Koselleck, edd., *Epochenschwelle und Epochenbewußtsein* (Munich) 131–51

Gabba, E. (1964) 'Un documento censorio in Dionigi d'Alicarnasso 1.74.5', in A. Guarino and L. Labruna, edd., *Synteleia: Vincenzo Arangio-Ruiz*, 2 vols (Naples) I.486–93

—— (1967) 'Considerazioni sulla tradizione letteraria sulle origini della repubblica', in *Les origines de la république romaine* (Entretiens sur l'Antiquité Classique XIII; Vandœuvres-Genève) 141–74

—— (1979) 'Proposta per l'elogio Tarquiniese di Velthur Spurinna', *NAC* 8: 143–7

—— (1981) 'True History and False History in Classical Antiquity', *JRS* 71: 50–62 (= this volume, Ch. 12)

—— (1982) '"La storia di Roma arcaica" di Dionigi d'Alicarnasso', *ANRW* II.30.1: 799–816

—— (1984) 'The Collegia of Numa: Problems of Method and Political Ideas', *JRS* 74: 81–6

—— (1991) *Dionysius and The History of Archaic Rome* (Berkeley–Los Angeles–London)

—— ed. (1983) *Tria Corda: Scritti in onore di A. Momigliano* (Como)

Galinsky, K. (1983) 'Aeneas in Latium: Archäologie, Mythos und Geschichte', in V. Pöschl, ed., *2000 Jahre Vergil: Ein Symposium* (*Wolfenbüttler Forschungen* 24; Wiesbaden) 37–62

Gardthausen, V. (1882) *Mastarna oder Servius Tullius: mit einer Einleitung über die Ausdehnung des Etruskerreiches* (Leipzig)

Gehrke, H.-J. (1976) *Phokion: Studien zur Erfassung seiner historichen Gestalt* (Munich)

—— (1986) *Jenseits von Athens und Sparta: Das Dritte Griechenland und seine Staatenwelt* (Munich)

—— (1990) *Geschichte des Hellenismus* (Munich)

—— (1994) 'Römischer mos und griechische Ethik: Überlegungen zum Zusammenhang von Akkulturation und politischer Ordnung im Hellenismus', *HZ* 258: 593–622

—— (2001) 'Myth, History and Collective Identity: Uses of the Past in Ancient Greece and Beyond', in Luraghi (2001b) 286–313

—— (2003) 'Was heißt und zu welchem Ende studiert man intentionale Geschichte? Marathon und Troja als fundierende Mythen', in G. Melville and K.-S. Rehberg, edd., *Gründungsmythen, Genealogien, Memorialzeichen: Beiträge zur institutionellen Konstruktion von Kontinuität* (Cologne) 21–36

—— (2005) 'Identität in der Alterität: Heroen als Grenzgänger zwischen Hellenen und Barbaren', in E. S. Gruen, ed., *Cultural Borrowings and Ethnic Appropriations in Antiquity* (Stuttgart) 50–67

—— (2007) 'Marathon: A European Charter Myth', *Palamedes* 2: 93–108

—— (2008) 'Vergangenheitsrepräsentation bei den Griechen', in *Internationales Jahrbuch für Hermeneutik* 7: 1–22; English trans. 'Greek Representations of the Past', forthcoming in L. Foxhall and N. Luraghi, edd., *Intentional History: Spinning Time* (Stuttgart)

—— and A. Möller, edd. (1996) *Vergangenheit und Lebenswelt: Soziale Kommunikation, Traditionsbildung, und historisches Bewusstsein* (Tübingen)

Gelzer, M. (1912) *Die Nobilität der römischen Republik* (Leipzig); reprinted with additions (Stuttgart 1983); English trans. Robin Seager (Oxford 1969)

—— (1933) 'Römische Politik bei Fabius Pictor', *Hermes* 68: 129–66; repr. in id. (1962–4) III.51–92

—— (1934) 'Der Anfang römischer Geschichtsschreibung', *Hermes* 69: 46–55; repr. in id. (1962–4) III.93–103

—— (1954) 'Nochmals über den Anfang der römischen Geschichtsschreibung', *Hermes* 82: 342–8; repr. in id. (1962–4) III.104–10

—— (1962–4) *Kleine Schriften*, 3 vols (Wiesbaden)

Gerhard, E. with A. Klügmann and G. Körte (1840–97) *Etruskische Spiegel*, 5 vols + Suppl. (Berlin)

Gernet, L. (1926) *Lysias: Discours*, 2 vols (Paris)

—— (1968) *La notion mythique de la valeur en Grèce* (Paris)

Giannini, A. (1963) 'Studi sulla paradossografia greca I. Da Omero a Callimaco: motivi e forme del meraviglioso', *RIL* 97: 247–66

—— (1964) 'Studi sulla paradossografia greca II. Da Callimaco all'età imperiale: la letteratura paradossografica, *Acme* 17: 99–140

—— (1967) *Paradoxographorum Graecorum Reliquiae* (Milan)

Giglioli, G. Q. (1935) *L'Arte Etrusca* (Milan)

Gill, C. (1993) 'Plato on Falsehood—Not Fiction', in Gill–Wiseman (1993) 38–87

—— ed. (1980) *Plato: the Atlantis Story* (Bristol)

—— and T. P. Wiseman, edd. (1993) *Lies and Fiction in the Ancient World* (Exeter–Austin)

Giovannini, G. (1943) 'The Connection between Tragedy and History in Ancient Criticism', *PhQ* 22: 308–14

Gjerstad, E. (1967) 'Discussions Concerning Early Rome, III', *Historia* 16: 257–78

Godley, A. D. (1920) *Herodotus*, vol. I (LCL; London)

Goeller, F. (1836) *Thucydidis de Bello Peloponnesiaco*, vol. 1² (Leipzig)

Goetze, A. (1947) 'Historical Allusions in Old Babylonian Omen Texts', *Journal of Cuneiform Studies* 1: 253–65

Gomme, A. W. (1954) *The Greek Attitude to Poetry and History* (Berkeley–Los Angeles)

—— (1962) 'The Old Oligarch', in id., *More Essays in Greek History and Literature* (Oxford) 38–69

Goody, J. (1977) *The Domestication of the Savage Mind* (Cambridge)

—— (1986) *The Logic of Writing and the Organization of Society* (Cambridge)

—— (1987) *The Interface between the Written and the Oral* (Cambridge)

—— ed. (1968) *Literacy in Traditional Societies* (Cambridge)

—— and I. Watt (1968) 'The Consequences of Literacy', in Goody (1968) 27–68

Goodyear, F. R. D. (1972) *The Annals of Tacitus Book I* (Cambridge)

Gossman, L. (1978) 'History and Literature', in R. H. Canary and H. Kozicki, edd., *The Writing of History: Literary Form and Historical Understanding* (Madison) 3–40

Gould, J. (1989) *Herodotus* (London–New York)

Graf, F. (1993) *Greek Mythology: An Introduction* (Baltimore–London); trans. T. Marier of *Griechische Mythologie: Eine Einführung* (Munich––Zurich, 1985)

Grafton, A. (1990) *Forgers and Critics* (London)

Grandazzi, A. (1991) *La fondation de Rome* (Paris)

Grayeff, F. (1955–6) 'The Problem of the Genesis of Aristotle's Text', *Phronesis* 1: 105–22

Greenwalt, W. (1985) 'The Introduction of Caranus into the Argead King List', *GRBS* 26: 43–9

Guarducci, M. (1980) 'La cosidetta fibula Praenestina', *MAL* 24: 413–574

Gugenberger, E. and R. Schweidlenka (1993) *Die Fäden der Normen: zur Macht der Mythen in politischen Bewegungen* (Vienna)

Haacke, C. F. F. (1831) *Thucydidis de Bello Peloponessiaco Libri Octo* (Leipzig)

Haedicke, W. (1936) *Die Gedanken der Griechen über Familienherkunft und Vererbung* (Halle)

Haffter, H. (1964) 'Rom und römische Ideologie bei Livius', *Gymnasium* 71: 236–50

Hainsworth, J. B. (1984) 'The Reliability of the Oral Tradition', in L. Foxhall and M. Davies, edd., *The Trojan War: its Historicity and Context* (Bristol) 111–35

Halbwachs, M. (1925) *Les cadres sociaux de la mémoire* (Paris); partial trans. L. A. Coser in *On Collective Memory* (Chicago–London, 1992)

—— (1950) *La mémoire collective* (Paris); English trans. F. J. Ditter, Jr., and Y. V. Ditter, *The Collective Memory* (Chicago–London 1980)

Hall, J. (1997) *Ethnic Identity in Greek Antiquity* (Cambridge)

—— (2002) *Hellenicity: Between Ethnicity and Culture* (Chicago–London)

Hammond, N. G. L. and G. T. Griffith (1979) *A History of Macedonia II: 550–336 B.C.* (Oxford)

Harris, W. V. (1971) *Rome in Etruria and Umbria* (Oxford)

Harrison, S. J., ed. (1990) *Oxford Readings in Vergil's* Aeneid (Oxford)

Hartog, F. (1980) *Le miroir d'Hérodote: Essai sur la representation de l'autre* (Paris); English trans. J. Lloyd, *The Mirror of Herodotus: The Representation of the Other in the Writing of History* (Berkeley–Los Angeles–London, 1988)

Havelock, E. A. (1982) *The Literate Revolution in Greece and its Cultural Consequences* (Princeton)

Hay, D. (1977) *Annalists and Historians: Western Historiography from the Eighth to the Eighteenth centuries* (London–New York)

Hedrick, C. W. (1993) 'The Meaning of Material Culture: Herodotus, Thucydides and their Sources', in R. Rosen and J. Farrell, edd., *Nomodeiktes: Greek Studies in Honor of Martin Ostwald* (Ann Arbor) 17–37

—— (1995) 'Thucydides and the Beginnings of Greek Archaeology', in D. Small, ed., *Methods in the Mediterranean: Historical and Archaeological Views on Texts and Archaeology* (Leiden–New York–Cologne) 45–88

Helbig, W. (1972) *Führer durch die öffentlichen Sammlungen klassicher Altertümer in Rom, IV*[4] (Tübingen)

Hemmerdinger, B. (1975) 'L'émigré (Pseudo-Xénophon, ΑΘΗΝΑΙΩΝ ΠΟΛΙΤΕΙΑ)', *REG* 88: 71–80

Henige, D. P. (1974) *The Chronology of Oral Tradition: Quest for a Chimera* (Oxford)

—— (1982) *Oral Historiography* (London–New York–Lagos)

Henz, G. J. (1974) 'Elemente einer Allgemeinen historischen Quellenkunde', *Archiv für Kulturgeschichte* 56: 1–24

Henze, H. (1899) *Quomodo Cicero de historia eiusque auctoribus iudicauerit* (diss. Jena)

Herkommer, E. (1968) *Die Topoi in den Proömien der römischen Geschichtswerke* (diss. Tübingen)

Heubeck, A. (1979) *Schrift* (*Archaeologia Homerica*, Bd. 3, Kap. X; Göttingen)

Heubeck, A. (1984) 'Homer und Mykene', *Gymnasium* 91: 1–14

—— (1986) 'Die Würzburger Alphabettafel', *WJA* 12: 7–20

Heubner, H. (1963–82) *Die Historien: Kommentar*, 5 vols (Heidelberg)

Heurgon, J. (1950) 'L'elogium d'un magistrat étrusque découvert à Tarquinia', *CRAI* 212–16

—— (1951) 'L'elogium d'un magistrat étrusque découvert à Tarquinia', *MEFR* 63: 119–137

—— (1953a) 'La vocation étruscologique de l'empereur Claude', *CRAI* 92–7

—— (1953b) 'Tarquitius Priscus et l'organisation de l'ordre des haruspices sous l'empereur Claude', *Latomus* 12: 402–17

—— (1957) 'L'État étrusque' *Historia* 6: 63–97

—— (1964a) 'L. Cincius et la loi du clavis annalis', *Athenaeum* 42: 432–7

—— (1964b) *Daily Life of the Etruscans*, English trans. J. Kirkup (London); French original, *La vie quotidienne chez les Etrusques* (Paris, 1961)

—— (1966) 'La coupe d'Aulus Vibenna', in *Mélanges d'archéologie, d'épigraphie et d'histoire offerts à J. Carcopino* (Paris) 515–28

—— (1969a) *Rome et la Méditerranée occidentale jusqu'aux guerres puniques* (Paris)

—— (1969b) 'Un addendum aux Elogia Tarquiniensia', *ArchClass* 21: 88–91

—— (1973) 'Les Graffites d'Aléria', in J. Jehasse and L. Jehasse, edd., *La nécropole préromaine d'Aléria (1960–1968)* (*Gallia* Suppl. 25; Paris) 547–76

Heuss, A. (1959) *Verlust der Geschichte* (Göttingen)

—— (1977) 'Alexander der Grosse und das Problem der historischen Urteilsbildung', *HZ* 225: 29–64

—— (1982) *Gedanken und Vermutungen zur frühen römischen Regierungsgewalt* (*NAWG* Jahrg. 1982, no. 10; Göttingen)

Hinks, D. A. G. (1936) 'Tria genera causarum', *CQ* 30: 170–76

Hobi, V. (1988) 'Kurze Einführing in die Grundlagen der Gedächtnispsychologie', in von Ungern-Sternberg–Reinau (1988) 9–33

Hobsbawm, E. J. (1983) 'Introduction: Inventing Traditions', in Hobsbawm–Ranger (1983) 1–14

—— (1990) *Nations and Nationalism since 1780: Programme, Myth, Reality* (Wiles Lectures; Cambridge)

—— and T. Ranger, edd. (1983) *The Invention of Tradition* (Cambridge)

Hoffmann, W. (1934) *Rom und die griechische Welt im 4. Jh.* (Leipzig)

Holford-Strevens, L. (1988/2003) *Aulus Gellius* (London–Chapel Hill; 2nd edn., Oxford)

Hölkeskamp, K.J. (1987) *Die Entstehung der Nobilität: Studien zur sozialen und politischen Geschichte der römischen Republik in 4. Jh. v. Chr.* (Stuttgart)

—— (1996) '*Exempla* und *mos maiorum*: Überlegungen zum kollektiven Gedächtnis der Nobilität', in Gehrke–Möller (1996) 301–38; repr. in

K.-J. Hölkeskamp, *Senatus Populusque Romanus*. *Die politische Kultur der Republik: Dimensionen und Deutungen* (Stuttgart, 2004) 169–198

Hölscher, T. (1978) 'Die Anfänge römischer Repräsentationskunst', *MDAI(R)* 85: 315–57

Homeyer, H. (1965) *Lukian: wie man Geschichte schreiben soll* (Munich)

Horsfall, N. (2003) *The Culture of the Roman Plebs* (London)

How, W. W. and J. Wells (1928) *A Commentary on Herodotus*², 2 vols (Oxford)

Howald, E. (1944) *Vom Geist antiker Geschichtsschreibung* (Munich; repr. 1964)

Humphreys, S. (1985) 'Lycurgus of Butadae: An Athenian Aristocrat', in J. Ober and J. W. Eadie, edd., *The Craft of the Ancient Historian: Essays in Honor of C. G. Starr* (Lanham, Md.–London) 199–252

—— (1997) 'Fragments, Fetishes, and Philosophies: Towards a History of Greek historiography after Thucydides,' in G. Most, ed., *Collecting Fragments/Fragmente Sammeln* (Göttingen) 207–24

Hunter, R., ed. (2005) *The Hesiodic Catalogue of Women: Constructions and Reconstructions* (Cambridge)

Hus, A. (1971) *Vulci étrusque et étrusco-romaine* (Paris)

Huss, W. (1985) *Geschichte der Karthager* (Munich)

Immerwahr, H. (1960) 'Ergon: On History as a Monument in Herodotus and Thucydides', *AJPh* 81: 261–90

Isnardi, M. (1955) 'τέχνη e ἦθος nella metodologia storiografica di Polibio', *SCO* 3: 102–10; repr. in German in K. Stiewe and N. Holzberg, edd., *Polybios* (*Wege der Forschung* 347; Darmstadt) 259–72

Jacoby, F. (1909) 'Über die Entwicklung der griechischen Historiographie und den Plan einer neuen Sammlung der griechischen Historikerfragmente', *Klio* 9: 80–123; repr. in id. (1956a) 16–64

—— (1912) 'Hekataios', *RE* VII: 2666–2769; repr. in id. (1956b) 185–237

—— (1913) 'Herodotos (7)', *RE Suppl.* II: 205–520; repr. in id. (1956b) 7–104

—— (1922) 'Kleitarchos', *RE* XI: 622–54; repr. in id. (1956b) 332–48

—— (1926) 'Griechische Geschichtschreibung', *Die Antike* 2: 1–29; repr. in id. (1956a) 73–99

—— (1940) 'Die Überlieferung von Ps.-Plutarchs *Parallela Minora* und die Schwindelautoren', *Mnemosyne*³ 8: 73–144, repr. in id. (1956a) 359–422

—— (1947) 'The First Athenian Prose Writer', *Mnemosyne* 13: 13–64; repr. in id. (1956a) 100–43

—— (1949) *Atthis: The Local Chronicles of Ancient Athens* (Oxford)

—— (1956a) *Abhandlungen zur griechischen Geschichtsschreibung*, ed. H. Bloch (Leiden)

—— (1956b) *Griechische Historiker* (Stuttgart)

Jeffery, L. (1961) *The Local Scripts of Archaic Greece* (Oxford)

—— (1976) *Archaic Greece: The City States c. 700–500 B.C.* (London–New York)

Jerome, T. S. (1923) *Aspects of the Study of Roman History* (New York–London)

Jocelyn, H. D. (1972) 'The Poems of Quintus Ennius', *ANRW* I.2: 987–1026

Johnson, A. (1926) *The Historian and Historical Evidence* (New York)

Johnson, W. A. (2000) 'Toward a Sociology of Reading in Classical Antiquity', *AJPh* 121: 593–627

Jones, C. P. (1999) *Kinship Diplomacy in the Ancient World* (Cambridge, Mass.–London)

Jördens, A. and G. Becht-Jördens (1994) 'Ein Eberunterkiefer als "Staatssymbol" des Aitolischen Bundes (*IG* XII 2.15): Politische Identitätssuche im Mythos nach dem Ende der spartanischen Hegemonie', *Klio* 76: 172–84

Jost, K. (1936) *Das Beispiel und Vorbild der Vorfahren bei den attischen Rednern und Geschichtsschreibern bis Demosthenes* (*Rhetorische Studien* 19; Paderborn)

Jüthner, J. and F. Brein (1965) *Die athletischen Leibesübungen der Griechen I* (Vienna)

Jüttner, C. (1979) *Gedächtnis: Grundlagen der psychologischen Gedächtnisforschung* (Munich)

Kahrstedt, U. (1953) 'Eine etruskische Stimme zur etruskischen Geschichte', *SO* 30: 68–76

Kalinka, E. (1913) *Die pseudoxenophontische Ἀθηναίων Πολιτεία: Einleitung, Übersetzung, Erklärung* (Leipzig)

Kappelmacher, W. (1926) 'Licinius (116a)', *RE* XIII.1: 436–43

Kebric, R. B. (1978) *In the Shadow of Macedon: Duris of Samos* (*Historia* Einzelschriften 29; Stuttgart)

Kelley, A. P. (1969) 'Historiography in Cicero' (diss., University of Pennsylvania)

Kennedy, G. (1972) *The Art of Rhetoric in the Roman World* (Princeton)

Kern, O. (1894) *Die Gründungsgeschichte von Magnesia am Mäandros* (Berlin)

—— ed. (1900) *Die Inschriften von Magnesia am Maeander* (Berlin)

Keyser, E. (1931) *Die Geschichtswissenschaft: Aufbau und Aufgaben* (Munich and Berlin)

Kienast, D. (1954) *Cato der Zensor* (Heidelberg; repr. Darmstadt, 1979)

Kierdorf, W. (1980a) *Laudatio Funebris: Interpretationen und Untersuchungen zur Entwicklung der römischen Leichenrede* (Meisenheim am Glan)

—— (1980b) 'Catos "Origines" und die Anfänge der römischen Geschichtsschreibung', *Chiron* 10: 205–24

—— (2002) 'Anfänge und Grundlagen der römischen Geschichtsschreibung', *Klio* 84: 400–13

Kilburn, K. (1959) *Lucian,* vol. 6 (LCL; London–Cambridge, Mass.)

Klein, R. (1962) 'Königtum und Königszeit bei Cicero' *(diss. Erlangen)*

Klingner, F. (1961) 'Cato Censorius und die Krisis des romischen Volkes', in id., *Römische Geisteswelt*⁴ (Munich) 34–65; orig. in *Die Antike* 10 (1934) 239–63

Kock, H. (1932) *Pronoia und Paideusis: Studien über Origenes und sein Verhältnis zum Platonismus* (Berlin)

Koenen, L. (1970) 'Die "Laudatio Funebris" des Augustus für Agrippa auf einem neuen Papyrus', *ZPE* 5: 217–83

Koestermann, E. (1963–8) *Cornelius Tacitus: Annalen,* 4 vols (Heidelberg)

Kopp, M. (1992) 'Mythische Genealogie und politische Identitäten: Studien zur Bedeutung des Mythos für die Entwicklung arkadischer Staaten' (diss., Freiburg i. Br.)

Kornemann, E. (1911) 'Die älteste Form der Ponifikalannalen', *Klio* 11: 245–57; repr. in Pöschl (1969) 59–76

—— (1960) *Römische Geschichte* I⁴ (Stuttgart)

Kornhardt, H. (1936) 'Exemplum' (diss., Göttingen)

Körte, G. (1897) 'Ein Wandgemälde von Vulci als Document zur römischen Königsgeschichte', *JDAI* 12: 57–80

Köves-Zulauf, Th. (1987) 'Die Eroberung von Gabii und die literarische Moral der römischen Annalistik', *WJA* 13: 121–47

Kraus, C. S., ed. (1999) *The Limits of Historiography: Genre and Narrative in Ancient Historical Texts* (Leiden–Boston–Cologne)

Kroll, W. (1913) *M. Tulli Ciceronis Orator* (Berlin)

—— (1924) *Studien zum Verständnis der römischen Literatur* (Stuttgart)

Krüger, K. W. (1823) *Dionysii Halicarnassensis Historiographica, h.e. Epistula ad Cn. Pompejum, ad Q. Aelium Tuberonem et Ad Ammaeum Altera* (Halle)

—— (1851) *Historisch Philologische Studien* I (Berlin)

—— (1860) Θουκυδίδου ξυγγραφή, *mit erklärenden Anmerkungen,* I.1³ (Berlin)

Kuch, H. (1989) *Der antike Roman* (Berlin)

Kunz, M. (1935) *Zur Beurteilung der Prooemien in Diodors historischer Bibliothek* (diss. Zurich)

La Regina, A. (1968) 'L'elogio di Scipione Barbato', *DArch* 2: 173–90

La Rocca, E. (1984) 'Fabio o Fannio: L'affresco media-republicano dell'Esquilino come riflesso dell'arte "rappresentativa" e come espressione di mobilità sociale', *DArch*³ 2: 31–53

Labruna, L. (1984) *Tito Livio e le istituzioni giuridiche e politiche dei Romani* (Naples)

LaCapra, D. (1985) *History and Criticism* (Ithaca)

Lachenaud, G. (1981) *De la malignité d'Hérodote*, in *Plutarque: Œuvres Morales*, Tome XII.1 (Budé; Paris) 105–258

Lacroix, B. (1951) *L'histoire dans l'Antiquité* (Montreal–Paris)

Laffi, U. (1980) 'La lex Arae Jovis Salonitanae', *Athenaeum* 58: 119–27

Laird, A. (1993) 'Fiction, Bewitchment and Story Worlds: The Implications of Claims to Truth in Apuleius', in Gill–Wiseman (1993) 147–74

Laistner, M. L. W. (1947) *The Greater Roman Historians* (Berkeley–Los Angeles)

Lamprechts, R. (1955) *Essai sur les magistratures des républiques étrusques* (Brussels–Rome)

Landfester, M. (1988) *Humanismus und Gesellschaft im 19 Jahrhundert: Untersuchungen zur politischen und gesellschaftlichen Bedeutung der humanistichen Bildung in Deutschland* (Darmstadt)

Laqueur, R. (1926) 'Lokalchronik', *RE* XIII.1: 1083–1110

Latacz, J. (1989) *Homer: der erste Dichter des Abenlandes*[2] (Munich)

—— ed. (1979) *Homer: Tradition und Neuerung* (*Wege der Forschung* 463; Darmstadt)

Latte, K. (1960) *Römische Religionsgeschichte* (Munich)

Lausberg, H. (1998) *Handbook of Literary Rhetoric*, trans. M. T. Bliss, A. Jansen, and D. E. Orton and ed. D. E. Orton and R. D. Anderson (Leiden–Boston–Cologne)

Leeman, A. D. (1955) 'Le genre et le style historique à Rome: théorie et pratique', *REL* 33: 183–208

—— (1963) *Orationis Ratio: the Stylistic Theories and Practices of the Roman Orators, Historians and Philosophers*, 2 vols (Amsterdam)

—— (1989) 'Antieke en moderne geschiedschrijving: Een misleidende Cicero-interpretatie', *Hermeneus* 61: 235–41

Legrand, Ph.-E. (1944) *Hérodote: Histoires Livre II* (Budé; Paris)

—— (1954) *Hérodote: Histoires Livre IX* (Budé; Paris)

Lehmann, G. A. (1974) 'Polybios und die ältere und zeitgenössische griechische Geschichtsschreibung: einige Bemerkungen', in E. Gabba, ed., *Polybe* (Entretiens sur l'Antiquité classique XX; Vandœuvres-Genève) 145–205

Lendon, J. E. (2009) 'Historians without History: Against Historiography', in Feldherr (2009) 41–61

Lenfant, D. (1999) 'Peut-on se fier aux "fragments" d'historiens? L'example des citations d'Hérodote', *Ktèma* 24: 103–21

Levene, D. S. (2005) 'Polybius on "Seeing" and "Hearing": 12.27', *CQ* 55: 627–9

Lewis, I. M. (1962) 'Historical Aspects of Genealogies in Northern Somali Social Structure', *Journal of African History* 3: 35–48

—— (1968) 'Literacy in a Nomadic Society: The Somali Case', in Goody (1968) 265–76

Linke, B. and M. Stemmler, edd. (2000) *Mos maiorum: Untersuchungen zu den Formen der Identitätsstiftung und Stabilisierung in der römischen Republik* (Stuttgart)

Lobeck, Chr. A. (1838) *Paralipomena Grammaticae Graecae* (Leipzig)

Loenen, D. (1926) 'De nobilitate apud Athenienses', *Mnemosyne* 54: 206–23

Lohmann, D. (1970) *Die Komposition der Reden in der Ilias* (Berlin)

Longo, O. (1978) 'Scrivere in Tucidide: comunicazione e ideologia', in E. Livrea and G. A. Privitera, edd., *Studi in onore di Anthos Ardizzoni* (Rome) 519–54

Loraux, N. (1976) 'Problèmes grecs de la démocration moderne', *Critique* 355: 1276–87

—— (1980) 'L'acropole comique', *AncSoc* 11–12: 119–50

—— (1986) *The Invention of Athens: the Funeral Oration in the Classical City*, English trans. A. Sheridan of *L'invention d'Athènes: Histoire de l'oraison funèbre dans la 'cité classique'* (Paris, 1983)

—— and P. Vidal-Naquet (1979) 'La formation de l'Athènes bourgeoise: essai d'historiographie 1750–1850', in R. R. Bolgar, ed., *Classical Influences on Western Thought* A.D. *1650–1870* (Cambridge) 169–222

Lowenthal, D. (1985) *The Past is a Foreign Country* (Cambridge)

Luce, T. J. (1977) *Livy: The Composition of his History* (Princeton)

—— (1988) 'Ancient Views on the Causes of Bias in Historical Writing', *CPh* 84: 16–31 (= this volume, Ch. 10)

—— (1991) 'Tacitus on 'History's Highest Function': *praecipuum munus annalium* (*Ann.* 3.65)', *ANRW* II.33.3: 2904–27

Luraghi, N. (2001a) 'Introduction', in Luraghi (2001b) 1–15

—— (2008) *The Ancient Messenians: Constructions of Ethnicity and Memory* (Cambridge)

—— ed. (2001b) *The Historian's Craft in the Age of Herodotus* (Oxford)

Luschnat, O. (1978) *Thukydides der Historiker* (Stuttgart); a corrected reprint of 'Thukydides der Historiker', *RE* Suppl. XII (1970) 1085–1354, together with 'Nachträge zu Suppl. Bd. XII S. 1085–1034', orig. in *RE* Suppl. XIV (1974) 760–86

Macan, R. W. (1908) *Herodotus VII–IX*, 3 vols (London)

MacLeod, M. D. (1991) *Lucian: A Selection* (Warminster)

Maggiani, A. (1996) 'Appunti sulle magistrature etrusche', *SE* 62: 95–137

Mahieu, W. de (1979) 'A l'intersection de temps et de l'espace du mythe et de l'histoire—les généalogies: l'exemple Komo', *Cultures et Développement* 11: 415–37

Malamar, A. (1992) 'Ursprünge und Frühgeschichte', in H. H. Ben-Sasson, ed., *Geschichte des jüdischen Volkes: von den Anfängen bis zur Gegenwart* (Munich) 35ff.

Malitz, J. (1990) 'Das Interesse an der Geschichte: Die griechischen Histor-iker und ihr Publikum', in Verdin–Schepens–de Keyser (1990) 323–49

Manganaro, G. (1974) 'Una biblioteca storica nel ginnasio a Tauromenio nel II sec. a.C.', *PP* 29: 389–409, repr. in Alföldi (1976) 83–96

Manthe, U. (1993) 'Stilistische Gemeinsamkeiten in den Fachsprachen der Juristen und Auguren der Römischen Republik', in K. Zimmermann, ed. *Der Stilbegriff in den Altertumswissenschaften* (Rostock) 69–74

Manuwald, G. (2001) *Fabulae pratextae: Spüren einer literarischen Gattung der Römer* (*Zetemata* 108; Munich)

Marchal, G. P. (1984) 'Das Meisterli von Emmenbrücke oder: Vom Aussa-gewert mündlicher Überlieferung', *Schweizerische Zeitschrift für Geschichte* 34: 521ff.

Marincola, J. (1994a) 'Plutarch's Refutation of Herodotus,' *AncW* 20: 191–203

—— (1994b) Review of Bowen (1993), *Ploutarchos* 10.2: 11–13

—— (1997) *Authority and Tradition in Ancient Historiography* (Cambridge)

—— (1999) 'Genre, Convention, and Innovation in Greco-Roman Histori-ography', in Kraus (1999) 281–324

—— (2007a) 'Odysseus and the Historians', *SylCl* 18: 1–79

—— ed. (2007b) *A Companion to Greek and Roman Historiography*, 2 vols (Oxford–Malden, Mass.)

Markowitsch, H. W. (2002) *Dem Gedächtnis auf der Spur: vom Erinnern und Vergessen* (Darmstadt)

Marquardt, J. (1886) *Das Privatleben der Römer*², 2 vols (Leipzig)

Marrou, H.-I. (1954) *De la connaissance historique* (Paris)

—— (1965) *Histoire de l'education dans l'Antiquité* (Paris)

—— (1977) *Décadence romaine ou Antiquité tardive? IIIe–VIe siècle* (Paris)

Martin, J. (1974) *Antike Rhetorik: Technik und Methode* (Handbuch der Altertumswissenschaften, 2.3; Munich)

Martínez-Pinna, J. (1996) *Tarquinio Prisco: ensayo histórico sobre Roma arcaica* (Madrid)

Marwick, A. (1970) *The Nature of History* (London–Basingstoke)

Mastrocinque, A. (1993) *Romolo (La fondazione di Roma tra storia e leggenda)* (Padua)

Mauersberger, A. (1966) *Polybios-Lexikon* I.3 (Berlin)

—— (2006) *Polybios-Lexikon*² I.3 (Berlin)

Mavrogiannis, T. (1989/90) *Roma e Pergamo: origini troiane e origini arcade* (Tesi di laurea, Università degli Studi di Perugia, Facoltà di Lettere e Filosofia)

—— (2003) *Aeneas und Euander: mythische Vergangenheit und Politik im Rom vom 6. Jh. v. Chr. bis zur Zeit des Augustus* (Naples)

Mazzarino, S. (1945) *Dalla monarchia allo stato repubblicano* (Catania)

—— (1966) *Il pensiero storico classico*, 3 vols (Bari)

McCullagh, C. B. (1984) *Justifying Historical Descriptions* (Cambridge)

McDonald, A. H. (1957) 'The Style of Livy', *JRS* 47: 155–72

—— (1968) 'The Roman Historians', in M. Platnauer, ed., *Fifty Years (and Twelve) of Classical Scholarship* (Oxford) 465–95

Meijering, R. (1987) *Literary and Rhetorical Theories in Greek Scholia* (Groningen)

Meissner, B. (1992) *Historiker zwischen Polis und Königshof: Studien zur Stellung der Geschichtsschreiber in der griechischen Gesellschaft in spätklassischer und hellenistischer Zeit* (Göttingen)

Meister, K. (1975) *Historische Kritik bei Polybios* (Wiesbaden)

—— (1990) *Die griechische Geschichtsschreibung: von den Anfängen bis zum Ende des Hellenismus* (Stuttgart)

Mensching, E. (1986) 'Zur Entstehung und Beurteilung von Ab urbe condita', *Latomus* 45: 572–89

Merkelbach, R. and M. L. West (1990) 'Fragmenta Selecta' in F. Solmsen, ed. *Hesiodi Theogonia, Opera et dies, Scutum*[3] (OCT; Oxford)

Messerschmidt, F. (1930a) *Nekropolen von Vulci* (*JDAI* Ergänzungsheft 12; Berlin)

—— (1930b) 'Probleme der etruskischen Malerei des Hellenismus', *JDAI* 45: 62–90

—— and A. von Gerkan (1930) *Nekropolen von Vulci* (Berlin)

Meyer, Ed. (1882) 'Untersuchungen über Diodors römische Geschichte', *Rh. Mus.* 37: 610–27

—— (1954) *Geschichte des Altertums* III[3] (Darmstadt)

Meyer, H. (1914) '*Imagines maiorum*', *RE* IX: 1099–1104

Miller, J. C., ed. (1980) *The African Past Speaks: Essays on Oral Tradition and History* (Folkestone–Hamden, Conn.)

Miller, P. N. (2007) *Momigliano and Antiquarianism: Foundations of the Modern Cultural Sciences* (Toronto–Los Angeles)

Mitchel, F. (1956) 'Herodotus' Use of Genealogical Chronology', *Phoenix* 10: 48–69

Mitchell, R. E. (1986) 'The Definition of *patres* and *plebs*: An End to the Struggle of the Orders', in Raaflaub (1986b) 130–74

Mitropoulou, E. (1993) 'The Origin and Significance of the Vergina Symbol', *Ancient Macedonia/Ἀρχαία Μακεδονία* 5: 843–958

Möller, A. (1996) 'Der Stammbaum der Philaiden—über Funktionen der Genealogie bei den Griechen', in M. Flashar, H.-J. Gehrke, and E. Heinrich, edd., *Retrospektive: Konzepte von Vergangenheit in der griechisch-römischen Antike* (Munich) 17–35

—— (2001) 'The Beginning of Chronography: Hellanicus' *Hiereiai*', in Luraghi (2001b) 241–62

Moles, J. L. (1993) 'Truth and Untruth in Herodotus and Thucydides', in Gill–Wiseman (1993) 88–121

Momigliano, A. (1957) 'Perizonius, Niebuhr and the Character of Early Roman Tradition', *JRS* 47: 107–14; repr. in id., *Secondo Contributo alla Storia degli Studi Classici e del Mondo Antico* (Rome 1960) 69–88

—— (1961) *Claudius: the Emperor and his Achievement*² (Cambridge)

—— (1966) 'Time in Ancient Historiography', *H&T* 6: 1–23; repr. in id. (1969) 13–41

—— (1967a) 'Osservazioni sulla distinzione fra patrizi e plebei', in: *Les origines de la république romaine* (Entretiens sur l'Antiquité Classique XIII; Vandœuvres-Genève) 197–221; repr. in id. (1969) 419–36

—— (1967b) Review of Alföldi (1965), *JRS* 57: 211–16; repr. in id. (1969) 487–99

—— (1969) *Quarto Contributo alla Storia degli Studi Classici e del Mondo Antico* (Rome)

—— (1972) 'Tradition and the Classical Historian', *H&T* 11: 279–93; repr. in id. (1975) I.14–31

—— (1974) 'Polybius' Reappearance in Western Europe', in *Polybe* (Entretiens sur l'Antiquité Classique XX; Vandœuvres-Genève) 347–72; repr. in id. (1980) I.103–23

—— (1975) *Quinto Contributo alla Storia degli Studi Classici e del Mondo Antico*, 2 vols (Rome)

—— (1977) 'Prolegomena a ogni futura metafisica sulla plebe romana', *Labeo* 23: 7–15; repr. in id. (1980) II.477–86

—— (1978) 'The Historians of the Classical World and their Audiences: Some Suggestions', *ANSP*³ 8: 59–75; repr. in id. (1980) I.361–76

—— (1980) *Sesto Contributo alla storia degli studi classici e del mondo antico*, 2 vols (Rome)

—— (1981) 'The Rhetoric of History and the History of Rhetoric', in E. S. Shaffer, ed., *Comparative Criticism: A Year Book*, vol. 3 (Cambridge) 259–68; repr. in id. (1984c) 49–59

—— (1984a) 'The Origins of Rome', in id. (1984c) 379–436; reprinted in *CAH*² VII.2: 52–112

—— (1984b) 'Georges Dumézil and the Trifunctional Approach to Roman Civilization', *H&T* 23: 312–30; repr. in id., *Ottavo Contributo alla storia degli studi classici e del mondo antico* (Rome, 1987) 135–59

—— (1984c) *Settimo Contributo alla Storia degli Studi Classici e del mondo antico* (Rome)

—— (1990) *The Classical Foundations of Modern Historiography* (Berkeley–Los Angeles–London

Momigliano, A. and A. Schiavone, edd. (1988) *Storia di Roma*, I (Turin)

Mommsen, Th. (1861) 'Mamilius Sura, Aemilius Sura, L. Manilius', *Rh. Mus.* 16: 282–7; repr. in id., *Gesammelte Schriften VII: Philologische Schriften* (Berlin, 1909) 70–6

—— (1870) 'Die Erzählung von Cn. Marcius Coriolanus', *Hermes* 4: 1–26, repr. in id. (1879) II.113–52, and in Pöschl (1969) 31–58

—— (1879) *Römische Forschungen*, 2 vols (Berlin)

—— (1881) 'Die Remuslegende', *Hermes* 16: 1–23; repr. in id. (1906–9) I.1–21

—— (1886) 'Die Tatiuslegende', *Hermes* 21: 570–84; repr. in id. (1906–9) I.22–35

—— (1887) *Römische Staatsrecht*³, 3 vols (Leipzig)

—— (1903) *Römische Geschichte*⁹ (Berlin)

—— (1906–9) *Gesammelte Schriften IV-VI: Historische Schriften*, 3 vols (Berlin)

—— (1920) *Römische Geschichte*, vol. I¹² (Munich)

Mora, F. (1999) *Fasti e schemi cronologici: la riorganizzazione annalistica del passato remoto romano* (Stuttgart)

Morgan, J. (1993) 'Make-Believe and Make Believe', in Gill–Wiseman (1993) 175–229

Morgan, T. (1998) *Literate Education in the Hellenistic and Roman Worlds* (Cambridge)

Mossé, Cl. (1969) 'Les utopies égalitaires à l'époque hellenistique', *RH* 93: 297–308

Moxon, I. S., J. D. Smart, and A. J. Woodman, edd. (1986) *Past Perspectives: Studies in Greek and Roman Historical Writing* (Cambridge)

Mühlmann, W. (1938) *Methodik der Völkerkunde* (Stuttgart)

Müller, K. O. and W. Deecke (1877) *Die Etrusker*, 2 vols (Stuttgart)

Müller-Karpe, H. (1962) *Zur Stadtwerdung Roms* (*MDAI(R)* Erg. Hft. VIII; Heidelberg)

Münzer, F. (1898) 'Caeles Vibenna und Mastarna', *Rh. Mus.* 53: 596–620

—— (1901) 'Cornelius (347)', *RE* IV: 1493

—— (1909) 'Fabius (126)', *RE* VI: 1836–41

Murray, O. (1987) 'Herodotus and Oral History', in H. Sancisi-Weerdenberg and A. Kuhrt, edd., *Achaemenid History II: The Greek Sources* (Leiden) 93–115; repr. in Luraghi (2001b) 16–44

Musti, D. (1972) 'Polibio negli studi dell'ultimo ventennio (1950–1970)', *ANRW* I.2: 1114–81

—— (1987) 'Etruria e Lazio arcaico nella tradizione (Demarato, Tarquinio, Mezenzio)', in Cristofani (1987) 139–55

Nelson, W. (1973) *Fact or Fiction: the Dilemma of the Renaissance Storyteller* (Cambridge, Mass.)

Nestle, W. (1911) 'Gab es eine jonische Sophistik?' *Philologus* 70: 242–66

Nicolai, R. (1992) *La storiografia nell'educazione antica* (Pisa)

Nicolet, C. (1977) *Polybe: Histoires Livre VI* (Paris)

Niebuhr, B. G. (1853) *History of Rome*, I, trans. C. Thirlwall (London)

—— (1969) 'Quellen der römischen Geschichte', in Pöschl (1969) 1–30; orig. published in B. G. Niebuhr, *Historische und Philologische Vorträge*, 1. Abt., Bd. 1 (Berlin 1846) 2–36

Nilsson, M. P. (1951) *Cults, Myths, Oracles and Politics in Ancient Greece* (Lund)

—— (1955) *Die hellenistische Schule* (Munich)

Nock, A. D. (1959) 'Posidonius', *JRS* 49: 1–15: repr. in id., *Essays on Religion and the Ancient World*, ed. Z. Stewart, 2 vols (Oxford–Cambridge, Mass. 1979) II.853–76

Nogara, B. (1933) *Gli Etruschi e la loro civiltà*, (Milan)

Nora, P. (1996) 'General Introduction: Between Memory and History', in id., ed., *Realms of Memory: Rethinking the French Past: I. Conflicts and Divisions* (New York–Chichester) 1–20; trans. A. Goldhammer of *Les lieux de mémoire* I (Paris 1984)

Norden, E. (1909) *Die Antike Kunstprosa²*, 2 vols (Stuttgart; repr. Darmstadt 1958)

Nörr, D. (1980) Review of d'Ippolito (1978), *ZRG* 97: 398–9

North, H. F. (1956) 'Rhetoric and Historiography', *Quarterly Journal of Speech* 42: 234–42

North, J. A. (1990) 'Diviners and Divination at Rome', in M. Beard and J. A. North, edd., *Pagan Priests* (London) 49–71

Northwood, S. J. (2008) 'Cicero, *de Oratore* 2.51–64 and Rhetoric in Historiography', *Mnemosyne* 61: 228–44

Nougayrol, J. (1955) 'Les rapports des haruspicines étrusque et assyro-babylonienne et le foie d'argile de Falerii Veteres', *CRAI* 309–517

Nutton, V. (2004) *Ancient Medicine* (London–New York)

O'Kelly, L. (1991) 'It's Dramatic, but it's not True', *The Independent* (12 May 1991) 15

O'Mara, M. (1971) 'The Structure of the *De Oratore*: a Study in Ciceronian Amplification' (diss., Univ. of North Carolina)

Oakley, S. P. (1997–2005) *A Commentary on Livy*, 4 vols (Oxford)

Ogilvie, R. M. (1965) *A Commentary on Livy* (Oxford; repr. with addenda, 1967)

—— and A. Drummond (1989) 'The Surviving Evidence', *CAH*² VII.2: 1–29

Oliver, R. (1955) 'The Traditional Histories of Buganda, Bunyoro and Ankole', *Journal of the Royal African Institute* 85: 111–17

Ong, W. J. (1982) *Orality and Literacy: The Technologizing of the Word* (London)

Pagliaro, A. (1953) *Saggi di critica semantica* (Messina–Florence)

Palacky, F. (1869) *Würdigung der alten böhmischen Geschichtsschreiber*² (Prague)

Pallottino, M. (1940) Review of Vetter (1940), *SE* 14: 462–6

—— (1947) *L'origine degli Etruschi* (Rome)

—— (1950/1) 'Uno spiraglio di luce sulla storia etrusca: gli elogia Tarquiniensia', *SE* 21: 147–71

—— (1954) *Testimonia Linguae Etruscae* (Florence)

—— (1955/6) 'Nuovi spunti di ricerca sul tema delle magistrature etrusche', *SE* 24: 45–72

—— (1969) 'L'ermeneutica etrusca tra due documenti-chiave', *SE* 37: 79–91

—— (1977) 'Servius Tullius à la lumière des nouvelles découvertes archéologiques et épigraphiques', *CRAI* 216–35

—— (1987) 'Il fregio dei Vibenna e le sue implicazioni storiche', in Buranelli (1987) 227–33

—— (1993) *Origini e storia primitiva di Roma* (Milan)

Palm, J. (1955) *Über Sprache und Stil des Diodoros von Sizilien* (Lund)

Palmer, R. E. A. (1969) *The King and the Comitium* (Wiesbaden)

Papantoniou, G. (1958–9) 'Θουκυδίδεια', *EEAth* 9: 404–30

Pareti, L. (1926) *Le origini etrusche* (Florence)

—— (1931a) 'La disiunione politica degli Etruschi e i suoi riflessi storici e archeologici', *RPAA* 7: 89–100

—— (1931b) 'Per la storia degli Etruschi', *SE* 5:147–61; repr. in id. (1958–69) I.305ff.

—— (1958–69) *Studi minori di storia antica*, 4 vols (Rome)

Pasquali, G. (1913) 'Die schriftstellerische Form des Pausanias', *Hermes* 48: 161–223

Patzek, B. (1992) *Homer und Mykene: Mündliche Dichtung und Geschichtsschreibung* (Munich)

Paul, G. M. (1982) '*Urbs capta*: Sketch of an Ancient Literary Motif', *Phoenix* 36: 144–55

Pearson, L. (1942) *The Local Historians of Attica* (Philadelphia)

—— (1960) *The Lost Histories of Alexander the Great* (New York–London)

—— (1965) 'On the Malice of Herodotus', in *Plutarch's Moralia XI* (LCL; London–Cambridge, Mass.) 1–129

—— (1975) 'Myth and *Archaeologia* in Italy and Sicily: Timaeus and his Predecessors', *YCS* 24: 171–95

Pédech, P. (1956) 'La géographie de Polybe. Structure et contenu du livre XXXIV des Histoires', *LEC* 24: 3–24

—— (1961) *Polybe: Histoires, Livre XII* (Budé; Paris)

—— (1964) *La methode historique de Polybe* (Paris)

—— (1970) 'Un historien nommé Cratippe', *REA* 72: 31–45

Pelling, C. B. R. (1990) 'Truth and Fiction in Plutarch's *Lives*', in D. A. Russell, ed., *Antonine Literature* (Oxford) 19–52

Peremans, W. (1950) *De historische kritiek toegepast op de bronnen van de Grieks-Romeinse Oudheid* (Meded. van de Kon. Vl. Acad. Wetensch. Lett. en Schone Kunsten van België, Klasse der Lett. XII 4; Brussels)

—— (1955) *Inleiding tot de bronnenstudie van de Grieks-Romeinse Geschiedenis* (Meded. van de Kon. Vl. Acad. Wetensch. Lett. en Schone Kunsten van België, Klasse der Lett. XVII 4; Brussels)

Perl, G. (1964) 'Der Anfang der römischen Geschichtsschreibung' *F&F* 38: 185–9, 213–18

Perry, B. E. (1967) *The Ancient Romances* (Berkeley)

Person, Y. (1972) 'Chronology and Oral Tradition', in M. A. Klein and G. W. Johnson, edd., *Perspectives on the African Past* (Boston) 3–16; orig. published as 'Tradition orale et chronologie' in *Cahiers d'études africaines* 7.3 (1962) 462–72

Peter, H. (1897) *Die geschichtliche Literatur über die römische Kaiserzeit*, 2 vols (Leipzig)

—— (1911) *Wahrheit und Kunst: Geschichtschreibung und Plagiat im klassischen Altertum* (Leipzig–Berlin)

Petersen, E. (1899) 'Caele Vibenna und Mastarna', *JDAI* 14: 43–9

Petzold, K.-E. (1969) *Studien zur Methode des Polybios und zu ihrer historischen Auswertung* (Munich)

—— (1972) 'Cicero und Historie', *Chiron* 2: 253–76; repr. in id. (1999) 86–108

—— (1991) 'Annales maximi und Annalen', in K. Herbers, ed., *Ex ipsis rerum documentis: Beiträge zur Mediävistik: Festschrift... Harald Zimmermann* (Sigmaringen) 3–16; repr. in Petzold (1999) 252–65

—— (1993) 'Zur Geschichte der römischen Annalistik', in W. Schuller, ed., *Livius: Aspekte seines Werkes* (Konstanz) 151–88; repr. in Petzold (1999) 184–221

—— (1999) *Geschichtsdenken und Geschichtsschreibung: Kleine Schriften zur griechischen und römischen Geschichte* (Stuttgart)

Pfeiffer, R. (1949) *Callimachus, Volumen I: Fragmenta* (Oxford)

Philippson, P. (1944) *Genealogie als mythische Form* (Basel)

Phillips, J. E. (1974) 'Form and Language in Livy's Triumph Notices', *CPh* 69: 265–73

Piderit, K. W. and O. Harnecker (1886–90) *De Oratore für den Schulgebrauch erklärt* [6], 3 vols (Leipzig)

Piérart, M. (1983) 'L'historien ancien face aux mythes et aux legends', *LEC* 51: 47–62, 105–115

Pina Polo, F. (2004) 'Die nützliche Erinnerung: Geschichtsschreibung, *mos maiorum* und die römische Identität', *Historia* 53: 147–72

Pippidi, D. M. (1944) *Autour de Tibère* (Bucharest)

Plumb, J. H. (1969) *The Death of the Past* (London)

Pólay, E. (1983) 'Das Jurisprudenzmonopol des Pontifikalkollegiums in Rom und seine Abschaffung', *ACD* 19: 49–56

Poma, G. (1984) *Tra legislatori e tiranni: problemi storici e storiografici sull'età delle XII tavole* (Bologna)

Poppo, E. F. (1831) *Thucydidis De Bello Peloponnesiaco libri octo. Pars III. Commentarii: v. 1: Adnotata ad librum I cum Stephani Proparasceue* (Leipzig)

—— (1866) *Thucydidis, de Bello Peloponnesiaco libri octo* I (Leipzig)

—— and J. M. Stahl (1875–83) *Thucydidis de Bello Peloponnesiaco Libri Octo*, 4 vols in 8 (Leipzig)

Porciani, L. (2001) *Prime forme della storiografia greca* (Stuttgart)

Porod, R. (2009) *Lukian und die antike Geschichtsmethodologische Debatte: Ein Kommentar zur Schrift über die Methoden der Geschichtsschreibung* (Habilitationsschrift, Graz)

Porter, H. (1984) *Lies, Damned Lies and Some Exclusives* (London)

Pöschl, V., ed. (1969) *Römische Geschichtsschreibung* (*Wege der Forschung* 90; Darmstadt)

Poucet, J. (1975) Review of Alföldi (1974), *AC* 44: 646–51

—— (1981) 'Préoccupations érudites dans la tradition du regne de Romulus', *AC* 50: 664–76

—— (1981/2) 'L'amplification narrative dans l'évolution de la geste de Romulus', *ACD* 17/18: 175–87

—— (1985) *Les origines de Rome: tradition et histoire* (Brussels)

—— (1986) 'Sur certains silences curieux dans le premier livre de Tite-Live', in Altheim-Stiehl–Rosenbach (1986) 212–31

—— (2000) *Les rois de Rome: tradition et histoire* (Brussels)

Powell, J. E. (1937) 'The Manuscript S of Herodotus', *CR* 51: 118–9

Prakken, D. W. (1943) *Studies in Greek Genealogical Chronology* (Lancaster)

Premerstein, A. von (1905) 'Elogium', *RE* V.2: 2440–52

Preuschen, E. (1903) *Origens Werke, Band IV: Der Johanneskommentar* (Leipzig)

Prinz, F. (1979) *Gründungsmythen und Sagenchronologie* (Munich)

Pritchett, W. K. (1975) *Dionysius of Halicarnassus: On Thucydides* (Berkeley–Los Angeles)

Puccioni, G. (1981) *Il problema della monografia storica latina* (Bologna)

Raaflaub, K. A. (1986a) 'The Conflict of the Orders in Archaic Rome: A Comprehensive and Comparative Approach', in Raaflaub (1986b) 1–51

—— ed. (1986b) *Social Struggles in Archaic Rome: New Perspectives on the Conflict of the Orders* (Berkeley–Los Angeles–London)

Radermacher, L. (1919) 'Kanon', *RE* X: 1873–8

Rambaud, M. (1953) *Cicéron et l'histoire Romaine* (Paris)

Ranouil, P.-Ch. (1975) *Recherches sur le patriciat (509–356 avant J.-C.)* (Paris)

Rawson, E. (1971) 'Prodigy Lists and the Use of the *Annales Maximi*', *CQ* 21: 158–69; repr. in ead. (1991) 1–15

—— (1972) 'Cicero the Historian and Cicero the Antiquarian', *JRS* 62: 33–45; repr. in ead. (1991) 58–79

—— (1978) 'Caesar, Etruria and the *disciplina Etrusca*', *JRS* 68: 132–52; repr. in ead. (1991) 289–323

—— (1985) *Intellectual Life in the Late Roman Republic* (London–Baltimore)

—— (1991) *Roman Culture and Society: Collected Papers* (Oxford)

Ray, R. (1980) 'Bede's *Vera Lex Historiae*', *Speculum* 55: 1–21

Rebuffat, R. (1966) 'Les Phéniciens à Rome', *MEFR* 78: 7–48

Reichert, H. (1985) *Niebelungenlied und Nibelungensage* (Vienna–Cologne)

Reinach, S. (1892) 'Exegetae', in C. Daremberg and E. Saglio, *Dictionnaire des Antiquités Grecques et Romans d'après les textes et les monuments* (Paris) II.883–6

Reisig, K. (1823) *Commentarii in Sophoclis Oedipum Coloneum: criticis commentationibus addita enarratione integri* (Jena)

Reitzenstein, R. (1906) *Hellenistische Wundererzählungen* (Lepizig)

Renan, E. (1882) *Qu'est-ce qu'une nation?: Conférence faite en Sorbonne, le 11 mars 1882* (Paris)

Rhodes, P. J. (1981) *A Commentary on the Aristotelian* Athenaion Politeia (Oxford; repr. with addenda, 1993)

—— (2007) 'Documents and the Greek Historians', in Marincola (2007b) 56–66

Richard, J.-C. (1983) 'L'oeuvre de Servius Tullius: essai de mise au point', *RD* 61: 181–93

—— (1986) 'Patricians and Plebeians: The Origin of a Social Dichotomy', in Raaflaub (1986b) 105–29

Ridley, R. T. (1980) 'Fastenkritik: A Stocktaking', *Athenaeum* 58: 264–98

—— (1983) '*Falsi triumphi, plures consulatus*', *Latomus* 42: 372–82

—— (1986) 'The Genesis of a Turning-Point: Gelzer's Nobilität', *Historia* 35: 474–502

Riemann, K.-A. (1967) *Das herodoteische Geschichtswerk in der Antike* (Munich)

Robertson, N. (1987) 'The Nones of July and Roman Weather Magic', *MH* 44: 8–41

Röhrich, L. (1988) 'Orale Traditionen als historische Quelle', in von Ungern-Sternberg–Reinau (1988) 79–99

Romanelli, P. (1948) 'Tarquinia: scavi e ricerche nell'area della città', *NSA* 73: 193–270

Romilly, J. de (1956) 'L'utilité de l'histoire selon Thucydide', in *Histoire et Historiens dans l'Antiquité* (Entretiens sur l'Antiquité classique IV; Vandœuvres-Genève) 41–81

—— (1959) *Histoire et raison chez Thucydide* (Paris)

—— (1966) 'Thucydide et l'idée de progrès', *ASNP* 35: 143–91

Romm, J. S. (1992) *The Edges of the Earth in Ancient Thought* (Princeton)

Roncalli, F. (1978–80) 'Osservazioni sui *libri lintei* degli Etruschi', *Rendiconti dell'Accademia Pontificia* 51.2: 3–21

—— (1980) 'Carbasinis voluminibus implicati libri: osservazioni sul liber linteus di Zagabria', *JDAI* 95: 227–64

Rondholz, E. (1993) 'Zankapfel Mazedonien: Historische Hintergründe des Streits zwischen Athen und Skopje', *Blätter für deutsche und internationale Politik* 7: 871–81

Roselli, A. (2002) 'ἐκ βιβλίου κυβερνήτης: i limiti dell'apprendimento dai libri nella formazione tecnica e filosofica (Galeno, Polibio, Filodemo)', *Vichiana* 4.1: 35–50

Rosen, K. (1985) 'Die falschen Numabücher: Politik, Religion und Literatur in Rom 181 v. Chr.', *Chiron* 15: 65–90

Rosenthal, J. T. (1975) 'Bede's Use of Miracles in "The Ecclesiastical History"', *Traditio* 31: 328–35

Roveri, A. (1963) *La nascita delle forme storiche da Ecateo ad Erodoto* (Studi pubblicati dall'Istituto di filologia classica, 13; Bologna)

—— (1964) *Studi su Polibio* (Bologna)

Rüpke, J. (1993) 'Livius, Priesternamen und die *annales maximi*', *Klio* 75: 155–179

—— (1995) '*Fasti:* Quellen oder Produkte römischer Geschichtsschreibung?', *Klio* 77: 184–202

Russell, D. A. (1967) 'Rhetoric and Criticism', *G&R* 14: 130–44

Russell, D. A. and M. Winterbottom, edd. (1972) *Ancient Literary Criticism: The Principal Texts in New Translations* (Oxford)

Sacks, K. (1981) *Polybius on the Writing of History* (University of California Publications in Classical Studies 24; Berkeley and Los Angeles)

Schacter, D. L. (1996) *Searching for Memory: the Brain, the Mind and the Past* (New York)

—— ed. (1995) *Memory Distortion: How Minds, Brains and Societies Reconstruct the Past* (Cambridge, Mass.)

Schanz, M. and C. Hosius (1922–35) *Geschichte der römischen Literatur*, 4 vols (Munich)

Schäublin, Ch. (1983) 'Sempronius Asellio Fr. 2', *WJA* 9: 147–55

Scheer, T. S. (1993) *Mythische Vorväter: zur Bedeutung griechischer Heroenmythen im Selbstverständnis kleinasiatischer Städte* (Münchener Arbeiten zur Alten Geschichte 7; Munich)

Schefold, K. (1989) *Die Sagen von den Argonauten: Theben und Troia in der klassischen und hellenistischen Kunst* (Munich)

Scheller, P. (1911) 'De hellenistica historiae conscribenda arte' (diss., Leipzig)

Schepens, G. (1970) 'Éphore sur la valeur de l'autopsie (*FGrHist* 70 F 110 = Polybe XII 27.7)', *AncSoc* 1: 163–182

—— (1974) 'The Bipartite and Tripartite Divisions of History in Polybius XII 25 & 27', *AncSoc* 5: 297–307

—— (1980) *L' 'autopsie' dans la méthode des historiens grecs du V^4 siècle avant J.-C.* (Verhand. Kon. Vlaamse Academie voor Wetenschappen, Letteren en Schone Kunsten van België, Klasse der Letteren 42, 1980, nr. 93; Brussels)

—— (1990) 'Polemic and Methodology in Polybius' Book XII', in Verdin–Schepens–de Keyser (1990) 39–61

—— (2006) 'Travelling Greek Historians', in M. G. A. Angeli Bertinelli and A. Donati, edd., *Le vie della storia: Migrazioni di popoli, viaggi di individui, circolazione di idee nel Mediterraneo antico, Atti del II Incontro Internazionale di Storia Antica, Genova 6–8 ottobre 2004* (*Serta Antiqua et Mediaevalia* 9; Rome) 81–102

—— (2007) 'History and *Historia*: Inquiry in the Greek Historians', in Marincola (2007b) 39–55

Schmid, W. and O. Stählin (1929–48) *Geschichte der griechischen Literatur*, 5 vols (Handbuch der Altertumswissenschaft VII.1.1–5; Munich)

Schmidt, S. J., ed. (1991) *Gedächtnis: Probleme und Perspektiven der interdisziplinären Gedächtnisforschung* (Frankfurt am Main)

Scholz, U. W. (1984) Review of C. Ulf, *Die römische Luperkalienfest* (Darmstadt 1982), *GGA* 236: 172–87

Schott, R. (1968) 'Das Geschichtsbewußtsein schriftloser Völker', *Archiv für Begriffgeschichte* 12: 166–205

Schramm, P. E. (1929) *Kaiser, Rom und Renovatio*, 2 vols (Leipzig)

Schröder, O. (1914) 'De laudibus Athenarum a poetis tragicis et ab oratoribus epidicticis excultis' (diss., Göttingen)

Schroeder, W. A. (1971) *M. Porcius Cato: Das erste Buch der Origines* (Meisenheim am Glan)

Schultze, C. (1986) 'Dionysius of Halicarnassus and his Audience', in Moxon–Smart–Woodman (1986) 121–41

Schuster, M. (1958) 'Vestricius Spurrina', *RE* VIII.A: 1791–7

—— (1988) 'Zur Konstruktion von Geschichte in Kulturen ohne Schrift', in von Ungern-Sternberg–Reinau (1988) 57–71

Schwartz, E. (1897) 'Die Berichte über die catilinarische Verschwörung', *Hermes* 32: 554–608

—— (1900) 'Kallisthenes' Hellenika', *Hermes* 35: 106–30

—— (1903) 'Diodoros', *RE* V.1: 663–704; repr. in id., *Griechische Geschichtschreiber* (Leipzig 1957) 35–97

—— (1909) 'Die Zeit des Ephoros', *Hermes* 44: 481–502

—— (1943) *Fünf Vorträge über den griechischen Roman* (Berlin)

Schwegler, A. (1853–76) *Römische Geschichte*, 5 vols (Tübingen–Berlin)

Scott, I. G. (1929) 'Early Roman Traditions in the Light of Archaeology', *MAAR* 7: 7–118

Scott-Kilvert, I. (1979) *Polybius: The Rise of Rome* (Harmondsworth)

Scullard, H. H. (1967) *The Etruscan Cities and Rome* (London and Ithaca, NY)

Sehlmeyer, M. (1999) *Stadtrömische Ehrenstatuen der republikanischen Zeit: Historizität und Kontext von symbolen nobilitären Standesbewusstseins* (Stuttgart)

Shackleton Bailey, D. R. (1980) *Cicero: Select Letters* (Cambridge)

Siewert, P. (1978) 'Die angebliche Übernahme solonischer Gesetze in die Zwölftafeln: Ursprung und Ausgestaltung einer Legende', *Chiron* 8: 331–44

Simon, Chr. (1988) 'Gelzer's "Nobilität der römischen Republik" als "Wendepunkt"', *Historia* 37: 222–40

Skutsch, O. (1985) *The Annals of Q. Ennius* (Oxford)

Slater, W. J. (1972) 'Asclepiades and History', *GRBS* 13: 317–33

Smarczyk, B. (1990) *Untersuchungen zur Religionspolitik und politischen Propaganda Athens im Delisch-Attischen Seebund* (Quellen und Forschungen zur Antiken Welt 5; Munich)

Smith, S. P. (1921) *Hawaiki, the Original Home of the Maori* (Auckland)

Snell, B. (1924) *Die Ausdrücke für den Begriff des Wissens in der vorplatonischen Philosophie* (Berlin)

—— (1973) 'Wie die Griechen lernten, was geistige Tätigkeit ist', *JHS* 93: 172–84

Snodgrass, A. M. (1971) *The Dark Age of Greece: An Archaeological Survey of the Eleventh to the Eight Centuries* (Edinburgh)

Söder, R. (1932) *Die apokryphen Apostolgeschichten und die romanhafte Literatur der Antike* (Stuttgart)

Solmsen, F. (1986) 'Aeneas Founded Rome with Odysseus', *HSCP* 90: 93–110

Spieler, K.-H. (1970) *Untersuchungen zu Johann Gustav Droysens 'Historik'* (Berlin)

Stahl, H.-P. (1966) *Thukydides: die Stellung des Menschen im geschichtlichen Prozess* (*Zetemata* 40; Munich); expanded English edn., *Thucydides: Man's Place in History* (Swansea 2003)

Starr, C. G. (1956) 'The Roman Emperor and the King of Ceylon', *CPh* 51: 27–30, repr. in id., *Essays in Ancient History* (Brill, 1979) 258–61

Staveley, E. S. (1986) Review of Poma (1984), *Gnomon* 58: 633–7

Stein, H. (1893–1908) *Herodotos, erklärt*[4–6], 7 vols (Berlin)

Steinberg, M., ed. (1991) *The Presence of the Historian: Essays in Memory of Arnaldo Momigliano* (*H&T Beiheft* 30; Middletown, Conn.)

Stibbe, C. M., G. Colonna, C. de Simone, and H. S. Versnel (1980) *Lapis Satricanus* (Gravenhage)

Stiehl, R. (1955) 'Polybios' Exkurs über die oberitalienischen Kelten', *Palaeologia* 4: 244–9

Stoneman, R. (1991) *The Greek Alexander Romance* (Harmondsworth)

Strasburger, H. (1956) 'Herodots Zeitrechnung', *Historia* 5: 129–61; repr. with corrections in id. (1982–90) II.627–75

—— (1958) 'Thukydides und die politische Selbstdarstellung der Athener', *Hermes* 86: 17–40; repr. in id. (1982–90) II.676–708; English trans., 'Thucydides and the Political Self-Portrait of the Athenians', in J. Rusten, ed., *Thucydides* (*Oxford Readings in Classical Studies*; Oxford 2009) 191–219

—— (1966) *Die Wesensbestimmung der Geschichte durch die antike Geschichtsschreibung* (Wiesbaden); repr. in id. (1982–90) II.963–1016

—— (1968) *Zur Sage von der Gründung Roms* (*SHAW* 1968, 5. Abt.; Heidelberg); repr. in id. (1982–90) II.1017–55

—— (1972) *Homer und die Geschichtsschreibung* (*SHAW* 1972, 1; Heidelberg); repr. in id. (1982–90) II.1057–97

—— (1977) 'Umblick in Trümmerfeld der griechischen Geschichtsschreibung', in *Historiographia Antiqua: Commentationes Lovanienses… W. Peremans* (Leuven) 3–52; repr. in id. (1982–90) III.169–218

—— (1982–90) *Studien zur Alten Geschichte*, 3 vols (Hildesheim–New York)

Straub, J. (1952) *Studien zur Historia Augusta* (Bern)

Stroheker, K. F. (1965) 'Studien zu den historischen-geographischen Grundlagen der Nibelungendichtung', in O. Gigon, ed. *Germanentum und Spätantike* (Zürich) 246–74

Stroud, R. S. (1971) 'Greek Inscriptions: Theozotides and the Athenian Orphans', *Hesperia* 40: 280–301

Strzelecki, W. (1963) 'Naevius and Roman Annalists', *RFIC* 91: 440–58

Stuveras, R. (1965) 'La vie politique au premier siècle de la République romaine à travers la tradition littéraire', *MEFR* 77: 35–67

Suerbaum, W. (1971) 'Der Historiker und die Freiheit des Wortes: Die Rede des Cremutius Cordus bei Tacitus, Ann. 4, 34–5', in G. Radke, ed., *Politik und literarische Kunst im Werke des Tacitus* (Stuttgart) 61–99

—— ed. (2002) *Die archaische Literatur von den Anfängen bis Sullas Tod. Die vorliterarische Periode und die Zeit von 240 bis 78 v. Chr.* (Handbuch der Altertumswissenschaft VIII.1; Munich)

Syme, R. (1958) *Tacitus*, 2 vols (Oxford)

—— (1968) *Ammianus and the Historia Augusta* (Oxford)

—— (1971) *Emperors and Biography* (Oxford)

—— (1982) *Greeks Invading the Roman Government* (Seventh Stephen J. Brademas Lecture; Brookline, Mass.); repr. in id., *Roman Papers IV* (Oxford 1988) 1–20

—— (1983) *Historia Augusta Papers* (Oxford)

—— (1984) *Fictional History Old and New: Hadrian* (James Bryce Memorial Lecture; Somerville College, Oxford); repr. in id., *Roman Papers VI* (Oxford 1991) 157–81

Täubler, E. (1927) *Die Archäologie des Thukydides* (Leipzig)

Thomas, R. (1989) *Oral Tradition and Written Record in Classical Athens* (Cambridge)

Thomsen, R. (1980) *King Servius Tullius: A Historical Synthesis* (Copenhagen)

Thomson, G. (1941) *Aeschylus and Athens: A Study in the Social Origins of Drama* (London)

Thulin, C. O. (1906–9) *Die etruskische Disciplin*, 3 vols (Göteborg)

—— (1912) 'Haruspices', *RE* VII.2: 2431–68

Timpe, D. (1970) *Arminius-Studien* (Heidelberg)

—— (1970/71) 'Le "Origini" di Catone e la storiografia latina', *AAPat* 83: 5–33; repr. in German in id. (2007) 182–208

—— (1972) 'Fabius Pictor und die Anfänge der römischen Historiographie', *ANRW* I.2: 928–69; repr. in id. (2007) 132–81

Timpe, D. (1973) 'Neue Gedanken zur Arminius-Geschichte', *Lippische Mitteilungen aus Geschichte und Landeskunde* 42: 5–30

—— (1979) 'Erwägungen zur jüngeren Annalistik', *A&A* 25: 97–119; repr. in id. (2007) 209–36

—— (1987a) 'Tacito e la realtà storica', in M. Pani, ed., *Epigrafia e territorio: politica e società* (Temi di antichità romane 2; Bari) 215–36

—— (1987b) 'Geschichtsschreibung und Prinzipatsopposition' in A. Giovannini, ed., *Opposition et résistances à l'empire d'Auguste à Trajan* (Entretiens sur l'Antiquité Classique XXXIII; Vandœuvres-Genève 1987) 65–102; repr. in Timpe (2007) 237–58

—— (1988) 'Mündlichkeit und Schriftlichkeit als Basis der frührömischen Überlieferung', in von Ungern-Sternberg–Reinau (1988) 266–286; repr. in Timpe (2007) 86–108

—— (1996) '*Memoria* und Geschichtsschreibung bei den Römern', in Gehrke–Möller (1996) 277–300; repr. in Timpe (2007) 64–85 (= this volume, Ch. 6)

—— (2007) *Antike Geschichtsschreibung: Studien zur Historiographie*, ed. U. Walter (Darmstadt)

Toepffer, J. (1889) *Attische Genealogie* (Berlin)

Toher, M. (1986) 'The Tenth Table and the Conflict of the Orders', in Raaflaub (1986b) 301–26

Tomberg, K.-H. (1968) *Die καινὴ ἱστορία des Ptolemaios Chennos* (Bonn)

Tonkin, E. (1992) *Narrating our Past: The Social Construction of Oral History* (Cambridge)

Too, Y. L., ed. (2001) *Education in Greek and Roman Antiquity* (Leiden)

Torelli, M. (1968) 'Un nuovo attacco fra gli Elogia Tarquiniensia', *SE* 36: 467–70

—— (1974/75) 'Tre studi di storia etrusca', *DArch* 8: 3–78

—— (1975) *Elogia Tarquiniensia* (Florence)

—— (1983) 'Ideologia e rappresentazione nelle tombe tarquiniesi dell'Orco I e II', *Dialoghi di Archeologia*[3] 1: 7–17

—— (1984) *Lavinio e Roma: riti iniziatici e matrimonio tra archeologia e storia* (Rome)

—— (1996) 'Riflessioni sulle registrazioni storiche in Etruria', *Eutopia* 5: 13–22

Toynbee, A. J., ed. (1924) *Greek Historical Thought* (London)

Trecsényi-Waldapfel, I. (1960) 'Poésie et réalité historique dans la théorie et la pratique littéraire de Cicéron', *Ann. Univ. Scient. Budap.* (Sect. Philol.) 2: 3–18

Tresp, A. (1914) *Die Fragmente der griechischen Kultschriftsteller* (Religionsgeschichtliche Versuche und Vorarbeiten, Band XV, Heft 1; Giessen)

Tulving, E. and W. Donaldson, edd. (1972) *Organization of Memory* (New York)

Turcan, R. (1976) 'Encore la prophétie de Végoia', in *L'Italie préromaine et la Rome républicaine. Mélanges offerts à Jacques Heurgon* (Rome) 1009–19

Ullman, B. L. (1942) 'History and Tragedy', *TAPhA* 73: 25–53

—— (1943) 'Sine ira et studio', *CJ* 38: 420–21

Ungern-Sternberg, J. von (1986) 'The Formation of the "Annalistic Tradition": The Example of the Decemvirate', in Raaflaub (1986b) 77–104

—— (1988) 'Überlegungen zur frühen römischen Überlieferung im Lichte der Oral-Tradition-Forschung', in von Ungern-Sternberg–Reinau (1988) 237–65; repr. in id. (2006b) 1–29 (= this volume, Ch. 5)

—— (1990) 'Die Wahrnehmung des "Standeskampfes" in der römischen Geschichtsschreibung', in W. Eder, ed., *Staat und Staatlichkeit in der frühen römischen Republik* (Stuttgart) 92–102; repr. in von Ungern-Sternberg (2006b) 170–80

—— (1993) 'Romulus-Bilder: Die Begründung der Republik im Mythos', in F. Graf, ed., *Mythos in mythenloser Gesellschaft: das Paradigma Roms* (Stuttgart) 88–108; repr. in von Ungern-Sternberg (2006b) 30–50

—— (2000) 'Eine Katastrophe wird verarbeitet: Die Gallier in Rom', in C. Bruun, ed., *The Roman Middle Republic: Politics, Religion and Historiography c. 400–133* (Rome) 207–22; repr. in von Ungern-Sternberg (2006) 113–31

—— (2006a) 'Hungersnöte und ihre Bewältigung im Rom des 5. Jh's v. Chr: Eine Studie zur mündlichen Überlieferung', in id. (2006b) 100–12

—— (2006b) *Römische Studien: Geschichtsbewußtsein–Zeitalter der Gracchen–Krise der Republik* (Munich–Leipzig)

—— and H. Reinau, edd. (1988) *Vergangenheit in mündlicher Überlieferung* (Stuttgart)

Usher, S. (1974–85) *Dionysius of Halicarnassus: Critical Essays*, 2 vols (LCL; Cambridge, Mass.–London)

Valentini, R. and G. Zucchetti (1940–53) *Codice Topografico della Città di Roma*, 4 vols (Rome)

van Baaren, T. P. (1972) 'The Flexibility of Myth', in *Ex orbe Religionum: Studia G. Widengren ... oblata*, 2 vols (Leiden) II.199–205

van Berchem, D. (1960) 'Trois cas d'asylie archaïque', *MH* 17: 21–33

—— (1966) 'Rome et le monde grec au VIe siècle avant notre ère', in R. Chevallier, ed., *Mélanges d'archéologie et d'histoire offerts à A. Piganiol* (Paris) II.739–48

—— (1967) 'Sanctuaires d'Hercule-Melqart', *Syria* 44: 307–38

—— (1980) 'La gérousie d'Ephèse', *MH* 37: 25–40

van Gennep, A. (1910) *La formation des legends* (Paris)

van Groningen, B. A. (1953) *In the Grip of the Past: An Essay on an Aspect of Greek Thought* (Leiden)

van Son, D. W. L. (1963) 'The Disturbances in Etruria during the Second Punic War', *Mnemosyne* 16: 267–74

Vansina, J. (1973) *Oral Tradition: A Study in Historical Methodology* (Harmondsworth); English trans. by H. M. Wright of *De la tradition orale: essai de methode historique* (Tervuren 1961)

—— (1985) *Oral Tradition as History* (London–Madison, Wisc.)

Vattuone, R. (1997) 'Una testimonianza dimenticata di Teopompo (Phot., *Bibl.*, 176, P. 121 A, 30–34): Note sul proemio dei *Philippika*', *Simblos* 2: 85–106

Veh, O. (1951) *Zur Geschichtsschreibung und Weltauffassung des Prokop von Caesarea*, 1. Teil (Wissenschaftliche Beilage zum Jahresbericht 1950/51, 1951/52 des Gymnasiums Bayreuth; Bayreuth)

Verdin, H. (1971) *De historisch-kritische methode van Herodotus* (Verhand. Kon. Vlaamse Academie voor Wetenschappen, Letteren en Schone Kunsten van België, Klasse der Letteren 33, 1971, nr. 69; Brussels)

—— G. Schepens, and E. de Keyser, edd. (1990) *Purposes of History: Studies in Greek Historiography from the 4th to the 2nd Centuries B.C.* (Studia Hellenistica 30; Leuven)

Verhaegen, B. (1970) 'Méthode et problèmes de l'histoire immédiate', *Cahiers économiques et sociaux* 8: 471–86

—— (1974) *Introduction à l'histoire immédiate: Essai de méthodologie qualitative* (Gembloux)

Vernant, J.-P. (1962) *Les origines de la pensée grecque* (Paris); English. trans. *The Origins of Greek Thought* (Ithaca, NY, 1982)

—— (1974) *Raison du mythe: mythe et société en Grèce ancienne* (Paris)

—— and P. Vidal-Naquet (1972) *Mythe et tragédie en grèce ancienne* (Paris); English trans. by J. Lloyd, *Tragedy and Myth in Ancient Greece* (Sussex–Atlantic Highlands, NJ, 1981)

Vernole, V. E. (2002) *Servius Tullius* (Rome)

Versnel, H. S. (1982) 'Die neue Inschrift von Satricum in historischer Sicht', *Gymnasium* 89: 193–235

Vetter, E. (1940) 'Literaturbericht 1935–1937: Etruskisch', *Glotta* 28: 117–231

—— (1955) 'Literaturbericht 1938–1953, Etruskisch: I. Neu veröffentlichte Inschriften', *Glotta* 34: 47–66

Veyne, P. (1984) *Writing History: Essay on Epistemology* (Middletown, Conn. and Manchester); translation by M. Moore-Rinvolucri of *Comment on écrit l'histoire: essai d'épistémologie* (Paris 1971)

—— (1988) *Did the Greeks Believe in their Myths?* (Chicago), trans. P. Wissing of *Les Grecs ont-ils cru à leurs mythes?* (Paris 1983)

Vidal-Naquet, P. (1963) 'Homère et le monde mycénien: à propos d'un livre recent et d'une polémique ancienne', *Annales ESC* 18: 703–19

—— (1964) 'Athènes et l'Atlantide: structure et signification d'un mythe platonicien', *REG* 77: 420–44

—— (1974) 'Les jeunes. Le cru. L'enfant grec et le cuit', in J. Le Goff and P. Nora, edd., *Faire de l'histoire*, 3 vols (Paris) III.137–68; English trans. A. Szegedy-Maszak, in *The Black Hunter: Forms of Thought and Forms of Society in the Greek World* (Baltimore–London, 1986) 129–56

—— (1978) 'Rites d'initiation et littérature', *Dossier du centre Thomas More, Table ronde sur l'initiation*, February 1977

—— (1980) 'Le texte, l'archéologue et l'histoire', in A. Schnapp, ed., *L'archéologie aujourd'hui* (Paris) 173–84

—— (1993) *Die griechische Demokratie von außen gesehen: I. Athen, Sparta, Atlantis* (Munich)

Virgilio, B. (1979) 'Logografia greca e storiografia locale: Pseudepigraphos in età ellenistica', *SCO* 29: 131–67

Vogt, J. (1936) 'Tacitus und die Unparteilichkeit des Historikers', *Würzburger Studien* 9: 1–20, repr. in V. Pöschl, ed., *Tacitus* (*Wege der Forschung* 97; Darmstadt, 1969) 39–59

Vogt-Spira, G., ed. (1989) *Studien zur vorliterarischen Periode im frühen Rom* (ScriptOralia 12; Tübingen)

—— (1990) *Strukturen der Mündlichkeit in der römischen Literatur* (ScriptOralia 19; Tübingen)

von Christ, W. (1920–34) *Geschichte der griechischen Literatur, Zweiter Teil: Die nachklassische Periode der griechischen Literatur*[7], 2 vols (Handbuch der Altertumswissenschaft VII.2.1–2; Munich)

von Fritz, K. (1950) 'The Reorganization of the Roman Government in 366 B.C. and the So-called Licinio-Sextian Laws', *Historia* 1: 3–44; repr. in id., *Schriften zur griechischen und römischen Verfassungsgeschichte und Verfassungstheorie* (Berlin 1976) 329–73

—— (1958) 'Die Bedeutung des Aristoteles für die Geschichtsschreibung', in *Histoire et historiens dans l'antiquité* (Entretiens sur l'Antiquité Classique IV; Vandœuvres-Genève, 1958) 83–145

—— (1967) *Die griechische Geschichtsschreibung von den Anfängen bis Thukydides*, 2 vols (Berlin)

—— (1969) Review of Strasburger (1966), *Gnomon* 41: 583–91

von Lübrow, U. (1986) 'Recht und Rechtswissenschaft im Rom der Frühzeit', in Altheim-Stiehl–Rosenbach (1986) 164–85 von Pohlmann, R. (1925) *Geschichte der sozialen Frage und des Sozialismus in der antiken Welt*³, 2 vols (Munich)

von Scala, R. (1890) *Die Studien des Polybios*, I (Stuttgart)

von Scheliha, R. (1931) *Die Wassergrenze im Altertum* (Historische Untersuchungen 8; Breslau)

Wachter, R. (1987) *Altlateinische Inschriften* (Bern)

Wade-Gery, H. T. (1952) *The Poet of the Iliad* (Cambridge)

Wagner, Ch. (1991) *Die Entwicklung Johann Gustav Droysens als Althistoriker* (diss., Bonn)

Walbank, F. W. (1955) 'Tragic History: A Reconsideration', *BICS* 2: 4–14

—— (1957) Review of Avenarius (1956), *Gnomon* 29: 416–9

—— (1960) 'History and Tragedy', *Historia* 9: 216–34; repr. in id. (1985) 224–41 (= this volume, Ch. 14)

—— (1962) 'Polemic in Polybius', *JRS* 52: 1–12; repr. in id. (1985) 262–79

—— (1972) *Polybius* (Berkeley–Los Angeles–London)

—— (2002) 'Polybian Studies, c. 1975–2000', in id., *Polybius, Rome and the Hellenistic World: Essays and Reflections* (Cambridge) 1–27

Walcot, P. (1973) 'The Funeral Speech: A Study of Values', *G&R* 20.111–21

—— (1978) *Envy and the Greeks: A Study of Human Behaviour* (Warminster)

Walsh, P. G. (1955) 'Livy's Preface and the Distortion of History', *AJPh* 76: 369–83

—— (1961) *Livy: His Historical Aims and Methods* (Cambridge)

Walter, U. (2004) *Memoria und res publica: zur Geschichtskultur im republikanischen Rom* (Frankfurt am Main)

Ward, B. (1976) 'Miracles and History: A Reconsideration of the Miracle Stories used by Bede', in G. Bonner, ed., *Famulus Christi: Essays in Commemoration of the Thirteenth Centenary of the Birth of the Venerable Bede* (London) 70–76

Waszink, J. H. (1972) 'Zum Anfangsstadium der römischen Literatur' *ANRW* I.2: 869–927

Wehrli, F. (1944) *Die Schule des Aristoteles: Dikaiarchos* (Basel; 2nd edn., 1967)

—— (1946) 'Der erhabene und der schlichte Stil in der poetisch-rhetorischen Theorie der Antike', in *Phyllobolia für Peter von der Mühll zum 60. Geburtstag* (Basel) 9–34

—— (1947) 'Die Geschichtsschreibung im Lichte der antiken Theorie', in *Eumusia: Festgabe für Ernst Howald zu 60. Geburtstag* (Erlenbach-Zurich) 54–71

Weil, R. (1975) 'Lire dans Thucydide', in J. Bingen et al., edd., *Le Monde Grec: Hommages à Claire Preaux* (Brussels) 162–8

Weinberg, J. (1988) *Where Three Civilizations Meet: A Tribute to the Life and Work of Arnaldo Dante Momigliano* (London)

Weiss, P. (1984) 'Lebendiger Mythos, Gründerheroen und städtische Gründungstraditionen im griechisch-römischen Osten' *WJA* 10: 179ff.

Weissthanner, A. (1954) 'Mittelalterliche Rompilgerführer: zur Überlieferung der Mirabilia und der Indulgentiae urbis Romae', *Archivalische Zeitschrift* 49: 39–64

Welzer, H. (2008) *Das kommunikative Gedächtnis: eine Theorie der Erinnerung*[2] (Munich)

Wenskus, R. (1961) *Stammesbildung und Verfassung* (Cologne)

Werner, J. (1962) 'Ὦτα ἀπιστότερα ὀφθαλμῶν', *Wiss. Zeitschr. der Karl Marx-Univ. Leipzig Sprachwiss. Reihe* 11: 577

Werner, R. (1963) *Der Beginn der römischen Republik* (Munich)

—— (1966) 'Zur Geschichte der Hunnen', *Jahrbücher für Geschichte Osteuropas* 14: 241–60

—— (1976a) Review of Ranouil (1975), *ZRG* 93: 346–50

—— (1976b) Review of Alföldi (1974), *HZ* 222: 146–51

—— (1982) Review of Thomsen (1980), *Gnomon* 54: 750–5

Wesch-Klein, G. (1993) *Funus Publicum: eine Studie zur öffentlichen Beisetzung und Gewährung von Ehrengräbern in Rom und den Westprovinzen* (Stuttgart)

West, D. A. (1987) *The Bough and the Gate* (Exeter)

—— and A. J. Woodman, edd. (1979) *Creative Imitation and Latin Literature* (Cambridge)

West, M. L. (1970) 'Epic Cycle', *OCD*[2] 388–9

—— (1985) *The Hesiodic Catalogue of Women* (Oxford)

—— (1996) 'Epic Cycle', *OCD*[3] 531

Westermann, C. (1974–82) *Genesis*, 3 vols (Neukirchen-Vluyn)

Weyman, C. (1908) '*Sine ira et studio*', *ALLG* 15: 278–9

Wheeldon, M. J. (1989) '"True Stories": the Reception of Historiography in Antiquity', in Cameron (1989b) 33–63

White, H. (1971) *Metahistory: The Historical Imagination in Nineteenth-Century Europe* (Baltimore–London)

—— (1978) 'The Fictions of Factual Representation', in id., *Tropics of Discourse* (Baltimore–London) 121–34

—— (1987) *The Content of the Form: Narrative Discourse and Historical Representation* (Baltimore–London)

Wickert-Micknat, G. (1986) 'Die Frage der Kontinuität: Bemerkungen zum Thema "Mykene und Homer"', *Gymnasium* 93: 337–47

Wieacker, F. (1967) 'Die XII Tafeln in ihrem Jahrhundert', in: *Les origines de la république romaine* (Entretiens sur l'Antiquité Classique XIII; Vandœuvres-Genève) 291–362

Wieacker, F. (1970) 'Die römischen Juristen in der politischen Gesellschaft des Zweiten vorchristlichen Jahrhunderts', in W. C. Becker and L. Schnorr von Carolsfeld, edd., *Sein und Werden im Recht: Festgabe für Ulrich von Lübtow* (Berlin) 183–214

—— (1988) *Römische Rechtsgeschichte*, I (Handbuch der Altertumswissenschaft 10.3.1; Munich)

Wilamowitz-Moellendorf, U. von (1893) *Aristoteles und Athen*, 2 vols (Berlin)

—— (1894) *Homerische Untersuchungen* (Berlin)

—— (1908) *Greek Historical Writing* (Oxford)

Wilkins, A. S. (1881) *Cicero: De Oratore II* (Oxford)

Will, E. (1972) *Le monde grec et l'orient I: le Vème siècle* (Paris)

Winter, U. (1983) *Frau und Göttin: exegetische und ikonographische Studien zum weiblichen Gottesbild im alten Israel und in dessen Umwelt* (Freiburg)

Wiseman, T. P. (1979) *Clio's Cosmetics: Three Studies in Greco-Roman Literature* (Leicester–Totowa, NJ)

—— (1981) 'Practice and Theory in Roman Historiography', *History* 66 (1981) 375–93; repr. in id. (1987) 244–62

—— (1983) 'The Credibility of the Roman Annalists', *LCM* 8: 20–22

—— (1985a) *Roman Political Life 90 BC–AD 69* (Exeter)

—— (1985b) *Catullus and his World* (Cambridge)

—— (1986) 'Monuments and the Roman Annalists', in Moxon–Smart–Woodman (1986) 87–100

—— (1987) *Roman Studies: Literary and Historical* (Liverpool)

—— (1989) 'Roman Legend and Oral Tradition', *JRS* 79: 129–37

—— (1998) *Roman Drama and Roman History* (Exeter)

Wissowa, G. (1912) *Religion und Kultus der Römer*² (Munich)

Wolf, J. G. (1980) *Die literarische Überlieferung der Publikation der Fasten und Legisaktionen durch Gnaeus Flavius* (*NAWG* Jhrg. 1980, no. 2; Göttingen)

Woodman, A. J. (1975) 'Questions of Date, Genre and Style in Velleius: Some Literary Answers', *CQ* 25: 272–306

—— (1977) *Velleius Paterculus: The Tiberian Narrative* (Cambridge)

—— (1979) 'Self-imitation and the Substance of History: Tacitus, *Annals* 1.61–5 and *Histories* 2.70, 5.14–15', in West–Woodman (1979) 143–55; repr. in Woodman (1998) 70–85

—— (1983a) *Velleius Paterculus: The Caesarian and Augustan Narrative* (Cambridge)

—— (1983b) 'From Hannibal to Hitler: the Literature of War', *Univ. of Leeds Review* 26: 107–24; repr. in id. (1998) 1–20

—— (1988) *Rhetoric in Classical Historiography: Four Studies* (London–Sydney–Portland)

—— (1998) *Tacitus Reviewed* (Oxford)

—— (2001) 'History', in T. O. Sloane, ed., *Encyclopedia of Rhetoric* (Oxford–New York) 337–47

—— (2007) 'Readers and Reception: A Text Case', in Marincola (2007b) 133–44

—— (2008) 'Cicero on Historiography: *De Oratore* 2.51–64', *CJ* 104: 23–31

Yates, F. A. (1966) *The Art of Memory* (Chicago)

Zecchini, G. (1991) 'Teoria e prassi del viaggio in Polibio', in G. Camassa and S. Fasce, edd., *Idea e realtà del viaggio: il viaggio nel mondo antico* (Genoa) 111–41

Ziegler, K. (1929) 'Der Ursprung der Exkurse im Thukydides', *Rh. Mus.* 78: 58–67

—— (1949) 'Paradoxographoi', *RE* XVIII: 1137–66

—— (1952) 'Polybios', *RE* XXI.2: 1440–1578

Acknowledgements

Permission to reprint the following items is gratefully acknowledged.

1. N. Loraux, 'Thucydide n'est pas un collègue': originally published in *Quaderni di Storia* 12 (1980) 55–81.

2. H.-J. Gehrke, 'Mythos, Geschichte, Politik–antik und modern': originally published in *Saeculum* 45 (1994) 239–64.

3. R. Thomas, 'Genealogy and the Genealogists': originally published as *Oral Tradition and Written Record in Classical Athens* (Cambridge, 1989) 173–95.

4. G. Schepens, 'Some Aspects of Source Theory in Greek Historiography': originally published in *Ancient Society* 6 (1975) 257–74.

5. J. von Ungern-Sternberg, 'Überlegungen zur frühen römischen Überlieferung im Lichte der Oral-Tradition-Forschung': originally published in J. von Ungern-Sternberg and H. Reinau, edd., *Vergangenheit in mündlicher Überlieferung*, Colloquium Rauricum, Band I (Stuttgart, 1988) 237–65.

6. D. Timpe, '*Memoria* und Geschichtsschreibung bei den Römern': originally published in H.-J. Gehrke and A. Möller, edd., *Vergangenheit und Lebenswelt: Soziale Kommunikation, Traditionsbildung und historisches Bewusstsein* (Tübingen, 1996) 277–300.

7. T. J. Cornell, 'Etruscan Historiography': originally published in *Annale della Scuola Normale di Pisa*, series 3, vol. 6.2 (1976) 411–39.

8. P. A. Brunt, 'Cicero and Historiography': originally published in *ΦΙΛΙΑΣ ΧΑΡΙΝ: Miscellanea di studi classici in onore di Eugenio Manni*, G. Bretschneider (Rome, 1980) I.311–340; repr. with minor additions in P. A. Brunt, *Studies in Greek History and Literature*, (Oxford, 1993) 181–209.

9. A. J. Woodman, 'Cicero and the Writing of History': originally published as *Rhetoric in Classical Historiography* (London–Sydney–Portland–Oregon, 1988) 70–116.

10. T. J. Luce, 'Ancient Views on the Causes of Bias in Historical Writing': originally published in *Classical Philology* 84 (1989) 16–31.

11. T. P. Wiseman, 'Lying Historians: Seven Types of Mendacity': originally published in C. Gill and T. P. Wiseman, edd. *Lies and Fiction in the Ancient World* edd (Exeter–Austin, Tex., 1993) 122–46.

12. E. Gabba, 'True History and False History in Classical Antiquity': originally published in *Journal of Roman Studies* 71 (1981) 50–62.

13. L. Canfora, 'Il "ciclo" storico': originally published in *Belfagor* 26 (1971) 653–70; reprinted in L. Canfora, *La storiografia greca* (Milan, 1999) 61–91.

14. F. W. Walbank, 'History and Tragedy': originally published in *Historia* 9 (1960) 216–34; reprinted in F. W. Walbank, *Selected Papers: Studies in Greek and Roman History and Historiography* (Cambridge, 1985) 224–41.

15. H. Funke, 'Poesia e storiografia': originally published in *Quaderni di Storia* 23 (1986) 71–93.

Index of Passages

I. Literary Sources